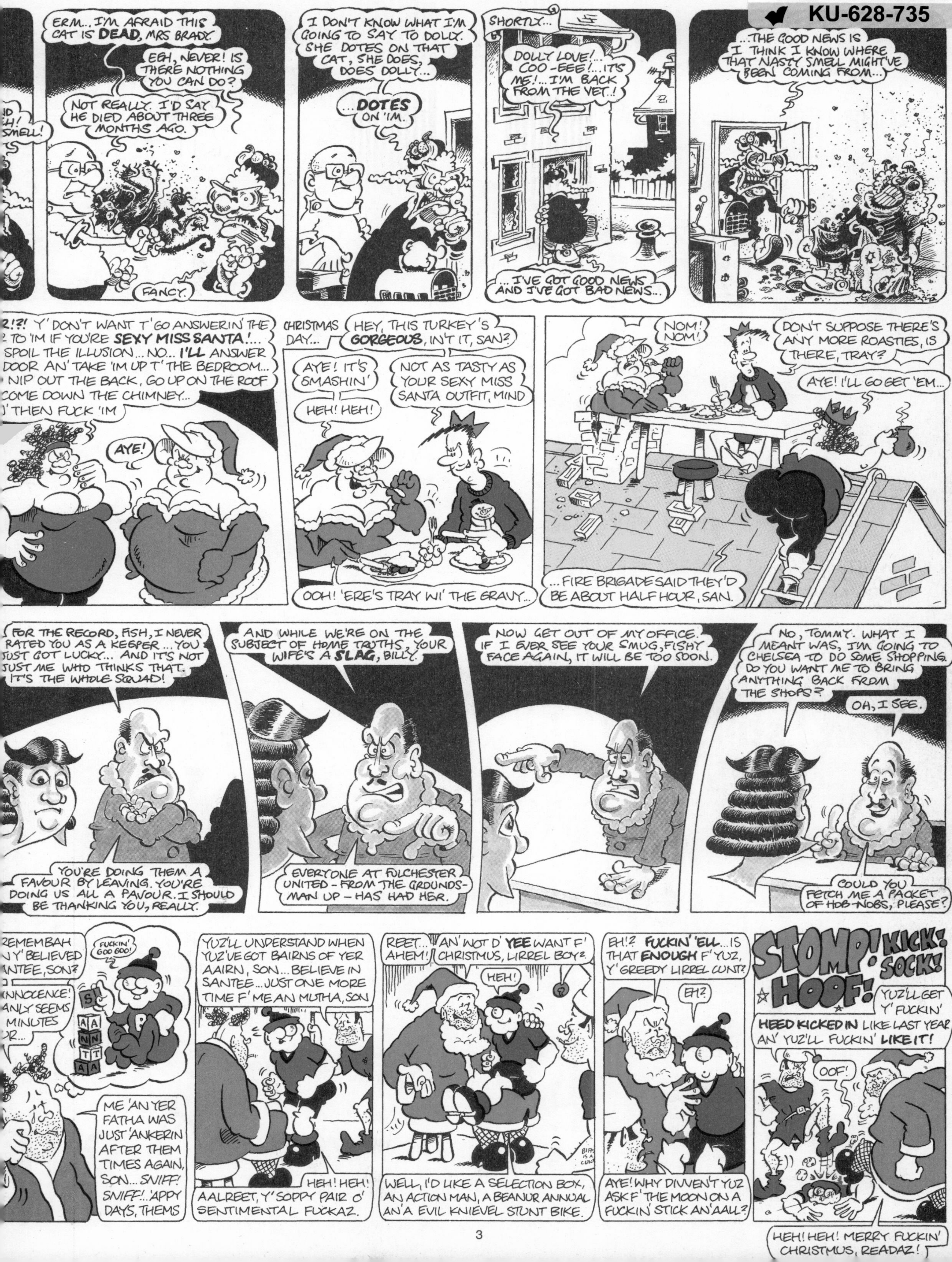
SMELL!
ERM... I'M AFRAID THIS CAT IS DEAD, MRS BRADY.
EEH, NEVER! IS THERE NOTHING YOU CAN DO?
NOT REALLY. I'D SAY HE DIED ABOUT THREE MONTHS AGO.
FANCY.
I DON'T KNOW WHAT I'M GOING TO SAY TO DOLLY. SHE DOTES ON THAT CAT, SHE DOES, DOES DOLLY...
...DOTES ON 'IM.
SHORTLY...
DOLLY LOVE!... COO-EEE!... IT'S ME!... I'M BACK FROM THE VET..!
...I'VE GOT GOOD NEWS AND I'VE GOT BAD NEWS...
...THE GOOD NEWS IS I THINK I KNOW WHERE THAT NASTY SMELL MIGHT'VE BEEN COMING FROM...
Y' DON'T WANT T'GO ANSWERIN' THE TO 'IM IF YOU'RE SEXY MISS SANTA!... SPOIL THE ILLUSION... NO... I'LL ANSWER DOOR AN' TAKE 'IM UP T' THE BEDROOM... NIP OUT THE BACK, GO UP ON THE ROOF COME DOWN THE CHIMNEY... THEN FUCK 'IM
AYE!
CHRISTMAS DAY...
HEY, THIS TURKEY'S GORGEOUS, IN'T IT, SAN?
AYE! IT'S SMASHIN'
NOT AS TASTY AS YOUR SEXY MISS SANTA OUTFIT, MIND
HEH! HEH!
OOH! 'ERE'S TRAY WI' THE GRAVY...
NOM! NOM!
DON'T SUPPOSE THERE'S ANY MORE ROASTIES, IS THERE, TRAY?
AYE! I'LL GO GET 'EM...
...FIRE BRIGADE SAID THEY'D BE ABOUT HALF HOUR, SAN.
FOR THE RECORD, FISH, I NEVER RATED YOU AS A KEEPER... YOU JUST GOT LUCKY... AND IT'S NOT JUST ME WHO THINKS THAT. IT'S THE WHOLE SQUAD!
YOU'RE DOING THEM A FAVOUR BY LEAVING. YOU'RE DOING US ALL A FAVOUR. I SHOULD BE THANKING YOU, REALLY.
AND WHILE WE'RE ON THE SUBJECT OF HOME TRUTHS, YOUR WIFE'S A SLAG, BILLY.
EVERYONE AT FULCHESTER UNITED - FROM THE GROUNDSMAN UP - HAS HAD HER.
NOW GET OUT OF MY OFFICE. IF I EVER SEE YOUR SMUG, FISHY FACE AGAIN, IT WILL BE TOO SOON.
NO, TOMMY. WHAT I MEANT WAS, I'M GOING TO CHELSEA TO DO SOME SHOPPING. DO YOU WANT ME TO BRING ANYTHING BACK FROM THE SHOPS?
OH, I SEE.
COULD YOU FETCH ME A PACKET OF HOB-NOBS, PLEASE?
REMEMBAH Y' BELIEVED ANTEE, SON? INNOCENCE! ANLY SEEMS MINUTES
FUCKIN' GOO GOO!
ME 'AN YER FATHA WAS JUST 'ANKERIN AFTER THEM TIMES AGAIN, SON... SNIFF! SNIFF!... 'APPY DAYS, THEMS
YUZ'LL UNDERSTAND WHEN YUZ'VE GOT BAIRNS OF YER AAIRN, SON... BELIEVE IN SANTEE... JUST ONE MORE TIME F' ME AN MUTHA, SON
HEH! HEH!
AALREET, Y' SOPPY PAIR O' SENTIMENTAL FUCKAZ.
REET... AHEM!
AN' WOT D' YEE WANT F' CHRISTMUS, LIRREL BOY?
HEH!
WELL, I'D LIKE A SELECTION BOX, AN ACTION MAN, A BEANUR ANNUAL AN' A EVIL KNIEVEL STUNT BIKE.
EH!? FUCKIN' 'ELL... IS THAT ENOUGH F' YUZ, Y' GREEDY LIRREL CUNT?
EH?
AYE! WHY DIVVEN'T YUZ ASK F' THE MOON ON A FUCKIN' STICK AN' AALL?
STOMP! KICK! SOCK! HOOF!
YUZ'LL GET Y' FUCKIN' HEED KICKED IN LIKE LAST YEAR AN' YUZ'LL FUCKIN' LIKE IT!
OOF!
HEH! HEH! MERRY FUCKIN' CHRISTMUS, READAZ!

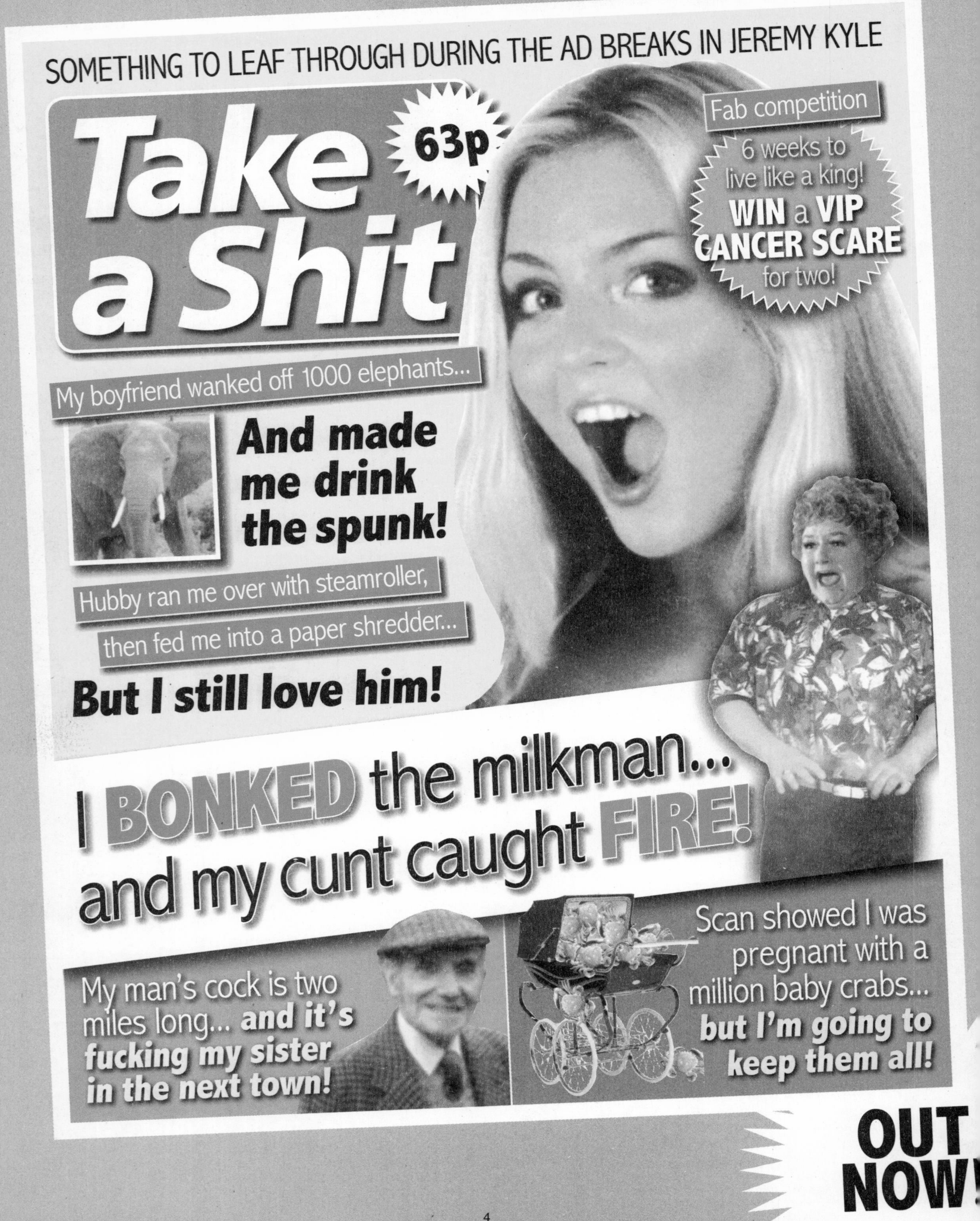
SOMETHING TO LEAF THROUGH DURING THE AD BREAKS IN JEREMY KYLE
Take a Shit
63p
Fab competition
6 weeks to live like a king! WIN a VIP CANCER SCARE for two!
My boyfriend wanked off 1000 elephants...
And made me drink the spunk!
Hubby ran me over with steamroller,
then fed me into a paper shredder...
But I still love him!
I BONKED the milkman... and my cunt caught FIRE!
My man's cock is two miles long... and it's fucking my sister in the next town!
Scan showed I was pregnant with a million baby crabs... but I'm going to keep them all!
OUT NOW!

Viz

THE
BILLPOSTER'S BUCKET

A Barber's Lather Pot Overflowing with
Mighty Wads of Junk from Issues 192~201

Buttered Buns

Graham Dury, Stevie Glover, Wayne Gamble, Davey Jones and Simon Thorp

Sloppy Seconds

Mark Bates, Julian Boffin, Tony Coffey, Alex Collier, Simon Ecob,
Tom Ellen, Barney Farmer, Robin Halstead, Jason Hazeley, Lee Healey,
James MacDougall, Christina Martin, Alex Morris, Joel Morris, Paul Palmer,
Will Reese, Terry Stickney, Lew Stringer and Cat Sullivan

Big Drips
Russell Blackman and Stephen Catherall

Pasted up by Dennis Flyposting Ltd
30 Cleveland Street, London W1T 4JD

ISBN 978-1-781060-90-2
First Printing Autumn 2012

Printed in the United Kingdom

Subscribe online at www.viz.co.uk

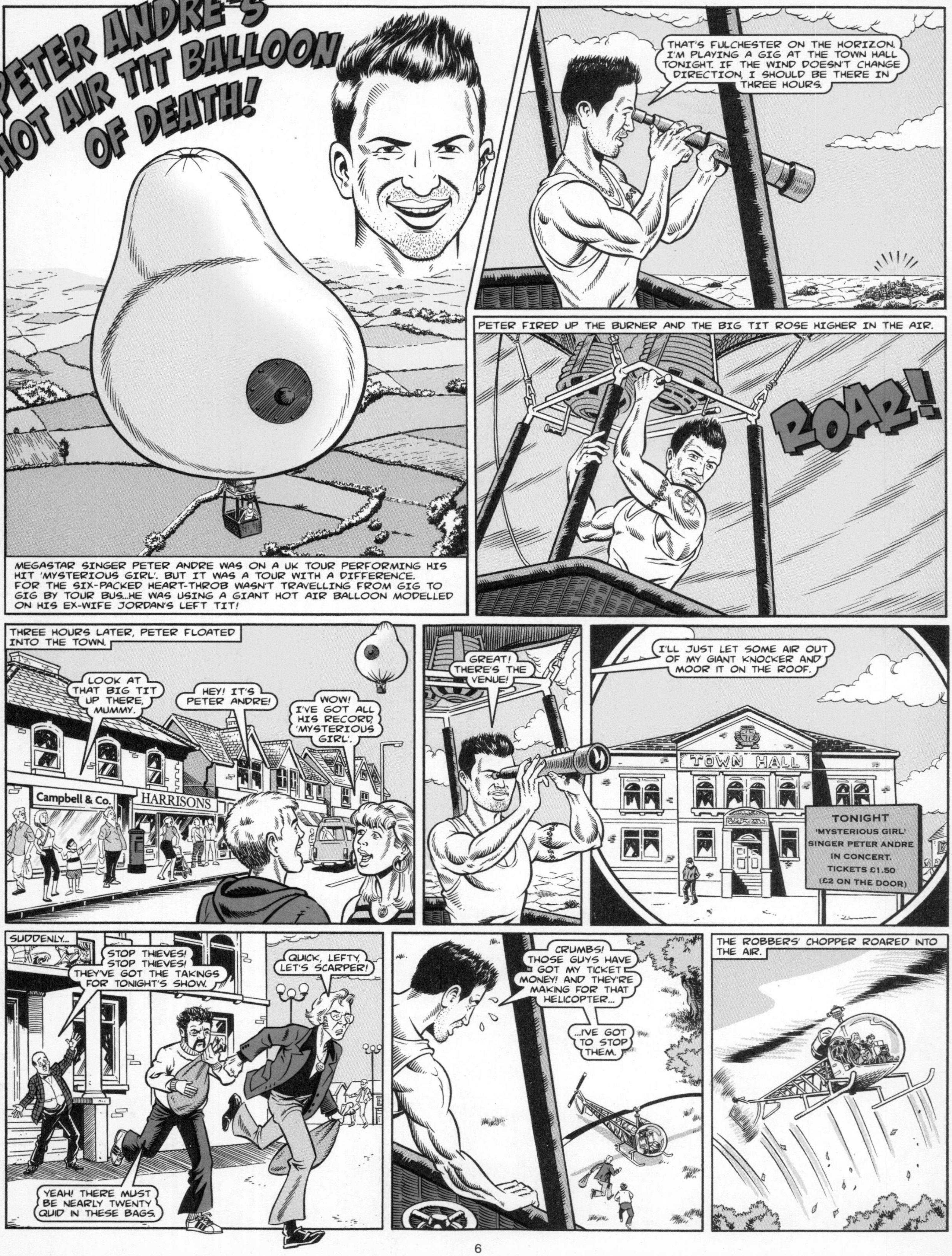
PETER ANDRE'S HOT AIR TIT BALLOON OF DEATH!
MEGASTAR SINGER PETER ANDRE WAS ON A UK TOUR PERFORMING HIS HIT 'MYSTERIOUS GIRL'. BUT IT WAS A TOUR WITH A DIFFERENCE. FOR THE SIX-PACKED HEART-THROB WASN'T TRAVELLING FROM GIG TO GIG BY TOUR BUS...HE WAS USING A GIANT HOT AIR BALLOON MODELLED ON HIS EX-WIFE JORDAN'S LEFT TIT!
THAT'S FULCHESTER ON THE HORIZON. I'M PLAYING A GIG AT THE TOWN HALL TONIGHT. IF THE WIND DOESN'T CHANGE DIRECTION, I SHOULD BE THERE IN THREE HOURS.
PETER FIRED UP THE BURNER AND THE BIG TIT ROSE HIGHER IN THE AIR.
ROAR!
THREE HOURS LATER, PETER FLOATED INTO THE TOWN.
LOOK AT THAT BIG TIT UP THERE, MUMMY.
HEY! IT'S PETER ANDRE!
WOW! I'VE GOT ALL HIS RECORD, 'MYSTERIOUS GIRL'.
Campbell & Co.
HARRISONS
GREAT! THERE'S THE VENUE!
I'LL JUST LET SOME AIR OUT OF MY GIANT KNOCKER AND MOOR IT ON THE ROOF.
TOWN HALL
TONIGHT
'MYSTERIOUS GIRL'
SINGER PETER ANDRE
IN CONCERT.
TICKETS £1.50
(£2 ON THE DOOR)
SUDDENLY...
STOP THIEVES! STOP THIEVES! THEY'VE GOT THE TAKINGS FOR TONIGHT'S SHOW.
QUICK, LEFTY, LET'S SCARPER!
YEAH! THERE MUST BE NEARLY TWENTY QUID IN THESE BAGS.
CRUMBS! THOSE GUYS HAVE GOT MY TICKET MONEY! AND THEY'RE MAKING FOR THAT HELICOPTER...
...I'VE GOT TO STOP THEM.
THE ROBBERS' CHOPPER ROARED INTO THE AIR.

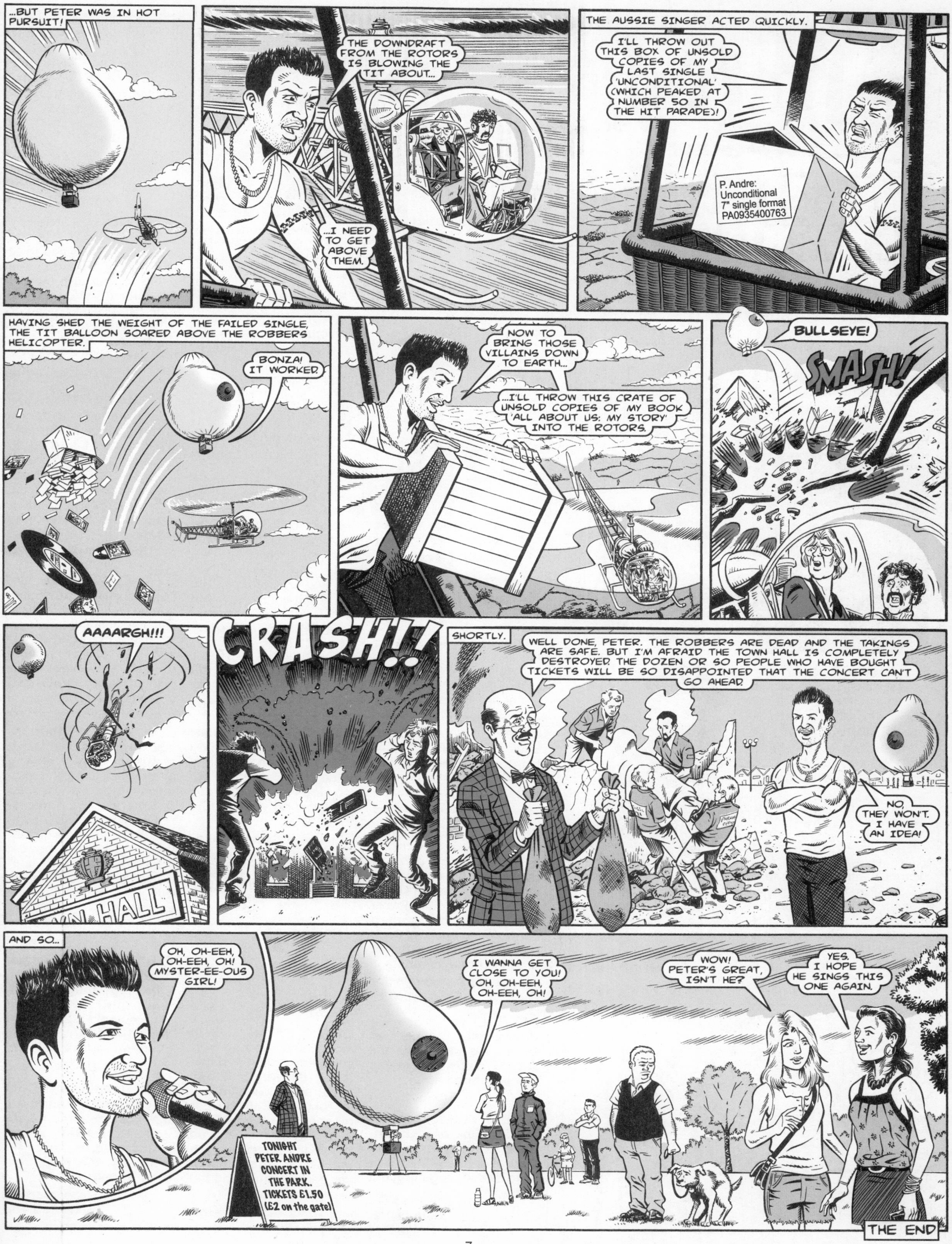
...BUT PETER WAS IN HOT PURSUIT!
THE DOWNDRAFT FROM THE ROTORS IS BLOWING THE TIT ABOUT...
...I NEED TO GET ABOVE THEM.
THE AUSSIE SINGER ACTED QUICKLY.
I'LL THROW OUT THIS BOX OF UNSOLD COPIES OF MY LAST SINGLE 'UNCONDITIONAL' (WHICH PEAKED AT NUMBER 50 IN THE HIT PARADE)!
P. Andre: Unconditional 7" single format PA0935400763
HAVING SHED THE WEIGHT OF THE FAILED SINGLE, THE TIT BALLOON SOARED ABOVE THE ROBBERS HELICOPTER.
BONZA! IT WORKED.
NOW TO BRING THOSE VILLAINS DOWN TO EARTH...
...I'LL THROW THIS CRATE OF UNSOLD COPIES OF MY BOOK 'ALL ABOUT US: MY STORY' INTO THE ROTORS.
BULLSEYE!
SMASH!
AAAARGH!!!
CRASH!!
SHORTLY.
WELL DONE, PETER. THE ROBBERS ARE DEAD AND THE TAKINGS ARE SAFE. BUT I'M AFRAID THE TOWN HALL IS COMPLETELY DESTROYED. THE DOZEN OR SO PEOPLE WHO HAVE BOUGHT TICKETS WILL BE SO DISAPPOINTED THAT THE CONCERT CAN'T GO AHEAD.
NO, THEY WON'T. I HAVE AN IDEA!
AND SO...
OH, OH-EEH, OH-EEH, OH! MYSTER-EE-OUS GIRL!
I WANNA GET CLOSE TO YOU! OH, OH-EEH, OH-EEH, OH!
WOW! PETER'S GREAT, ISN'T HE?
YES. I HOPE HE SINGS THIS ONE AGAIN.
TONIGHT PETER ANDRE CONCERT IN THE PARK. TICKETS £1.50 (£2 on the gate)
THE END

LetterbOcks

VIZ COMIC
PO Box 841
Whitley Bay
NE26 9EQ

STAR LETTER

IT DOES irritate me when people say "If we had lost the war we'd all be speaking German by now". I'm currently taking night classes in German, and it would have saved me a lot of time and money.

Christina Martin, London

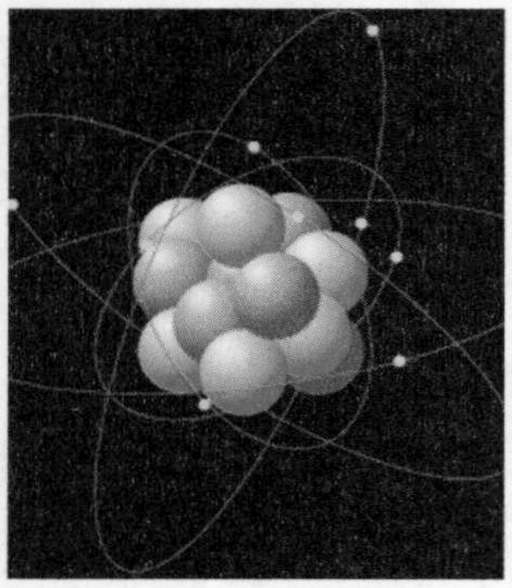

I DON'T know why scientists make such a fuss about splitting the atom. Atoms are tiny. Splitting a big fuck-off rock the size of a house would be much more impressive.

Popey Mike, e-mail

A TAG attached to the front of my new shirt reads "We hope you enjoy wearing this garment as much as we enjoyed creating it." Bearing in mind that the shirt cost £7.99 and the label inside it states that it was made in Bangladesh, I'm not really expecting to enjoy wearing it very much at all.

Spud, Luton

NASA needn't waste millions of dollars every year looking for life elsewhere in the Universe. I can tell them now that there isn't any. I had a look through my mate Dave's telescope last night when we were both pissed, and I couldn't see fuck all.

Justin Reeder, e-mail

IT WOULDN'T surprise me if someone somewhere was being stopped from doing something as a result of the over-zealous application of Health and Safety legislation. If this is indeed the case, then it will be just another case of political correctness gone mad.

Mrs Edna Mansfield, Surrey

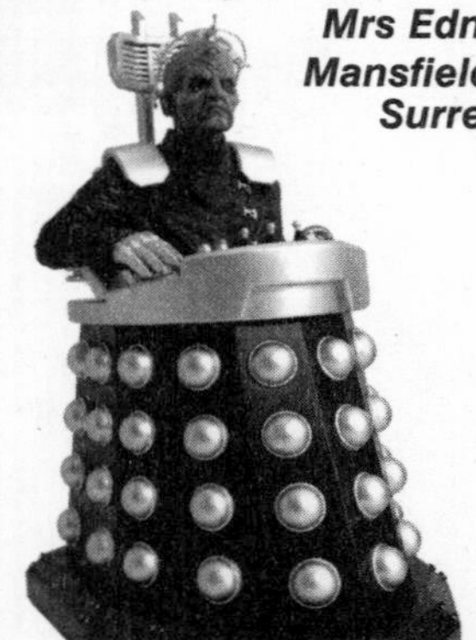

CAN ANY Doctor Who fans confirm what Davros did if he wanted a shit? I reckon his Dalek arse was fitted with a 'crumb tray' like you get with some toasters.

Stu Mandry, e-mail

A LOT of people have "had a go" at Johnny Rotten for apparently abandoning his punk principles in order to do those Country Life Commercials. But to give him his due he's right, it is nice butter.

M Spiers, Stapeley

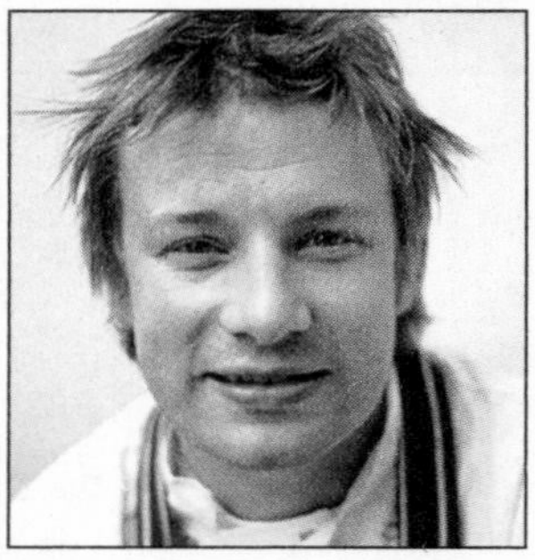

I THINK Jamie Oliver should be the first TV chef to go into space, whether the little fucker wants to or not.

Mr Crosby, Merseyside

IN THE final scene of Titanic, Kate Winslet says "I'll never let go, Jack!" to Leonardo Di Caprio. She then proceeds to let go of his hand and watch him sink to the bottom of the Atlantic. You'd think an experienced director like James Cameron would have spotted this glaring blooper before allowing the film to go on general release.

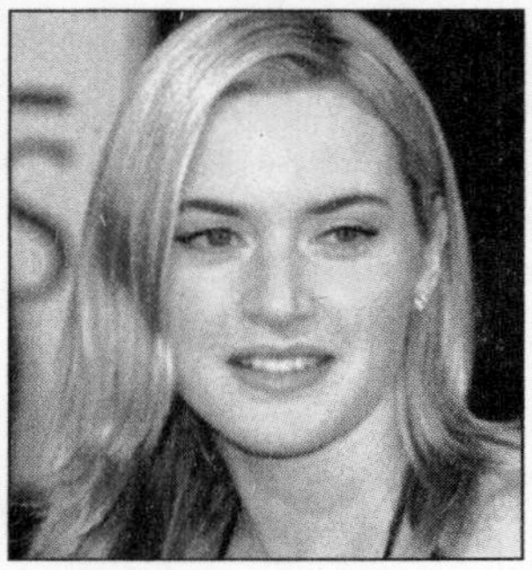

M. Ireland, Warwick

ACCORDING to their tourist board's TV adverts, "A long weekend in Yorkshire isn't long enough". Upon hearing this, I immediately cancelled the long weekend in Yorkshire that I had booked. Thanks for the heads-up, lads.

C Martin, London

TO THE tall man in the newsagents on Stamford Street, SE1 on Monday November 30th. Buying a copy of GQ with an issue of Razzle tucked inside doesn't make you look any less of a wanker than if it was the other way round.

Pete Macphail, Codsall

WOULDN'T IT it be refreshing if the television companies could provide some sort of platform for members of the general public to showcase their talents? There must be dozens of individuals out there with unique skills and lovely singing voices just waiting to prove what they can do. Come on TV bosses, give us ordinary people a chance.

Chorlton Penfold, Manchester

WHILST watching a re-run of *The Crystal Maze*, I was intrigued to see that the Futuristic Zone didn't contain such things as flat screen TV displays, or even half-decent computers. What is going to go wrong in the future, I wonder, to re-turn us to 1980s technology?

J Bayliss, e-mail

HOW IS IT it, despite all the millions of dollars at the make-up department's disposal, no Hollywood film has ever been able to produce a "waking up" scene where the character looks even half as fucked as I do when I go for a piss at seven in the morning?

Steve Rowland, e-mail

NO WONDER there's so many paedophiles around when art galleries and stately homes seem only too happy to cover their walls with old master paintings of nude cherubims. In my opinion, the authorities ought to station a policeman in

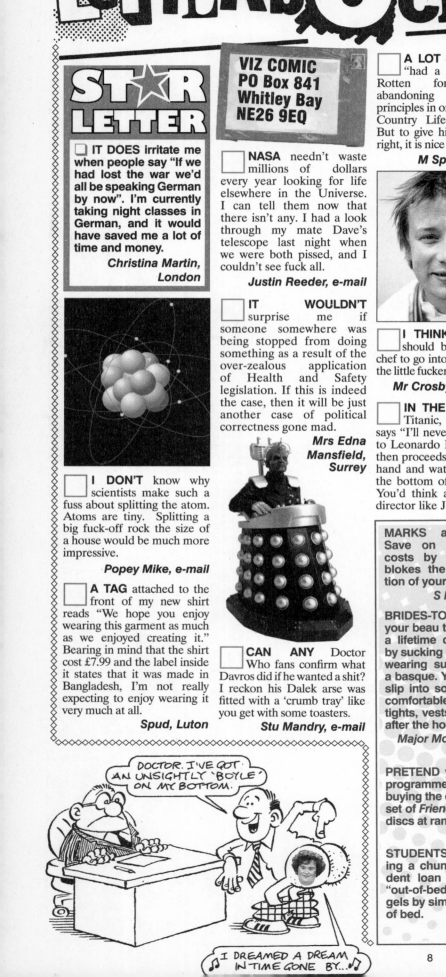

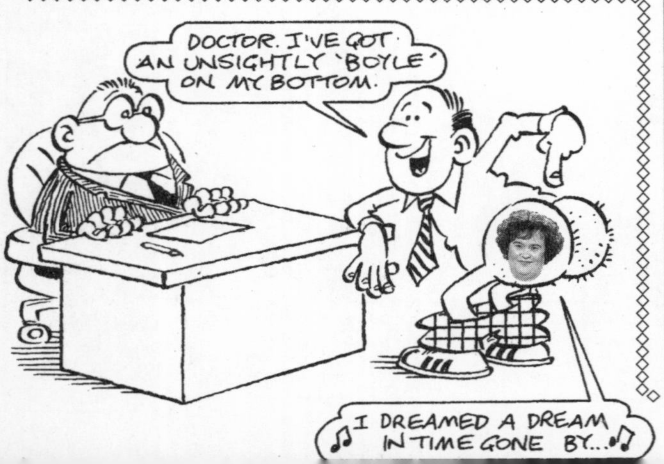
DOCTOR. I'VE GOT AN UNSIGHTLY 'BOYLE' ON MY BOTTOM.
I DREAMED A DREAM IN TIME GONE BY...

TOP TIPS

MARKS and Spencer. Save on your printing costs by only sending blokes the lingerie section of your catalogue.

S Mencer, e-mail

BRIDES-TO-BE. Convince your beau that he is in for a lifetime of A1 banging by sucking his cock whilst wearing suspenders and a basque. You can always slip into something more comfortable such as thick tights, vests and pyjamas after the honeymoon.

Major McKidderminster Kidderminster

PRETEND you are an E4 programme planner by buying the entire DVD box set of *Friends* and playing discs at random.

Smiffy, e-mail

STUDENTS. Avoid spending a chunk of your student loan on expensive "out-of-bed-look" hair gels by simply getting out of bed.

Chris Preston, Manchester

MOTORISTS. Avoid costly MOTs by simply booking an MOT test on every day of the year. Then if the police stop you, you can say you were on your way to get an MOT.

J Barnes, e-mail

LADY Drivers. Save money by ordering your shopping online and having it delivered. It only costs a fiver, which is a lot less than all the petrol you use trying to park your tiny car in a great big space whilst bringing the whole supermarket car park to a fucking halt every Saturday.

V. Higham, e-mail

CONVINCE neighbours you are a multi-instrumentalist by having a guitar, piano, saxophone, some drums, speakers and microphones and lots of recording equipment delivered to your house. Then open all your windows and play something by Mike Oldfield very loudly.

Eric Underpants, Lupset

ELECTRICITY companies. Please ensure that, following a power cut, the supply is restored at precisely 12.00 so I don't have to re-set the clock on my microwave.

D Booth, e-mail

PUB landlords. Convince your customers that you are not an alcoholic by walking round with a mug of coffee for the first twenty minutes after opening.

Grant Warner, New Zealand

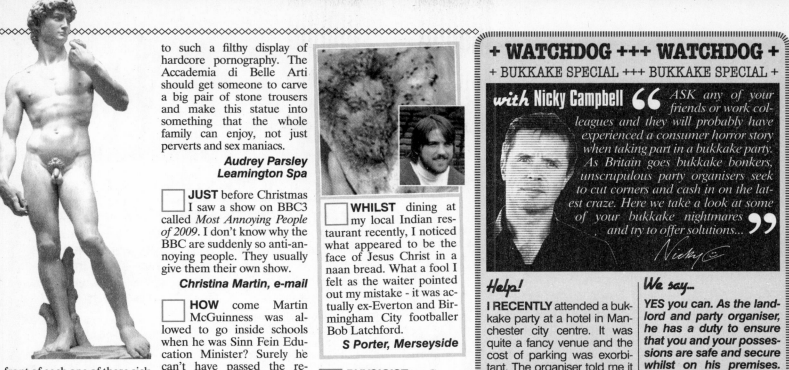

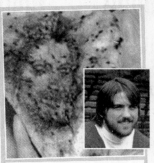

front of each one of these sick so-called "works of art" with instructions to apprehend anyone who stops to take a look at the babies' bottoms or tassels and put them on the sex offenders' register.

Heather Ptarmigan, Hull

I AGREE with the sentiments of Mrs Ptarmigan's letter *(above)*. I took my children to see Michelangelo's David in Florence. Imagine my disgust when we arrived to find that the sculpture wasn't wearing any clothes and you could clearly see his whatnot and his thingy-bag. Now I'm as broad-minded as the next person, but I vomited. My son and daughter, who are fourteen and seventeen respectively, were in tears at being exposed to such a filthy display of hardcore pornography. The Accademia di Belle Arti should get someone to carve a big pair of stone trousers and make this statue into something that the whole family can enjoy, not just perverts and sex maniacs.

***Audrey Parsley
Leamington Spa***

JUST before Christmas I saw a show on BBC3 called *Most Annoying People of 2009*. I don't know why the BBC are suddenly so anti-annoying people. They usually give them their own show.

Christina Martin, e-mail

HOW come Martin McGuinness was allowed to go inside schools when he was Sinn Fein Education Minister? Surely he can't have passed the required Criminal Records Bureau check.

Ada Smallbury, Luton

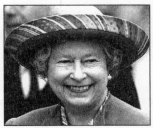

IF THE Queen was any kind of monarch she'd kill herself during the next final of *The X-Factor,* causing the major channels to go to rolling news coverage, thus sparing us the pain of this television programme. Come on, Ma'am, your subjects need you.

Joel Young, e-mail

WHILST dining at my local Indian restaurant recently, I noticed what appeared to be the face of Jesus Christ in a naan bread. What a fool I felt as the waiter pointed out my mistake - it was actually ex-Everton and Birmingham City footballer Bob Latchford.

S Porter, Merseyside

PHYSICIST George Johnston Storey is credited in 1891 with determining that electricity is made friom electrons. Given the similarity in the two terms, quite frankly I'm surprised that nobody realised this earlier.

Magnus Mbanu, e-mail

AFTER my recent redundancy, my girlfriend took a second job to help pay for Christmas. I felt lonely and abandoned with her working until 10 o'clock each night, so after two nights I started having an affair with the neighbour, which she found out about on Christmas Day. Now she wants me back and has apologised, but I'm not sure that I can trust her.

Duncan, e-mail

THING
JOKE
CHECKED
CRAP
No. 30745/26/b
MONDAY...
BUS STOP
TUESDAY...
WEDNESDAY...
THURSDAY...
FRIDAY...
ICES
SATURDAY...
SUNDAY...
THERE'S A THING YOU DON'T SEE EVERY DAY.

+ WATCHDOG +++ WATCHDOG +

+ BUKKAKE SPECIAL +++ BUKKAKE SPECIAL +

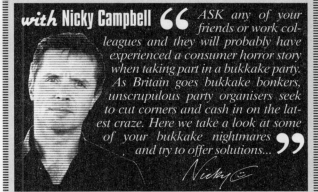

with Nicky Campbell

"ASK any of your friends or work colleagues and they will probably have experienced a consumer horror story when taking part in a bukkake party. As Britain goes bukkake bonkers, unscrupulous party organisers seek to cut corners and cash in on the latest craze. Here we take a look at some of your bukkake nightmares and try to offer solutions..."

Nicky

Help!

I RECENTLY attended a bukkake party at a hotel in Manchester city centre. It was quite a fancy venue and the cost of parking was exorbitant. The organiser told me it should take no longer than 2 hours and guaranteed me 2 shots. In fact, the event was a shambles and I didn't go off because I was so worried about exceeding the meter limit. I eventually made it back to my car 3 hours later and got a parking ticket for £30. The party organiser said that he was not responsible for parking charges.

We say...

UNFORTUNATELY, this is an all too frequent story, but I'm afraid that the organiser is within his rights. Bukkake parties held at swanky hotels will always incur high parking charges. A good tip is to pop out to your car in between cumshots and move it to a different space. Also, check beforehand with the hotel reception to see if they offer free parking facilities for bukkake participants. If not, consider going by public transport. Or perhaps you could car share with your fellow facial masturbators.

Help!

I ATTENDED a bukkake party last week above a pub in Acton. It was well attended and the woman we wanked on was very nice, so I have no complaints about the party. However, when it finished and I went to get dressed, I found that someone had taken my shoes. I had to walk home in my socks and tell the wife that I had been mugged. The pub landlord who organised the party said he was not responsible. Can I force him to pay for a new pair?

We say...

YES you can. As the landlord and party organiser, he has a duty to ensure that you and your possessions are safe and secure whilst on his premises. However, his obligation is only to replace like for like. ie he is not obliged to replace the shoes with new ones if the pair you lost were old. Have a chat and see if you can come to an arrangement about him making a contribution towards a replacement pair. If you cannot reach an agreement, I'm afraid you may have to get a solicitor involved.

Help!

TWO weeks ago I booked a place at a bukkake party in a prefab on the edge of a trading estate. However, when I got there, the organiser told me that the bukkake lady was ill and had had to cancel. He said that he would reschedule the party for 3 weeks' time and to come back then. However, I cannot attend the re-organised date as my daughter is getting married that day. He is refusing to give me my money back claiming to have fulfilled his obligations. What can I do?

We say...

TECHNICALLY he is in the right. He cancelled the party through no fault of his own and offered you an alternative day. If this is not convenient for you, he should offer you a credit note which will allow you to attend a future party. It is also a good idea to pay for any bukkake party event by plastic as if things go wrong, you will be covered by the credit card company.

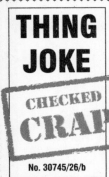

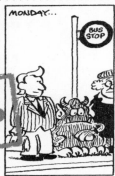

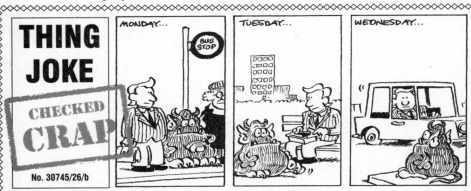

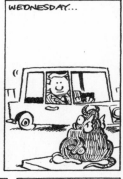

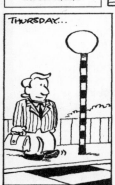

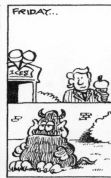

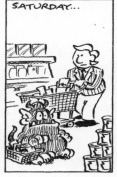

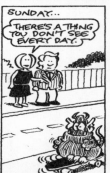

OPEN ALL YEARS

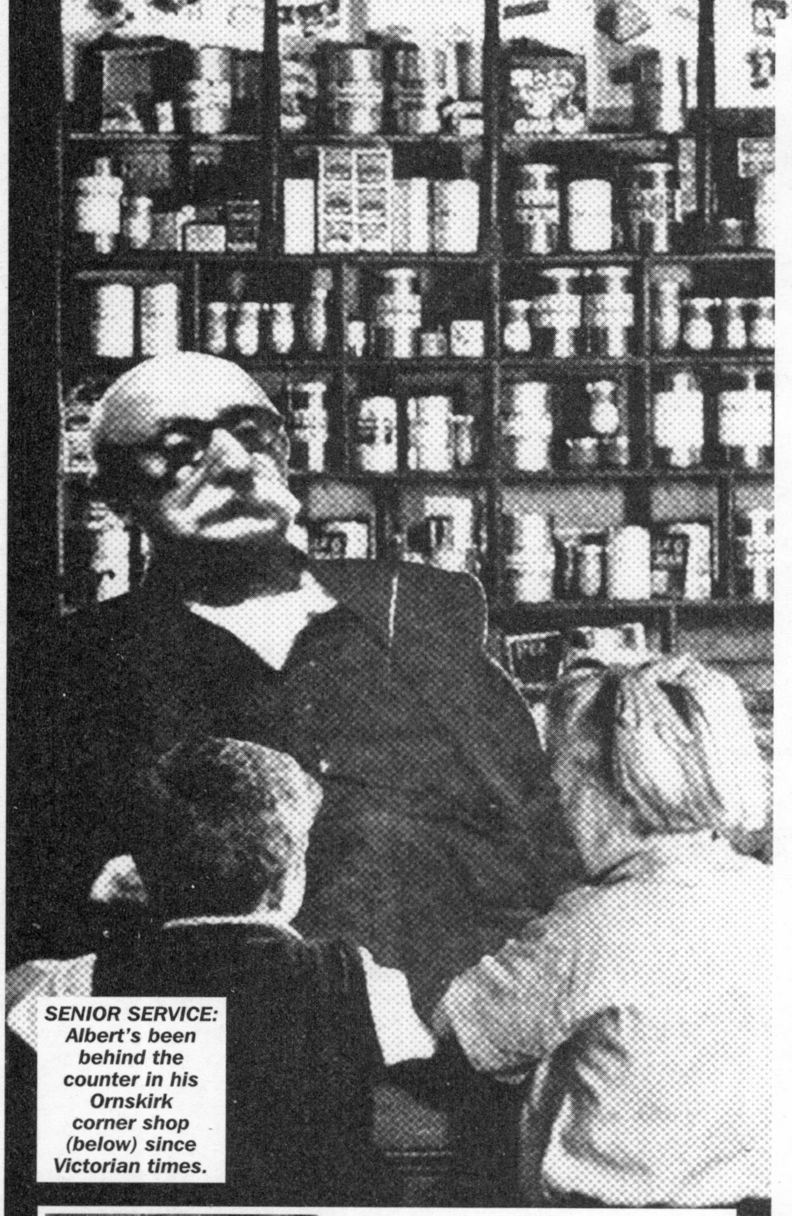

SENIOR SERVICE: *Albert's been behind the counter in his Ornskirk corner shop (below) since Victorian times.*

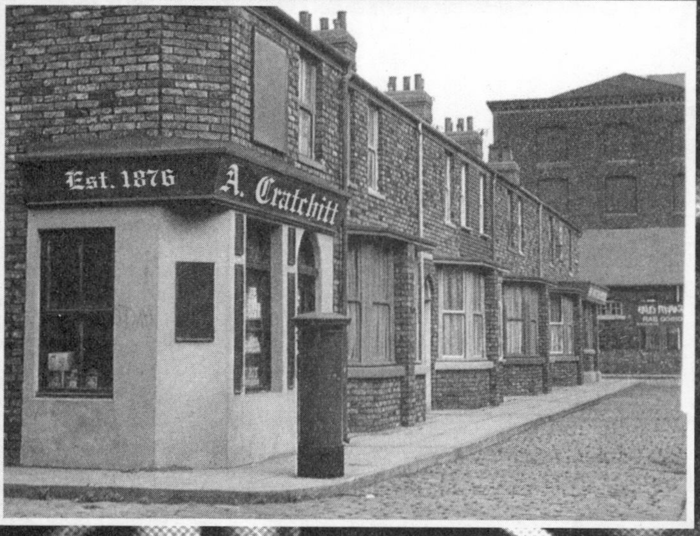

Est. 1876
A. Cratchitt

Gong for Ormskirk's Oldest Shopkeeper

MEET ALBERT CRATCHITT, the shopkeeper who makes Arkwright from TV's *Open All Hours* look like a part-timer. For Albert has been behind the till of his corner shop in Ormskirk, Lancashire for an incredible 134 years... *and he's never had a day off in all that time!*

By AEROGEL INGLEHURST

When Albert opened the doors to his first customers on June 4th 1876, Queen Victoria was still on the throne, General Custer was fighting Red Indians on the other side of the Atlantic and powered flight was still a quarter of a century in the future. Back then a pound of sausages cost just a penny, a loaf of bread was a farthing and a penny-farthing would set you back just sixpence.

HARD WORK

Albert puts down his staying power to good old-fashioned hard work. "I've never had a holiday since the shop opened. I've never felt the need for one," he says. "And I've never had a day off sick, either. What would my customers do if I decided not to open up one morning just because I had the sniffles?"

Not even two World Wars could stop Cratchitt serving his local community with their groceries and general household supplies. In 1914, Albert was 58 and too old to join up. And even following a direct hit on his shop from a German doodlebug one night in 1942, it was still business as usual the next morning, as he served his customers from amidst the smoking rubble.

And the rise of giant out-of-town megastores has done little to dent Albert's profits. "I know all my customers by name," he says. "And they all know that I'm open every day from six in the morning till midnight. You simply don't get that sort of service in a big supermarket."

Not even his own death at the ripe old age of 98 could keep Albert from opening up as usual, just like he had done seven days a week for the previous 78 years. "In 1954 I had a stroke and died whilst asleep in my little flat above the shop," he remembers.

BARRY GEORGE

For any other shopkeeper dying might be a chance to put his feet up, but not for Albert. "I wasn't going to let a little thing like that stop me, and I was in my brown shopcoat and stood behind the counter as usual the next day," he says. "I just got on with it."

"Well, you had to in those days," he smiles. "I even put a jokey sign on the door - 'Open due to bereavement'!"

Many of the locals in the quiet Lancashire town have been his loyal customers for years. "Albert's a real old character," says Mavis DuPont, 67, who has lived in the same street all her life. "I can remember him dying when I was in my teens, and how we were all amazed when he simply opened up as usual the following morning."

"Most people just throw in the towel when their hearts stop beating," agrees neighbour Herbert Posidrive. "They just seem to shrivel up and you never see them again."

BOY GEORGE

"But not Albert. He's an inspiration to everyone who's dead," he says.

Now Cratchitt's oustanding service to his local community has been officially recognised. He has been awarded the CBE in the Birthday Honours. A local funeral director has already volunteered to transport Albert's corpse to Buckingham Palace for the investiture ceremony.

So could it be that the shop will have to close for the first time in nearly a century-and-a-half, so that Cratchitt can go to London and meet the Queen? "Don't talk so daft," chuckles Albert as he serves yet another customer. "My younger sister Beattie, who died in the Spanish flu pandemic of 1919, will be coming over and minding the till while I'm away."

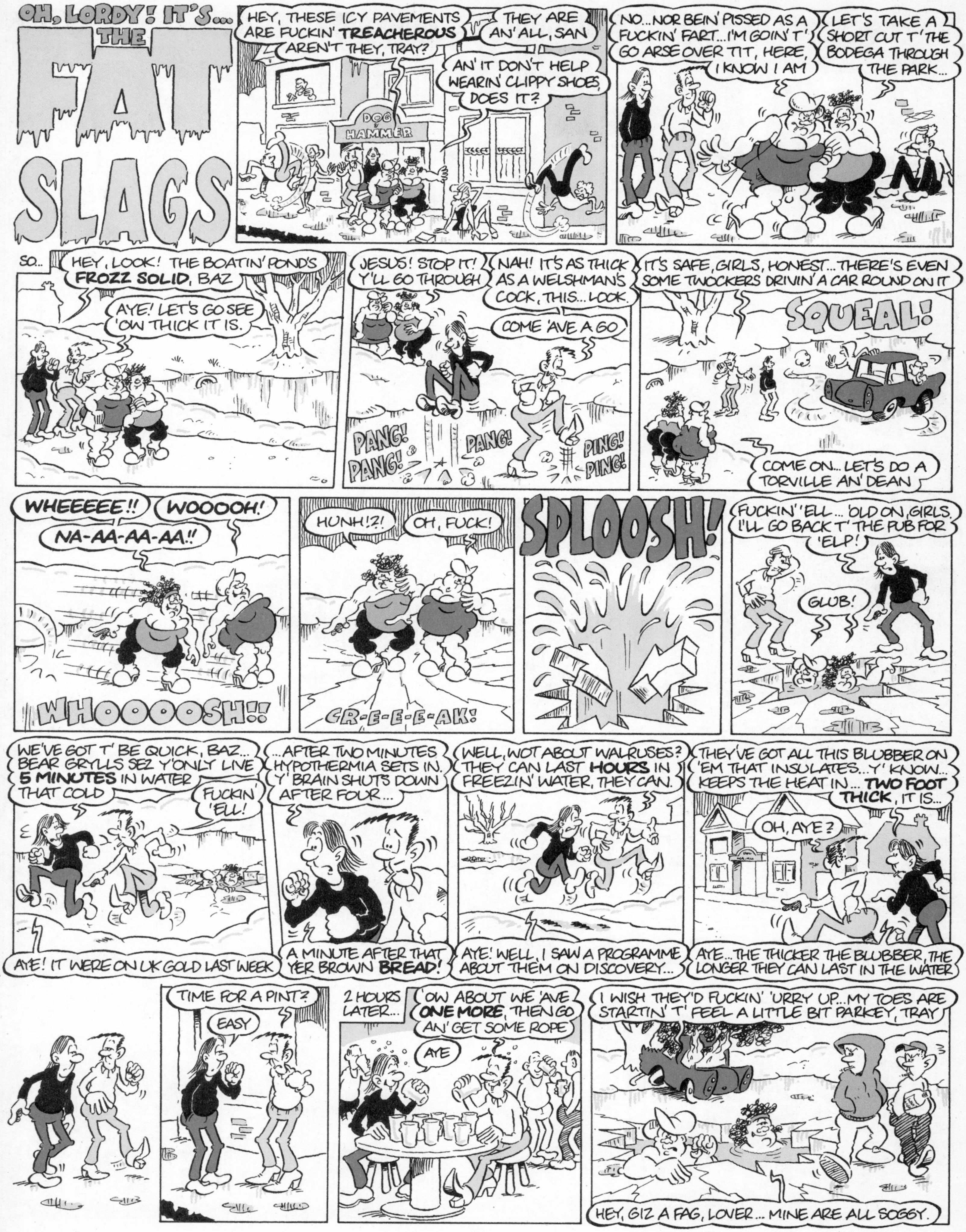
OH, LORDY! IT'S... THE FAT SLAGS
HEY, THESE ICY PAVEMENTS ARE FUCKIN' TREACHEROUS AREN'T THEY, TRAY?
THEY ARE AN' ALL, SAN
AN' IT DON'T HELP WEARIN' CLIPPY SHOES, DOES IT?
DOG & HAMMER
NO... NOR BEIN' PISSED AS A FUCKIN' FART... I'M GOIN' T' GO ARSE OVER TIT, HERE, I KNOW I AM
LET'S TAKE A SHORT CUT T' THE BODEGA THROUGH THE PARK...
SO...
HEY, LOOK! THE BOATIN' POND'S FROZZ SOLID, BAZ
AYE! LET'S GO SEE 'OW THICK IT IS.
JESUS! STOP IT! Y'LL GO THROUGH
NAH! IT'S AS THICK AS A WELSHMAN'S COCK, THIS... LOOK.
COME 'AVE A GO
PANG! PANG! PANG! PING! PING!
IT'S SAFE, GIRLS, HONEST... THERE'S EVEN SOME TWOCKERS DRIVIN' A CAR ROUND ON IT
SQUEAL!
COME ON... LET'S DO A TORVILLE AN' DEAN
WHEEEEE!!
WOOOOH!
NA-AA-AA-AA!!
WHOOOOOSH!!
HUNH!?!
OH, FUCK!
CR-E-E-E-AK!
SPLOOSH!
FUCKIN' 'ELL... 'OLD ON, GIRLS. I'LL GO BACK T' THE PUB FOR 'ELP!
GLUB!
WE'VE GOT T' BE QUICK, BAZ... BEAR GRYLLS SEZ Y'ONLY LIVE 5 MINUTES IN WATER THAT COLD
FUCKIN' 'ELL!
AYE! IT WERE ON UK GOLD LAST WEEK
...AFTER TWO MINUTES HYPOTHERMIA SETS IN. Y' BRAIN SHUTS DOWN AFTER FOUR...
A MINUTE AFTER THAT YER BROWN BREAD!
WELL, WOT ABOUT WALRUSES? THEY CAN LAST HOURS IN FREEZIN' WATER, THEY CAN.
AYE! WELL, I SAW A PROGRAMME ABOUT THEM ON DISCOVERY...
THEY'VE GOT ALL THIS BLUBBER ON 'EM THAT INSULATES... Y' KNOW... KEEPS THE HEAT IN... TWO FOOT THICK, IT IS...
OH, AYE?
AYE... THE THICKER THE BLUBBER, THE LONGER THEY CAN LAST IN THE WATER
TIME FOR A PINT?
EASY
2 HOURS LATER...
'OW ABOUT WE 'AVE ONE MORE, THEN GO AN' GET SOME ROPE
AYE
I WISH THEY'D FUCKIN' 'URRY UP... MY TOES ARE STARTIN' T' FEEL A LITTLE BIT PARKEY, TRAY
HEY, GIZ A FAG, LOVER... MINE ARE ALL SOGGY.

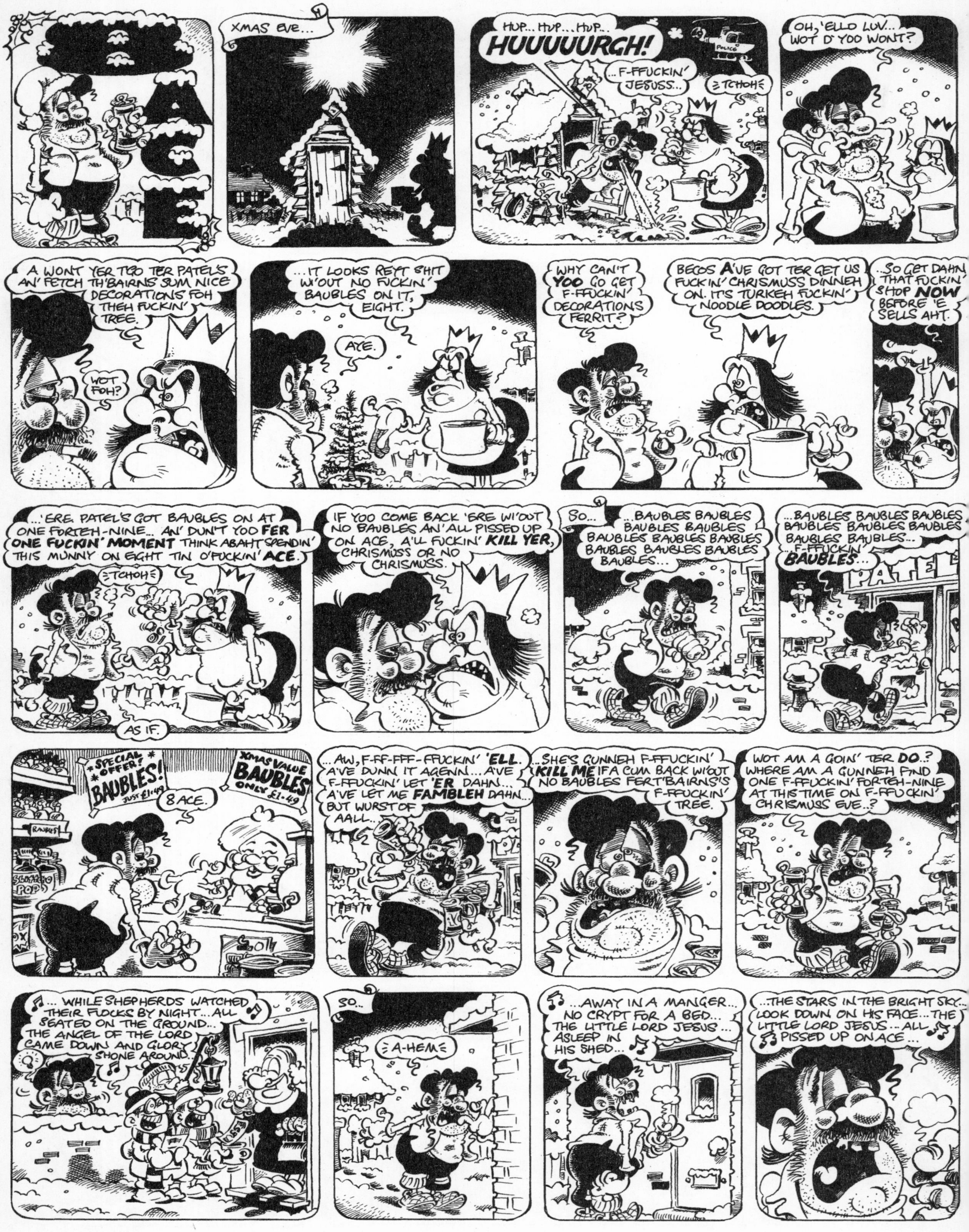
ACE
XMAS EVE...
HUP... HUP... HUP...
HUUUUURGH!
...F-FFUCKIN' JESUSS...
TCHOH
POLICE
OH, 'ELLO LUV... WOT D' YOO WONT?
A WONT YER TGO TER PATEL'S AN' FETCH TH'BAIRNS SUM NICE DECORATIONS FOH THEH FUCKIN' TREE.
WOT FOH?
...IT LOOKS REYT SHIT WI'OUT NO FUCKIN' BAUBLES ON IT, EIGHT.
AYE.
WHY CAN'T YOO GO GET F-FFUCKIN' DECORATIONS FERRIT?
BECOS A'VE GOT TER GET US FUCKIN' CHRISMUSS DINNEH ON. IT'S TURKEH FUCKIN' NOODLE DOODLES.
...SO GET DAHN THAT FUCKIN' SHOP NOW BEFORE 'E SELLS AHT.
...'ERE. PATEL'S GOT BAUBLES ON AT ONE FORTEH-NINE... AN' DUN'T YOO FER ONE FUCKIN' MOMENT THINK ABAHT SPENDIN' THIS MUNNY ON EIGHT TIN O'FUCKIN' ACE.
TCHOH
AS IF.
IF YOO COME BACK 'ERE WI'OUT NO BAUBLES AN' ALL PISSED UP ON ACE, A'LL FUCKIN' KILL YER, CHRISMUSS OR NO CHRISMUSS.
SO...
...BAUBLES BAUBLES BAUBLES BAUBLES BAUBLES BAUBLES BAUBLES BAUBLES BAUBLES BAUBLES BAUBLES BAUBLES...
...BAUBLES BAUBLES BAUBLES BAUBLES BAUBLES BAUBLES BAUBLES BAUBLES... ...F-FFUCKIN' BAUBLES...
PATEL
SPECIAL OFFER! BAUBLES! JUST £1.49
XMAS VALUE BAUBLES ONLY £1.49
8 ACE.
...AW, F-FF-FFF-FFUCKIN' 'ELL. A'VE DUNN IT AGENN... A'VE F-FFUCKIN' LET 'ER DAHN... A'VE LET ME FAMBLEH DAHN... BUT WURST OF AALL...
...SHE'S GUNNEH F-FFUCKIN' KILL ME IF A CUM BACK WI'OUT NO BAUBLES FER T'BAIRNS'S F-FFUCKIN' TREE.
WOT AM A GOIN' TER DO..? WHERE AM A GUNNEH FIND ONE F-FFUCKIN' FORTEH-NINE AT THIS TIME ON F-FFUCKIN' CHRISMUSS EVE..?
... WHILE SHEPHERDS WATCHED THEIR FLOCKS BY NIGHT... ALL SEATED ON THE GROUND... THE ANGEL OF THE LORD CAME DOWN AND GLORY SHONE AROUND...
SO...
A-HEM
...AWAY IN A MANGER... NO CRYPT FOR A BED... THE LITTLE LORD JESUS... ASLEEP IN HIS SHED...
...THE STARS IN THE BRIGHT SKY... LOOK DOWN ON HIS FACE... THE LITTLE LORD JESUS... ALL PISSED UP ON ACE...

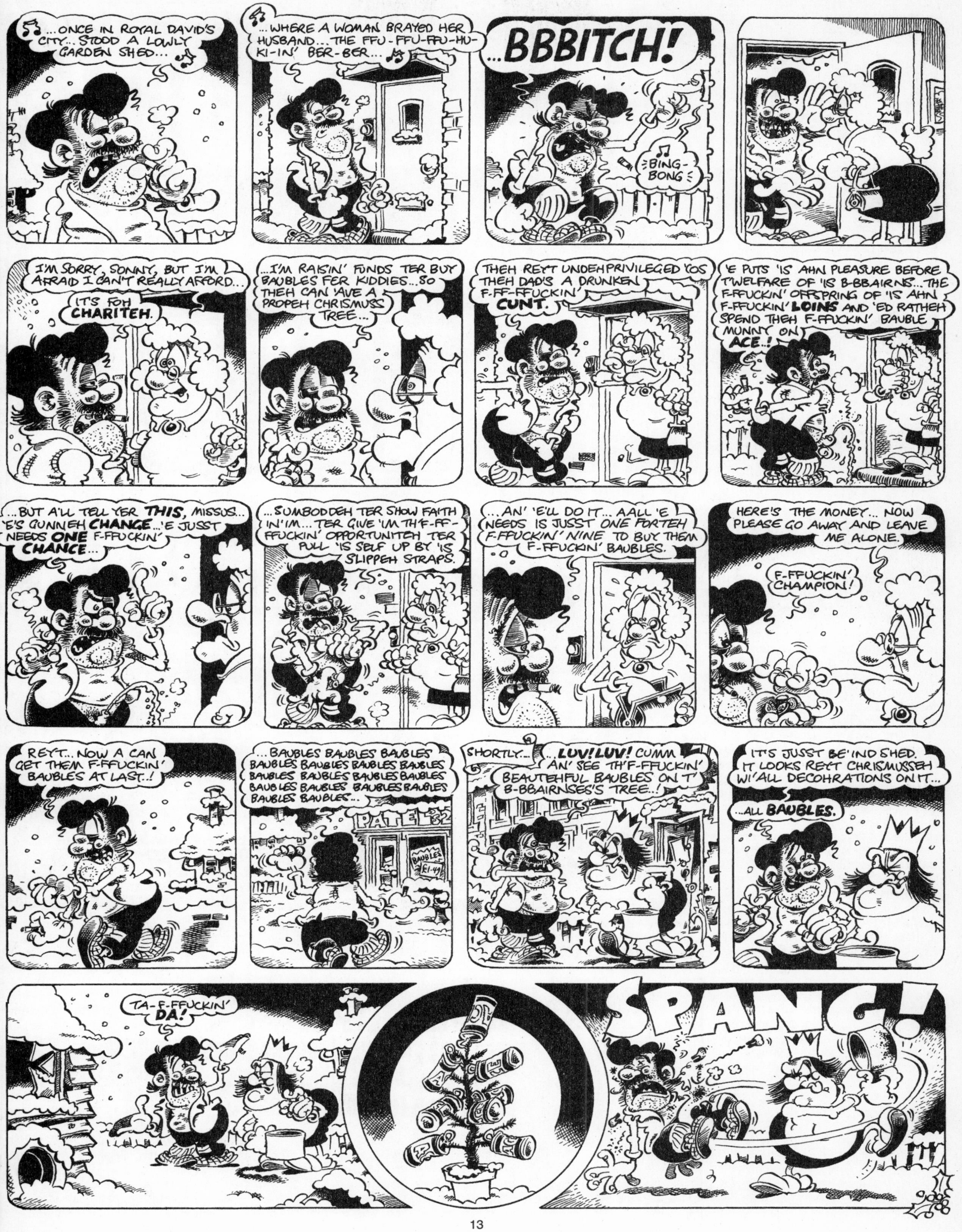
...ONCE IN ROYAL DAVID'S CITY... STOOD A LOWLY GARDEN SHED...
...WHERE A WOMAN BRAYED HER HUSBAND... THE FFU-FFU-FFU-HU-KI-IN' BER-BER...
...BBBITCH!
BING-BONG
I'M SORRY, SONNY, BUT I'M AFRAID I CAN'T REALLY AFFORD...
IT'S FOH CHARITEH.
...I'M RAISIN' FUNDS TER BUY BAUBLES FER KIDDIES... SO THEH CAN 'AVE A PROPEH CHRISMUSS TREE...
THEH REYT UNDEHPRIVILEGED 'COS THEH DAD'S A DRUNKEN F-FF-FFUCKIN' CUNT.
'E PUTS 'IS AHN PLEASURE BEFORE T'WELFARE OF 'IS B-BBAIRNS... THE F-FFUCKIN' OFFSPRING OF 'IS AHN F-FFUCKIN' LOINS AND 'ED RATHEH SPEND THEH F-FFUCKIN' BAUBLE MUNNY ON ACE..!
...BUT A'LL TELL YER THIS, MISSUS... 'E'S GUNNEH CHANGE... 'E JUSST NEEDS ONE F-FFUCKIN' CHANCE...
...SUMBODDEH TER SHOW FAITH IN 'IM... TER GIVE 'IM TH'F-FF-FFUCKIN' OPPORTUNITEH TER PULL 'IS SELF UP BY 'IS SLIPPEH STRAPS.
...AN' 'E'LL DO IT... AALL 'E NEEDS IS JUSST ONE FORTEH F-FFUCKIN' NINE TO BUY THEM F-FFUCKIN' BAUBLES.
HERE'S THE MONEY... NOW PLEASE GO AWAY AND LEAVE ME ALONE.
F-FFUCKIN' CHAMPION!
REYT... NOW A CAN GET THEM F-FFUCKIN' BAUBLES AT LAST..!
...BAUBLES BAUBLES BAUBLES BAUBLES BAUBLES BAUBLES BAUBLES BAUBLES BAUBLES BAUBLES BAUBLES BAUBLES BAUBLES BAUBLES BAUBLES BAUBLES BAUBLES...
PATEL'S
BAUBLES £1.49
SHORTLY...
...LUV! LUV! CUMM AN' SEE TH'F-FFUCKIN' BEAUTEHFUL BAUBLES ON T' B-BBAIRNSES'S TREE..!
IT'S JUSST BE'IND SHED. IT LOOKS REYT CHRISMUSSEH WI' ALL DECOHRATIONS ON IT...
...ALL BAUBLES.
TA-F-FFUCKIN' DA!
SPANG!

SEX AND DRUGS AND ROCKET ROLF

A FORMER NASA astronaut is offering Yorkshire ladies the chance to blast off into the heavens on board his home-built interplanetary rocket... and experience *NOOKIE* in the weightless void of space!

Ex Space Shuttle pilot **ROLF BANNISTER**, 58, is a veteran of over 500 space missions, many with lady astronauts on board, and he has this message for the ladies of his home town of Todmorden: "Believe me, sex in space is out of this world!"

Rocket Rolf has lost count of the close encounters he's had with heavenly bodies. And now he's written a no-black-holes barred account of his randy adventures beyond the stars.

"When the word astronaut is mentioned, most people think of the likes of Neil Armstrong and Buzz Aldrin - clean cut, level-headed and scientifically-minded men," says Bannister.

"But let me tell you, NASA back in the 60s was more like party central. Free love, swinging, and drugs...let me tell you, it was all going on on the launch pad. And once the rockets lifted off, the parties really got going."

"I've bonked on Mars, I've had a blow job on Haley's Comet, and I've even had a threes-up whilst traveling at the speed of light. You name it, I've done it," boasts Rolf.

And in this series of *EXCLUSIVE* extracts from his new biography, **The Million Mile High Club** (Weetabix Books, £2.99), Rolf lifts the lid on the steamy side of the space race.

THE MILLION MILE HIGH CLUB

ROLF BANNISTER

SPACE RACEY MEMOIRS: *Rolf's book, yesterday.*

Todmorden man lifts lid on saucy adventures amongst the stars

In 1967, Rolf was a 15-year-old school leaver with no qualifications, and he was expected to follow his father into the scrap metal business. But pictures of American astronauts on the TV captivated the young boy who longed to be part of the space race. The fact that his NASA heroes were never seen without a pretty girl on their arm added to the appeal. So he decided to abandon a steady career in scrap and reach for the stars. A week later he arrived at Cape Canaveral.

"I was a young lad with an eye for the girls, and I fancied the glamour of the astronaut's life. When I got to NASA headquarters, they liked the look of me and offered me a job straight away. I was thrilled, and decided to go out for a drink that night with the other astronauts to pull a bird. But I was in for a bit of a shock when they told me that my first space mission was the very next day. I was going to the moon for a couple of weeks in one of the rockets. My heart sank, because in the early days, astronauts were always male, and me and my two other crew members, Neil Armstrong and Buzz Aldrin, were not looking forward to a fortnight without a bit of rumpy pumpy.

I needn't have worried!

The rocket blasted off for the moon the following day. When the seatbelt light went off, Neil stood up and announced that he had a surprise for us. He opened a cupboard door in the command module, and out floated three gorgeous women, dressed in saucy underwear. He told me and Buzz that he picked them up at a party in Cape Canaveral the night before and asked them if they fancied a trip to the moon. How he managed to smuggle them aboard our rocket past tight NASA security, I'll never know. But I'm glad that he did.

We all had a gravity-free gang bang that I'll never forget as long as I live. All three of us had all the girls every way you could imagine, and thanks to the weightlessness, probably a few that you can't!

Halfway to the Moon, we received a worried call from Mission Control. They said that their navigation computers showed that the rocket was bouncing up and down on its trajectory like a kangaroo on a pogo stick. We told them that we were having trouble with the gyroscopes, but it was nothing we couldn't handle.

> **"All three of us had all the girls every way you could imagine, and thanks to the weightlessness, probably a few that you can't!"**

And it wasn't the only time, I can tell you. During that two-week mission, we had exactly the same trouble with the gyroscopes... about five times a day!"

Back on earth, Bannister's new found career as a spaceman ensured his success with the ladies. He dated a string of beauties, including Hollywood actresses, bra models and Miss Worlds. But NASA's 'no ladies' policy meant that space was officially still a 'sex-free zone'. Or so they thought.

"Later on in my career, I was posted to the orbiting space station Skylab

BANNISTER: *Offering ladies a stairway to heaven.*

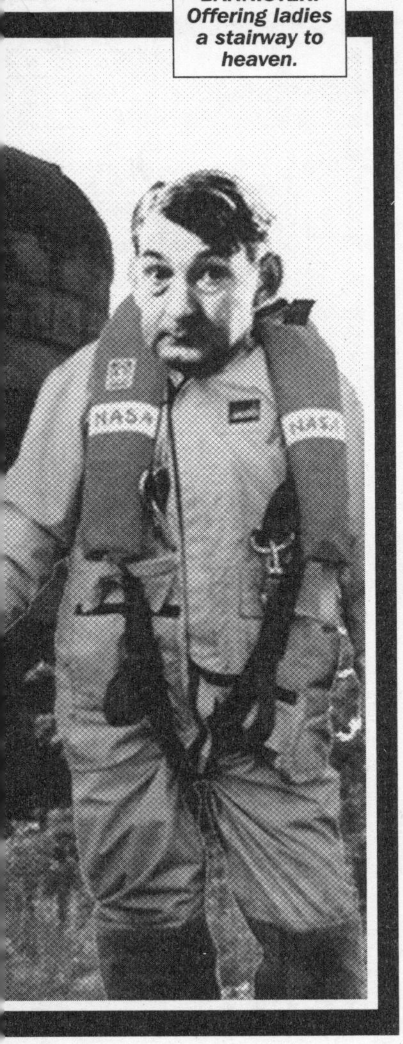

for four weeks. The rocket that took me there was very small and there was no way I could of smuggled any birds on board, so it looked like it was going to be a lonely, bonk-free month. However, on the first night, I went for a space walk outside the station and bumped into a couple of Russian lady cosmonauts who were out walking their space dog. We got chatting and I invited them back to Skylab for a nightcap.

Back on board, they explained how they'd been orbiting the Earth in their Sputnik for six months, and that they hadn't seen a man in all that time. I asked them how they passed the time, but they said that their English wasn't good enough to explain, so they'd show me instead.

My eyes nearly popped out of their orbits when they slowly peeled off their bulky space suits. And believe me, their underwear left *cosmonaut* to the imagination!

To cut a long story short, they put on a sizzling lesbian show that was made even more erotic because of being in the vacuum of space. After they had brought themselves to a pair of earth-shattering climaxes, they turned to me. "Remind us, comrade astronautski, what it is like to be with a man, da?" they said. As you can imagine, I didn't need asking twice, and within minutes I was parting their iron curtains.

They say that in space, no one can hear you scream. But let me tell you, I had no difficulty hearing their screams of ecstasy as I brought them to dizzy heights of sexual delirium again and again. Our interstellar love-in only came to an end when their dog Laika started scratching at the capsule door to go out for a shit."

Bannister became regular on the NASA missions and in the early 80s was promoted to starship commander. At the same time, the space agency finally gave way to pressure from feminists about their recruiting policy for the space programme.

"By this time, NASA were operating an equal opportunities policy, so they were sending birds into space too. It was a good move on their part, as it meant that we didn't have to go through the farce of smuggling girls on board the rockets. And I well remember the first time I was blasted into space with a bird. I had been chosen to drive a two man rocket to Mars to get some soil samples and I had been assigned a female co-pilot. Mars is about three weeks there and back, so I was quite excited. However, when she turned up, the first thing I noticed was that her tits were as flat as Saturn's rings. I was really disappointed.

But first and foremost I was an astronaut and I had a job to do, so I just got on with it.

However, when we landed on the red planet and climbed down onto the surface, I was in for a nice surprise. The atmosphere on Mars is only an eighth as strong as the earth's. This meant that as she stepped outside the rocket, my female co-pilot's knockers blew up to eight times their normal size!

"There was nothing I could do and I was stuck in the vinegar strokes... for three weeks!"

On Earth, her chest size was a paltry 28A tops, but on Mars she was a 38 double D at least, and then some. Giving way under the sudden expansion, her bra pinged off and landed on the front of my space helmet. I looked at her standing on Mars, admiring her newly ample charms, and I had never felt so randy.

And neither had she. Because unbeknownst to me, the atmosphere had had the same effect on my lunchbox, and she couldn't take her eyes off it. Needless to say, the soil sampling would have to wait. They call Mars the Red planet, but let me tell you, we were set to turn it BLUE that day!

We found a secluded crater, stripped off and were soon at it like knives. And it was then we got another surprise. We've all seen the shots of the astronauts bouncing on the moon where everything happens in slow motion - well bonking on Mars was just the same. Each push lasted twice as long as it would of done on earth, and our climaxes were twice as shattering. The only downside was, after I had shot my bolt, I had to wait 40 minutes to get a bone on again, twice as long as back on my home planet!"

"On Earth, her chest size was a paltry 28A tops, but on Mars she was a 38 double D at least!"

Rolf's sexploits in outer space are the kind of adventures most of us can only dream of. But on one occasion, something happened that left even a seasoned astronaut like Rolf scratching his head.

"I'd been asked to captain a space ship on a trip to another galaxy to look for some mineral or other, and my co pilot was a gorgeous blonde. The galaxy we were going to was so far away that it would have taken millions of years to get there, but I worked out that if I drove at the speed of light, we could get there in about three weeks.

Anyway, we blasted off, and we had just got out of the earth's atmosphere when my co-pilot asked me if I fancied a quickie. Well, I didn't need asking twice. I set the controls to auto pilot and we got down to business. It was a little cramped in the cockpit, but it was absolutely fantastic. She was a real stunner and I must admit that I got a bit excited.

In fact, I got a little over-excited, and as I approached the vinegar strokes, I lost control and my arse hit the throttle leaver on the dashboard. The rocket immediately shot into warp drive and we hit the speed of light.

Now I was never very good at physics when I was at school, but I did know that according to Albert Einstein, strange things happen at the speed of light. Space becomes curved and gravity gets all heavy. But the strangest thing is that time stands still! And that's exactly what happened. Outside, my rocket was hurtling through space at warp factor one. But inside, time was standing still. I looked at my watch and saw that it had stopped. There was nothing I could do and I was stuck in the vinegar strokes... for three weeks!

I don't need to tell you how frustrating it was being on the brink of orgasm for 21 days solid. When we finally reached our destination, the rocket slowed down, time started up again and I went off.

I must admit, I was relieved to say the least. The 'quickie' had turned into the longest bonk of my life and I was pretty exhausted. It was a really sexy experience, but one which I wouldn't want to repeat in a hurry."

In 2006, the space race ended and NASA began to make cutbacks. Rolf was kept on as a Space Shuttle pilot, but was eventually made redundant in 2009. He returned to Todmorden in Yorkshire and began work at his father's scrap metal business.

"My astronaut days were fun, but the Challenger disaster put paid to them," he says. "I miss going into space, but above all, I miss nookie amongst the stars. Believe me, once you've had it up there, nothing else will do." And undaunted, Bannister is planning to go back into space under his own steam to pursue his passion for interplanetary intercourse.

Using his knowledge of aeronautics and his contacts in the scrap metal industry, the former spaceman has constructed a 30-foot-long rocket which he says is capable of reaching space, orbiting the earth a couple of times and returning to his garden. And he has issued an open invitation to any women who want to experience sex in space.

"It's all kitted out inside with a mattress and a small fridge stocked with drinks," he says. "I haven't put any windows in it because, quite frankly, any lady will be having too good a time inside to want to look out. And it's so smooth a take off and landing, that she won't know it's moving."

"In fact, it will only be because the sex is so mind blowing that she'll know she's been in space."

Bannister plans to launch his rocket every Friday and Saturday night. "I hope to be having regular blasts off every weekend," he says. "Any lady who fancies a little trip into space should meet me outside The Jolly Boatman in Todmorden at about 11.30. The more the merrier."

NEXT WEEK Rolf and a Space Shuttle stewardess share a night of passion on Mercury... *where the nights are 115 days long!*

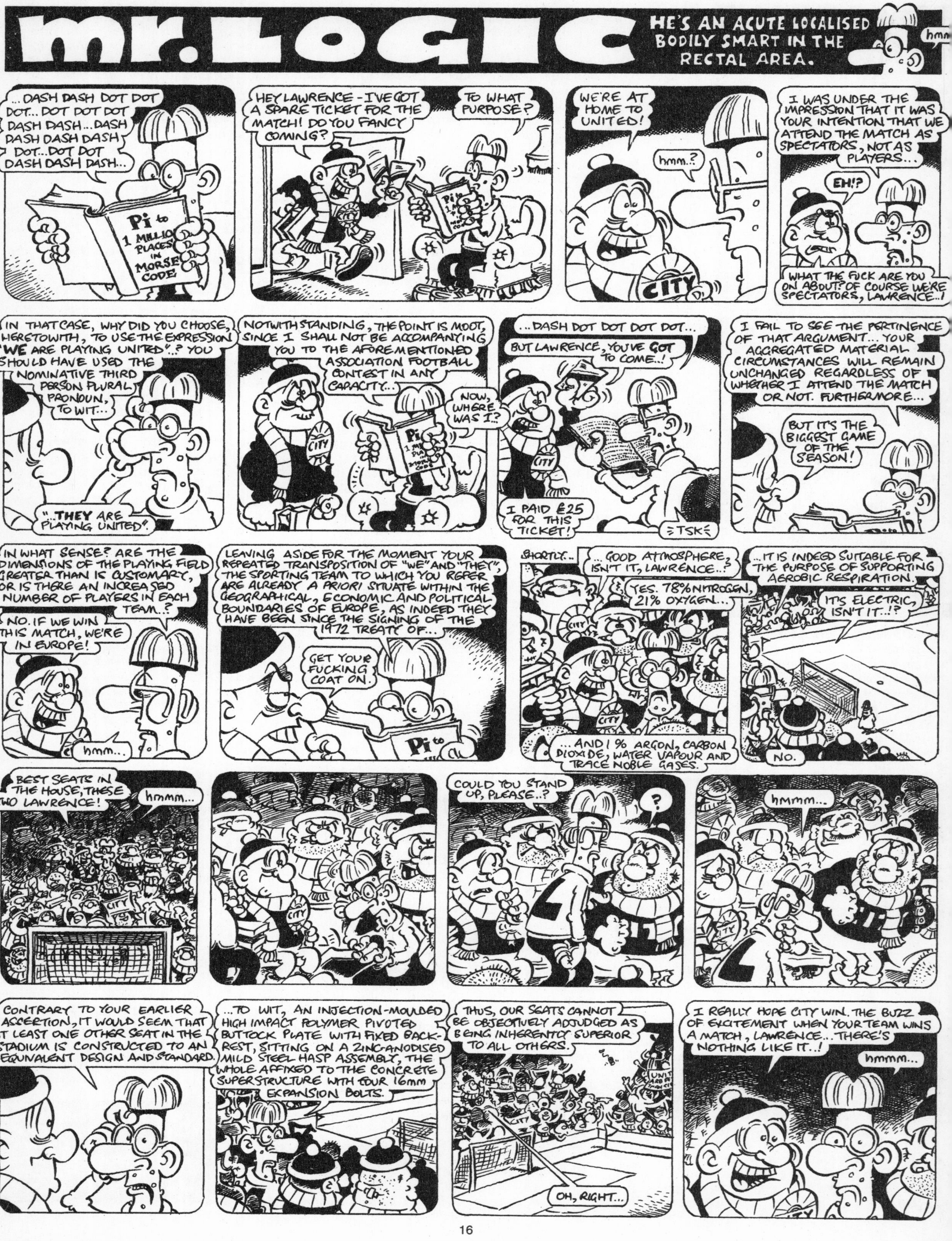
mr. LOGIC
HE'S AN ACUTE LOCALISED BODILY SMART IN THE RECTAL AREA.
hmm
...DASH DASH DOT DOT DOT... DOT DOT DOT DASH DASH...DASH DASH DASH DASH DOT...DOT DOT DASH DASH DASH...
Pi to 1 MILLION PLACES IN MORSE CODE
HEY LAWRENCE - I'VE GOT A SPARE TICKET FOR THE MATCH! DO YOU FANCY COMING?
TO WHAT PURPOSE?
WE'RE AT HOME TO UNITED!
hmm..?
CITY
I WAS UNDER THE IMPRESSION THAT IT WAS YOUR INTENTION THAT WE ATTEND THE MATCH AS SPECTATORS, NOT AS PLAYERS...
EH!?
WHAT THE FUCK ARE YOU ON ABOUT? OF COURSE WE'RE SPECTATORS, LAWRENCE..!
IN THAT CASE, WHY DID YOU CHOOSE, HERETOWITH, TO USE THE EXPRESSION "WE ARE PLAYING UNITED"..? YOU SHOULD HAVE USED THE NOMINATIVE THIRD PERSON PLURAL PRONOUN, TO WIT...
"..THEY ARE PLAYING UNITED".
NOTWITHSTANDING, THE POINT IS MOOT, SINCE I SHALL NOT BE ACCOMPANYING YOU TO THE AFOREMENTIONED ASSOCIATION FOOTBALL CONTEST IN ANY CAPACITY...
NOW, WHERE WAS I..?
...DASH DOT DOT DOT DOT...
BUT LAWRENCE, YOU'VE GOT TO COME..!
I PAID £25 FOR THIS TICKET!
TSK
I FAIL TO SEE THE PERTINENCE OF THAT ARGUMENT... YOUR AGGREGATED MATERIAL CIRCUMSTANCES WILL REMAIN UNCHANGED REGARDLESS OF WHETHER I ATTEND THE MATCH OR NOT. FURTHERMORE...
BUT IT'S THE BIGGEST GAME OF THE SEASON!
IN WHAT SENSE? ARE THE DIMENSIONS OF THE PLAYING FIELD GREATER THAN IS CUSTOMARY, OR IS THERE AN INCREASED NUMBER OF PLAYERS IN EACH TEAM..?
NO. IF WE WIN THIS MATCH, WE'RE IN EUROPE!
hmm...
LEAVING ASIDE FOR THE MOMENT YOUR REPEATED TRANSPOSITION OF "WE" AND "THEY", THE SPORTING TEAM TO WHICH YOU REFER ARE ALREADY A PRIORI SITUATE WITHIN THE GEOGRAPHICAL, ECONOMIC AND POLITICAL BOUNDARIES OF EUROPE, AS INDEED THEY HAVE BEEN SINCE THE SIGNING OF THE 1972 TREATY OF...
GET YOUR FUCKING COAT ON.
SHORTLY...
...GOOD ATMOSPHERE, ISN'T IT, LAWRENCE..?
YES. 78% NITROGEN, 21% OXYGEN...
...AND 1% ARGON, CARBON DIOXIDE, WATER VAPOUR AND TRACE NOBLE GASES.
...IT IS INDEED SUITABLE FOR THE PURPOSE OF SUPPORTING AEROBIC RESPIRATION.
IT'S ELECTRIC, ISN'T IT..!?
NO.
BEST SEATS IN THE HOUSE, THESE TWO LAWRENCE!
hmmm...
COULD YOU STAND UP, PLEASE..?
?
hmmm...
CONTRARY TO YOUR EARLIER ASSERTION, IT WOULD SEEM THAT AT LEAST ONE OTHER SEAT IN THE STADIUM IS CONSTRUCTED TO AN EQUIVALENT DESIGN AND STANDARD.
...TO WIT, AN INJECTION-MOULDED HIGH IMPACT POLYMER PIVOTED BUTTOCK PLATE WITH FIXED BACK-REST, SITTING ON A ZINC-ANODISED MILD STEEL HASP ASSEMBLY, THE WHOLE AFFIXED TO THE CONCRETE SUPERSTRUCTURE WITH FOUR 16mm EXPANSION BOLTS.
THUS, OUR SEATS CANNOT BE OBJECTIVELY ADJUDGED AS BEING INHERENTLY SUPERIOR TO ALL OTHERS.
OH, RIGHT...
I REALLY HOPE CITY WIN. THE BUZZ OF EXCITEMENT WHEN YOUR TEAM WINS A MATCH, LAWRENCE... THERE'S NOTHING LIKE IT..!
hmmm...

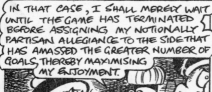

IN THAT CASE, I SHALL MERELY WAIT UNTIL THE GAME HAS TERMINATED BEFORE ASSIGNING MY NOTIONALLY PARTISAN ALLEGIANCE TO THE SIDE THAT HAS AMASSED THE GREATER NUMBER OF GOALS, THEREBY MAXIMISING MY ENJOYMENT.

NO, **NO**. IT DOESN'T WORK THAT WAY, LAWRENCE. THEY'RE **YOUR** TEAM, YOU SEE...

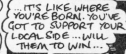

...IT'S LIKE WHERE YOU'RE BORN. YOU'VE GOT TO SUPPORT YOUR LOCAL SIDE...WILL THEM TO WIN...

ERM...

...OOH, LOOK-THEY'RE ABOUT TO KICK OFF!

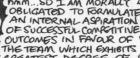

HMM...SO I AM MORALLY OBLIGATED TO FORMULATE AN INTERNAL ASPIRATION OF SUCCESSFUL COMPETITIVE OUTCOMES IN FAVOUR OF THE TEAM WHICH EXHIBITS THE GREATEST DEGREE OF GEOGRAPHICAL PROXIMITY TO THE LOCUS OF THE POINT WHERE I EXITED MY MOTHER'S VAGINA..?

♪ PHEEP! ♪

COME ON! COME ON THE LADS!

SEND IT! PLAY IT WIDE!

FUCKIN' COME ON!

TAKE HIM ON! ...THAT'S IT..! PULL THE TRIGGER...! GO ON... **GO ON..!**

DOOOH! JESUS! HOW DID HE MISS THAT..!?

HARD LUCK, CITY! STRAIGHT BACK ON IT!

FUCKIN' **COME ON!** GET IT SORTED!

COME ON, LAWRENCE DON'T SIT THERE LIKE A TWAT... JOIN IN, MAN!

IN WHAT SENSE..?

WELL, IF CITY LOOK LIKE SCORING, SHOUT OUT SOME ENCOURAGEMENT! TELL 'EM WHAT TO DO!

HMMM...

♪ PHEEEP! ♪

PENALTY TO CITY!

YESSS!

THIS IS IT, LAWRENCE! ONE-NIL TO US HERE, YOU JUST WATCH..!

HUSH!

♪ PEEEP! ♪

COME ON! ENDEAVOUR TO DIRECT THE BALL IN AN ACCURATE MANNER TOWARDS A PARTICULAR PART OF THE DESIGNATED SCORING AREA WHILST SIMULTANEOUSLY LEADING THE OPPOSING GOALKEEPER TO INFER THAT YOUR DIRECTIONAL INTENTIONS FOR THE BALL ARE DIAMETRICALLY CONTRARY TO THE ACTUALITY..!

SPOON!

!?

..AND FURTHERMORE, DO YOUR UTMOST TO CONTINUE SO TO DO THROUGHOUT THE DESIGNATED PLAYING PERIOD, WITH THE AIM OF AMASSING A TALLY OF GOALS THAT IS NUMERICALLY SUPERIOR TO THAT OF YOUR OPPOSING COUNTERPARTS..!

NER! NER! NER! NER!

LOOKS LIKE HE WAS RIGHT AFTER ALL, EH LAWRENCE..?

FUCKING AMBULANCE

ON THE CONTRARY...

YOU'RE GOING HOME IN A FUCKIN' AMBULANCE, PAL...

HMM...YOUR ASSERTION IS FACTUALLY INACCURATE...

I SHALL, IN FACT, BE RETURNING TO MY PLACE OF DOMICILE VIA THE MUNICIPAL PUBLIC TRANSPORT NETWORK, TO WIT...

MY ASSAILANT VOUCHSAFED THAT I WAS GOING **HOME** IN A FUCKING AMBULANCE, WHEREAS MY ACTUAL DESTINATION IN THIS VEHICLE IS THE SEVERE TRAUMA UNIT OF FULCHESTER GENERAL INFIRMARY...

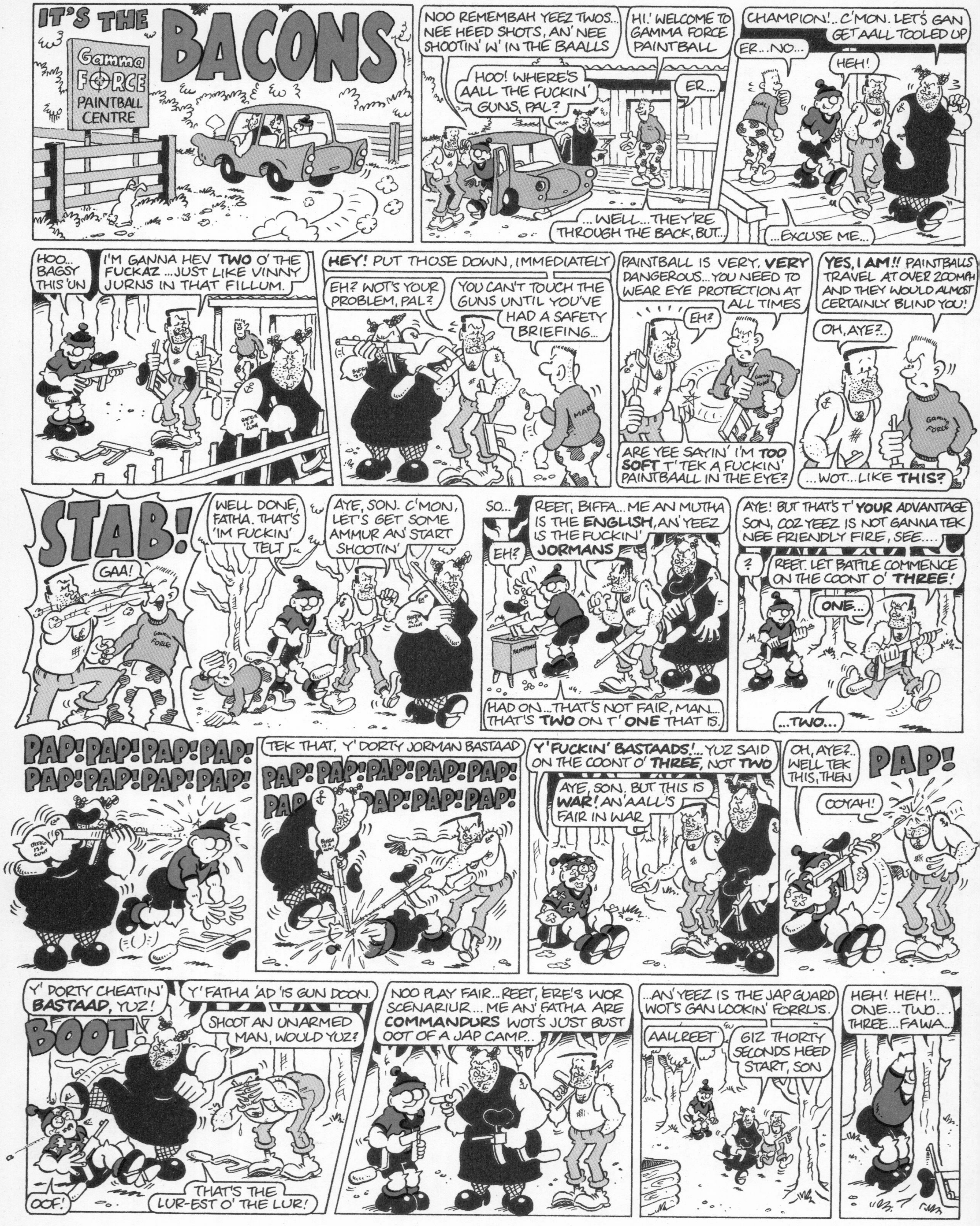
IT'S THE BACONS
Gamma FORCE PAINTBALL CENTRE
NOO REMEMBAH YEEZ TWOS... NEE HEED SHOTS, AN' NEE SHOOTIN' W' IN THE BAALLS
HI! WELCOME TO GAMMA FORCE PAINTBALL
HOO! WHERE'S AALL THE FUCKIN' GUNS, PAL?
ER...
...WELL... THEY'RE THROUGH THE BACK, BUT...
CHAMPION!... C'MON. LET'S GAN GET AALL TOOLED UP
ER... NO...
HEH!
...EXCUSE ME...
HOO... BAGSY THIS 'UN
I'M GANNA HEV TWO O' THE FUCKAZ ... JUST LIKE VINNY JURNS IN THAT FILLUM.
HEY! PUT THOSE DOWN, IMMEDIATELY
EH? WOT'S YOUR PROBLEM, PAL?
YOU CAN'T TOUCH THE GUNS UNTIL YOU'VE HAD A SAFETY BRIEFING...
PAINTBALL IS VERY, VERY DANGEROUS... YOU NEED TO WEAR EYE PROTECTION AT ALL TIMES
EH?
ARE YEE SAYIN' I'M TOO SOFT T' TEK A FUCKIN' PAINTBAALL IN THE EYE?
YES, I AM!! PAINTBALLS TRAVEL AT OVER 200MPH AND THEY WOULD ALMOST CERTAINLY BLIND YOU!
OH, AYE?..
...WOT... LIKE THIS?
STAB!
GAA!
WELL DONE, FATHA. THAT'S 'IM FUCKIN' TELT
AYE, SON. C'MON, LET'S GET SOME AMMUR AN' START SHOOTIN'
SO...
REET, BIFFA... ME AN MUTHA IS THE ENGLISH, AN' YEEZ IS THE FUCKIN' JORMANS
EH?
HAD ON... THAT'S NOT FAIR, MAN... THAT'S TWO ON T' ONE THAT IS.
AYE! BUT THAT'S T' YOUR ADVANTAGE SON, COZ YEEZ IS NOT GANNA TEK NEE FRIENDLY FIRE, SEE....
?
REET. LET BATTLE COMMENCE ON THE COONT O' THREE!
ONE...
...TWO...
PAP! PAP! PAP! PAP! PAP! PAP! PAP! PAP!
TEK THAT, Y' DORTY JORMAN BASTAAD
PAP! PAP! PAP! PAP! PAP! PAP! PAP! PAP! PAP!
Y' FUCKIN' BASTAADS!... YUZ SAID ON THE COONT O' THREE, NOT TWO
AYE, SON. BUT THIS IS WAR! AN' AALL'S FAIR IN WAR
OH, AYE?.. WELL TEK THIS, THEN
PAP!
OOYAH!
Y' DORTY CHEATIN' BASTAAD, YUZ!
BOOT
Y' FATHA 'AD 'IS GUN DOON.
SHOOT AN UNARMED MAN, WOULD YUZ?
OOF!
THAT'S THE LUR-EST O' THE LUR!
NOO PLAY FAIR... REET, ERE'S WOR SCENARIUR... ME AN' FATHA ARE COMMANDURS WOT'S JUST BUST OOT OF A JAP CAMP...
...AN' YEEZ IS THE JAP GUARD WOT'S GAN LOOKIN' FORRUS.
AALLREET
GIZ THORTY SECONDS HEED START, SON
HEH! HEH!.. ONE... TWO... THREE... FAWA...

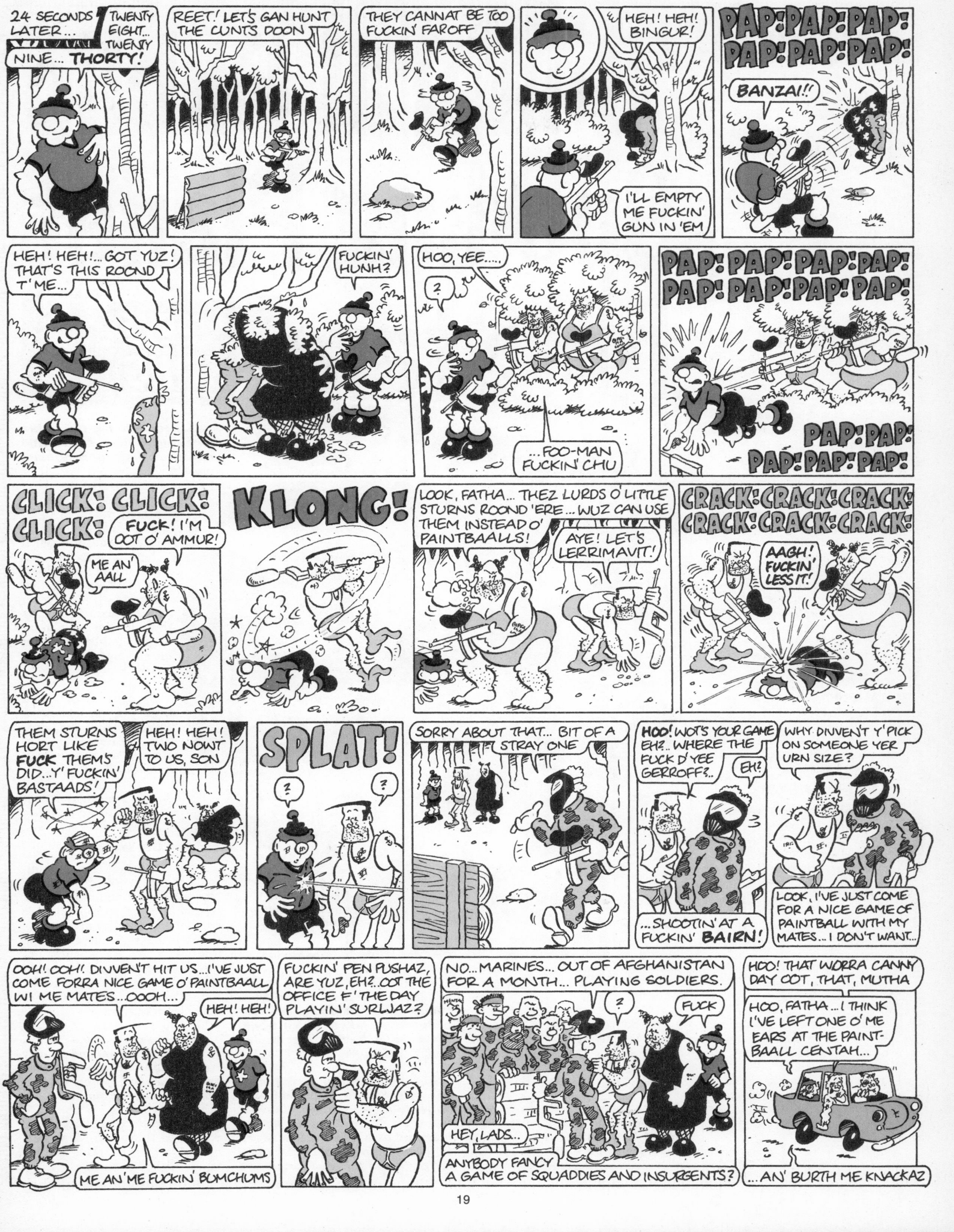
24 SECONDS LATER...
TWENTY EIGHT... TWENTY NINE... THORTY!
REET! LET'S GAN HUNT THE CUNTS DOON
THEY CANNAT BE TOO FUCKIN' FAR OFF
HEH! HEH! BINGUR!
I'LL EMPTY ME FUCKIN' GUN IN 'EM
PAP! PAP! PAP! PAP! PAP! PAP! PAP!
BANZAI!!
HEH! HEH!... GOT YUZ! THAT'S THIS ROOND T'ME...
FUCKIN' HUNH?
HOO, YEE.....
?
...FOO-MAN FUCKIN' CHU
PAP! PAP! PAP! PAP! PAP! PAP! PAP! PAP!
PAP! PAP! PAP! PAP! PAP!
CLICK! CLICK! CLICK!
FUCK! I'M OOT O' AMMUR!
ME AN' AALL
KLONG!
LOOK, FATHA... THEZ LURDS O' LITTLE STURNS ROOND 'ERE... WUZ CAN USE THEM INSTEAD O' PAINTBAALLS!
AYE! LET'S LERRIMAVIT!
CRACK! CRACK! CRACK! CRACK! CRACK! CRACK!
AAGH! FUCKIN' LESS IT!
THEM STURNS HORT LIKE FUCK THEM'S DID... Y' FUCKIN' BASTAADS!
HEH! HEH! TWO NOWT TO US, SON
SPLAT!
?
?
SORRY ABOUT THAT... BIT OF A STRAY ONE
HOO! WOT'S YOUR GAME EH?.. WHERE THE FUCK D'YEE GERROFF?..
EH?
...SHOOTIN' AT A FUCKIN' BAIRN!
WHY DIVVEN'T Y' PICK ON SOMEONE YER URN SIZE?
LOOK, I'VE JUST COME FOR A NICE GAME OF PAINTBALL WITH MY MATES... I DON'T WANT...
OOH! OOH! DIVVEN'T HIT US... I'VE JUST COME FORRA NICE GAME O' PAINTBAALL WI ME MATES... OOOH...
HEH! HEH!
ME AN' ME FUCKIN' BUMCHUMS
FUCKIN' PEN PUSHAZ, ARE YUZ, EH?.. OOT THE OFFICE F' THE DAY PLAYIN' SORJAZ?
NO... MARINES... OUT OF AFGHANISTAN FOR A MONTH... PLAYING SOLDIERS.
?
FUCK
HEY, LADS...
ANYBODY FANCY A GAME OF SQUADDIES AND INSURGENTS?
HOO! THAT WORRA CANNY DAY OOT, THAT, MUTHA
HOO, FATHA... I THINK I'VE LEFT ONE O' ME EARS AT THE PAINT-BAALL CENTAH...
...AN' BURTH ME KNACKAZ

'General Public Spoiling Planet for Stars' ~ says STING

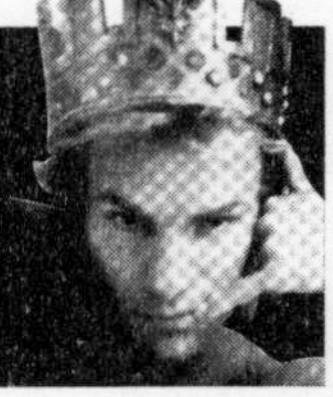

ENVIRONMENTAL campaigner STING has launched an attack on people who squander the earth's resources with no thought for the effects of their actions on celebs.

According to the musician, housing projects, industrial developments and roads have urbanised the British landscape, spoiling the view for megastars from the worlds of music, film and television.

GREEN

"Not too long ago, I could look out of the window of any of my enormous houses and see nothing but rolling green fields and woodland," said the 58-year-old former Police frontman. "Now, due to the selfishness and ignorance of the British public, I can see the roofs of a couple of houses in the distance from one of my turrets," he added.

"I have a dreadful fear that if things go on unchecked, my children will grow up in a world where two or three houses will be visible on the far horizon, using powerful binoculars," he continued.

Sting, real name Gordon O'Dowd, was addressing the Rio de Janiero S20 Summit, a gathering of the world's 20 biggest celebrities. A glittering array of A-listers including ***BONO***, ***GEORGE CLOONEY***, ***MADONNA*** and ***BRAD PITT*** listened to the Geordie lute-enthusiast as he outlined his plans for a sustainable future for the planet's megastars.

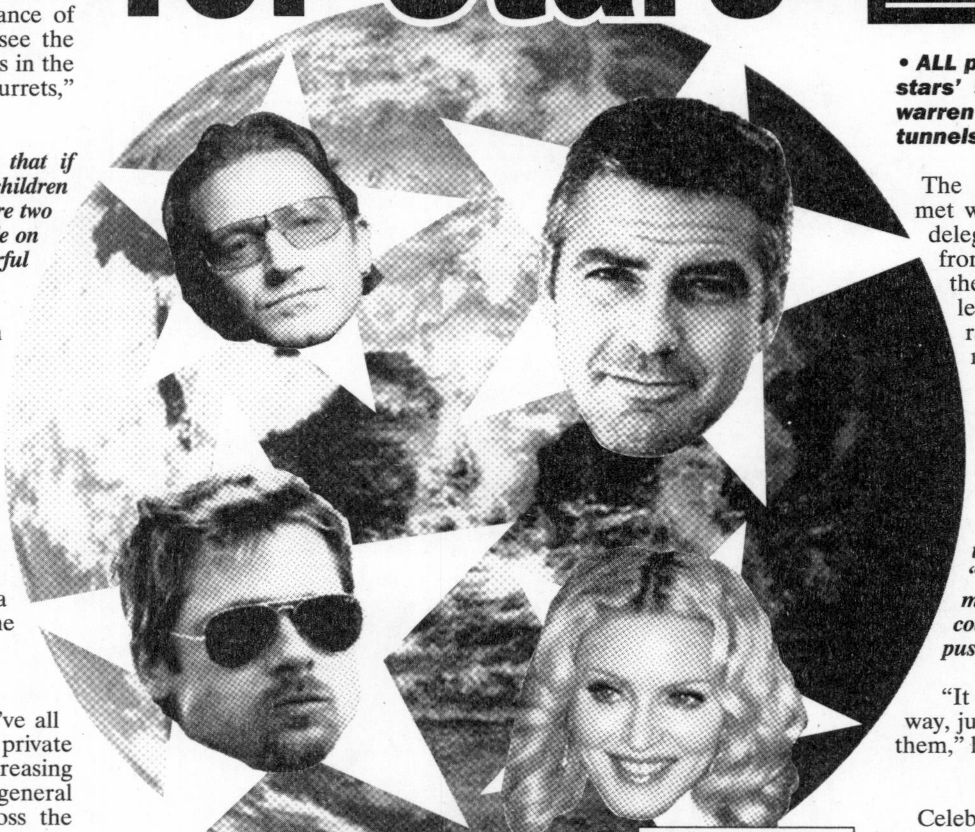

BLAME IT ON RIO: *Top stars were attending summit in Brazilian capital..*

NIAL JINKS

He told delegates: "We've all looked down from our private jets and seen the ever-increasing sprawl of suburbia. The general public are spreading across the face of the planet like a cancer, building dismal little houses to live in and offices and shops to work in. What right do they have to impose their buildings on our views?"

"It's arrogance of the worst sort," he added.

And the rocker-turned-environmentalist painted a picture of a bleak future for his fellow glitterati: "If things go on the way they are, by the end of this decade we will be virtually living cheek-by-jowl with non-celebrities," he said.

"We will be forced to smell their Findus Crispy Pancakes cooking every evening, and we will have no choice but to see cheap, supermarket clothes flapping on their washing lines. We have to act now or it will be too late. We are teetering on the brink of an abyss," he warned.

The pop legend, whose hits include *An Englishman in New York* and *De Do Do Do, De Da Da Da*, outlined a 10-point plan to rescue the planet for the stars, including:

- ***UGLY housing estates, industrial sites and towns to be bulldozed and turned into forests, populated with endangered species such as koala bears, parrots and white rhionoceroses***
- ***PROVINCIAL cities such as Birmingham, Manchester and Newcastle to be flooded, creating picturesque lakes, which would serve as a habitat for whales and dolphins***
- ***ALL roads to be turfed over to discourage unnecessary non-celebrity journeys. Current transport infrastructure to be replaced with a network of tastefully-landscaped helicopter landing pads and private jet runways***
- ***ALL people to live out of the stars' sight in a nationwide warren of dark, underground tunnels***

The controversial measures met with approval from other delegates at the summit. U2 front-twat Bono welcomed the plans to force non-celebrities to live a subterranean existence. He told reporters: "It may seem a little draconian, but it's the only way to guarantee a beautiful world for me and my fellow stars to enjoy."

"I don't know what they'd eat," he continued. "Probably soil and dead moles, like worms do. They could even eat each other if push came to shove."

"It doesn't really matter anyway, just as long as we can't see them," he added.

TOM MORLEY

Celebrity expert Boyd Pointless, editor of *Heat* magazine, also gave the thumbs-up to the scheme. "Sting's proposals are contentious, but they're definitely a step in the right direction," he told us. "If we are going to ensure a picturesque, idyllic world for our megastars to enjoy in the future, we're all going to have to make sacrifices now."

"If that means going to live underground, eating soil and possibly becoming a blind cannibal, then that's a price that I for one am prepared to pay," he continued.

"We have to remember that we don't own this world, we merely hold it in trust for Sting and his famous pals," he added.

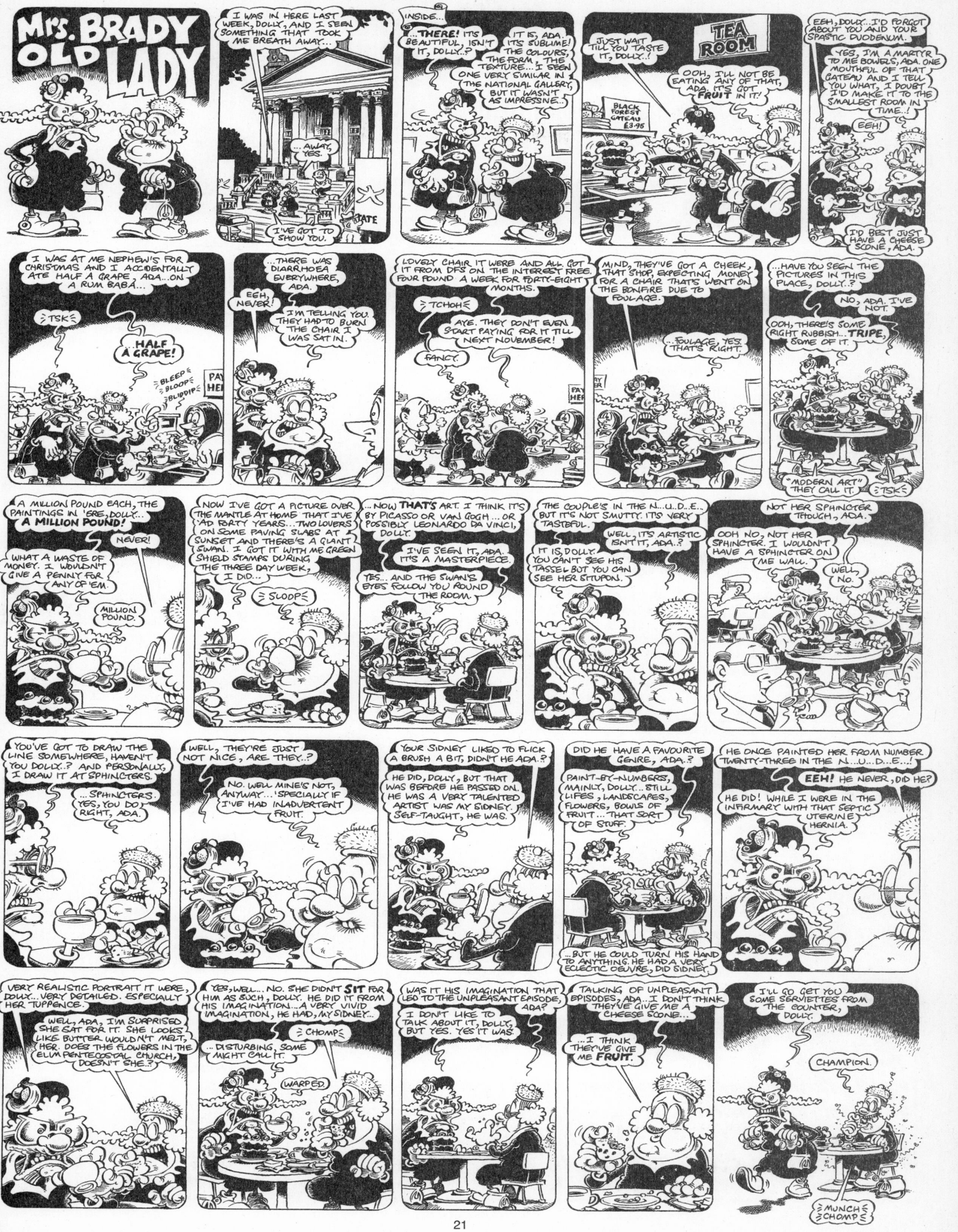
Mrs. BRADY OLD LADY
I WAS IN HERE LAST WEEK, DOLLY, AND I SEEN SOMETHING THAT TOOK ME BREATH AWAY...
...AWAY, YES.
I'VE GOT TO SHOW YOU.
INSIDE...
...THERE! IT'S BEAUTIFUL, ISN'T IT, DOLLY..?
IT IS, ADA. IT'S SUBLIME! THE COLOURS, THE FORM, THE TEXTURE... I SEEN ONE VERY SIMILAR IN THE NATIONAL GALLERY, BUT IT WASN'T AS IMPRESSIVE...
TEA ROOM
JUST WAIT TILL YOU TASTE IT, DOLLY..!
OOH, I'LL NOT BE EATING ANY OF THAT, ADA. IT'S GOT FRUIT IN IT!
BLACK FOREST GATEAU £3.95
EEH, DOLLY... I'D FORGOT ABOUT YOU AND YOUR SPASTIC DUODENUM.
YES, I'M A MARTYR TO ME BOWELS, ADA. ONE MOUTHFUL OF THAT GATEAU AND I TELL YOU WHAT, I DOUBT I'D MAKE IT TO THE SMALLEST ROOM IN TIME..!
EEH!
I'D BEST JUST HAVE A CHEESE SCONE, ADA.
I WAS AT ME NEPHEW'S FOR CHRISTMAS AND I ACCIDENTALLY ATE HALF A GRAPE, ADA... ON A RUM BABA...
TSK
...HALF A GRAPE!
BLEEP BLOOP BLIDDIP
...THERE WAS DIARRHOEA EVERYWHERE, ADA.
EEH, NEVER!
I'M TELLING YOU. THEY HAD TO BURN THE CHAIR I WAS SAT IN.
LOVELY CHAIR IT WERE AND ALL. GOT IT FROM DFS ON THE INTEREST FREE. FOUR POUND A WEEK FOR FORTY-EIGHT MONTHS.
TCHOH
AYE. THEY DON'T EVEN START PAYING FOR IT TILL NEXT NOVEMBER!
FANCY.
MIND, THEY'VE GOT A CHEEK, THAT SHOP, EXPECTING MONEY FOR A CHAIR THAT'S WENT ON THE BONFIRE DUE TO FOULAGE.
...FOULAGE, YES. THAT'S RIGHT.
...HAVE YOU SEEN THE PICTURES IN THIS PLACE, DOLLY..?
NO, ADA. I'VE NOT.
OOH, THERE'S SOME RIGHT RUBBISH... TRIPE, SOME OF IT.
"MODERN ART" THEY CALL IT.
TSK
A MILLION POUND EACH, THE PAINTINGS IN 'ERE, DOLLY... A MILLION POUND!
NEVER!
WHAT A WASTE OF MONEY. I WOULDN'T GIVE A PENNY FOR ANY OF 'EM.
MILLION POUND.
NOW I'VE GOT A PICTURE OVER THE MANTLE AT HOME THAT I'VE 'AD FORTY YEARS... TWO LOVERS ON SOME PAVING SLABS AT SUNSET AND THERE'S A GIANT SWAN. I GOT IT WITH ME GREEN SHIELD STAMPS DURING THE THREE DAY WEEK, I DID...
SLOOP
...NOW THAT'S ART. I THINK IT'S BY PICASSO OR VAN GOGH... OR POSSIBLY LEONARDO DA VINCI, DOLLY.
I'VE SEEN IT, ADA. IT'S A MASTERPIECE.
YES... AND THE SWAN'S EYES FOLLOW YOU ROUND THE ROOM.
THE COUPLE'S IN THE N...U...D...E... BUT IT'S NOT SMUTTY. IT'S VERY TASTEFUL.
WELL, IT'S ARTISTIC ISN'T IT, ADA..?
IT IS, DOLLY. YOU CAN'T SEE HIS TASSEL BUT YOU CAN SEE HER SITUPON.
NOT HER SPHINCTER THOUGH, ADA.
OOH NO, NOT HER SPHINCTER. I WOULDN'T HAVE A SPHINCTER ON ME WALL.
WELL, NO.
YOU'VE GOT TO DRAW THE LINE SOMEWHERE, HAVEN'T YOU DOLLY..? AND PERSONALLY, I DRAW IT AT SPHINCTERS.
...SPHINCTERS. YES, YOU DO RIGHT, ADA.
WELL, THEY'RE JUST NOT NICE, ARE THEY..?
NO. WELL MINE'S NOT, ANYWAY... 'SPECIALLY IF I'VE HAD INADVERTENT FRUIT.
YOUR SIDNEY LIKED TO FLICK A BRUSH A BIT, DIDN'T HE ADA..?
HE DID, DOLLY, BUT THAT WAS BEFORE HE PASSED ON. HE WAS A VERY TALENTED ARTIST WAS MY SIDNEY. SELF-TAUGHT, HE WAS.
DID HE HAVE A FAVOURITE GENRE, ADA..?
PAINT-BY-NUMBERS, MAINLY, DOLLY... STILL LIFES, LANDSCAPES, FLOWERS, BOWLS OF FRUIT... THAT SORT OF STUFF.
...BUT HE COULD TURN HIS HAND TO ANYTHING. HE HAD A VERY ECLECTIC OEUVRE, DID SIDNEY.
HE ONCE PAINTED HER FROM NUMBER TWENTY-THREE IN THE N...U...D...E...!
EEH! HE NEVER, DID HE?
HE DID! WHILE I WERE IN THE INFIRMARY WITH THAT SEPTIC UTERINE HERNIA.
VERY REALISTIC PORTRAIT IT WERE, DOLLY... VERY DETAILED. ESPECIALLY HER TUPPENCE.
WELL, ADA, I'M SURPRISED SHE SAT FOR IT. SHE LOOKS LIKE BUTTER WOULDN'T MELT, HER. DOES THE FLOWERS IN THE ELIM PENTECOSTAL CHURCH, DOESN'T SHE..?
YES, WELL... NO. SHE DIDN'T SIT FOR HIM AS SUCH, DOLLY. HE DID IT FROM HIS IMAGINATION... A VERY VIVID IMAGINATION, HE HAD, MY SIDNEY...
CHOMP
...DISTURBING, SOME MIGHT CALL IT.
WARPED.
WAS IT HIS IMAGINATION THAT LED TO THE UNPLEASANT EPISODE, ADA?
I DON'T LIKE TO TALK ABOUT IT, DOLLY, BUT YES. YES IT WAS.
TALKING OF UNPLEASANT EPISODES, ADA... I DON'T THINK THEY'VE GIVE ME A CHEESE SCONE...
...I THINK THEY'VE GIVE ME FRUIT.
I'LL GO GET YOU SOME SERVIETTES FROM THE COUNTER, DOLLY.
CHAMPION.
MUNCH CHOMP

Letterbocks

...viz Comic, PO Box 841, Whitley Bay, NE26 9EQ ...e-mail letters@viz.co.uk

ST★R LETTER

AS A DEVOUT Christian with an unshakeable faith in God and His Eternal Kingdom of Heaven, what a delight it is to contemplate the afterlife. Upon my demise, I'll never again have to look at my missus's crabbit old hatchet face nor listen to her incessant whinging and moaning. 'Til Death Do Us Part' was the deal we made at the altar, and I won't be renewing that contract at the Pearly Gates, I can tell you.

Bert Trautman, e-mail

I GET tired of your magazine constantly having a go at pop star Bono, so I want to be the first to write in and stand up for him. Alright, he's an utter twat with a high opinion of himself and a bit of a shortarse, but come on. Give the man a break.

M Plywod, Rhyll

AMID all the tragedy and horror that the eartquake in Haiti has caused, it was heartwarming to see that a visiting group of Christian Missionaries were safe and sound. Although shocked, it was a relief to discover they felt well enough to leave Haiti for home on the first plane. Their comments that they were 'leaving in body, but not in spirit' must have been a great comfort to those left behind.

Christian Barnyard, Totnes

COULD I just say thank you to the young man who picked up my shopping and helped me to my feet when I slipped on some ice in the recent cold weather.

Ethel Acetate, Surrey

I USED to think that Stephen Fry looked awful when he was all fat, bloated and unhealthy looking. So I was delighted to hear last year that he had sorted out his diet and started taking exercise. To his credit, he shed

six-and-a-half stones, but unfortunately, I think that he now looks all gaunt and unwell. Perhaps he should try being a weight somewhere between the two so I can see if that looks any better.

Florado Mybridge, Stanford

ACCORDING to Lance Armstrong's autobiography, 'it's not about the bike.' While there may be some truth in that, I would like to have seen him try to win five Tour de Frances on a Raleigh Chopper.

Craig W, e-mail

I WOULD like to say a big thank you to the gentleman who helped me after I slipped on some ice and smashed my pelvis during the recent cold snap. He even waited with me until the ambulance arrived.

Edna Sodium, Corbridge

I NOTICED on my bottle of shampoo the instructions 'lather, rinse, repeat.' Could somebody please tell me when I should stop, only I've been washing my hair for about three weeks now. Surely it must be clean.

Alex Freak, e-mail

WITH BEES nearing extinction, wouldn't it be nice if wasps cleaned up their act a bit and took over the honey-making duties?

Ed O'Meara, e-mail

I SAT down with my family last night to watch a film called *British Bukkake Babes*, and I have to say, we didn't laugh once.

R Tarpaulin, e-mail

I DON'T know much about art, but I know what I like - cheese and onion sandwiches, football and brass bands.

Major A Hepscott-Whyte, York

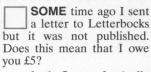

SOME time ago I sent a letter to Letterbocks but it was not published. Does this mean that I owe you £5?

Andy Cross, Australia

✱ *Yes, Andy, but the £5 from your letter enquiring about it cancels it out. Any other readers who have failed to have letter printed in Letterbocks should send £5 per letter to the usual address. Mark your envelope 'Letterbocks Non Publication Fee.'*

WE ARE led to believe that if the polar ice-caps were to melt, the sea would rise and flood half of Britain. But when we and half of Europe were under two feet of snow and ice, did the sea levels go down? No. I for one would like these so-called experts to explain that one.

S MacRat, e-mail

MY FAVOURITE painting is that one of the bloke with his ear cut off. And I like the one of the old-fashioned cart stuck in the canal as well, because it's dead realistic.

Brian Sewell, London

COULD I say a big thank you to the man who called the emergency services when I died after slipping on some ice and cracking my skull on the kerb. It's nice to see that there are some gentlemen still around in this day and age.

Doris Salts, Leeds

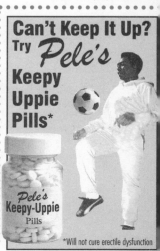
22

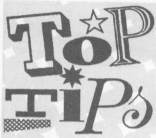

TOP TIPS

A WARM stream of piss makes an excellent lightsabre for slaying snowmen who have fallen to the dark side.

Adrian Garford, e-mail

MOTHS dipped in lighter fuel and released into a room lit by candles suspended from the ceiling make an effective and inexpensive indoor firework display.

Mike Y, e-mail

AMATEUR pool players. Appear more skilfull than you actually are by grimacing and sounding disappointed after every misplaced shot.

Andrew Fox, e-mail

GREEN pet owners. The filter from a tipped cigarette when shoved up a cat's arse makes an ideal 'catalytic converter' to remove the environmentally harmful methane from their farts.

Stu Mandry, e-mail

HOMEOWNERS. When going upstairs, walk up two and then back one. That way your neighbours will think you have more stairs than them.

Hiapop, e-mail

MEN. When asked by your wife "do you prefer this one... or this one?" simply choose any outfit at random because she won't pay any attention to your decision. It'll just be a complete waste of your fucking time.

J Wipp, Australia

WOMEN. Discourage men from looking at your breasts by wearing a skirt short enough to see your knickers.

Dick Swindles, e-mail

POLICE officers on ITV's The Bill. Avoid giving suspect criminals a 100-yard head start by not shouting "Oi!" when you see them at that distance.

Berry, e-mail

LIAM Gallagher. When singing, lower the microphone a bit so as it's in front of your mouth. This will prevent any unnecessary neck strain. How you could stop being a cunt, though, is beyond me, I'm afraid.

Gary Parslow, e-mail

PREVENT the inconvenience of waiting for energy saving fluorescent lightbulbs to brighten up by simply leaving them switched on all the time.

Matt Salisbury, e-mail

OFFICE party goers. Impress your colleagues when photocopying your genitals by setting the machine to enlarge by 400%. This works for men only, as the results are less impressive for women.

Eskimo Pope, e-mail

GIVE your kitchen a more spacious feel by putting a pile of sprouts at one end and pretending they are far-off cabbages.

Louis Lawson, Croydon

FOOL your neighbours into believing you somehow run a private harbour or port by blowing a low A on a baritone saxophone every 15 minutes and emitting high-pitched squeals to emulate seagulls.

Gregory Reuland, e-mail

BINGE drinking seems to be getting out of control in Britain. Why don't the government encourage people to slow down and enjoy their favourite tipples more consistently over a longer period of time? They could take advantage of the normally unpopular drinking hours of the morning and early afternoon.

John Paul Des, e-mail

GEORGE Michael recently said he was embarrassed about the hooped earings he wore in the 80s. Which when compared to being caught by a *News of the World* reporter sucking off a tramp on Hampstead Heath doesn't seem so bad.

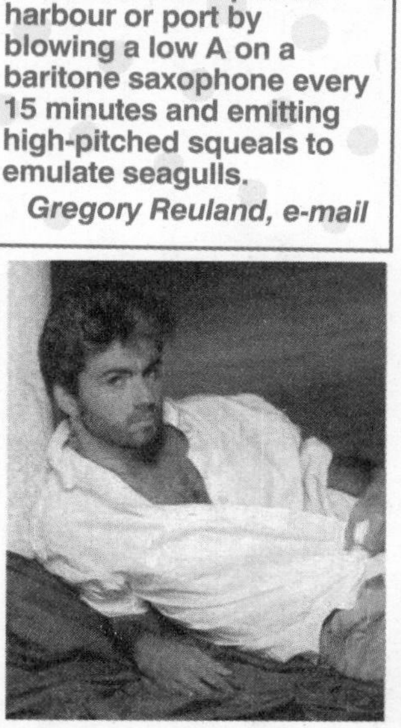

Paul Richards, Sussex

CONSTIPATION STREET No. 6

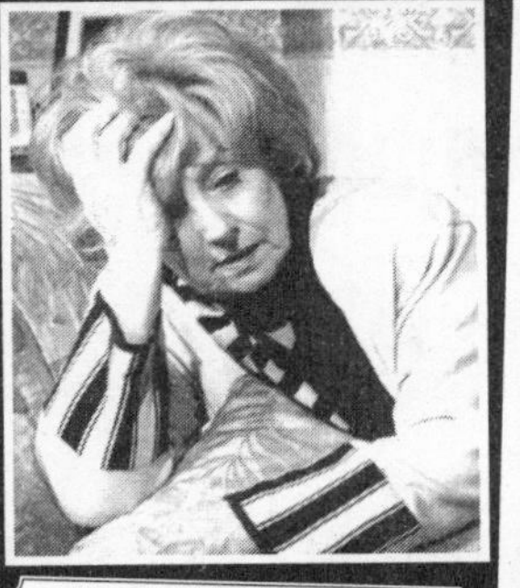

RITA FAIRCLOUGH
14 boiled eggs and a treacle tart.

IF THE waitress at the Ashworth High Street Pizza Hut is reading this, could she come over and take my order? Only she's given me a massive bone on and I couldn't possibly hazard a walk up to the counter in my present condition.

Todjer Andrews, e-mail

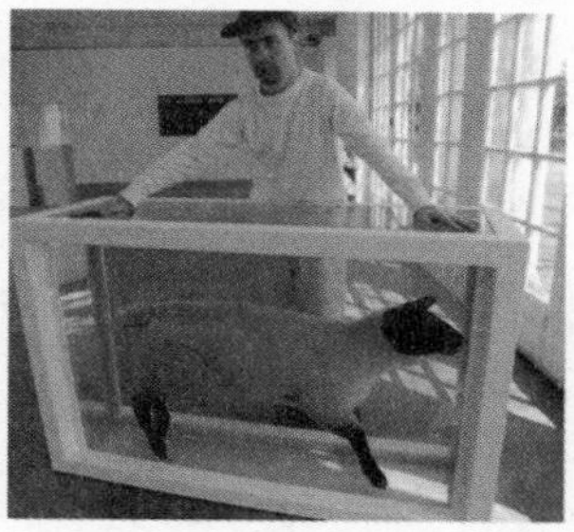

HE CLAIMS to be an artist, but I bet Damien Hirst can't draw the back legs of a horse. I don't think anybody should be allowed to call themselves an artist unless they can draw the back legs of a horse.

P M Cafferty, Yeovil

DO ANY of your readers, like me, reckon that Hobbits probably have really thick cocks? It is certainly never alluded to in *The Lord of the Rings* trilogy, it's just something I feel to be true.

Umberto Bongo, Congo

WHY ON earth do we only send Christmas cards in December? I think we should send them in June or July as well. It would give everyone some much-needed festive cheer.

Tommy Robinson, e-mail

I'VE just seen an advert for Magnet asking customers to tell them what happens in their kitchen. I don't know how telling them that my pet rabbit tries to shag the cat while it's eating will help them design a kitchen, but I'm willing to give it a go.

Jum, e-mail

WHILST dining at my local greasy spoon cafe recently I noticed (once again) what appeared to be the face of Jesus Christ in a Marmite lid. What a fool I felt as the waiter (once again) pointed out out my mistake-it was actually ex-Everton and Birmingham City footballer Bob Latchford.

S Porter, Merseyside

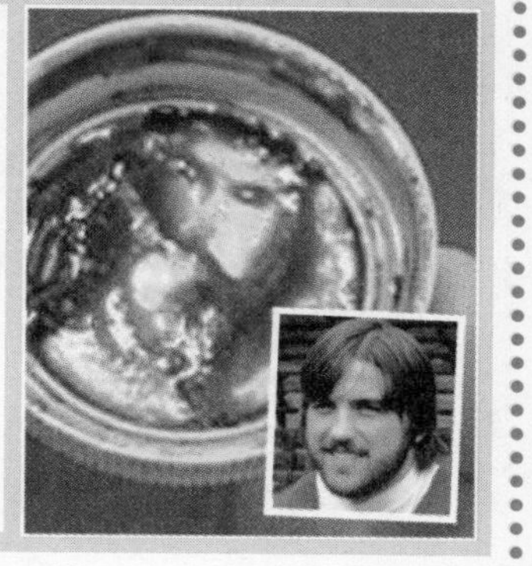

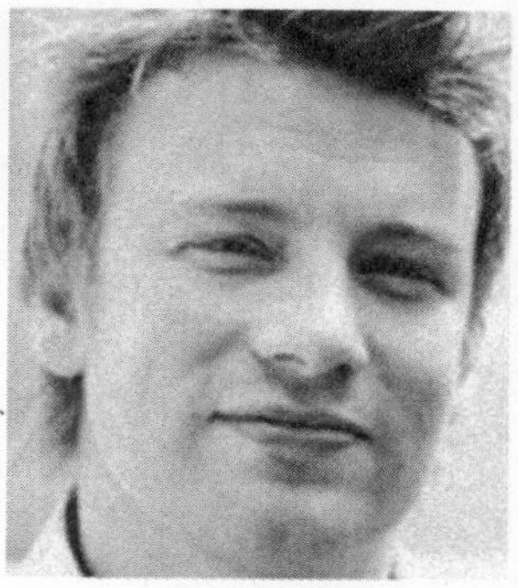

I THOUGHT your readers may be interested to know that if Jamie Oliver ever turns up on my doorstep, I will turn my back on him, pull my pants down, squat on my haunches and shit on his shoes and the front of his trousers. I must admit, I'm not a fan.

Ben Margerison, e-mail

THOSE Fairtrade products in the supermarket are a con. Their tea bags cost a quid more than Tesco value. Doesn't seem very fair to me.

Ryan Pooh, e-mail

A KLEENEZE catalogue gets put through my letterbox every month, and a couple of days later a lady calls to collect it. This has been going on for years now. Wouldn't it be easier if they just sent it to her in the first place?

Doug Roberts, e-mail

Job '*Too Small*' for 'No Job Too Small' Handyman EXCLUSIVE!

A LEEDS pensioner was left fuming yesterday when a local handyman claimed a job she had requested him to do was "too small", despite claims in his advertising that "No Job is Too Small."

Mrs Nancy Bouys, 79, claimed that handyman Martin Gill came round to give a quote for some work. "When he visited my bungalow, he said he couldn't do it because the job was 'too small,'" she fumed. "He claimed it wasn't worth getting the tools out of his van."

backlash

Gill, who quips in his adverts that he is *'Licenced to Drill'* has been forced to employ PR Guru Max Clifford to handle the inevitable backlash.

Speaking from outside his London office, Clifford said:

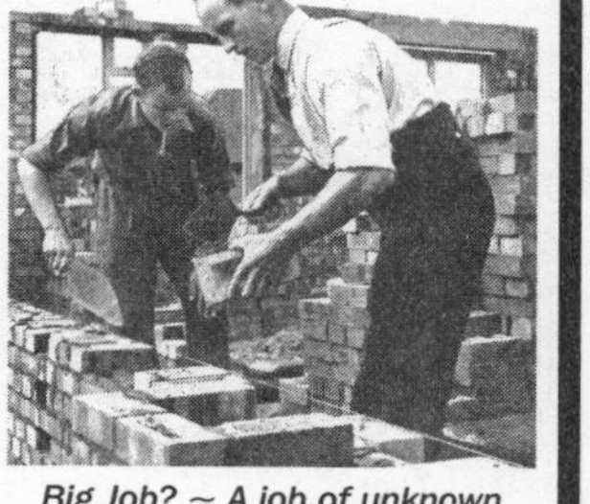

Big Job? ~ A job of unknown size being attempted, yesterday

"My client assumed that he was going to Mrs Bouys' bungalow to quote on a small job which might grow into a little job. On assessing the size of the job, however, he soon realised that it was not small. It was much smaller than that."

"In light of events, my client acknowledges that his 'No Job to Small' claim may be misleading and has vowed to alter his advertising strategy. In future, he will claim that 'No Job is Too Large,'" he added.

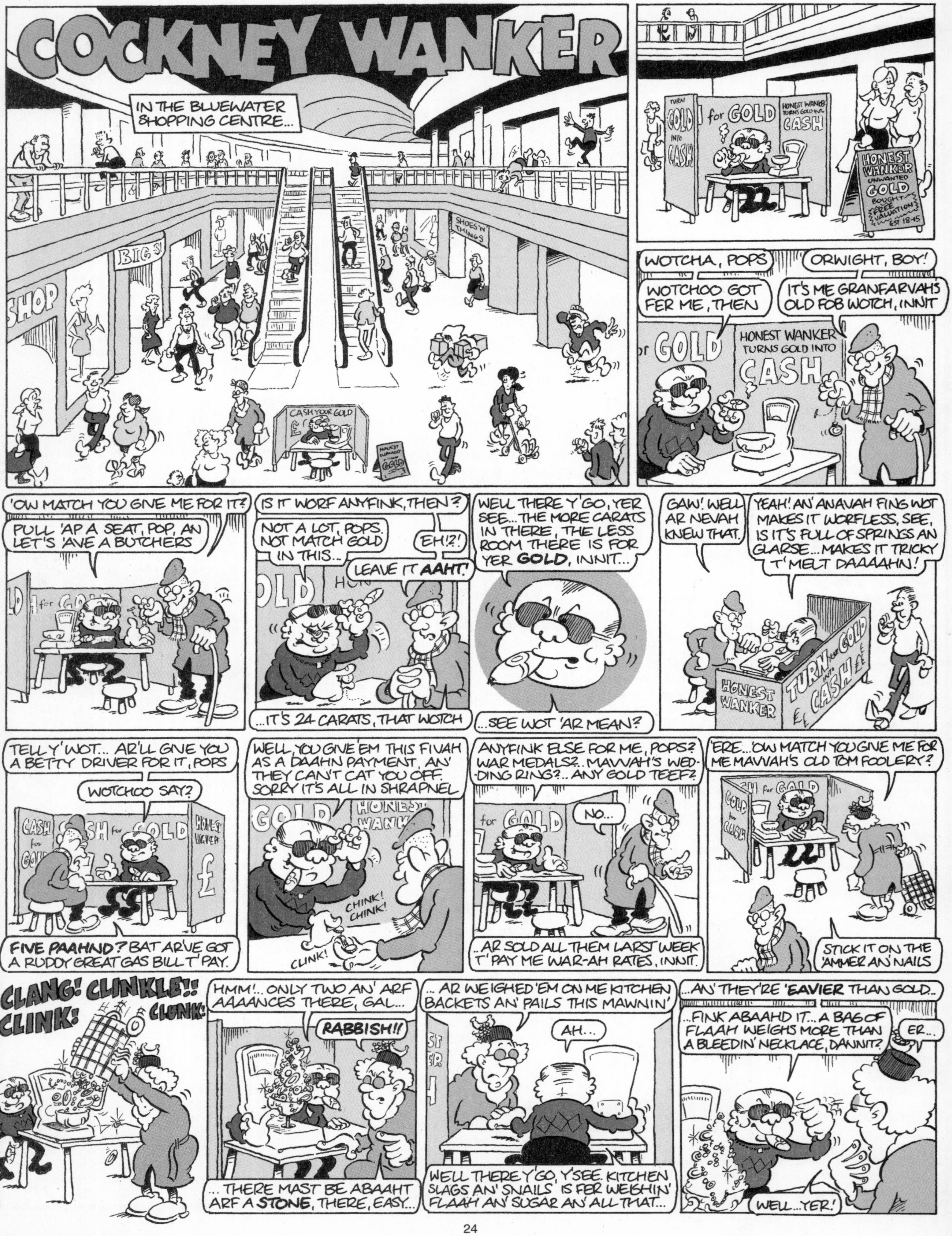
COCKNEY WANKER
IN THE BLUEWATER SHOPPING CENTRE...
BIG $!
SHOP
SHOES 'N' THINGS
CASH YOUR GOLD
TURN GOLD INTO CASH
for GOLD
HONEST WANKER TURNS GOLD INTO CASH
HONEST WANKER UNWANTED GOLD BOUGHT FREE VALUATION EST 18-45
WOTCHA, POPS
ORWIGHT, BOY!
WOTCHOO GOT FER ME, THEN
IT'S ME GRANFARVAH'S OLD FOB WOTCH, INNIT
HONEST WANKER TURNS GOLD INTO CASH
'OW MATCH YOU GIVE ME FOR IT?
PULL 'AP A SEAT, POP, AN LET'S 'AVE A BUTCHERS
IS IT WORF ANYFINK, THEN?
NOT A LOT, POPS. NOT MATCH GOLD IN THIS...
EH!?!
LEAVE IT AAHT!
...IT'S 24 CARATS, THAT WOTCH
WELL THERE Y'GO, YER SEE... THE MORE CARATS IN THERE, THE LESS ROOM THERE IS FOR YER GOLD, INNIT...
...SEE WOT 'AR MEAN?
GAW! WELL AR NEVAH KNEW THAT.
YEAH! AN' ANAVAH FING WOT MAKES IT WORFLESS, SEE, IS IT'S FULL OF SPRINGS AN GLARSE... MAKES IT TRICKY T'MELT DAAAAHN!
HONEST WANKER
TURN GOLD INTO CASH
TELL Y' WOT... AR'LL GIVE YOU A BETTY DRIVER FOR IT, POPS
WOTCHOO SAY?
FIVE PAAHND? BAT AR'VE GOT A RUDDY GREAT GAS BILL T' PAY.
WELL, YOU GIVE 'EM THIS FIVAH AS A DAAHN PAYMENT, AN' THEY CAN'T CAT YOU OFF. SORRY IT'S ALL IN SHRAPNEL
CHINK! CHINK!
CLINK!
ANYFINK ELSE FOR ME, POPS? WAR MEDALS?.. MAVVAH'S WED-DING RING?.. ANY GOLD TEEF?
NO...
..AR SOLD ALL THEM LARST WEEK T' PAY ME WAR-AH RATES, INNIT.
'ERE...'OW MATCH YOU GIVE ME FOR ME MAVVAH'S OLD TOM FOOLERY?
STICK IT ON THE 'AMMER AN' NAILS
CLANG! CLINKLE!! CLINK! CLUNK!
HMM!... ONLY TWO AN' ARF AAAANCES THERE, GAL...
RABBISH!!
... THERE MAST BE ABAAHT ARF A STONE, THERE, EASY...
... AR WEIGHED 'EM ON ME KITCHEN BACKETS AN' PAILS THIS MAWNIN'
AH...
WELL THERE Y'GO, Y'SEE. KITCHEN SLAGS AN' SNAILS IS FER WEIGHIN' FLAAH AN' SUGAR AN' ALL THAT...
...AN' THEY'RE 'EAVIER THAN GOLD...
...FINK ABAAHD IT... A BAG OF FLAAH WEIGHS MORE THAN A BLEEDIN' NECKLACE, DANNIT?
ER...
WELL...YER!

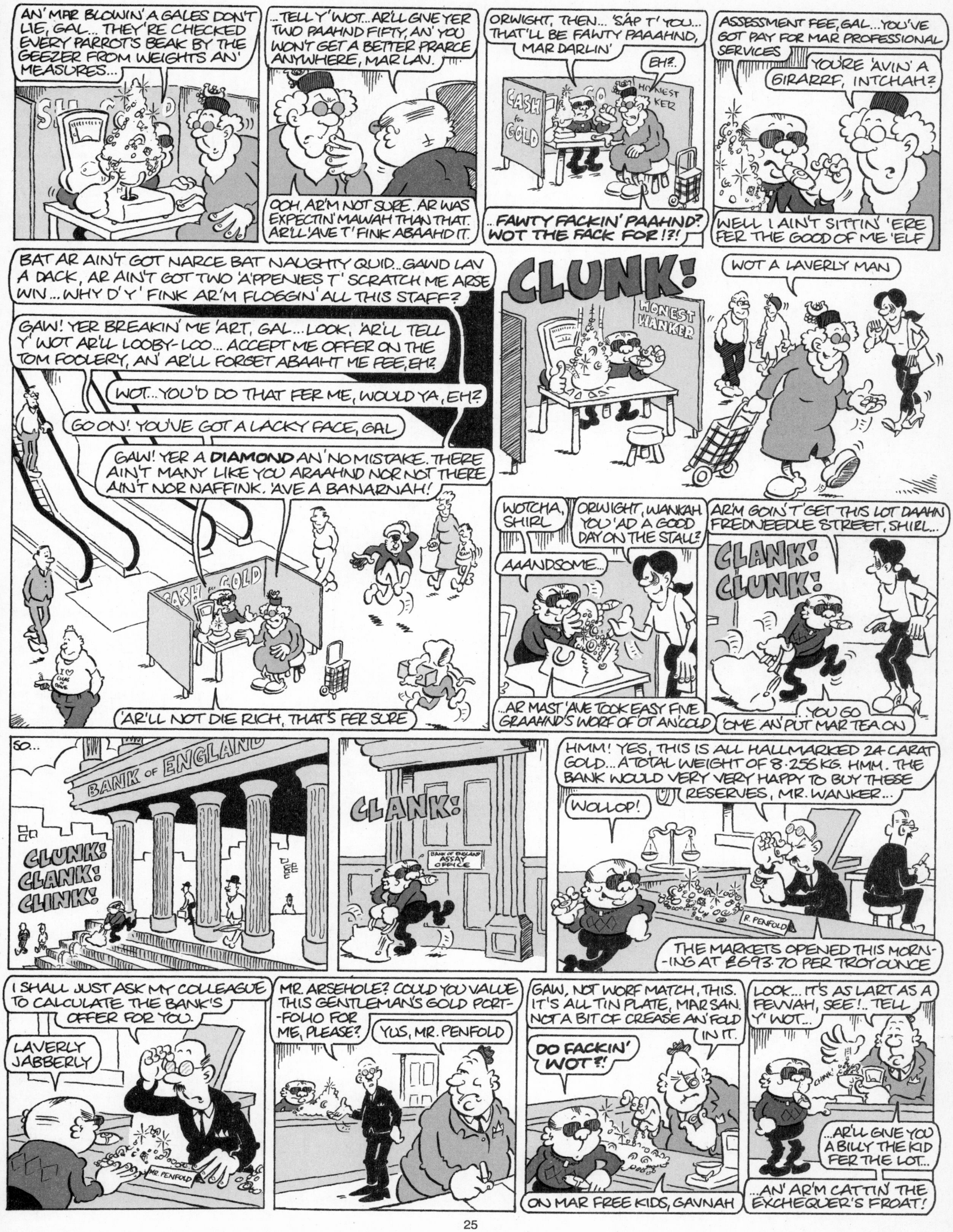
AN' MAR BLOWIN' A GALES DON'T LIE, GAL... THEY'RE CHECKED EVERY PARROT'S BEAK BY THE GEEZER FROM WEIGHTS AN' MEASURES...
...TELL Y' WOT... AR'LL GIVE YER TWO PAAHND FIFTY, AN' YOU WON'T GET A BETTER PRARCE ANYWHERE, MAR LAV.
OOH, AR'M NOT SURE. AR WAS EXPECTIN' MAWAH THAN THAT. AR'LL 'AVE T' FINK ABAAHD IT.
ORWIGHT, THEN... 'SÁP T' YOU... THAT'LL BE FAWTY PAAAHND, MAR DARLIN'
EH?..
CASH for GOLD
...FAWTY FACKIN' PAAHND? WOT THE FACK FOR!?!
ASSESSMENT FEE, GAL... YOU'VE GOT PAY FOR MAR PROFESSIONAL SERVICES
YOU'RE 'AVIN' A GIRARRF, INTCHAH?
WELL I AIN'T SITTIN' 'ERE FER THE GOOD OF ME 'ELF
BAT AR AIN'T GOT NARCE BAT NAUGHTY QUID... GAWD LAV A DACK, AR AIN'T GOT TWO 'A'PPENIES T' SCRATCH ME ARSE WIV... WHY D'Y' FINK AR'M FLOGGIN' ALL THIS STAFF?
GAW! YER BREAKIN' ME 'ART, GAL... LOOK, 'AR'LL TELL Y' WOT AR'LL LOOBY-LOO... ACCEPT ME OFFER ON THE TOM FOOLERY, AN' AR'LL FORGET ABAAHT ME FEE, EH?
WOT... YOU'D DO THAT FER ME, WOULD YA, EH?
GO ON! YOU'VE GOT A LACKY FACE, GAL
GAW! YER A **DIAMOND** AN' NO MISTAKE. THERE AIN'T MANY LIKE YOU ARAAHND NOR NOT THERE AIN'T NOR NAFFINK. 'AVE A BANARNAH!
CASH for GOLD
'AR'LL NOT DIE RICH, THAT'S FER SURE
CLUNK!
HONEST WANKER
WOT A LAVERLY MAN
WOTCHA, SHIRL
ORWIGHT, WANKAH. YOU 'AD A GOOD DAY ON THE STALL?
AAANDSOME...
...AR MAST 'AVE TOOK EASY FIVE GRAAHND'S WORF OF OT AN' COLD
AR'M GOIN' T' GET THIS LOT DAAHN FREDNEEDLE STREET, SHIRL...
CLANK! CLUNK!
...YOU GO 'OME AN' PUT MAR TEA ON
SO...
BANK OF ENGLAND
CLUNK! CLANK! CLINK!
CLANK!
BANK OF ENGLAND ASSAY OFFICE
HMM! YES, THIS IS ALL HALLMARKED 24 CARAT GOLD... A TOTAL WEIGHT OF 8·256 KG. HMM. THE BANK WOULD VERY VERY HAPPY TO BUY THESE RESERVES, MR. WANKER...
WOLLOP!
R. PENFOLD
THE MARKETS OPENED THIS MORN- -ING AT £693·70 PER TROY OUNCE
I SHALL JUST ASK MY COLLEAGUE TO CALCULATE THE BANK'S OFFER FOR YOU.
LAVERLY JABBERLY
MR. PENFOLD
MR. ARSEHOLE? COULD YOU VALUE THIS GENTLEMAN'S GOLD PORT- -FOLIO FOR ME, PLEASE?
YUS, MR. PENFOLD
GAW, NOT WORF MATCH, THIS. IT'S ALL TIN PLATE, MAR SAN. NOT A BIT OF CREASE AN' FOLD IN IT.
DO FACKIN' WOT?!
ON MAR FREE KIDS, GAVNAH
LOOK... IT'S AS LART AS A FEWAH, SEE!.. TELL Y' WOT...
CHINK!
...AR'LL GIVE YOU A BILLY THE KID FER THE LOT...
...AN' AR'M CATTIN' THE EXCHEQUER'S FROAT!

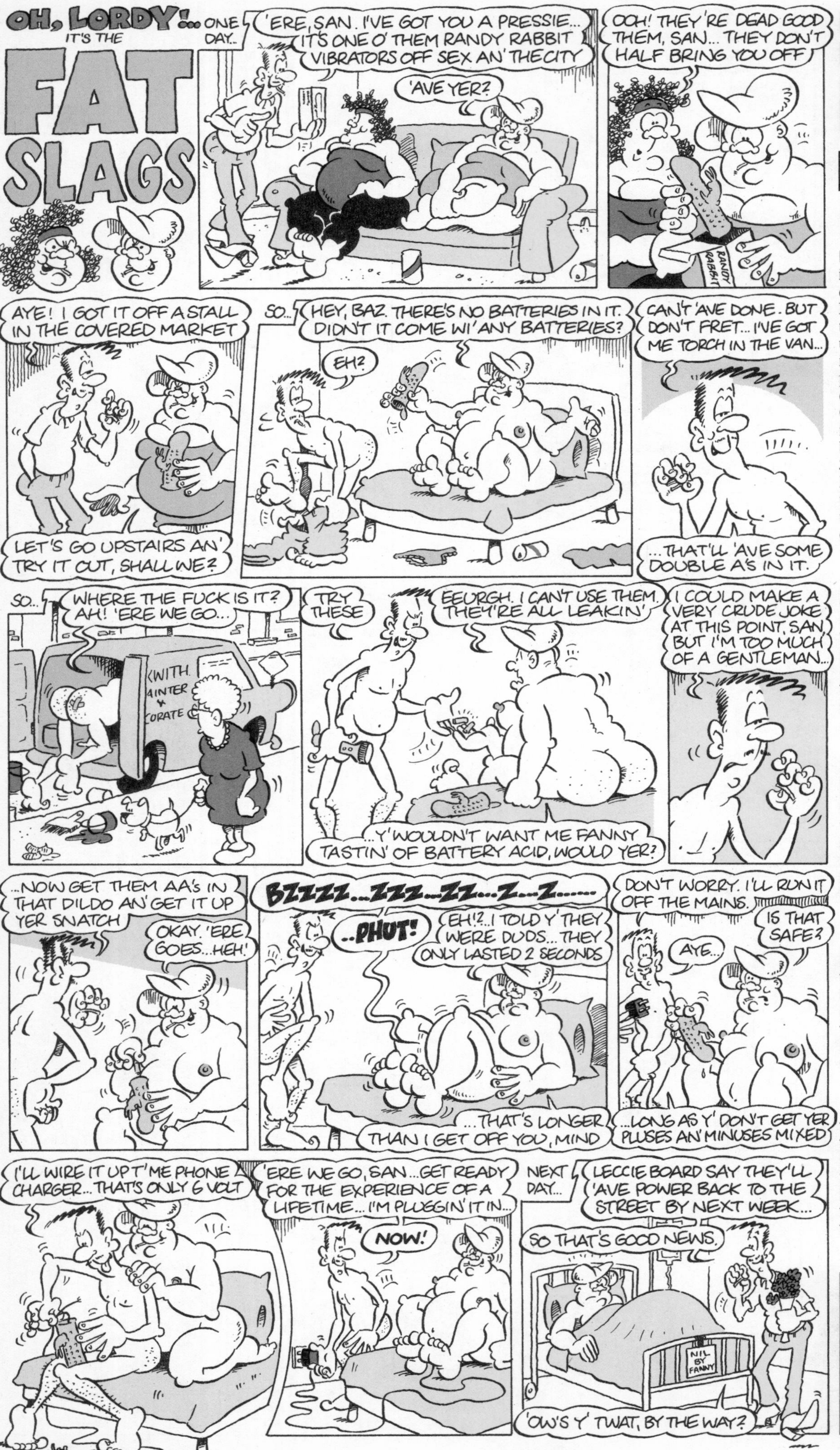
OH, LORDY!... IT'S THE
FAT SLAGS
ONE DAY...
'ERE, SAN. I'VE GOT YOU A PRESSIE... IT'S ONE O' THEM RANDY RABBIT VIBRATORS OFF SEX AN' THE CITY
'AVE YER?
OOH! THEY'RE DEAD GOOD THEM, SAN... THEY DON'T HALF BRING YOU OFF
RANDY RABBIT
AYE! I GOT IT OFF A STALL IN THE COVERED MARKET
LET'S GO UPSTAIRS AN' TRY IT OUT, SHALL WE?
SO...
HEY, BAZ. THERE'S NO BATTERIES IN IT. DIDN'T IT COME WI' ANY BATTERIES?
EH?
CAN'T 'AVE DONE. BUT DON'T FRET... I'VE GOT ME TORCH IN THE VAN...
...THAT'LL 'AVE SOME DOUBLE A'S IN IT.
SO...
WHERE THE FUCK IS IT? AH! 'ERE WE GO...
TRY THESE
EEURGH. I CAN'T USE THEM. THEY'RE ALL LEAKIN'
...Y'WOULDN'T WANT ME FANNY TASTIN' OF BATTERY ACID, WOULD YER?
I COULD MAKE A VERY CRUDE JOKE AT THIS POINT, SAN BUT I'M TOO MUCH OF A GENTLEMAN...
...NOW GET THEM AA's IN THAT DILDO AN' GET IT UP YER SNATCH
OKAY. 'ERE GOES...HEH!
BZZZZZ...ZZZ...ZZ...Z...Z......
..PHUT!
EH!?..I TOLD Y' THEY WERE DUDS... THEY ONLY LASTED 2 SECONDS
...THAT'S LONGER THAN I GET OFF YOU, MIND
DON'T WORRY. I'LL RUN IT OFF THE MAINS.
IS THAT SAFE?
AYE...
...LONG AS Y' DON'T GET YER PLUSES AN' MINUSES MIXED
I'LL WIRE IT UP T'ME PHONE CHARGER... THAT'S ONLY 6 VOLT
'ERE WE GO, SAN... GET READY FOR THE EXPERIENCE OF A LIFETIME... I'M PLUGGIN' IT IN...
NOW!
NEXT DAY...
LECCIE BOARD SAY THEY'LL 'AVE POWER BACK TO THE STREET BY NEXT WEEK...
SO THAT'S GOOD NEWS.
NIL BY FANNY
'OW'S Y' TWAT, BY THE WAY?

Saints 'n' Greavesie

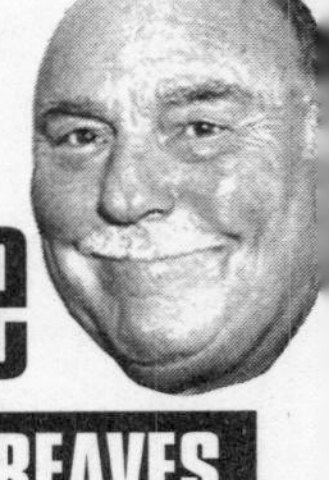

with JIMMY GREAVES

Dear Greavesie,

I'M REALLY fed up because my iPod nano has gone a bit haywire. It doesn't recognise some of the tunes I've got on my computer. Even though they're in my iTunes, they don't show up in the iPod menu after I've synced it. As a devout catholic, I intend to pray to get the problem fixed, but I don't know which Saint to approach. Cecilia is the obvious choice as she is the Patron Saint of Musicians, but since she was martyred in the 3rd century AD it's unlikely that she knows anything about digital electronics. Do any readers have suggestions about to whom I should pray in order to get my iPod fixed?

Dermott O'Murphy, Liverpool

...SINCE the records are in the iTunes catalogue but aren't showing up on his iPod, they are clearly getting lost somewhere in the syncing process, perhaps by being misdirected into the wrong playlist. I suggest Mr O'Murphy prays to Saint Anthony, the Patron Saint of lost things, who should be able to help.

Gloria Antrobus, Chelsea

...IS MR O'Murphy a chimney sweep? If so, he could do worse to pray to the Patron saint of chimney sweeps, Saint Florian. I am a chimney sweep and I always pray to Saint Florian, whatever the problem. My prayers are sometimes answered, but not the really difficult ones. If he's not a chimney sweep, I really don't know what to suggest.

Bert Poppins, London

...IT'S A long shot, but perhaps a caterpillar might have crawled into your iPod through the headphone socket. Its furry legs might be shorting out some of the contacts inside, in which case a prayer to Saint Magnus of Fussen, the Patron Saint against caterpillars might well bring results.

Mrs Ricicles, Bowl

...MR O'Murphy should pray to the Apostle Peter, the head Saint, briefly outlining the problems he is having. Peter may not intercede and repair it personally, as he is very busy, but he will know which member of the Heavenly Host would be best at fixing iPods and will pass your details on to the relevant Saint.

Father T Abrahams, Wimbledon

Do YOU have a problem and don't know to which Catholic Saint to pray to get it sorted? Send your query to: *Jimmy Greaves's Saints and Greavesie, c/o Viz Comic, PO Box 656, North Shields NE30 4XX*.

Ghost Stories for Christmas

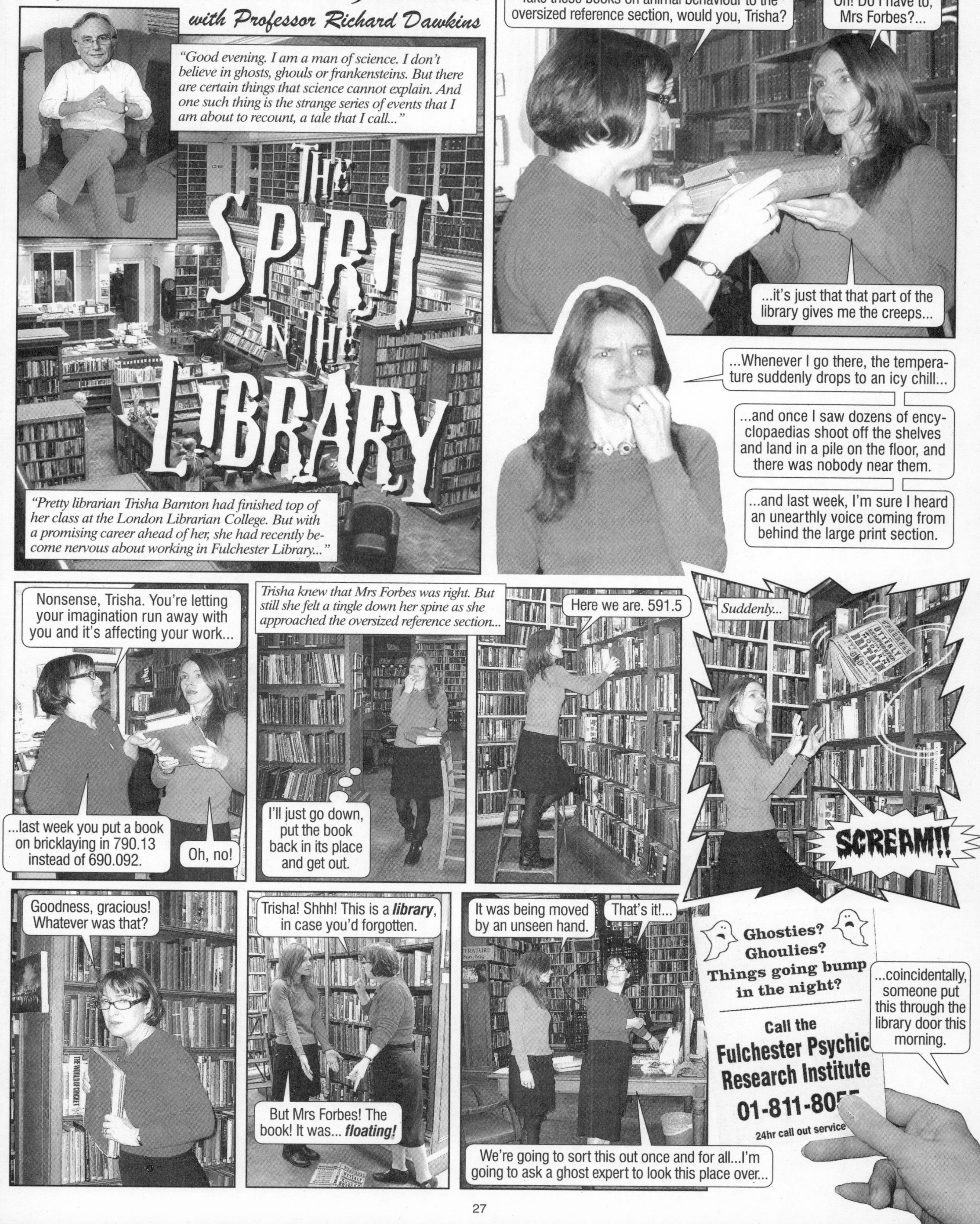
with Professor Richard Dawkins
"Good evening. I am a man of science. I don't believe in ghosts, ghouls or frankensteins. But there are certain things that science cannot explain. And one such thing is the strange series of events that I am about to recount, a tale that I call..."
THE SPIRIT IN THE LIBRARY
"Pretty librarian Trisha Barnton had finished top of her class at the London Librarian College. But with a promising career ahead of her, she had recently become nervous about working in Fulchester Library..."
Take these books on animal behaviour to the oversized reference section, would you, Trisha?
Oh! Do I have to, Mrs Forbes?...
...it's just that that part of the library gives me the creeps...
...Whenever I go there, the temperature suddenly drops to an icy chill...
...and once I saw dozens of encyclopaedias shoot off the shelves and land in a pile on the floor, and there was nobody near them.
...and last week, I'm sure I heard an unearthly voice coming from behind the large print section.
Nonsense, Trisha. You're letting your imagination run away with you and it's affecting your work...
...last week you put a book on bricklaying in 790.13 instead of 690.092.
Oh, no!
Trisha knew that Mrs Forbes was right. But still she felt a tingle down her spine as she approached the oversized reference section...
I'll just go down, put the book back in its place and get out.
Here we are. 591.5
Suddenly...
SCREAM!!
Goodness, gracious! Whatever was that?
Trisha! Shhh! This is a ***library***, in case you'd forgotten.
But Mrs Forbes! The book! It was... ***floating!***
It was being moved by an unseen hand.
That's it!...
We're going to sort this out once and for all...I'm going to ask a ghost expert to look this place over...
Ghosties?
Ghoulies?
Things going bump in the night?
Call the
Fulchester Psychic Research Institute
01-811-805
24hr call out service
...coincidentally, someone put this through the library door this morning.

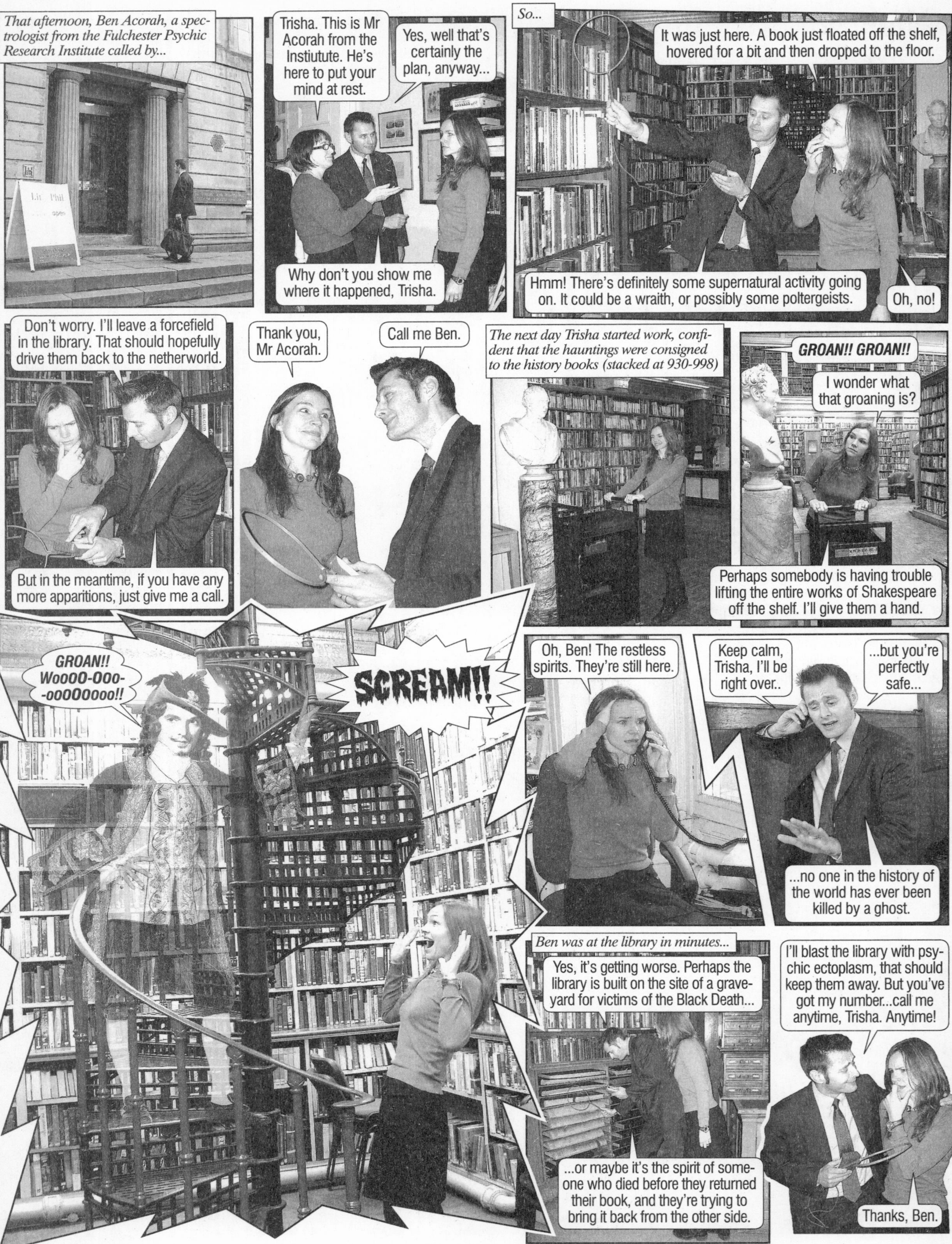
That afternoon, Ben Acorah, a spectrologist from the Fulchester Psychic Research Institute called by...
Lit Phil
open
Trisha. This is Mr Acorah from the Instiutute. He's here to put your mind at rest.
Yes, well that's certainly the plan, anyway...
Why don't you show me where it happened, Trisha.
So...
It was just here. A book just floated off the shelf, hovered for a bit and then dropped to the floor.
Hmm! There's definitely some supernatural activity going on. It could be a wraith, or possibly some poltergeists.
Oh, no!
Don't worry. I'll leave a forcefield in the library. That should hopefully drive them back to the netherworld.
But in the meantime, if you have any more apparitions, just give me a call.
Thank you, Mr Acorah.
Call me Ben.
The next day Trisha started work, confident that the hauntings were consigned to the history books (stacked at 930-998)
GROAN!! GROAN!!
I wonder what that groaning is?
Perhaps somebody is having trouble lifting the entire works of Shakespeare off the shelf. I'll give them a hand.
GROAN!! WooOO-OOO--ooOOOooo!!
SCREAM!!
Oh, Ben! The restless spirits. They're still here.
Keep calm, Trisha, I'll be right over..
...but you're perfectly safe...
...no one in the history of the world has ever been killed by a ghost.
Ben was at the library in minutes...
Yes, it's getting worse. Perhaps the library is built on the site of a graveyard for victims of the Black Death...
...or maybe it's the spirit of someone who died before they returned their book, and they're trying to bring it back from the other side.
I'll blast the library with psychic ectoplasm, that should keep them away. But you've got my number...call me anytime, Trisha. Anytime!
Thanks, Ben.

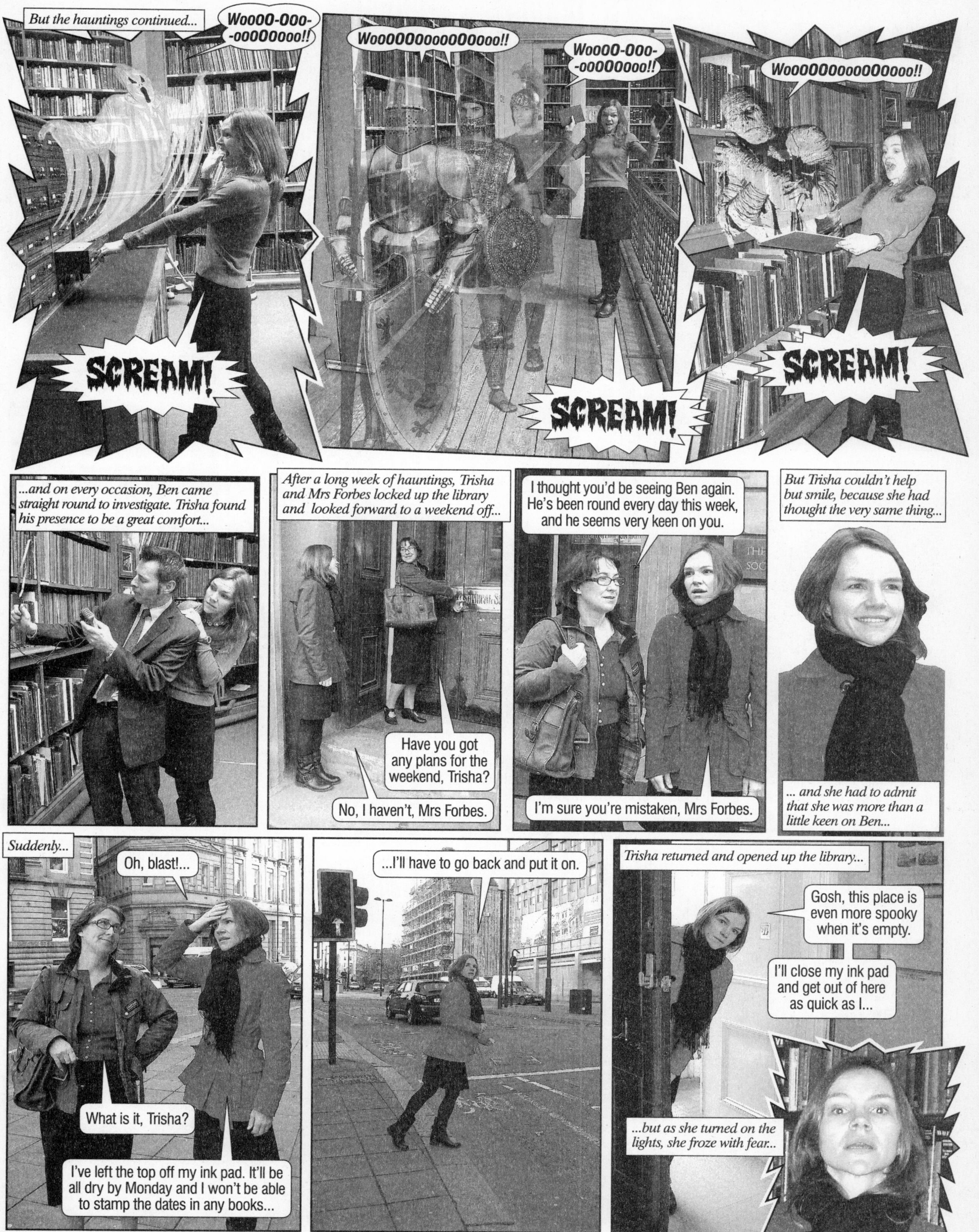
But the hauntings continued...
WoooO-OOO-
-ooOOOooo!!
SCREAM!
WoooOOOoooOOOoooo!!
WoooO-OOO-
-ooOOOooo!!
SCREAM!
WoooOOOoooOOOoooo!!
SCREAM!
...and on every occasion, Ben came straight round to investigate. Trisha found his presence to be a great comfort...
After a long week of hauntings, Trisha and Mrs Forbes locked up the library and looked forward to a weekend off...
Have you got any plans for the weekend, Trisha?
No, I haven't, Mrs Forbes.
I thought you'd be seeing Ben again. He's been round every day this week, and he seems very keen on you.
I'm sure you're mistaken, Mrs Forbes.
But Trisha couldn't help but smile, because she had thought the very same thing...
... and she had to admit that she was more than a little keen on Ben...
Suddenly...
Oh, blast!...
What is it, Trisha?
I've left the top off my ink pad. It'll be all dry by Monday and I won't be able to stamp the dates in any books...
...I'll have to go back and put it on.
Trisha returned and opened up the library...
Gosh, this place is even more spooky when it's empty.
I'll close my ink pad and get out of here as quick as I...
...but as she turned on the lights, she froze with fear...

Ben!?! What are **YOU** doing here?...

Trisha!?!

Oh! I... erm...

...the library is closed. And what's all this stuff?

I... I won't lie to you, Trisha. The truth is that the library isn't haunted. And it never was.

What!?... But the ghosts... I... I don't understand...

There **were** no ghosts, Trisha. I've been sneaking in here at night when everybody has gone and creating the illusions of ghosts...

...using this ciné projector, a tape recorder, a tin of luminous paint...

...some magnets and a fan-type motor.

But why, Ben?... Why did you do it?

To see **YOU**, Trisha...

You've been in my thoughts ever since I saw you go into the library a month ago. And whilst you thought the library was haunted, I always had an excuse to come in and see you.

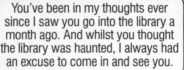

Oh, Ben. Why on earth didn't you just come in and borrow a book?

No, Trisha...

That would have been impossible...you see, I'm not a member of this library.

But now I have told you everything, Trisha, do you... do you think you could ever **love** me?

Oh, Ben, Yes. yes, I could of... but I'm afraid it's too late...

...and you're wrong about the library not being haunted.

What do you mean?

I mean, there **is** a ghost in the library...

...you see, as I ran back here to put the top on my ink pad, I was ran over by a bus and killed.

Oh, my God! **NO!**

Goodbye, Ben. Goodbye forever.

Trisha!...

"Science is very good at explaining chemical reactions, electrical circuits and gravity. But some things defy scientific explaination - the tears on a young baby's cheek... the flash of a kingfisher's wing... the delicate bloom of a rose. Science cannot explain ghosts. And it cannot explain love..."

"See you next Christmas, Ghost Stories for Christmas lovers."

THE EN

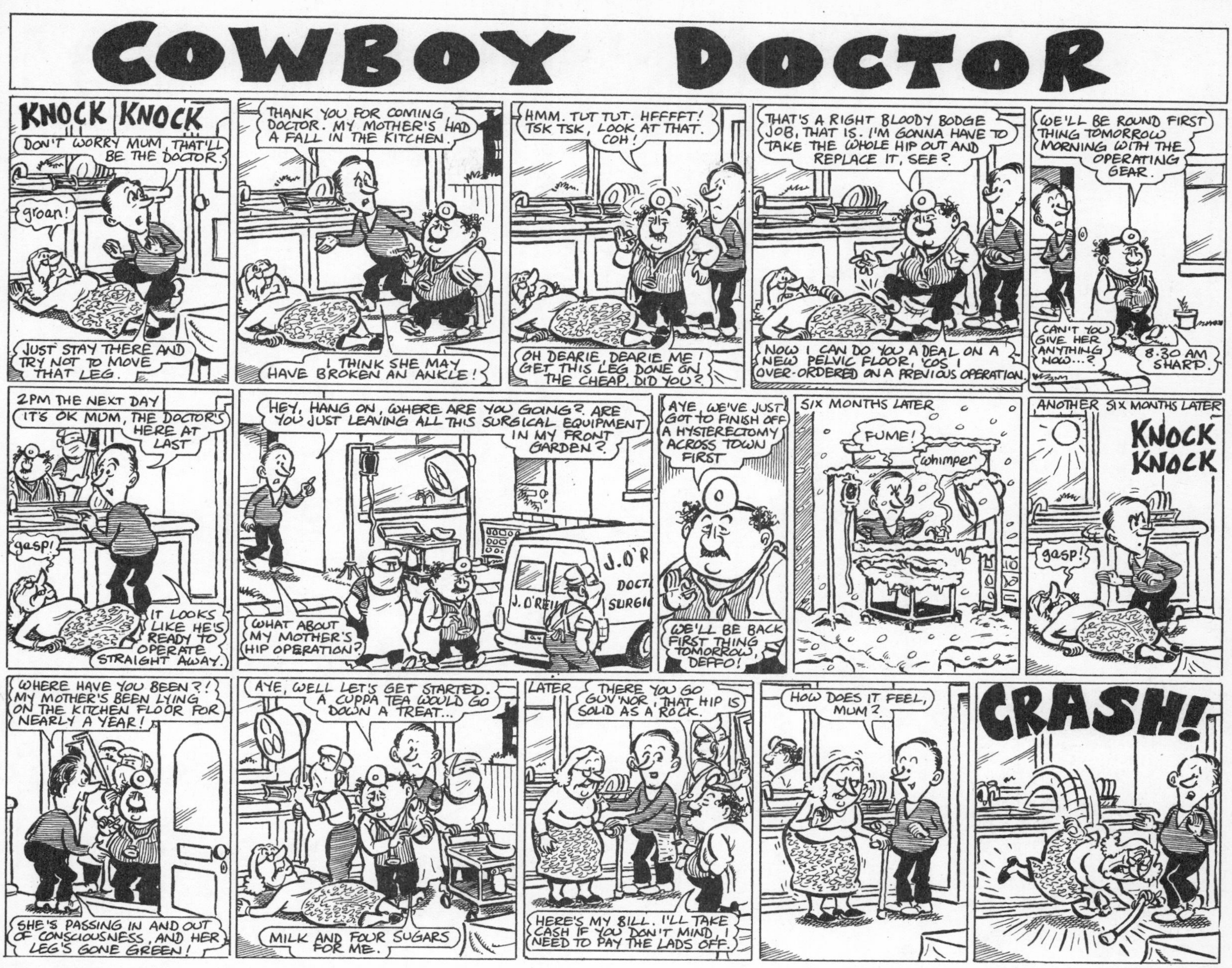
COWBOY DOCTOR
KNOCK KNOCK
DON'T WORRY MUM, THAT'LL BE THE DOCTOR.
groan!
JUST STAY THERE AND TRY NOT TO MOVE THAT LEG.
THANK YOU FOR COMING DOCTOR. MY MOTHER'S HAD A FALL IN THE KITCHEN.
I THINK SHE MAY HAVE BROKEN AN ANKLE!
HMM. TUT TUT. HFFFFT! TSK TSK, LOOK AT THAT. OOH!
OH DEARIE, DEARIE ME! GET THIS LEG DONE ON THE CHEAP, DID YOU?
THAT'S A RIGHT BLOODY BODGE JOB, THAT IS. I'M GONNA HAVE TO TAKE THE WHOLE HIP OUT AND REPLACE IT, SEE?
NOW I CAN DO YOU A DEAL ON A NEW PELVIC FLOOR, 'COS I OVER-ORDERED ON A PREVIOUS OPERATION.
WE'LL BE ROUND FIRST THING TOMORROW MORNING WITH THE OPERATING GEAR.
CAN'T YOU GIVE HER ANYTHING NOW...?
8.30 AM SHARP.
2PM THE NEXT DAY
IT'S OK MUM, THE DOCTOR'S HERE AT LAST
gasp!
IT LOOKS LIKE HE'S READY TO OPERATE STRAIGHT AWAY.
HEY, HANG ON, WHERE ARE YOU GOING? ARE YOU JUST LEAVING ALL THIS SURGICAL EQUIPMENT IN MY FRONT GARDEN?
WHAT ABOUT MY MOTHER'S HIP OPERATION?
AYE, WE'VE JUST GOT TO FINISH OFF A HYSTERECTOMY ACROSS TOWN FIRST
WE'LL BE BACK FIRST THING TOMORROW, DEFFO!
SIX MONTHS LATER
FUME!
whimper
ANOTHER SIX MONTHS LATER
KNOCK KNOCK
gasp!
WHERE HAVE YOU BEEN?! MY MOTHER'S BEEN LYING ON THE KITCHEN FLOOR FOR NEARLY A YEAR!
SHE'S PASSING IN AND OUT OF CONSCIOUSNESS, AND HER LEG'S GONE GREEN!
AYE, WELL LET'S GET STARTED. A CUPPA TEA WOULD GO DOWN A TREAT...
MILK AND FOUR SUGARS FOR ME.
LATER
THERE YOU GO GUV'NOR, THAT HIP IS SOLID AS A ROCK.
HERE'S MY BILL. I'LL TAKE CASH IF YOU DON'T MIND, I NEED TO PAY THE LADS OFF.
HOW DOES IT FEEL, MUM?
CRASH!

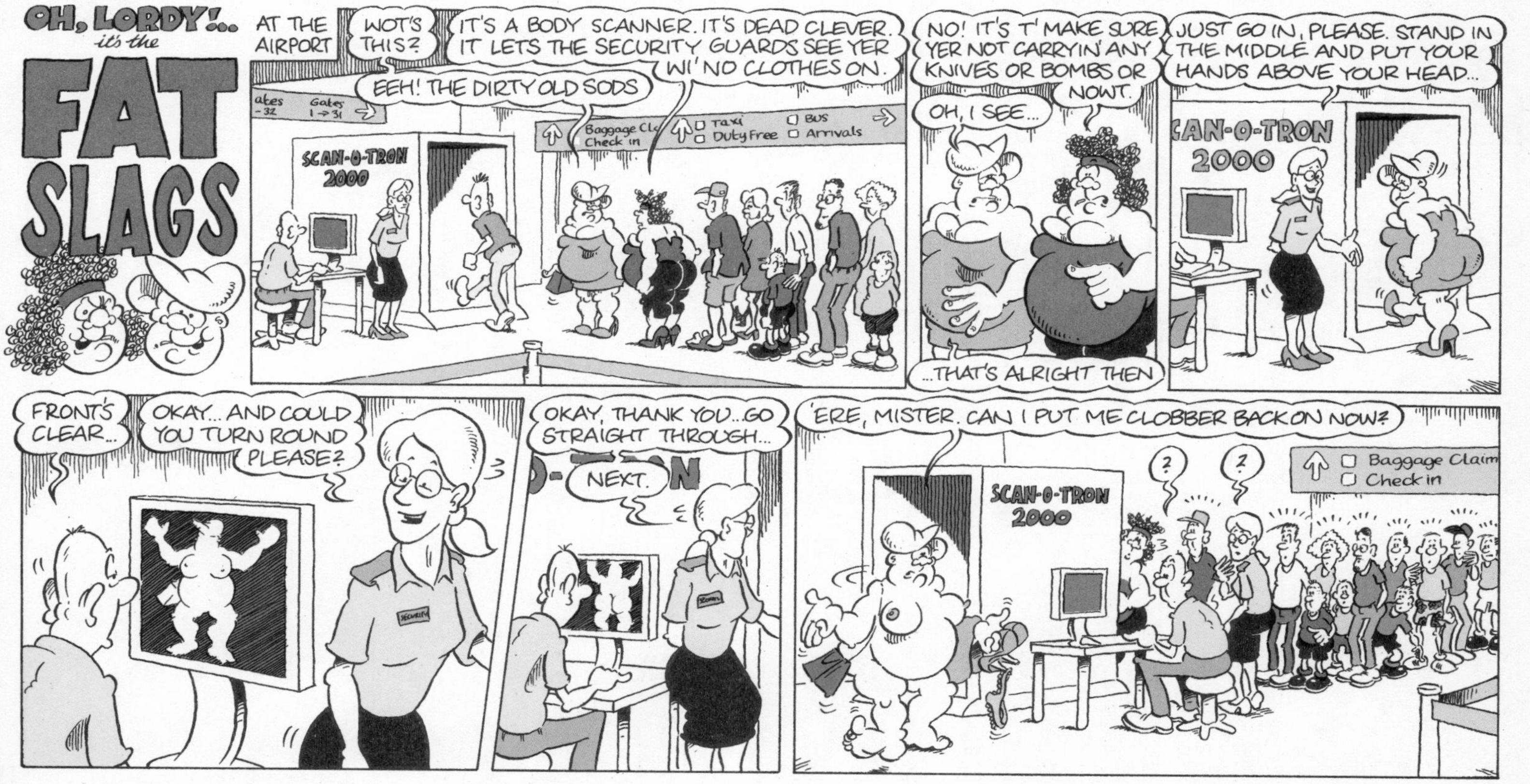
OH, LORDY!.. it's the
FAT SLAGS
AT THE AIRPORT
WOT'S THIS?
IT'S A BODY SCANNER. IT'S DEAD CLEVER. IT LETS THE SECURITY GUARDS SEE YER WI' NO CLOTHES ON.
EEH! THE DIRTY OLD SODS
Gates 1→31
Baggage Claim Check in
Taxi Bus Duty Free Arrivals
SCAN-O-TRON 2000
NO! IT'S T' MAKE SURE YER NOT CARRYIN' ANY KNIVES OR BOMBS OR NOWT.
OH, I SEE...
...THAT'S ALRIGHT THEN
JUST GO IN, PLEASE. STAND IN THE MIDDLE AND PUT YOUR HANDS ABOVE YOUR HEAD...
FRONT'S CLEAR...
OKAY... AND COULD YOU TURN ROUND PLEASE?
OKAY, THANK YOU... GO STRAIGHT THROUGH...
NEXT.
'ERE, MISTER. CAN I PUT ME CLOBBER BACK ON NOW?
?
?
Baggage Claim
Check in

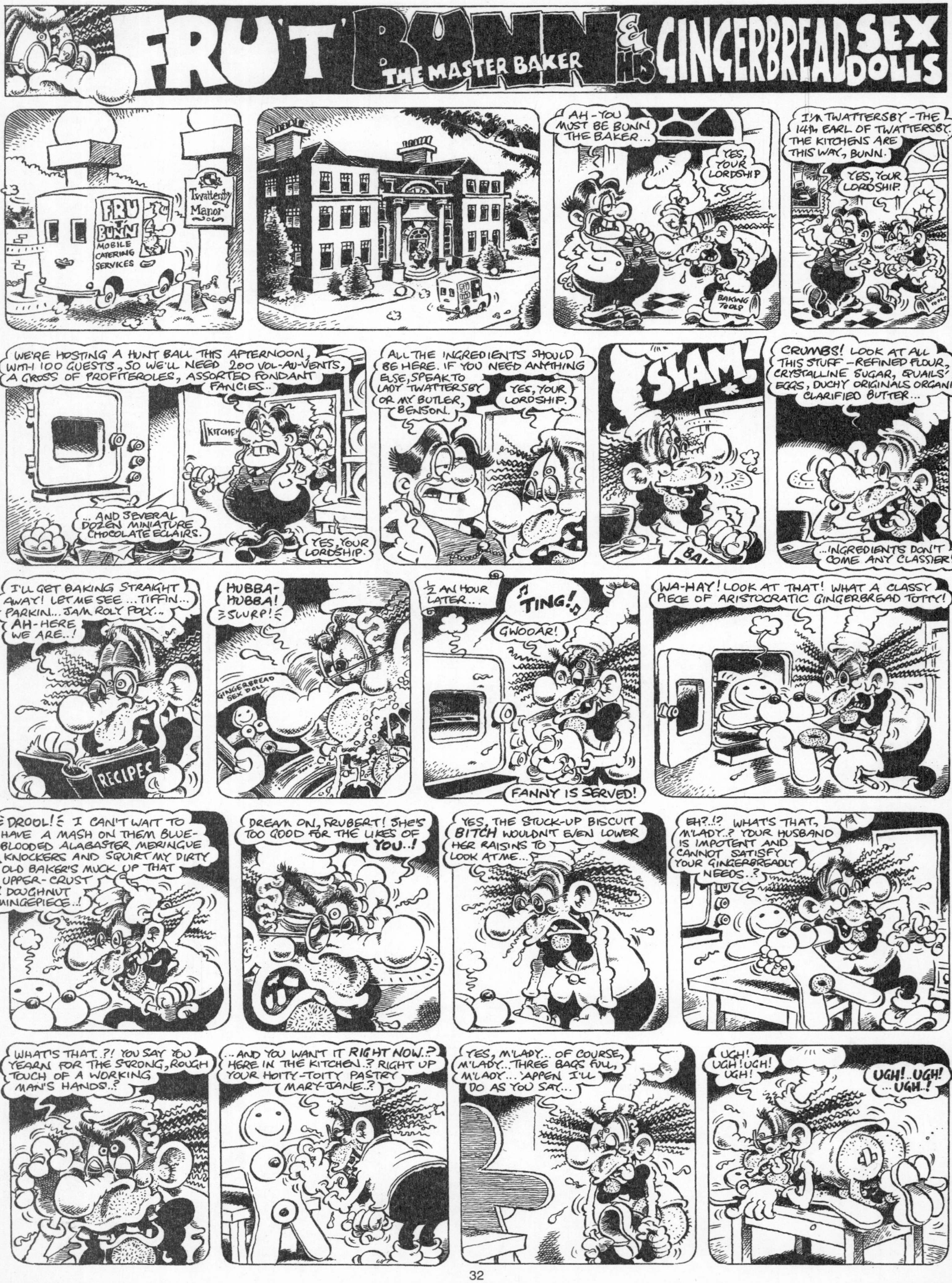
FRU'T BUNN THE MASTER BAKER & HIS GINGERBREAD SEX DOLLS
FRU 'T' BUNN MOBILE CATERING SERVICES
Twattersby Manor
AH - YOU MUST BE BUNN THE BAKER...
YES, YOUR LORDSHIP
BAKING TOOLS
I'M TWATTERSBY - THE 14th EARL OF TWATTERSBY. THE KITCHENS ARE THIS WAY, BUNN.
YES, YOUR LORDSHIP.
WE'RE HOSTING A HUNT BALL THIS AFTERNOON, WITH 100 GUESTS, SO WE'LL NEED 200 VOL-AU-VENTS, A GROSS OF PROFITEROLES, ASSORTED FONDANT FANCIES...
KITCHEN
...AND SEVERAL DOZEN MINIATURE CHOCOLATE ECLAIRS.
YES, YOUR LORDSHIP.
ALL THE INGREDIENTS SHOULD BE HERE. IF YOU NEED ANYTHING ELSE, SPEAK TO LADY TWATTERSBY OR MY BUTLER, BENSON.
YES, YOUR LORDSHIP.
SLAM!
CRUMBS! LOOK AT ALL THIS STUFF - REFINED FLOUR, CRYSTALLINE SUGAR, QUAILS' EGGS, DUCHY ORIGINALS ORGANIC CLARIFIED BUTTER...
...INGREDIENTS DON'T COME ANY CLASSIER!
I'LL GET BAKING STRAIGHT AWAY! LET ME SEE... TIFFIN... PARKIN... JAM ROLY POLY... AH - HERE WE ARE...!
RECIPES
HUBBA-HUBBA!
SLURP!
GINGERBREAD SEX DOLL
1/2 AN HOUR LATER...
TING!
GWOOAR!
FANNY IS SERVED!
WA-HAY! LOOK AT THAT! WHAT A CLASSY PIECE OF ARISTOCRATIC GINGERBREAD TOTTY!
DROOL! I CAN'T WAIT TO HAVE A MASH ON THEM BLUE-BLOODED ALABASTER MERINGUE KNOCKERS AND SQUIRT MY DIRTY OLD BAKER'S MUCK UP THAT UPPER-CRUST DOUGHNUT MINGEPIECE..!
DREAM ON, FRUBERT! SHE'S TOO GOOD FOR THE LIKES OF YOU..!
YES, THE STUCK-UP BISCUIT BITCH WOULDN'T EVEN LOWER HER RAISINS TO LOOK AT ME...
EH?..!? WHAT'S THAT, M'LADY..? YOUR HUSBAND IS IMPOTENT AND CANNOT SATISFY YOUR GINGERBREADLY NEEDS..?
WHAT'S THAT..?! YOU SAY YOU YEARN FOR THE STRONG, ROUGH TOUCH OF A WORKING MAN'S HANDS..?
...AND YOU WANT IT RIGHT NOW..? HERE IN THE KITCHEN..? RIGHT UP YOUR HOITY-TOITY PASTRY MARY-JANE..?
YES, M'LADY... OF COURSE, M'LADY... THREE BAGS FULL, M'LADY... 'APPEN I'LL DO AS YOU SAY...
UGH! UGH! UGH! UGH!
UGH!..UGH! ...UGH..!

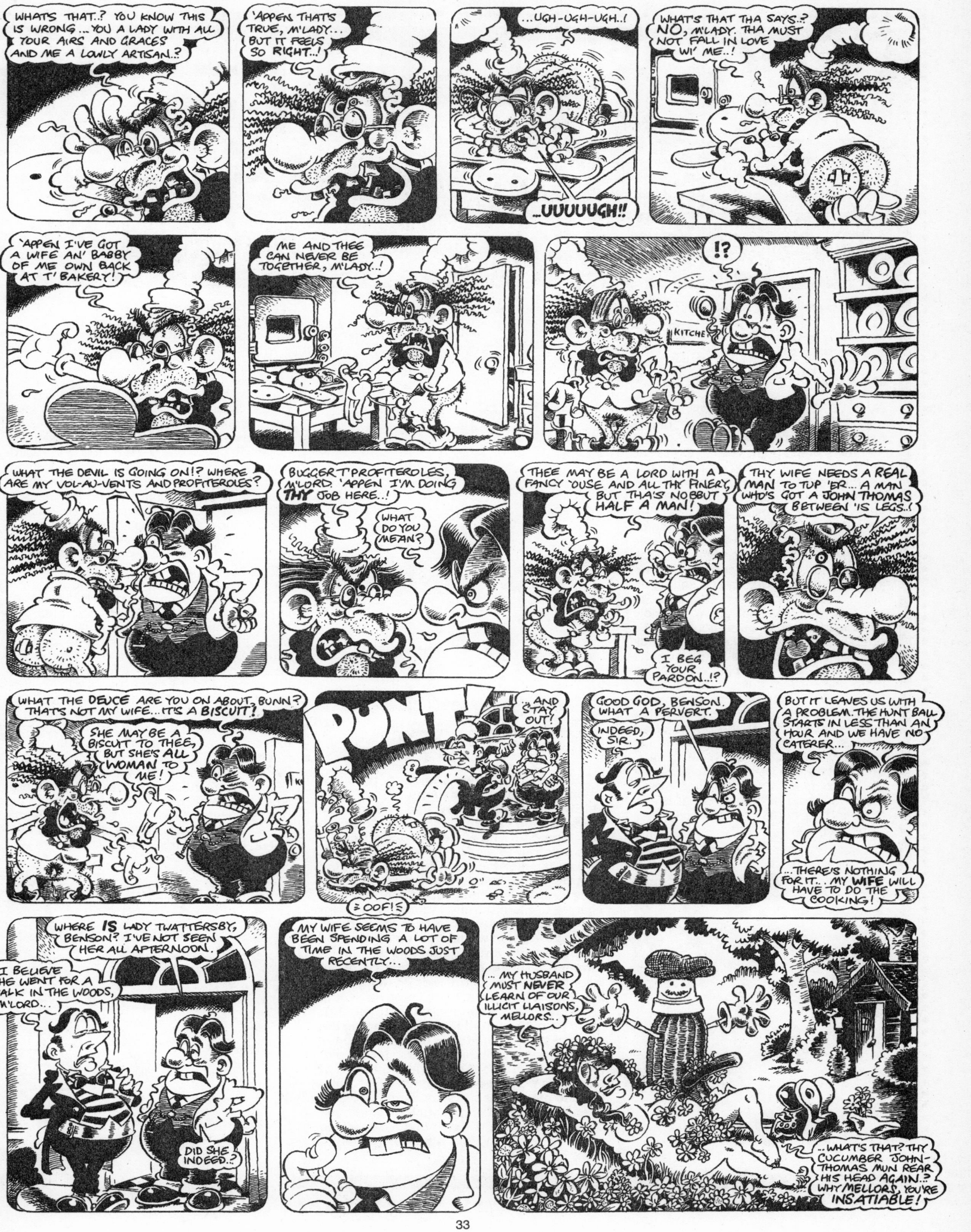
WHAT'S THAT..? YOU KNOW THIS IS WRONG... YOU A LADY WITH ALL YOUR AIRS AND GRACES AND ME A LOWLY ARTISAN..?
'APPEN THAT'S TRUE, M'LADY... BUT IT FEELS SO RIGHT..!
...UGH-UGH-UGH..!
...UUUUUGH!!
WHAT'S THAT THA SAYS..? NO, M'LADY. THA MUST NOT FALL IN LOVE WI' ME..!
'APPEN I'VE GOT A WIFE AN' BABBY OF ME OWN BACK AT T' BAKERY!
ME AND THEE CAN NEVER BE TOGETHER, M'LADY..!
!?
WHAT THE DEVIL IS GOING ON!? WHERE ARE MY VOL-AU-VENTS AND PROFITEROLES?
BUGGER T' PROFITEROLES, M'LORD. 'APPEN I'M DOING THY JOB HERE..!
WHAT DO YOU MEAN?
THEE MAY BE A LORD WITH A FANCY 'OUSE AND ALL THY FINERY, BUT THA'S NOBBUT HALF A MAN!
I BEG YOUR PARDON..!?
THY WIFE NEEDS A REAL MAN TO TUP 'ER... A MAN WHO'S GOT A JOHN THOMAS BETWEEN 'IS LEGS..!
WHAT THE DEUCE ARE YOU ON ABOUT, BUNN? THAT'S NOT MY WIFE... IT'S A BISCUIT!
SHE MAY BE A BISCUIT TO THEE, BUT SHE'S ALL WOMAN TO ME!
PUNT!
...AND STAY OUT!
OOF!
GOOD GOD, BENSON. WHAT A PERVERT.
INDEED, SIR.
BUT IT LEAVES US WITH A PROBLEM. THE HUNT BALL STARTS IN LESS THAN AN HOUR AND WE HAVE NO CATERER...
...THERE'S NOTHING FOR IT... MY WIFE WILL HAVE TO DO THE COOKING!
WHERE IS LADY TWATTERSBY, BENSON? I'VE NOT SEEN HER ALL AFTERNOON.
I BELIEVE SHE WENT FOR A WALK IN THE WOODS, M'LORD...
DID SHE INDEED..?
MY WIFE SEEMS TO HAVE BEEN SPENDING A LOT OF TIME IN THE WOODS JUST RECENTLY...
... MY HUSBAND MUST NEVER LEARN OF OUR ILLICIT LIAISONS, MELLORS...
...WHAT'S THAT? THY CUCUMBER JOHN-THOMAS MUN REAR HIS HEAD AGAIN..? WHY MELLORS, YOU'RE INSATIABLE!

WOT'S NEXT

SHOWBIZ star Jonathan Ross's decision not to renew his lucrative BBC contract came as a massive shock to everyone - including Ross himself. Why anyone would want to give up a 3-day-a-week, £6 million-a-year job is hard to comprehend. But after 25 years at the top of the entertainment tree, perhaps the cockney chat show king felt that he was stuck in a rut. After all, there are only so many times you can interview Ricky Gervais and Lee Evans, (about 8 to be precise), and maybe he was looking for a new career challenge.

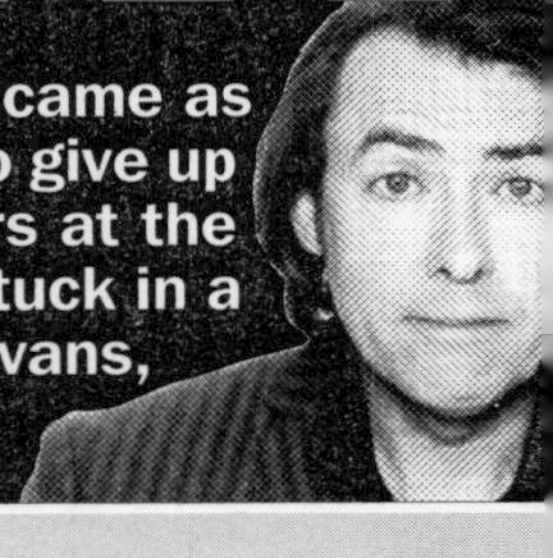

JOB: British Gas Call Centre Operative
SALARY: £8.35 per hour
HOURS: 38 p/w

EVERYONE knows that Wossy has the gift of the gab, so it would seem that he might be suited to this job. Cold calling members of the public and trying to sell them overpriced, unnecessary service contract schemes would be a doddle for the chatty 48-year-old. Over the years as a chat show host, he has demonstrated the ability to weedle personal information out of such famous guests as Ricky Gervais and Lee Evans. These skills could be put to good use charming bank account details and setting up direct debits from British Gas customers. However, Ross has an irrepressibly mischievous sense of humour, and it's doubtful that he could keep it in check for long. Whilst talking to a pensioner, he would sooner or later blurt out that his mate had fucked their grand-daughter. Since British Gas record all phonecalls for training purposes, Ross's four-letter tirade would come to the notice of his bosses. Just like at the BBC, he would probably be punished by being suspended for three months on full pay. But unable to resist the temptation again, his days would be numbered at British Gas, and he would quickly find himself signing on again.

JOB: Market Researcher
SALARY: £5.20 per hour
HOURS: 16-20 p/w

WORKING in a busy shopping precinct, asking strangers questions about what kind of detergents they use sounds like the ideal job for an affable motor-mouth like Jonathan. And whilst shoppers usually take a detour to avoid market researchers, Ross's familiar face and friendly outgoing manner would draw potential survey subjects to him like bees round a honey pot. Thanks to his naturally inquisitive manner and 25 years behind his chat show desk, the conversation would flow easily and the answer sheets would quickly fill up with information. However, it would not be about washing powder, cornflakes or margerine. For regular viewers of his shows would know that Ross cannot chat to anyone for more than 30 seconds without bringing the conversation round to his favourite subject - masturbation. His employers, faced with reams of data about the wanking habits of shoppers would no doubt have a few questions to ask themselves, such as is it worth keeping such an unproductive employee on the payroll? It is likely that Ross would soon be swapping his stack of questionaires for a P45.

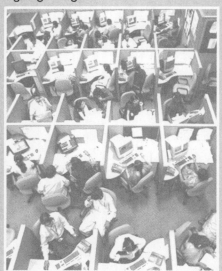

JOB: Porn Star
SALARY: £200 per film + £50 pop shot bonus
HOURS: variable

IT IS NO secret that Jonathan Ross is a great fan of erotica of all sorts. A man of natural appetites, he is believed to have an extensive collection of raunchy DVDs on top of the wardrobe in the bedroom of his Hampstead mansion. Couple his love for these films with his easy, uninhibited manner in front of the camera, and you might think that a career as an adult movie star beckons. Although nearly 50, Ross is still highly-sexed and makes no secret of the fact that he enjoys regular intercourse with his young wife Jane. So there would be no danger of him failing to rise to the occasion during a steamy hardcore clinch on set. Indeed, it's possible that Ross could manage three or even four pop shots in an afternoon, making him one of Britan's most sought after scud studs. However, there is nothing worse on a porn shoot than an actor or actress getting an attack of the giggles, and with Ross on set, the chances of that happening are high. With his trademark speech impediment, delivering a line like "I'm gonna ram my rock-hard rod right up your red-hot ringpiece, baby," would reduce cast and crew alike to fits of hysterics. Hours would be lost setting up the scene again, and as with any other business, time is money. Ross would end up blowing the budget instead of blowing his stack up his co-star's back, and would very quickly find himself on the dole again.

FOR WOSSY?

So what next for Wossy? When he leaves Broadcasting House for the last time in September, Ross will turn up to gn on at the White City DSS. But with a large family and houses in Hampstead, Devon and Florida, he'll find that s £26.75 per week Jobseeker's Allowance won't keep him in the lifestyle to which he is accustomed. Jonathan is oing to have to get another job... and quick.

But just exactly what will he do? We popped down the local Job Centre and checked the boards to see if there were ny situations vacant that Jonathan could fill...

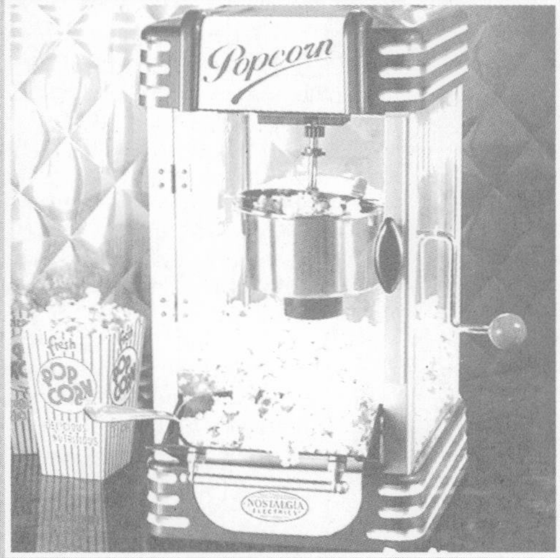
Popcorn

JOB: Multiplex Cinema Popcorn Seller
SALARY: £5.20 p/hr + 2 cinema tickets p/wk
HOURS: 16 p/weekend

JONATHAN **Ross's passion for all aspects of cinema is second to none, so selling overpriced snacks in the foyer of a sticky-carpeted warehouse on the edge of a trading estate would seem like an ideal job for the ex-*Film 2010* host. What's more, Ross is well known for his outlandish fashion sense, and is often pictured at premiers wearing ridiculous clothing designed by the likes of Vivienne Westwood and Alexander McQueen, so he wouldn't feel at all uncomfortable donning the blue nylon pinafore and cardboard Thunderbirds hat of a multiplex popcorn vendor. But his very enthusiasm for the silver screen could prove his undoing in this chosen career. This business depends on a fast turnover as hungry customers buy popcorn before heading in to see their chosen movie. With Ross on duty, long queues of frustrated customers would soon build up as the *Film 2010* host insisted on giving each customer a detailed critique, plot synopsis and star rating of the movie they were about to watch. This would be followed by a run down of the Top10 US films, based on box office receipts that week. Doubtless it wouldn't be long before Jonathan's new cinema career ended up on the cutting room floor.**

JOB: Assistant Ferret Keeper at Dudley Zoo
SALARY: £280 p/wk
HOURS: 35 p/wk

ALTHOUGH listeners to Jonathan's Saturday morning Radio 2 show won't have heard many records, they will have heard all about his fondness for animals. Ross's endless anecdotes about his pet dogs, cats, snakes, ferrets and pot-bellied pigs paint a picture of a man who is never happier than when he is surrounded by animals. So you might imagine that this job - second in charge of the ferrets at a busy Midlands zoo - would be the ideal move for an ex-celebrity looking to make a mid-life career change. However, on his first shift, Ross could well realise that he has made a big mistake. The glamorous part of the job - feeding and handling the ferrets and organising their popular daily tea-party - is the responsibility of the Chief Ferret Keeper. His assistant - Ross's lowly post - is merely employed to shovel up barrow-load after barrow-load of their foetid excrement. The fashion-conscious former TV dandy would no doubt refuse to don the keeper's regulation overalls and wellies, insisting instead on wearing his own snazzy designer gear. Unwilling to ruin an exclusive made-to-measure £8000 Norman Hartnell designer suit each day by getting ferret shit on it, he would quickly resign.

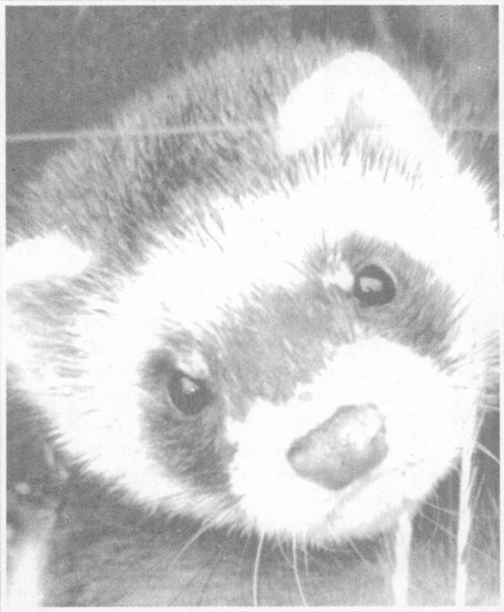

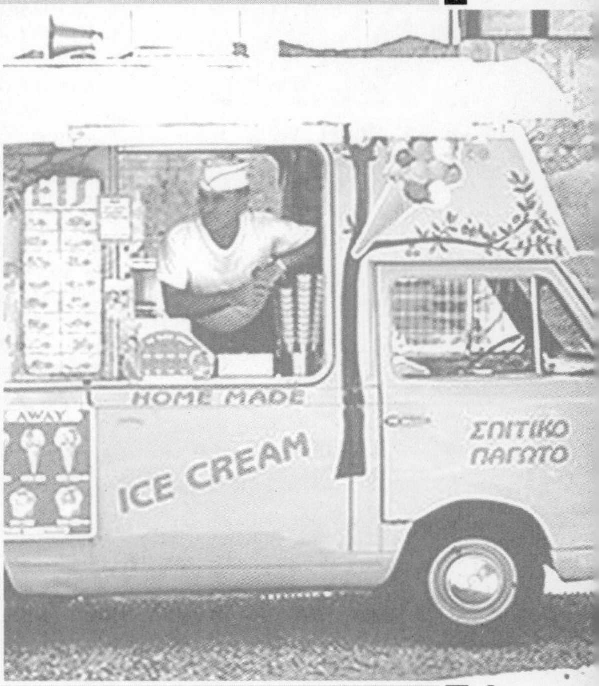
HOME MADE
ICE CREAM

JOB: Ice Cream Seller
SALARY: £230 p/wk
HOURS: 48 to suit

JONATHAN **Ross has hosted the British Comedy Awards for more years than his audience cares to remember. The crowd of drunken comedians are notoriously unruly, but Ross handles them with ease as he dispenses their prizes. This being the case, you would think handing out ice creams and lollies to a gaggle of badly-behaved children from the back of a Commer van would be a job that suited him down to the ground. However, by force of habit, between handing over each ice cream, Ross would feel compelled to deliver a 5-minute comedy monologue peppered with in-jokes of interest solely to people intimately acquainted with the TV programme commissioning process. The ice creams would melt before he handed them over, and his jibes about the poor BARB ratings for the third series of Gavin and Stacey would likely go over the heads of the impatient queue of toddlers.**

LETTERBOCKS

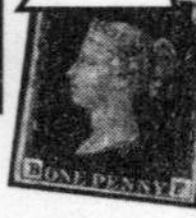

Viz Comic
PO Box 841
Whitley Bay
NE26 9EQ

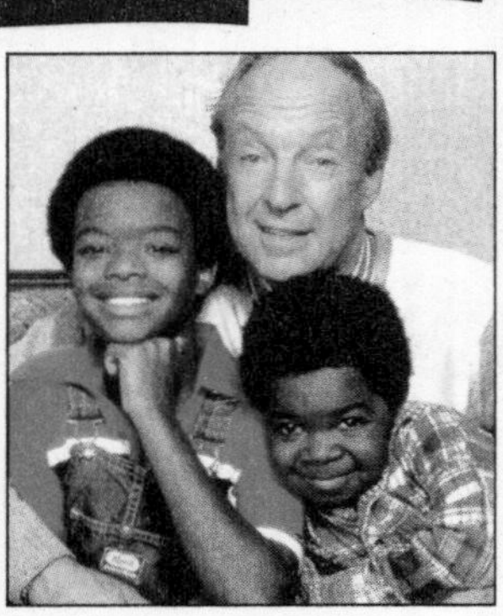

☐ **I WISH** Willis from *Diff'rent Strokes* would explain himself more clearly. That way, his little brother wouldn't have to say 'wotchoo talkin' 'bout?' a dozen times every episode.

S Porter, Merseyside

☐ **I SAW** several signs on the London Underground saying that due to engineering works on the Circle Line, that trains would not be running, but there was a replacement bus service running in their place. Well, I might be missing something, but if a train can't get down the tunnel because of engineering works, I don't see how a bus is going to manage it.

Alan Heath, e-mail

STAR LETTER

☐ **HOW** I panicked the other morning when I slept in until a quarter to nine. When I put my glasses on I realised I was looking at a tub of E45 on my bedside table, and that my alarm hadn't gone off yet.

Craig Eddie, e-mail

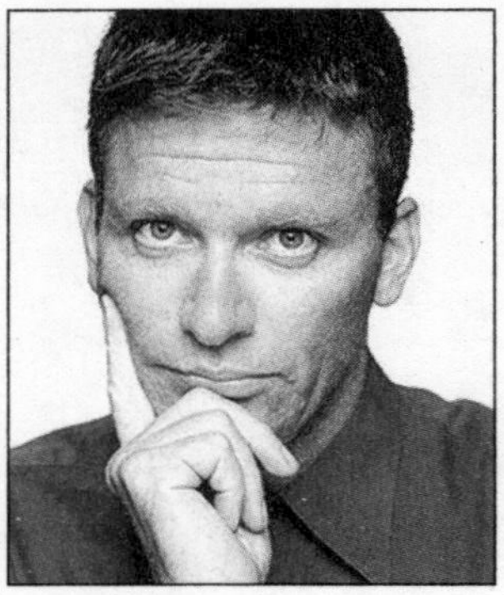

☐ **THE** number of times the guests on the Jeremy Kyle show are confirmed as lying by the Lie Dectector, and they claim they are telling the truth. Honestly, he wants to get that ruddy machine fixed.

John Cohen, e-mail

☐ **THIS** morning I was having a soak in the bath when my bell-end emerged out of the water looking like a faceless Sontaran off *Dr. Who*, or a Sontaran with his back to me. Either way I was quite scared.

Ralphie K, e-mail

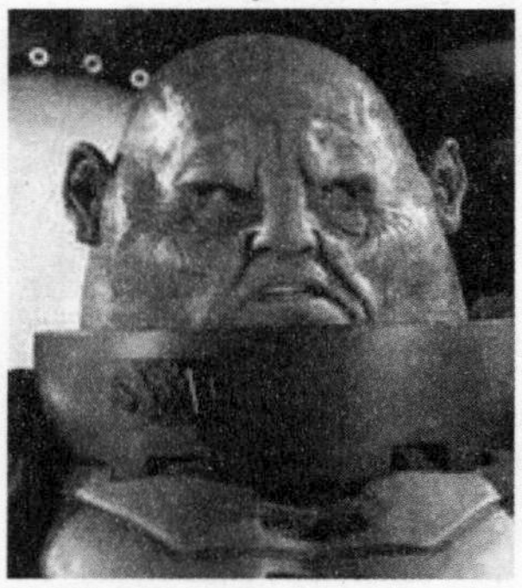

☐ **MY LOCAL** Sainsbury's had a sign up saying 'All our fresh chickens are 100% British.' Imagine being that racist.

Christina Martin, e-mail

☐ **I WAS** watching the news the other day when I saw a report about how Muslim extremists had tried to murder a Danish cartoonist who drew depictions of the prophet Mohammed. I thought to myself that with all the injustice in the world, how pathetic it was that people could get so angry over a cartoon. But then I remembered how radge I went when they first introduced that fucking Scrappy Doo into the Scooby Doo show when I was a kid. So maybe they do have a point.

Matt McCann, e-mail

☐ **EVERYONE** loves sausages, but large, clumsy 'sausage fingers' are generally considered an unattractive feature. Let's see the so called 'experts' explain that one.

R Jeremy, e-mail

☐ **WHEN** the local paper reported on a recent fire at my home, they said that I had awoken to smoke. These journalists never get their facts right. I wanted a piss.

Ben Rigsby, e-mail

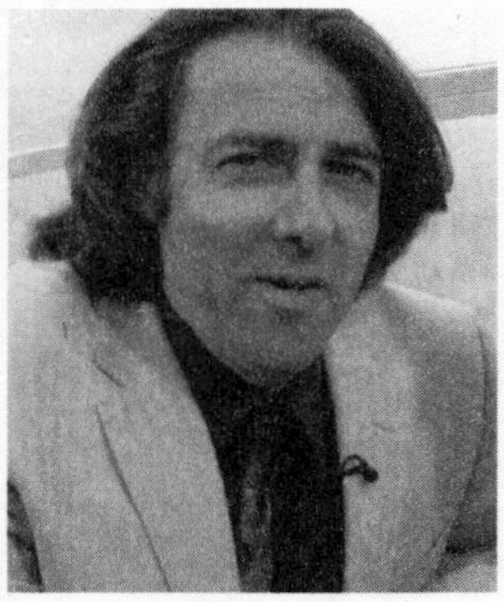

☐ **I READ** that during his enforced absence from the BBC, Jonathan Ross used his free time to learn Japanese. As a British chat show host, I would have thought learning top speak English proberly would have been a better use of his time.

Kenny Clarke, e-mail

☐ **I CAN'T** help thinking what a waste of money the recent snow has been. Surely taxpayers' money would have been better spent on the NHS or schools than wasted buying snow, which just melts anyway.

E Bamyasi, Cyberspace

☐ **IN A** recent BBC interview, Alan Sugar was asked if he should be referred to as 'Sir Alan' or 'Lord Sugar,' to which he replied, "Either one is fine, I'm not bothered." You've got to applaud his modesty.

Colin Stalin, e-mail

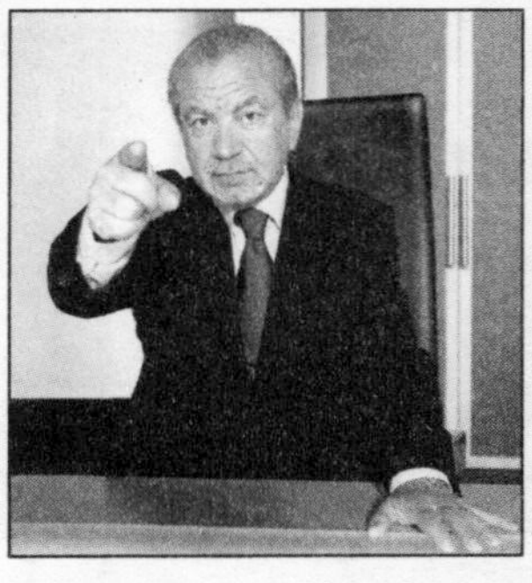

☐ **I SEE** Welsh ex-rugby international JPR Williams has been prosecuted for drink driving and tried to beat the breathalyser by sucking pennies in the back of the police car. How ridiculous for an educated man like him to believe that this urban myth would work. What he should have done was knock the policeman's hat off. That way the officer would technically have been 'out of uniform' and unable to make an arrest.

A man in a pub, London

☐ **CAN** anyone explain why God wants me to wait until 11.00am to buy a hammer on a Sunday? I can't find anything about it in the Bible.

Naich, e-mail

☐ **I BOUGHT** a 7-year-old Polo recently, and had to return it to the garage a week later as the oil warning light was on and the engine was knocking and rattling. The sympathetic man at the garage said I had been making too many short journeys, and that 'they all do that.' It certainly put my mind at rest.

Billy Bloodorange, e-mail

☐ **IT'S** good to see that the NHS are offering free chlamydia tests to anyone who wants one, but I was a

People Who You'd Never Get Tired of Punching...

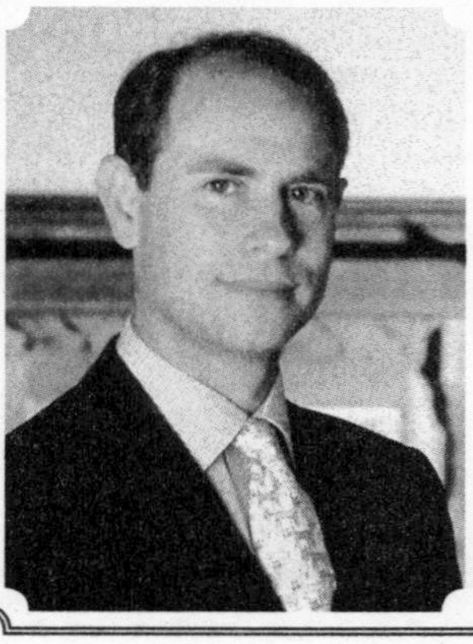

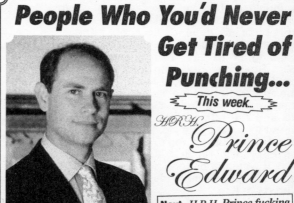

This week...

H.R.H. Prince Edward

Next week: *H.R.H. Prince fucking Edward again*

EUCLIDEAN PLANAR SHOPPING INTEREST

You'll only find ROUND things at ROUNDLAND

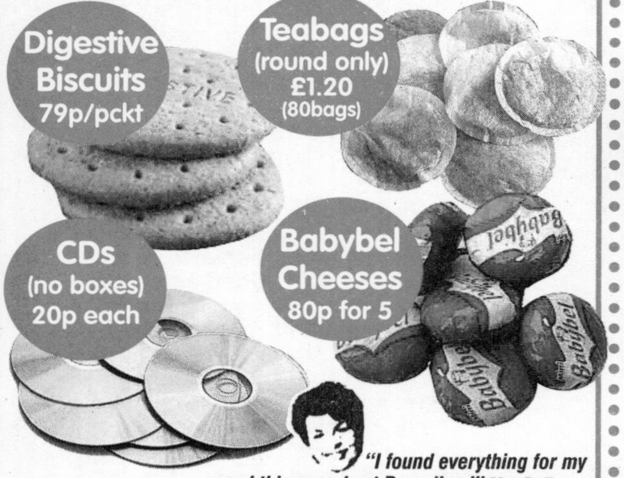

Digestive Biscuits 79p/pckt
Teabags (round only) £1.20 (80bags)
CDs (no boxes) 20p each
Babybel Cheeses 80p for 5

"I found everything for my round thing needs at Roundland" Mrs B, Essex

ROUNDLAND MONEY-BACK PROMISE!

"If you find something more round in any other store, we'll give you your money back! No Quibbles!"

ROUND or SPHERE You'll find it HERE!

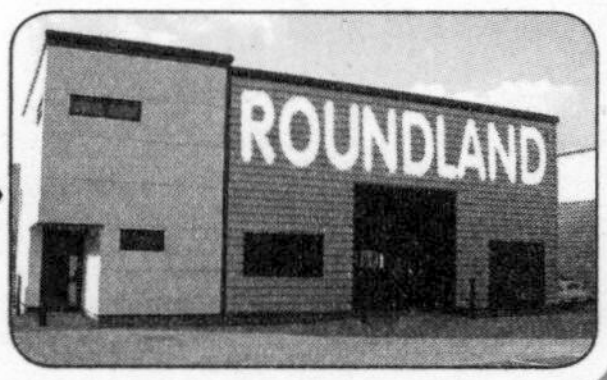

ROUNDLAND

little alarmed when I learned that we are being encouraged to send urine samples through the post for testing. When I sent Noel Edmonds a turd in an envelope via the Royal Mail, I was given 100 hours community service.

S Hummer, Grimsby

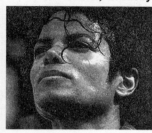

WHEN they make the inevitable film of Michael Jackson's life story, will they use a black actor and lighten him up towards the end of the film, or a white actor who will start the film blacked up?

G Ulfstatic, e-mail

THANK goodnes for Oatso Simple. Gone are the tiresome days of having to add milk to porridge and heat it up every morning. Now all I do is add milk to Oatso Simple and heat it up.

G Ramsay, e-mail

I SAW a toy on Amazon called 'My First Castle'. I assume that this is a niche item aimed at the children of royalty. Unless I am underestimating how many people grow up to own castles.

Martin Christian, e-mail

Top Tips

OLD people. Feeling lonely, isolated and ignored? Simply advertise a car in the *Autotrader* for £2000 below the list price and Hey Presto! Your phone won't stop ringing for a month.

Peter Britton, e-mail

WIDOWER motorists. Place your SatNav on a long plank of wood protruding from the back of your car. The spoken directional instructions will then be delivered at the exact moment you have missed your intended turning, thus bringing back fond memories of your late wife's attempts at map reading.

Larry Olden, e-mail

HOUSEWIVES. Don't waste kitchen roll mopping up spilt milk. Simply place a Weetabix in the centre of the puddle to soak it up and pop it in the fridge for the following day's breakfast.

Penny Chew, e-mail

SEAN Connery. Over-emphasise your Scottishness by rolling your Rs and occasionally wearing a kilt and nobody will remember that you haven't lived there for years.

GS Hickman, e-mail

TWO ladybirds glued together make an ideal bowling ball for a doll's house bowling alley.

T Wardrobe, e-mail

CRIMINALS. Keep a handkerchief in yor back pocket. When the police put handcuffs on you, simply cover your hands with the handkerchief for a few seconds. When you remove it, the cuffs will be unlocked and off. I have seen magicians do this many times and it always works.

Pat Roig, New Orleans

KEEN on owning a hamster? Simply urinate in the corner of your room and make a nick in the end of your finßger with a kitchen knife every couple of weeks for 18 months.

Jon, e-mail

HOUSEWIVES. Prevent multinational supermarkets from knowing everything about you by simply filling your shopping trolley with things you don't need or want.

Dan Baker, e-mail

AQUARIUM owners. Slow your fish down to a more therapeutic pace by filling your tank with clear hair gel.

Craig Eddie, e-mail

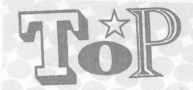

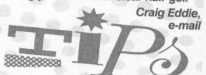

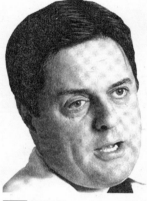

WHEN that Nick Griffin appeared on *Question Time* last year, the programme's ratings went through the roof. Seeing as he's so popular, why don't the BBC put him on other shows? He could appear on *SpringWatch* moaning about migrating birds or the grey squirrel.

S Noble, e-mail

SHOULDN'T the telly channel E4+1 simply be called E5?

Popey, e-mail

WITH reference to Popey's letter (above). I am a professor of maths at a university somewhere, and I can tell Mr Popey that E4+1 does not necessarily equal E5, except in the circumstance where E=1. The expression E4+1 is mathematically (E x 4)+1, but since we do not know the value of E, the expression cannot be simplified. E4+E = E5, however, which is perhaps where Mr Popey's confusion comes from.

Prof. W. Schnell University somewhere

WITH our 20th Wedding Anniversary approaching next month, my wife told me last night that she consevatively estimates that I have farted in bed 73,000 times since we said "I do."

Orangeman, e-mail

MAY I be the first to congratulate Chris Moyles after transforming himself from a fat cunt into

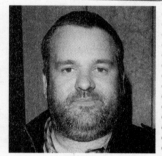

merely a cunt. Well done, Chris, you are an inspiration.

David Hammond, e-mail

DO ANY of your readers know if chimps drink tea anymore? Or move pianos?

David Hammond, e-mail

+++ West Yorkshire Explorers News Roundup +++ West Yorkshire Explorers News Roundup +++

NEW MOUNTAIN FOUND

EXPLORERS have discovered a mountain one-and-a-half times higher than Everest... *in West Yorkshire!*

BY'ECKSCLUSIVE!

The snow-topped peak, named Mount Boycott by its discoverers, stands over 36,000 feet high and incredibly has lain undiscovered in a field alongside the A645 between Wakefield and Featherstone for countless millennia.

LONG

"We don't know how we missed it for so long," admitted a red-faced Eric Mytholmroyd, head of the Featherstone Tourist Board. "But now we've found it, we're certainly going to make the most of it."

Local bed and breakfast owners are gearing up for an influx of sightseers and daytrippers, all eager to look at the jagged 7 mile-high peak.

BATTERSBY

Meanwhile businesses in the area are working round the clock producing tea-towels, paperweights and souvenir fudge, all featuring The Lost Mountain of Yorkshire.

MISERABLES

Featherstone Tourist Board last hit the headlines in 2009, when explorers discovered a mysterious lost valley filled with giant dinosaurs and pterodactyls, also alongside the A645, about half a mile out of Purston.

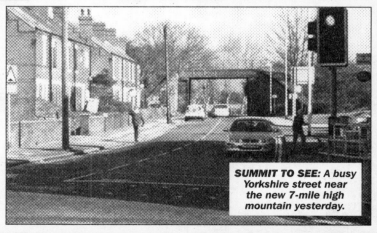

***SUMMIT TO SEE:* A busy Yorkshire street near the new 7-mile high mountain yesterday.**

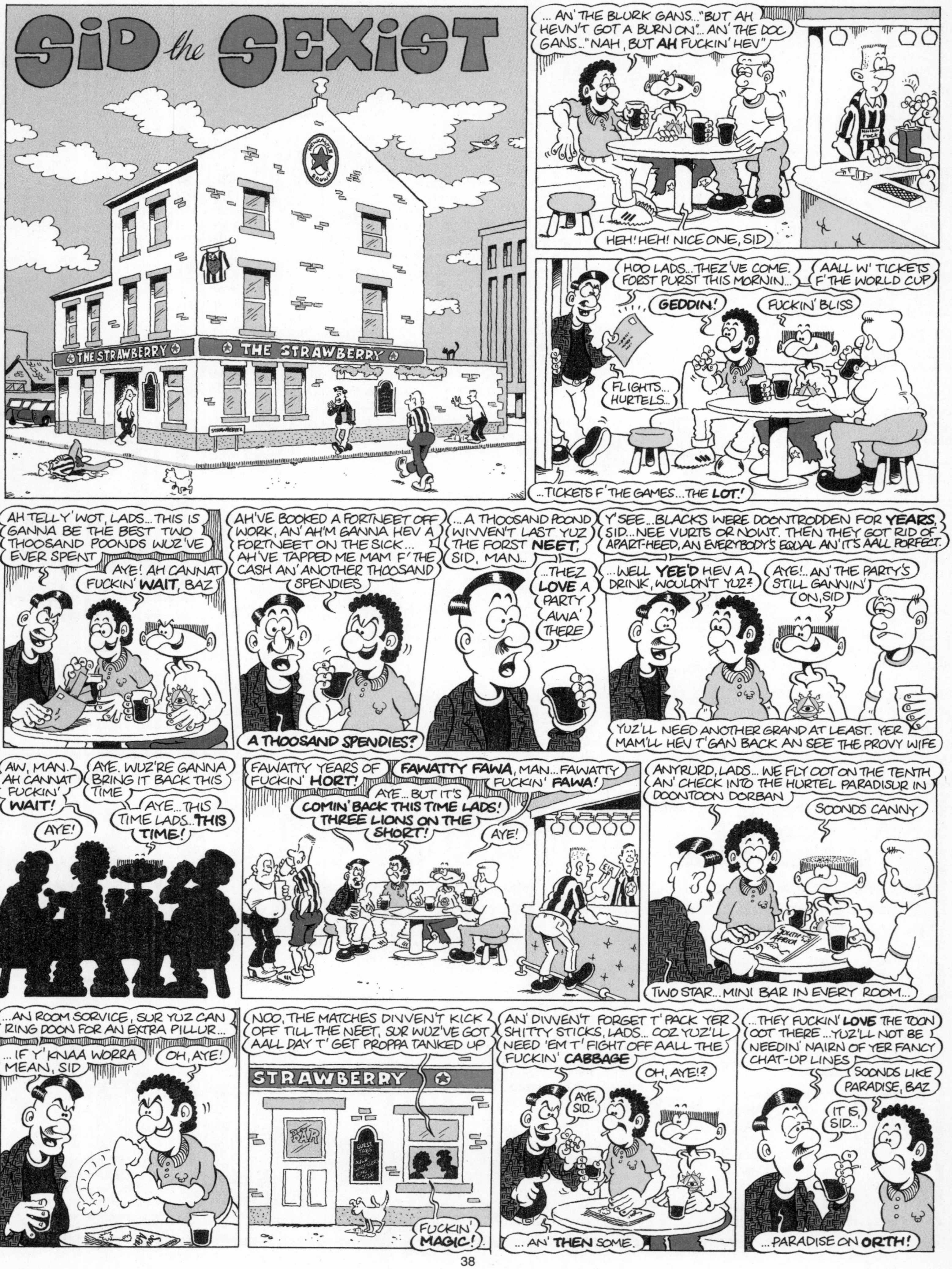
SID the SEXIST
THE STRAWBERRY
THE STRAWBERRY
... AN' THE BLURK GANS... "BUT AH HEVN'T GOT A BURN ON"... AN' THE DOC GANS... "NAH, BUT AH FUCKIN' HEV"
HEH! HEH! NICE ONE, SID
HOO LADS... THEZ'VE COME. FORST PURST THIS MORNIN...
AALL W' TICKETS F' THE WORLD CUP
GEDDIN!
FUCKIN' BLISS
FLIGHTS... HURTELS...
...TICKETS F' THE GAMES... THE LOT!
AH TELL Y' WOT, LADS... THIS IS GANNA BE THE BEST TWO THOOSAND POONDS WUZ'VE EVER SPENT
AYE! AH CANNAT FUCKIN' WAIT, BAZ
AH'VE BOOKED A FORTNEET OFF WORK, AN' AH'M GANNA HEV A FORTNEET ON THE SICK... AH'VE TAPPED ME MAM F' THE CASH AN' ANOTHER THOOSAND SPENDIES
A THOOSAND SPENDIES?
... A THOOSAND POOND WIVVEN'T LAST YUZ THE FORST NEET, SID, MAN...
...THEZ LOVE A PARTY AWA' THERE
Y' SEE... BLACKS WERE DOONTRODDEN FOR YEARS, SID... NEE VURTS OR NOWT. THEN THEY GOT RID OF APART-HEED, AN EVERYBODY'S EQUAL AN' IT'S AALL PORFECT.
...WELL YEE'D HEV A DRINK, WOULDN'T YUZ?
AYE!... AN' THE PARTY'S STILL GANNIN' ON, SID
YUZ'LL NEED ANOTHER GRAND AT LEAST. YER MAM'LL HEV T'GAN BACK AN SEE THE PROVY WIFE
AW, MAN. AH CANNAT FUCKIN' WAIT!
AYE. WUZ'RE GANNA BRING IT BACK THIS TIME
AYE!
AYE... THIS TIME LADS... THIS TIME!
FAWATTY YEARS OF FUCKIN' HORT!
FAWATTY FAWA, MAN... FAWATTY FUCKIN' FAWA!
AYE... BUT IT'S COMIN' BACK THIS TIME LADS! THREE LIONS ON THE SHORT!
AYE!
ANYRURD, LADS... WE FLY OOT ON THE TENTH AN' CHECK INTO THE HURTEL PARADISUR IN DOONTOON DORBAN
SOONDS CANNY
SOUTH AFRICA
TWO STAR... MINI BAR IN EVERY ROOM...
...AN ROOM SORVICE, SUR YUZ CAN RING DOON FOR AN EXTRA PILLUR...
... IF Y' KNAA WORRA MEAN, SID
OH, AYE!
NOO, THE MATCHES DIVVEN'T KICK OFF TILL THE NEET, SUR WUZ'VE GOT AALL DAY T' GET PROPPA TANKED UP
STRAWBERRY
BAR
FUCKIN' MAGIC!
AN' DIVVEN'T FORGET T' PACK YER SHITTY STICKS, LADS... COZ YUZ'LL NEED 'EM T' FIGHT OFF AALL THE FUCKIN' CABBAGE
AYE, SID...
OH, AYE!?
... AN' THEN SOME.
...THEY FUCKIN' LOVE THE TOON OOT THERE ...YUZ'LL NOT BE NEEDIN' NAIRN OF YER FANCY CHAT-UP LINES
SOONDS LIKE PARADISE, BAZ
IT IS, SID...
... PARADISE ON ORTH!

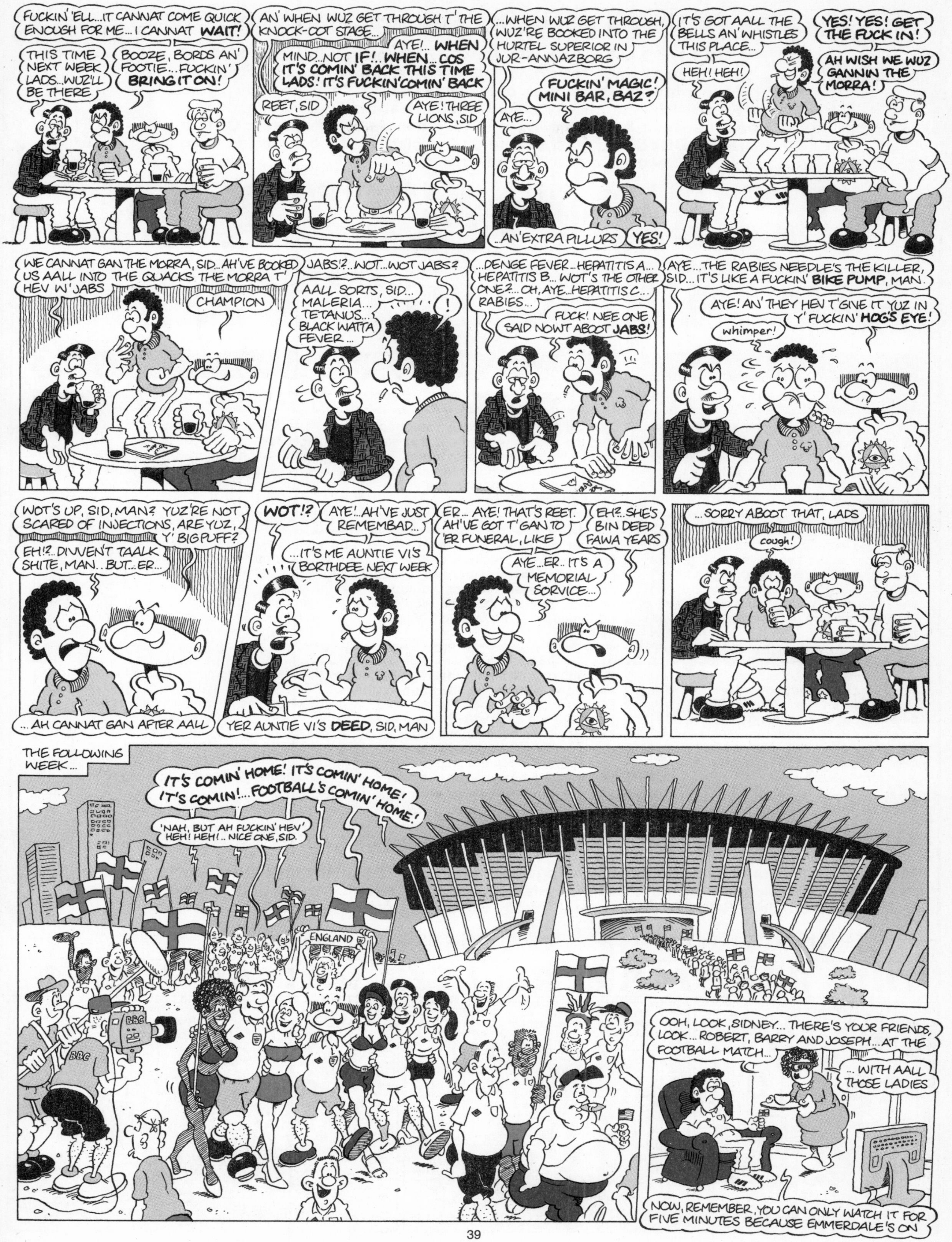
FUCKIN' 'ELL...IT CANNAT COME QUICK ENOUGH FOR ME... I CANNAT WAIT!
THIS TIME NEXT WEEK LADS...WUZ'LL BE THERE
BOOZE, BORDS AN' FOOTIE...FUCKIN' BRING IT ON!
AN' WHEN WUZ GET THROUGH T' THE KNOCK-OOT STAGE...
AYE!... WHEN
MIND..NOT IF!..WHEN...COS IT'S COMIN' BACK THIS TIME LADS! IT'S FUCKIN' COMIN' BACK
REET, SID
AYE! THREE LIONS, SID
...WHEN WUZ GET THROUGH, WUZ'RE BOOKED INTO THE HURTEL SUPERIOR IN JUR-ANNAZBORG
FUCKIN' MAGIC! MINI BAR, BAZ?
AYE...
...AN' EXTRA PILLURS
YES!
IT'S GOT AALL THE BELLS AN' WHISTLES THIS PLACE...
HEH! HEH!
YES! YES! GET THE FUCK IN!
AH WISH WE WUZ GANNIN THE MORRA!
WE CANNAT GAN THE MORRA, SID...AH'VE BOOKED US AALL INTO THE QUACKS THE MORRA T' HEV W' JABS
CHAMPION
JABS!?...WOT...WOT JABS?
AALL SORTS, SID... MALERIA... TETANUS... BLACK WATTA FEVER...
!
...DENGE FEVER...HEPATITIS A... HEPATITIS B... WOT'S THE OTHER ONE?...OH, AYE...HEPATITIS C... RABIES...
FUCK! NEE ONE SAID NOWT ABOOT JABS!
AYE...THE RABIES NEEDLE'S THE KILLER, SID...IT'S LIKE A FUCKIN' BIKE PUMP, MAN.
AYE! AN' THEY HEV T'GIVE IT YUZ IN Y' FUCKIN' HOG'S EYE!
whimper!
WOT'S UP, SID, MAN? YUZ'RE NOT SCARED OF INJECTIONS, ARE YUZ, Y' BIG PUFF?
EH!?...DIVVEN'T TAALK SHITE, MAN...BUT...ER...
...AH CANNAT GAN AFTER AALL
WOT!?
AYE!...AH'VE JUST REMEMBAD...
...IT'S ME AUNTIE VI'S BORTHDEE NEXT WEEK
YER AUNTIE VI'S DEED, SID, MAN
ER... AYE! THAT'S REET. AH'VE GOT T' GAN TO 'ER FUNERAL, LIKE
EH?...SHE'S BIN DEED FAWA YEARS
AYE...ER...IT'S A MEMORIAL SORVICE...
...SORRY ABOOT THAT, LADS
cough!
THE FOLLOWING WEEK...
IT'S COMIN' HOME! IT'S COMIN' HOME! IT'S COMIN!...FOOTBALL'S COMIN' HOME!
'NAH, BUT AH FUCKIN' HEV' HEH! HEH!...NICE ONE, SID.
ENGLAND
BBC
OOH, LOOK, SIDNEY... THERE'S YOUR FRIENDS, LOOK... ROBERT, BARRY AND JOSEPH...AT THE FOOTBALL MATCH...
...WITH AALL THOSE LADIES
NOW, REMEMBER, YOU CAN ONLY WATCH IT FOR FIVE MINUTES BECAUSE EMMERDALE'S ON

It's the debate that's splitting the nation down the middle!

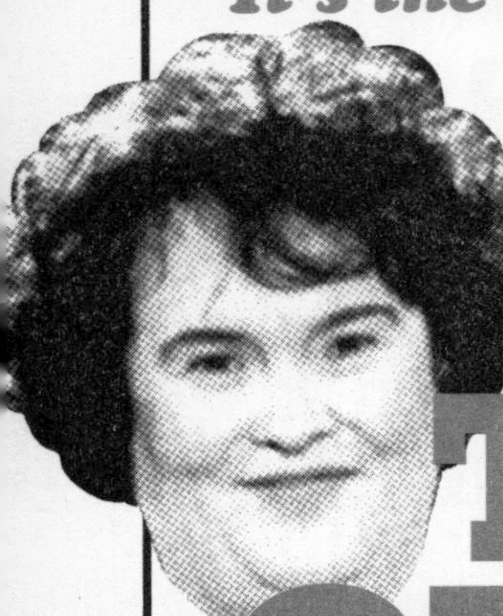

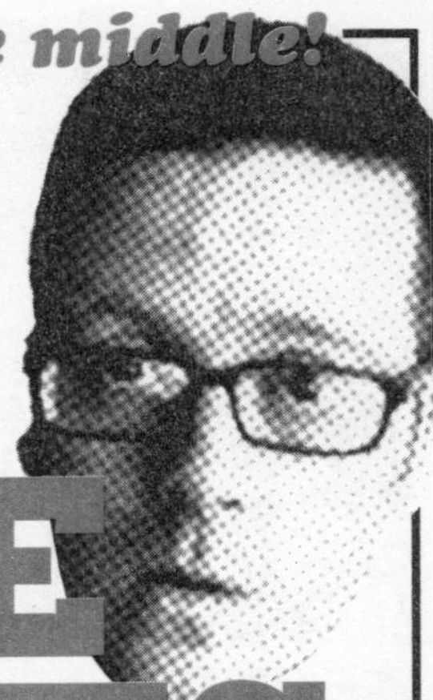

JUST *WHO* is Britain's best Boyle? Perhaps you think it's **SUSAN** - the hairy angel of *Britain's Got Talent,* whose beautiful singing brought tears to the eyes of the whole world. Or maybe you'd vote for **FRANKIE** - the cheeky comic whose near-the-knuckle humour on *Mock the Week* has us crying with laughter week after week. Or is it **ROBERT BOYLE** - the 17th century physicist? It's time to decide once and for all. Seconds out for Round One of...

THE BATTLE OF THE BOYLES

SUSAN		FRANKIE		ROBERT	
FOUNDING THE ROYAL SOCIETY					
Susan Boyle's performance of the song *I Dreamed a Dream* from Les Miserables was a worldwide YouTube hit, but sadly she was born 400 years too late to be a founder member of the Royal Society.	0	**Frankie Boyle famously quipped that the Queen was so old that her vagina was infested with moths. To be associated with the Royal Society would be against his anti-establishment principles.**	0	The Charter of Incorporation for the Royal Society - a group of scientists, philosophers and thinkers - was granted by Charles II in 1663 and named Robert Boyle as a founder member.	10
REPEALING HENRY IV'S ANTI-ALCHEMY STATUTE					
Susan Boyle's album *I Dreamed a Dream* went gold within two days of its release, but with her busy touring and promotion schedule, it is unlikely that she has time to give much thought to the transmutation of base metals into gold.	0	**Former alcoholic Frankie is clearly not impressed by precious metals, as he made tongue-in-cheek jokes about swimmer Rebecca Adlington despite the fact that she won five gold medals at the Beijing Olympics in 2008.**	0	In 1689, Robert Boyle successfully lobbied Parliament to turn over Henry IV's long-standing law of 1422 which forbade the transmutation of common metals into gold or silver. This allowed him to continue his scientific experiments.	10
FORMULATING BOYLE'S LAW					
When Susan walked out onto the Britain's Got Talent stage, nobody knew what her talent would turn out to be. In the end, it turned out to be singing *I Dreamed a Dream* rather than formulating laws governing the relationship between gas pressure and volume at a constant temperature.	0	**No subject is off limits in fearless Frankie's studiedly outrageous stand-up routines. Disability, paedophilia, incest and HIV/AIDS are all grist to his comical mill. However, even he has probably never made jokes about the inversely proportional relationship between the pressure and volume of a gas!**	0	As every schoolboy knows, in 1662 Robert formulated his famous law, which can be expressed as $pV = k$, where p is the pressure in the system, V is the volume of the gas in the system and k is a constant value. The law is true for all closed systems where the temperature remains unchanged.	10
TOTALS					
SUSAN: 0		FRANKIE: 0		ROBERT: 30	

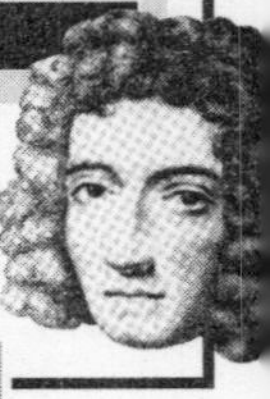

SUBO may have dreamed a dream of winning this contest, but that dream has turned into a nightmare. And taboo-breaking funnyman **FRANKIE** isn't laughing now, either. They've both had a proper pasting from rank outsider **ROBERT**, who is still "on the Boyle" despite having been dead for 319 years!

NEXT WEEK Who's the Best Bacon - Hollywood star Kevin, Radio 5 bad boy Richard or 17th century physicist Sir Francis?

THE POSTMAN ALWAYS WRINGS FLEISS

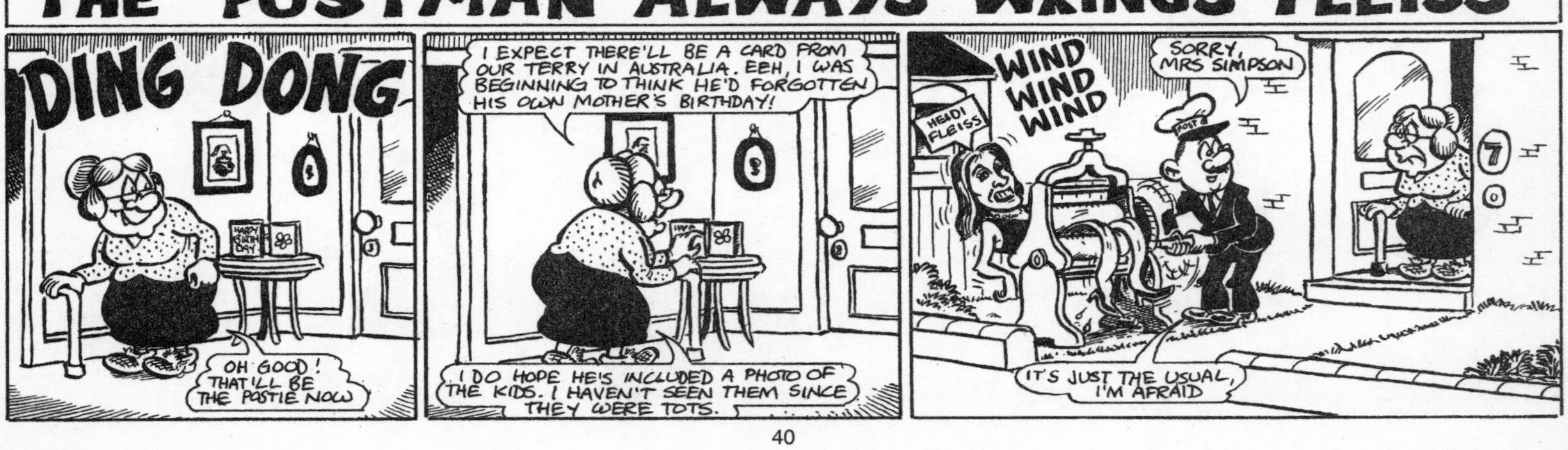
DING DONG
OH GOOD! THAT'LL BE THE POSTIE NOW
I EXPECT THERE'LL BE A CARD FROM OUR TERRY IN AUSTRALIA. EEH, I WAS BEGINNING TO THINK HE'D FORGOTTEN HIS OWN MOTHER'S BIRTHDAY!
I DO HOPE HE'S INCLUDED A PHOTO OF THE KIDS. I HAVEN'T SEEN THEM SINCE THEY WERE TOTS.
WIND WIND WIND
SORRY, MRS SIMPSON
HEIDI FLEISS
IT'S JUST THE USUAL, I'M AFRAID

Posh Spice Solves Engine Knock Riddle

VICTORIA BECKHAM yesterday unveiled her latest product - and this time it's not a pair of shoes, a perfume or some sparkly earrings - it's a revolutionary device to reduce engine knock.

The phenomenon, also known as pinking, is caused when small pockets of air/fuel mixture ignite at the wrong point of the combustion cycle, leading to excess fuel consumption, premature wear on the pistons and stress on the engine block. Now the 36-year-old singer, whose hits include *Really Really Want*, *Wannabe* and *Zig-a-zig-aah*, believes she has cracked it once and for all.

HONEYCOMB

"I have approached the problem in a revolutionary way," she told a charity lunch raising money for dolphin poverty. *"My solution is to warm up the fuel/air mixture with heat from the exhaust gases by passing it through a honeycomb complex mounted inside the exhaust manifold before it is injected into the cylinder."*

"This warming makes the mixture more combustible, ensuring a clean, single burn on the ignition stroke, increasing horse-power whilst reducing fuel consumption and emissions," she continued. "This engine will rev all the way up to the red line without pinking."

BROWN

The new gadgets are expected to go on sale in November, when they will be offered as a £100,000 optional extra on the Beckhams' signature Range Rover Evoque model.

Beckham's agent told us: "That may sound like a lot of money, but these devices are made of solid gold, and they've got David and Victoria's monograms picked out on the top in Swarovski crystals."

STRACHAN

Posh explained how the engineering project had taken up all her spare time for the past four years. "Solving the engine knock problem meant that I had to put many other potential schemes on hold," she told diners at the Ritz. "So I'm raring to get to work on some of the things I've had to leave on the back burner since 2006."

Beckham now intends to start developing a series of children's books about a school for pony wizards, a range of colour-coordinated lipsticks and tights, and research to find a monoclonal antibody to identify the gene responsible for Huntington's Chorea.

GIRL POWER: Posh (*right*) promises improved torque curve for new Range Rover (*left*).

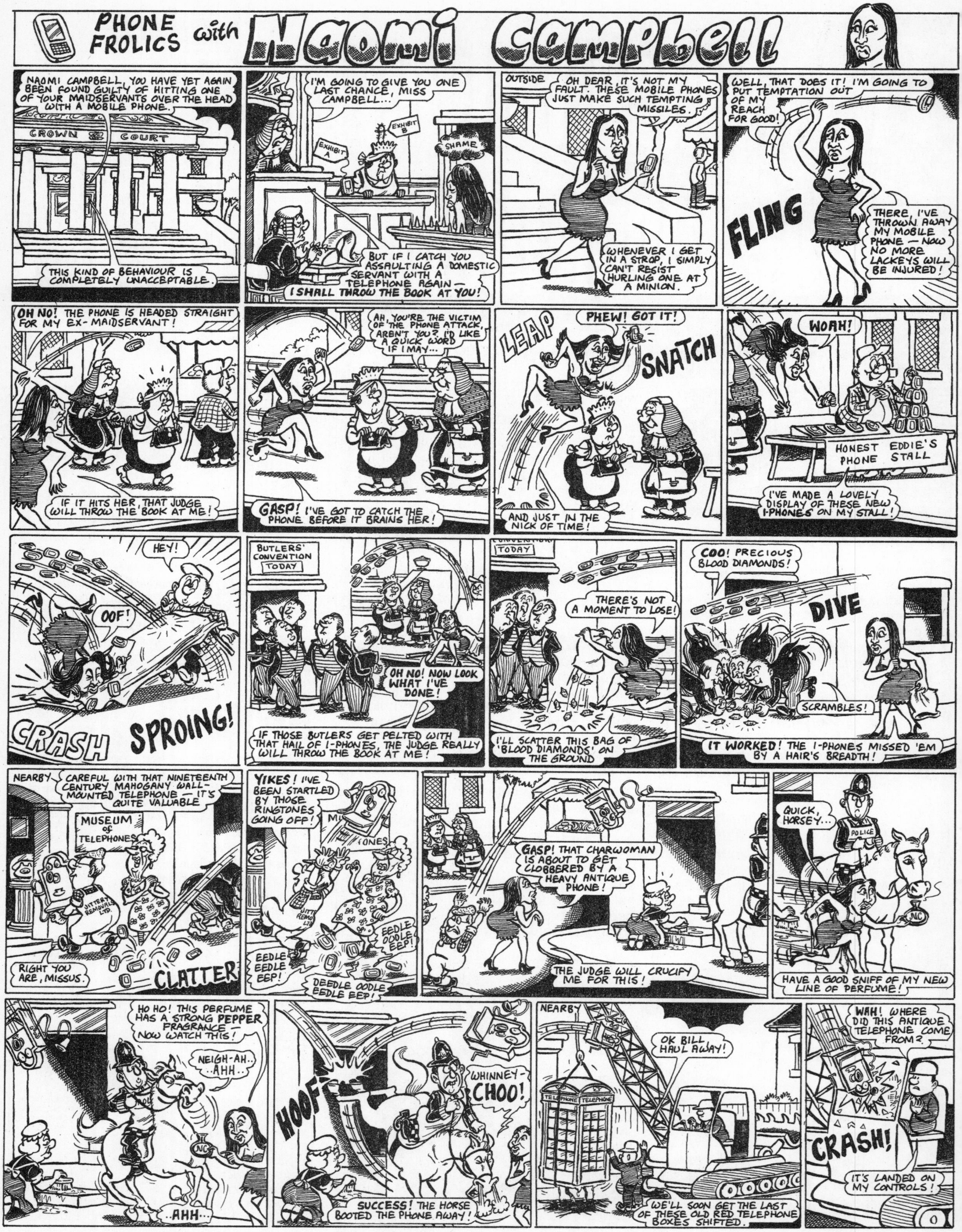
PHONE FROLICS with Naomi Campbell
NAOMI CAMPBELL, YOU HAVE YET AGAIN BEEN FOUND GUILTY OF HITTING ONE OF YOUR MAIDSERVANTS OVER THE HEAD WITH A MOBILE PHONE.
CROWN COURT
THIS KIND OF BEHAVIOUR IS COMPLETELY UNACCEPTABLE.
I'M GOING TO GIVE YOU ONE LAST CHANCE, MISS CAMPBELL...
EXHIBIT B
EXHIBIT A
SHAME
BUT IF I CATCH YOU ASSAULTING A DOMESTIC SERVANT WITH A TELEPHONE AGAIN — I SHALL THROW THE BOOK AT YOU!
OUTSIDE
OH DEAR, IT'S NOT MY FAULT. THESE MOBILE PHONES JUST MAKE SUCH TEMPTING MISSILES.
WHENEVER I GET IN A STROP, I SIMPLY CAN'T RESIST HURLING ONE AT A MINION.
WELL, THAT DOES IT! I'M GOING TO PUT TEMPTATION OUT OF MY REACH FOR GOOD!
FLING
THERE, I'VE THROWN AWAY MY MOBILE PHONE — NOW NO MORE LACKEYS WILL BE INJURED!
OH NO! THE PHONE IS HEADED STRAIGHT FOR MY EX-MAIDSERVANT!
IF IT HITS HER, THAT JUDGE WILL THROW THE BOOK AT ME!
AH, YOU'RE THE VICTIM OF THE PHONE ATTACK, AREN'T YOU? I'D LIKE A QUICK WORD IF I MAY...
GASP! I'VE GOT TO CATCH THE PHONE BEFORE IT BRAINS HER!
LEAP
PHEW! GOT IT!
SNATCH
AND JUST IN THE NICK OF TIME!
WOAH!
HONEST EDDIE'S PHONE STALL
I'VE MADE A LOVELY DISPLAY OF THESE NEW I-PHONES ON MY STALL!
HEY!
OOF!
CRASH
SPROING!
BUTLERS' CONVENTION TODAY
OH NO! NOW LOOK WHAT I'VE DONE!
IF THOSE BUTLERS GET PELTED WITH THAT HAIL OF I-PHONES, THE JUDGE REALLY WILL THROW THE BOOK AT ME!
TODAY
THERE'S NOT A MOMENT TO LOSE!
I'LL SCATTER THIS BAG OF 'BLOOD DIAMONDS' ON THE GROUND
COO! PRECIOUS BLOOD DIAMONDS!
DIVE
SCRAMBLES!
IT WORKED! THE I-PHONES MISSED 'EM BY A HAIR'S BREADTH!
NEARBY
CAREFUL WITH THAT NINETEENTH CENTURY MAHOGANY WALL-MOUNTED TELEPHONE — IT'S QUITE VALUABLE
MUSEUM of TELEPHONES
JITTERS REMOVALS LTD.
RIGHT YOU ARE, MISSUS.
CLATTER
YIKES! I'VE BEEN STARTLED BY THOSE RINGTONES GOING OFF!
EEDLE EEDLE EEP!
EEDLE OODLE EEP!
DEEDLE OODLE EEDLE EEP!
GASP! THAT CHARWOMAN IS ABOUT TO GET CLOBBERED BY A HEAVY ANTIQUE PHONE!
THE JUDGE WILL CRUCIFY ME FOR THIS!
QUICK, HORSEY...
POLICE
NC
HAVE A GOOD SNIFF OF MY NEW LINE OF PERFUME!
HO HO! THIS PERFUME HAS A STRONG PEPPER FRAGRANCE — NOW WATCH THIS!
NEIGH-AH.. ..AHH..
..AHH..
HOOF
WHINNEY-CHOO!
SUCCESS! THE HORSE BOOTED THE PHONE AWAY!
NEARBY
OK BILL HAUL AWAY!
TELEPHONE TELEPHONE
WE'LL SOON GET THE LAST OF THESE OLD RED TELEPHONE BOXES SHIFTED.
WAH! WHERE DID THIS ANTIQUE TELEPHONE COME FROM?
CRASH!
IT'S LANDED ON MY CONTROLS!

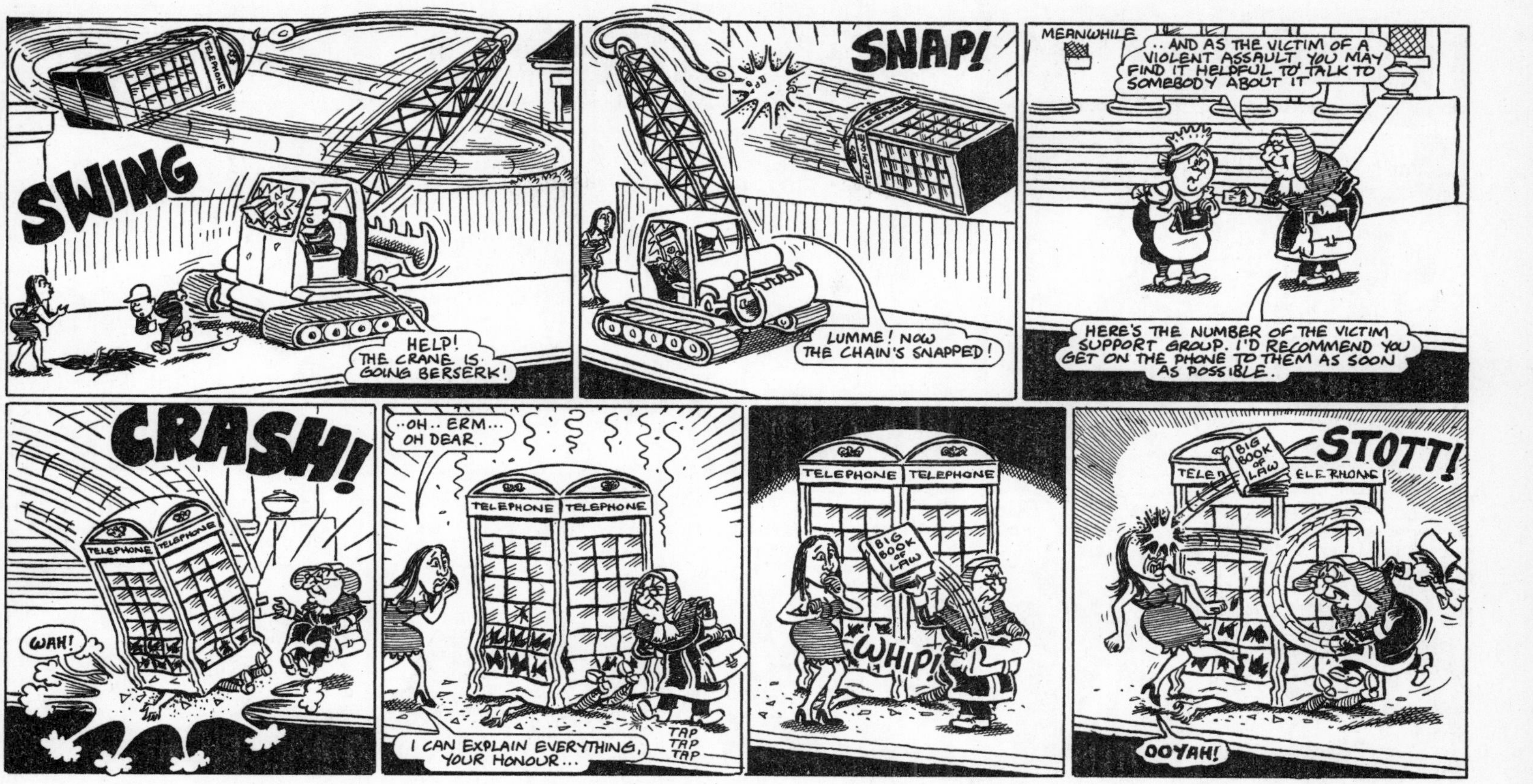
SWING
HELP! THE CRANE IS GOING BERSERK!
SNAP!
LUMME! NOW THE CHAIN'S SNAPPED!
MEANWHILE
.. AND AS THE VICTIM OF A VIOLENT ASSAULT YOU MAY FIND IT HELPFUL TO TALK TO SOMEBODY ABOUT IT
HERE'S THE NUMBER OF THE VICTIM SUPPORT GROUP. I'D RECOMMEND YOU GET ON THE PHONE TO THEM AS SOON AS POSSIBLE.
CRASH!
TELEPHONE TELEPHONE
WAH!
..OH.. ERM... OH DEAR.
TELEPHONE TELEPHONE
I CAN EXPLAIN EVERYTHING, YOUR HONOUR...
TAP TAP TAP
TELEPHONE TELEPHONE
BIG BOOK OF LAW
WHIP!
STOTT!
BIG BOOK OF LAW
OOYAH!

Spacemen flee orbiting lab after ghostly goings-on

THE SPACE WRAITH

NASA bosses have denied rumours that petrified astronauts fled the International Space Station last week after claiming that the multi-billion pound orbiting science lab is *HAUNTED!*

A premature evacuation of the 400m long research unit was ordered on Tuesday after boffins announced that an unexpected increase in solar activity could place the thirteen strong crew in serious danger. But a secret NASA source has admitted that the mission was aborted when the crew threatened to mutiny after witnessing a chilling series of paranormal events which left them too scared to sleep or work alone.

The source, who wished to remain nameless, told our reporter that the experienced team of 10 men and 3 women had reported seeing large objects such as a frying pan and a Corgi trouser press floating in mid air. And other normally static items were seen to move through the capsule as if of their own free will.

egg-heads

The rocketeers were ordered to sleep while egg-heads at mission control ran checks on the station's mainframe computers believing sun spots to be the cause of the disturbances. But the following morning senior flight staff demanded to come home after waking up to find themselves hovering a full six inches above their bed sheets. "It was as if they were being held aloft by some strange invisible force," the insider told us.

He continued: "The final straw came when Commander Alan Poindexter attempted to calm shattered nerves by making everyone a nice cup of tea. The already jittery crew froze in horror as he turned the tap only to see the water to flow upwards into the air rather than down into the kettle."

call my bluff

"At this point the entire crew ran screaming from the main living quarters and back onto the Space Shuttle, barricading the air-lock behind them with a wooden chair. The crew spent two nights in the cramped conditions, sleeping with all the lights on. NASA chiefs were concerned that their actions would run the ageing spacecraft's battery flat, and at that point they had no-option but to allow an early return to earth."

Speaking from the agency's headquarters in Houston a NASA spokesman promised a full investigation into the incident. However, he admitted that this isn't the first time a space mission has come close to disaster due to fears of the supernatural.

only connect

"The 1969 Apollo 11 moon landing was almost scuppered when Buzz Aldrin got all scared because he could see the famous 'face' on Mars from his bedroom window," he said.

"He was all spooked up because Command Module pilot Michael Collins had been telling him ghost stories on the way to the moon. Neil Armstrong had to issue Collins with an official warning and swap bedrooms with Aldrin," he added.

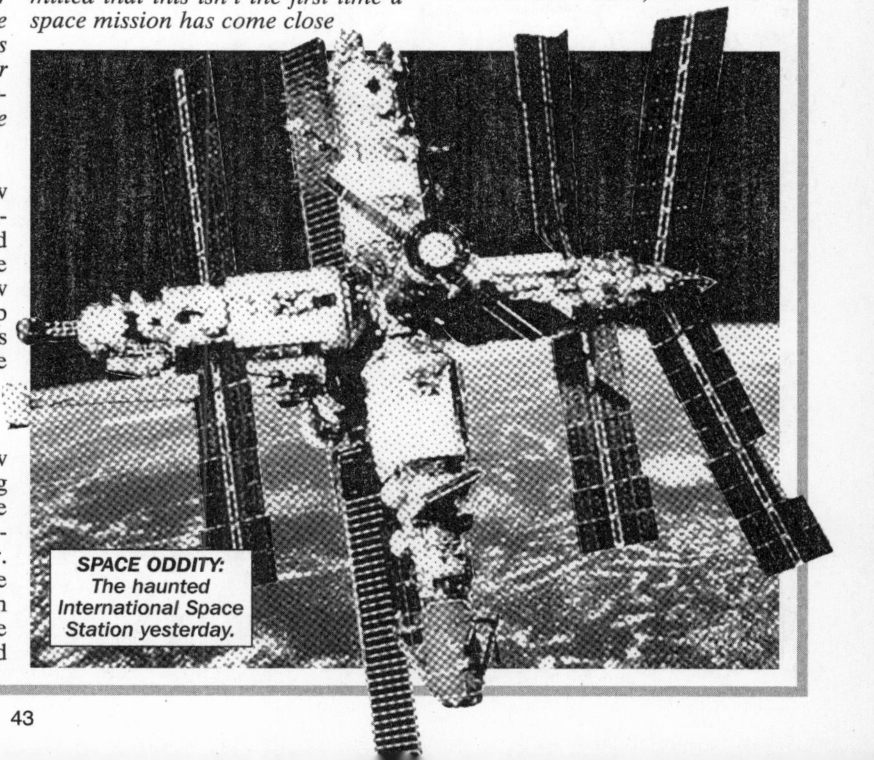

SPACE ODDITY: The haunted International Space Station yesterday.

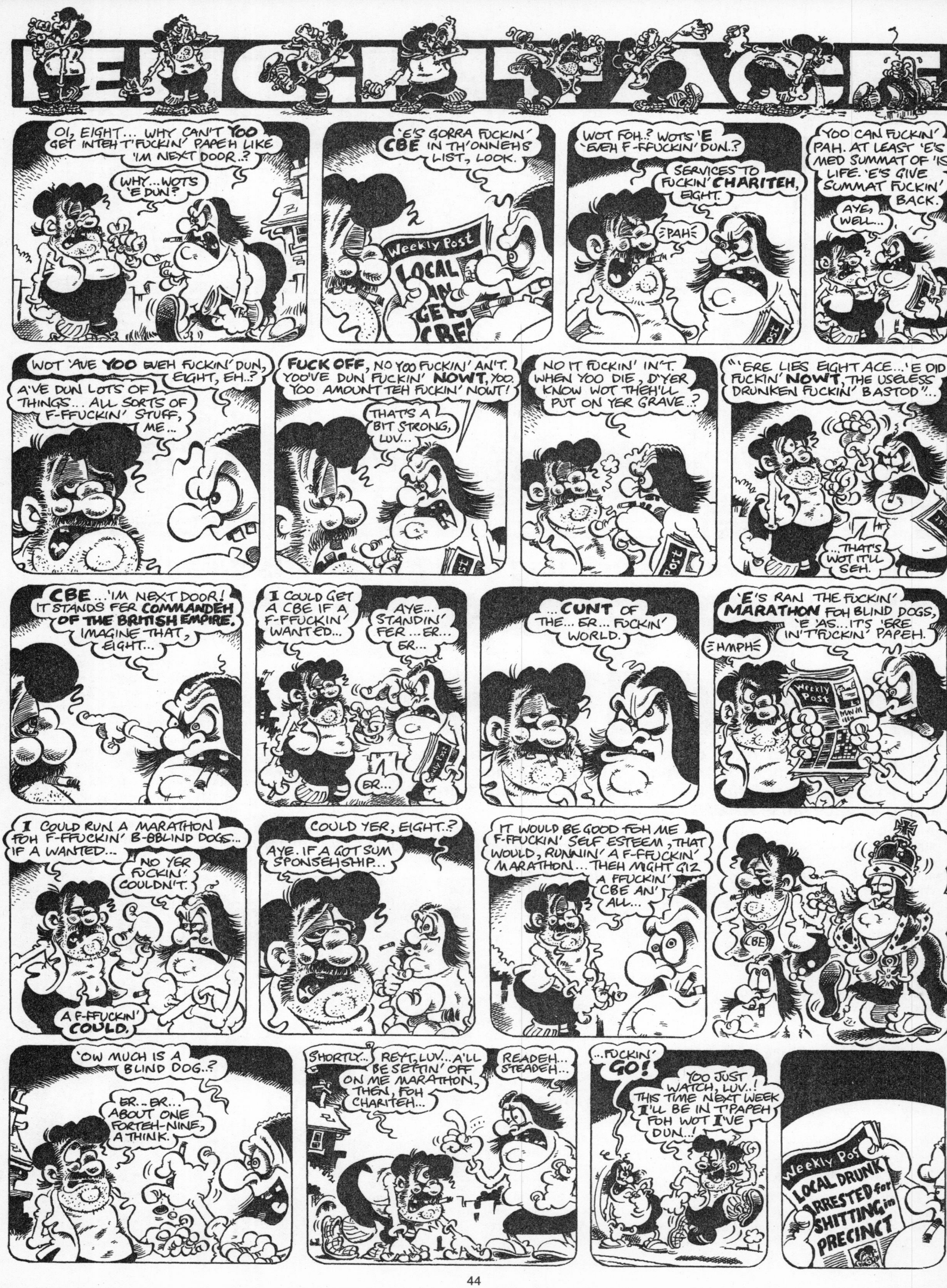

OI, EIGHT... WHY CAN'T YOO GET INTEH T'FUCKIN' PAPE'H LIKE 'IM NEXT DOOR..?
WHY... WOT'S 'E DUN?
'E'S GORRA FUCKIN' CBE IN TH'ONNEH'S LIST, LOOK.
Weekly Post
WOT FOH..? WOT'S 'E 'EVEH F-FFUCKIN' DUN..?
SERVICES TO FUCKIN' CHARITEH, EIGHT.
PAH
YOO CAN FUCKIN' PAH. AT LEAST 'E'S MED SUMMAT OF 'IS LIFE. 'E'S GIVE SUMMAT FUCKIN' BACK.
AYE, WELL...
WOT 'AVE YOO EVEH FUCKIN' DUN, EIGHT, EH..?
A'VE DUN LOTS OF THINGS... ALL SORTS OF F-FFUCKIN' STUFF, ME...
FUCK OFF, NO YOO FUCKIN' AN'T. YOO'VE DUN FUCKIN' NOWT, YOO. YOO AMOUNT TEH FUCKIN' NOWT!
THAT'S A BIT STRONG, LUV...
NO IT FUCKIN' IN'T. WHEN YOO DIE, D'YER KNOW WOT THEH'LL PUT ON YER GRAVE..?
"'ERE LIES EIGHT ACE... 'E DID FUCKIN' NOWT, THE USELESS DRUNKEN FUCKIN' BASTOD"...
...THAT'S WOT IT'LL SEH.
CBE... 'IM NEXT DOOR! IT STANDS FER COMMANDEH OF THE BRITISH EMPIRE. IMAGINE THAT, EIGHT...
I COULD GET A CBE IF A F-FFUCKIN' WANTED...
AYE... STANDIN' FER... ER... ER...
ER...
...CUNT OF THE... ER... FUCKIN' WORLD.
'E'S RAN THE FUCKIN' MARATHON FOH BLIND DOGS, 'E 'AS... IT'S 'ERE IN'T'FUCKIN' PAPEH.
HMPH
Weekly Post
I COULD RUN A MARATHON FOH F-FFUCKIN' B-BBLIND DOGS... IF A WANTED...
NO YER FUCKIN' COULDN'T.
A F-FFUCKIN' COULD.
COULD YER, EIGHT..?
AYE. IF A GOT SUM SPONSEHSHIP...
IT WOULD BE GOOD FOH ME F-FFUCKIN' SELF ESTEEM, THAT WOULD, RUNNIN' A F-FFUCKIN' MARATHON... THEH MIGHT GIZ A FFUCKIN' CBE AN' ALL...
CBE
'OW MUCH IS A BLIND DOG..?
ER... ER... ABOUT ONE FORTEH-NINE, A THINK.
SHORTLY...
REYT, LUV... A'LL BE SETTIN' OFF ON ME MARATHON, THEN, FOH CHARITEH...
READEH... STEADEH...
...FUCKIN' GO!
YOO JUST WATCH, LUV..! THIS TIME NEXT WEEK I'LL BE IN T'PAPEH FOH WOT I'VE DUN..!
Weekly Pos
LOCAL DRUNK ARRESTED for SHITTING in PRECINCT

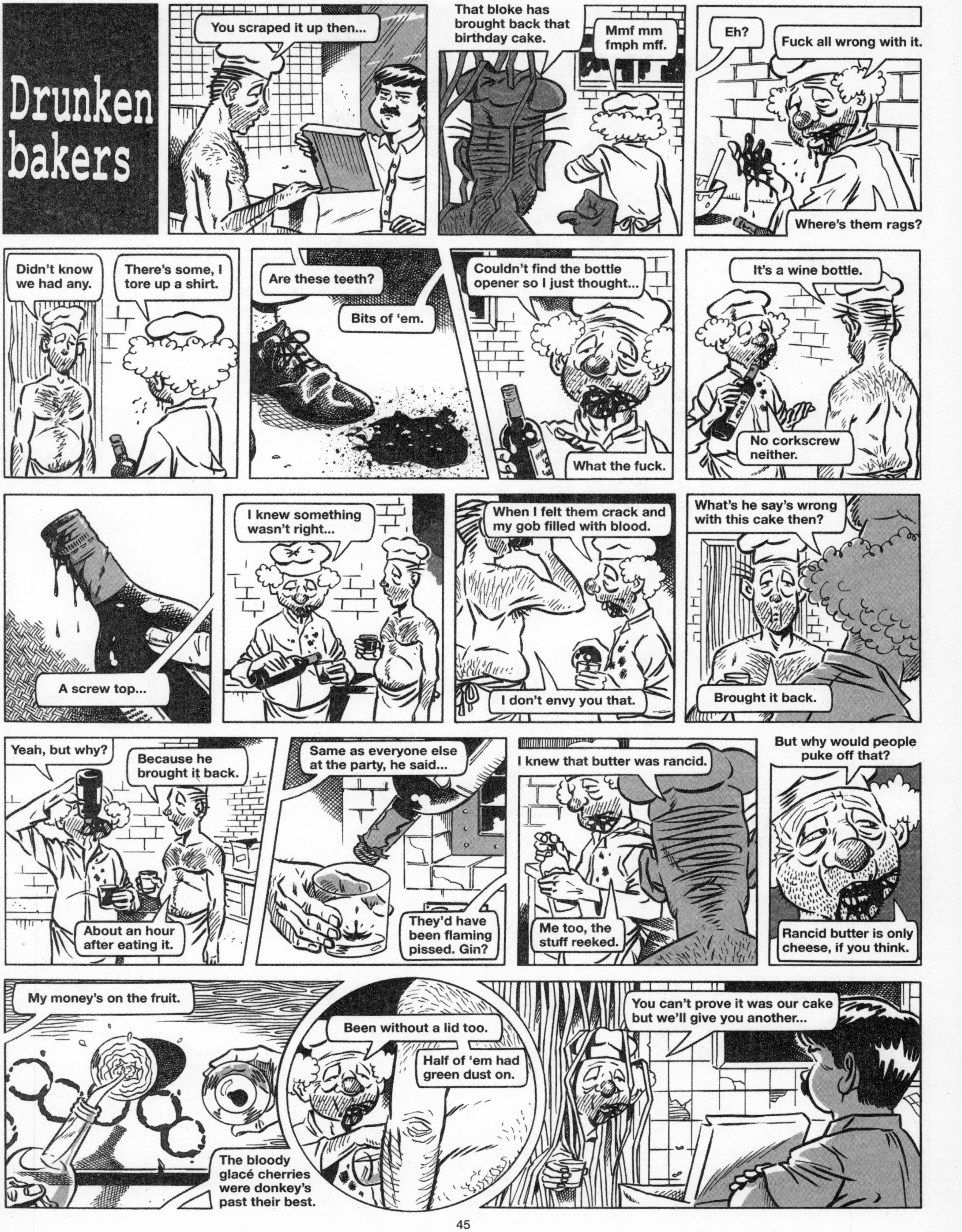
Drunken bakers
You scraped it up then...
That bloke has brought back that birthday cake.
Mmf mm fmph mff.
Eh?
Fuck all wrong with it.
Where's them rags?
Didn't know we had any.
There's some, I tore up a shirt.
Are these teeth?
Bits of 'em.
Couldn't find the bottle opener so I just thought...
What the fuck.
It's a wine bottle.
No corkscrew neither.
A screw top...
I knew something wasn't right...
When I felt them crack and my gob filled with blood.
I don't envy you that.
What's he say's wrong with this cake then?
Brought it back.
Yeah, but why?
Because he brought it back.
About an hour after eating it.
Same as everyone else at the party, he said...
They'd have been flaming pissed. Gin?
I knew that butter was rancid.
Me too, the stuff reeked.
But why would people puke off that?
Rancid butter is only cheese, if you think.
My money's on the fruit.
Been without a lid too.
Half of 'em had green dust on.
The bloody glacé cherries were donkey's past their best.
You can't prove it was our cake but we'll give you another...

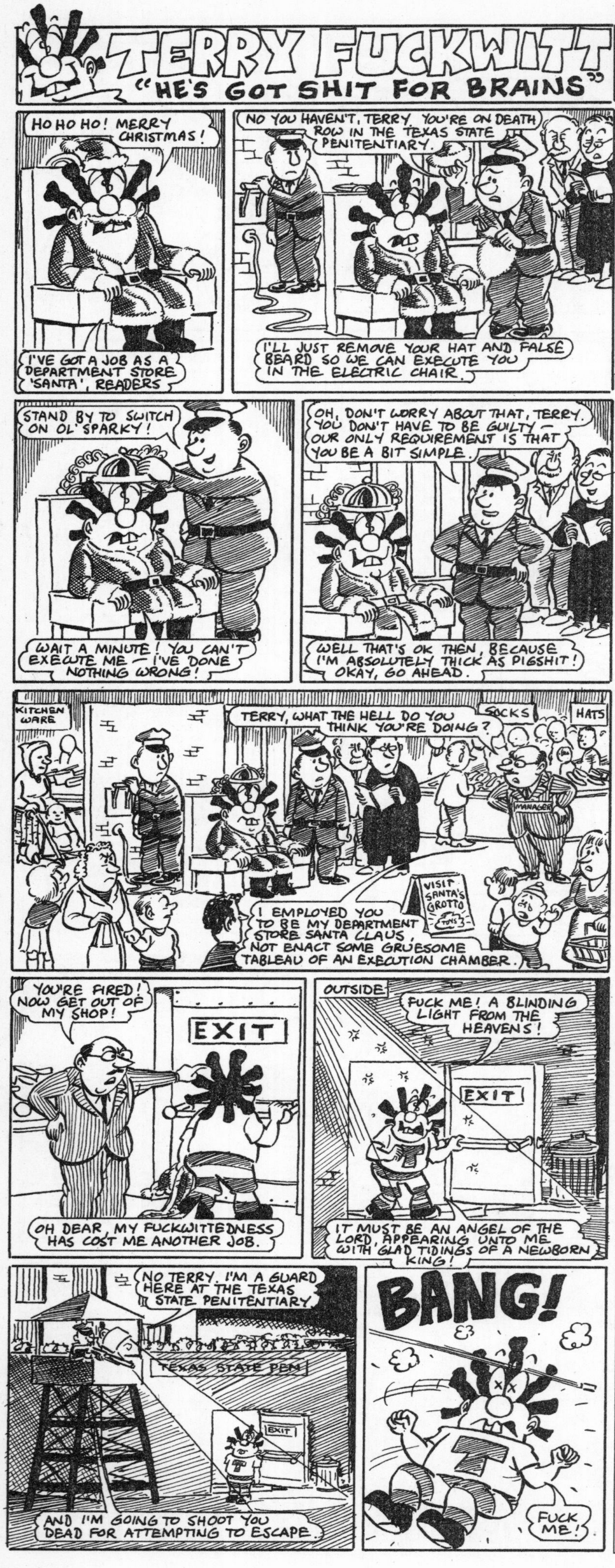

TERRY FUCKWITT
"HE'S GOT SHIT FOR BRAINS"
HO HO HO! MERRY CHRISTMAS!
I'VE GOT A JOB AS A DEPARTMENT STORE 'SANTA', READERS
NO YOU HAVEN'T, TERRY. YOU'RE ON DEATH ROW IN THE TEXAS STATE PENITENTIARY.
I'LL JUST REMOVE YOUR HAT AND FALSE BEARD SO WE CAN EXECUTE YOU IN THE ELECTRIC CHAIR.
STAND BY TO SWITCH ON OL' SPARKY!
WAIT A MINUTE! YOU CAN'T EXECUTE ME — I'VE DONE NOTHING WRONG!
OH, DON'T WORRY ABOUT THAT, TERRY. YOU DON'T HAVE TO BE GUILTY — OUR ONLY REQUIREMENT IS THAT YOU BE A BIT SIMPLE.
WELL THAT'S OK THEN, BECAUSE I'M ABSOLUTELY THICK AS PIGSHIT! OKAY, GO AHEAD.
KITCHEN WARE
SOCKS
HATS
TERRY, WHAT THE HELL DO YOU THINK YOU'RE DOING?
MANAGER
VISIT SANTA'S GROTTO
I EMPLOYED YOU TO BE MY DEPARTMENT STORE SANTA CLAUS, NOT ENACT SOME GRUESOME TABLEAU OF AN EXECUTION CHAMBER.
YOU'RE FIRED! NOW GET OUT OF MY SHOP!
EXIT
OH DEAR, MY FUCKWITTEDNESS HAS COST ME ANOTHER JOB.
OUTSIDE
FUCK ME! A BLINDING LIGHT FROM THE HEAVENS!
EXIT
IT MUST BE AN ANGEL OF THE LORD, APPEARING UNTO ME WITH GLAD TIDINGS OF A NEWBORN KING!
NO TERRY. I'M A GUARD HERE AT THE TEXAS STATE PENITENTIARY.
TEXAS STATE PEN
EXIT
AND I'M GOING TO SHOOT YOU DEAD FOR ATTEMPTING TO ESCAPE.
BANG!
FUCK ME!

TONY PARSEHOLE

Why our lives have no meaning now the Hurricane is gone

ALEX HIGGINS. Mr Alex Higgins. Mr Alex Higgins Esquire. Mr Alexander Higgins Esquire. He went by many names, but we knew him by a single word. The Hurricane. Alex "The Hurricane" Higgins.

Snooker has lost its brightest star. A star that burnt brighter than a million lightbulbs. Proper hundred watt lightbulbs. Not the energy-saving ones like you get nowadays.

And energy was something The Hurricane had in abundance. When he hit that green beige, he was like a tsunami of snooker. A typhoon of billiards. A whirlwind of pool.

He wielded his queue like a wizard wielded a wand. And with that queue he brought magic to the world of snooker, making the balls disappear one after another.

A red. Then a black. Then another red. Then black again. Red. Black. Red. Black. Red. Black. Red. Black. Red. Black. Red. Black. Red. Black. Red. Black. Red. Black. Red. Black. Red. Black. Red. Black. Red. Black.

Then yellow. Then Green. Brown. Blue.

Pink.

Then Black.

The world gasped as The Hurricane cleared the table quicker than the eye could see. He was so fast, he was like lightning. He wielded his queue like a conductor wielded his orchestra stick thing.

He was a lightning conductor, forging a symphony of snooker across the green beige. The red balls was his violins. The white ball was his trumpets and flutes. The coloured balls were the other members of the orchestra, such as clarinets, oboes, bassoons and trombones.

He made music with his balls. And it was heavenly music like a choir of angels singing upon the hallowed turf of that green beige. We listened with our eyes and it was beautiful.

His genius was more than a million Mozarts. Bigger than a billion Beethovens. Tremendouser than a trillion Tchaikovskys.

When I heard the news that he had died, I cried more tears than if I had peeled a million onions. I cried myself to sleep.

And in the morning I cried myself awake. And then I cried again. All day. I am still crying.

And I'm not ashamed to admit that I wept when I heard that the

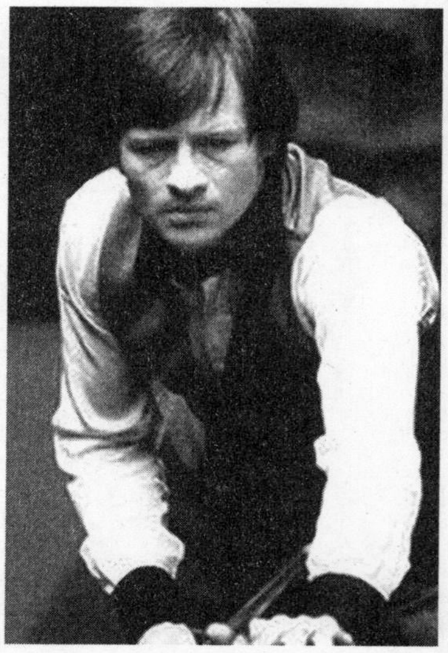

Hurricane had blown out his own candle. He had so much more to give. He had so many more balls to pot. So many more queues to wipe chalk on the end of.

He truly was the greatest human being who ever lived. Greater than Gandhi. Greater than Shakespeare. Greater even than Lady Diana Spencer.

Yes. Lady Di herself could not hold a candle to the wind of the Hurricane.

Higgins was the true People's Princess. A People's Princess of Snooker of Hearts. He was an Irish rose and now that rose has been plucked to play a final frame on God's own snooker table.

Like all roses, he blossomed in the sun. The sunshine of his own prodigious talent. But now that sun has gone behind the clouds in heaven and his petals have there that's 750 words. Make cheque payable to T. Parsehole.

NEXT WEEK : *Why I'd give my life to save 'Last of the Summer Wine'*

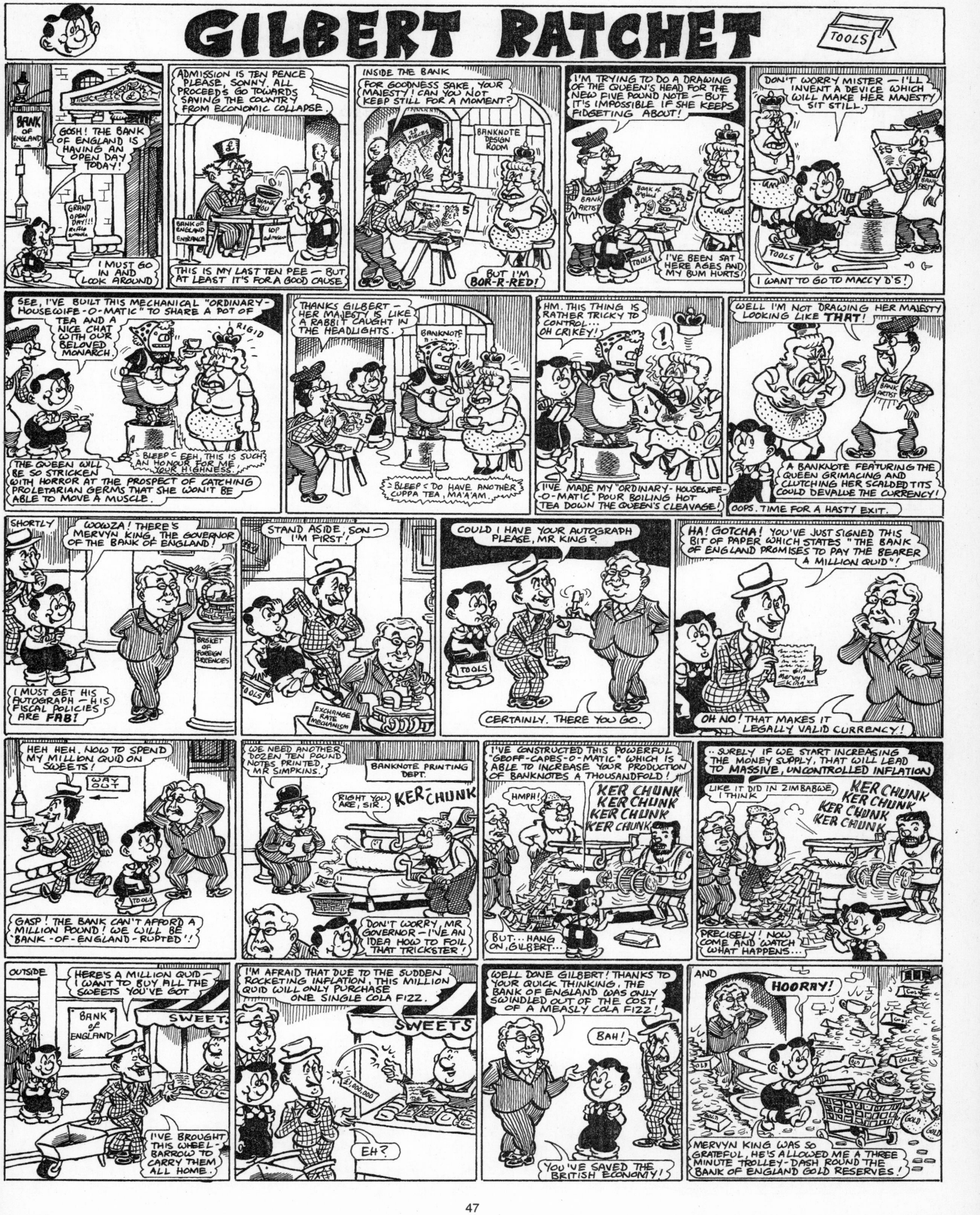
GILBERT RATCHET
TOOLS
BANK OF ENGLAND
GOSH! THE BANK OF ENGLAND IS HAVING AN OPEN DAY TODAY!
GRAND OPEN DAY!!!
I MUST GO IN AND LOOK AROUND
ADMISSION IS TEN PENCE PLEASE, SONNY. ALL PROCEEDS GO TOWARDS SAVING THE COUNTRY FROM ECONOMIC COLLAPSE.
THANK YOU
BANK OF ENGLAND ENTRANCE
THIS IS MY LAST TEN PEE — BUT AT LEAST IT'S FOR A GOOD CAUSE.
INSIDE THE BANK
FOR GOODNESS SAKE, YOUR MAJESTY! CAN YOU NOT KEEP STILL FOR A MOMENT?
2P PIECES
BANKNOTE DESIGN ROOM
BUT I'M BOR-R-RED!
I'M TRYING TO DO A DRAWING OF THE QUEEN'S HEAD FOR THE NEW FIVE POUND NOTE — BUT IT'S IMPOSSIBLE IF SHE KEEPS FIDGETING ABOUT!
BANK ARTIST
TOOLS
I'VE BEEN SAT HERE AGES AND MY BUM HURTS!
DON'T WORRY MISTER — I'LL INVENT A DEVICE WHICH WILL MAKE HER MAJESTY SIT STILL.
TOOLS
I WANT TO GO TO MACCY D'S!
SEE, I'VE BUILT THIS MECHANICAL "ORDINARY-HOUSEWIFE-O-MATIC" TO SHARE A POT OF TEA AND A NICE CHAT WITH OUR BELOVED MONARCH.
RIGID
THE QUEEN WILL BE SO STRICKEN WITH HORROR AT THE PROSPECT OF CATCHING PROLETARIAN GERMS THAT SHE WON'T BE ABLE TO MOVE A MUSCLE.
BLEEP EEH, THIS IS SUCH AN HONOUR FOR ME, YOUR HIGHNESS.
THANKS GILBERT — HER MAJESTY IS LIKE A RABBIT CAUGHT IN THE HEADLIGHTS.
BANKNOTE
BLEEP DO HAVE ANOTHER CUPPA TEA, MA'A'AM.
HM. THIS THING IS RATHER TRICKY TO CONTROL... OH CRIKEY!
I'VE MADE MY "ORDINARY-HOUSEWIFE-O-MATIC" POUR BOILING HOT TEA DOWN THE QUEEN'S CLEAVAGE!
WELL I'M NOT DRAWING HER MAJESTY LOOKING LIKE THAT!
BANK ARTIST
A BANKNOTE FEATURING THE QUEEN GRIMACING AND CLUTCHING HER SCALDED TITS COULD DEVALUE THE CURRENCY!
OOPS. TIME FOR A HASTY EXIT.
SHORTLY
WOWZA! THERE'S MERVYN KING, THE GOVERNOR OF THE BANK OF ENGLAND!
BASKET OF FOREIGN CURRENCIES
I MUST GET HIS AUTOGRAPH — HIS FISCAL POLICIES ARE FAB!
STAND ASIDE, SON — I'M FIRST!
TOOLS
EXCHANGE RATE MECHANISM
COULD I HAVE YOUR AUTOGRAPH PLEASE, MR KING?
TOOLS
CERTAINLY. THERE YOU GO.
HA! GOTCHA! YOU'VE JUST SIGNED THIS BIT OF PAPER WHICH STATES "THE BANK OF ENGLAND PROMISES TO PAY THE BEARER A MILLION QUID"!
OH NO! THAT MAKES IT LEGALLY VALID CURRENCY!
HEH HEH. NOW TO SPEND MY MILLION QUID ON SWEETS!
WAY OUT
TOOLS
GASP! THE BANK CAN'T AFFORD A MILLION POUND! WE WILL BE "BANK-OF-ENGLAND-RUPTED"!
WE NEED ANOTHER DOZEN TEN POUND NOTES PRINTED, MR SIMPKINS.
BANKNOTE PRINTING DEPT.
RIGHT YOU ARE, SIR.
KER-CHUNK
DON'T WORRY, MR GOVERNOR — I'VE AN IDEA HOW TO FOIL THAT TRICKSTER!
I'VE CONSTRUCTED THIS POWERFUL "GEOFF-CAPES-O-MATIC" WHICH IS ABLE TO INCREASE YOUR PRODUCTION OF BANKNOTES A THOUSANDFOLD!
HMPH!
KER CHUNK KER CHUNK KER CHUNK KER CHUNK
BUT... HANG ON, GILBERT...
.. SURELY IF WE START INCREASING THE MONEY SUPPLY, THAT WILL LEAD TO MASSIVE, UNCONTROLLED INFLATION
LIKE IT DID IN ZIMBABWE, I THINK
KER CHUNK KER CHUNK KER CHUNK KER CHUNK
PRECISELY! NOW COME AND WATCH WHAT HAPPENS...
OUTSIDE
HERE'S A MILLION QUID — I WANT TO BUY ALL THE SWEETS YOU'VE GOT
BANK of ENGLAND
SWEETS
I'VE BROUGHT THIS WHEEL-BARROW TO CARRY THEM ALL HOME.
I'M AFRAID THAT DUE TO THE SUDDEN ROCKETING INFLATION, THIS MILLION QUID WILL ONLY PURCHASE ONE SINGLE COLA FIZZ.
SWEETS
£1,000,000
EH?
WELL DONE GILBERT! THANKS TO YOUR QUICK THINKING, THE BANK OF ENGLAND WAS ONLY SWINDLED OUT OF THE COST OF A MEASLY COLA FIZZ!
BAH!
YOU'VE SAVED THE BRITISH ECONOMY!
AND
HOORAY!
GOLD
MERVYN KING WAS SO GRATEFUL, HE'S ALLOWED ME A THREE MINUTE TROLLEY-DASH ROUND THE BANK OF ENGLAND GOLD RESERVES!

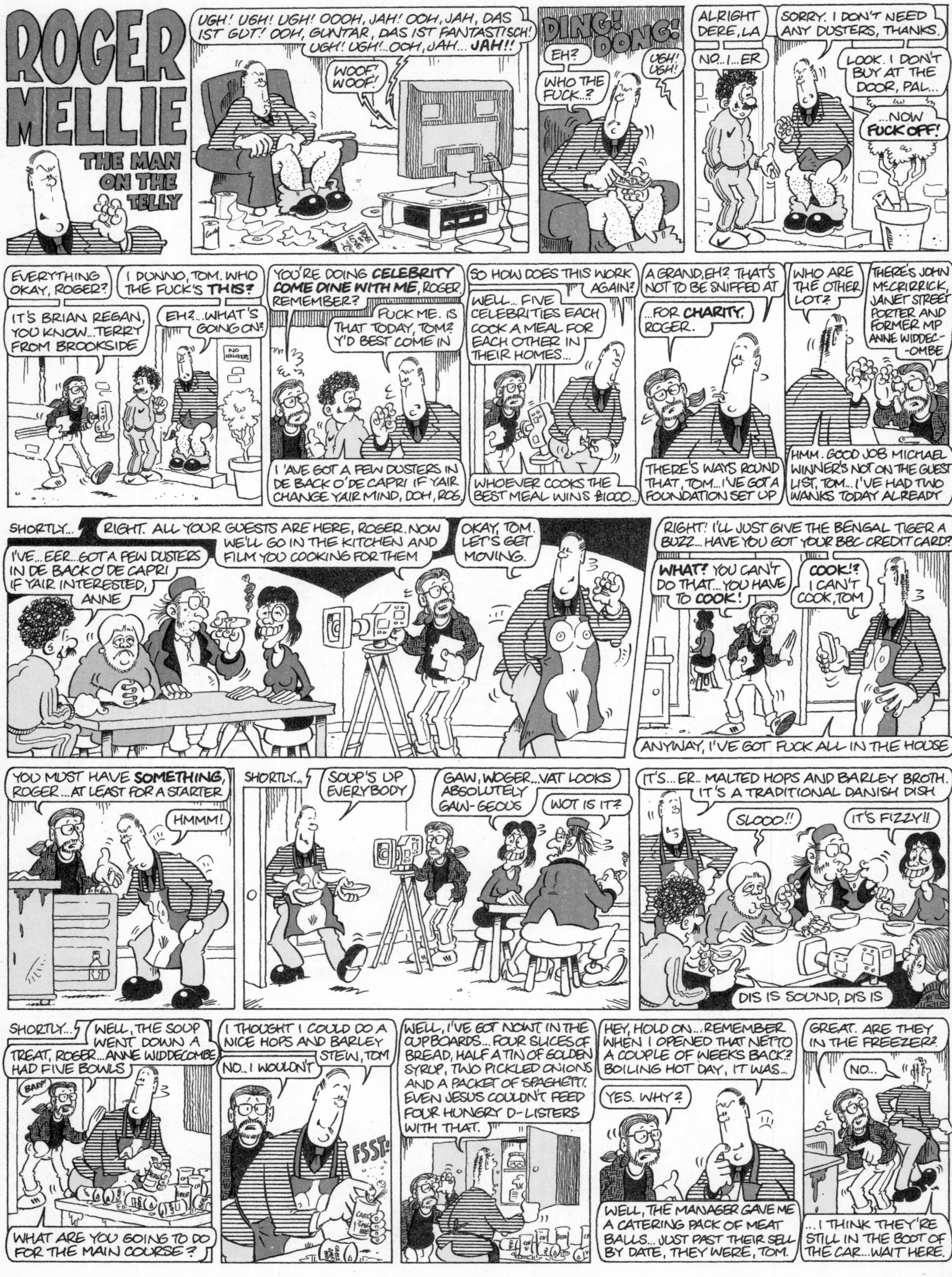
ROGER MELLIE
THE MAN ON THE TELLY
UGH! UGH! UGH! OOOH, JAH! OOH, JAH, DAS IST GUT! OOH, GUNTAR, DAS IST FANTASTISCH! UGH! UGH!.. OOH, JAH... JAH!!
WOOF! WOOF!
DING! DONG!
EH?
WHO THE FUCK..?
UGH! UGH!
ALRIGHT DERE, LA
SORRY. I DON'T NEED ANY DUSTERS, THANKS.
NO... I... ER
LOOK. I DON'T BUY AT THE DOOR, PAL...
...NOW FUCK OFF!
EVERYTHING OKAY, ROGER?
I DUNNO, TOM. WHO THE FUCK'S THIS?
IT'S BRIAN REGAN, YOU KNOW... TERRY FROM BROOKSIDE
EH?... WHAT'S GOING ON?
NO HAWKERS
YOU'RE DOING CELEBRITY COME DINE WITH ME, ROGER REMEMBER?
FUCK ME. IS THAT TODAY, TOM? Y'D BEST COME IN
I 'AVE GOT A FEW DUSTERS IN DE BACK O'DE CAPRI IF YAIR CHANGE YAIR MIND, DOH, ROG
SO HOW DOES THIS WORK AGAIN?
WELL... FIVE CELEBRITIES EACH COOK A MEAL FOR EACH OTHER IN THEIR HOMES...
WHOEVER COOKS THE BEST MEAL WINS £1000...
A GRAND, EH? THAT'S NOT TO BE SNIFFED AT
...FOR CHARITY, ROGER.
THERE'S WAYS ROUND THAT, TOM... I'VE GOT A FOUNDATION SET UP
WHO ARE THE OTHER LOT?
THERE'S JOHN McCRIRRICK, JANET STREET PORTER AND FORMER MP ANNE WIDDEC--OMBE
HMM. GOOD JOB MICHAEL WINNER'S NOT ON THE GUEST LIST, TOM... I'VE HAD TWO WANKS TODAY ALREADY
SHORTLY...
RIGHT. ALL YOUR GUESTS ARE HERE, ROGER. NOW WE'LL GO IN THE KITCHEN AND FILM YOU COOKING FOR THEM
I'VE... EER... GOT A FEW DUSTERS IN DE BACK O'DE CAPRI IF YAIR INTERESTED, ANNE
OKAY, TOM. LET'S GET MOVING.
RIGHT! I'LL JUST GIVE THE BENGAL TIGER A BUZZ... HAVE YOU GOT YOUR BBC CREDIT CARD?
WHAT? YOU CAN'T DO THAT... YOU HAVE TO COOK!
COOK!? I CAN'T COOK, TOM
ANYWAY, I'VE GOT FUCK ALL IN THE HOUSE
YOU MUST HAVE SOMETHING, ROGER... AT LEAST FOR A STARTER
HMMM!
SHORTLY...
SOUP'S UP EVERYBODY
GAW, WOGER... VAT LOOKS ABSOLUTELY GAW-GEOUS
WOT IS IT?
IT'S... ER... MALTED HOPS AND BARLEY BROTH. IT'S A TRADITIONAL DANISH DISH
SLOOO!!
IT'S FIZZY!!
DIS IS SOUND, DIS IS
SHORTLY...
WELL, THE SOUP WENT DOWN A TREAT, ROGER... ANNE WIDDECOMBE HAD FIVE BOWLS
BARP!
WHAT ARE YOU GOING TO DO FOR THE MAIN COURSE?
I THOUGHT I COULD DO A NICE HOPS AND BARLEY STEW, TOM
NO.. I WOULDN'T
FSST!
WELL, I'VE GOT NOWT IN THE CUPBOARDS... FOUR SLICES OF BREAD, HALF A TIN OF GOLDEN SYRUP, TWO PICKLED ONIONS AND A PACKET OF SPAGHETTI. EVEN JESUS COULDN'T FEED FOUR HUNGRY D-LISTERS WITH THAT.
HEY, HOLD ON... REMEMBER WHEN I OPENED THAT NETTO A COUPLE OF WEEKS BACK? BOILING HOT DAY, IT WAS...
YES. WHY?
WELL, THE MANAGER GAVE ME A CATERING PACK OF MEAT BALLS... JUST PAST THEIR SELL BY DATE, THEY WERE, TOM.
GREAT. ARE THEY IN THE FREEZER?
NO...
... I THINK THEY'RE STILL IN THE BOOT OF THE CAR... WAIT HERE.

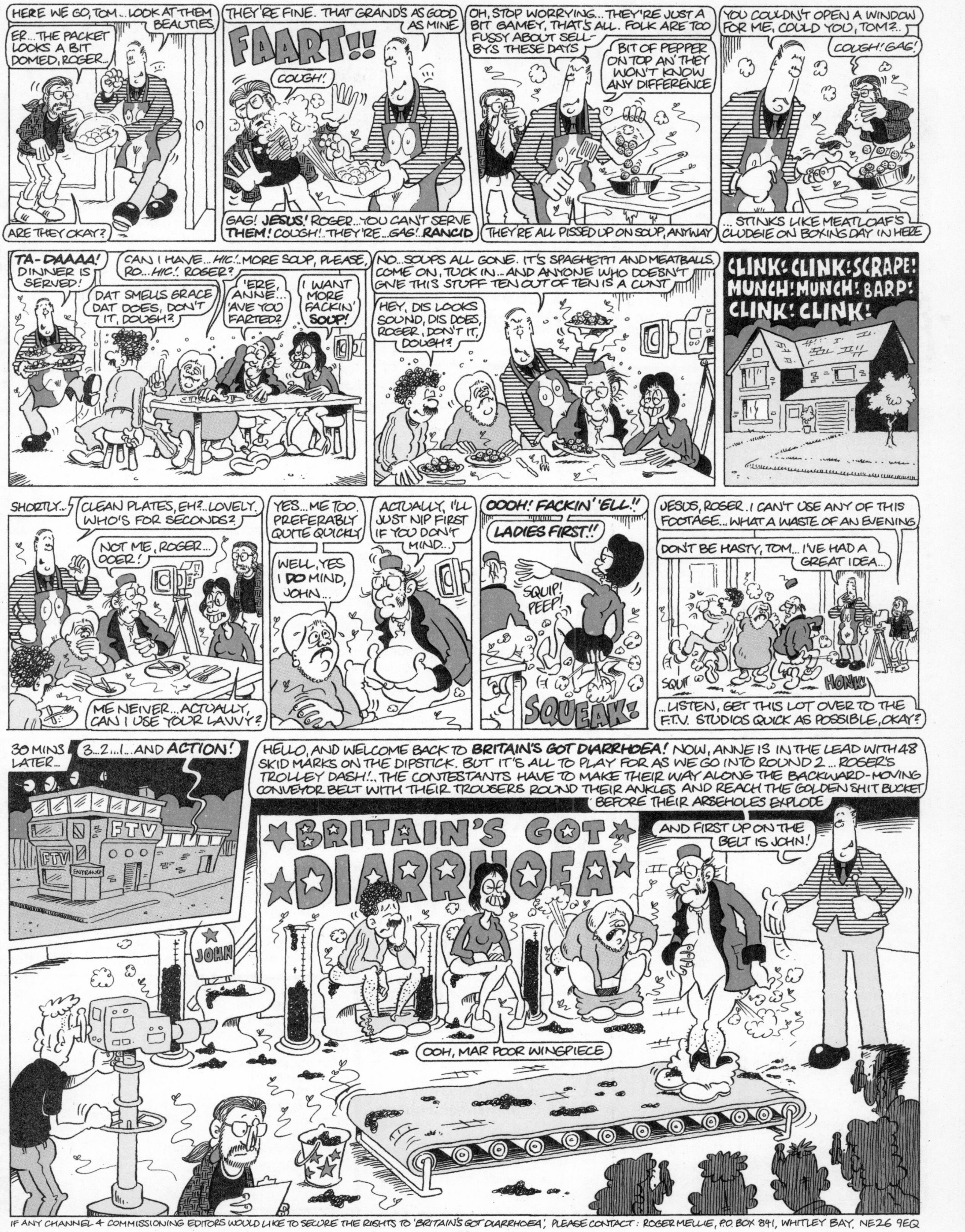
HERE WE GO, TOM... LOOK AT THEM BEAUTIES
ER... THE PACKET LOOKS A BIT DOMED, ROGER...
ARE THEY OKAY?
THEY'RE FINE. THAT GRAND'S AS GOOD AS MINE
FAART!!
COUGH!
GAG! JESUS! ROGER... YOU CAN'T SERVE THEM! COUGH!.. THEY'RE... GAG!.. RANCID
OH, STOP WORRYING... THEY'RE JUST A BIT GAMEY, THAT'S ALL.. FOLK ARE TOO FUSSY ABOUT SELL-BY'S THESE DAYS
BIT OF PEPPER ON TOP AN' THEY WON'T KNOW ANY DIFFERENCE
THEY'RE ALL PISSED UP ON SOUP, ANYWAY
YOU COULDN'T OPEN A WINDOW FOR ME, COULD YOU, TOM?..
COUGH! GAG!
... STINKS LIKE MEATLOAF'S CLUDGIE ON BOXING DAY IN HERE
TA-DAAAA! DINNER IS SERVED!
CAN I HAVE... HIC!.. MORE SOUP, PLEASE, RO... HIC!.. ROGER?
DAT SMELLS GRACE DAT DOES, DON'T IT, DOUGH?
'ERE, ANNE... 'AVE YOU FARTED?
I WANT MORE FACKIN' SOUP!
NO... SOUPS ALL GONE. IT'S SPAGHETTI AND MEATBALLS. COME ON, TUCK IN... AND ANYONE WHO DOESN'T GIVE THIS STUFF TEN OUT OF TEN IS A CUNT
HEY, DIS LOOKS SOUND, DIS DOES, ROGER, DON'T IT, DOUGH?
CLINK! CLINK! SCRAPE! MUNCH! MUNCH! BARP! CLINK! CLINK!
SHORTLY...
CLEAN PLATES, EH?.. LOVELY. WHO'S FOR SECONDS?
NOT ME, ROGER... OOER!
ME NEIVER... ACTUALLY, CAN I USE YOUR LAVVY?
YES... ME TOO. PREFERABLY QUITE QUICKLY
ACTUALLY, I'LL JUST NIP FIRST IF YOU DON'T MIND...
WELL, YES I DO MIND, JOHN...
OOOH! FACKIN' 'ELL!!
LADIES FIRST!!
SQUIP! PEEP!
SQUEAK!
JESUS, ROGER.. I CAN'T USE ANY OF THIS FOOTAGE... WHAT A WASTE OF AN EVENING
DON'T BE HASTY, TOM... I'VE HAD A GREAT IDEA...
SQUIT
HONK!
... LISTEN, GET THIS LOT OVER TO THE F.T.V. STUDIOS QUICK AS POSSIBLE, OKAY?
30 MINS LATER...
3...2...1... AND ACTION!
FTV
FTV
ENTRANCE
HELLO, AND WELCOME BACK TO BRITAIN'S GOT DIARRHOEA! NOW, ANNE IS IN THE LEAD WITH 48 SKID MARKS ON THE DIPSTICK. BUT IT'S ALL TO PLAY FOR AS WE GO INTO ROUND 2 ... ROGER'S TROLLEY DASH!.. THE CONTESTANTS HAVE TO MAKE THEIR WAY ALONG THE BACKWARD-MOVING CONVEYOR BELT WITH THEIR TROUSERS ROUND THEIR ANKLES AND REACH THE GOLDEN SHIT BUCKET BEFORE THEIR ARSEHOLES EXPLODE
BRITAIN'S GOT DIARRHOEA
AND FIRST UP ON THE BELT IS JOHN!
JOHN
OOH, MAR POOR WINGPIECE

IF ANY CHANNEL 4 COMMISSIONING EDITORS WOULD LIKE TO SECURE THE RIGHTS TO 'BRITAIN'S GOT DIARRHOEA', PLEASE CONTACT: ROGER MELLIE, P.O. BOX 841, WHITLEY BAY, NE26 9EQ

Letterbocks

PO Box 841,
Whitley Bay,
NE26 9EQ

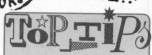

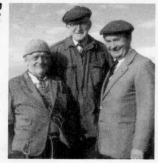

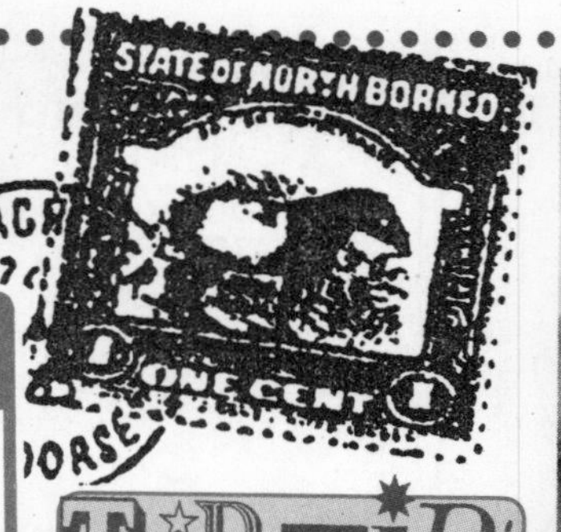

STATE OF NORTH BORNEO
ONE CENT

I FELL out with my best friend Irene after a pointless argument over a sausage roll, and we didn't speak for years. After 25 years, I was really missing the good times that we used to have, but by then we had lost touch with each other. But last year, whilst on holiday in Australia with my husband, I recognised a familiar voice beside the hotel pool. It was Irene, who by coincidence was also on holiday with her husband. We immediately began chatting about the old days, and it was soon clear that she had missed me as much as I had missed her. We decided that fate had brought us together again and we would now stay friends forever. However, the next morning at breakfast, she took the last piece of bacon at the buffet. So if I ever see her again it will be too soon.

Edna Cockscombe Cheshire

TOP TIPS

GIRLS. Embarrassing noises? Leave an empty trombone stand outside the lavatory door and people will think that you are just practising.

A Non, Lost

IF YOU are over 10 metres in front of someone, don't hold the door open for them. You're not doing them a favour, you're just making them run.

Christina Martin, e-mail

MEN. Pretend you have a sex drive until your girlfriend moves in with you. Then wear 15-year-old band T-shirts in bed whilst reading Tintin books.

Rabbit's Best Friend, e-mail

DON'T throw away the lids off yoghurt pots. Simply stick them onto the top of dowdy shoes to jazz them up.

Toby Yarwood, Thirsk

STAR LETTER

I HAD been happily married to my husband Frank for forty years when he tragically died of cancer over eight years ago. All I had left for company was our cocker spaniel Rex, and it was that dog who brought me love when I thought I had lost it. For, a couple of years after my husband's death, I was walking Rex in the park when his lead got tangled with that of a Yorkshire terrier who was being walked by an elderly gentleman. I got chatting to the dog's owner and I suddenly realised that it was my husband Frank. To cut a long story short, it turned out that he hadn't died after all, and Rex had brought us back together again.

Dolly Prentice, Leeds

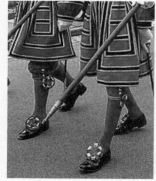

I AM a Beefeater at the Tower of London. There is a very strict dress code which includes bright red tights as part of our uniform. However, for years I have worn bright red stockings and suspenders without any of my colleagues knowing. They are far more practical as they are less likely to sag and cause chaffing around the crotch during the long periods I spend standing around guarding the Crown Jewels and watching ravens.

Yeoman Albert Tower of London

I HAVE been watching a lot of films about Cosa Nostra gangsters lately - *The Godfather, Goodfellas, Scarface* etc. I enjoyed them so much that I decided to start my own crime family. My 8-year-old daughter and grandmother were quite keen to join in, but my parents did not think it was such a good idea and my wife was absolutely furious when I told her. Do any other gangland bosses have this sort of difficulty with their families?

Alan Heath, e-mail

FOR years now, I have thought that the tawdry goings-on from the likes of Jordan, Peter Andre and Kerry Katona were nothing but a shallow, publicity-seeking sham. However, yesterday I saw on the cover of a magazine that Pete was planning to start a family with her off the Iceland adverts. Can I use your letters page to apologise publicly for ever doubting their sincerity?

James Brown Edinburgh

DO HOUSES in China have chimneys? I only ask because I have never seen any Chinese chimney sweeps.

B. von Philipenhausen, e-mail

WITH reference to Mr Philipenhausen's letter *(above)*. We had our chimney swept last week, and I think the sweep may have been a Chinaman as he was quite short. However, I couldn't say for certain as he was covered in soot.

Mrs Sheila Maddox, Leigh

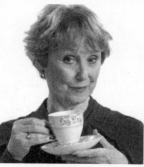

YOU know that rumour about Una Stubbs? Well apparently it's true. Do I win £5?

Dr Heather Jenkinson, e-mail

WHAT I don't understand about Quidditch in *Harry Potter*, is that whichever team gets the snitch wins the game, regardless of how many goals they have scored. There are effectively two separate games going on and the result of one has no effect on the overall outcome. If I was captain, I'd just tell all my team to forget throwing balls through hoops and go after the snitch. You can tell JK Rowling doesn't understand ball games. I think she should give all the money she has made back.

Clive Wildesmith, Dundee

TOP TIPS

A FEW flat black and white pieces of Lego sandwiched together maker ideal liquorice allsorts for people who don't like eating them very much.

Claude Balls, e-mail

CONVINCE your nan that she is losing her marbles by moving the bookmark in her Barbara Cartland novel 10 pages back when she isn't looking.

M Coxlong, e-mail

A FEW conkers threaded on an old bootlace makes an inexpensive 'love bead' sex toy to surprise your wife with on her next birthday.

Philip O'Carroll, e-mail

HAS anyone else noticed that all the actors in *Last of the Summer Wine* are all elderly and usually male? It's just another case of BBC discrimination in action. They should let some young, female actors play Compo, Clegg and Foggy for once.

Ron Johnson, e-mail

WHILST I don't go in for it myself, I can see how others might get a little kick from a bit of spanking during sex. I can even see how a bit of bondage and role play might turn people on. But when it comes to couples shitting on each other for thrills, I'm afraid that goes right over my head. Try as I might, I just cannot see an erotic link between sex and turds. I wonder if there are any German readers who could write in and explain the appeal of such a practice? Or perhaps David Cameron could ask Angela Merkel what it's all about when he sees her next at a G8 conference.

Sine Nomine, e-mail

I ALSO like to wear a bra.

Yeoman Albert Tower of London

MY MUM used to say that you should always wear clean underwear in case you ever get knocked over and I always followed her advice. But he other week I was hit by a bus, and after looking at the open fracture on my shin, I shat my pants anyway. And pissed them.

Craig Eddie, e-mail

I RECENTLY made the mistake of watching *Jackass 2* before I had watched the first movie. Consequently, I had no idea what was going on. Could

I AM gaining a great deal of knowledge from BBC2's *Wonders of the Solar System*, perhaps most notably the fact that part of the surface of Mars looks like an extremely unkempt, violently jizzing cock.

David Whyte London

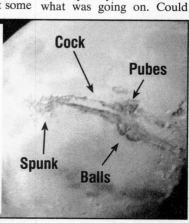

Cock
Pubes
Spunk
Balls

HAS anyone seen a more symmetrical nun than this one that I snapped having tea with my nan and her sister?

George Bakewell
Buxton

**WELL readers, have you spotted a Bride of Christ displaying a greater degree of reflexive bilateral uniformity? Write in to the usual address and let us know. Mark your envelope 'Symmetrical Nuns'.*

any of your readers fill me in on the plot of the first film so I can enjoy this movie fully?

R Perv, London

I JUST pissed a fly out of mid-air in the toilet. After getting himself in the wrong place at the wrong time, he dodged a few sprays but was eventually no match for my accurate urine-gun and succumbed to his watery grave. Mr Miyagi eat your heart out.

Steve Parsons, e-mail

WHILST I was very impressed with Mr Parson's ability to piss a fly out of mid-air (letter above), I was even more impressed with his ability to identify the sex of the thing whilst he did it.

H Fibreboard, Luton

WHILST watching a close-run horse race, the commentator announced that there would be a photo for second place. What a thoughtful gift, and a nice way to make up for the disappointment of not winning.

Mike Cooper, e-mail

I'VE JUST watched *World War II: The Complete Story* on the Discovery Channel. Complete story, my arse. Not once did they mention the time when my grandad was serving in Egypt and he shot a camel.

Matt McCann, e-mail

I HAD reason to attend a Catholic church service recently, where the priest declared before communion: "This is my body, and this is my blood." I was a little disappointed that in this day and age they do not offer a vegetarian option.

TPE Martin, e-mail

MY MATE Stan was once chased by an emu. Can any of your readers beat that?

Prothero Fitzgibbon, e-mail

**WELL, readers, do YOU know anyone who has been chased by a large, flightless bird? Perhaps your brother has been pursued by an ostrich, or maybe a rhea once ran after your boss. Or perhaps your gran once had to leg it from a cassowary. Write in and let us know. Mark your envelope 'I know someone who's been chased by a large flightless bird.'*

INSTEAD of drivers having to check their blind spot all the time, why don't car manufacturers just make the wing mirrors bigger? If cars are going to have mirrors there, they might as well show me everything I need to see and save me having to turn my head any further.

James B Derby, e-mail

TOP TIPS

A DOG turd bent into a U shape makes a great magnet for flies.

S Nutkin, Stoke

ALL YOUR bowls in the dishwasher? An old trilby hat turned upside down makes an ideal salad bowl for dry salad. For soup, try the appropriately-named 'bowler' hat, but line it first with a real bowl to stop the soup seeping out.

Renton Boyce, Torquay

BODYBUILDERS. Strands of cooked spaghetti draped all over your body give your muscles that 'ripped' look that will be the envy of everyone at the gym.

Spud, Luton

SMOKERS. When non-smokers visit your house, ask them to stand outside in the cold whilst you have a fag.

Desi Friel, e-mail

TOP STORY "How I Got Ripped In Just 4 Weeks..."

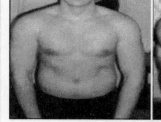

I WAS surfing the net recently, when I came upon this advert which claimed to give you a completely ripped body in just four weeks. It must be a fantastic technique, because according to the before and after pictures, it also gives you a completely different shaped chin.

Hector Wallbottle, Scunthorpe

PLAY 1 TO 3 COINS

COULD the next actor who gets a bit part in *EastEnders* please press the Star button on the fruit machine in the Queen Vic? I'm sure it's about to pay out.

Will Gatley, e-mail

MOST HAUNTED recently did a live show in Prague. I was sitting at home scoffing at how convenient it was that the 16th century Czech ghosts could speak English, but then the presenters explained that when you die there is a universal language of ghosts. Boy, oh boy, did I feel silly.

Christina Martin, e-mail

I WAS wondering if your readers can help me out with something that has been puzzling me recently? Every single human being I have come across in every walk of life when asked, has agreed with me that Noel Edmonds is a complete cunt. Every single one. Yet Channel 4 manages to find an entire audience every day that not only tolerate, but actually seem to like the man. Am I missing something?

David Hammond, e-mail

ARE grey squirrels not just old red squirrels?

Stu the Gasman, e-mail

TOP TIPS

ALARM clock owners. Save money on batteries by drinking 12 pints of ale the night before, then setting your arse to fart loudly in a sleep/snooze pattern between 7.00 and 8.00 o'clock the following morning.

Marc Rats, e-mail

BENT politicians. Conduct interviews in the nude. This will encourage reporters to strip as well, revealing any hidden cameras and tape recorders that could catch you out offering to ask questions for cash or whatever it is you do.

L Aney, e-mail

DON'T throw out that old record player. It makes an ideal revolving serving platter for cakes, where diners can pick a cake as it spins by. Set it to 33rpm for rock cakes and scones, 45rpm for Eccles cakes and Battenburg and 78 rpm for Danish pastries.

Betty Prolapse, Pontyprydd

A LADDER turned upside-down can be used for climbing down off things.

Dr Camel, via Twitter

Benson & Hedges

ARTIST FAGS

Government Health Warning

SMOKING ARTIST FAGS MAY CAUSE JUXTAPOSITION OF FORM & CONTENT, LEADING THE VIEWER TO QUESTION ACCEPTED NOTIONS OF TWO-DIMENSIONAL REPRESENTATION OF THREE-DIMENSIONAL SPACE, IF YOU WILL.

6mg Tar 0.5mg Nicotine 32mg Pretentious bollocks

HAVE YOUR "ovision" SAY

ONCE again, we have been humiliated in the Eurovision Song Contest. The British entry *Sounds Good to Me* was penned by million-selling hit-man Pete Waterman, but garnered a measly ten votes during the Oslo spectacular and finished in last place. So what went wrong? Was Josh Dubovie's performance to blame, or have we been the victims of political voting once more? Is it time to call it a day and pull out of the competition or should we redouble our efforts and come out fighting in 2011? British pop music leads the world, so why can't we win a crappy song contest? You've been writing in your droves to let us know what YOU think. Here's a selection of your letters.

WHY DOES our song always have to be performed by someone you've never heard of? Why don't we get our biggest star Cliff Richard to represent us in this important international event? After all, Cliff's an expert - he won the competition twice in the past - with *Congratulations* in 1968 and *Power to All Our Friends* in 1973!

Mrs Hartley, Seaton Delaval

OUR LEADERS should have foreseen Germany's future dominance in this contest many years ago. Measures should have been included in the 1919 Treaty of Versailles or the Potsdam Agreement of 1945 to make them perform their entries to any future international song contests on instruments that would severely hamper their chances of success, such as washboards, kazoos and bagpipes.

Col. A Hepscott-Whyte, Aldershot

I THOUGHT that our song this year was by far the best. We only lost because everyone else in Europe hates us and they've ganged up against us. It's institutionalised bullying, pure and simple. Everybody in Britain should kill themselves, and then they'll be sorry. I'm going to put my head in the gas oven tonight, and I suggest everyone else in the country does the same.

Renton Stibworth, Leeds

I LOVE Wogan's twinkly Irish commentary during Eurovision. His affectionate mickey-taking of the various foreign songs has always been the highlight of the competition for me. However, this year I thought Sir Terry sounded quite camp - even effeminate. I was just wondering whether he hasn't been well, or whether he's simply decided to become "one of those".

Hector Leviathan, Holmfirth

MY HUSBAND just pointed out to me that, contrary to my earlier comment, Cliff Richard has NEVER won the Eurovision song contest. He came second in 1968 and did even worse five years later, when he came in a poor third. So bollocks to him. We should get the Brotherhood of Man back.

Mrs Hartley, Seaton Delaval

THE REST of Europe can stick their contest up their arse. Next year we should have our own "Englandovision Song Contest" with no foreigners allowed to take part. Not even the Scotch or Welsh. Jim Davidson or Richard Littlejohn could present it and we could scramble the signal so other nationalities couldn't watch the show even if they wanted to. Our songs might not be very good, but at least we'd be guaranteed to win it every year.

J Gaunt, Cirencester

FOLLOWING on from Mrs Hartley's letter *(above)*, why was Cliff Richard given a knighthood, when he has clearly brought shame upon his country not just once, but twice? Why don't we go the whole hog and give Josh Dubovie a peerage for his out-of-tune caterwauling in Oslo? Honestly, you couldn't make it up.

Jack Bollocks, Cuntingford

NEXT YEAR, we should just get Johnny Vegas to get up on the stage, drop his trousers and do a great big shit. At worst, it could only score ten marks less than this year's entry did. And the Germans, who like that sort of thing, might well give us twelve points.

Dr M Butcher, Trainwhistle

BRITAIN should do what the Balkans did and have a huge civil war which results in the formation of dozens of tiny countries. Then all our little states could give us loads of points and we would win the contest for once.

Paddy Ashdown, Devon

I UNDERSTAND that Cyprus was represented by a man from Wales in this year's contest. Not only that, but he managed to beat his own country by fourteen places. If that had happened in the war, this traitor would of been hung from piano wire in the Tower of London for treason. Don't get me wrong, I'm not for a moment suggesting that Jon Lilygreen should be subjected to such a barbaric punishment for this betrayal of his homeland. There are far more humane ways of executing criminals these days - such as lethal injection, a firing squad or sitting him in a bath of water and pushing an electric fire in.

Mrs Hercules, Uttoxeter

WE SHOULD get back to the old days of Eurovision, when the winning songs were always called something like Bing-a-bang-a-bong, Ding-a-dang a-dong or Clang-a-dang-a-ding-dong. Next year we should enter a song with just noises in the title. And we should get someone whose name is also just noises, like Lulu, Kajagoogoo or Chumbawumba to perform it.

Mr Jism, Yeovil

WHAT IS the point of spending a hundred billion pounds on Trident if we can't even use it to intimidate our enemies into giving twelve points to Josh Dubovie? We should scrap this pointless submarine missile defence system and spend the money on getting Barry Manilow or Michael Bolton to perform our song in next year's contest.

Mrs Asquith, Chester

MY GRANDAD spent the First World War sat in a rat-infested French trench getting mustard-gassed and shelled by the Hun. If he'd known then that the country he was risking his life to defend would, ninety-six years later, give Germany three points and Britain zero in the 2010 Eurovision song contest, he would have packed up and gone home.

Rupert Triangle, Bermuda

IT MAKES my blood boil that practically every song in this year's competition was performed in English. These foreigners are quite prepared to steal our beautiful mother tongue from us, but they refuse to do the decent thing in return and vote for our entry. Next year, all these foreign countries should be forced to sing in their own jibber-jabber languages. Let's see how good they sound then.

D'Arcy London, London

MY GRANDAD was one of Montgomery's desert rats, who fought his way through North Africa to free the world from German tyranny. He sat and watched this year's Eurovision Song Contest with glee, cheering on Josh Dubovie's performance, but had a massive stroke and died just before the voting started. I am glad that he didn't live to see the Europe he fought so hard to liberate finally hand victory to the Nazis.

Colin Trubshaw, Arsebury

WE'VE PUSSYFOOTED around for long enough, and now Germany have come out on top. We should have done to Eurovision what we did to Dresden in 1945 - and carpet-bombed it into submission. Then we'd see who's the best at singing.

Wing Commander Bob Harris, Testwhistle

HOW DEPRESSING to read all these comments from people who are still obsessed with the war. It's about time we drew a line under the events of sixty years ago and moved on. Let's face it, we were simply beaten by a better song this year - an *Über Leistüng* if you will - sung by a member of a superior Aryan race - *der Herrenvolk auf dem Vaterland*. I honestly can't see anybody beating us, I mean them, in the Eurovision song contest for a thousand years. Seig Heil.

Dr J McMengele, Hull

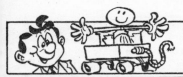

TINRIBS
11-YEAR OLD TOMMY TAYLOR'S BEST PAL WAS AN INCREDIBLE ROBOT NAMED TINRIBS
AT SCHOOL
AH, MR SNODWORTHY. I HAVE DEVELOPED AN EROTIC FIXATION FOR WORDS LIKE "MANAGEMENT STRATEGY" AND "BUDGET."
SCHOOL BUSINESS MANAGER
HEAD MASTER
THEREFORE, TO FACILITATE MY ERECTIONS, I HAVE APPOINTED A SCHOOL BUSINESS MANAGER. THIS IS MR GNATSARSE.
I SHALL BE HANDLING THE SCHOOL'S FINANCES, AND ENSURING THAT WE OPERATE MORE EFFICIENTLY, AND WITHIN BUDGET.
OOH.... "BUDGET."
IN ORDER TO CARRY OUT MY JOB, I'VE GOT THIS BRAND NEW MILLION POUND SOLID GOLD MINK-LINED DESK FOR MY OFFICE.
NOW, LET'S TAKE A LOOK AT THE SCHOOL'S ACCOUNTS...
ACCOUNTS
GOOD LORD! YOU HAVE APPARENTLY JUST SPENT A MILLION POUNDS ON A DESK! WHAT AN APPALLING WASTE OF RESOURCES!
WE MUST IMPLEMENT SOME DRASTIC CUTBACKS IMMEDIATELY!
IT'S HIGH TIME THIS SCHOOL WAS RUN MORE LIKE A BUSINESS, AND LESS LIKE SOME AIRY-FAIRY "PLACE FOR EDUCATING CHILDREN."
LOOK AT THAT, FOR INSTANCE — AN ELECTRIC SCHOOL BELL!
CLANG-A-LANG-A-LANG
EVERY TIME IT RINGS, WE'RE THROWING MONEY AWAY ON THE ELECTRICITY BILL!
HEADMASTER, MY ROBOT CHUM CAN PROVIDE YOU WITH A SCHOOL BELL THAT USES NO ELECTRICITY WHATSOEVER!
HI. I'M BARBIE. I LOVE YOU VERY MUCH.
SEE, I'VE REMOVED MR SNODWORTHY'S TROUSERS AND NAILED HIM TO THE WALL — LIKE SO.
HEY!
NOW YOU CAN USE HIS DANGLING TESTICLES AS A BELL — AND TINRIBS'S WOODEN ARMPIECE FOR THE CLAPPER!
COME ALONG CHILDREN, TIME FOR YOUR LESSONS!
GAH!
DING-A-LING A-LING-A-LING
WELL DONE, THAT ROBOT! WE'VE MADE A SUBSTANTIAL SAVING!
SHORTLY, IN CLASS
TUT TUT! THESE PROFLIGATE PUPILS ARE USING EXERCISE BOOKS AND PENS TO DO THEIR SCHOOLWORK!
EXERCISE BOOKS AND PENS COST MONEY, YOU KNOW!
2+2 =
MY ELECTRONIC PAL CAN HELP REDUCE THE SCHOOL'S STATIONERY COSTS, MR GNATSARSE.
EEP!
I'LL SLICE SOME RECTANGLES OF SKIN OFF MR SNODWORTHY'S BODY WITH ONE OF TINRIBS'S SOUP-CAN SUPPORTS ~ THEY'LL MAKE AN INEXPENSIVE ALTERNATIVE TO PAPER.
NEXT I'LL CHOP OFF MR SNODWORTHY'S FINGERS, WHICH WILL PROVIDE US WITH TEN COST-EFFECTIVE 'PENS'.
CHUNK!
SIMPLY PRESS DOWN ON THE SEVERED FINGER, AND BLOOD WILL OOZE OUT FROM UNDER THE FINGERNAIL LIKE INK.
WELL DONE, YOUNG TAYLOR! THESE "FINGER PENS" ARE RATHER GOOD...
the headmaster is 2kill
OH BLAST! I'VE BLOTTED THE PAGE! I'D BETTER GET SOME TIPPEX CORRECTION FLUID...
NO NEED TO SQUANDER MONEY ON EXPENSIVE TIPPEX, HEADMASTER ~ I'M SURE MR SNODWORTHY CAN FURNISH YOU WITH SOME KIND OF CUT-PRICE SUBSTITUTE...
EH?
AND SO
COME ON, SNODWORTHY, HURRY UP WITH THAT TIPPEX SUBSTITUTE!
TUG TUG
~GROAN~ I'M TRYING, HEADMASTER, BUT IT'S NOT EASY WITHOUT ANY FINGERS!
LATER
HOORAY! IT'S DINNERTIME, TINRIBS — HOPE WE GET CHICKEN AND CHIPS TODAY!
DINNER HALL
HI, I'M BARBIE — I LOVE YOU VERY MUCH.
BUT
HUNH? WHAT'S THIS?
DINING HALL
AS A FURTHER COST-CUTTING EXERCISE, PUPILS AND TEACHERS WILL NOW BE GETTING A SPOONFUL OF SOIL FOR THEIR DINNER.
FORTUNATELY, THE CUTBACKS DON'T APPLY TO DINNERS FOR HEADMASTERS AND BUSINESS MANAGERS.
CHICKEN AND CHIPS
ANOTHER GLASS OF 1787 CHATEAU LAFITE, MR GNATSARSE?
HUH! I'M NOT EATING SOIL! WE'LL HAVE TO GET RID OF THAT BUSINESS MANAGER!
FOR ONCE I AGREE WITH YOU, TAYLOR! AND WE'LL NEED YOUR ROBOT PAL TO DO IT...
AND LATER
FIRE EXIT
~AHEM~ GOODNESS ME! THERE'S AN EXCELLENT OPPORTUNITY FOR CUTBACKS OUTSIDE THIS DOOR!
WHERE? LET ME SEE!
I LOVE OPPORTUNITIES FOR CUTBACKS!
SEE, IF SOMEONE WERE TO RUSH OUT OF THIS DOOR AND STEP ONTO THAT CAREFULLY POSITIONED SKATEBOARD....
WAH!
WHIZZ!
...THEN BE CATAPULTED THROUGH THE AIR AND LAND HEAVILY ON A COUPLE OF JAGGED SOUP TINS...
AAGH! MY SPINE!
...THEN THEY'D HAVE AN EXCELLENT OPPORTUNITY TO SUSTAIN A SEVERELY CUT BACK!
MR GNATSARSE, COME BACK! I NEED YOU TO SAY "BUDGETARY CONTROL POLICY" AND MAKE MY WINKLE GROW STIFF!
SPINAL LACERATION CLINIC
SHAKE HANDS, TINRIBS — WE'RE RID OF THAT BUSINESS MANAGER FOR GOOD!
HI. I'M BARBIE. I LOVE YOU VERY MUCH.

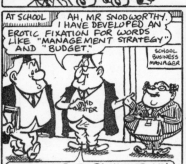

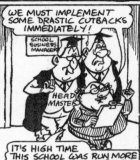

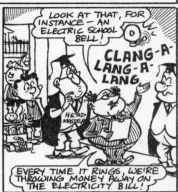

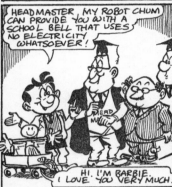

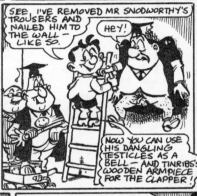

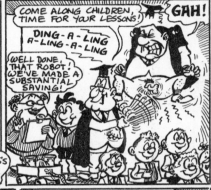

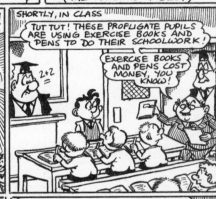

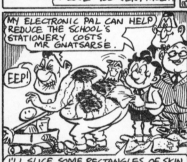

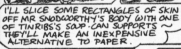

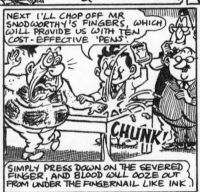

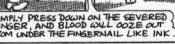

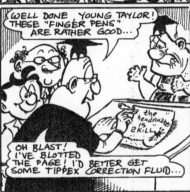

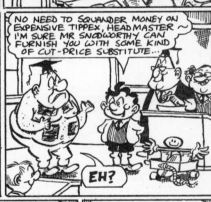

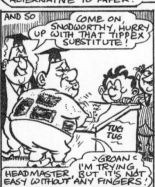

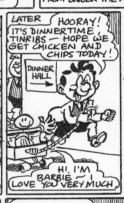

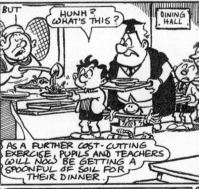

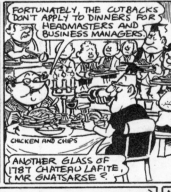

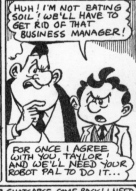

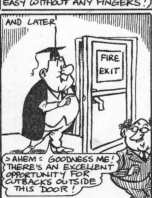

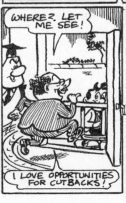

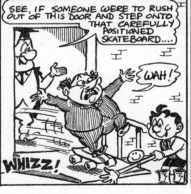

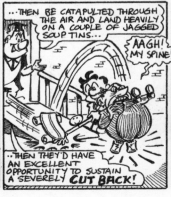

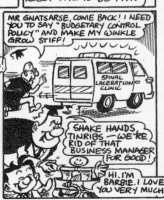

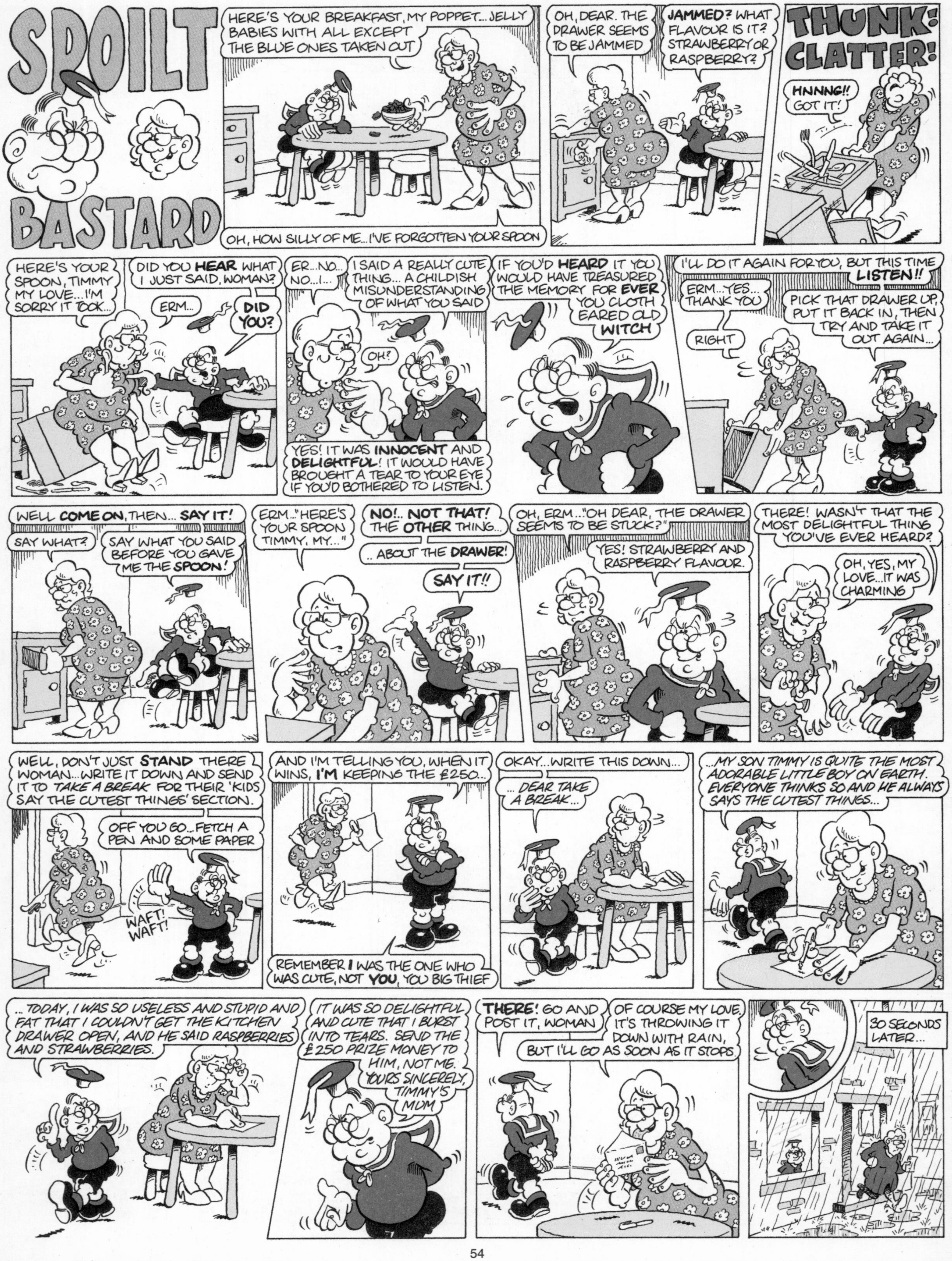
SPOILT BASTARD
HERE'S YOUR BREAKFAST, MY POPPET... JELLY BABIES WITH ALL EXCEPT THE BLUE ONES TAKEN OUT
OH, HOW SILLY OF ME... I'VE FORGOTTEN YOUR SPOON
OH, DEAR. THE DRAWER SEEMS TO BE JAMMED
JAMMED? WHAT FLAVOUR IS IT? STRAWBERRY OR RASPBERRY?
THUNK! CLATTER!
HNNNG!! GOT IT!
HERE'S YOUR SPOON, TIMMY MY LOVE... I'M SORRY IT TOOK...
DID YOU HEAR WHAT I JUST SAID, WOMAN?
ERM...
DID YOU?
ER... NO... NO... I...
I SAID A REALLY CUTE THING... A CHILDISH MISUNDERSTANDING OF WHAT YOU SAID
OH?
YES! IT WAS INNOCENT AND DELIGHTFUL! IT WOULD HAVE BROUGHT A TEAR TO YOUR EYE IF YOU'D BOTHERED TO LISTEN.
IF YOU'D HEARD IT YOU WOULD HAVE TREASURED THE MEMORY FOR EVER YOU CLOTH EARED OLD WITCH
I'LL DO IT AGAIN FOR YOU, BUT THIS TIME LISTEN!!
ERM... YES... THANK YOU
PICK THAT DRAWER UP, PUT IT BACK IN, THEN TRY AND TAKE IT OUT AGAIN...
RIGHT
WELL COME ON, THEN... SAY IT!
SAY WHAT?
SAY WHAT YOU SAID BEFORE YOU GAVE ME THE SPOON!
ERM... "HERE'S YOUR SPOON TIMMY, MY..."
NO!.. NOT THAT! THE OTHER THING...
.. ABOUT THE DRAWER!
SAY IT!!
OH, ERM... "OH DEAR, THE DRAWER SEEMS TO BE STUCK?"
YES! STRAWBERRY AND RASPBERRY FLAVOUR.
THERE! WASN'T THAT THE MOST DELIGHTFUL THING YOU'VE EVER HEARD?
OH, YES, MY LOVE... IT WAS CHARMING
WELL, DON'T JUST STAND THERE WOMAN... WRITE IT DOWN AND SEND IT TO TAKE A BREAK FOR THEIR 'KIDS SAY THE CUTEST THINGS' SECTION.
OFF YOU GO... FETCH A PEN AND SOME PAPER
WAFT! WAFT!
AND I'M TELLING YOU, WHEN IT WINS, I'M KEEPING THE £250...
REMEMBER I WAS THE ONE WHO WAS CUTE, NOT YOU, YOU BIG THIEF
OKAY... WRITE THIS DOWN...
... DEAR TAKE A BREAK...
...MY SON TIMMY IS QUITE THE MOST ADORABLE LITTLE BOY ON EARTH. EVERYONE THINKS SO AND HE ALWAYS SAYS THE CUTEST THINGS...
... TODAY, I WAS SO USELESS AND STUPID AND FAT THAT I COULDN'T GET THE KITCHEN DRAWER OPEN, AND HE SAID RASPBERRIES AND STRAWBERRIES.
IT WAS SO DELIGHTFUL AND CUTE THAT I BURST INTO TEARS. SEND THE £250 PRIZE MONEY TO HIM, NOT ME. YOURS SINCERELY, TIMMY'S MUM
THERE! GO AND POST IT, WOMAN
OF COURSE MY LOVE, IT'S THROWING IT DOWN WITH RAIN, BUT I'LL GO AS SOON AS IT STOPS
30 SECONDS LATER...

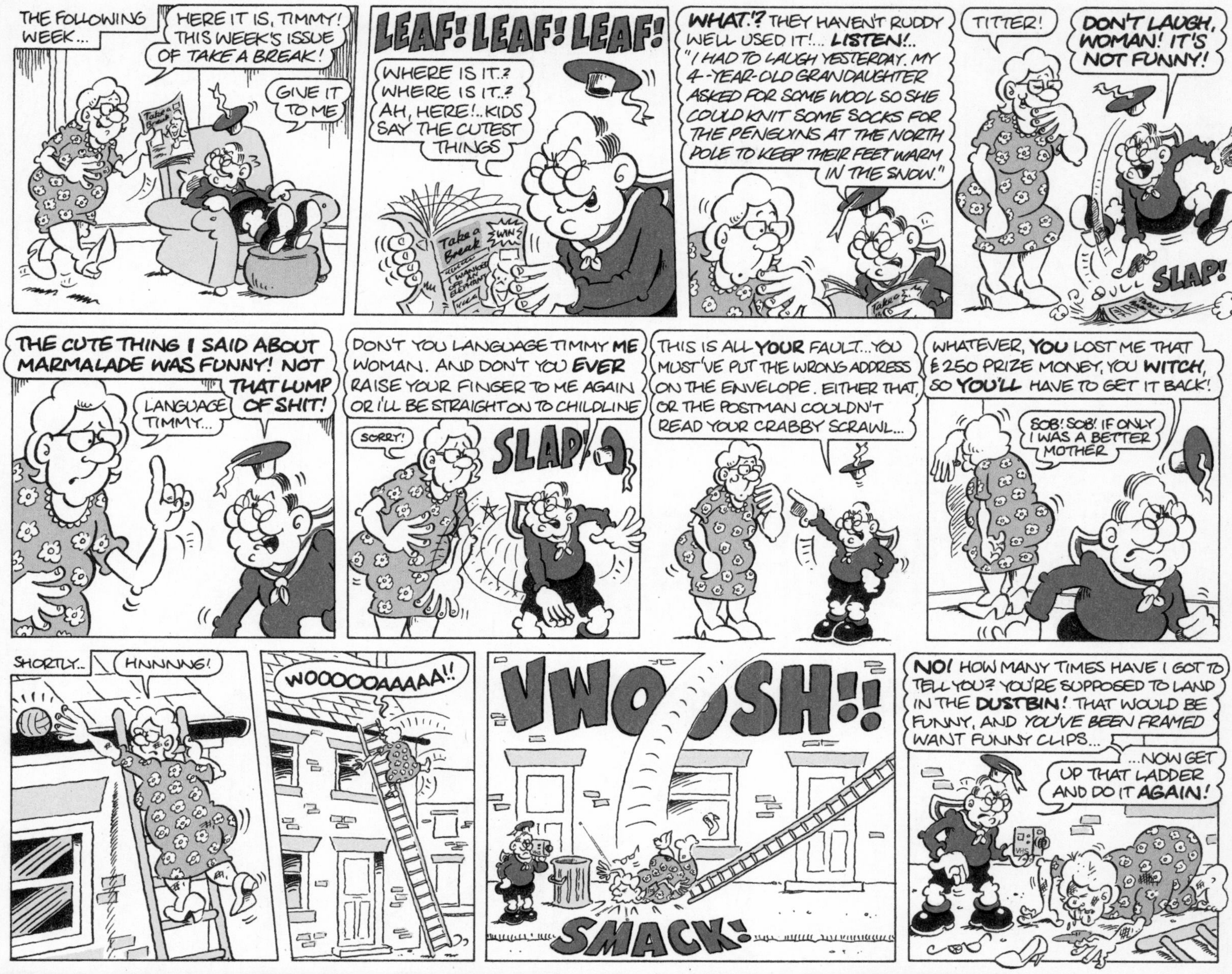
THE FOLLOWING WEEK...
HERE IT IS, TIMMY! THIS WEEK'S ISSUE OF TAKE A BREAK!
GIVE IT TO ME
LEAF! LEAF! LEAF!
WHERE IS IT..? WHERE IS IT..? AH, HERE!.. KIDS SAY THE CUTEST THINGS
WHAT!? THEY HAVEN'T RUDDY WELL USED IT!... LISTEN!...
"I HAD TO LAUGH YESTERDAY. MY 4-YEAR-OLD GRANDAUGHTER ASKED FOR SOME WOOL SO SHE COULD KNIT SOME SOCKS FOR THE PENGUINS AT THE NORTH POLE TO KEEP THEIR FEET WARM IN THE SNOW."
TITTER!
DON'T LAUGH, WOMAN! IT'S NOT FUNNY!
SLAP!
THE CUTE THING I SAID ABOUT MARMALADE WAS FUNNY! NOT THAT LUMP OF SHIT!
LANGUAGE TIMMY...
DON'T YOU LANGUAGE TIMMY ME WOMAN. AND DON'T YOU EVER RAISE YOUR FINGER TO ME AGAIN OR I'LL BE STRAIGHT ON TO CHILDLINE
SORRY!
SLAP!
THIS IS ALL YOUR FAULT... YOU MUST'VE PUT THE WRONG ADDRESS ON THE ENVELOPE. EITHER THAT, OR THE POSTMAN COULDN'T READ YOUR CRABBY SCRAWL...
WHATEVER, YOU LOST ME THAT £250 PRIZE MONEY, YOU WITCH, SO YOU'LL HAVE TO GET IT BACK!
SOB! SOB! IF ONLY I WAS A BETTER MOTHER
SHORTLY...
HNNNNG!
WOOOOOAAAAA!!
VWOOSH!!
SMACK!
NO! HOW MANY TIMES HAVE I GOT TO TELL YOU? YOU'RE SUPPOSED TO LAND IN THE DUSTBIN! THAT WOULD BE FUNNY, AND YOU'VE BEEN FRAMED WANT FUNNY CLIPS...
...NOW GET UP THAT LADDER AND DO IT AGAIN!

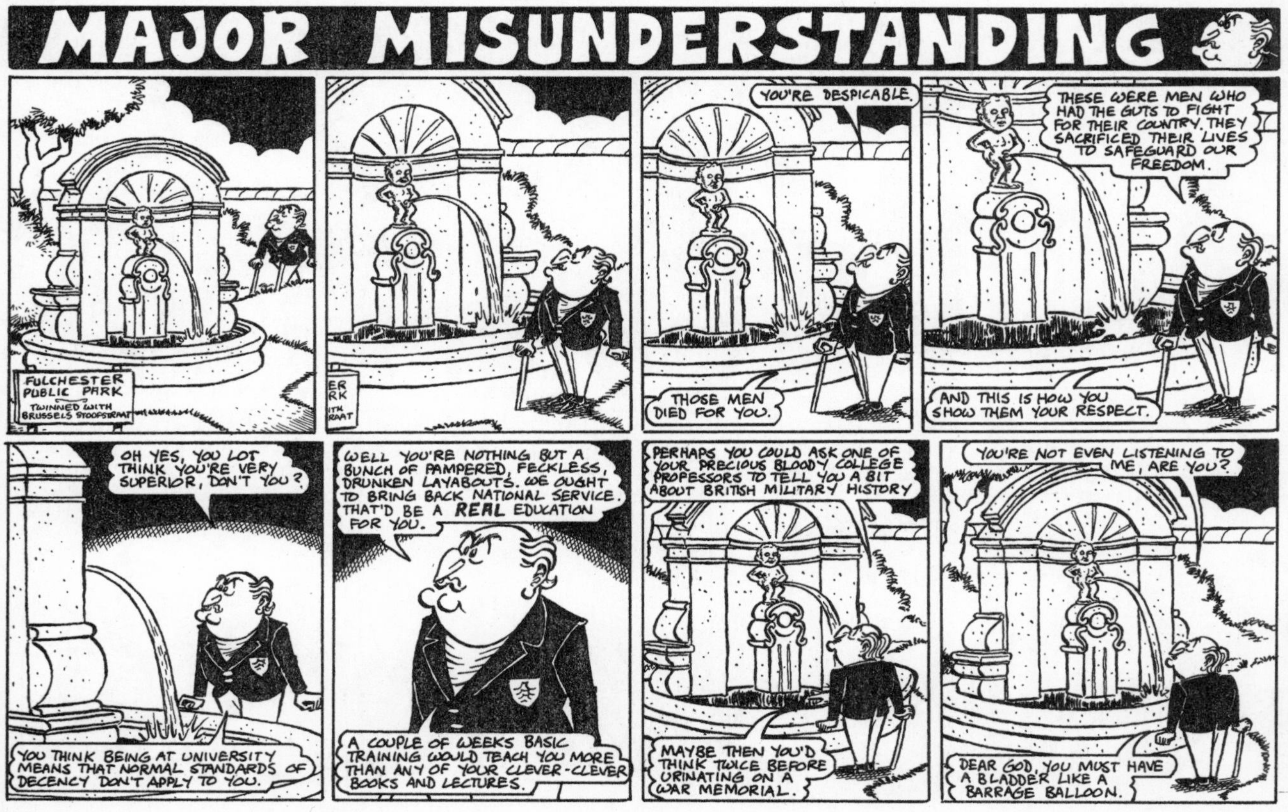
MAJOR MISUNDERSTANDING
FULCHESTER PUBLIC PARK
TWINNED WITH BRUSSELS STOOPSTRAAT
YOU'RE DESPICABLE.
THOSE MEN DIED FOR YOU.
THESE WERE MEN WHO HAD THE GUTS TO FIGHT FOR THEIR COUNTRY. THEY SACRIFICED THEIR LIVES TO SAFEGUARD OUR FREEDOM.
AND THIS IS HOW YOU SHOW THEM YOUR RESPECT.
OH YES, YOU LOT THINK YOU'RE VERY SUPERIOR, DON'T YOU?
YOU THINK BEING AT UNIVERSITY MEANS THAT NORMAL STANDARDS OF DECENCY DON'T APPLY TO YOU.
WELL YOU'RE NOTHING BUT A BUNCH OF PAMPERED, FECKLESS, DRUNKEN LAYABOUTS. WE OUGHT TO BRING BACK NATIONAL SERVICE. THAT'D BE A REAL EDUCATION FOR YOU.
A COUPLE OF WEEKS BASIC TRAINING WOULD TEACH YOU MORE THAN ANY OF YOUR CLEVER-CLEVER BOOKS AND LECTURES.
PERHAPS YOU COULD ASK ONE OF YOUR PRECIOUS BLOODY COLLEGE PROFESSORS TO TELL YOU A BIT ABOUT BRITISH MILITARY HISTORY
MAYBE THEN YOU'D THINK TWICE BEFORE URINATING ON A WAR MEMORIAL.
YOU'RE NOT EVEN LISTENING TO ME, ARE YOU?
DEAR GOD, YOU MUST HAVE A BLADDER LIKE A BARRAGE BALLOON.

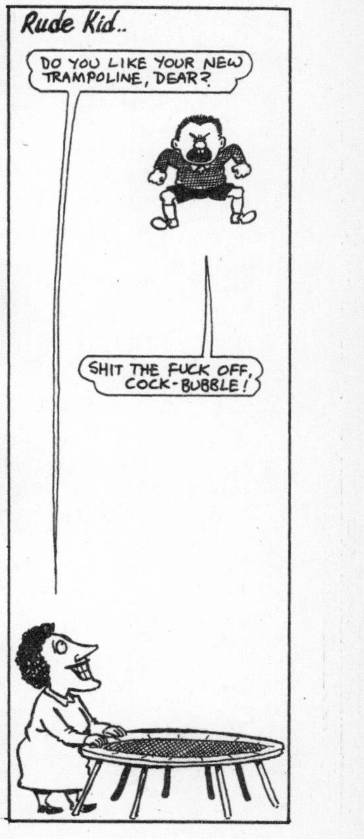
Rude Kid..
DO YOU LIKE YOUR NEW TRAMPOLINE, DEAR?
SHIT THE FUCK OFF, COCK-BUBBLE!

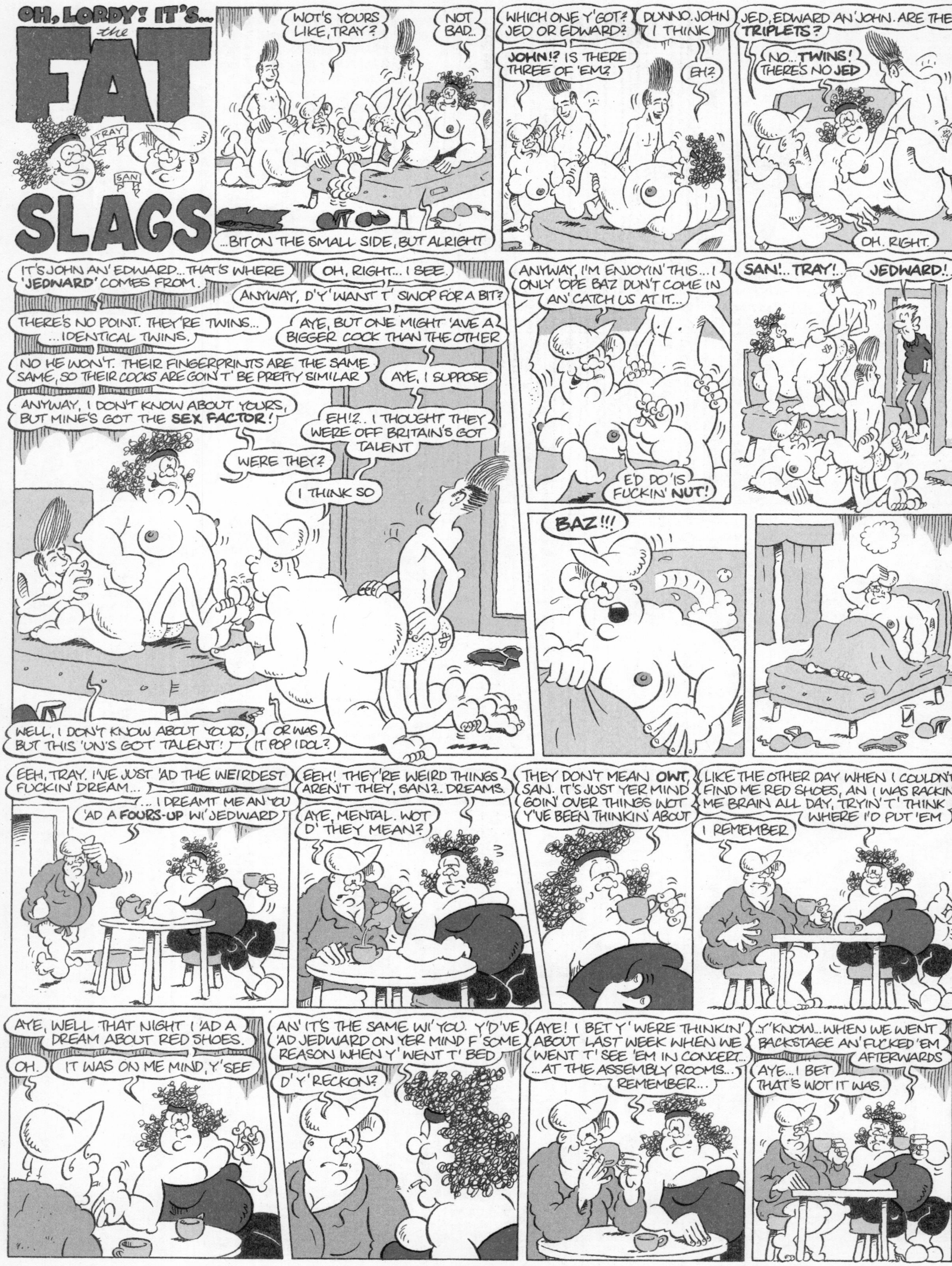
OH, LORDY! IT'S... the FAT SLAGS
TRAY
SAN
WOT'S YOURS LIKE, TRAY?
NOT BAD...
...BIT ON THE SMALL SIDE, BUT ALRIGHT
WHICH ONE Y'GOT? JED OR EDWARD?
DUNNO. JOHN I THINK
JOHN!? IS THERE THREE OF 'EM?
EH?
JED, EDWARD AN' JOHN. ARE THEY TRIPLETS?
NO... TWINS! THERE'S NO JED
OH. RIGHT.
IT'S JOHN AN' EDWARD... THAT'S WHERE 'JEDWARD' COMES FROM.
OH, RIGHT... I SEE.
ANYWAY, D'Y' WANT T' SWOP FOR A BIT?
THERE'S NO POINT. THEY'RE TWINS... ...IDENTICAL TWINS.
AYE, BUT ONE MIGHT 'AVE A BIGGER COCK THAN THE OTHER
NO HE WON'T. THEIR FINGERPRINTS ARE THE SAME SAME, SO THEIR COCKS ARE GOIN' T' BE PRETTY SIMILAR
AYE, I SUPPOSE
ANYWAY, I DON'T KNOW ABOUT YOURS, BUT MINE'S GOT THE SEX FACTOR!
EH!?.. I THOUGHT THEY WERE OFF BRITAIN'S GOT TALENT
WERE THEY?
I THINK SO
WELL, I DON'T KNOW ABOUT YOURS, BUT THIS 'UN'S GOT TALENT!
OR WAS IT POP IDOL?
ANYWAY, I'M ENJOYIN' THIS... I ONLY 'OPE BAZ DON'T COME IN AN' CATCH US AT IT...
ED DO 'IS FUCKIN' NUT!
SAN!.. TRAY!..
JEDWARD!..
BAZ!!!
EEH, TRAY. I'VE JUST 'AD THE WEIRDEST FUCKIN' DREAM...
...I DREAMT ME AN' YOU 'AD A FOURS-UP WI' JEDWARD
EEH! THEY'RE WEIRD THINGS AREN'T THEY, SAN?.. DREAMS.
AYE, MENTAL. WOT D' THEY MEAN?
THEY DON'T MEAN OWT, SAN. IT'S JUST YER MIND GOIN' OVER THINGS WOT Y'VE BEEN THINKIN' ABOUT
LIKE THE OTHER DAY WHEN I COULDN'T FIND ME RED SHOES, AN I WAS RACKIN' ME BRAIN ALL DAY, TRYIN' T' THINK WHERE I'D PUT 'EM
I REMEMBER
AYE, WELL THAT NIGHT I 'AD A DREAM ABOUT RED SHOES.
OH.
IT WAS ON ME MIND, Y'SEE
AN' IT'S THE SAME WI' YOU. Y'D'VE 'AD JEDWARD ON YER MIND F' SOME REASON WHEN Y' WENT T' BED
D'Y'RECKON?
AYE! I BET Y' WERE THINKIN' ABOUT LAST WEEK WHEN WE WENT T' SEE 'EM IN CONCERT... ...AT THE ASSEMBLY ROOMS... REMEMBER...
...Y'KNOW... WHEN WE WENT BACKSTAGE AN' FUCKED 'EM AFTERWARDS
AYE... I BET THAT'S WOT IT WAS.

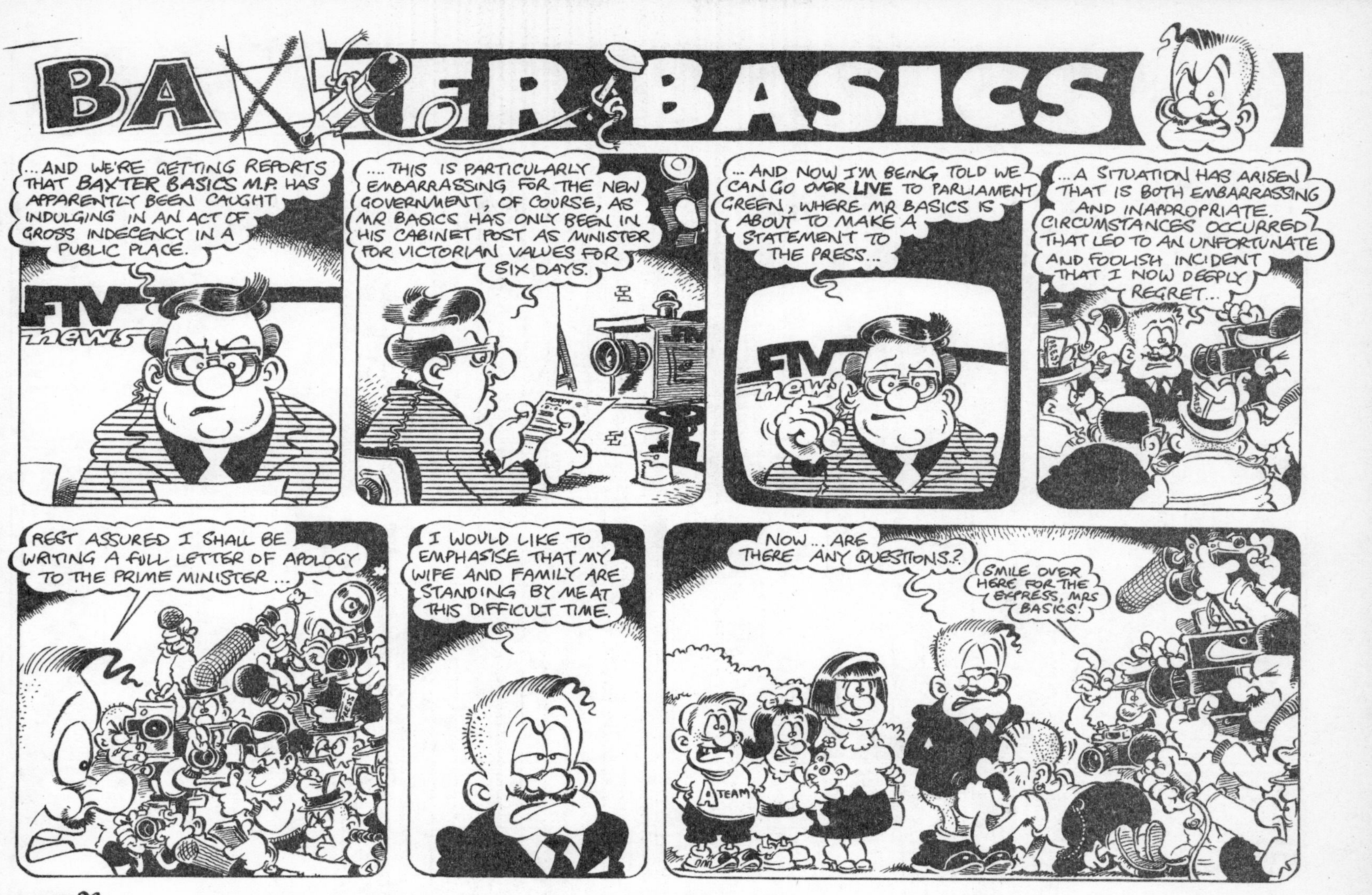
...AND WE'RE GETTING REPORTS THAT BAXTER BASICS M.P. HAS APPARENTLY BEEN CAUGHT INDULGING IN AN ACT OF GROSS INDECENCY IN A PUBLIC PLACE.
FTV news
....THIS IS PARTICULARLY EMBARRASSING FOR THE NEW GOVERNMENT, OF COURSE, AS MR BASICS HAS ONLY BEEN IN HIS CABINET POST AS MINISTER FOR VICTORIAN VALUES FOR SIX DAYS.
...AND NOW I'M BEING TOLD WE CAN GO OVER LIVE TO PARLIAMENT GREEN, WHERE MR BASICS IS ABOUT TO MAKE A STATEMENT TO THE PRESS...
FTV news
...A SITUATION HAS ARISEN THAT IS BOTH EMBARRASSING AND INAPPROPRIATE. CIRCUMSTANCES OCCURRED THAT LED TO AN UNFORTUNATE AND FOOLISH INCIDENT THAT I NOW DEEPLY REGRET...
REST ASSURED I SHALL BE WRITING A FULL LETTER OF APOLOGY TO THE PRIME MINISTER...
I WOULD LIKE TO EMPHASISE THAT MY WIFE AND FAMILY ARE STANDING BY ME AT THIS DIFFICULT TIME.
NOW... ARE THERE ANY QUESTIONS..?
SMILE OVER HERE FOR THE EXPRESS, MRS BASICS!
A TEAM

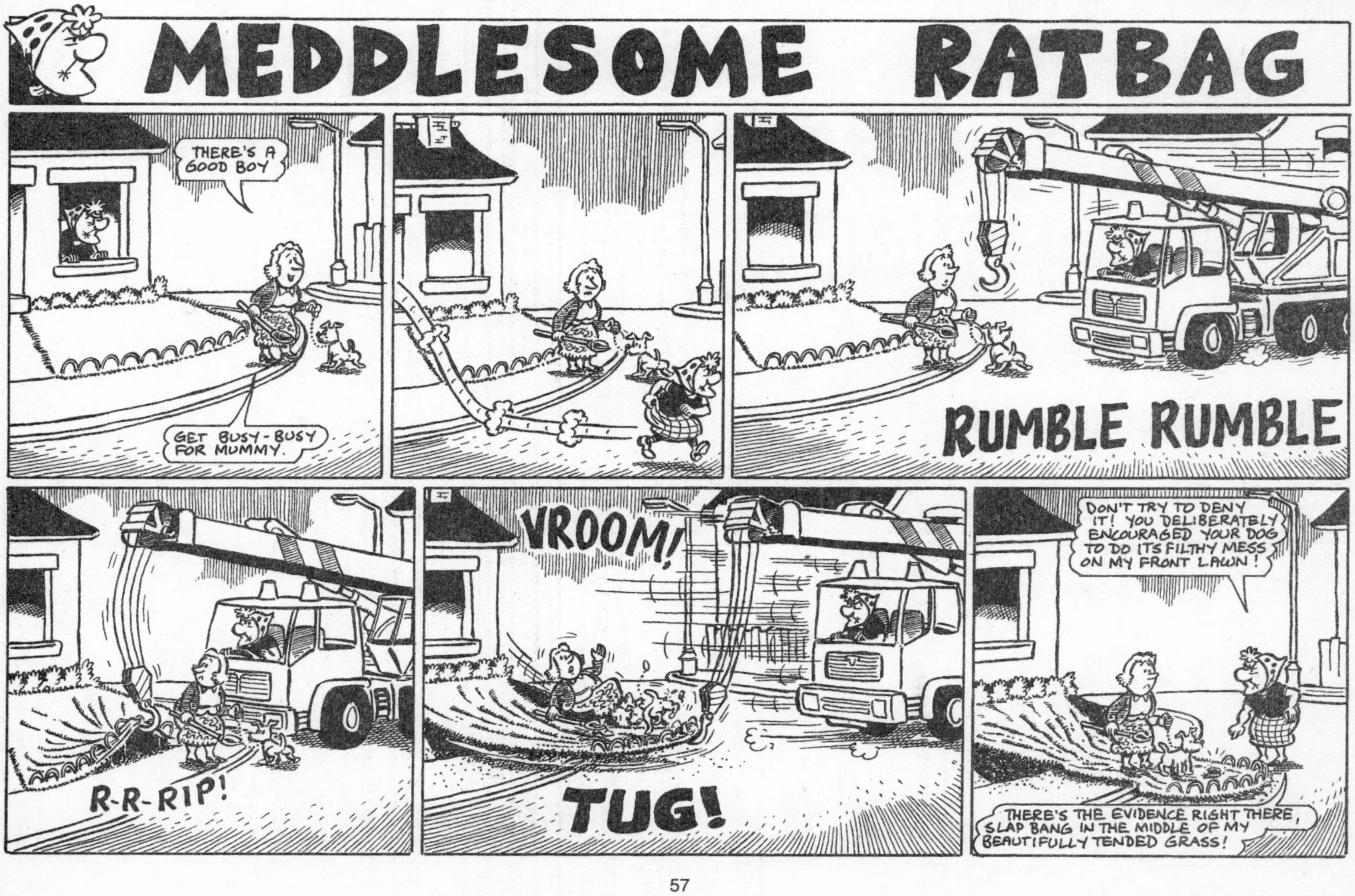
MEDDLESOME RATBAG
THERE'S A GOOD BOY
GET BUSY-BUSY FOR MUMMY.
RUMBLE RUMBLE
R-R-RIP!
VROOM!
TUG!
DON'T TRY TO DENY IT! YOU DELIBERATELY ENCOURAGED YOUR DOG TO DO ITS FILTHY MESS ON MY FRONT LAWN!
THERE'S THE EVIDENCE RIGHT THERE, SLAP BANG IN THE MIDDLE OF MY BEAUTIFULLY TENDED GRASS!

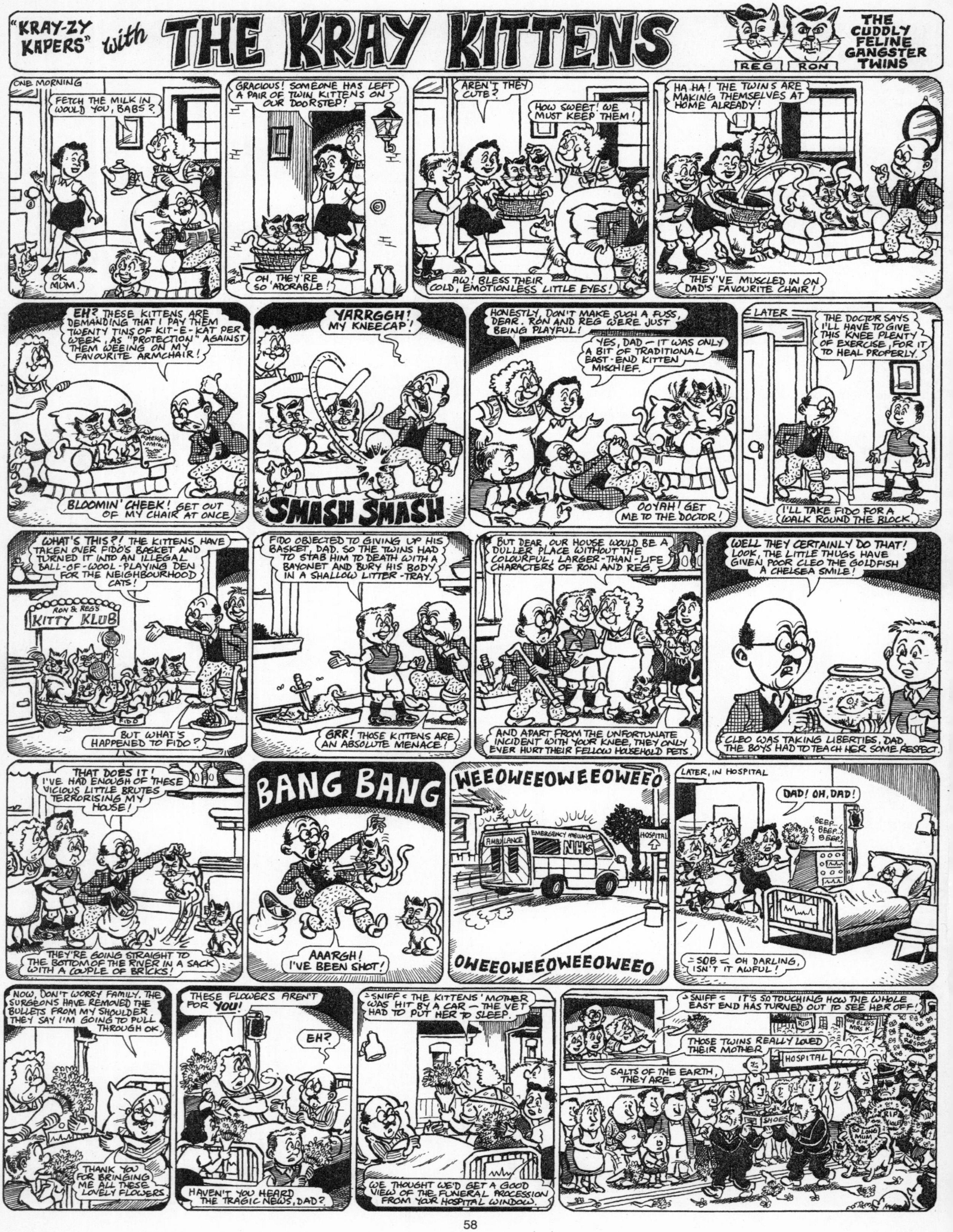

"KRAY-ZY KAPERS" with
THE KRAY KITTENS
REG
RON
THE CUDDLY FELINE GANGSTER TWINS
ONE MORNING
FETCH THE MILK IN WOULD YOU, BABS?
OK MUM.
GRACIOUS! SOMEONE HAS LEFT A PAIR OF TWIN KITTENS ON OUR DOORSTEP!
OH, THEY'RE SO ADORABLE!
AREN'T THEY CUTE?
HOW SWEET! WE MUST KEEP THEM!
AW! BLESS THEIR COLD, EMOTIONLESS LITTLE EYES!
HA HA! THE TWINS ARE MAKING THEMSELVES AT HOME ALREADY!
THEY'VE MUSCLED IN ON DAD'S FAVOURITE CHAIR!
EH? THESE KITTENS ARE DEMANDING THAT I PAY THEM TWENTY TINS OF KIT-E-KAT PER WEEK, AS "PROTECTION" AGAINST THEM WEEING ON MY FAVOURITE ARMCHAIR!
Protekshun contract
BLOOMIN' CHEEK! GET OUT OF MY CHAIR AT ONCE
YARRGGH! MY KNEECAP!
SMASH SMASH
HONESTLY, DON'T MAKE SUCH A FUSS, DEAR. RON AND REG WERE JUST BEING PLAYFUL!
YES, DAD — IT WAS ONLY A BIT OF TRADITIONAL EAST-END KITTEN MISCHIEF.
OOYAH! GET ME TO THE DOCTOR!
LATER
THE DOCTOR SAYS I'LL HAVE TO GIVE THIS KNEE PLENTY OF EXERCISE, FOR IT TO HEAL PROPERLY.
I'LL TAKE FIDO FOR A WALK ROUND THE BLOCK.
WHAT'S THIS?! THE KITTENS HAVE TAKEN OVER FIDO'S BASKET AND TURNED IT INTO AN ILLEGAL BALL-OF-WOOL-PLAYING DEN FOR THE NEIGHBOURHOOD CATS!
RON & REG'S
KITTY KLUB
FIDO
BUT WHAT'S HAPPENED TO FIDO?
FIDO OBJECTED TO GIVING UP HIS BASKET, DAD. SO THE TWINS HAD TO STAB HIM TO DEATH WITH A BAYONET AND BURY HIS BODY IN A SHALLOW LITTER-TRAY.
GRR! THOSE KITTENS ARE AN ABSOLUTE MENACE!
BUT DEAR, OUR HOUSE WOULD BE A DULLER PLACE WITHOUT THE COLOURFUL, LARGER-THAN-LIFE CHARACTERS OF RON AND REG.
AND APART FROM THE UNFORTUNATE INCIDENT WITH YOUR KNEE, THEY ONLY EVER HURT THEIR FELLOW HOUSEHOLD PETS.
WELL THEY CERTAINLY DO THAT! LOOK, THE LITTLE THUGS HAVE GIVEN POOR CLEO THE GOLDFISH A CHELSEA SMILE!
CLEO WAS TAKING LIBERTIES, DAD. THE BOYS HAD TO TEACH HER SOME RESPECT.
THAT DOES IT! I'VE HAD ENOUGH OF THESE VICIOUS LITTLE BRUTES TERRORISING MY HOUSE!
THEY'RE GOING STRAIGHT TO THE BOTTOM OF THE RIVER IN A SACK WITH A COUPLE OF BRICKS!
BANG BANG
AAARGH! I'VE BEEN SHOT!
WEEOWEEOWEEOWEEO
AMBULANCE
EMERGENCY AMBULANCE
NHS
HOSPITAL
OWEEOWEEOWEEOWEEO
LATER, IN HOSPITAL
DAD! OH, DAD!
BEEP... BEEP... BEEP...
>SOB< OH DARLING, ISN'T IT AWFUL!
NOW, DON'T WORRY FAMILY. THE SURGEONS HAVE REMOVED THE BULLETS FROM MY SHOULDER. THEY SAY I'M GOING TO PULL THROUGH OK.
THANK YOU FOR BRINGING ME ALL THESE LOVELY FLOWERS.
THESE FLOWERS AREN'T FOR YOU!
EH?
HAVEN'T YOU HEARD THE TRAGIC NEWS, DAD?
>SNIFF< THE KITTENS' MOTHER WAS HIT BY A CAR — THE VET HAD TO PUT HER TO SLEEP.
WE THOUGHT WE'D GET A GOOD VIEW OF THE FUNERAL PROCESSION FROM YOUR HOSPITAL WINDOW.
>SNIFF< IT'S SO TOUCHING HOW THE WHOLE EAST END HAS TURNED OUT TO SEE HER OFF!
RIP
GOD BLESS MRS K.
With Respect
THOSE TWINS REALLY LOVED THEIR MOTHER
HOSPITAL
SALTS OF THE EARTH, THEY ARE.

Unlucky Pete

"I'm JINXED" ~ says Jailed Sutcliffe

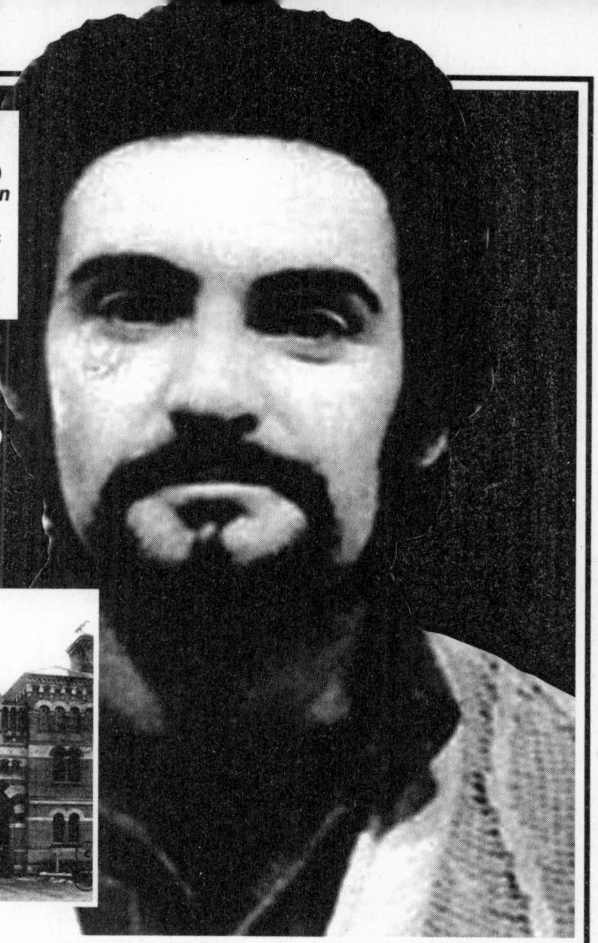

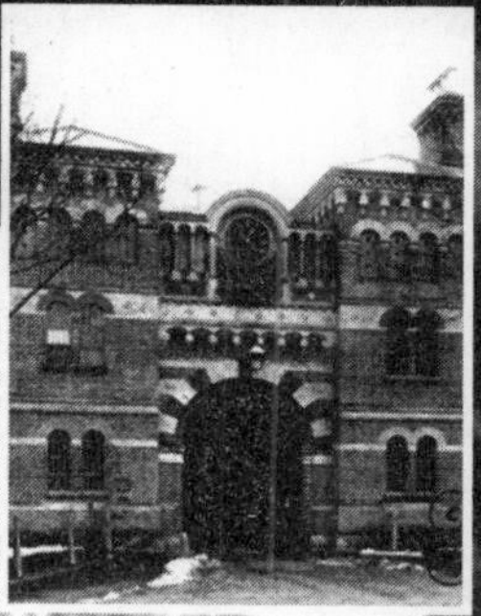

YORKSHIRE PUDDING: *Ripper (right) says he's been plagued by daft mishaps whilst in Broadmoor (inset).*

MASS murderer PETER SUTCLIFFE thinks he must have broken four mirrors in a previous life, for over the last twenty-eight years he has endured an incredible run of bad luck.

Since receiving a life sentence for the murder of thirteen women, the former Yorkshire Ripper has suffered a string of bizarre calamities and madcap mishaps in prison. And now his incredible run of ill-fortune has led to him being voted Britain's Unluckiest Man by the readers of *Heat* magazine.

total

The 64-year-old former lorry driver took the title after his jail bosses totted up a total of over ***THREE HUNDRED*** separate entries in the accident book at Broadmoor Hospital for the Criminally Insane.

Since his conviction, Sutcliffe has been a regular visitor to the prison nurse thanks to his crazy, accident-prone capers which include

*** A FALL from a tree in the exercise yard whilst trying to retrieve a football**

*** A TUMBLE down a fire escape after stepping on a roller skate**

*** A BROKEN nose after treading on a rake in the prison allotments**

*** 20 STITCHES in a head wound after running into a patio door**

*** A SINGED beard and burnt chin after getting his tie caught in an automatic toaster**

Sutcliffe's most recent visit to the sick bay came just a week ago when the bearded serial killer plummeted nearly forty feet down a laundry chute whilst working in the maximum security unit's wash-house, fracturing two ribs and bruising his buttocks.

The Ripper, who is suspected of committing many unsolved crimes across the North of England in the 1970s and early 1980s, told the BBC's *One Show* that he didn't know what he'd done to deserve such bad luck. "Everything that can go wrong does go wrong for me," he joked with the bloke who took over from Adrian Chiles. "I'm always in matron's room, getting my various cuts stitched and bumps bandaged."

And the vicious monster revealed how his run of misfortune isn't just confined to slapstick accidents. "Last month I decided to buy a lottery ticket for the first time," he explained. "It was a Saturday Double Rollover Jackpot, and I had worked out all my numbers using family birthdays."

water

"I was just about to pop down to the corner shop to buy my ticket when I suddenly remembered I had been locked up in a high security prison for nearly thirty years, so I wasn't allowed out to buy one," he continued.

Sutcliffe recalled how, whilst watching the lottery draw from his cell later that night, he had rubbed his eyes in disbelief as his six numbers popped out of the machine one after another. He told us: "You really couldn't make it up. It was just my luck!"

bear

"I'm telling you, if I didn't have bad luck, I don't think I'd have any luck at all."

Nursing a black eye that he'd received whilst winding a cuckoo clock in the prison chapel, Sutcliffe explained that he will be coming up for parole next year. He said: "I'm on my best behaviour and I'm keeping my fingers crossed."

"But knowing my luck, perhaps I should also cross my toes, eyes, legs and everything else!" he added.

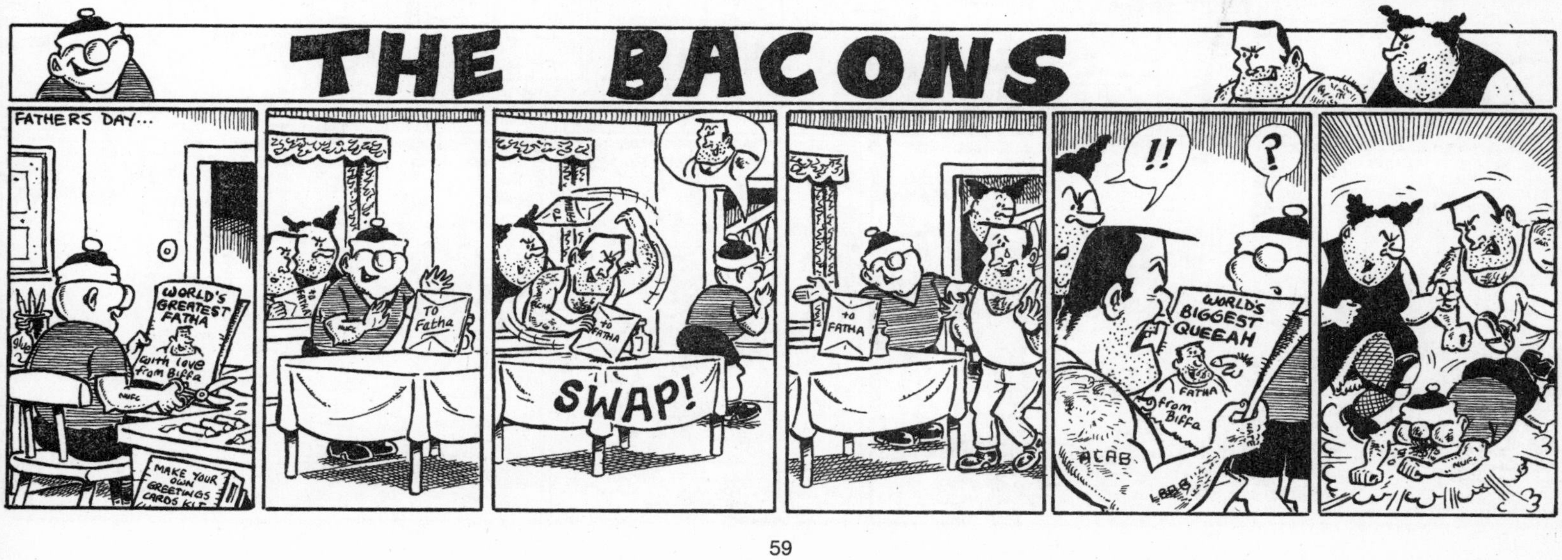
THE BACONS
FATHERS DAY...
WORLD'S GREATEST FATHA
with love from Biffa
MAKE YOUR OWN GREETINGS CARDS KIT
TO Fatha
to FATHA
SWAP!
to FATHA
!!
?
WORLD'S BIGGEST QUEEAH
FATHA
from Biffa
ACAB

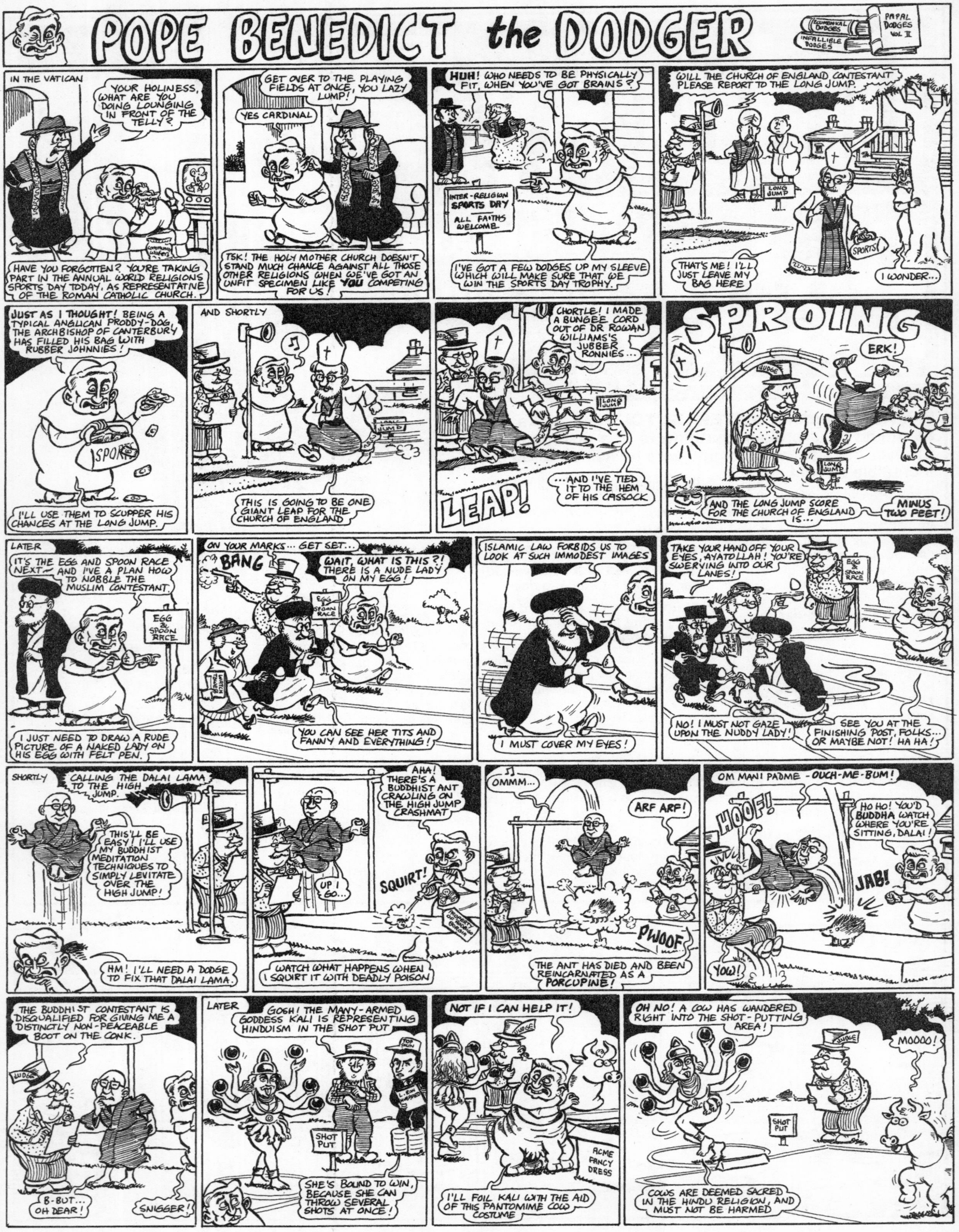
POPE BENEDICT the DODGER
ECUMENICAL DODGES
INFALLIBLE DODGES
PAPAL DODGES VOL II
IN THE VATICAN
YOUR HOLINESS, WHAT ARE YOU DOING LOUNGING IN FRONT OF THE TELLY?
COMMUNION WAFERS
HAVE YOU FORGOTTEN? YOU'RE TAKING PART IN THE ANNUAL WORLD RELIGIONS SPORTS DAY TODAY, AS REPRESENTATIVE OF THE ROMAN CATHOLIC CHURCH.
GET OVER TO THE PLAYING FIELDS AT ONCE, YOU LAZY LUMP!
YES CARDINAL
TSK! THE HOLY MOTHER CHURCH DOESN'T STAND MUCH CHANCE AGAINST ALL THOSE OTHER RELIGIONS WHEN WE'VE GOT AN UNFIT SPECIMEN LIKE YOU COMPETING FOR US!
HUH! WHO NEEDS TO BE PHYSICALLY FIT, WHEN YOU'VE GOT BRAINS?
INTER-RELIGION SPORTS DAY ALL FAITHS WELCOME
I'VE GOT A FEW DODGES UP MY SLEEVE WHICH WILL MAKE SURE THAT WE WIN THE SPORTS DAY TROPHY.
WILL THE CHURCH OF ENGLAND CONTESTANT PLEASE REPORT TO THE LONG JUMP.
LONG JUMP
THAT'S ME! I'LL JUST LEAVE MY BAG HERE
SPORTS
I WONDER...
JUST AS I THOUGHT! BEING A TYPICAL ANGLICAN PRODDY-DOG, THE ARCHBISHOP OF CANTERBURY HAS FILLED HIS BAG WITH RUBBER JOHNNIES!
SPORTS
I'LL USE THEM TO SCUPPER HIS CHANCES AT THE LONG JUMP.
AND SHORTLY
LONG JUMP
THIS IS GOING TO BE ONE GIANT LEAP FOR THE CHURCH OF ENGLAND
CHORTLE! I MADE A BUNGEE CORD OUT OF DR ROWAN WILLIAMS'S JUBBER RONNIES...
LONG JUMP
...AND I'VE TIED IT TO THE HEM OF HIS CASSOCK
LEAP!
SPROING
ERK!
JUDGE
LONG JUMP
AND THE LONG JUMP SCORE FOR THE CHURCH OF ENGLAND IS...
MINUS TWO FEET!
LATER
IT'S THE EGG AND SPOON RACE NEXT — AND I'VE A PLAN HOW TO NOBBLE THE MUSLIM CONTESTANT.
EGG & SPOON RACE
I JUST NEED TO DRAW A RUDE PICTURE OF A NAKED LADY ON HIS EGG WITH FELT PEN.
ON YOUR MARKS... GET SET...
BANG
WAIT, WHAT IS THIS?! THERE IS A NUDE LADY ON MY EGG!
EGG & SPOON RACE
WATCH TOWER
YOU CAN SEE HER TITS AND FANNY AND EVERYTHING!
ISLAMIC LAW FORBIDS US TO LOOK AT SUCH IMMODEST IMAGES
I MUST COVER MY EYES!
TAKE YOUR HAND OFF YOUR EYES, AYATOLLAH! YOU'RE SWERVING INTO OUR LANES!
EGG & SPOON RACE
NO! I MUST NOT GAZE UPON THE NUDDY LADY!
SEE YOU AT THE FINISHING POST, FOLKS... OR MAYBE NOT! HA HA!
SHORTLY
CALLING THE DALAI LAMA TO THE HIGH JUMP.
THIS'LL BE EASY! I'LL USE MY BUDDHIST MEDITATION TECHNIQUES TO SIMPLY LEVITATE OVER THE HIGH JUMP!
HM! I'LL NEED A DODGE TO FIX THAT DALAI LAMA.
AHA! THERE'S A BUDDHIST ANT CRAWLING ON THE HIGH JUMP CRASHMAT
UP I GO...
SQUIRT!
WATCH WHAT HAPPENS WHEN I SQUIRT IT WITH DEADLY POISON
OMMM...
ARF ARF!
PWOOF
THE ANT HAS DIED AND BEEN REINCARNATED AS A PORCUPINE!
OM MANI PADME -OUCH-ME-BUM!
HOOF!
HO HO! YOU'D BUDDHA WATCH WHERE YOU'RE SITTING, DALAI!
JAB!
YOW!
THE BUDDHIST CONTESTANT IS DISQUALIFIED FOR GIVING ME A DISTINCTLY NON-PEACEABLE BOOT ON THE CONK.
JUDGE
B-BUT... OH DEAR!
SNIGGER!
LATER
GOSH! THE MANY-ARMED GODDESS KALI IS REPRESENTING HINDUISM IN THE SHOT PUT
SHOT PUT
SHE'S BOUND TO WIN, BECAUSE SHE CAN THROW SEVERAL SHOTS AT ONCE!
NOT IF I CAN HELP IT!
JUDGE
ACME FANCY DRESS
I'LL FOIL KALI WITH THE AID OF THIS PANTOMIME COW COSTUME
OH NO! A COW HAS WANDERED RIGHT INTO THE SHOT-PUTTING AREA!
JUDGE
MOOOO!
SHOT PUT
COWS ARE DEEMED SACRED IN THE HINDU RELIGION, AND MUST NOT BE HARMED

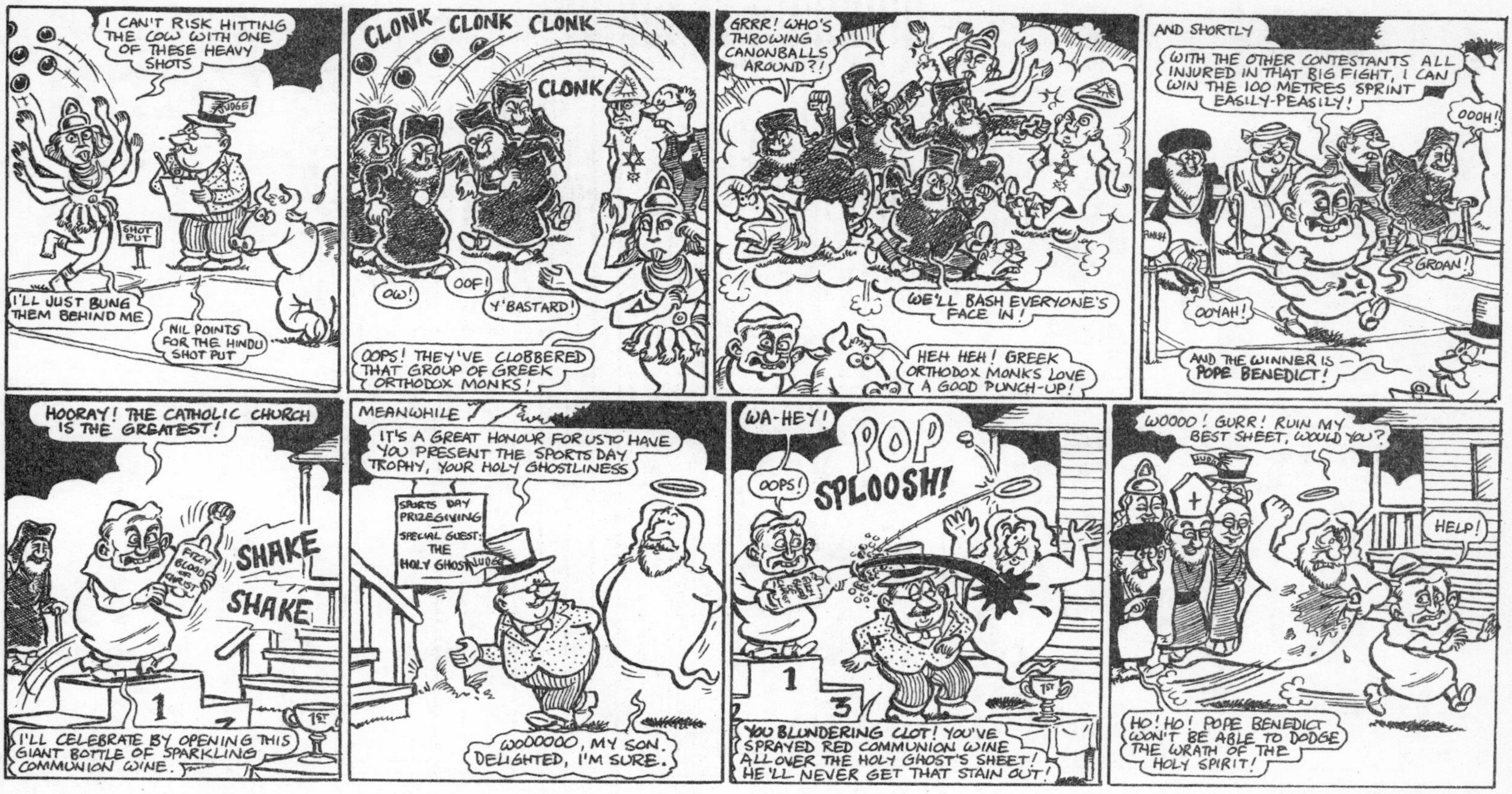

I CAN'T RISK HITTING THE COW WITH ONE OF THESE HEAVY SHOTS
JUDGE
SHOT PUT
I'LL JUST BUNG THEM BEHIND ME
NIL POINTS FOR THE HINDU SHOT PUT
CLONK CLONK CLONK
CLONK
OW!
OOF!
Y'BASTARD!
OOPS! THEY'VE CLOBBERED THAT GROUP OF GREEK ORTHODOX MONKS!
GRRR! WHO'S THROWING CANONBALLS AROUND?!
WE'LL BASH EVERYONE'S FACE IN!
HEH HEH! GREEK ORTHODOX MONKS LOVE A GOOD PUNCH-UP!
AND SHORTLY
WITH THE OTHER CONTESTANTS ALL INJURED IN THAT BIG FIGHT, I CAN WIN THE 100 METRES SPRINT EASILY-PEASILY!
OOOH!
GROAN!
OOYAH!
AND THE WINNER IS – POPE BENEDICT!
HOORAY! THE CATHOLIC CHURCH IS THE GREATEST!
SHAKE
SHAKE
I'LL CELEBRATE BY OPENING THIS GIANT BOTTLE OF SPARKLING COMMUNION WINE.
MEANWHILE
IT'S A GREAT HONOUR FOR US TO HAVE YOU PRESENT THE SPORTS DAY TROPHY, YOUR HOLY GHOSTLINESS
SPORTS DAY PRIZEGIVING SPECIAL GUEST: THE HOLY GHOST
WOOOOOO, MY SON. DELIGHTED, I'M SURE.
WA-HEY!
POP
OOPS!
SPLOOSH!
YOU BLUNDERING CLOT! YOU'VE SPRAYED RED COMMUNION WINE ALL OVER THE HOLY GHOST'S SHEET! HE'LL NEVER GET THAT STAIN OUT!
WOOOO! GURR! RUIN MY BEST SHEET, WOULD YOU?
HELP!
HO! HO! POPE BENEDICT WON'T BE ABLE TO DODGE THE WRATH OF THE HOLY SPIRIT!

Ken Barlow - "I fear being typecast"

THE ACTOR formerly known as that man who plays *Coronation Street*'s KEN BARLOW spoke yesterday of his fear of being typecast in the role he has played for half a century.

EXCLUSIVE!

In a keynote speech at a packed NUT Conference in Brighton, Barlow told delegates that being best known for portraying a mild-mannered former school teacher could prevent him from getting different, more diverse roles.

Barlow, who has been played by that actor since the first episode of the soap in 1960, explained that he wanted to avoid the common actor's pitfall of getting too comfortable with a role and becoming typecast.

"You only have to look at the likes of Joe Pesci and Robert DeNiro to see how easy it is to fall into that trap," he said.

"They will only ever be known for playing Italian mobsters. I don't want to become a one-trick-pony like them."

Addressing a group of confused A-Level students at South Trafford College later the same day, Barlow outlined his desire to play more exciting roles.

"I'd like to play a British spy who's actually a Russian double agent, or maybe a detective who bends the rules but always gets results.

"Having said that, the holidays you get as a retired teacher being played by that man are very good," he said.

But he also explained how he felt it was important to stay fresh and not let the grass grow under his feet.

"Maybe I'll branch out next year," he said. "I'll probably start off by playing a doctor or policeman or maybe even an enthused amateur local historian. Yes, that's what I'll do, right after I've written to the *Weatherfield Gazette* about the proposed changes to Key Stage 8 marking guidelines."

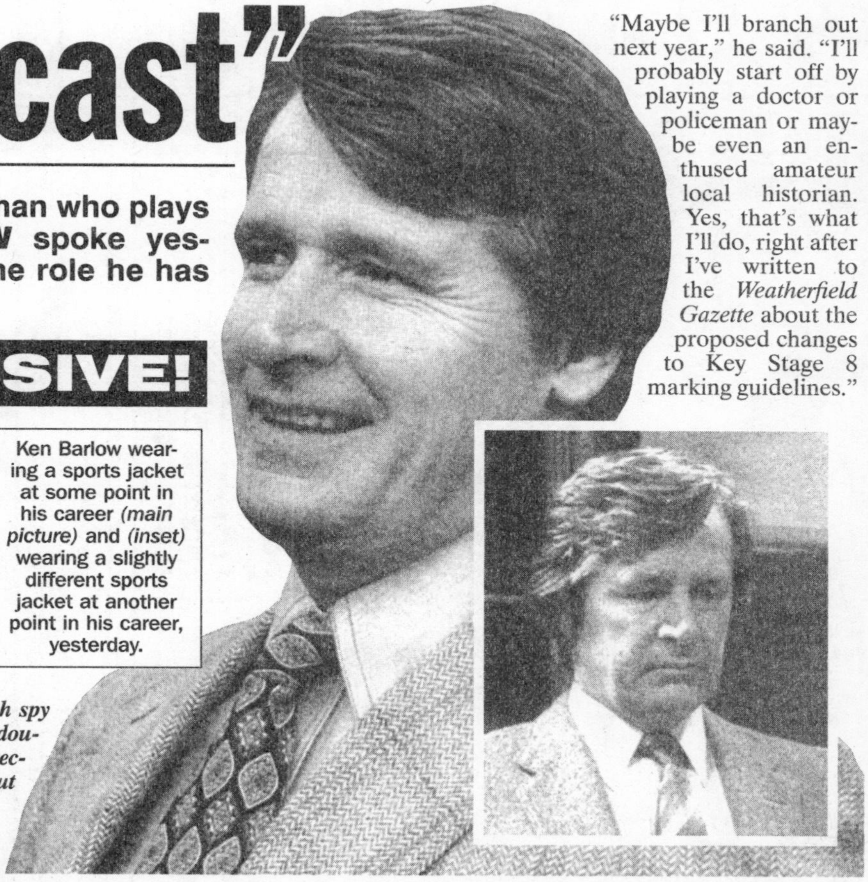

Ken Barlow wearing a sports jacket at some point in his career *(main picture)* and *(inset)* wearing a slightly different sports jacket at another point in his career, yesterday.

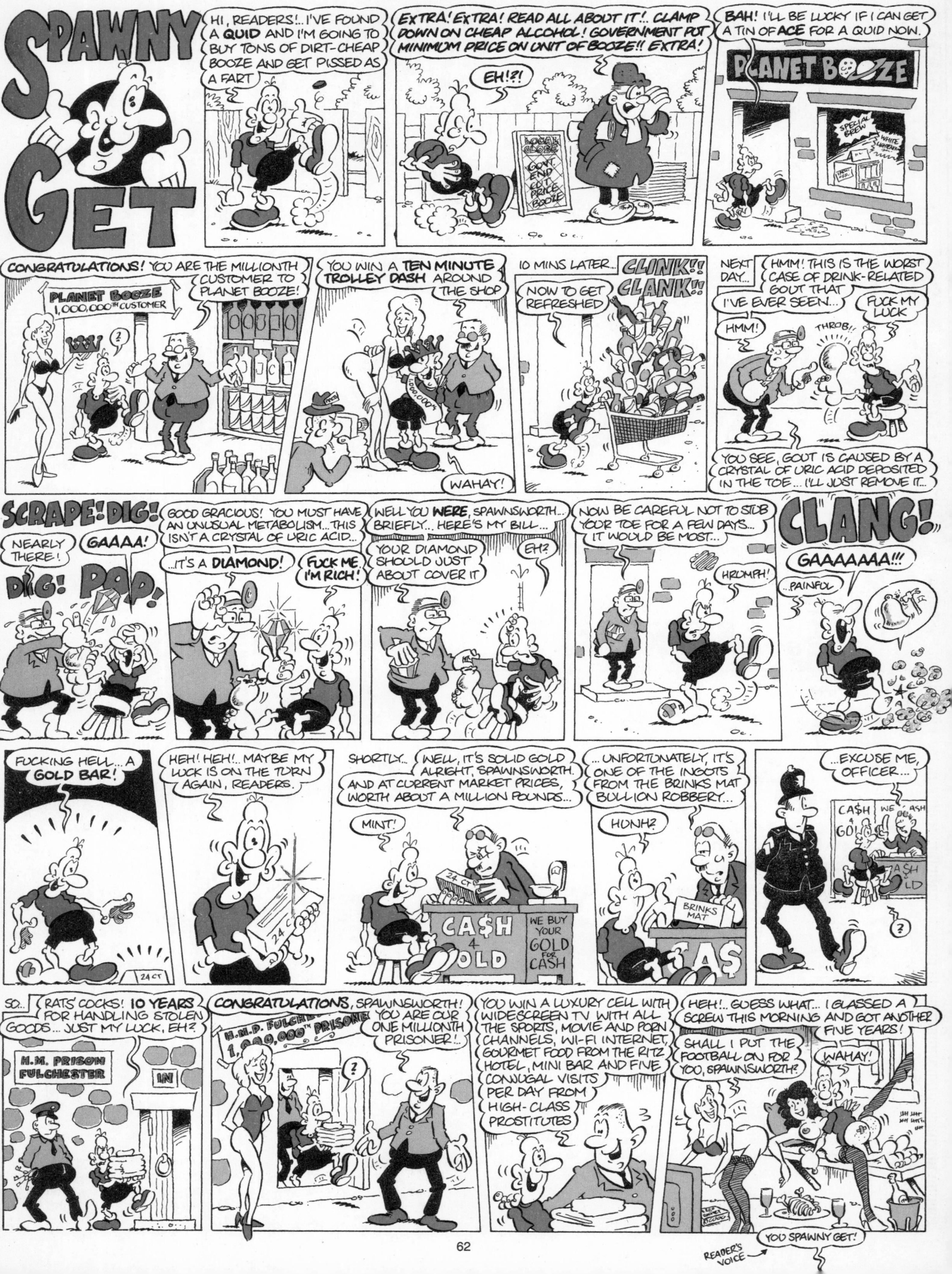
SPAWNY GET
HI, READERS!... I'VE FOUND A QUID AND I'M GOING TO BUY TONS OF DIRT-CHEAP BOOZE AND GET PISSED AS A FART
EXTRA! EXTRA! READ ALL ABOUT IT!.. CLAMP DOWN ON CHEAP ALCOHOL! GOVERNMENT PUT MINIMUM PRICE ON UNIT OF BOOZE!! EXTRA!
EH!?!
LOCAL GLOBE
GOVT. END CUT PRICE BOOZE
BAH! I'LL BE LUCKY IF I CAN GET A TIN OF ACE FOR A QUID NOW.
PLANET BOOZE
SPECIAL BREW
WHITE LIGHTNING
CONGRATULATIONS! YOU ARE THE MILLIONTH CUSTOMER TO PLANET BOOZE!
PLANET BOOZE 1,000,000TH CUSTOMER
?
YOU WIN A TEN MINUTE TROLLEY DASH AROUND THE SHOP
1,000,000TH
WAHAY!
10 MINS LATER...
CLINK!! CLANK!!
NOW TO GET REFRESHED
NEXT DAY...
HMM! THIS IS THE WORST CASE OF DRINK-RELATED GOUT THAT I'VE EVER SEEN...
FUCK MY LUCK
HMM!
THROB!!
YOU SEE, GOUT IS CAUSED BY A CRYSTAL OF URIC ACID DEPOSITED IN THE TOE... I'LL JUST REMOVE IT...
SCRAPE! DIG!
NEARLY THERE!
GAAAA!
DIG! POP!
GOOD GRACIOUS! YOU MUST HAVE AN UNUSUAL METABOLISM... THIS ISN'T A CRYSTAL OF URIC ACID...
...IT'S A DIAMOND!
FUCK ME I'M RICH!
WELL YOU WERE, SPAWNSWORTH... BRIEFLY... HERE'S MY BILL...
YOUR DIAMOND SHOULD JUST ABOUT COVER IT
EH?
NOW BE CAREFUL NOT TO STUB YOUR TOE FOR A FEW DAYS... IT WOULD BE MOST...
HROMPH!
CLANG!
GAAAAAAA!!!
...PAINFUL
FUCKING HELL... A GOLD BAR!
24 CT
HEH! HEH!.. MAYBE MY LUCK IS ON THE TURN AGAIN, READERS.
24 CT
SHORTLY...
WELL, IT'S SOLID GOLD ALRIGHT, SPAWNSWORTH. AND AT CURRENT MARKET PRICES, WORTH ABOUT A MILLION POUNDS...
MINT!
24 CT
CA$H 4 GOLD
WE BUY YOUR GOLD FOR CASH
...UNFORTUNATELY, IT'S ONE OF THE INGOTS FROM THE BRINKS MAT BULLION ROBBERY...
HUNH?
BRINKS MAT
CA$
...EXCUSE ME, OFFICER...
?
SO...
RATS' COCKS! 10 YEARS FOR HANDLING STOLEN GOODS... JUST MY LUCK, EH?
H.M. PRISON FULCHESTER
IN
CONGRATULATIONS, SPAWNSWORTH! YOU ARE OUR ONE MILLIONTH PRISONER!..
1,000,000TH PRISONER
?
YOU WIN A LUXURY CELL WITH WIDESCREEN TV WITH ALL THE SPORTS, MOVIE AND PORN CHANNELS, WI-FI INTERNET, GOURMET FOOD FROM THE RITZ HOTEL, MINI BAR AND FIVE CONJUGAL VISITS PER DAY FROM HIGH-CLASS PROSTITUTES
HEH!.. GUESS WHAT... I GLASSED A SCREW THIS MORNING AND GOT ANOTHER FIVE YEARS!
SHALL I PUT THE FOOTBALL ON FOR YOU, SPAWNSWORTH?
WAHAY!
READER'S VOICE
YOU SPAWNY GET!

Bishop Mauled by Bear

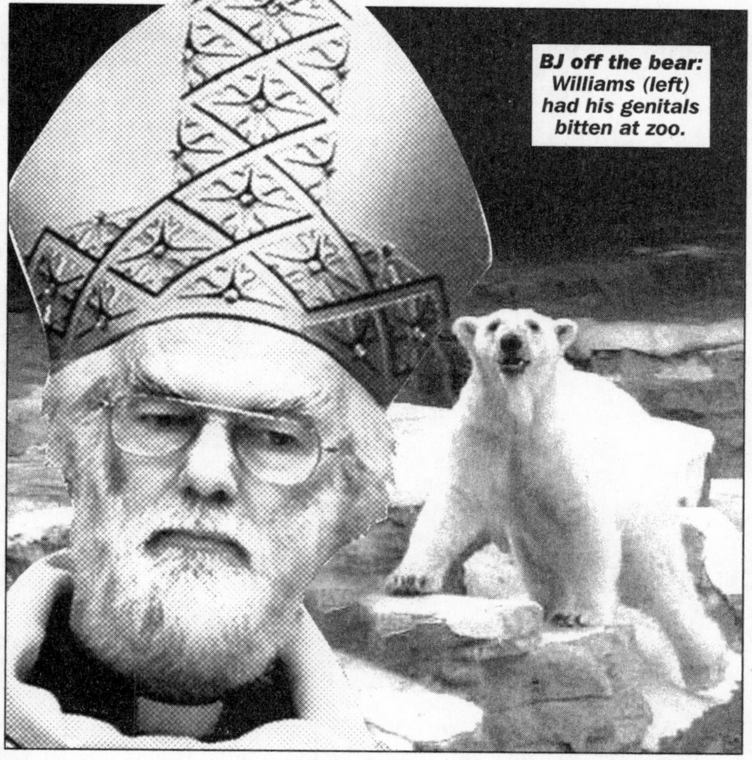

BJ off the bear: Williams (left) had his genitals bitten at zoo.

ARCHBISHOP of Canterbury DR ROWAN WILLIAMS was recovering in hospital last night after being attacked by a polar bear at Whipsnade Zoo.

Details of the incident are still sketchy, but it is believed that Williams, 60, was attacked by the 2-ton carnivore after apparently climbing over a safety barrier and pushing his testicles through the bars of its cage.

ACTING

Witnesses said that the archbishop, who was dressed in his full ceremonial regalia, had been acting strangely in the minutes leading up to the accident. Primary school teacher Maureen Mimblehulme, who was visiting the zoo with her class of 6-year-olds, said: "Dr Williams looked very agitated. He was pacing up and down in front of the bear enclosure mumbling to himself."

"He kept putting his hands under his cassock. He appeared to be fiddling with something," she added.

The archbishop then apparently vaulted across a safety fence and approached the bear's cage. "He was breathing heavily and his face was red," said Mrs Mimblehulme. "Then he seemed to lift his robes, pull his underpants down and start pushing his crotch through the bars. I couldn't believe what I was seeing."

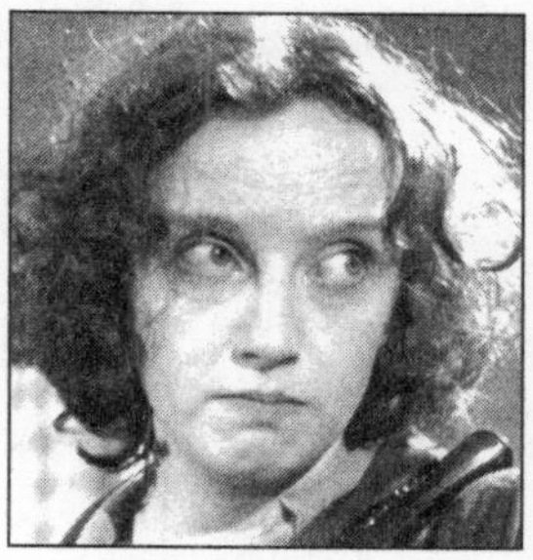

***SHOCKED:* Maureen Mimblehulme**

"He was shouting something that sounded like 'Come on, Momma bear! Lick 'em! Lick 'em!'," she added.

Zoo visitors then watched in horror as Nell, a 22-year-old polar bear who has lived in the zoo since 1995, grabbed the archbishop's scrotum in her jaws and began shaking it from side to side. "Williams was shouting out in agony and vainly trying to hit the bear with his bishop's crook, but it wouldn't release its grip," said one shocked eyewitness.

EXCLUSIVE!

After several minutes, a zoo keeper arrived and managed to beat Nell off using a sweeping brush. Dr Williams received first aid at the scene before being taken to Dunstable General Hospital where he was said to be stable but in agony.

A Church of England spokesman said: "Dr Williams would like to thank the many well-wishers who have sent kind messages and remembered him in their prayers at this difficult time. He would like to make it clear that he was in no way attempting to get a polar bear to perform a sex act on his person at the time of the mishap. Although it may have looked like he was, he was actually doing another thing that might have given the impression that that was what he was doing. But it wasn't."

SHRUNKEN

He continued: "Dr Williams has been under a lot of stress recently after taking on a very heavy workload. Services at Christmas, New Year blessings and preparations for Easter have left him exhausted, which is why it may have appeared that he did what he did. Which he didn't."

Dr Williams is not the first Archbishop of Canterbury to suffer at the jaws of Nell the polar bear. His predecessor Dr George Carey suffered lacerations to his glans in 2002 after slipping whilst "attempting to feed Nell a sausage." And Dr Robert Runcie, who retired as Archbishop in 1991, required 300 stitches in his taint after he used a workman's ladder to enter her enclosure after smearing his buttocks with fish paste in 1998.

A zoo spokesman said: "Safety barriers are put in place for a reason. Anyone who crosses them in order to get closer to an animal is putting not only themselves, but also zoo staff at risk of serious injury."

GIVING

"Nell may look cute and cuddly, but she is a wild animal. We would urge Archbishops of Canterbury to resist the temptation to get close to her," he added.

Benson & Hedges

CRAB FAGS

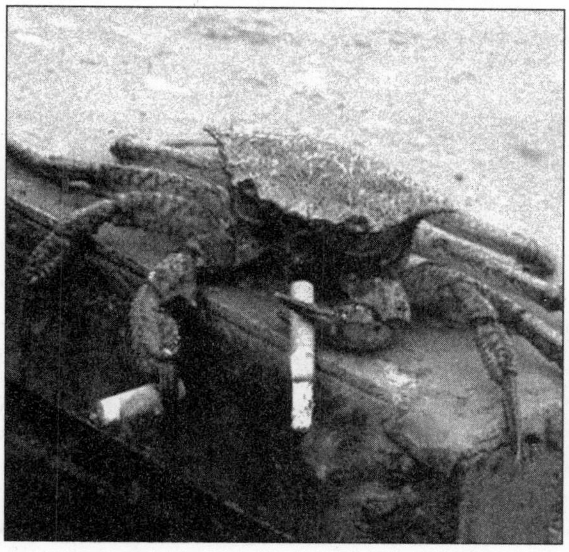

Government Health Warning

SMOKING CRAB FAGS CAN LEAD TO GETTING BOILED ALIVE OR SMASHED WITH A SPADE BY A BORED TODDLER

6mg Tar 0.5mg Nicotine 3mg Side salad

LETTERBOCKS

Viz Comic, PO Box 841
Whitley Bay, NE26 9EQ
e-mail: letters@viz.co.uk

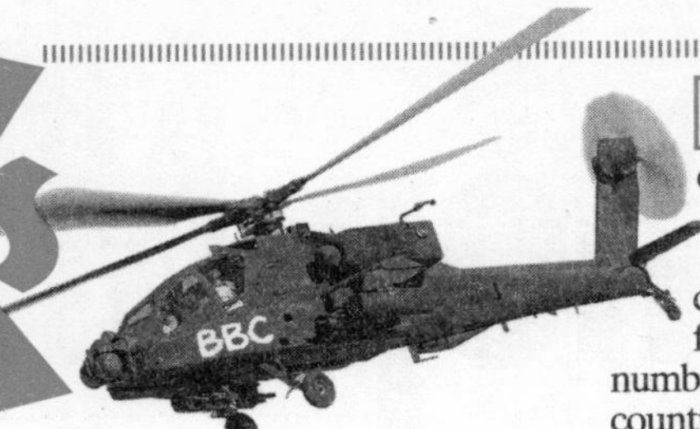
BBC

I DON'T mind having somebody doing sign language in the bottom right hand corner of my television screen on certain programmes for the benefit of the hard of hearing. But why don't the broadcasters have a topless woman doing it so people with normal hearing can get something out of it?

Wayne Statham, e-mail

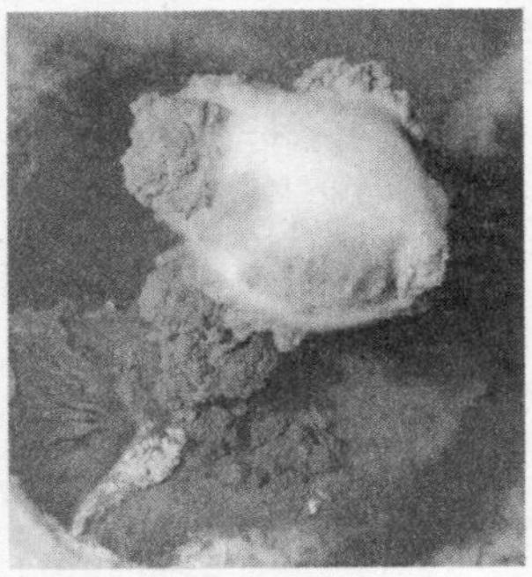

IF ICELAND can't be trusted not to let their volcanoes off, then they shouldn't be allowed to have them.

Dean Moncaster, e-mail

THE 'first past the post' voting system certainly needs to be rethought after the confusion of this general election. But other systems such as proportional representation are not without their flaws. Why don't we have a system whereby the electorate simply vote for which leader's wife they would most like to bang? This would have led to a landslide victory for Nick Clegg this time round, and it would ensure that future ambitious politicians would not go round marrying old boots.

Milton Penninger, Carlisle

STAR LETTER

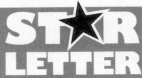

FORREST Gump's mother famously said, 'life is like a box of chocolates - you never know what you're going to get.' Well I can't help thinking that Mrs Gump was buying the wrong chocolates. The ones I get come with a little card that shows you which centres are which.

Martin Williams, e-mail

I CAN'T see that those voters locked out of the polling booths at the last election have anything to complain about. They knew that voting closed at 10 o'clock, and I'm afraid that if they don't own a watch or are unable to tell the time, then they simply don't deserve a vote.

Nelson Spears, e-mail

WITH reverence to Mr Spears's letter *(above)*, I think that the voters who were locked out of the polling booths on election night should be allowed to have two votes in the next election, plus another one for the inconvenience caused.

Celia Huvit, Torquay

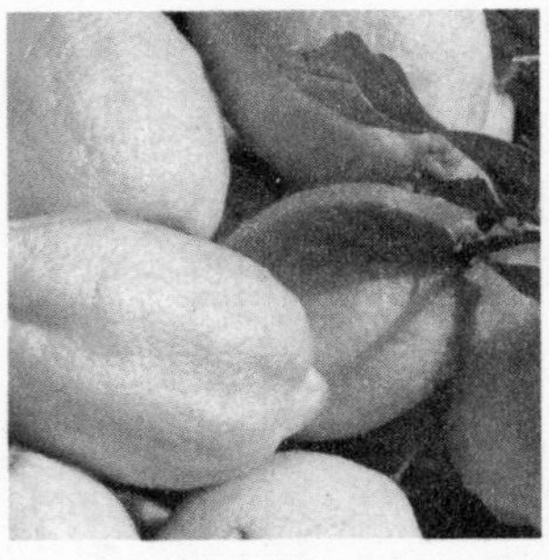

WHY IS lemon juice made with artificial flavour and lemon washing-up liquid made with real lemons?

Ant Hands, e-mail

WHY did the BBC have a helicopter hovering over Downing Street waiting for Gordon Brown to come out and resign? Did they think he was going to come out onto the roof and start throwing slates down or something? I don't pay my licence fee so the BBC staff can play around in helicopters. Not since Noel Edmonds left anyway.

B Barnfather, e-mail

MR BARNFATHER *(above letter)* is talking nonsense about the BBC helicopter being a waste of public cash. Gorden Brown was Prime Minister for nearly three years and his resignation was a pivotal moment in British politics. Thanks to the BBC, when political commentators look back on his premiership, they will know exactly what the top of his head looked like on that day.

Hector Ashcloud, Dorset

A FEW days ago I had a rather disturbing nightmare in which I was standing in the bathroom, when I saw someone outside the window carrying a spade. All of a sudden, I realised that it was myself, and that I was in the process of digging my own grave. It was very curious indeed, particularly as I don't actually own a spade.

Wayne Redhart, e-mail

ACCORDING to the senior Iranian cleric Hojatoleslam Kazem Sedighi, women wearing revealing clothing are responsible for an increase in the number of earthquakes in his country. Evidently, Mr Sedighi has been too busy copping an eyeful to find time to read up on plate tectonics. The dirty rascal.

Jimmy Dale, e-mail

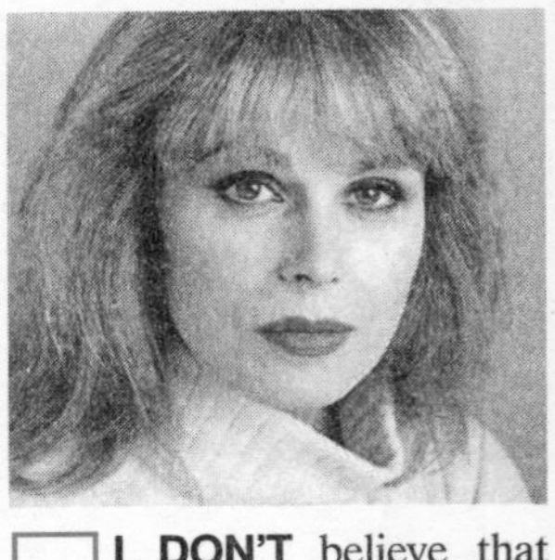

I DON'T believe that rumour about Joanna Lumley having a plastic arse, because I recently saw her on a television show where she was sitting quite close to a camp fire. Well you simply wouldn't do that if your nipsy was made of polythene.

Vincent Puckett, e-mail

AS A long-term customer, I have to say I am really enjoying watching these Halifax adverts where their staff pretend to run a radio station. It makes a welcome change from watching them pretend to run a fucking building society.

Dr Tim Walker, e-mail

I READ in an earlier *Letterbocks* page that

Dragons Sort Out Pothole Crisis

TV entrepreneurs on mission to fix UK roads

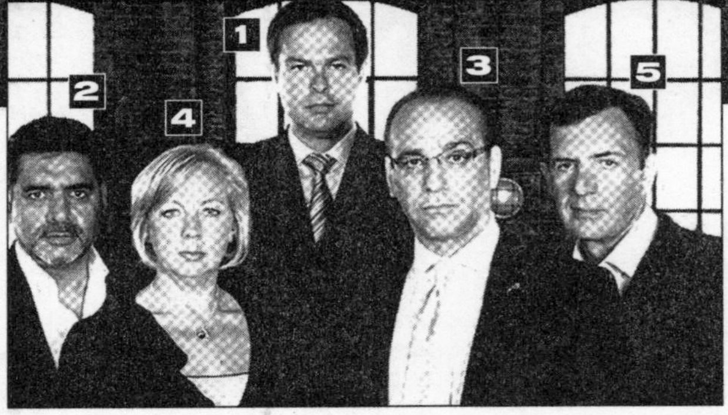
1
2
3
4
5

BIG-HEARTED stars of TV's *Dragons' Den* have agreed to step in and sort out Britain's spiralling pothole crisis by filling them all in... with gold! And that's not all, because any profits the 5 millionaires make from the venture will be handed straight over to charity!

Britain has been in the grip of a pothole crisis since the record cold snap ruined roads in the new year. And it's a problem that was playing on the mind of Duncan 'I'm out of it' Bannatyne.

"I was sat round in Theo Pathitis's massive caravan one night drinking a £14 bottle of wine when a report came on the TV about the large increase in potholes," he told reporters at a press conference in the Grosvenor House Hotel.

He continued: "Theo and myself are tough men. We've drunk room temperature Pinot Grigot and used lavatories that don't flush. But we were moved to tears by the sight of grim-faced motorists having to take their small cars to garages to have minor suspension repairs carried out. It certainly made us feel lucky to be drinking moderately-priced wine and wearing £50 shoes."

And it was this sight that led Bannatyne to act. "I said to Theo 'Let's fill those potholes with gold and put a smile back on the face of Britain's motorists'".

The Dragons met the following day in the Palace of Versailles to finalise details. And after a £2000 a head lunch of lark eggs and turtle soup, they came up with an ambitious plan to fill all of the holes on Britain's treacherous road network... in just 24 hours! All five Dragons will be taking part in relay with the help of celebrity pals.

"It's a for good cause, and hopefully it's going to be a bit of a laugh. And we also want a 51% equity of Britain's roads for doing it," Bannatyne told reporters. And he invited members of the public to join in the fun by staying as far out of their way as possible and avoiding all eye contact.

1 PETER JONES will drive round the country at high-speed in his expensive car with co-driver Prince Andrew. The pair will take photos of all the potholes while dressed in casual clothes.

2 JAMES CAAN will drive the 'Dragons' Den Pothole Busters' truck laden with liquid gold to the sites identified by Jones. He will then fill in each hole with the help of celebrity handyman Tommy Walsh.

3 THEO PATHITIS will then make use of his considerable contacts in the stationery business to write down each pothole location on gilded paper as it is filled in alongside close pal, the late Rod Hull and Emu.

4 DEBORAH MEADEN will then stand and give the thumbs up to the cameras wearing an unconvincing hard hat and wellies as each hole is sealed.

5 DUNCAN BANNATYNE will then complete the marathon by flying over each pothole in his private jet, piloted by John Travolta, scattering 'Caution: Drying Gold' leaflets over the surrounding countryside.

UP THE ARSE CORNER

Alan Sugar is so laid back that he doesn't mind if we call him Sir Alan or Lord Sugar. Now it appears that he is equally at ease if mere mortals address him as Baron of Clapton as well. It's nice to have people like him to remind us that that celebrities are people too.

James Conway, e-mail

CRIMEWATCH is getting a bit far fetched these days. I know the BBC are struggling to beat *The Bill* in the ratings, but some of the storylines are frankly ridiculous.

Peter Crumpet, e-mail

NOT THAT I watch it much, but surely BBC3's *Snog, Marry, Avoid* is crying out for a fourth option.

Paddy Milner, Kent

WHILST boozing in a Liverpool pub recently, I was informed by the barmaid that I might get a better reception on my mobile in the 'beer garden.' Do any of your readers know a less appealing sanctuary for alfresco drinking?

S Porter, Merseyside

'WE'D ALL be speaking German if we'd lost the war,' as the old saying goes. But is that really true? Because they're not speaking English in Germany and they lost the bloody thing unless I'm very much mistaken.

Brendan Stitch, e-mail

IT SEEMS that on her latest single *Rude Boy*, R&B singer Rihanna seems to be requesting that someone smashes her back doors in whilst pulling her hair and smacking her on the bottom. Could I use the pages of your magazine to let her know that I would like to help out with her request? Not Thursdays, though, as it's darts night.

Jon Creasy, e-mail

I CAN'T help thinking that these so called Formula 1 drivers are a little over-rated. Yesterday I watched Lewis Hamilton crash into a wall of tyres after suffering a puncture as he was unable to 'get the car home.' yet my wife suffered a puncture in her Clio last week, but managed to drive 45 miles down the M4 to get home before she even noticed.

Rich Lewis, e-mail

I'M TRYING to organise a Flash Mob to take place at Liverpool Street Station one day next week during the rush hour. There will be no singing, dancing or choreography involved, but participants will be required to shuffle around hastily looking at the ground or ignorantly shove other participants out of the way before catching the train home.

Bobby Harrison, e-mail

A RECENT edition of the *Daily Mail* complained that a primary school was failing because the pupils there spoke 27 languages. Now call me picky, but I call that an astonishing feat for anybody, let alone young children.

Rooster, e-mail

CAR PARK

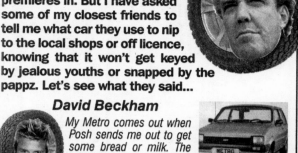

HI, THERE. Petrolhead *Jeremy Clarkson* here. We all know what cars our stars drive to film premieres in. But I have asked some of my closest friends to tell me what car they use to nip to the local shops or off licence, knowing that it won't get keyed by jealous youths or snapped by the pappz. Let's see what they said...

David Beckham

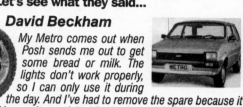

My Metro comes out when Posh sends me out to get some bread or milk. The lights don't work properly, so I can only use it during the day. And I've had to remove the spare because it was bald. You can't get nicked for having no spare tyre, but you can if you've got one and it's bald.

Johnny Depp

The Allegro is the girl for me. When I'm not in my pirate fancy dress costume, I like to pop down to my local Lidl with her. The heater is stuck on hot, so I have to drive with the windows open. The handbrake is fucked and the garage wanted forty quid to fix it, so when I park up I have to leave it in gear.

Daniel Craig

When I'm in films, I drive really fast cars. When I'm popping down to the petrol station to buy sweets, nothing is better than my Morris Minor. It's so old that it doesn't have seatbelts which means I can look cool and not get into trouble with the filth. After five backfires in the morning, she's good to go.

Fiona Bruce

Mr Bruce is always calling me his princess. So for my last birthday he bought me this one. It can move off from second gear and has the loudest Colonel Bogey air horns ever. My neighbours love to be woken in the mornings when I forget to unarm the car before opening the door with a butter knife.

Jacko out of Brush Strokes

I don't drive a car because the insurance companies won't insure me as I can't recall my real name. For keeping out of the limelight and nipping to the local shops, I use this electric box of shite. It has a couple of pedals for when the battery is fucked and a brolly for rainy days.

POST OFFICE counter staff. If the queue in your post office is too small, try to sell insurance, mobile phone top ups and any other useless shite you can think of to anyone who just wants to buy a stamp. In no time at all you'll have the poor buggers queueing out of the door and down the street again.

John Smith, e-mail

TEENAGERS. Shave minutes off your daily routine by forcing your face into a collander to burst your acne.

Lund Humphries, e-mail

OUT OF WORK actors. Simply pretend that you have a job and, hey presto! You're working.

Ben Margerison, e-mail

KEEP wooden chip shop forks, plastic holly decorations and broken birthday candles somewhere handy. We keep ours at the back of the tea towel drawer.

Ed Surname, e-mail

CONVINCE people that you are a secret service agent by attaching a piece of curly telephone cable to your ear and occasionally raising your hand to it while frowning.

Martyn Goodram, Bolton

CRAFT cheese slices make ideal patches for heavy cheese eaters who are trying to cut down.

Fish, Axminster

COUNTDOWN contestants. Always choose consonants for your first three letters so that sad, unemployed male viewres can get a good view of Rachael's bottom as she twists to lift them.

Hugh Beaforte, e-mail

HAYFEVER sufferers. Don't waste money on expensive pills and nasal sprays. Simply glue a bee to your upper lip. The insect workaholic will grab all stray pollen heading towards your nostrils and transform it into delicious honey for your morning toast.

Stu the Gasman, e-mail

FOOL your girlfriend into thinking that you don't fancy her identical twin sister by telling her that you think she is ugly.

John W, e-mail

VIBRATING cock rings make excellent shock collars for naughty ferrets and other small rodents.

Naomi Willett, e-mail

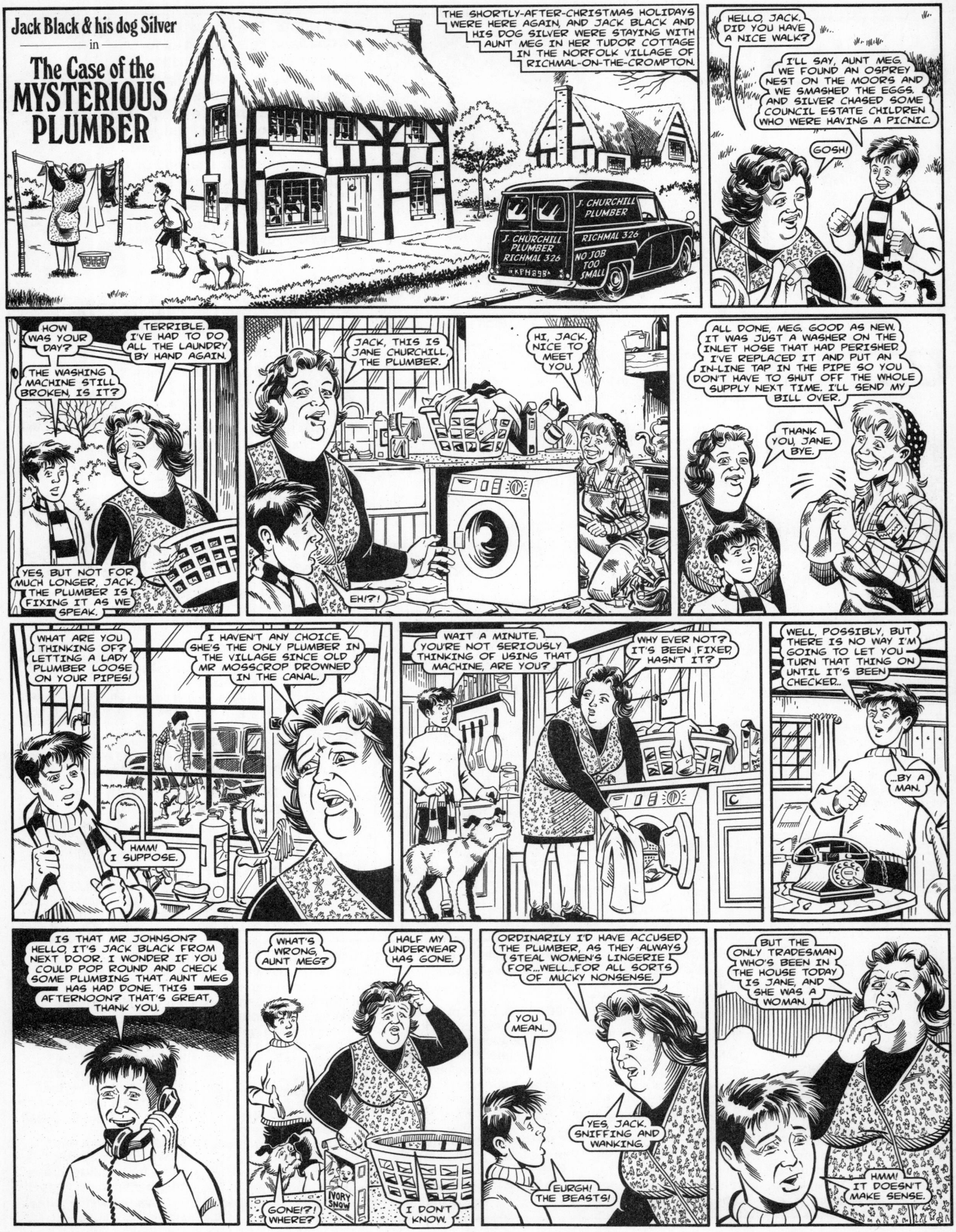

Jack Black & his dog Silver
in
The Case of the MYSTERIOUS PLUMBER
THE SHORTLY-AFTER-CHRISTMAS HOLIDAYS WERE HERE AGAIN, AND JACK BLACK AND HIS DOG SILVER WERE STAYING WITH AUNT MEG IN HER TUDOR COTTAGE IN THE NORFOLK VILLAGE OF RICHMAL-ON-THE-CROMPTON.
J. CHURCHILL PLUMBER
J. CHURCHILL PLUMBER RICHMAL 326
RICHMAL 326
NO JOB TOO SMALL
KPH 398
HELLO, JACK. DID YOU HAVE A NICE WALK?
I'LL SAY, AUNT MEG. WE FOUND AN OSPREY NEST ON THE MOORS AND WE SMASHED THE EGGS. AND SILVER CHASED SOME COUNCIL ESTATE CHILDREN WHO WERE HAVING A PICNIC.
GOSH!
HOW WAS YOUR DAY?
TERRIBLE. I'VE HAD TO DO ALL THE LAUNDRY BY HAND AGAIN.
THE WASHING MACHINE STILL BROKEN, IS IT?
YES, BUT NOT FOR MUCH LONGER, JACK. THE PLUMBER IS FIXING IT AS WE SPEAK.
JACK, THIS IS JANE CHURCHILL, THE PLUMBER.
HI, JACK. NICE TO MEET YOU.
EH!?!
ALL DONE, MEG. GOOD AS NEW. IT WAS JUST A WASHER ON THE INLET HOSE THAT HAD PERISHED. I'VE REPLACED IT AND PUT AN IN-LINE TAP IN THE PIPE SO YOU DON'T HAVE TO SHUT OFF THE WHOLE SUPPLY NEXT TIME. I'LL SEND MY BILL OVER.
THANK YOU, JANE. BYE.
WHAT ARE YOU THINKING OF? LETTING A LADY PLUMBER LOOSE ON YOUR PIPES!
I HAVEN'T ANY CHOICE. SHE'S THE ONLY PLUMBER IN THE VILLAGE SINCE OLD MR MOSSCROP DROWNED IN THE CANAL.
HMM! I SUPPOSE.
WAIT A MINUTE. YOU'RE NOT SERIOUSLY THINKING OF USING THAT MACHINE, ARE YOU?
WHY EVER NOT? IT'S BEEN FIXED, HASN'T IT?
WELL, POSSIBLY, BUT THERE IS NO WAY I'M GOING TO LET YOU TURN THAT THING ON UNTIL IT'S BEEN CHECKED...
...BY A MAN.
IS THAT MR JOHNSON? HELLO, IT'S JACK BLACK FROM NEXT DOOR. I WONDER IF YOU COULD POP ROUND AND CHECK SOME PLUMBING THAT AUNT MEG HAS HAD DONE. THIS AFTERNOON? THAT'S GREAT, THANK YOU.
WHAT'S WRONG, AUNT MEG?
HALF MY UNDERWEAR HAS GONE.
IVORY SNOW
GONE!?! WHERE?
I DON'T KNOW.
ORDINARILY I'D HAVE ACCUSED THE PLUMBER, AS THEY ALWAYS STEAL WOMEN'S LINGERIE FOR...WELL...FOR ALL SORTS OF MUCKY NONSENSE.
YOU MEAN...
YES, JACK. SNIFFING AND WANKING.
EURGH! THE BEASTS!
BUT THE ONLY TRADESMAN WHO'S BEEN IN THE HOUSE TODAY IS JANE, AND SHE WAS A WOMAN.
HMM! IT DOESN'T MAKE SENSE.

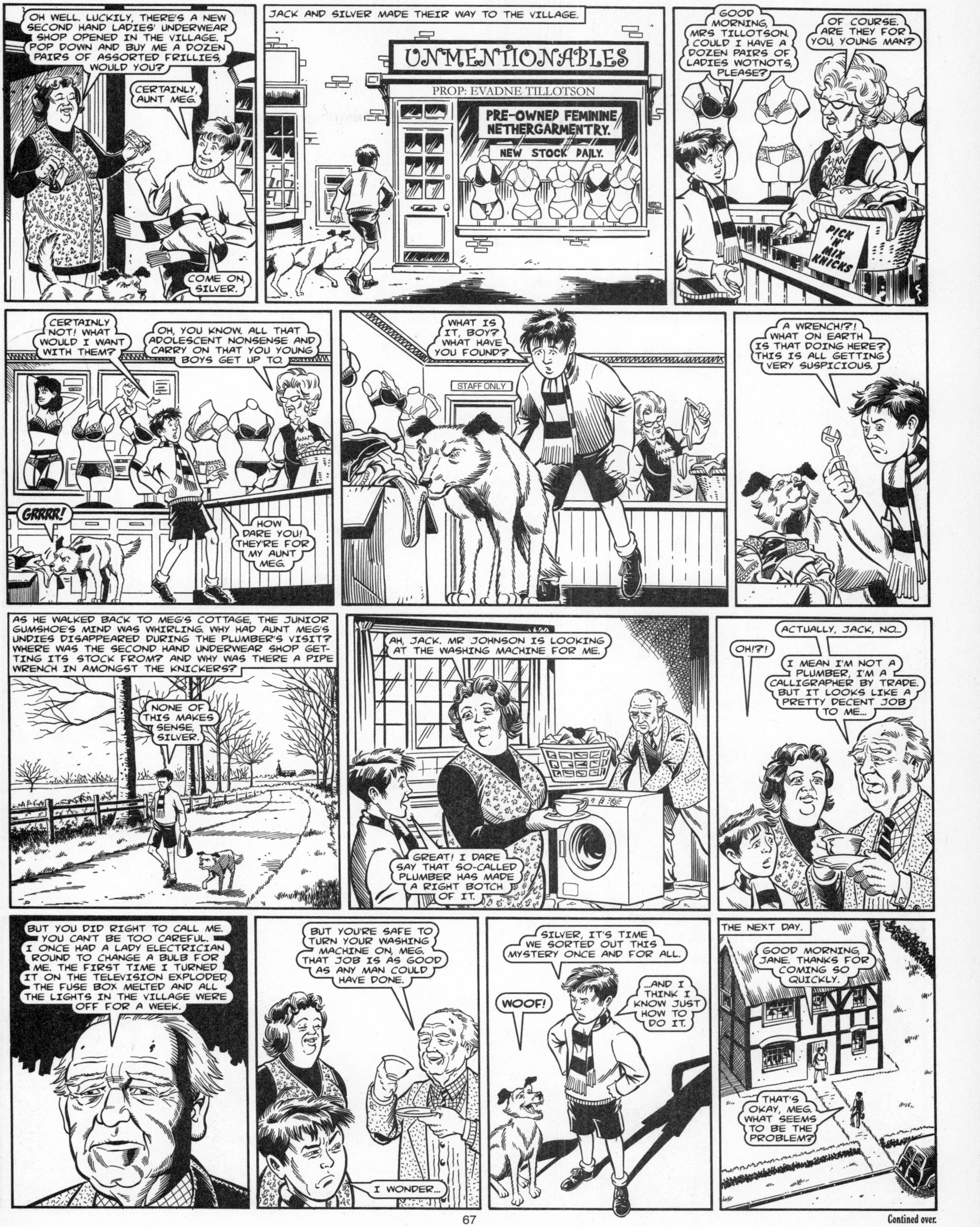
OH WELL. LUCKILY, THERE'S A NEW SECOND HAND LADIES' UNDERWEAR SHOP OPENED IN THE VILLAGE. POP DOWN AND BUY ME A DOZEN PAIRS OF ASSORTED FRILLIES, WOULD YOU?
CERTAINLY, AUNT MEG.
COME ON, SILVER.
JACK AND SILVER MADE THEIR WAY TO THE VILLAGE.
UNMENTIONABLES
PROP: EVADNE TILLOTSON
PRE-OWNED FEMININE NETHERGARMENTRY.
NEW STOCK DAILY.
GOOD MORNING, MRS TILLOTSON. COULD I HAVE A DOZEN PAIRS OF LADIES WOTNOTS, PLEASE?
OF COURSE. ARE THEY FOR YOU, YOUNG MAN?
PICK 'N' MIX KNICKS
CERTAINLY NOT! WHAT WOULD I WANT WITH THEM?
OH, YOU KNOW. ALL THAT ADOLESCENT NONSENSE AND CARRY ON THAT YOU YOUNG BOYS GET UP TO.
GRRRR!
HOW DARE YOU! THEY'RE FOR MY AUNT MEG.
WHAT IS IT, BOY? WHAT HAVE YOU FOUND?
STAFF ONLY
A WRENCH!?! WHAT ON EARTH IS THAT DOING HERE? THIS IS ALL GETTING VERY SUSPICIOUS.
AS HE WALKED BACK TO MEG'S COTTAGE, THE JUNIOR GUMSHOE'S MIND WAS WHIRLING. WHY HAD AUNT MEG'S UNDIES DISAPPEARED DURING THE PLUMBER'S VISIT? WHERE WAS THE SECOND HAND UNDERWEAR SHOP GETTING ITS STOCK FROM? AND WHY WAS THERE A PIPE WRENCH IN AMONGST THE KNICKERS?
NONE OF THIS MAKES SENSE, SILVER.
AH, JACK. MR JOHNSON IS LOOKING AT THE WASHING MACHINE FOR ME.
GREAT! I DARE SAY THAT SO-CALLED PLUMBER HAS MADE A RIGHT BOTCH OF IT.
ACTUALLY, JACK, NO...
OH!?!
I MEAN I'M NOT A PLUMBER, I'M A CALLIGRAPHER BY TRADE. BUT IT LOOKS LIKE A PRETTY DECENT JOB TO ME...
BUT YOU DID RIGHT TO CALL ME. YOU CAN'T BE TOO CAREFUL. I ONCE HAD A LADY ELECTRICIAN ROUND TO CHANGE A BULB FOR ME. THE FIRST TIME I TURNED IT ON THE TELEVISION EXPLODED, THE FUSE BOX MELTED AND ALL THE LIGHTS IN THE VILLAGE WERE OFF FOR A WEEK.
BUT YOU'RE SAFE TO TURN YOUR WASHING MACHINE ON, MEG. THAT JOB IS AS GOOD AS ANY MAN COULD HAVE DONE.
I WONDER...
SILVER, IT'S TIME WE SORTED OUT THIS MYSTERY ONCE AND FOR ALL.
WOOF!
...AND I THINK I KNOW JUST HOW TO DO IT.
THE NEXT DAY.
GOOD MORNING, JANE. THANKS FOR COMING SO QUICKLY.
THAT'S OKAY, MEG. WHAT SEEMS TO BE THE PROBLEM?

Contined over.

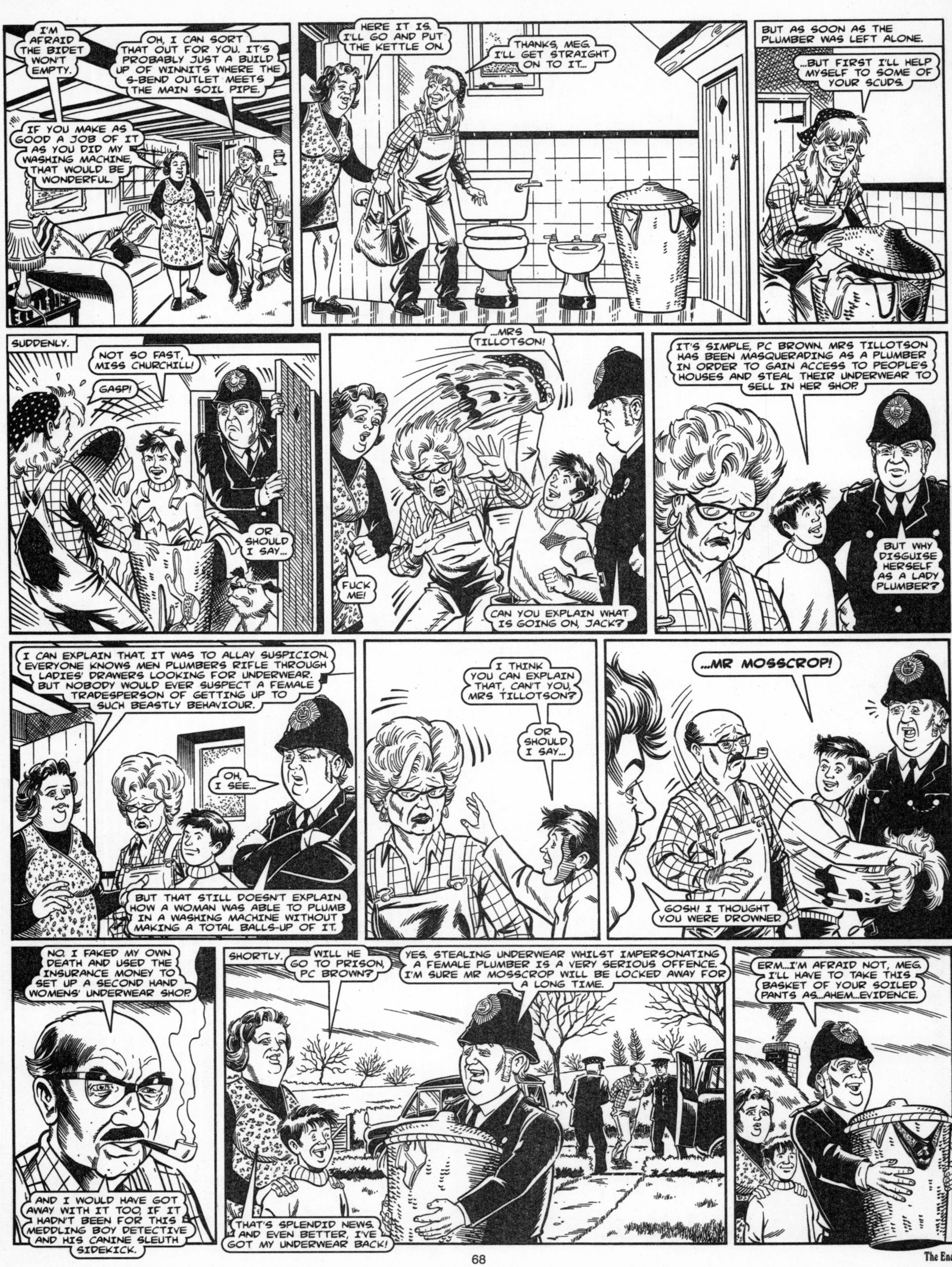
I'M AFRAID THE BIDET WON'T EMPTY.
OH, I CAN SORT THAT OUT FOR YOU. IT'S PROBABLY JUST A BUILD UP OF WINNITS WHERE THE S-BEND OUTLET MEETS THE MAIN SOIL PIPE.
IF YOU MAKE AS GOOD A JOB OF IT AS YOU DID MY WASHING MACHINE, THAT WOULD BE WONDERFUL.
HERE IT IS. I'LL GO AND PUT THE KETTLE ON.
THANKS, MEG. I'LL GET STRAIGHT ON TO IT...
BUT AS SOON AS THE PLUMBER WAS LEFT ALONE.
...BUT FIRST I'LL HELP MYSELF TO SOME OF YOUR SCUDS.
SUDDENLY.
NOT SO FAST, MISS CHURCHILL!
GASP!
OR SHOULD I SAY...
...MRS TILLOTSON!
FUCK ME!
CAN YOU EXPLAIN WHAT IS GOING ON, JACK?
IT'S SIMPLE, PC BROWN. MRS TILLOTSON HAS BEEN MASQUERADING AS A PLUMBER IN ORDER TO GAIN ACCESS TO PEOPLE'S HOUSES AND STEAL THEIR UNDERWEAR TO SELL IN HER SHOP.
BUT WHY DISGUISE HERSELF AS A LADY PLUMBER?
I CAN EXPLAIN THAT. IT WAS TO ALLAY SUSPICION. EVERYONE KNOWS MEN PLUMBERS RIFLE THROUGH LADIES' DRAWERS LOOKING FOR UNDERWEAR. BUT NOBODY WOULD EVER SUSPECT A FEMALE TRADESPERSON OF GETTING UP TO SUCH BEASTLY BEHAVIOUR.
OH, I SEE...
BUT THAT STILL DOESN'T EXPLAIN HOW A WOMAN WAS ABLE TO PLUMB IN A WASHING MACHINE WITHOUT MAKING A TOTAL BALLS-UP OF IT.
I THINK YOU CAN EXPLAIN THAT, CAN'T YOU, MRS TILLOTSON?
OR SHOULD I SAY...
...MR MOSSCROP!
GOSH! I THOUGHT YOU WERE DROWNED.
NO. I FAKED MY OWN DEATH AND USED THE INSURANCE MONEY TO SET UP A SECOND HAND WOMENS' UNDERWEAR SHOP.
AND I WOULD HAVE GOT AWAY WITH IT TOO, IF IT HADN'T BEEN FOR THIS MEDDLING BOY DETECTIVE AND HIS CANINE SLEUTH SIDEKICK.
SHORTLY.
WILL HE GO TO PRISON, PC BROWN?
YES. STEALING UNDERWEAR WHILST IMPERSONATING A FEMALE PLUMBER IS A VERY SERIOUS OFFENCE. I'M SURE MR MOSSCROP WILL BE LOCKED AWAY FOR A LONG TIME.
THAT'S SPLENDID NEWS. AND EVEN BETTER, I'VE GOT MY UNDERWEAR BACK!
ERM...I'M AFRAID NOT, MEG. I'LL HAVE TO TAKE THIS BASKET OF YOUR SOILED PANTS AS...AHEM...EVIDENCE.

The End.

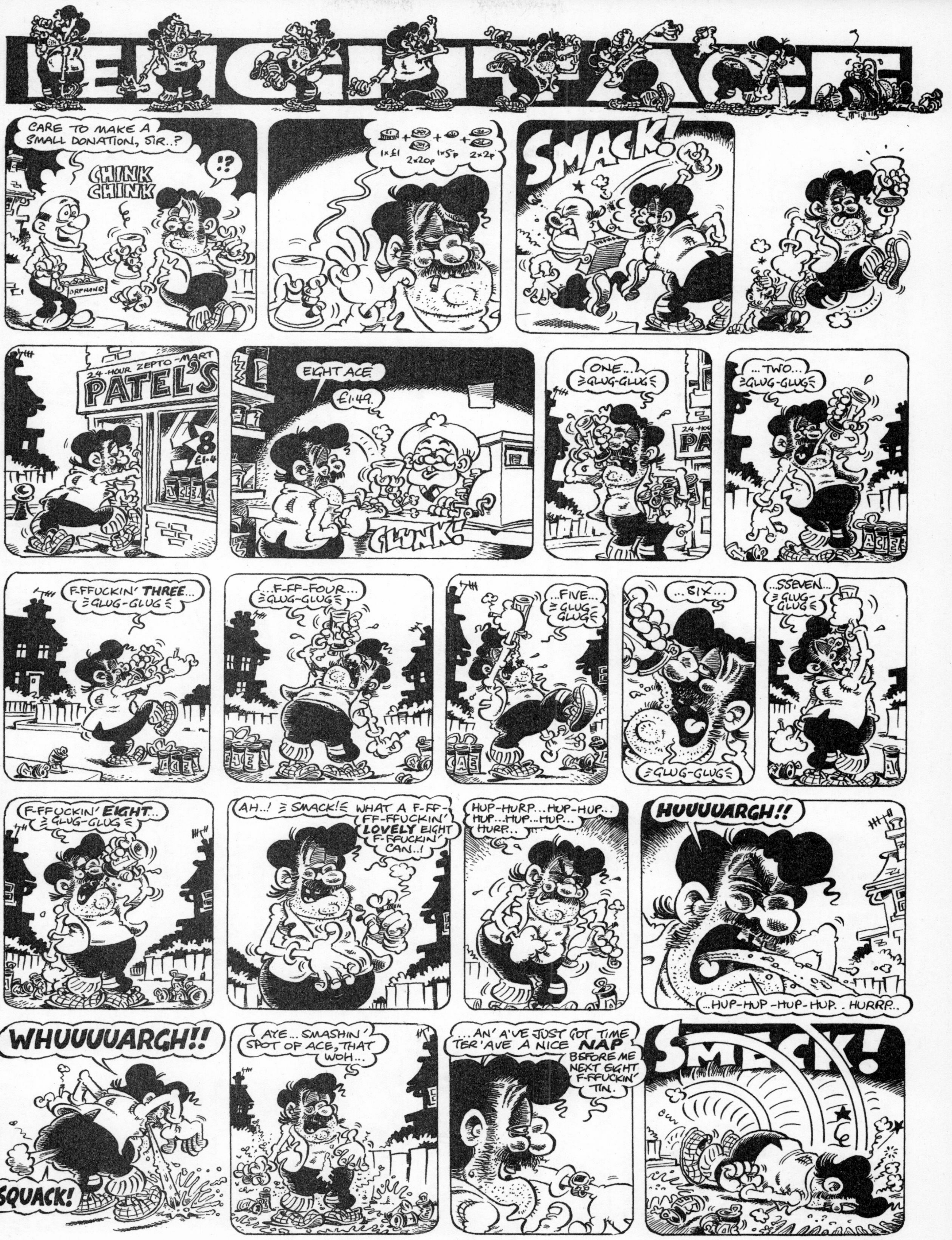
CARE TO MAKE A SMALL DONATION, SIR..?
CHINK CHINK
!?
ORPHANS
1×£1 2×20p 1×5p 2×2p
SMACK!
24-HOUR ZEPTO-MART PATEL'S
EIGHT ACE.
£1.49.
CLUNK!
ONE... GLUG-GLUG
...TWO... GLUG-GLUG
F-FFUCKIN' THREE... GLUG-GLUG
...F-FF-FOUR... GLUG-GLUG
...FIVE... GLUG GLUG
...SIX...
GLUG-GLUG
...SSEVEN... GLUG-GLUG
F-FFUCKIN' EIGHT... GLUG-GLUG
AH..! SMACK! WHAT A F-FF-FF-FFUCKIN' LOVELY EIGHT F-FFUCKIN' CAN..!
HUP-HURP...HUP-HUP... HUP...HUP...HUP... HURP..
HUUUUARGH!!
...HUP-HUP-HUP-HUP.. HURRP..
WHUUUUARGH!!
SQUACK!
AYE... SMASHIN' SPOT OF ACE, THAT WOH...
...AN' A'VE JUST GOT TIME TER 'AVE A NICE NAP BEFORE ME NEXT EIGHT F-FFUCKIN' TIN.
SMECK!
OW

CONTINUED OVER

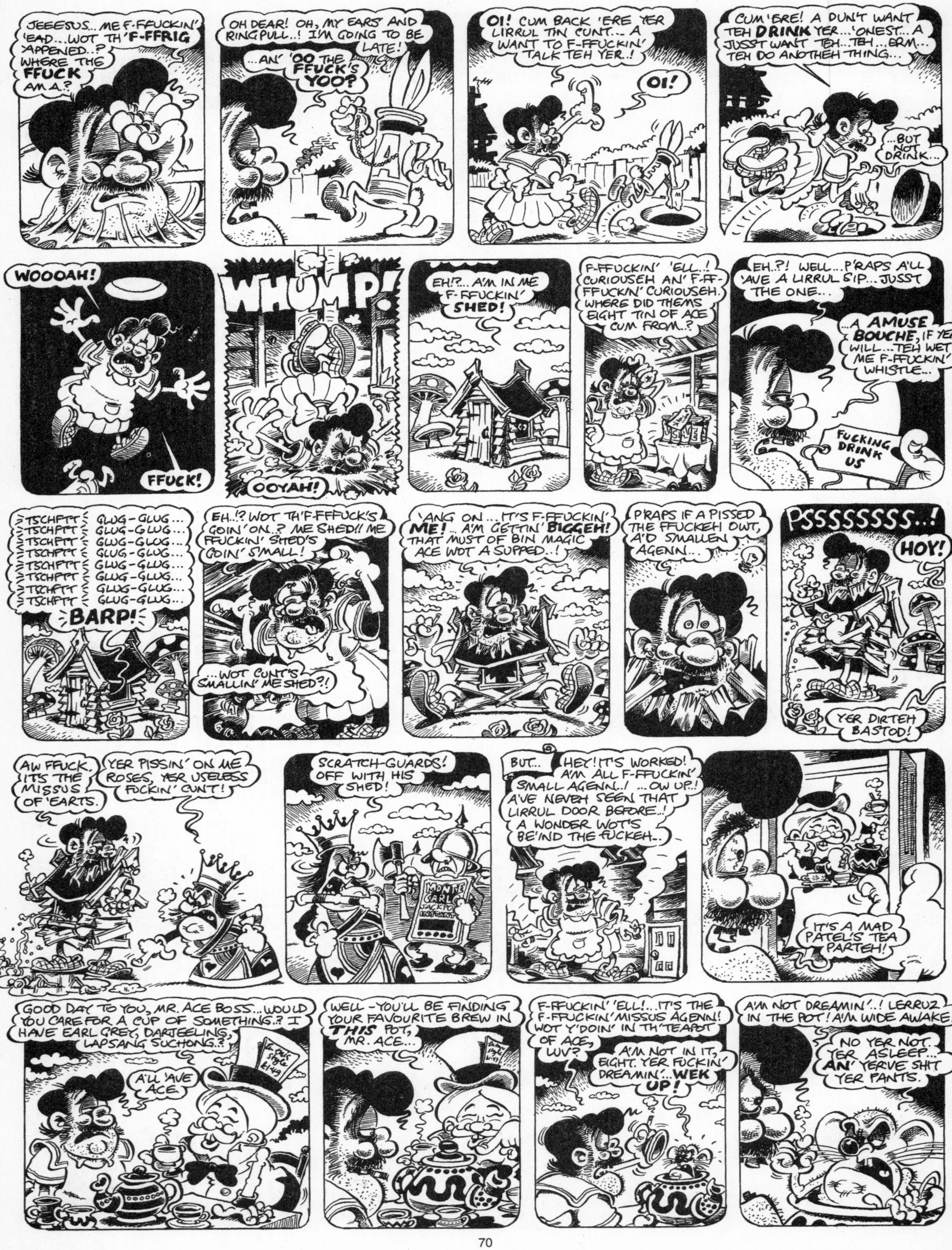
JEEESUS... ME F-FFUCKIN' 'EAD... WOT TH' F-FFRIG 'APPENED..? WHERE THE FFUCK AM A..?
OH DEAR! OH, MY EARS AND RINGPULL..! I'M GOING TO BE LATE!
...AN' 'OO THE FFUCK'S YOO?
OI! CUM BACK 'ERE YER LIRRUL TIN CUNT... A WANT TO F-FFUCKIN' TALK TEH YER..!
OI!
CUM 'ERE! A DUN'T WANT TEH DRINK YER... 'ONEST... A JUSST WANT TEH... TEH... ERM... TEH DO ANOTHEH THING...
...BUT NOT DRINK...
WOOOAH!
FFUCK!
WHUMP!
OOYAH!
EH!?... A'M IN ME F-FFUCKIN' SHED!
F-FFUCKIN' 'ELL..! CURIOUSEH AN' F-FF-FFUCKIN' CURIOUSEH. WHERE DID THEMS EIGHT TIN OF ACE CUM FROM..?
EH..?! WELL... P'RAPS A'LL 'AVE A LIRRUL SIP... JUSST THE ONE...
...A AMUSE BOUCHE, IF YER WILL... TEH WET ME F-FFUCKIN' WHISTLE...
FUCKING DRINK US
TSCHFTT GLUG-GLUG... TSCHFTT GLUG-GLUG... TSCHFTT GLUG-GLUG... TSCHFTT GLUG-GLUG... TSCHFTT GLUG-GLUG... TSCHFTT GLUG-GLUG... TSCHFTT GLUG-GLUG... TSCHFTT GLUG-GLUG...
BARP!
EH..!? WOT TH'F-FFFUCK'S GOIN' ON..? ME SHED!! ME FFUCKIN' SHED'S GOIN' SMALL!
...WOT CUNT'S SMALLIN' ME SHED?!
'ANG ON... IT'S F-FFUCKIN' ME!... A'M GETTIN' BIGGEH! THAT MUST OF BIN MAGIC ACE WOT A SUPPED..!
P'RAPS IF A PISSED THE FFUCKEH OWT, A'D SMALLEN AGENN...
PSSSSSSSS..!
HOY!
YER DIRTEH BASTOD!
AW FFUCK. IT'S THE MISSUS OF 'EARTS.
YER PISSIN' ON ME ROSES, YER USELESS FUCKIN' CUNT!
SCRATCH-GUARDS! OFF WITH HIS SHED!
MONTE CARLO JACKPOT INSTANT
BUT...
HEY! IT'S WORKED! A'M ALL F-FFUCKIN' SMALL AGENN..! ...OW UP..! A'VE NEVEH SEEN THAT LIRRUL DOOR BEFORE..! A WONDER WOT'S BE'IND THE FUCKEH...
IT'S A MAD PATEL'S TEA PARTEH!
GOOD DAY TO YOU, MR. ACE BOSS... WOULD YOU CARE FOR A CUP OF SOMETHING..? I HAVE EARL GREY, DARJEELING, LAPSANG SUCHONG..?
A'LL 'AVE ACE.
WELL - YOU'LL BE FINDING YOUR FAVOURITE BREW IN THIS POT, MR. ACE...
F-FFUCKIN' 'ELL!... IT'S THE F-FFUCKIN' MISSUS AGENN! WOT Y'DOIN' IN TH' TEAPOT OF ACE, LUV?
A'M NOT IN IT, EIGHT. YER FUCKIN' DREAMIN'... WEK UP!
A'M NOT DREAMIN'..! LERRUZ IN THE POT! A'M WIDE AWAKE!
NO YER NOT. YER ASLEEP... AN' YERVE SHIT YER PANTS.

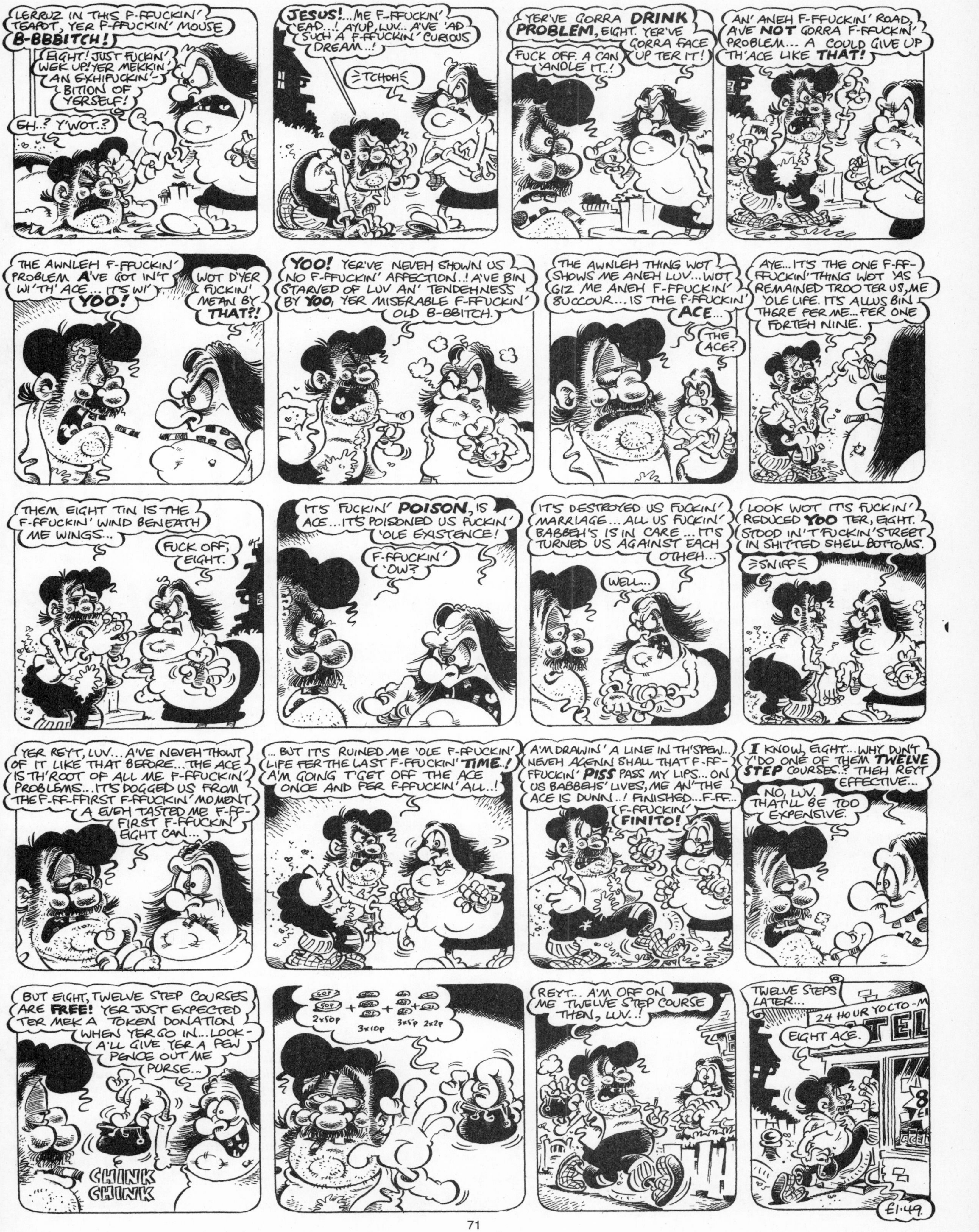
LERRUZ IN THIS F-FFUCKIN' TEAPOT, YER F-FFUCKIN' MOUSE B-BBBITCH!
EIGHT! JUST FUCKIN' WEK UP! YER MEKKIN AN EXHIFUCKIN'-BITION OF YERSELF!
EH..? Y'WOT..?
JESUS!... ME F-FFUCKIN' 'EAD..! AYUP, LUV... A'VE 'AD SUCH A F-FFUCKIN' CURIOUS DREAM..!
TCHOH
YER'VE GORRA DRINK PROBLEM, EIGHT. YER'VE GORRA FACE UP TER IT!
FUCK OFF. A CAN 'ANDLE IT..!
AN' ANEH F-FFUCKIN' ROAD, A'VE NOT GORRA F-FFUCKIN' PROBLEM... A COULD GIVE UP TH'ACE LIKE THAT!
THE AWNLEH F-FFUCKIN' PROBLEM A'VE GOT IN'T WI' TH' ACE... IT'S WI' YOO!
WOT D'YER FUCKIN' MEAN BY THAT?!
YOO! YER'VE NEVEH SHOWN US NO F-FFUCKIN' AFFECTION..! A'VE BIN STARVED OF LUV AN' TENDEHNESS BY YOO, YER MISERABLE F-FFUCKIN' OLD B-BBITCH.
THE AWNLEH THING WOT SHOWS ME ANEH LUV... WOT GIZ ME ANEH F-FFUCKIN' SUCCOUR... IS THE F-FFUCKIN' ACE...
THE ACE?
AYE... IT'S THE ONE F-FF-FFUCKIN' THING WOT 'AS REMAINED TROO TER US, ME 'OLE LIFE. IT'S ALLUS BIN THERE FER ME... FER ONE FORTEH NINE.
THEM EIGHT TIN IS THE F-FFUCKIN' WIND BENEATH ME WINGS...
FUCK OFF, EIGHT.
IT'S FUCKIN' POISON, IS ACE... IT'S POISONED US FUCKIN' 'OLE EXISTENCE!
F-FFUCKIN' 'OW?
IT'S DESTROYED US FUCKIN' MARRIAGE... ALL US FUCKIN' BABBEH'S IS IN CARE... IT'S TURNED US AGAINST EACH OTHEH...
WELL...
LOOK WOT IT'S FUCKIN' REDUCED YOO TER, EIGHT. STOOD IN'T FUCKIN' STREET IN SHITTED SHELL BOTTOMS.
SNIFF
YER REYT, LUV... A'VE NEVEH THOWT OF IT LIKE THAT BEFORE... THE ACE IS TH' ROOT OF ALL ME F-FFUCKIN' PROBLEMS... IT'S DOGGED US FROM THE F-FF-FFIRST F-FFUCKIN' MOMENT A EVEH TASTED ME F-FF-FIRST F-FFUCKIN' EIGHT CAN...
...BUT IT'S RUINED ME 'OLE F-FFUCKIN' LIFE FER THE LAST F-FFUCKIN' TIME..! A'M GOING T'GET OFF THE ACE ONCE AND FER F-FFUCKIN' ALL..!
A'M DRAWIN' A LINE IN TH'SPEW... NEVEH AGENN SHALL THAT F-FF-FFUCKIN' PISS PASS MY LIPS... ON US BABBEHS' LIVES, ME AN' THE ACE IS DUNN..! FINISHED... F-FF...
F-FFUCKIN' FINITO!
I KNOW, EIGHT... WHY DUN'T Y'DO ONE OF THEM TWELVE STEP COURSES..? THEH REYT EFFECTIVE...
NO, LUV. THAT'LL BE TOO EXPENSIVE.
BUT EIGHT, TWELVE STEP COURSES ARE FREE! YER JUST EXPECTED TER MEK A TOKEN DONATION WHEN YER GO IN... LOOK-A'LL GIVE YER A FEW PENCE OUT ME PURSE...
CHINK CHINK
2×50p + 3×10p + 3×5p 2×2p
REYT... A'M OFF ON ME TWELVE STEP COURSE THEN, LUV..!
TWELVE STEPS LATER...
24 HOUR YOCTO-M
TEL
EIGHT ACE.
£1.49.

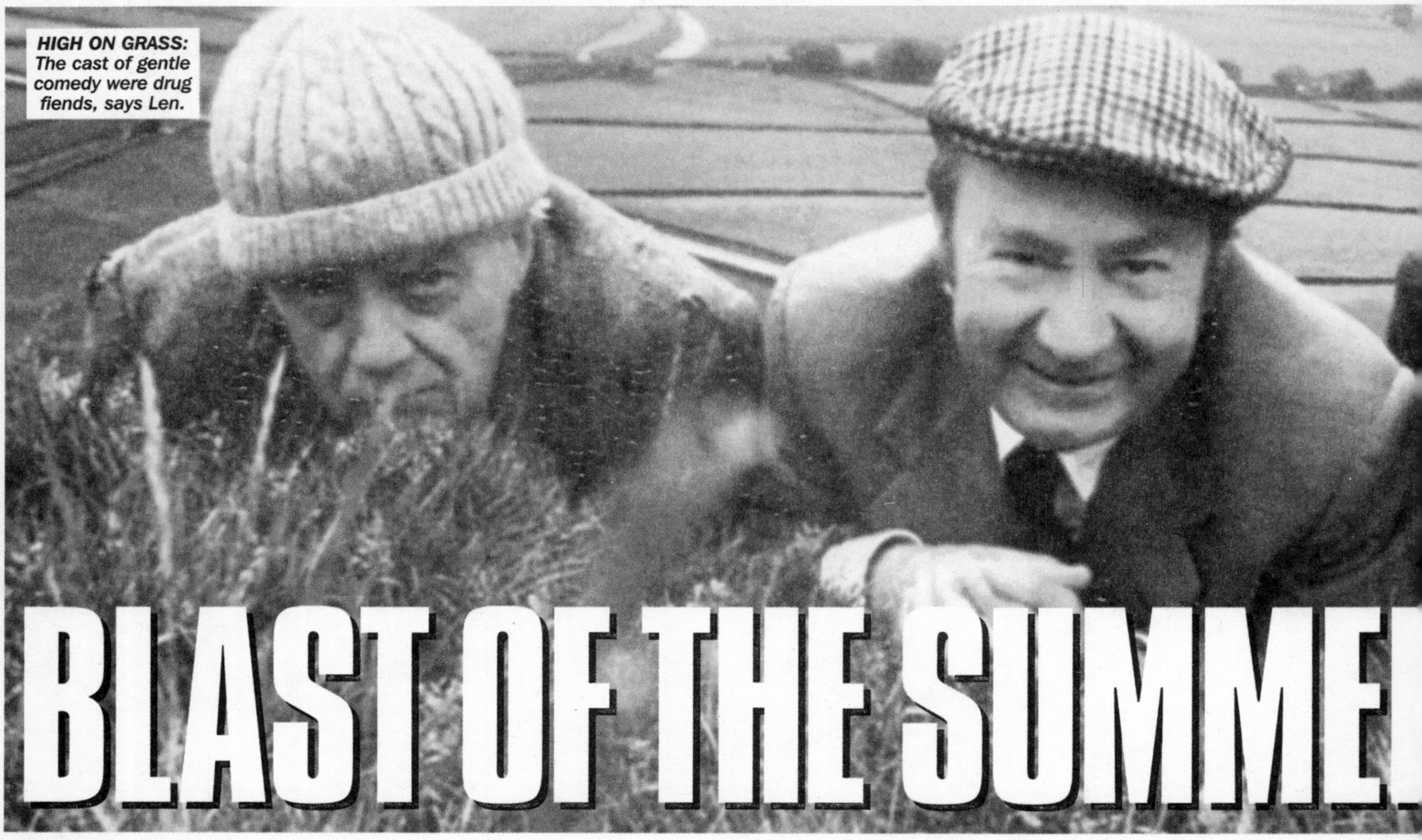

HIGH ON GRASS: The cast of gentle comedy were drug fiends, says Len.

BLAST OF THE SUMMER

Drugs shame of long-running BBC comedy

THE BBC was last night at the centre of a new scandal following revelations that a much-loved family show was a hotbed of drug use. Former assistant location caterer LEN SCARBOROUGH claims that he was sacked from his part-time job on *Last of the Summer Wine* after threatening to lift the beans on the debauched scenes he had witnessed on the set of the popular gentle sitcom.

And now he has decided to spill the whistle on the stars' wild behind-the-scenes antics in a no-holds-barred internet blog that has received over 33 hits in as many weeks.

On his site *www.thembastardsatthebbc.freewebs.net*, Len writes: "The viewers know them as Compo, Cleggy and Foggy Dewhurst, three old codgers bumbling about the Yorkshire countryside, but the reality could not be further away from the truth. If the show's viewers could see the way they carried on the moment the cameras stopped rolling, it would turn their hair even whiter than it already is."

"It's time the public found out how their TV licences are being spent."

Scarborough, 61, had his eyes opened to the stars' debauched goings-on when he turned up to start work on the pensioners' favourite comedy.

"My first assignment was to take a bacon sandwich and a cup of tea to Compo's caravan. I had to knock two or three times before he finally answered the door. He was rubbing his eyes and looked scruffy and unshaven.

I thought he must of already of been in make-up, but it turned out he'd been partying all night. There were empty booze bottles and drugs paraphernalia on every surface in the caravan, and I couldn't help noticing that there was a great big bong bubbling away on the lid of his porta-potty.

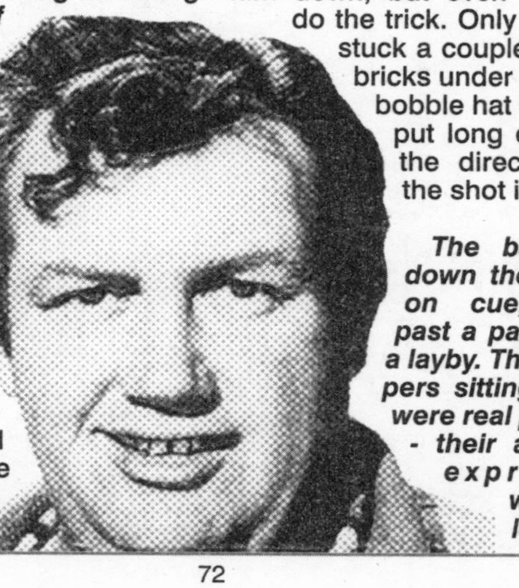

The scene being filmed that morning involved him being rolled down a hill in a bath-tub on wheels. As the crew got ready for the first take, Compo just stood at the side of the set, puffing on a giant doobie. By the time they'd sorted out the cameras and lighting, the elderly actor was completely caned. His eyes were whirring round in their sockets and he didn't know where he was.

But that wasn't the problem. When it was time to start filming, they couldn't keep him in the bath. Compo was so high, he just kept floating out of the tub like a balloon!

They tried filling his pockets and wellies with gravel to weigh him down, but even that didn't do the trick. Only when they stuck a couple of house-bricks under his famous bobble hat did he stay put long enough for the director to get the shot in the can.

The bath rolled down the hill right on cue, straight past a panda car in a layby. The two coppers sitting inside it were real policemen - their astonished expressions were priceless and made it into the final show. But it wasn't the rolling bath that had amazed them - it was the sight of one of Britain's best known OAPs whipped to his tits on drugs!"

But Compo wasn't the only cast-member who treated the sleepy Pennine town of Holmfirth as party central, as Scarborough found out when he took a snack to another *Last of the Summer Wine* stalwart - Foggy Dewhurst.

"Shooting had been held up because battleaxe Nora Batty - real-life ugly actress Kathy Staff - couldn't find one of her trademark wrinkled stockings. She was making quite a fuss, insisting that someone must of broken into her caravan and stolen it.

A runner had been sent into Huddersfield to buy a replacement, but meanwhile the producer ordered an early lunch so we wouldn't lose too much shooting time. My boss handed me a sausage roll and told me to take it to Foggy Dewhurst - real life Porridge actor Mr Barraclough.

Of course I'd seen him on the

teeth bit her squarely on the bottom. Her face was a picture! It was a classic *Last of the Summer Wine* moment, but unfortunately the cameras didn't catch it so the public missed out on one of the funniest bloopers they never got to see.

Eventually, Foggy gave up looking for a vein in his arm and mainlined his smack into the shaft of his penis instead. Compared with the priceless moment of comedy I'd witnessed just moments before, watching Foggy slump unconscious into a drug-induced stupor with that empty syringe hanging out of his whatnot was a tragic sight to see. It is a sight I will never forget and one that I never hope to live to see again.

The longest-serving member of the show's cast is *Wallace & Gromit*-voiced octogenarian actor Peter Sallis, who plays loveable pensioner Clegg.

"Cleggie's so mild-mannered on screen, you'd think that butter wouldn't melt. But the moment the director shouts 'Cut!', he transforms into the wild man of Holmfirth. Believe you me, his insatiable appetite for narcotics makes Keith Moon look like a Sunday School teacher.

Production of the show was constantly being interrupted by the arrival on set of heavily-armed Columbian drugs dealers, bringing him suitcases stuffed with packets of cocaine. Clegg would halt filming while he sliced one open and used his finger to rub the white crystals into his gums before nodding and handing over thick wads of twenty-pound notes.

Most of the time, he'd be so wired after taking a hit that he'd deliver

the rest of his lines at breakneck speed. In the editing suite, they often had to slow the film down to a third of its normal speed before his words became intelligible.

I remember one scene in the cafe. Compo, Foggy and Clegg were sitting at a table in the cafe, putting the world to rights over a cup of tea. But let me tell you, it wasn't sugar in that sugar bowl ... it was Grade A Charlie! During the scene, whenever the camera was on his co-stars, Clegg took the opportunity to toot another spoonful of his favourite drug up his nose.

By the middle of the afternoon's shooting, the sugar bowl was completely empty - the veteran character had snorted the lot. Then, disaster struck. Cleggie sneezed and his nose fell off.

The show was going out in a few hours so there was no time to rush him to hospital for reconstructive surgery. The director and the producer had to think quickly. In the end, Clegg delivered the rest of his lines whilst holding a teacup up in front of his face to conceal the gaping hole where his nose had been."

The drug-fuelled excesses of the three main characters are shocking enough. But they literally pale into insignificance next to the outrageous behaviour of the oldest actor in the show - Joe Gladwin, who played Wally Batty short-sighted, long-suffering husband of Nora.

"Famous for his flat cap, thick glasses and big ears, hen-pecked Wally looked like he wouldn't say boo to a goose. Yet his put-upon demeanour disguised an insatiable appetite for any sort of drugs he could get his hands on. Amphetamines, Es, smack, angel dust, PCPs, ecstasy, crystal meths, crack or meow meow. You name it, Wally had took it.

By the time I started working on the show, Wally had already developed an £1000-a-day drugs habit. And like all addicts, he got the money anywhere he could. Other cast members often returned after a day's filming to discover that their caravans had been broken into and ransacked. Anything of value would be stolen and sold in a desperate bid to fund his hunger for illicit highs.

Batty was also often to be seen turning tricks in Dunsley Bank, Holmfirth's notorious red light district, where he would sell his drug-ravaged body for £10 to buy a wrap of Ketamine or a wobbly egg.

After several overdoses and even more near misses, Wally decided that enough was enough and announced his intention to get himself clean. 'Me and the junk are finished. I'm going to kick this bugger before it kicks me,' he told his fellow cast and crew. He started going cold turkey during filming that very afternoon.

That day's scene was set in Nora Batty's kitchen. By the time that shooting got underway, Wally was rattling. His withdrawal symptoms left him shaking, sweating and scratching imaginary spiders that were crawling round under his skin. In the end, the director had to call 'cut' and order a last-minute plot change.

In the re-written script, Compo had asked Batty to look after his flea circus, but the lid had come off the tobacco tin in which it was kept.

Wally's frantic scratching kept the audience in stitches. However, if they'd only known the mental torment that the actor in front of them was going through, I doubt they'd have laughed as hard."

WINE

telly, so I thought I knew what to expect. Dewhurst was a retired military man with a very strait-laced attitude to life and I assumed he would be much the same off-screen. But I had a rude awakening in store when I met him for the first time.

The caravan was parked in a corner of the set. I knocked and opened the door. It was immediately clear where his nickname of Foggy came from when a huge, cloud of white smoke billowed out. It was so thick it made my eyes water. I knew immediately from the smell that it was heroin. What's more, the whereabouts of Nora Batty's missing stocking was a mystery no more.

One end was tied round Dewhurst's upper arm whilst he was gripping the other end in his teeth, pulling it tight. In his other hand he held the biggest syringe I'd ever seen - the drugs in it must of had a street value of a million pounds at least. He was trying to find a vein to inject them into but he was having no luck. His arm looked like a Swiss cheese, there were so many needle holes in it.

In his desperation to jack up, Foggy pulled the stockings tighter and tighter until, suddenly, his false teeth shot out of his mouth. I couldn't believe my eyes as they flew out the window. As luck would have it, Ivy from the cafe was bending over outside, patting a Yorkshire Terrier, and the

SHOWBIZ SHERBET DIPPY: Cokehead Compo kept floating away, says Scarborough (facing page).

A *Last of the Summer Wine* spokesman last night dismissed the claim that there was a culture of drug abuse on the long-running show. And he accused the former catering assistant of spreading deliberate untruths in revenge for being dismissed from his post.

He told us: "A week after Mr Scarborough took up his temporary post, there was a serious outbreak of food poisoning on the set. The source was eventually traced back to Mr Scarborough."

"We found out that he hadn't been washing his hands after he'd been for a shit," the spokesman said.

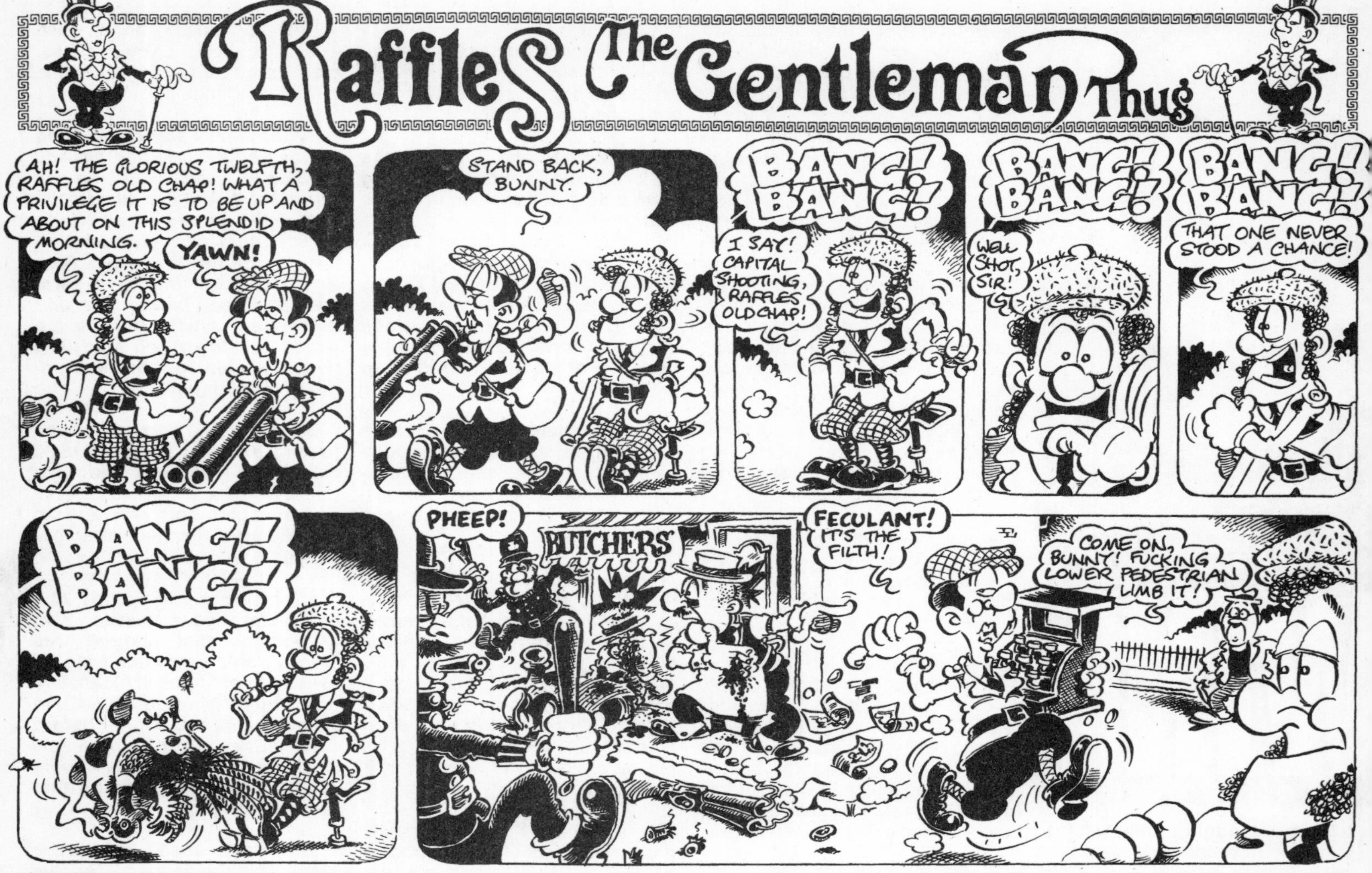
Raffles The Gentleman Thug
AH! THE GLORIOUS TWELFTH, RAFFLES OLD CHAP! WHAT A PRIVILEGE IT IS TO BE UP AND ABOUT ON THIS SPLENDID MORNING.
YAWN!
STAND BACK, BUNNY.
BANG! BANG!
I SAY! CAPITAL SHOOTING, RAFFLES OLD CHAP!
BANG! BANG!
WELL SHOT, SIR!
BANG! BANG!
THAT ONE NEVER STOOD A CHANCE!
BANG! BANG!
PHEEP!
BUTCHERS
FECULANT! IT'S THE FILTH!
COME ON, BUNNY! FUCKING LOWER PEDESTRIAN LIMB IT!

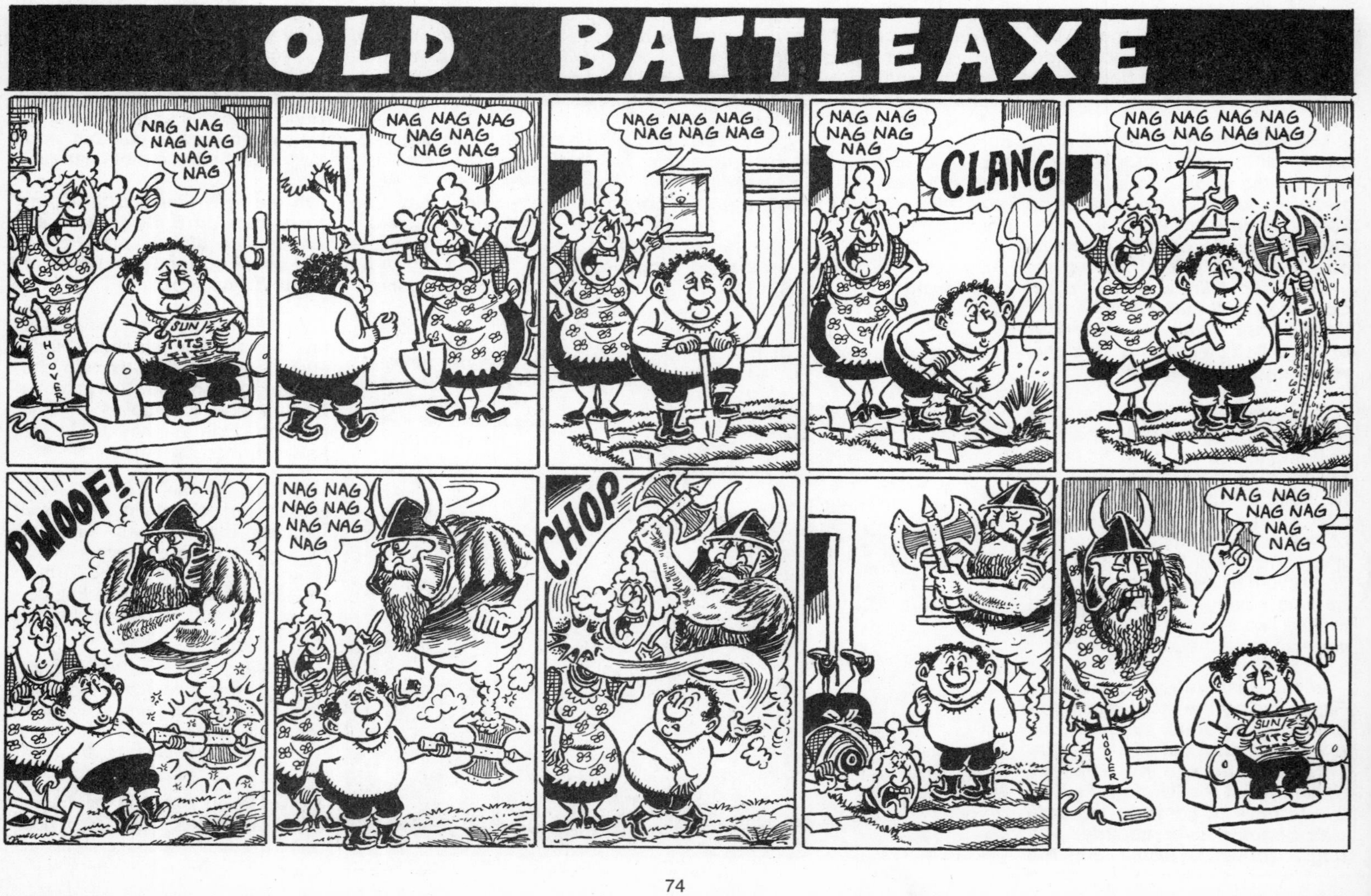
OLD BATTLEAXE
NAG NAG NAG NAG NAG NAG
SUN TITS
HOOVER
NAG NAG NAG NAG NAG NAG NAG
NAG NAG NAG NAG NAG NAG
NAG NAG NAG NAG NAG
CLANG
NAG NAG NAG NAG NAG NAG NAG NAG
PWOOF!
NAG NAG NAG NAG NAG NAG NAG
CHOP
NAG NAG NAG NAG NAG NAG
SUN TITS
HOOVER

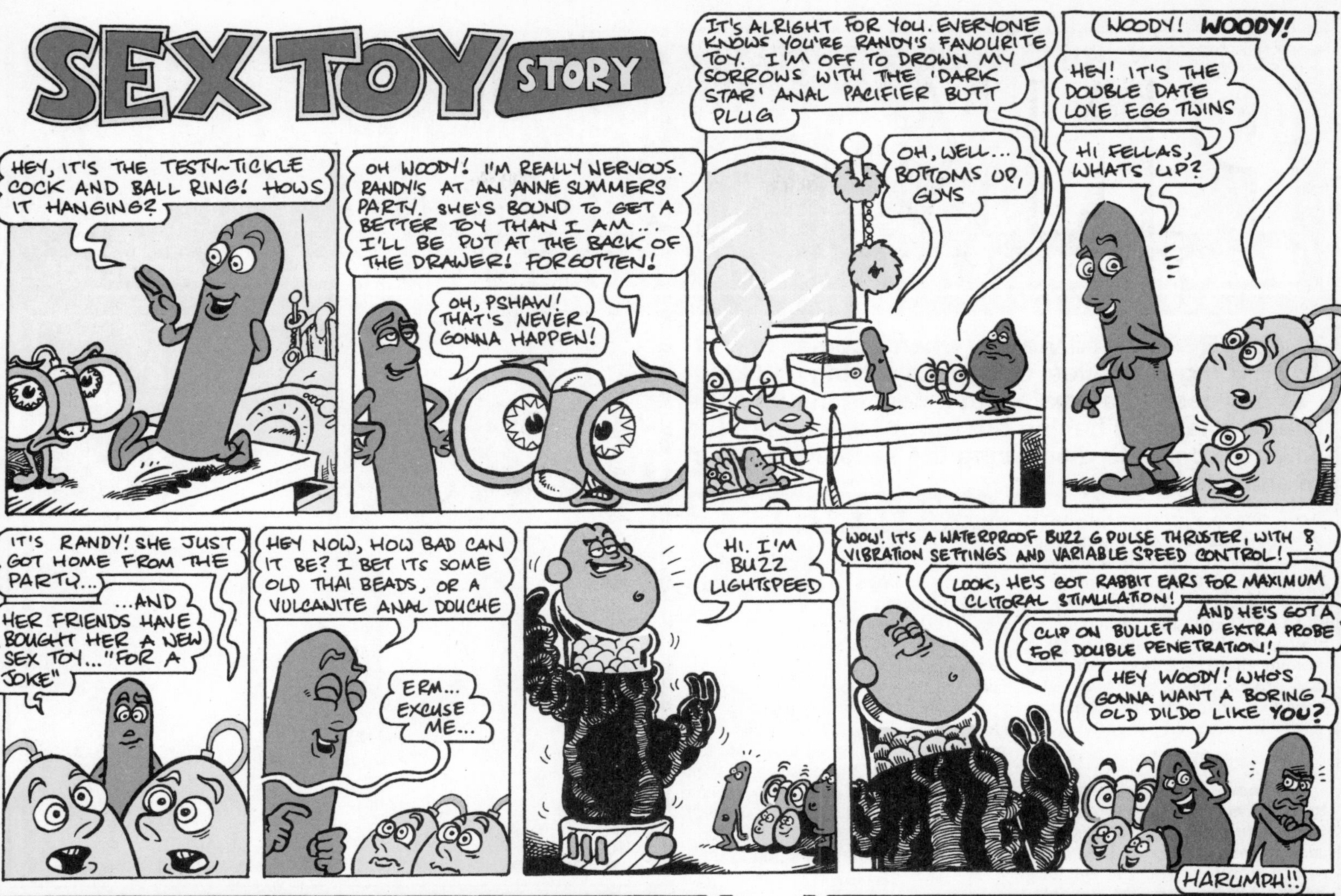
SEX TOY STORY
HEY, IT'S THE TESTY~TICKLE COCK AND BALL RING! HOWS IT HANGING?
OH WOODY! I'M REALLY NERVOUS. RANDY'S AT AN ANNE SUMMERS PARTY. SHE'S BOUND TO GET A BETTER TOY THAN I AM... I'LL BE PUT AT THE BACK OF THE DRAWER! FORGOTTEN!
OH, PSHAW! THAT'S NEVER GONNA HAPPEN!
IT'S ALRIGHT FOR YOU. EVERYONE KNOWS YOU'RE RANDY'S FAVOURITE TOY. I'M OFF TO DROWN MY SORROWS WITH THE 'DARK STAR' ANAL PACIFIER BUTT PLUG
OH, WELL... BOTTOMS UP, GUYS
WOODY! WOODY!
HEY! IT'S THE DOUBLE DATE LOVE EGG TWINS
HI FELLAS, WHATS UP?
IT'S RANDY! SHE JUST GOT HOME FROM THE PARTY...
...AND HER FRIENDS HAVE BOUGHT HER A NEW SEX TOY..."FOR A JOKE"
HEY NOW, HOW BAD CAN IT BE? I BET ITS SOME OLD THAI BEADS, OR A VULCANITE ANAL DOUCHE
ERM... EXCUSE ME...
HI. I'M BUZZ LIGHTSPEED
WOW! IT'S A WATERPROOF BUZZ G PULSE THRUSTER, WITH 8 VIBRATION SETTINGS AND VARIABLE SPEED CONTROL!
LOOK, HE'S GOT RABBIT EARS FOR MAXIMUM CLITORAL STIMULATION!
AND HE'S GOT A CLIP ON BULLET AND EXTRA PROBE FOR DOUBLE PENETRATION!
HEY WOODY! WHO'S GONNA WANT A BORING OLD DILDO LIKE YOU?
HARUMPH!!

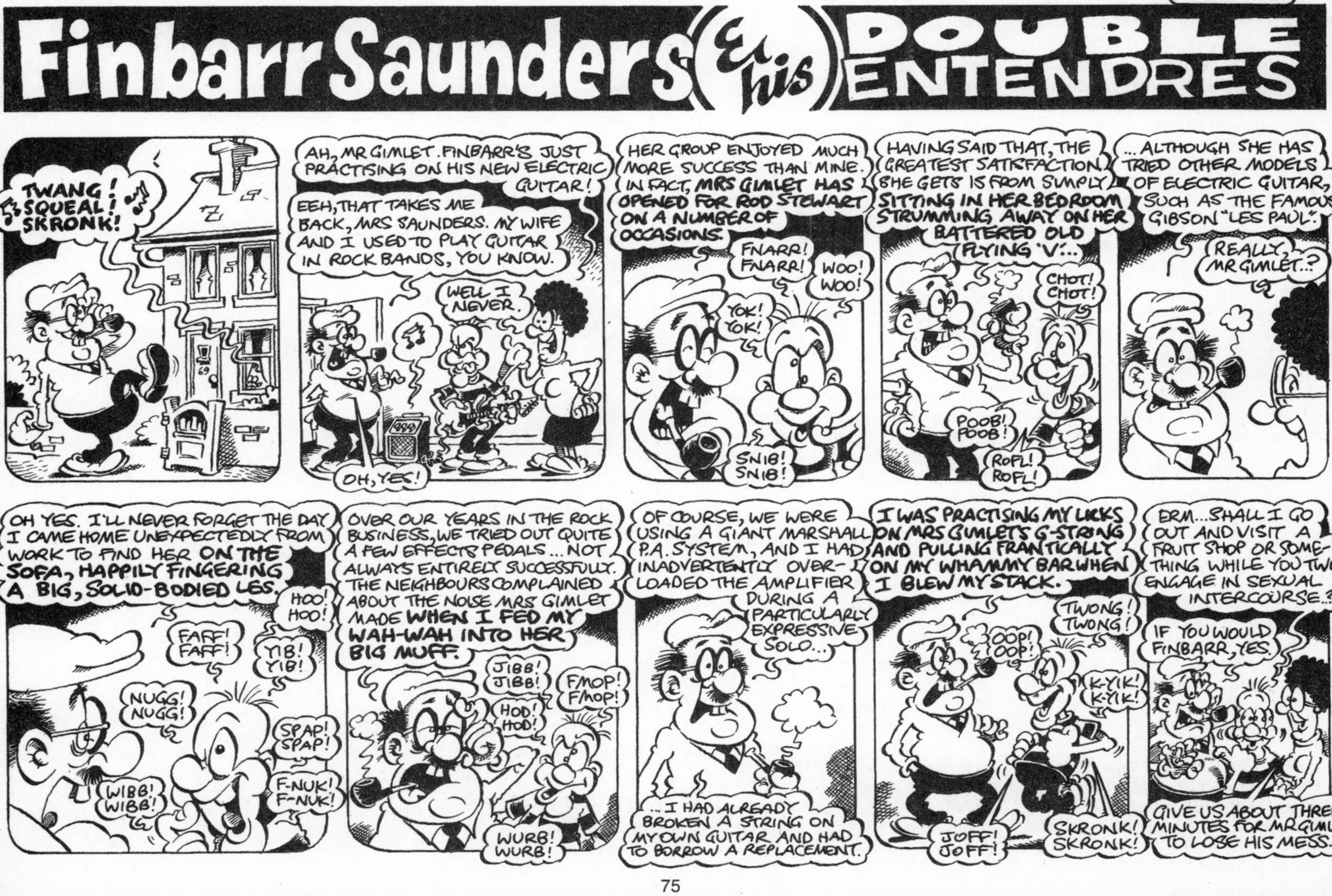
Finbarr Saunders (& his) DOUBLE ENTENDRES
TWANG! SQUEAL! SKRONK!
AH, MR GIMLET. FINBARR'S JUST PRACTISING ON HIS NEW ELECTRIC GUITAR!
EEH, THAT TAKES ME BACK, MRS SAUNDERS. MY WIFE AND I USED TO PLAY GUITAR IN ROCK BANDS, YOU KNOW.
WELL I NEVER.
OH, YES!
HER GROUP ENJOYED MUCH MORE SUCCESS THAN MINE. IN FACT, MRS GIMLET HAS OPENED FOR ROD STEWART ON A NUMBER OF OCCASIONS.
FNARR! FNARR!
WOO! WOO!
YOK! YOK!
SNIB! SNIB!
HAVING SAID THAT, THE GREATEST SATISFACTION SHE GETS IS FROM SIMPLY SITTING IN HER BEDROOM STRUMMING AWAY ON HER BATTERED OLD 'FLYING 'V'...
CHOT! CHOT!
POOB! POOB!
ROFL! ROFL!
...ALTHOUGH SHE HAS TRIED OTHER MODELS OF ELECTRIC GUITAR, SUCH AS THE FAMOUS GIBSON "LES PAUL".
REALLY, MR GIMLET..?
OH YES. I'LL NEVER FORGET THE DAY I CAME HOME UNEXPECTEDLY FROM WORK TO FIND HER ON THE SOFA, HAPPILY FINGERING A BIG, SOLID-BODIED LES.
HOO! HOO!
FAFF! FAFF!
YIB! YIB!
NUGG! NUGG!
SPAP! SPAP!
WIBB! WIBB!
F-NUK! F-NUK!
OVER OUR YEARS IN THE ROCK BUSINESS, WE TRIED OUT QUITE A FEW EFFECTS PEDALS... NOT ALWAYS ENTIRELY SUCCESSFULLY. THE NEIGHBOURS COMPLAINED ABOUT THE NOISE MRS GIMLET MADE WHEN I FED MY WAH-WAH INTO HER BIG MUFF.
JIBB! JIBB!
F/MOP! F/MOP!
HOD! HOD!
WURB! WURB!
OF COURSE, WE WERE USING A GIANT MARSHALL P.A. SYSTEM, AND I HAD INADVERTENTLY OVER-LOADED THE AMPLIFIER DURING A PARTICULARLY EXPRESSIVE SOLO...
...I HAD ALREADY BROKEN A STRING ON MY OWN GUITAR AND HAD TO BORROW A REPLACEMENT.
I WAS PRACTISING MY LICKS ON MRS GIMLET'S G-STRING AND PULLING FRANTICALLY ON MY WHAMMY BAR WHEN I BLEW MY STACK.
TWONG! TWONG!
OOP! OOP!
K-YIK! K-YIK!
JOFF! JOFF!
SKRONK! SKRONK!
ERM...SHALL I GO OUT AND VISIT A FRUIT SHOP OR SOME-THING WHILE YOU TWO ENGAGE IN SEXUAL INTERCOURSE..?
IF YOU WOULD FINBARR, YES.
GIVE US ABOUT THREE MINUTES FOR MR GIMLET TO LOSE HIS MESS.

PINK or BROWN?

Snooker stars help break taboo about anal bleaching

WE MAY lead the way when it comes to waiting in queues, courteous driving and kindness to animals, but it seems that bashful Brits are lagging behind our European neighbours when it comes to discussing the sensitive subject of anal bleaching.

According to a government survey, 98% of Brits are too shy to bring up the subject of freckle shade with members of their own family or work colleagues. Most go through life feeling that the dark colouration around their anal sphincter is holding them back both personally and professionally, especially after spending many hours inspecting pornstars' polished poopers.

STIGMA

But now a new government scheme is hoping to break the stigma surrounding changing the skin pigmentation of the anus. And it has received the backing of the World Snooker Association.

Former World Champion and long-time anal bleaching campaigner Dennis Taylor explained: "Twenty years ago, Britons' bottoms were in a terrible state, all dark through natural staining following a lifetime of excreting bodily waste.

The average light-skinned Brit's anus was a sight for sore eyes. Since then we have made some inroads into dispelling the scare stories about the dangers of changing the colouring of your balloon knot."

MAGMA

Taylor continued: "Myself, Eddie Charlton and Mike Hallet have spent most of our careers bending over tables with our nipsies exposed to public scrutiny – albeit with shiny black trousers on. So we know how embarrassing it can be to think your ringpiece is less than aesthetically pleasing. I only found out that other were suffering as well when Tony Drago broke down in tears about it at a ranking event in Prestatyn".

And the upside down-bespectacled cuesmith hoped that the newly formed organisation of snooker players would get the

EXCLUSIVE

message across to the public that no one has to be stuck with a brown bumhole.

"I heard a story about a gentleman who was ridiculed by housemates for his dark anal colouring when they returned home early one night to find him trying to reset his freeview box while naked and on all fours. He felt too embarrassed to discuss it with anyone and ended up trying to bleach his own anus by smearing it with toothpaste," said Taylor. "This kind of thing should never happen again."

SMEGMA

He continued: "We'll be playing a series of exhibition matches around the UK in venues like Sheffield's Crucible Theatre and The Hexagon, Reading. Between frames, myself and the other snooker stars will be chatting with the audience, answering questions about anal bleaching. At the end of the evening we'll be handing out leaflets that will give the audience the facts, and the fiction, about lightening the tea-towel holder," he added.

But even with the help of the world's top snooker stars, the government admits that it will be difficult to change British attitudes towards peroxiding their ringpieces.

A spokesperson for the Department of Health explained: "Our national reserve means it's going to be a difficult subject to get people talking about."

But he told reporters that the government would be leading by example. "In an effort to get the public talking, Local Government Minister Eric Pickles will be having his anus bleached live on the BBC Parliament channel. Afterwards, he will discuss the procedure in an interactive web forum with viewers," he said.

> "Eric Pickles is getting his anus bleached on live TV."

TO BLEACH HIS OWN: Taylor (main picture) and Pickles (inset) are set to sort out their anii.

JOHNNY FARTPANTS QUACK

ME AND DAD ARE IN SOUTH AFRICA TO SEE THE WORLD CUP, READERS.

FOOTBALL STADIUM

HOW ABOUT **THAT** FOR A TOPICALLY-THEMED CARTOON?

OH DEAR. ALL 40,000 OF US SPECTATORS HAVE FORGOTTEN TO BRING OUR VUVUZELAS WITH US TO THE MATCH.

STADIUM

HOW ARE WE GOING TO RECREATE THE SOUND OF 40,000 VUVUZELAS BEING BLOWN AT ONCE?

THAT'LL BE NO PROBLEM - PUMP POWER TO THE RESCUE!

CURRIED EGGY SPROUTS

VOOOOOOOOOT

AN EXTRA-SLOW RELEASED CHUFF INTO THIS TIN SAUCEPAN SHOULD DO THE TRICK!

BETTER HAVE SOME MORE CURRIED EGGY SPROUTS, JOHNNY- LOOKS LIKE WE'LL GO INTO EXTRA TIME.

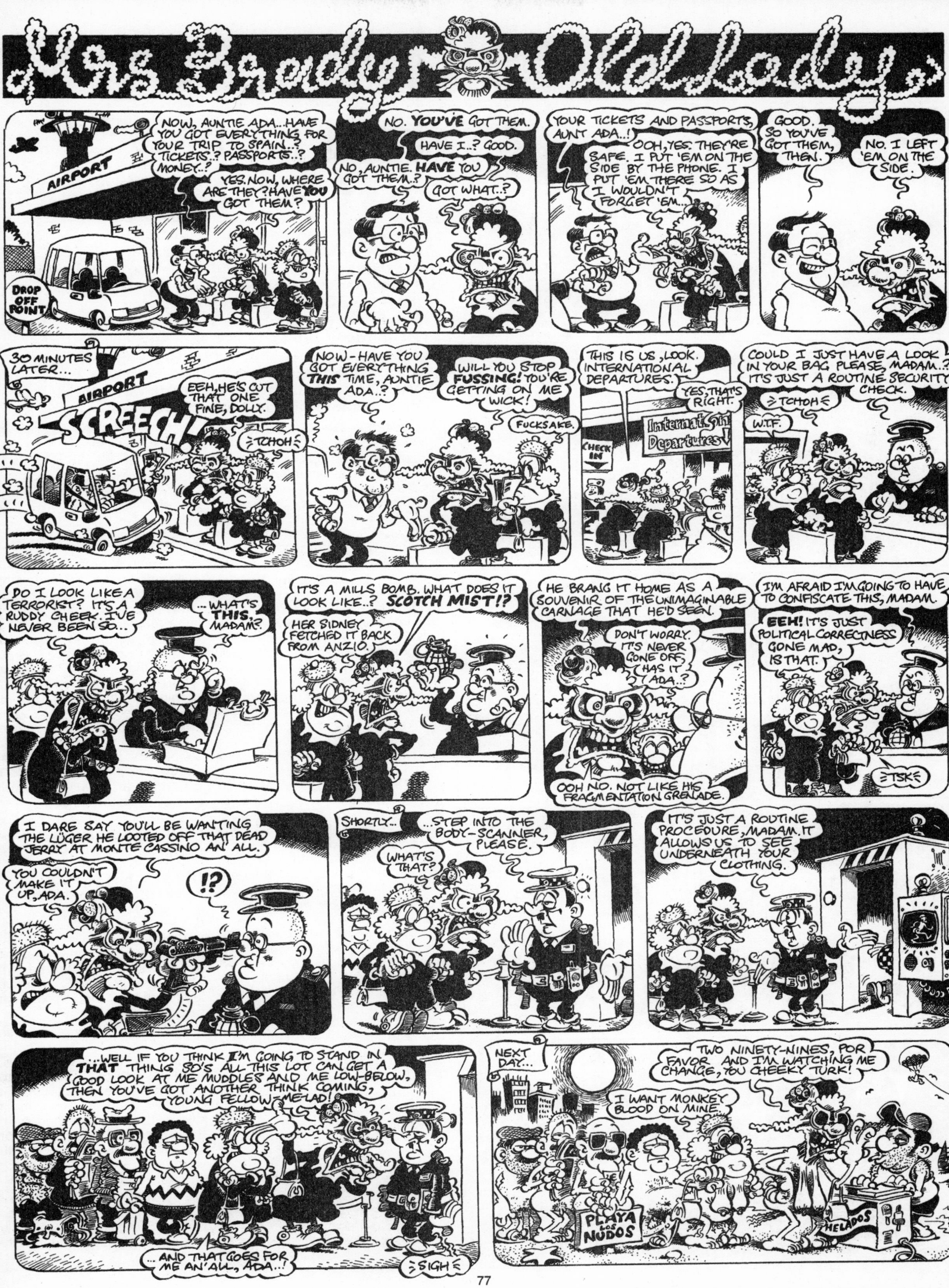
Mrs Brady Old Lady
AIRPORT
NOW, AUNTIE ADA...HAVE YOU GOT EVERYTHING FOR YOUR TRIP TO SPAIN..? TICKETS..? PASSPORTS..? MONEY..?
YES. NOW, WHERE ARE THEY? HAVE YOU GOT THEM?
DROP OFF POINT
NO. YOU'VE GOT THEM.
HAVE I..? GOOD.
NO, AUNTIE. HAVE YOU GOT THEM..?
GOT WHAT..?
YOUR TICKETS AND PASSPORTS, AUNT ADA..!
OOH, YES. THEY'RE SAFE. I PUT 'EM ON THE SIDE BY THE PHONE. I PUT 'EM THERE SO AS I WOULDN'T FORGET 'EM...
GOOD. SO YOU'VE GOT THEM, THEN.
NO. I LEFT 'EM ON THE SIDE.
30 MINUTES LATER...
AIRPORT
SCREECH!
EEH, HE'S CUT THAT ONE FINE, DOLLY.
TCHOH
NOW- HAVE YOU GOT EVERYTHING THIS TIME, AUNTIE ADA..?
WILL YOU STOP FUSSING! YOU'RE GETTING ON ME WICK!
FUCKSAKE.
THIS IS US, LOOK. INTERNATIONAL DEPARTURES.
YES, THAT'S RIGHT.
International Departures
CHECK IN
COULD I JUST HAVE A LOOK IN YOUR BAG PLEASE, MADAM..? IT'S JUST A ROUTINE SECURITY CHECK.
TCHOH
W.T.F.
DO I LOOK LIKE A TERRORIST? IT'S A RUDDY CHEEK. I'VE NEVER BEEN SO...
...WHAT'S THIS, MADAM?
IT'S A MILLS BOMB. WHAT DOES IT LOOK LIKE..? SCOTCH MIST!?
HER SIDNEY FETCHED IT BACK FROM ANZIO.
HE BRANG IT HOME AS A SOUVENIR OF THE UNIMAGINABLE CARNAGE THAT HE'D SEEN.
DON'T WORRY. IT'S NEVER GONE OFF, HAS IT ADA..?
OOH NO. NOT LIKE HIS FRAGMENTATION GRENADE.
I'M AFRAID I'M GOING TO HAVE TO CONFISCATE THIS, MADAM.
EEH! IT'S JUST POLITICAL CORRECTNESS GONE MAD, IS THAT.
TSK
I DARE SAY YOU'LL BE WANTING THE LÜGER HE LOOTED OFF THAT DEAD JERRY AT MONTE CASSINO AN' ALL.
YOU COULDN'T MAKE IT UP, ADA.
!?
SHORTLY...
...STEP INTO THE BODY-SCANNER, PLEASE.
WHAT'S THAT?
IT'S JUST A ROUTINE PROCEDURE, MADAM. IT ALLOWS US TO SEE UNDERNEATH YOUR CLOTHING.
...WELL IF YOU THINK I'M GOING TO STAND IN THAT THING SO'S ALL THIS LOT CAN GET A GOOD LOOK AT ME MUDDLES AND ME LOW-BELOW, THEN YOU'VE GOT ANOTHER THINK COMING, YOUNG FELLOW-ME-LAD!
...AND THAT GOES FOR ME AN' ALL, ADA..!
SIGH
NEXT DAY...
TWO NINETY-NINES, POR FAVOR. AND I'M WATCHING ME CHANGE, YOU CHEEKY TURK!
I WANT MONKEY BLOOD ON MINE.
PLAYA LOS NUDOS
HELADOS

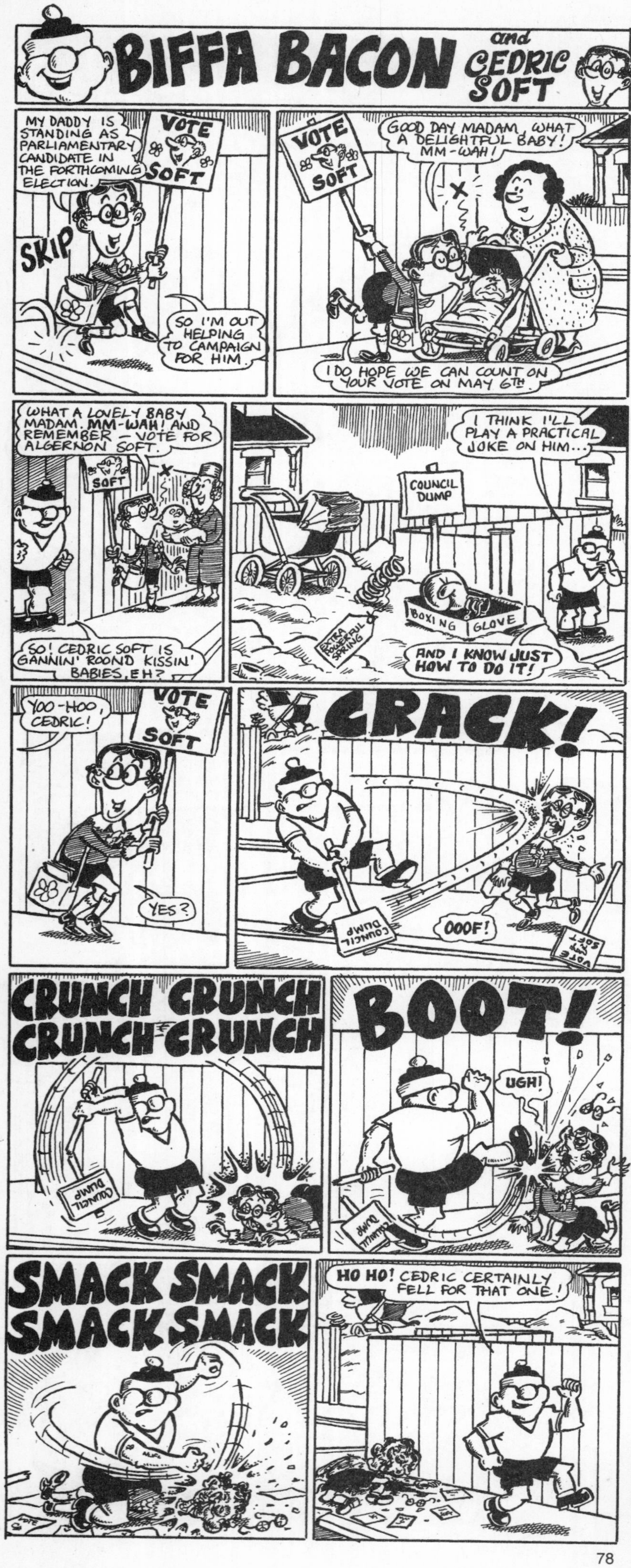
BIFFA BACON and CEDRIC SOFT
MY DADDY IS STANDING AS PARLIAMENTARY CANDIDATE IN THE FORTHCOMING ELECTION.
VOTE SOFT
SKIP
SO I'M OUT HELPING TO CAMPAIGN FOR HIM.
VOTE SOFT
GOOD DAY MADAM, WHAT A DELIGHTFUL BABY! MM-WAH!
I DO HOPE WE CAN COUNT ON YOUR VOTE ON MAY 6TH.
WHAT A LOVELY BABY MADAM. MM-WAH! AND REMEMBER — VOTE FOR ALGERNON SOFT.
SOFT
SO! CEDRIC SOFT IS GANNIN' ROOND KISSIN' BABIES, EH?
I THINK I'LL PLAY A PRACTICAL JOKE ON HIM...
COUNCIL DUMP
BOXING GLOVE
EXTRA POWERFUL SPRING
AND I KNOW JUST HOW TO DO IT!
YOO-HOO, CEDRIC!
VOTE SOFT
YES?
CRACK!
COUNCIL DUMP
OOOF!
VOTE SOFT
CRUNCH CRUNCH CRUNCH CRUNCH
BOOT!
UGH!
SMACK SMACK SMACK SMACK
HO HO! CEDRIC CERTAINLY FELL FOR THAT ONE!

PRINCE ON MINCE

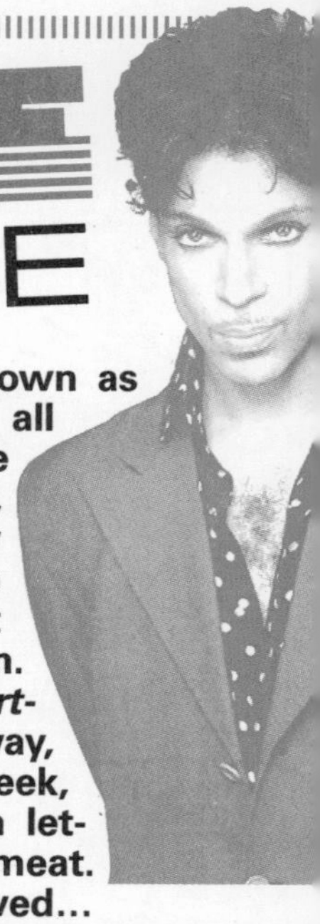

HI. The artist formerly known as Prince here. Now you all know that I love the Minnesota Vikings, Jehova's Witnessing and absolutely anything purple. But did you also know that I'm a sod for mince? Or at least I was before I became a vegan. I suppose you could say I'm *"the artist formerly prone to mince"*! Anyway, enough of this larking about. This week, my postbag has been bulging with letters about your favourite shredded meat. Here's a few of the best that I've received...

I FANCIED making a bolognese the other day, so I sent my husband to the shops to buy some minced meat. Imagine my surprise when he returned with some *mincemeat*, the sweet, raisin-based filling material for Christmas pies. How we laughed. He'll not make that mistake again.

Edna Migraine, Dawlish

I'M THE vaguely well-known comedian Robin Ince, and I absolutely love mince. I can't get enough of it and I eat it every day for my breakfast, dinner and tea. I like it so much that I started to write a limerick about how much I love it.

There was a young fellow called Ince,
Who had quite a penchant for mince,

That's as far as I've managed to get so far, and I'm afraid I'm struggling to think of the next bit. If any other mince fans could think of the last three lines, I really would appreciate it. If it's any help, the last line could end with rinse.

Robin Ince, Swindon

I AM emeritus professor of mince at Oxford University, and it really boils my piss when I hear people talking about "turkey mince". The term "mince" refers to ground or macerated beef and nothing else, so "turkey mince" is a meaningless oxymoron. I suggest that the producers of this misnomenclatured foodstuff should, in future, adopt the term "minced turkey" as a more accurate description of their product.

Prof AJ Gowans-Whyte, Dewhurst College, Oxford

MINCE FACTZ

ALBERT Einstein ate nothing but raw mince from 1902 until 1938. After that, he ate frozen sweetcorn and Quavers.

MINCE FACTZ

THE Ukranian town of Minsk is named after the Russian word for mince. The technique of grinding meat in a mincer was discovered there in 1963.

AS emeritus professor of applied mince at Cambridge University, I feel I must take issue with Professor Gowans-Whyte's letter *(above)*. Whilst I fully take his point about the misuse of the term "turkey mince", his assertion that "mince" refers to "ground or macerated beef and nothing else" is wrong. Ground or macerated lamb may also be correctly referred to as mince; for example when preparing a shepherd's pie. The professor should check his facts before leaping into print with such sweeping statements.

Prof H Cushion, Hickory House College, Cambridge

I FANCIED making a shepherd's pie the other day, so I sent my husband to the shops to buy a pound of mince. Imagine my surprise when he returned with a bag of humbugs. he had misheard me and thought I had asked for *mints*. How we laughed. He'll not make that mistake again.

Edna Migraine, Dawlish

MINCE may come *FROM* cows, but I have to go *TO* Cowes to get it. That's because I live just outside Cowes on the Isle of Wight, and my butcher is in the town! I've lived here for fifty years and I still weep with laughter for hours on end every time this ironic fact strikes me.

Archie Vulva, East Cowes

MY HUSBAND and I recently went out to a posh dinner party

Ask a MINCE EXPERT

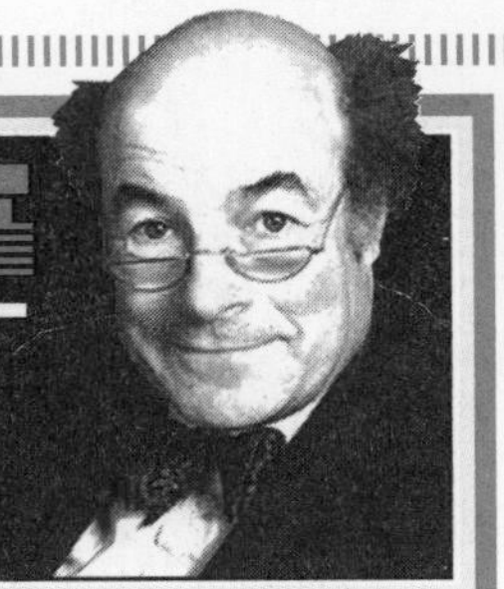

DR. HEINZ MEINTSZ ANSWERS YOUR QUESTIONS ABOUT MINCE

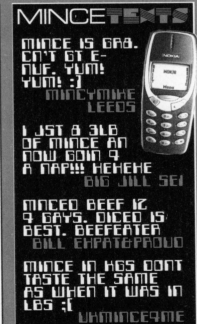

WHAT is the point of burgers? Why go to the bother of mincing up a slab of meat, only to then re-form it into another slab?

@MrsEtherington, Airedale

The reason *that burger manufacturers go to the trouble of mincing slabs of meat, only to mould the mince back into a different slab, is to make the meat into circles so that they fit nicely in a bap.*

A FRIEND recently told me that cockneys refer to their eyes as their "mince pies". Where does this expression come from?

@MrsHomunculus, Goole

During *the First World War, people from London who were in the trenches used to suck large round mints to keep their spirits up. The soldiers thought the sweets looked like eyeballs, and began to refer to their own eyeballs as "mints". Over the years, this became "mint spies" and eventually "mince pies".*

WHAT was the biggest bit of some mince in the world?

@UmbertoEco, Bologna

For the *opening ceremony of the Texas World Fair in 1936, they had some mince that weighed over 8 tons and was as big as a double decker bus. It was estimated that if it had been used to make a spag bol, the spaghettis would have to of been as thick as a man's leg and the height of Nelson's Column, and you would have to of had enough tomato sauce to fill an Olympic-sized swimming pool as large as a Wembley Stadium full of St Paul's Cathedrals ... to the Moon and back!*

TWEET YOUR MINCE QUERIES TO: DR HEINZ MEINTSZ, VIZ COMIC, PO BOX 841, WHITLEY BAY, NE26 9EQ

MINCE FACTZ

NASA boffins are working on a mincer that can work in a weightless environment, so that astronauts can enjoy spaghetti bolognese in space.

...and had mince and dumplings. It was so delicious we asked for seconds. As he served up the extra portions, our host quipped: "Here's your after dinner mince." My husband laughed so hard that he had an accident in his trousers. Needless to say, my evening was ruined.

Ada Elsan, Beverley

I FANCIED making a lasagne the other day, so I sent my husband to the shops with strict instructions to come back with a little mince. Imagine my surprise when he walked back up the path empty-handed, but with a slightly effeminate gait. How we laughed. He'll not make that mistake again.

Edna Migraine, Dawlish

WHO says shepherd's pies have to contain mince? I'm a shepherd and the other day I had an apple & blackberry pie.

Davey the Shepherd, Hereford

I LOVE mince, but I can't eat it because I once saw it being made. All those little wiggly worms of meat coming out of the metal holes in the mincer looked just like long turds being shat out of loads of tiny robots' bottoms. Just thinking about it now is making me retch.

Dr M Candlestickmaker, Halftimewhistle

I ONLY eat mince because my mother told me it was the one meat that the butcher couldn't interfere with sexually.

June Medford, Plywood-on-Stour

WITH reference to June Medford's letter *(above)*, I am a butcher. Whilst it is true that other sorts of meat are easier to interfere with sexually - chickens, turkey crowns and sausages, for example - it is not impossible to molest mince. It can be moulded into a variety of shapes (for example vagina, mouth, anus etc), or simply masturbated into, then mixed up a bit.

Hampton Cleftbridge, Cleftbridge & Sons of Bartlepool, Family Butchers since 1910

MINCE FACTZ

THE tiniest ever bit of mince was eaten by the world's smallest man Calvin Phillips. It was served up on a shirt button plate, with dumplings the size of hundreds and thousands.

MINCE ...Jokes...

Q Which mince is the Minister for Trade and Industry?
A Mince Cable (Vince Cable).

J Bronowski, Gravesend

Q What mince is in danger of falling over?
A Lean mince.

D Attenborough, London

Q What is the difference between a plate of good quality steak mince and the photosynthetic organs of the plant Phaseolus?
A One of them is a "lean beef" and the other is a "bean leaf".

D Bellamy, Durham

MINCE TEXTS

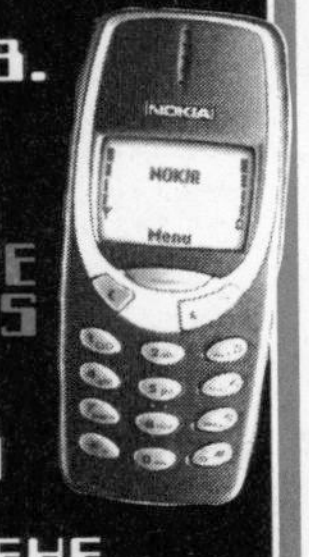

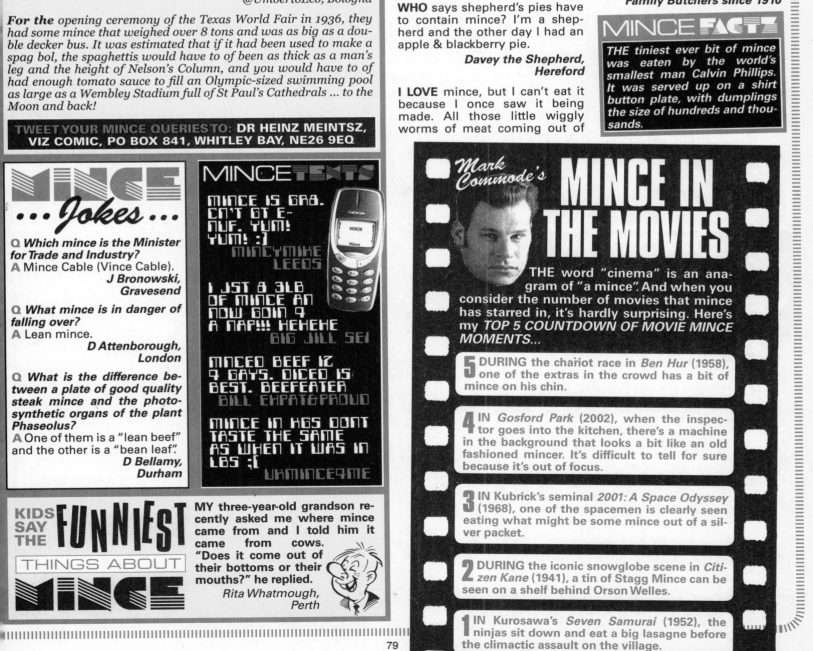

MINCE IS GR8. CN'T GT E-NUF. YUM! YUM! :)
MINCYMIKE LEEDS

I JST 8 3LB OF MINCE AN NOW GOIN 4 A NAP!!! HEHEHE
BIG JILL SE1

MINCED BEEF IZ 4 GAYS. DICED IS BEST. BEEFEATER
BILL EXPAT&PROUD

MINCE IN KGS DONT TASTE THE SAME AS WHEN IT WAS IN LBS :(
UKMINCE4ME

KIDS SAY THE FUNNIEST THINGS ABOUT MINCE

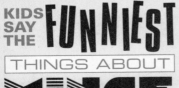

MY three-year-old grandson recently asked me where mince came from and I told him it came from cows. "Does it come out of their bottoms or their mouths?" he replied.

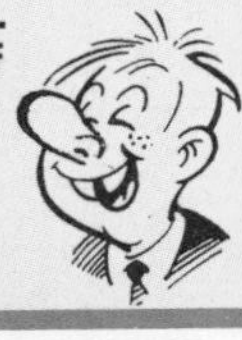

Rita Whatmough, Perth

Mark Commode's MINCE IN THE MOVIES

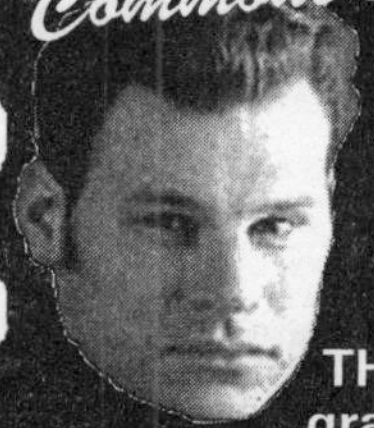

THE word "cinema" is an anagram of "a mince". And when you consider the number of movies that mince has starred in, it's hardly surprising. Here's my *TOP 5 COUNTDOWN OF MOVIE MINCE MOMENTS...*

5 DURING the chariot race in *Ben Hur* (1958), one of the extras in the crowd has a bit of mince on his chin.

4 IN *Gosford Park* (2002), when the inspector goes into the kitchen, there's a machine in the background that looks a bit like an old fashioned mincer. It's difficult to tell for sure because it's out of focus.

3 IN Kubrick's seminal *2001: A Space Odyssey* (1968), one of the spacemen is clearly seen eating what might be some mince out of a silver packet.

2 DURING the iconic snowglobe scene in *Citizen Kane* (1941), a tin of Stagg Mince can be seen on a shelf behind Orson Welles.

1 IN Kurosawa's *Seven Samurai* (1952), the ninjas sit down and eat a big lasagne before the climactic assault on the village.

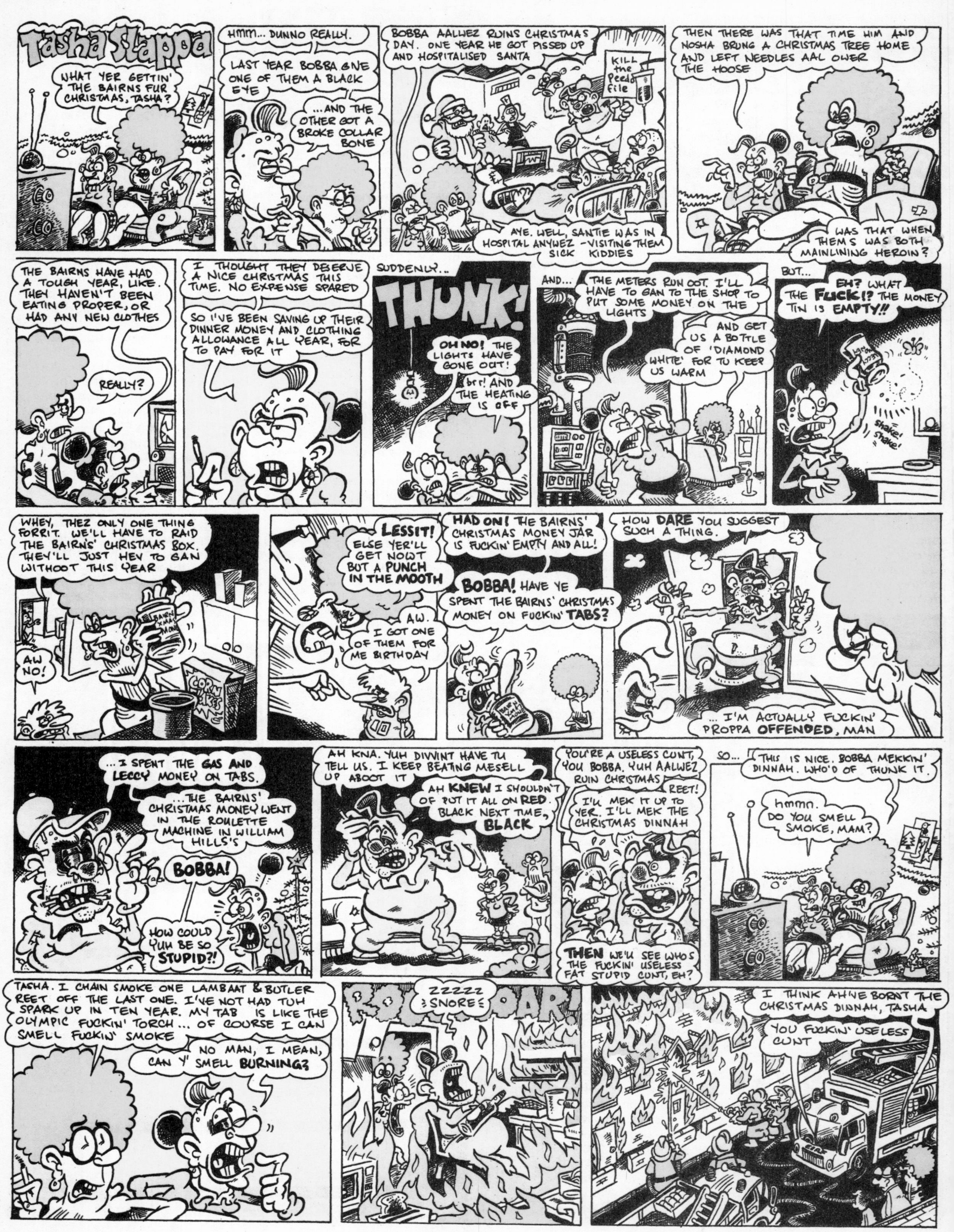
Tasha Slappa
WHAT YER GETTIN' THE BAIRNS FUR CHRISTMAS, TASHA?
HMM... DUNNO REALLY.
LAST YEAR BOBBA GIVE ONE OF THEM A BLACK EYE
...AND THE OTHER GOT A BROKE COLLAR BONE
BOBBA AALWEZ RUINS CHRISTMAS DAY. ONE YEAR HE GOT PISSED UP AND HOSPITALISED SANTA
KILL the Peedo file
AYE. WELL, SANTIE WAS IN HOSPITAL ANYWEZ - VISITING THEM SICK KIDDIES
THEN THERE WAS THAT TIME HIM AND NOSHA BRUNG A CHRISTMAS TREE HOME AND LEFT NEEDLES AAL OWER THE HOOSE
WAS THAT WHEN THEM'S WAS BOTH MAINLINING HEROIN?
THE BAIRNS HAVE HAD A TOUGH YEAR, LIKE. THEY HAVEN'T BEEN EATING PROPER, OR HAD ANY NEW CLOTHES
REALLY?
I THOUGHT THEY DESERVE A NICE CHRISTMAS THIS TIME. NO EXPENSE SPARED
SO I'VE BEEN SAVING UP THEIR DINNER MONEY AND CLOTHING ALLOWANCE ALL YEAR, FOR TO PAY FOR IT
SUDDENLY...
THUNK!
OH NO! THE LIGHTS HAVE GONE OUT!
brr! AND THE HEATING IS OFF
AND...
THE METERS RUN OOT. I'LL HAVE TO GAN TO THE SHOP TO PUT SOME MONEY ON THE LIGHTS
AND GET US A BOTTLE OF 'DIAMOND WHITE' FOR TU KEEP US WARM
BUT...
EH? WHAT THE FUCK!? THE MONEY TIN IS EMPTY!!
shake! shake!
WHEY, THEZ ONLY ONE THING FORRIT. WE'LL HAVE TO RAID THE BAIRNS' CHRISTMAS BOX. THEY'LL JUST HEV TO GAN WITHOOT THIS YEAR
AW NO!
LESSIT! ELSE YER'LL GET NOWT BUT A PUNCH IN THE MOOTH
AW. I GOT ONE OF THEM FOR ME BIRTHDAY
HAD ON! THE BAIRNS' CHRISTMAS MONEY JAR IS FUCKIN' EMPTY AND ALL!
BOBBA! HAVE YE SPENT THE BAIRNS' CHRISTMAS MONEY ON FUCKIN' TABS?
HOW DARE YOU SUGGEST SUCH A THING.
...I'M ACTUALLY FUCKIN' PROPPA OFFENDED, MAN
...I SPENT THE GAS AND LECCY MONEY ON TABS.
...THE BAIRNS' CHRISTMAS MONEY WENT IN THE ROULETTE MACHINE IN WILLIAM HILLS'S
BOBBA!
HOW COULD YUH BE SO STUPID?!
AH KNA. YUH DIVVINT HAVE TU TELL US. I KEEP BEATING MESELL UP ABOOT IT
AH KNEW I SHOULDN'T OF PUT IT ALL ON RED. BLACK NEXT TIME, BLACK
YOU'RE A USELESS CUNT, YOU BOBBA. YUH AALWEZ RUIN CHRISTMAS
REET! I'LL MEK IT UP TO YER. I'LL MEK THE CHRISTMAS DINNAH
THEN WE'LL SEE WHO'S THE FUCKIN' USELESS FAT STUPID CUNT, EH?
SO...
THIS IS NICE. BOBBA MEKKIN' DINNAH. WHO'D OF THUNK IT.
hmmn. DO YOU SMELL SMOKE, MAM?
TASHA. I CHAIN SMOKE ONE LAMBAAT & BUTLER REET OFF THE LAST ONE. I'VE NOT HAD TUH SPARK UP IN TEN YEAR. MY TAB IS LIKE THE OLYMPIC FUCKIN' TORCH... OF COURSE I CAN SMELL FUCKIN' SMOKE
NO MAN, I MEAN, CAN Y' SMELL BURNING?
ZZZZZ SNORE
I THINK AH'VE BORNT THE CHRISTMAS DINNAH, TASHA
YOU FUCKIN' USELESS CUNT

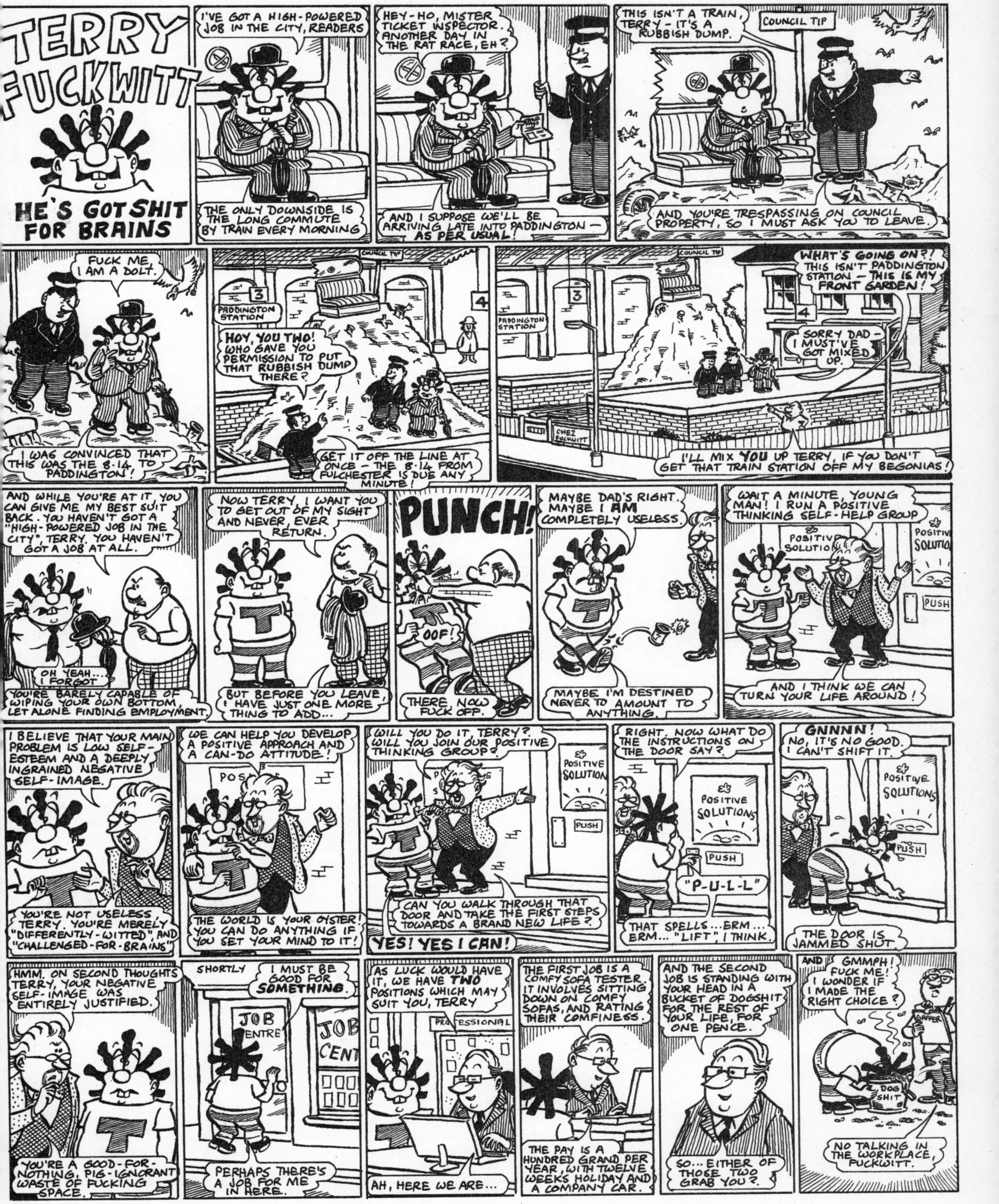
TERRY FUCKWITT
HE'S GOT SHIT FOR BRAINS
I'VE GOT A HIGH-POWERED JOB IN THE CITY, READERS
THE ONLY DOWNSIDE IS THE LONG COMMUTE BY TRAIN EVERY MORNING
HEY-HO, MISTER TICKET INSPECTOR. ANOTHER DAY IN THE RAT RACE, EH?
AND I SUPPOSE WE'LL BE ARRIVING LATE INTO PADDINGTON — AS PER USUAL!
THIS ISN'T A TRAIN, TERRY - IT'S A RUBBISH DUMP.
COUNCIL TIP
AND YOU'RE TRESPASSING ON COUNCIL PROPERTY, SO I MUST ASK YOU TO LEAVE.
FUCK ME. I AM A DOLT.
I WAS CONVINCED THAT THIS WAS THE 8.14 TO PADDINGTON!
COUNCIL TIP
PADDINGTON STATION
HOY, YOU TWO! WHO GAVE YOU PERMISSION TO PUT THAT RUBBISH DUMP THERE?
GET IT OFF THE LINE AT ONCE - THE 8.14 FROM FULCHESTER IS DUE ANY MINUTE!
COUNCIL TIP
PADDINGTON STATION
WHAT'S GOING ON?! THIS ISN'T PADDINGTON STATION - THIS IS MY FRONT GARDEN!
SORRY DAD - I MUST'VE GOT MIXED UP.
CHEZ FUCKWITT
I'LL MIX YOU UP TERRY, IF YOU DON'T GET THAT TRAIN STATION OFF MY BEGONIAS!
AND WHILE YOU'RE AT IT, YOU CAN GIVE ME MY BEST SUIT BACK. YOU HAVEN'T GOT A "HIGH-POWERED JOB IN THE CITY", TERRY. YOU HAVEN'T GOT A JOB AT ALL.
OH YEAH... I FORGOT
YOU'RE BARELY CAPABLE OF WIPING YOUR OWN BOTTOM, LET ALONE FINDING EMPLOYMENT.
NOW TERRY, I WANT YOU TO GET OUT OF MY SIGHT AND NEVER, EVER RETURN.
BUT BEFORE YOU LEAVE, I HAVE JUST ONE MORE THING TO ADD...
PUNCH!
OOF!
THERE. NOW FUCK OFF.
MAYBE DAD'S RIGHT. MAYBE I AM COMPLETELY USELESS.
MAYBE I'M DESTINED NEVER TO AMOUNT TO ANYTHING.
WAIT A MINUTE, YOUNG MAN! I RUN A POSITIVE THINKING SELF-HELP GROUP
POSITIVE SOLUTIONS
PUSH
AND I THINK WE CAN TURN YOUR LIFE AROUND!
I BELIEVE THAT YOUR MAIN PROBLEM IS LOW SELF-ESTEEM AND A DEEPLY INGRAINED NEGATIVE SELF-IMAGE.
YOU'RE NOT USELESS, TERRY. YOU'RE MERELY "DIFFERENTLY-WITTED", AND "CHALLENGED-FOR-BRAINS"
WE CAN HELP YOU DEVELOP A POSITIVE APPROACH AND A CAN-DO ATTITUDE!
THE WORLD IS YOUR OYSTER! YOU CAN DO ANYTHING IF YOU SET YOUR MIND TO IT!
WILL YOU DO IT, TERRY? WILL YOU JOIN OUR POSITIVE THINKING GROUP?
POSITIVE SOLUTION
PUSH
CAN YOU WALK THROUGH THAT DOOR AND TAKE THE FIRST STEPS TOWARDS A BRAND NEW LIFE?
YES! YES I CAN!
RIGHT. NOW WHAT DO THE INSTRUCTIONS ON THE DOOR SAY?
POSITIVE SOLUTIONS
PUSH
"P-U-L-L"
THAT SPELLS... ERM... ERM... "LIFT", I THINK.
GNNNN! NO, IT'S NO GOOD. I CAN'T SHIFT IT.
POSITIVE SOLUTIONS
PUSH
THE DOOR IS JAMMED SHUT.
HMM. ON SECOND THOUGHTS TERRY, YOUR NEGATIVE SELF-IMAGE WAS ENTIRELY JUSTIFIED.
YOU'RE A GOOD-FOR-NOTHING, PIG-IGNORANT WASTE OF FUCKING SPACE.
SHORTLY
I MUST BE GOOD FOR SOMETHING.
JOB CENTRE
JOB CENT
PERHAPS THERE'S A JOB FOR ME IN HERE.
AS LUCK WOULD HAVE IT, WE HAVE TWO POSITIONS WHICH MAY SUIT YOU, TERRY
PROFESSIONAL
AH, HERE WE ARE...
THE FIRST JOB IS A COMFY SOFA TESTER. IT INVOLVES SITTING DOWN ON COMFY SOFAS, AND RATING THEIR COMFINESS.
THE PAY IS A HUNDRED GRAND PER YEAR, WITH TWELVE WEEKS HOLIDAY AND A COMPANY CAR.
AND THE SECOND JOB IS STANDING WITH YOUR HEAD IN A BUCKET OF DOGSHIT FOR THE REST OF YOUR LIFE, FOR ONE PENCE.
SO... EITHER OF THOSE TWO GRAB YOU?
AND
GMMPH! FUCK ME! I WONDER IF I MADE THE RIGHT CHOICE?
DOG SHIT
NO TALKING IN THE WORKPLACE, FUCKWITT.

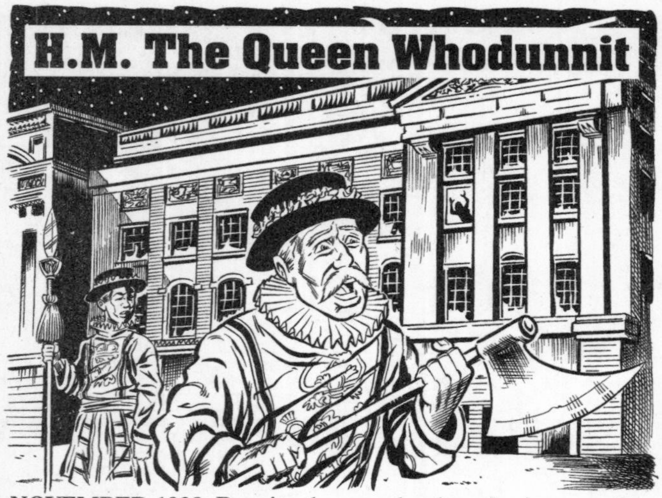
H.M. The Queen Whodunnit

NOVEMBER 1938. Despite the war clouds gathering over Europe, Britain slept soundly under the benign protection its beloved King George VI and his radiant wife Queen Elizabeth. Suddenly, the peaceful night air outside Buckingham Palace was shattered by a blood-curdling scream from the Queen's private dressing room. Awoken by the commotion, the members of the royal household rushed to see what had happened.

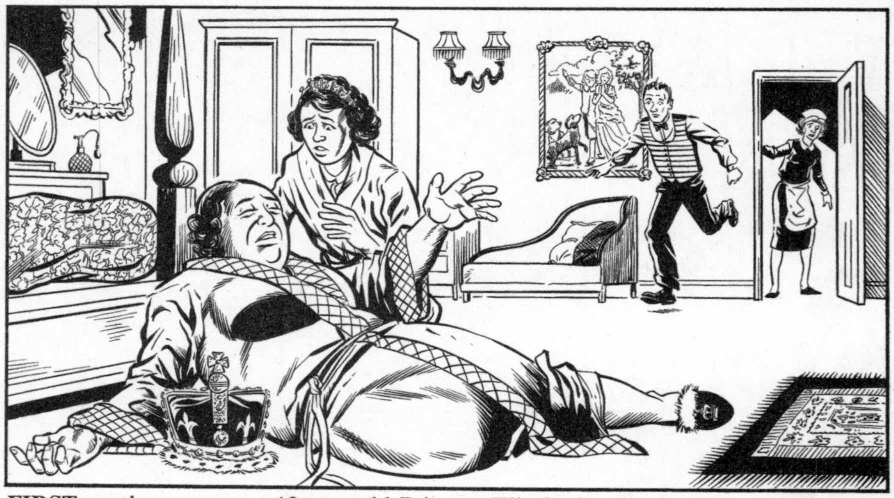

FIRST on the scene was 12-year-old Princess Elizabeth, who found her mother the Queen collapsed on the floor. "Mama! Mama! What happened?" she cried, cradling her mother's head. The majestic Princess craned forward to hear her mother's faint voice. "One of the footmen," the Queen gasped. "He brought me my evening gin and tonic... but as he left... he...he... he...didn't... didn't... *bow!*" As the horrifying words left her lips, the Queen lapsed into unconsciousness. "The Queen! The Queen! Somebody help my mother the Queen," screamed the little Princess.

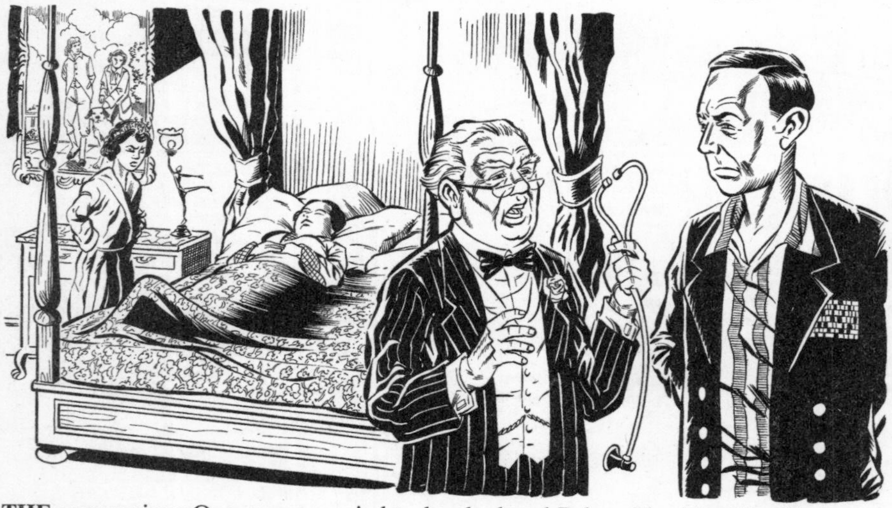

THE unconscious Queen was carried to her bed and Palace Physician Sir Gladstone Gamble was summoned. The anxious King George was taken to one side as the doctor delivered his diagnosis. "Her majesty has suffered a terrible shock, sir," explained the medical man. "The horror of her experience has put her into a serious coma from which she may never awake. All we can do is wait and pray that she recovers," he added gravely. But little Lilibet was determined to identify the evil footman who had brought her beloved mother so close to death. "I shall find the footman responsible," she vowed. "I shall find him and make sure he is brought to justice."

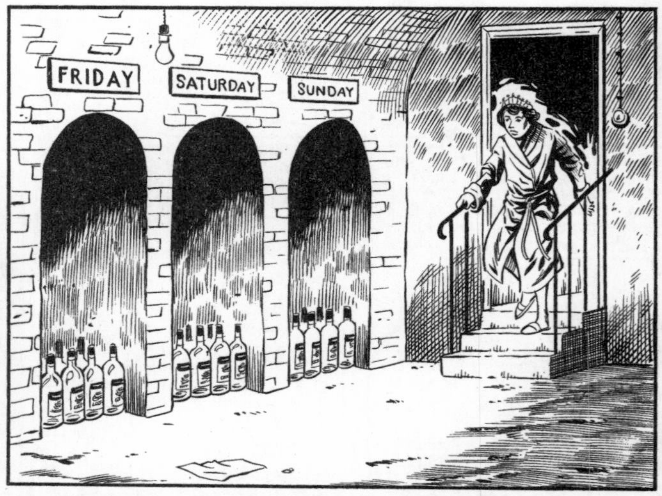
FRIDAY
SATURDAY
SUNDAY

AND Lillibet knew exactly where to start her search for the offending minion. "My mother, the Queen, said that the footman was bringing her gin when he committed the crime," she thought to herself. So off she set for the Queen's private gin cellar. It was below stairs, which was a part of the palace she had never been to before - the realm of servants and lackies. The walls were stark and bare. There was not a piece of gold or velvet to be seen and she shuddered at the lack of opulence around her. But bravely she pressed on. And as she entered the cellar, lying on the floor by that day's gin supply she spotted a small slip of paper.

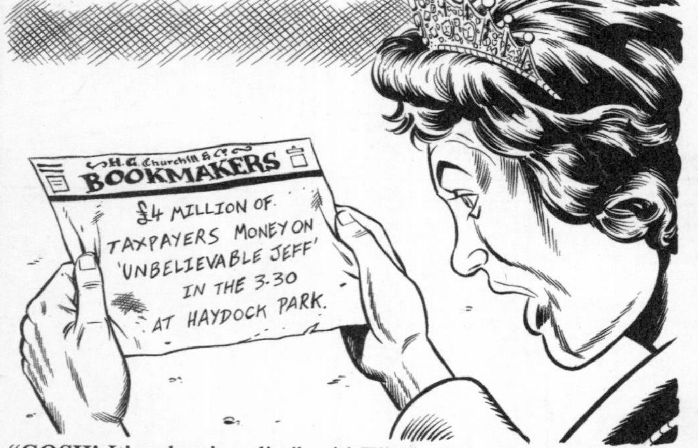
BOOKMAKERS
£4 MILLION OF TAXPAYERS MONEY ON 'UNBELIEVABLE JEFF' IN THE 3.30 AT HAYDOCK PARK.

"GOSH! It's a betting slip," said Elizabeth as she examined the scrap of paper. "This must be a clue. It means that the footman who brought Mama's gin was the same one who took her betting slips to the bookmaker in Picadilly High Street." The little Princess had started to unravel the mystery. But which footman was it? She knew her Mother would never be able to identify him by sight, as all common people looked the same. She had to have a name.

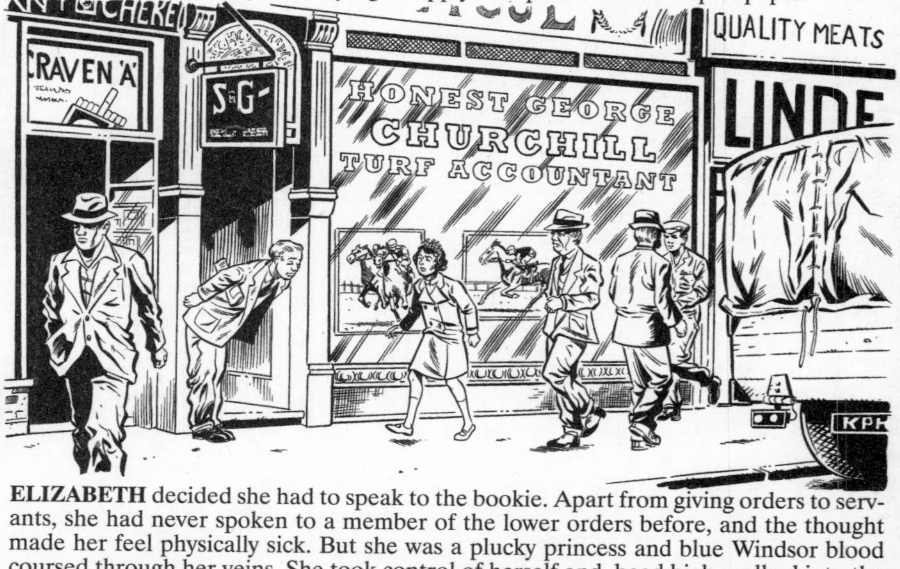
QUALITY MEATS
CRAVEN 'A'
HONEST GEORGE CHURCHILL TURF ACCOUNTANT
LINDE

ELIZABETH decided she had to speak to the bookie. Apart from giving orders to servants, she had never spoken to a member of the lower orders before, and the thought made her feel physically sick. But she was a plucky princess and blue Windsor blood coursed through her veins. She took control of herself and, head high, walked into the den of commoners.

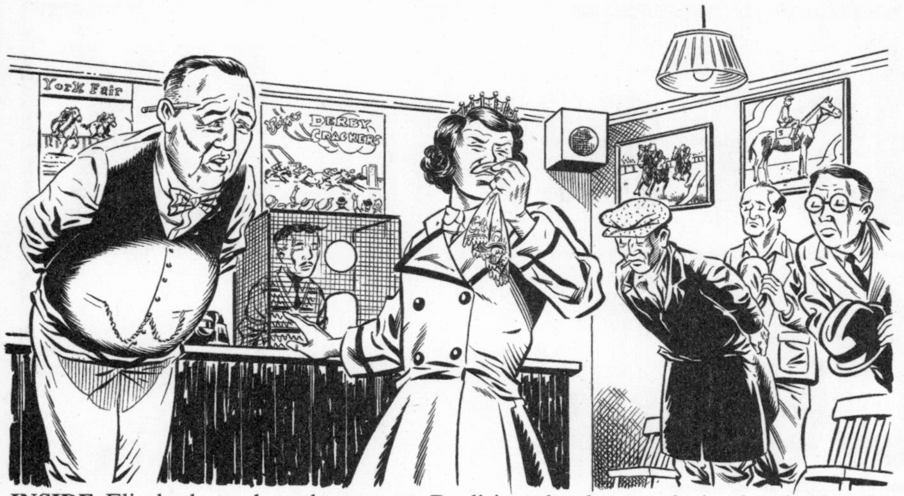
York Fair
DERBY CRACKERS

INSIDE, Elizabeth strode to the counter. Realising who she was, the bookmaker bowed low, quivering before her regal majesty. "Your R.. R.. Royal Highness," he stammered. "What an honour." Elizabeth looked at him with disgust. His watch was gold-plated, and his shirt, although clean, clearly cost less than a hundred guineas. She felt her gorge rise. "Who placed a bet here yesterday for my Mama, Her Majesty the Queen?" she demanded haughtily. "I... I don't know, you Highness," he replied. "A... a... footman. He didn't tell me his name. But I do remember that he appeared to be in some pain. He said something about his bad back playing up."

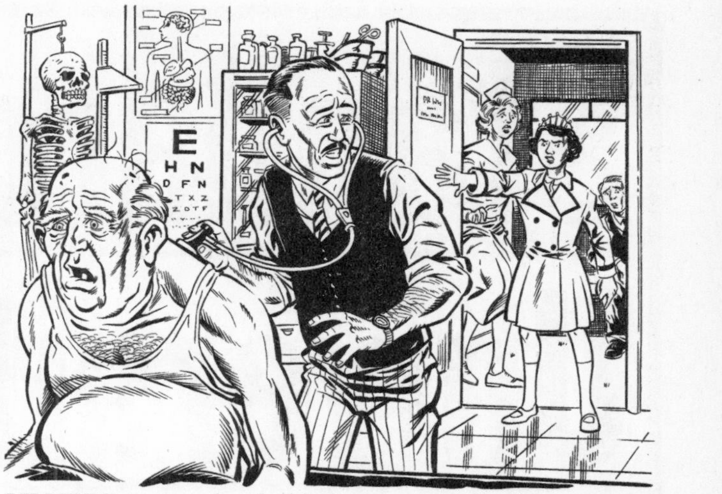

LILLIBET was now faced with the prospect of having to pay another visit to a commoner. The doctor who treated the palace footmen for their aches and pains would provide the final piece of the jigsaw. "I want to see all your medical records," she proclaimed as she burst through the door. "I am sorry your Highness," ventured the doctor. "Medical records are private and may not be seen, not even by the highest in the land." The little princess was outraged. Never had she encountered such disrespect and insolence!

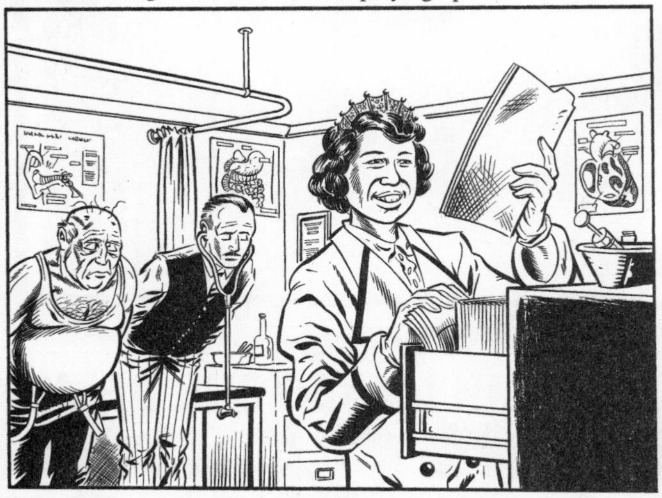

"BOW! BOW to your future Sovereign!" she hollered with regal dignity. "And do NOT rise until I, Princess Elizabeth, give my Royal permission." Such was the majesty of her voice, that the doctor did immediately as he was commanded. And as the physician stood in a respectful stoop, Lillibet stepped lightly over to the filing cabinet and began to go through his confidential records. A minute's searching was all it took. She finally had her answer.

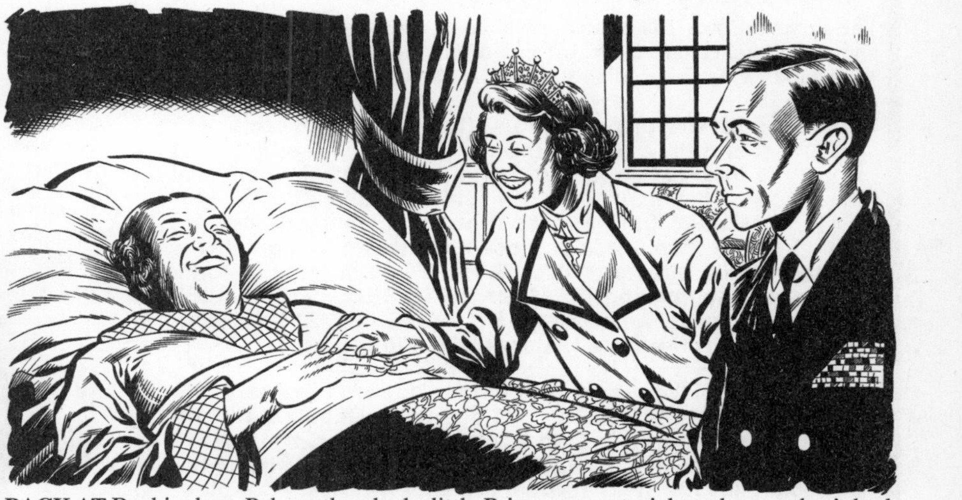

BACK AT Buckingham Palace, the plucky little Princess ran straight to her mother's bed chamber where her father the King was keeping a vigil by her bed. "Mama, Mama," she whispered. "I have found the identity of the footman who did this to you." Both the king and Lillibet saw the faintest glimmer of a smile play across the Queen's majestic lips and her regal eyelids flickered. The King looked at his daughter with pride. "I think she's going to be alright, Lillibet," he said. "Thanks to you, my little princess."

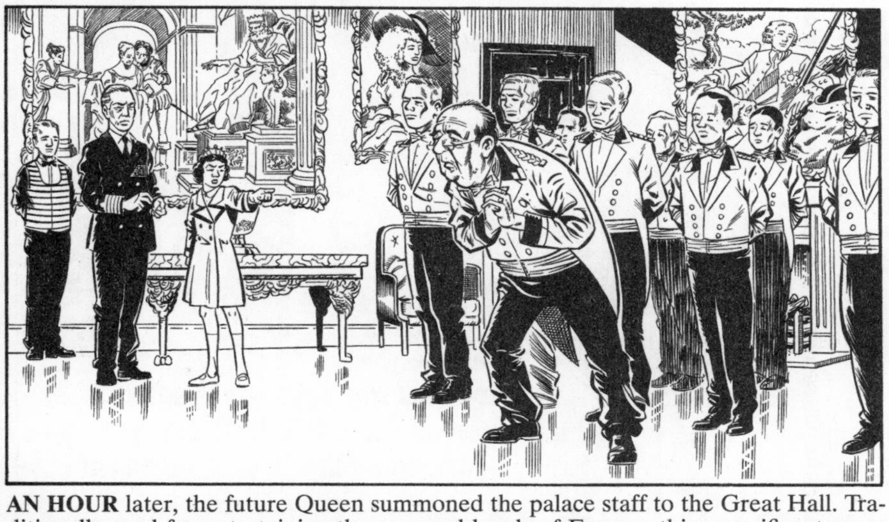

AN HOUR later, the future Queen summoned the palace staff to the Great Hall. Traditionally used for entertaining the crowned heads of Europe, this magnificent room was now to be used to unmask a criminal. Elizabeth held the crowd in her thrall as she explained how the perpetrator of the crime had the betting slip, and how she had subsequently discovered he had a bad back. And she revealed that a search through the medical records showed a footman had visited his doctor with back pain that same day. "Step forward, Albert Pastry," she called. An old, bent footman timidly approached her.

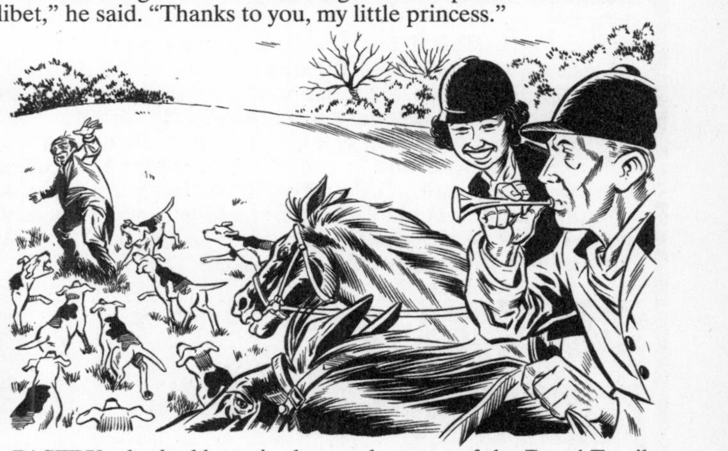

PASTRY, who had been in the employment of the Royal Family since he was 2 years old, immediately confessed. He explained that crippling lumbar arthritis that caused excruciating pain whenever he bent, and he cravenly begged their Majesties' forgiveness. "What shall we do, Lillibet?" asked the King. "As you discovered him, you shall sentence him." Elizabeth showed the compassion and empathy with the common people that would in future serve her well as Queen. "I think he should be given a chance," she said with a gracious smile. So, after breakfast the following day, the footman was given a three minute head start before the Palace Hunt chased him down and tore him to pieces.

Standards Fall in UK Universities

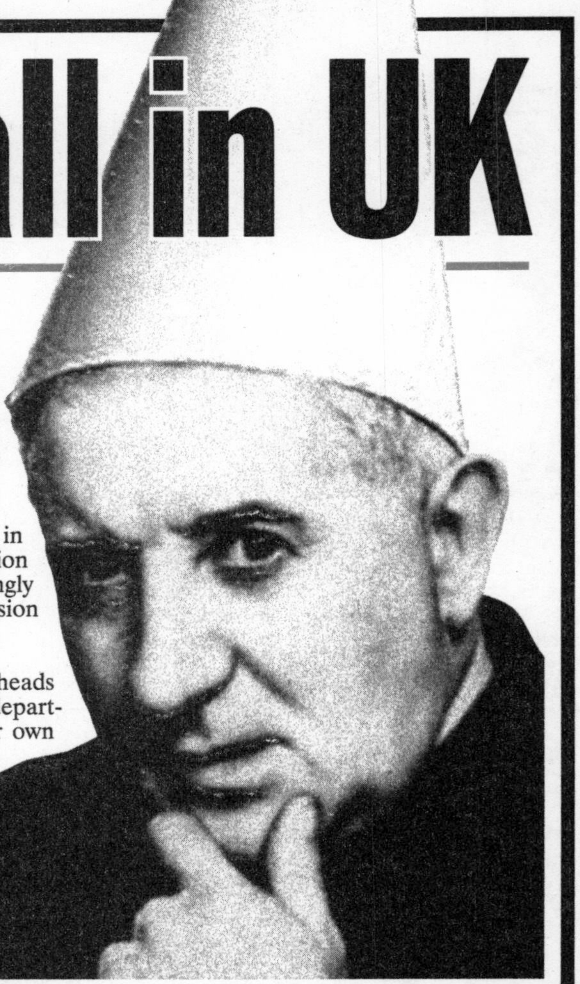

A SHOCKING survey released today reveals that 80% of elderly academics are unable to correctly identify well-known figures from the world of TV. And a staggering 97% are unable to name a single character from a daytime soap.

The survey of over 100 academics, philosophers and intellectuals from British Universities makes sobering reading and reinforces the belief that the people in charge of higher education and research are increasingly out of touch with television celebrities.

We buttonholed eggheads coming out of academic departments all over the country and gave them our own test. The results were a sad indictment of education in this country...

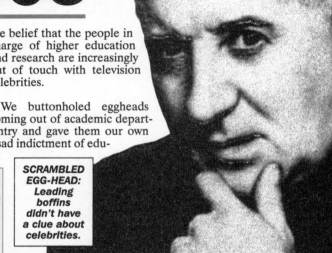

***SCRAMBLED EGG-HEAD:* Leading boffins didn't have a clue about celebrities.**

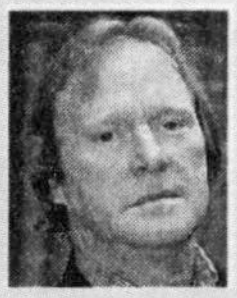

SHOW any schoolboy (from the 1980s) this face and they will instantly to tell you all the facts and information about Dennis Waterman's portrayal of fictional dogsbody and hardman TERRY McCANN from *Minder*. Not so our elderly academics. Two thirds of those interviewed thought it was german Opera director WERNER HERZOG, with the majority of the rest suggesting BERTRAND RUSSELL or KINGSLEY AMIS. The closest answer was SYLVESTER STALLONE, suggested by a Professor of History at Cambridge.

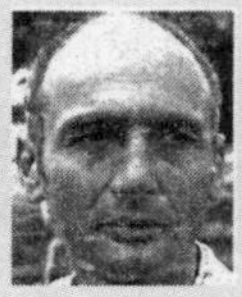

NEXT up is smooth former *Howard's Way* lothario KEN MASTERS - not the most difficult of historical figures you would think. Think again! "I haven't got a clue," said one Oxford egghead who unbelievably held a Nobel Prize for physics! Four other academics questioned suggested SAMUEL PEPYS. Another two struggled before coming up with a desperate RUDOLPH HESS and ISAAC NEWTON. And when told the answer, 83% of these so-called boffins claimed never to have heard of *Howard's Way*. Incredible.

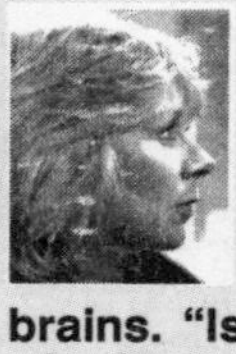

SURELY our academics can't fail to identify Ken Barlow's 1990 on screen lover WENDY CROZIER. The *Corrie* couple's affair briefly gripped the nation before being replaced with another storyline, but poor Ken will be turning in his slacks when he hears of the impact it made on the lives of our top brains. "Is..is..is..it JOAN OF ARC?" stammered one award-winning mathematician. The other answers were equally poor, with 45% of respondees suggesting QUEEN BOUDICEA and 20% believing it to be WILLAM GLADSTONE.

Are YOU an academic with your finger on Britain's pulse?

Simply identify the three famous faces and fill in the form stating your qualifications and academic institute.

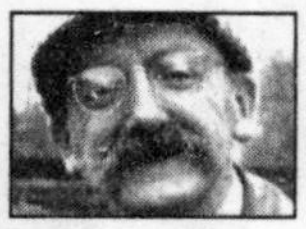

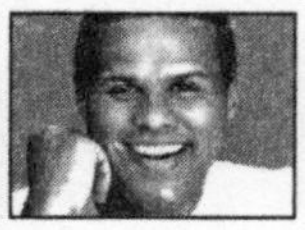

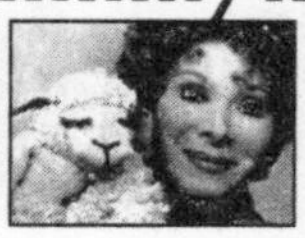

ANSWERS
a) .... **b)** .... **c)** ....

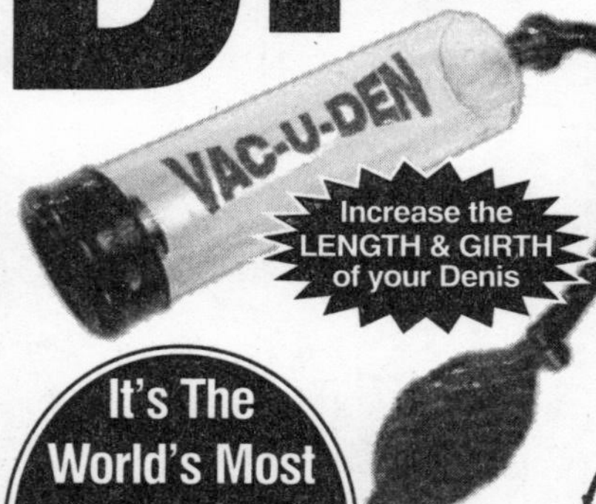

Name: Dr/Prof *(delete as applicable)*..
Field of Study: ....
Academic Institution: ....
No. of Nobel Prizes: ....

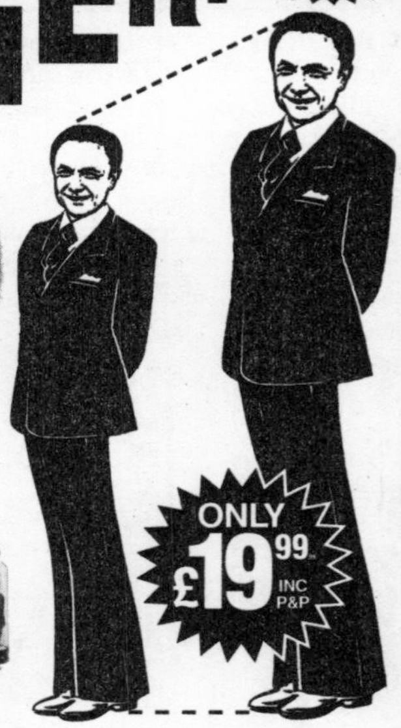

Send your completed entries to: *Viz University Challenge, PO Box 656, North Shields, NE30 4XX.*

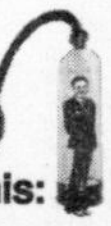

The first entry out of the Viz mortar board wins a fantastic spotty dickie bow & a pile of dusty books.

DENIS ENLARGEMENT

NOW YOU CAN MAKE YOUR DENIS BIGGER!

REALLY WORKS!

VAC-U-DEN

Increase the LENGTH & GIRTH of your Denis

It's The World's Most Effective Denile Enlargement Device!

ONLY £19.99 INC P&P

Works on any small Denis:
• *Wise* • *Waterman*
• *Law* • *Taylor etc.*

Any lady who says she is satisfied by a small Denis is LYING! Now you can add solid inches to your Denis with...

THE MIGHTY

VAC-U-DEN

P.O. Box 887, Leeds

BEFORE

AFTER

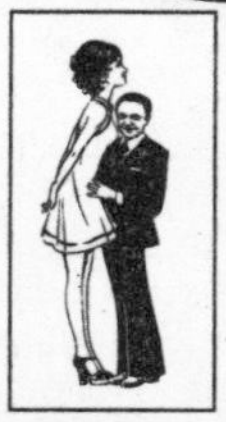

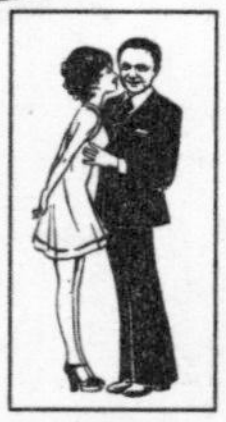

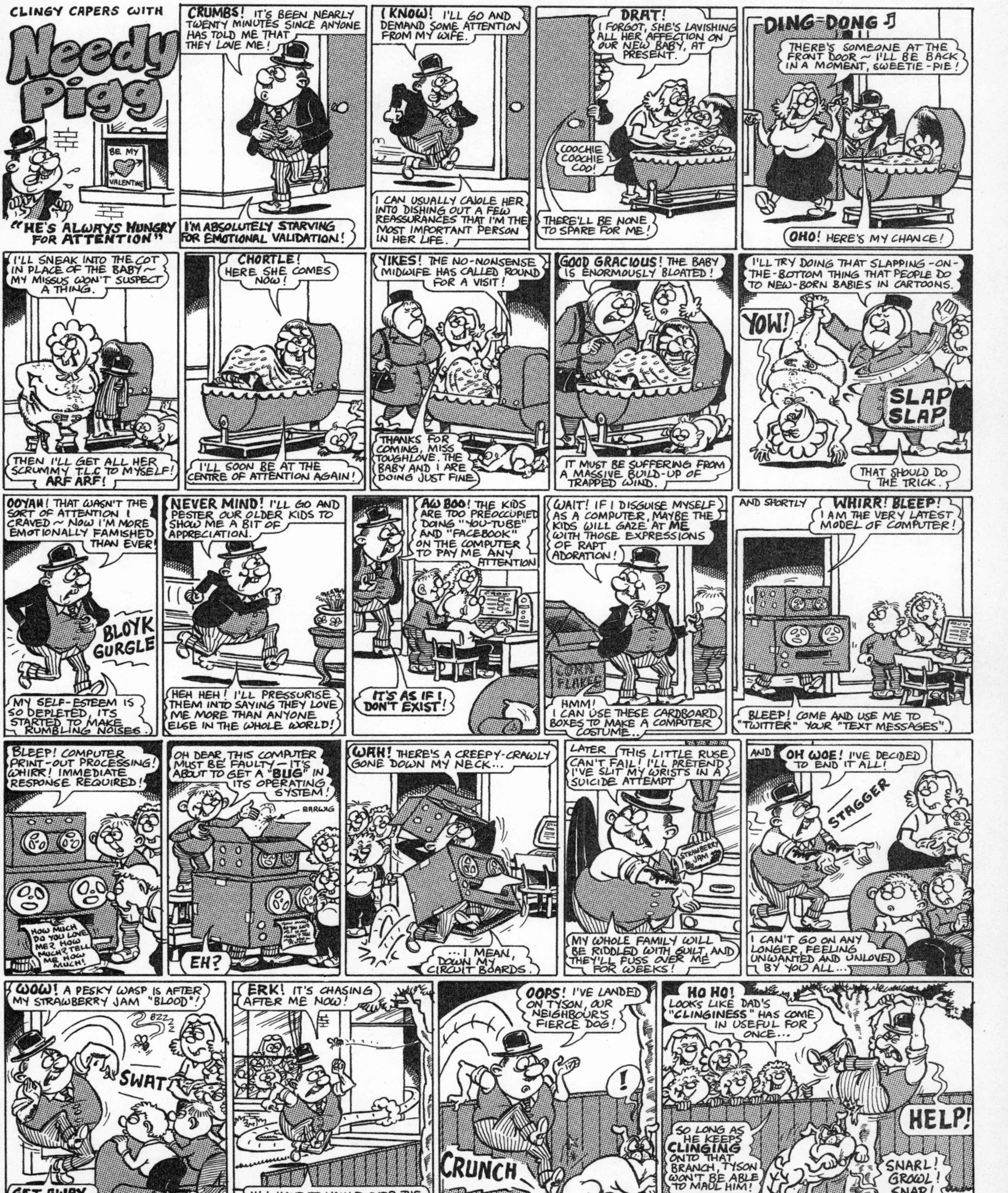
CLINGY CAPERS WITH
Needy Pigg
BE MY VALENTINE
"HE'S ALWAYS HUNGRY FOR ATTENTION"
CRUMBS! IT'S BEEN NEARLY TWENTY MINUTES SINCE ANYONE HAS TOLD ME THAT THEY LOVE ME!
I'M ABSOLUTELY STARVING FOR EMOTIONAL VALIDATION!
I KNOW! I'LL GO AND DEMAND SOME ATTENTION FROM MY WIFE.
I CAN USUALLY CAJOLE HER INTO DISHING OUT A FEW REASSURANCES THAT I'M THE MOST IMPORTANT PERSON IN HER LIFE.
DRAT! I FORGOT, SHE'S LAVISHING ALL HER AFFECTION ON OUR NEW BABY, AT PRESENT.
COOCHIE COOCHIE COO!
THERE'LL BE NONE TO SPARE FOR ME!
DING-DONG
THERE'S SOMEONE AT THE FRONT DOOR ~ I'LL BE BACK IN A MOMENT, SWEETIE-PIE!
OHO! HERE'S MY CHANCE!
I'LL SNEAK INTO THE COT IN PLACE OF THE BABY ~ MY MISSUS WON'T SUSPECT A THING.
THEN I'LL GET ALL HER SCRUMMY T.L.C TO MYSELF! ARF ARF!
CHORTLE! HERE SHE COMES NOW!
I'LL SOON BE AT THE CENTRE OF ATTENTION AGAIN!
YIKES! THE NO-NONSENSE MIDWIFE HAS CALLED ROUND FOR A VISIT!
THANKS FOR COMING, MISS TOUGHLOVE. THE BABY AND I ARE DOING JUST FINE.
GOOD GRACIOUS! THE BABY IS ENORMOUSLY BLOATED!
IT MUST BE SUFFERING FROM A MASSIVE BUILD-UP OF TRAPPED WIND.
I'LL TRY DOING THAT SLAPPING-ON-THE-BOTTOM THING THAT PEOPLE DO TO NEW-BORN BABIES IN CARTOONS.
YOW!
SLAP SLAP
THAT SHOULD DO THE TRICK.
OOYAH! THAT WASN'T THE SORT OF ATTENTION I CRAVED ~ NOW I'M MORE EMOTIONALLY FAMISHED THAN EVER!
BLOYK GURGLE
MY SELF-ESTEEM IS SO DEPLETED, ITS STARTED TO MAKE RUMBLING NOISES.
NEVER MIND! I'LL GO AND PESTER OUR OLDER KIDS TO SHOW ME A BIT OF APPRECIATION.
HEH HEH! I'LL PRESSURISE THEM INTO SAYING THEY LOVE ME MORE THAN ANYONE ELSE IN THE WHOLE WORLD!
AW BOO! THE KIDS ARE TOO PREOCCUPIED DOING "YOU-TUBE" AND "FACEBOOK" ON THE COMPUTER TO PAY ME ANY ATTENTION
IT'S AS IF I DON'T EXIST!
WAIT! IF I DISGUISE MYSELF AS A COMPUTER, MAYBE THE KIDS WILL GAZE AT ME WITH THOSE EXPRESSIONS OF RAPT ADORATION!
CORN FLAKES
HMM! I CAN USE THESE CARDBOARD BOXES TO MAKE A COMPUTER COSTUME...
AND SHORTLY
WHIRR! BLEEP! I AM THE VERY LATEST MODEL OF COMPUTER!
BLEEP! COME AND USE ME TO "TWITTER" YOUR "TEXT MESSAGES".
BLEEP! COMPUTER PRINT-OUT PROCESSING! WHIRR! IMMEDIATE RESPONSE REQUIRED!
HOW MUCH DO YOU LOVE ME? HOW MUCH? TELL ME HOW MUCH!
OH DEAR, THIS COMPUTER MUST BE FAULTY — IT'S ABOUT TO GET A "BUG" IN ITS OPERATING SYSTEM!
EARWIG
EH?
WAH! THERE'S A CREEPY-CRAWLY GONE DOWN MY NECK...
...I MEAN, DOWN MY CIRCUIT BOARDS.
LATER
THIS LITTLE RUSE CAN'T FAIL! I'LL PRETEND I'VE SLIT MY WRISTS IN A SUICIDE ATTEMPT
STRAWBERRY JAM
MY WHOLE FAMILY WILL BE RIDDLED WITH GUILT, AND THEY'LL FUSS OVER ME FOR WEEKS!
AND
OH WOE! I'VE DECIDED TO END IT ALL!
STAGGER
I CAN'T GO ON ANY LONGER, FEELING UNWANTED AND UNLOVED BY YOU ALL...
WOW! A PESKY WASP IS AFTER MY STRAWBERRY JAM "BLOOD"!
BZZ
SWAT
GET AWAY FROM ME, WASP!
ERK! IT'S CHASING AFTER ME NOW!
I'LL HAVE TO VAULT OVER THE FENCE INTO NEXT DOOR'S GARDEN, TO ESCAPE!
OOPS! I'VE LANDED ON TYSON, OUR NEIGHBOUR'S FIERCE DOG!
!
CRUNCH
HO HO! LOOKS LIKE DAD'S "CLINGINESS" HAS COME IN USEFUL FOR ONCE...
SO LONG AS HE KEEPS CLINGING ONTO THAT BRANCH, TYSON WON'T BE ABLE TO MAUL HIM!
HELP!
SNARL! GROWL! SNAP!

The Nolan Sisters's

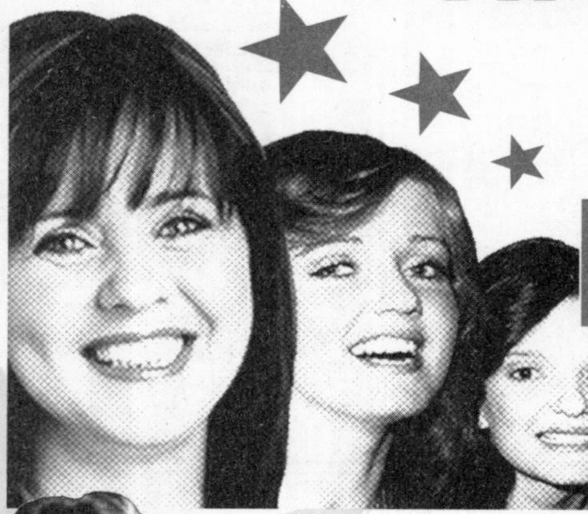

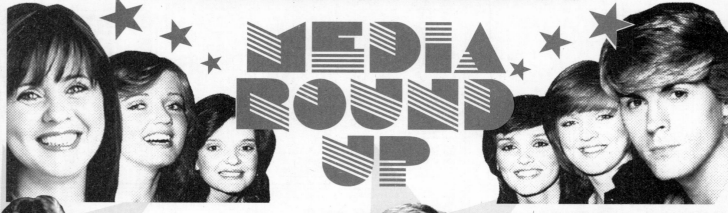

MEDIA ROUND UP

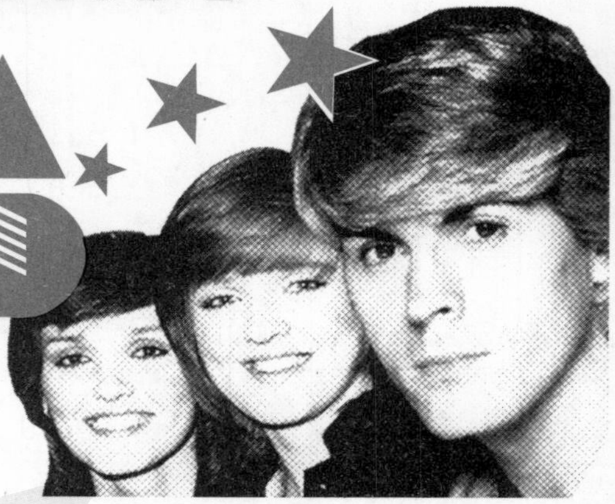

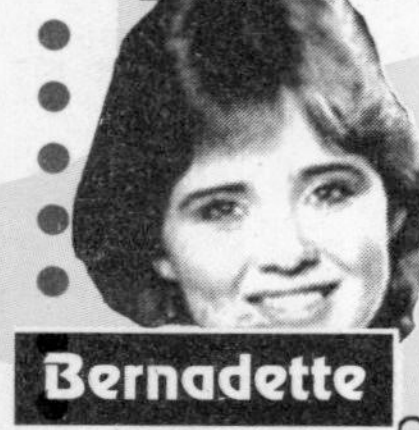
Bernadette

RADIO

IN A MOVE that is set to raise the blood pressure of its listeners, venerable Radio 4 soap *The Archers* is set to air its first scene of bestiality. In the episode, to be broadcast next May, farmer Eddie Grundy will be heard bumming one of his chickens in the bar of the Black Bull. "It's a great plot," says the show's new producer Rupert Golightly. "Eddie loses a bet with Marjorie Antrobus and has to bum the chicken as a forfeit. This episode may ruffle a few feathers, not least of all the ones round the chicken's arse, but The Archers is an everyday story of country life and it has always reflected what goes on in rural communities," he added.

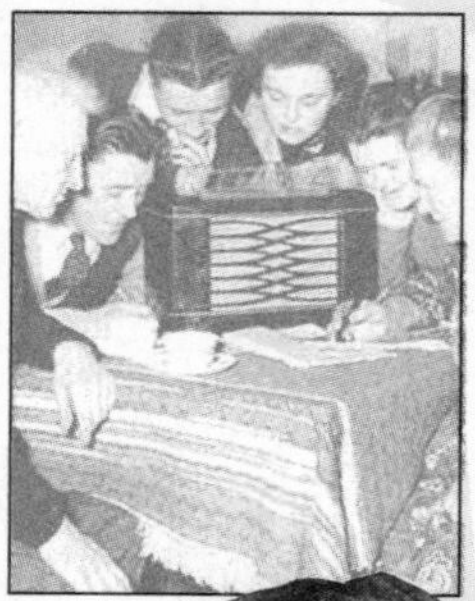

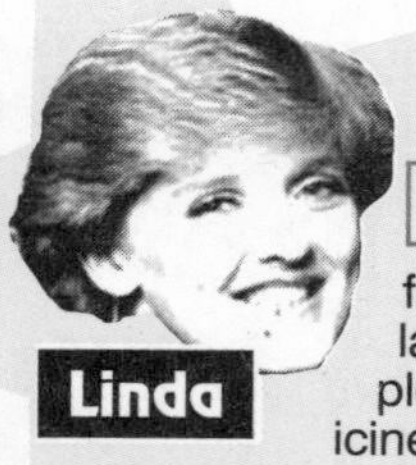
Linda

ADVERTISING

THAT FUCKING meerkat advert is now officially the world's most favourite thing. The fucking advert with its hilarious catchphrase "Simples" beat democracy, medicine and clean drinking water to take the coveted title of Best Thing in the World. The director of the fucking ad, Terry Shitcrumbs, was in New York yesterday to receive a huge gold award from United Nations Secretary General Banksy Moon. "I love that fucking meerkat ad, me," said Moon. "Honestly, when the rat thing says 'simples'" and does that little click, I just piss myself," he added.

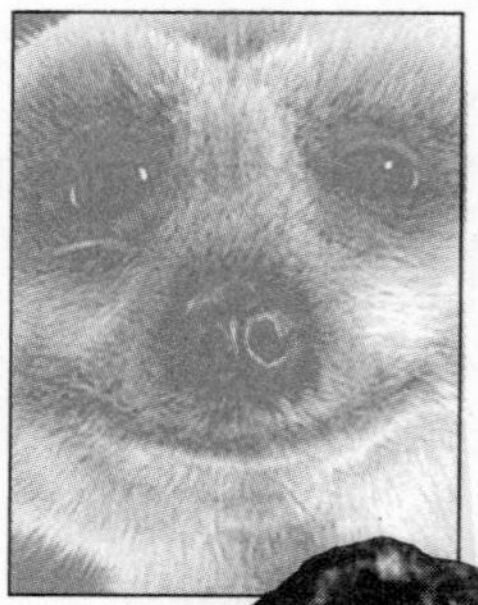

LIFESTYLE

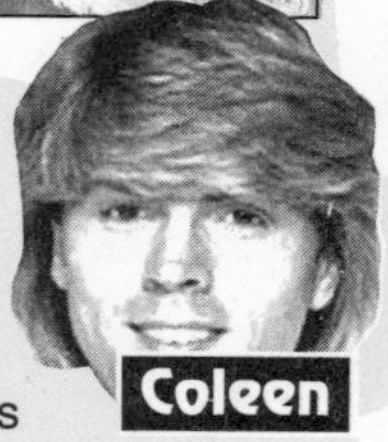
Coleen

AN EXPLOSION in the population of celebrity chefs is causing concern amongst broadcasters, after scientists predicted that there would not be enough studio space on the planet to accommodate them by the year 2015. "40 years ago there was just Fanny Craddock and the Galloping Gourmet," said Office of TV Chef Statistics head Dr Harvey Furniture. "Following the TV cooking boom of the 80s, their numbers started growing exponentially. Soon, there won't be enough ingredients to meet their recipe needs." A report produced by a controversial TV Chef Think Tank suggests that the best way to keep a healthy population of TV chefs is to cull the weak ones, such as James Martin and the one who looks like Rene off *'Allo 'Allo*.

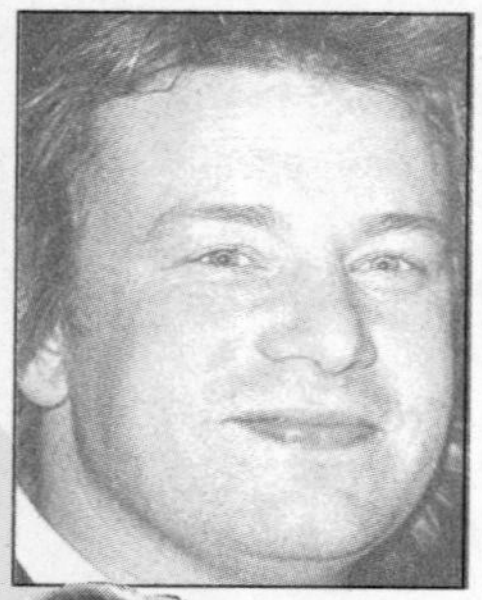

FILM

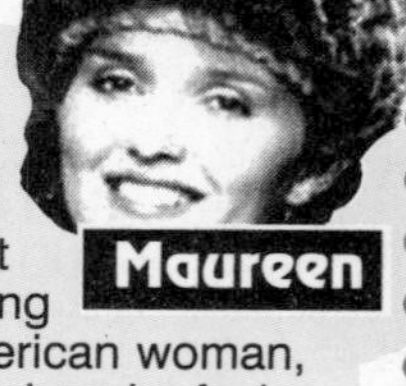
Maureen

AFTER THE commercial failure of his last film *The Boat That Rocked*, writer Richard Curtis has revealed details of his next movie project. "It's about a successful scriptwriter who churns out the same film over and over again where a bumbling Englishman falls for a seemingly unattainable American woman, but is too diffident to tell her how he feels. Bored of this and seeking a new challenge, he decides to write a completely different type of film. However, it bombs at the box office and he is forced to go back to writing the other sort of film," he told Entertainment News. The new film, provisionally entitled *Oh, Gosh! Crumbs!* is set to star Hugh Grant as screenwriter Curtis Richards and Andi McDowell as Roberta Julius, an unattainable American literary agent with whom he falls in love but is too diffident to tell her how he feels.

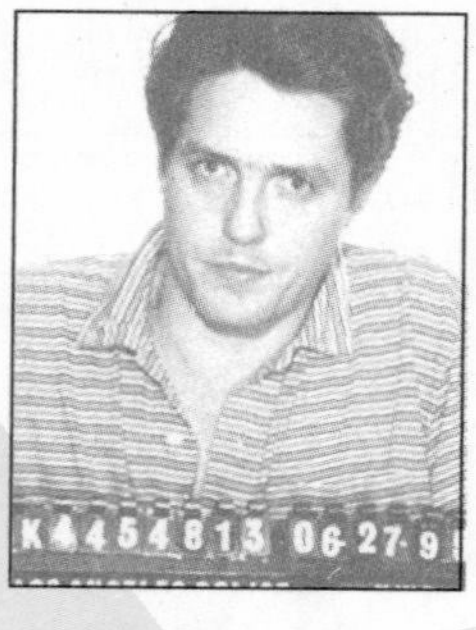
K4454813 06 27 9

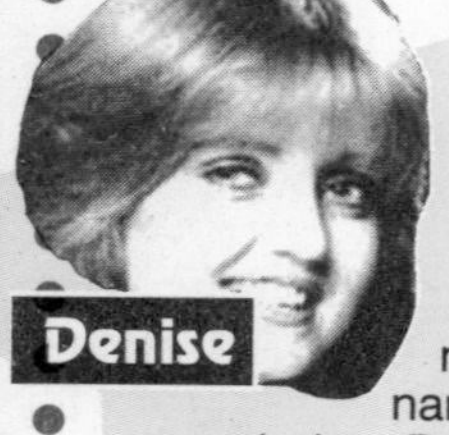
Denise

TV DRAMA

COLIN BAKER has been voted the most popular Dr Who of all time in a survey carried out by Colin Baker. The actor questioned 5 members of his family as to which was their favourite incarnation of the famous timelord, and nearly two thirds named him as their number one choice. Baker, who occupied the Tardis from 1984 to 1986, said he was delighted and honoured with the accolade. "My wife and two of my daughters all thought I was the best," he told reporters. "The other two probably got confused and voted for Tom Baker by mistake. But it doesn't matter, I still won." Baker's findings contradict a survey conducted last year by Sylvester McCoy, which found that 100% of 2 people polled thought Sylvester McCoy was the number one Doctor of all time.

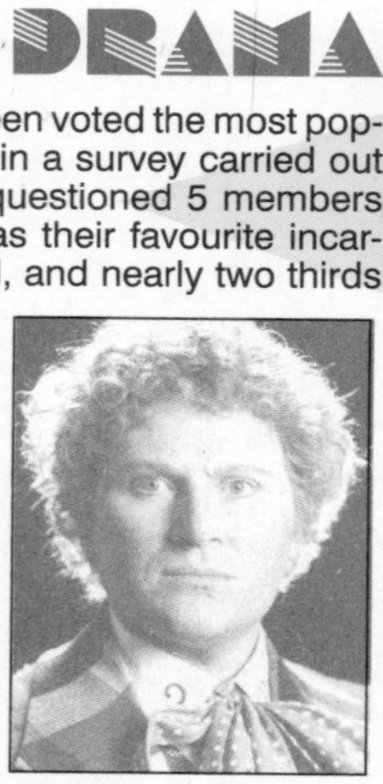

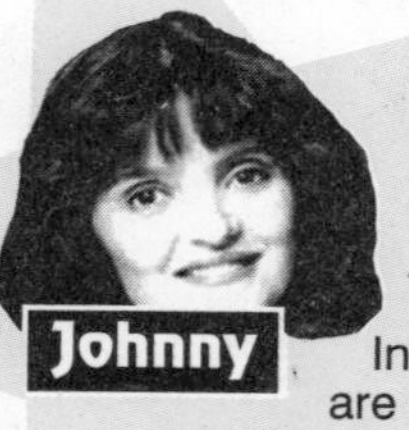
Johnny

CURRENT AFFAIRS

FOLLOWING the Met Office's wildly inaccurate predictions for 2009, which promised an Indian summer followed by a mild winter, the BBC are to experiment with a new weather forecasting system. "We've borrowed a baboon from London Zoo, and we're going to make it wank onto a map of Britain at the end of the news," said BBC head of weather Hampton Mingebandit. "Wherever the spunk lands on the map, that's where the nicest weather is going to be. The new technique might not have a scientific basis, but it's going to be at least as accurate as the current system," he added. "And it'll be more entertaining than watching Rob McElwee farting about."

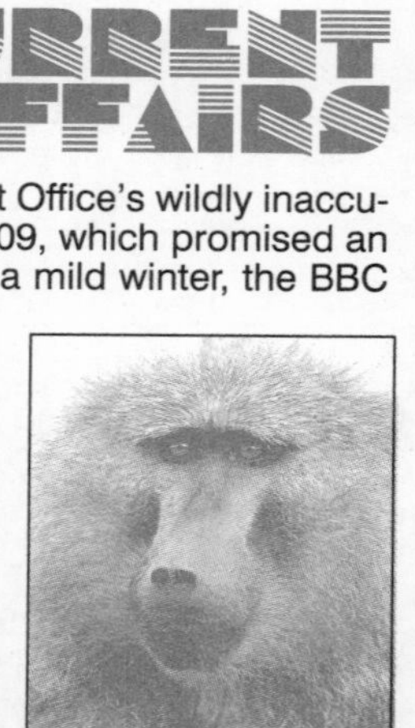

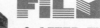

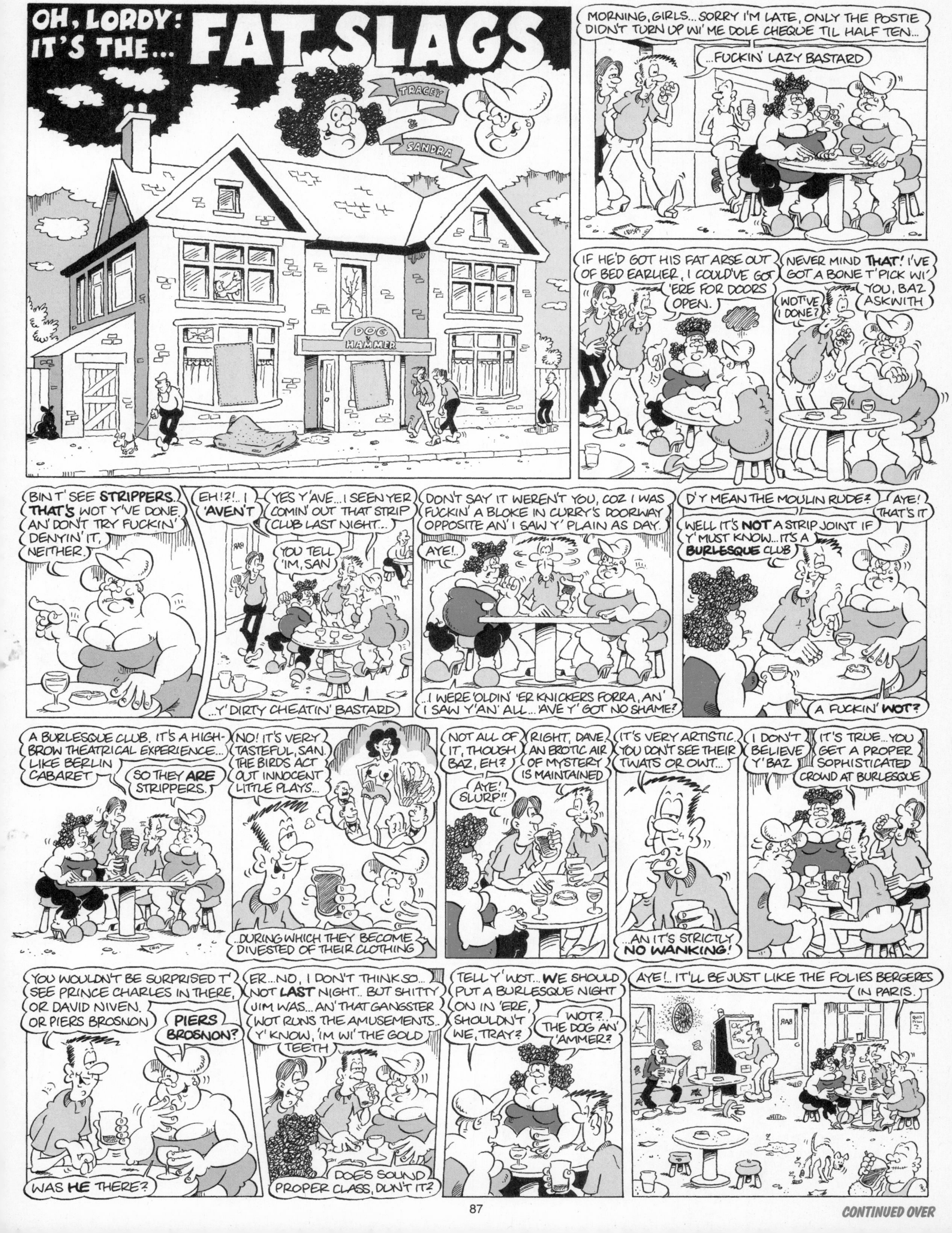
OH, LORDY: IT'S THE... FAT SLAGS
TRACEY
&
SANDRA
DOG & HAMMER
MORNING, GIRLS... SORRY I'M LATE, ONLY THE POSTIE DIDN'T TURN UP WI' ME DOLE CHEQUE TIL HALF TEN...
...FUCKIN' LAZY BASTARD
IF HE'D GOT HIS FAT ARSE OUT OF BED EARLIER, I COULD'VE GOT 'ERE FOR DOORS OPEN.
NEVER MIND THAT! I'VE GOT A BONE T' PICK WI' YOU, BAZ ASKWITH
WOT'VE I DONE?
BIN T' SEE STRIPPERS. THAT'S WOT Y'VE DONE, AN' DON'T TRY FUCKIN' DENYIN' IT, NEITHER.
EH!?!.. I 'AVEN'T
YES Y'AVE... I SEEN YER COMIN' OUT THAT STRIP CLUB LAST NIGHT...
YOU TELL 'IM, SAN
...Y' DIRTY CHEATIN' BASTARD
DON'T SAY IT WEREN'T YOU, COZ I WAS FUCKIN' A BLOKE IN CURRY'S DOORWAY OPPOSITE AN' I SAW Y' PLAIN AS DAY.
AYE!..
...I WERE 'OLDIN' 'ER KNICKERS FORRA, AN' I SAW Y' AN' ALL... 'AVE Y' GOT NO SHAME?
D'Y MEAN THE MOULIN RUDE?
AYE! THAT'S IT
WELL IT'S NOT A STRIP JOINT IF Y' MUST KNOW... IT'S A BURLESQUE CLUB
A FUCKIN' WOT?
A BURLESQUE CLUB. IT'S A HIGH-BROW THEATRICAL EXPERIENCE... LIKE BERLIN CABARET
SO THEY ARE STRIPPERS.
NO! IT'S VERY TASTEFUL, SAN. THE BIRDS ACT OUT INNOCENT LITTLE PLAYS...
...DURING WHICH THEY BECOME DIVESTED OF THEIR CLOTHING
NOT ALL OF IT, THOUGH BAZ, EH?
RIGHT, DAVE. AN EROTIC AIR OF MYSTERY IS MAINTAINED
AYE! SLURP!!
IT'S VERY ARTISTIC. YOU DON'T SEE THEIR TWATS OR OWT...
...AN IT'S STRICTLY NO WANKING!
I DON'T BELIEVE Y' BAZ
IT'S TRUE... YOU GET A PROPER SOPHISTICATED CROWD AT BURLESQUE
YOU WOULDN'T BE SURPRISED T' SEE PRINCE CHARLES IN THERE, OR DAVID NIVEN. OR PIERS BROSNON
PIERS BROSNON?
WAS HE THERE?
ER... NO, I DON'T THINK SO... NOT LAST NIGHT.. BUT SHITTY JIM WAS... AN' THAT GANGSTER WOT RUNS THE AMUSEMENTS.. Y' KNOW, 'IM WI' THE GOLD TEETH
DOES SOUND PROPER CLASS, DUN'T IT?
TELL Y' WOT... WE SHOULD PUT A BURLESQUE NIGHT ON IN 'ERE, SHOULDN'T WE, TRAY?
WOT?.. THE DOG AN' 'AMMER?
AYE!.. IT'LL BE JUST LIKE THE FOLIES BERGERES IN PARIS.

CONTINUED OVER

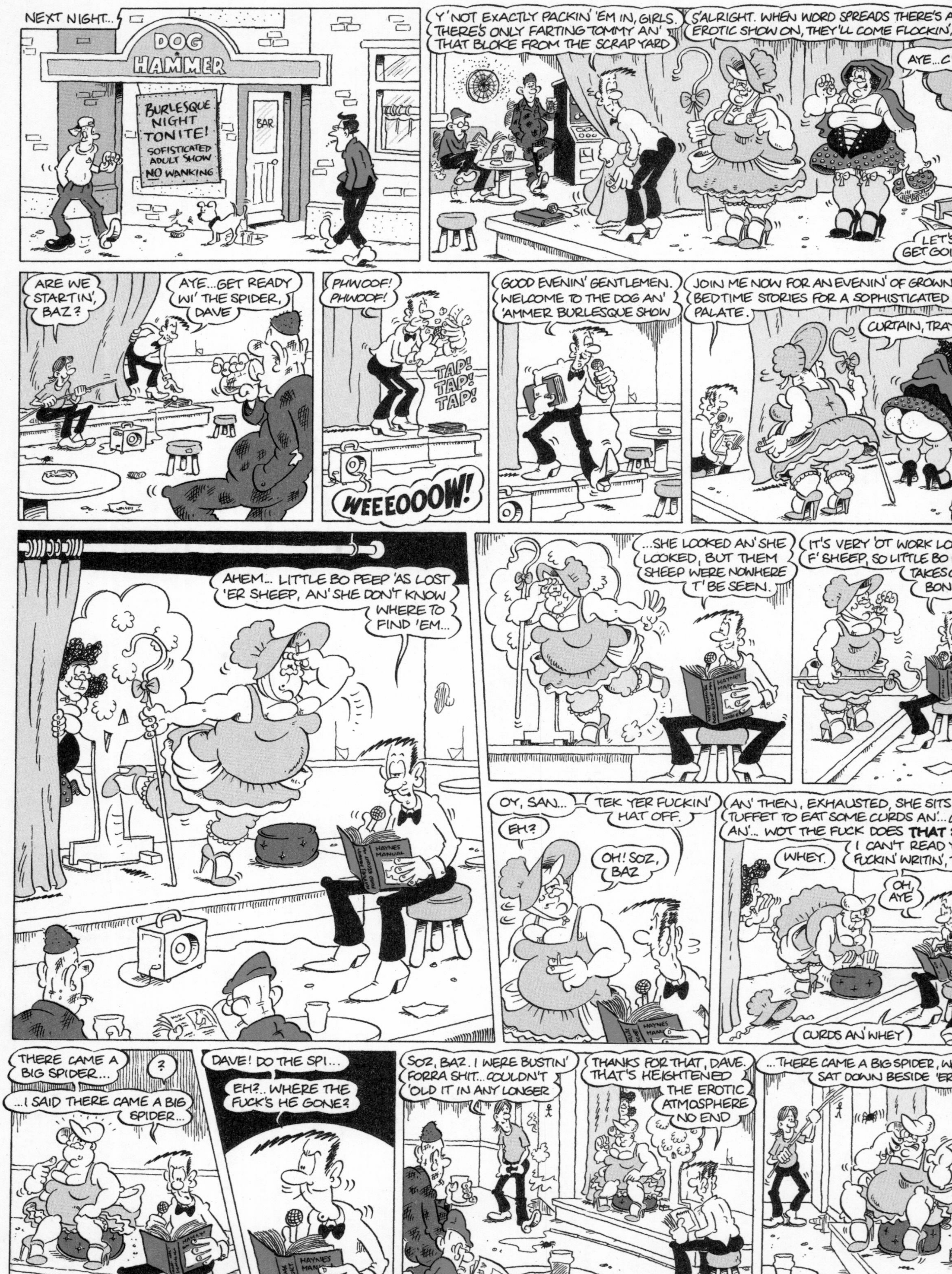
NEXT NIGHT...
DOG HAMMER
BURLESQUE NIGHT TONITE! SOFISTICATED ADULT SHOW NO WANKING
BAR
Y' NOT EXACTLY PACKIN' 'EM IN, GIRLS. THERE'S ONLY FARTING TOMMY AN' THAT BLOKE FROM THE SCRAP YARD
S'ALRIGHT. WHEN WORD SPREADS THERE'S A CLASSY EROTIC SHOW ON, THEY'LL COME FLOCKIN', BAZ.
AYE...C'MON...
LET'S GET GOIN'
ARE WE STARTIN', BAZ?
AYE...GET READY WI' THE SPIDER, DAVE
PHWOOF! PHWOOF!
TAP! TAP! TAP!
WEEEOOOW!
GOOD EVENIN' GENTLEMEN. WELCOME TO THE DOG AN' 'AMMER BURLESQUE SHOW
JOIN ME NOW FOR AN EVENIN' OF GROWN-UP BEDTIME STORIES FOR A SOPHISTICATED ADULT PALATE.
CURTAIN, TRAY
AHEM... LITTLE BO PEEP 'AS LOST 'ER SHEEP, AN' SHE DON'T KNOW WHERE TO FIND 'EM...
HAYNES MANUAL
...SHE LOOKED AN' SHE LOOKED, BUT THEM SHEEP WERE NOWHERE T' BE SEEN.
IT'S VERY 'OT WORK LOOKIN' F' SHEEP, SO LITTLE BO PEEP TAKES OFF 'ER BONNET...
OY, SAN...
TEK YER FUCKIN' HAT OFF.
EH?
OH! SOZ, BAZ
AN' THEN, EXHAUSTED, SHE SITS ON A TUFFET TO EAT SOME CURDS AN'... CURDS AN'... WOT THE FUCK DOES **THAT** SAY? I CAN'T READ YOUR FUCKIN' WRITIN', TRAY.
WHEY.
OH, AYE
CURDS AN' WHEY
THERE CAME A BIG SPIDER...
?
...I SAID THERE CAME A BIG SPIDER...
DAVE! DO THE SPI...
EH?. WHERE THE FUCK'S HE GONE?
SOZ, BAZ. I WERE BUSTIN' FORRA SHIT...COULDN'T 'OLD IT IN ANY LONGER
THANKS FOR THAT, DAVE. THAT'S HEIGHTENED THE EROTIC ATMOSPHERE NO END
...THERE CAME A BIG SPIDER, WOT SAT DOWN BESIDE 'ER...

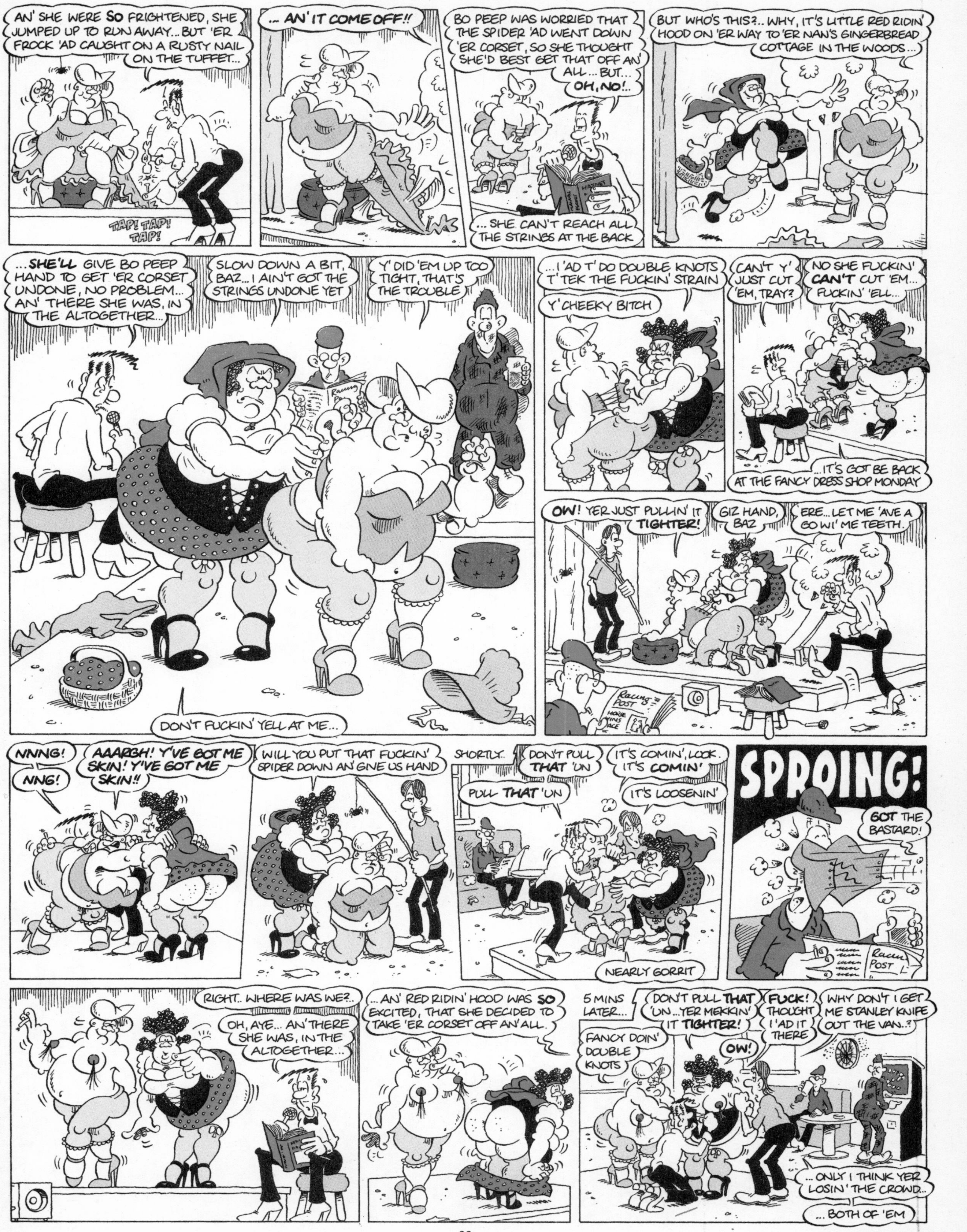
AN' SHE WERE SO FRIGHTENED, SHE JUMPED UP TO RUN AWAY... BUT 'ER FROCK 'AD CAUGHT ON A RUSTY NAIL ON THE TUFFET...
TAP! TAP! TAP!
... AN' IT COME OFF!!
BO PEEP WAS WORRIED THAT THE SPIDER 'AD WENT DOWN 'ER CORSET, SO SHE THOUGHT SHE'D BEST GET THAT OFF AN' ALL... BUT...
OH, NO!..
... SHE CAN'T REACH ALL THE STRINGS AT THE BACK
BUT WHO'S THIS?.. WHY, IT'S LITTLE RED RIDIN' HOOD ON 'ER WAY TO 'ER NAN'S GINGERBREAD COTTAGE IN THE WOODS...
... SHE'LL GIVE BO PEEP HAND TO GET 'ER CORSET UNDONE, NO PROBLEM... AN' THERE SHE WAS, IN THE ALTOGETHER...
SLOW DOWN A BIT, BAZ... I AIN'T GOT THE STRINGS UNDONE YET
Y' DID 'EM UP TOO TIGHT, THAT'S THE TROUBLE
DON'T FUCKIN' YELL AT ME...
... I 'AD T' DO DOUBLE KNOTS T' TEK THE FUCKIN' STRAIN
Y' CHEEKY BITCH
CAN'T Y' JUST CUT 'EM, TRAY?
NO SHE FUCKIN' CAN'T CUT 'EM... FUCKIN' 'ELL...
... IT'S GOT BE BACK AT THE FANCY DRESS SHOP MONDAY
OW! YER JUST PULLIN' IT TIGHTER!
GIZ HAND, BAZ
'ERE... LET ME 'AVE A GO WI' ME TEETH.
RACING POST
NNNG!
NNG!
AAARGH! Y'VE GOT ME SKIN! Y'VE GOT ME SKIN!!
WILL YOU PUT THAT FUCKIN' SPIDER DOWN AN' GIVE US HAND
SHORTLY...
DON'T PULL THAT 'UN
PULL THAT 'UN
IT'S COMIN', LOOK. IT'S COMIN'
IT'S LOOSENIN'
NEARLY GORRIT
SPROING!
GOT THE BASTARD!
RACING POST
RIGHT.. WHERE WAS WE?..
OH, AYE... AN' THERE SHE WAS, IN THE ALTOGETHER...
... AN' RED RIDIN' HOOD WAS SO EXCITED, THAT SHE DECIDED TO TAKE 'ER CORSET OFF AN' ALL.
5 MINS LATER...
DON'T PULL THAT 'UN... YER MEKKIN' IT TIGHTER!
FANCY DOIN' DOUBLE KNOTS
OW!
FUCK! THOUGHT I 'AD IT THERE
WHY DON'T I GET ME STANLEY KNIFE OUT THE VAN..?
... ONLY I THINK YER LOSIN' THE CROWD...
... BOTH OF 'EM

CONTINUED OVER

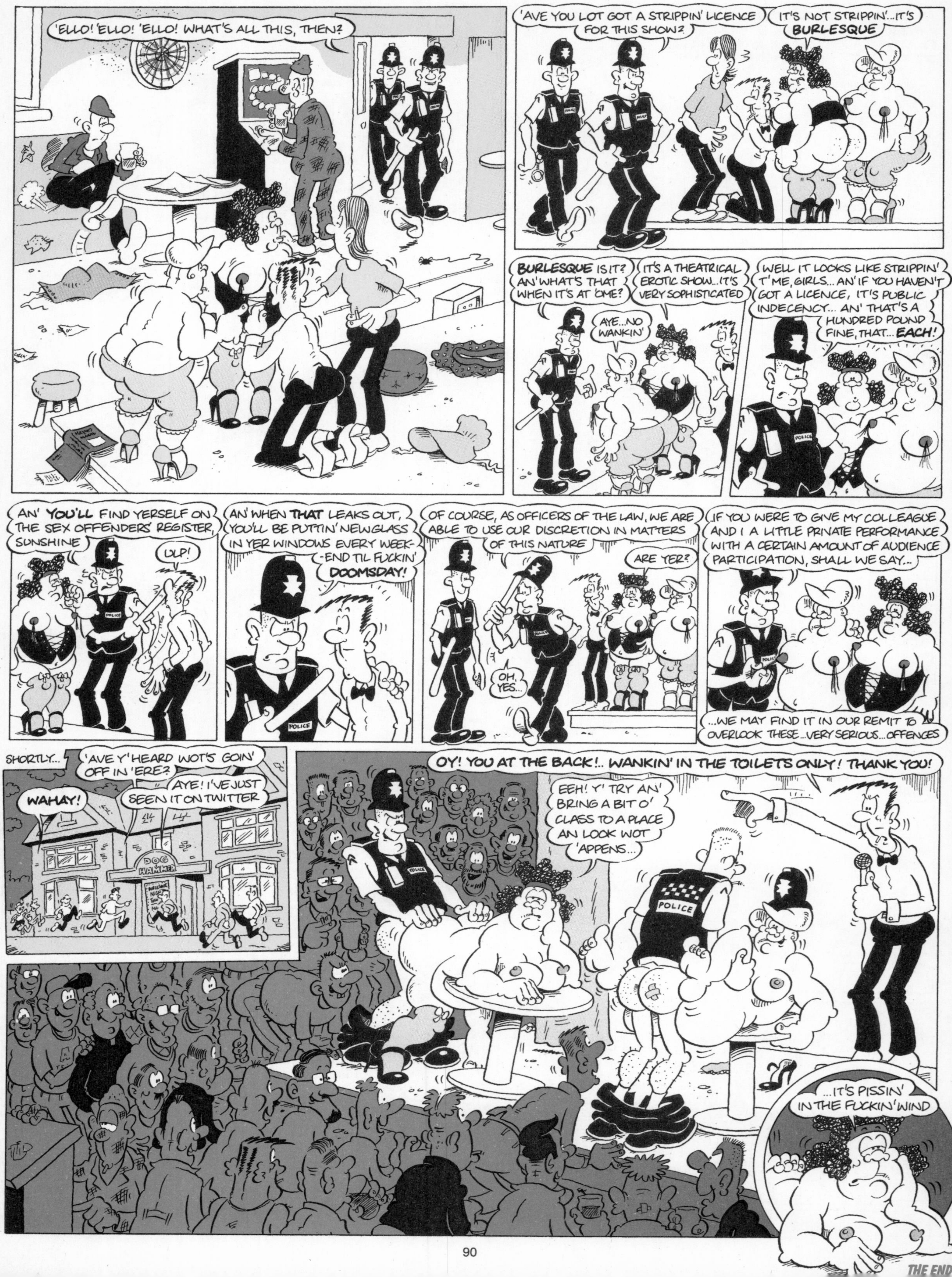
'ELLO! 'ELLO! 'ELLO! WHAT'S ALL THIS, THEN?
'AVE YOU LOT GOT A STRIPPIN' LICENCE FOR THIS SHOW?
IT'S NOT STRIPPIN'...IT'S BURLESQUE
BURLESQUE IS IT? AN' WHAT'S THAT WHEN IT'S AT 'OME?
IT'S A THEATRICAL EROTIC SHOW...IT'S VERY SOPHISTICATED
AYE...NO WANKIN'
WELL IT LOOKS LIKE STRIPPIN' T'ME, GIRLS... AN' IF YOU HAVEN'T GOT A LICENCE, IT'S PUBLIC INDECENCY... AN' THAT'S A HUNDRED POUND FINE, THAT... EACH!
AN' YOU'LL FIND YERSELF ON THE SEX OFFENDERS' REGISTER, SUNSHINE
ULP!
AN' WHEN THAT LEAKS OUT, YOU'LL BE PUTTIN' NEW GLASS IN YER WINDOWS EVERY WEEK-END TIL FUCKIN' DOOMSDAY!
OF COURSE, AS OFFICERS OF THE LAW, WE ARE ABLE TO USE OUR DISCRETION IN MATTERS OF THIS NATURE
ARE YER?
OH, YES...
...IF YOU WERE TO GIVE MY COLLEAGUE AND I A LITTLE PRIVATE PERFORMANCE WITH A CERTAIN AMOUNT OF AUDIENCE PARTICIPATION, SHALL WE SAY...
...WE MAY FIND IT IN OUR REMIT TO OVERLOOK THESE...VERY SERIOUS...OFFENCES
SHORTLY...
'AVE Y' HEARD WOT'S GOIN' OFF IN 'ERE?
AYE! I'VE JUST SEEN IT ON TWITTER
WAHAY!
DOG HAMMER
POLICE
OY! YOU AT THE BACK!.. WANKIN' IN THE TOILETS ONLY! THANK YOU!
EEH! Y' TRY AN' BRING A BIT O' CLASS TO A PLACE AN LOOK WOT 'APPENS...
...IT'S PISSIN' IN THE FUCKIN' WIND
THE END

"Bigotgate" woman to launch perfume

GILLIAN DUFFY, the woman at the centre of the "Bigotgate" scandal during the election campaign, is to launch her own range of perfumes.

Mrs Duffy shot to fame when a candid recording of former Prime Minister Gordon Brown referring to her as "a bigoted woman" was broadcast by Sky News. She is believed to have received a £20 million advance from a major scent manufacturer for the rights to her new perfume, Umbrage.

Speaking from her modest Rochdale home, Mrs Duffy, 65, told us: "Ever since I was a little girl I've wanted to release my own range of celebrity colognes. Being slagged off behind my back by Mr Brown made me into a household name, and Umbrage is the result."

"It's a very subtle fragrance, combining high tones of lavender and sandalwood with undercurrents of juniper and a hint of lemongrass. It's very me," she added.

Former Labour voter Duffy is thought to have raked in an incredible £500 million in endorsements and advertising deals since her on-air spat with the ex-premier. PR guru Max Clifford reckons there's plenty more where that came from. "If she plays her cards right, Gillian could easily become the first shitstorm-in-a-teacup billionaire," he told us.

As well as Mrs Duffy's perfume, a range of lingerie, several children's books, an autobiography and a CD album of her favourite songs are all selling like hot-cakes on the high street. In August, she is flying to America to begin a 100-date tour on the lucrative US lecture circuit.

And while she's stateside, the Rochdale grandmother is expected to take time out to visit Hollywood and finalise a seven-figure deal with Steven Spielberg. The *Jaws* director is planning to shoot a blockbuster biopic about her life, starring Kiera Knightley as Mrs Duffy and Morgan Freeman as Gordon Brown.

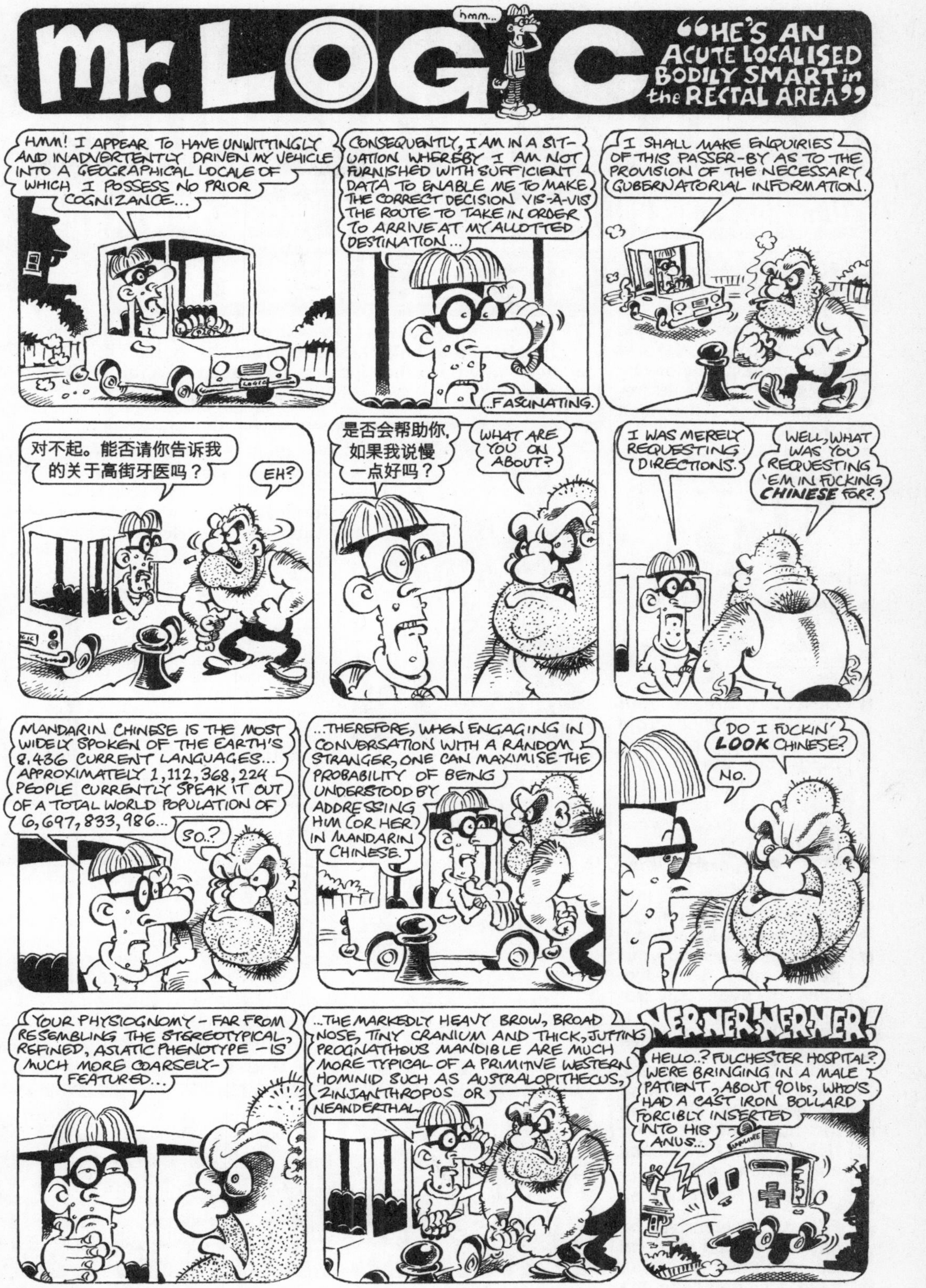
hmm...
Mr. LOGIC
"HE'S AN ACUTE LOCALISED BODILY SMART in the RECTAL AREA"
HMM! I APPEAR TO HAVE UNWITTINGLY AND INADVERTENTLY DRIVEN MY VEHICLE INTO A GEOGRAPHICAL LOCALE OF WHICH I POSSESS NO PRIOR COGNIZANCE...
CONSEQUENTLY, I AM IN A SITUATION WHEREBY I AM NOT FURNISHED WITH SUFFICIENT DATA TO ENABLE ME TO MAKE THE CORRECT DECISION VIS-A-VIS THE ROUTE TO TAKE IN ORDER TO ARRIVE AT MY ALLOTTED DESTINATION...
...FASCINATING.
I SHALL MAKE ENQUIRIES OF THIS PASSER-BY AS TO THE PROVISION OF THE NECESSARY GUBERNATORIAL INFORMATION.
对不起。能否请你告诉我的关于高街牙医吗？
EH?
是否会帮助你，如果我说慢一点好吗？
WHAT ARE YOU ON ABOUT?
I WAS MERELY REQUESTING DIRECTIONS.
WELL, WHAT WAS YOU REQUESTING 'EM IN FUCKING CHINESE FOR?
MANDARIN CHINESE IS THE MOST WIDELY SPOKEN OF THE EARTH'S 8,436 CURRENT LANGUAGES... APPROXIMATELY 1,112,368,224 PEOPLE CURRENTLY SPEAK IT OUT OF A TOTAL WORLD POPULATION OF 6,697,833,986...
SO..?
...THEREFORE, WHEN ENGAGING IN CONVERSATION WITH A RANDOM STRANGER, ONE CAN MAXIMISE THE PROBABILITY OF BEING UNDERSTOOD BY ADDRESSING HIM (OR HER) IN MANDARIN CHINESE.
DO I FUCKIN' LOOK CHINESE?
NO.
YOUR PHYSIOGNOMY - FAR FROM RESEMBLING THE STEREOTYPICAL, REFINED, ASIATIC PHENOTYPE - IS MUCH MORE COARSELY-FEATURED...
...THE MARKEDLY HEAVY BROW, BROAD NOSE, TINY CRANIUM AND THICK, JUTTING PROGNATHOUS MANDIBLE ARE MUCH MORE TYPICAL OF A PRIMITIVE WESTERN HOMINID SUCH AS AUSTRALOPITHECUS, ZINJANTHROPUS OR NEANDERTHAL...
NERNER! NERNER!
HELLO..? FULCHESTER HOSPITAL? WE'RE BRINGING IN A MALE PATIENT, ABOUT 90lbs, WHO'S HAD A CAST IRON BOLLARD FORCIBLY INSERTED INTO HIS ANUS...

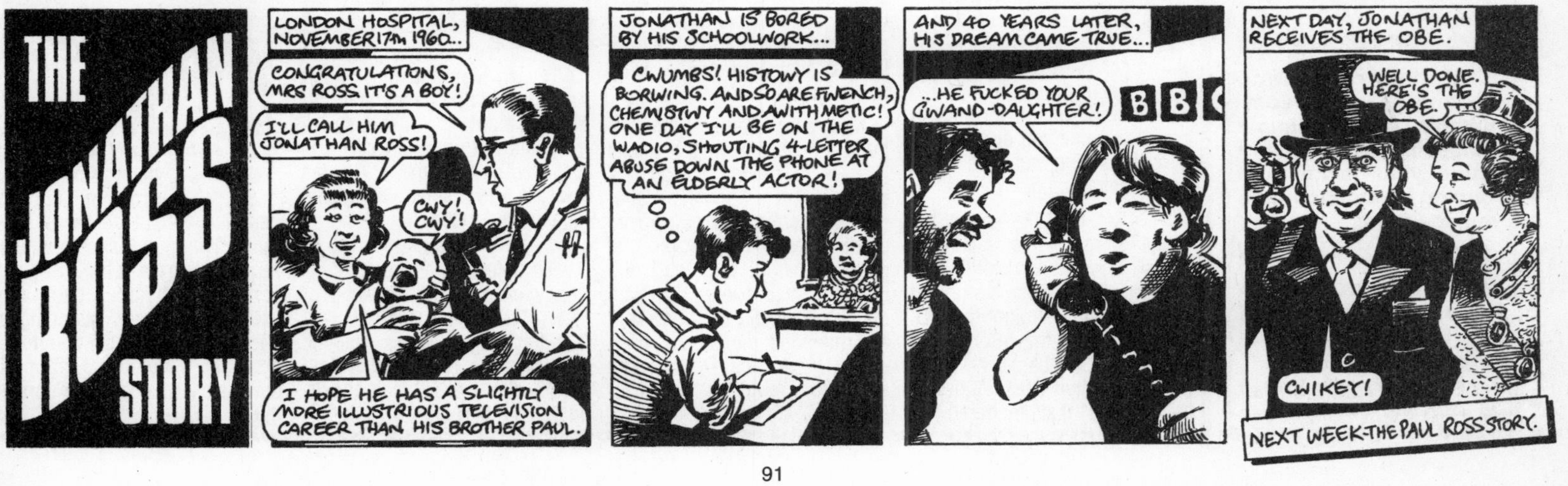
THE JONATHAN ROSS STORY
LONDON HOSPITAL, NOVEMBER 17th 1960...
CONGRATULATIONS, MRS ROSS. IT'S A BOY!
I'LL CALL HIM JONATHAN ROSS!
CWY! CWY!
I HOPE HE HAS A SLIGHTLY MORE ILLUSTRIOUS TELEVISION CAREER THAN HIS BROTHER PAUL.
JONATHAN IS BORED BY HIS SCHOOLWORK...
CWUMBS! HISTOWY IS BORWING. AND SO ARE FWENCH, CHEMISTWY AND AWITHMETIC! ONE DAY I'LL BE ON THE WADIO, SHOUTING 4-LETTER ABUSE DOWN THE PHONE AT AN ELDERLY ACTOR!
AND 40 YEARS LATER, HIS DREAM CAME TRUE...
...HE FUCKED YOUR GWAND-DAUGHTER!
BBC
NEXT DAY, JONATHAN RECEIVES THE OBE.
WELL DONE. HERE'S THE OBE.
CWIKEY!
NEXT WEEK-THE PAUL ROSS STORY.

Letterbocks

VIZ COMIC, PO Box 841, Whitley Bay, NE26 9EQ | letters@viz.co.uk

FOOTBALL commentators. When a player is mouthing off at the referee, make people think you are cleverer than you actually are by insisting that he is 'remonstrating' rather than arguing.

R Clemence, e-mail

Top Tips

GIRLS. Recreate your favourite scenes from *Sex & The City* by strapping your tits to your knees and going to a café to talk utter bollocks with three of your mates.

Kirk Jones, e-mail

A DOUBLE oven mitt draped over your dog's back makes ideal 'saddle bags' enabling your pet to carry items like cans of beer, telly remote controls, etc.

Steve White, e-mail

EAST Sussex Council. Save money on cleaning up grafitti by changing the name of the River Uck to the River Fuck and be done with.

Christina Martin, e-mail

FELLAS. Pretend to be gay so you can befriend lesbian couples. Then have an affair with the cute one.

M Butch, e-mail

FOOL the police into thinking you have committed a crime by simply concealing one hand inside your jacket and running away each time you see them.

Michael Colling, e-mail

WIVES of darts players. Put an oche in front of the toilet to minimise careless spraying.

Leftin Frefall, e-mail

STAR LETTER

IF ornithologists are so scared of birds that they have to build hides to avoid being seen by them, why don't they just stay at home and shut the curtains?

Rob Chingford, e-mail

I MET the comedian Arthur Smith at a house party in Finchley in the early 90s and he seemed like quite a nice bloke. However, I am going to reserve judgement until I've met him a few more times.

Steven Chambers, e-mail

I READ in the paper that 42 people are killed in accidents on South Africa's roads every day. Why don't they simply get a bus with 42 murderers in it and drive it off a cliff each morning? That way, the roads would be perfectly safe for everyone else for the rest of the day.

Ralph Gonads, Goole

WHEN it came to the taboo issue of death, my nan used to always say 'You just don't know the day.' Well I'm afraid she's wrong. My day is the 21st of July, 2014.

S Porter, Death Row Mississippi State Pen.

I CAN'T help thinking that these so-called 'copycat killers' are over reacting. When I was in the 5th year at school, I sat next to Roy Sneer , and he was always copying my maths answers. Although I found it slightly annoying, I never felt the urge to murder him.

Tony Fenlon, e-mail

ONE OF my mates recently confessed that whilst hung over, he resorted to a drawing of the Fat Slags as a visual stimulus for masturbating. Have any readers resorted to material less erotic than this when knocking one out?

P Gorman, e-mail

JUST because Russell Crowe is a fat, cantankerous Antipodean twat doesn't make him a bad actor. It's his acting that does that.

T Rustling, e-mail

SO David Cameron is claiming that his new government is going to be 'radical'. Since when was that allowed? It seems like ther's one rule for cobbled together coalitions of convenience and another for violent religeois fundamentalists. And another for the rest of us, I shouldn't wonder.

N Barnard, Willesden

WHILE working the other day, I was listening to a jazz station on the radio when the Dave Brubeck tune *Take 5* came on. So I did just that. And a very nice rest it was too. Have any other readers had similar experiences where they have done what they were told by a piece of music?

S. Bradley, Southampton

* Well, readers, have YOU followed the orders of a piece of music? Perhaps you've done a stupid gait after listening to Walk Like An Egyptian by the Bangles, or maybe you've lept from a bridge after you heard Van Halan's Jump. Did you inflate a tyre on your bike after listening to Elvis Costello's Pump It Up? Write in to the usual address and let us know.

WIZARDS' hats are really pointy, and so are policemen's. If JK Rowling had put wizard police in her Harry Potter stories, just think how pointy their hats would have been.

M Plank, Luton

TODAY I discovered that if you put the word 'banana' in a string of hahas, no one notices the difference. For two days now I have been texting

EXECUTIVE DECISION

HOLLYWOOD actor STEVEN SEAGAL's films are to be humanely destroyed after an investigation by Trading Standards concluded that they were 'not fit for purpose'. And the landmark court ruling could pave the way for the destruction of the back catalogues of other D-list action movie stars.

Seagal held unfussy cinema goers' attention for up to an hour-and-a-half in the 1990s with a series of improbable action films that usually involved a seemingly spiritual former CIA operative punching and kicking a never-ending succession of mullet-haired thugs.

failure

But Seagal's later failure to secure a new studio distribution deal saw him release a string of truly appalling 'straight to DVD' films in which the 58-year-old actor could be barely arsed to mouth his own lines. And it is these films that triggered an investigation by Trading Standards after a complaint was made by a member of the public that they were neither films not entertainment.

Seagal's defence team argued that it was in the public interest to be fed a constant barrage of superficial scenarios where eastern European criminals would be kicked and punched about the head and body by their client. However, the panel upheld the complaint and deemed films such as *Mercenary for Justice*, *Fight of Fury* and *Driven to Kill* as "not fit for purpose".

By our straight-to-video correspondent
ERNEST WHITELEY & Co.

The films, including unsold DVD, .avi files and the master tapes will all be incinerated, although a date for their destruction has not yet been set. It is believed that Seagal, a 7th dan martial arts master, will appeal against the ruling.

box

His defence attorney has already enlisted the services of Jean-Claude Van Damme, Dolf Lundgren and Wings Hauser, who fear the ruling could lead to a similar fate for their shockingly poor film output.

Seagal ~ films to be humanely destroyed, say bosses

Seagal was not in court to hear the verdict as he is currently filming in Bulgaria, where he is playing a retired Special Forces agent forced back into action kicking and punching a succession of people about the head and body after a group of terrorists kill his friend or something.

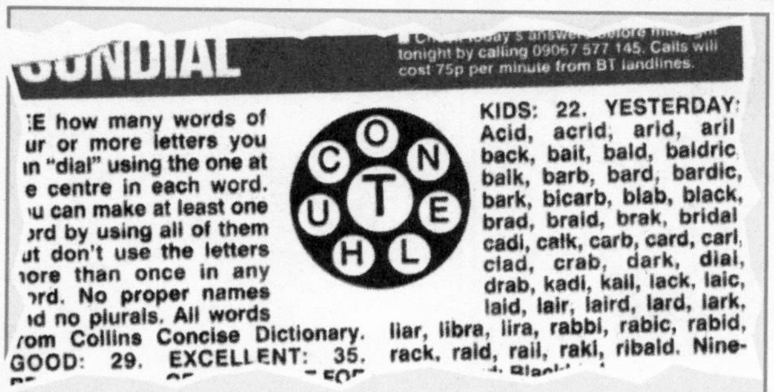

SUNDIAL

Check today's answers before phone in tonight by calling 09067 577 145. Calls will cost 75p per minute from BT landlines.

SEE how many words of four or more letters you can make in "dial" using the one at the centre in each word. You can make at least one word by using all of them but don't use the letters more than once in any word. No proper names and no plurals. All words from Collins Concise Dictionary. GOOD: 29. EXCELLENT: 35.

KIDS: 22. YESTERDAY: Acid, acrid, arid, aril, back, bait, bald, baldric, balk, barb, bard, bardic, bark, bicarb, blab, black, brad, braid, brak, bridal, cadi, calk, carb, card, carl, clad, crab, dark, dial, drab, kadi, kail, lack, laic, laid, lair, laird, lard, lark, liar, libra, lira, rabbi, rabic, rabid, rack, raid, rail, raki, ribald. Nine-...

I HAVE been enjoying the Sun's 'Sundial' puzzle with my mum since childhood, providing some healthy competition between us. The mood was somewhat soured recently in our household when it became apparent that, due to the longevity of the game, new depths were being plumbed in search of words they'd yet to use. I got it within ten seconds, unsurprisingly. Just ahead of my mum.

Andy Slocombe, e-mail

hahahahahahahbananahaha to people and no one has noticed.

M Livingstone, e-mail

I RECENTLY discovered that my local priest is not a paedophile. Can any of your readers beat that?

Maurice East, e-mail

* *Well, readers, CAN you beat Mr East's non-paedophile priest? Maybe your postie isn't a thief, or perhaps you know a copper who's not a racist. You might even have met a builder who hasn't rifled through your wife's underwear draw and put a pair of her knickers on her head.*

WHAT'S the point in having a Queen Mother Chase in horse racing? It's not going to be very difficult for them to catch a 101 year old woman. And a dead one at that. Surely a Usain Bolt chase would be far more entertaining and certainly last longer.

H Woodpecker, Crewe

I THINK our star the Sun is highly overrated. At least the Moon gives a bit of light off at night. The Sun only shines in the daytime, when it's light anyway.

Alan Skewer, e-mail

REMEMBER how *The Really Wild Show* used to bang on about how ants were the strongest animals in the world? Well, I'm in Afghanistan at the moment, and I've just watched 6 indigenous fire ants attempting to lift half a polo mint between them and failing miserably. Does anyone share my sense of outrage at being lied to by terry Nutkins and Michaela Strachan for so many years?

Jimbob, e-mail

I HAVE a friend who is the spitting double of Steve Guttenberg out of the *Police Academy* films, but I've never seen anyone ask him for his autograph.

Adrian, e-mail

I READ today that a British stamp has just sold for £400,000. Well, if the Royal Mail think they are offering value for money they can think again. I'm not paying 20 years' wages to send my nephew in Gloucester a bithday card.

Eugene Guthbert, Bristol

COULD you please print 'Ste Porter is about to have a bath' on your Letterbocks page? It's just that I don't have a Facebook account, so I've no way of letting everyone know such mundane, pointless and tedious facts.

Stephen Porter, e-mail

ARE you aware that Big Vern is moonlighting as a plain clothes cop in the Ukraine? The attached pic shows him in action. Are his underworld associates aware he is an undercover cop?

Paul Atherton, Blackburn

COULD everyone from the South East please tell me where they plan to holiday this year so I can make other arrangements?

Mr Burns, e-mail

BADLY DRAWN CURTAINS

THOSE DON'T LOOK ANYTHING LIKE REAL CURTAINS.

NO. AND THEY'RE NOT EVEN SHUT PROPERLY EITHER.

Cox, not cocks!

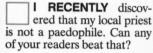

The page that's about SCIENCE, not COCKS!

" Hello, I'm **BRIAN COX**, I look like I've just got off stage but don't let that fool you. I'm a serious scientist. I'm here today to answer the general public's science questions and hopefully expand your knowledge of life and the Universe. Remember though, please no questions about cocks or male genitalia, let's keep it strictly science! "

Hello Brian,

THE guys down the pub tell me that Pioneer 10 was the first man-made object to leave the solar system and is now believed to be passing through the heliosphere. I heard that it could take another 1.7 million years to reach the nearest star which may have planets in its orbit that harbour life. The probe contains directions to our solar system and earth's whereabouts in relation to other planets as well as records and proof of our civilsation. Don't you think aliens will all think we have small cocks when they look at the picture of a naked man that was sent up with it? As it took off in the late early 70s shouldn't they have taken a picture of King Dong or John Holmes instead to make us look better?

John, Leeds

HEY, less of the cock talk! I'll let that one go for now, but you have to pull you up on one thing. I checked in my big book of science and there is no such thing as Pioneer 10 or the heliosphere things, you must must be mistaken. I tell you who was a pioneer though, Marshall Jefferson who harnessed the underground house groove of Chicago and made it his own with driving bass grooves and 4-4 rhythm!

Hello Brian,

I WORK in a sorting office in Morecambe and am a big fan of string theory. At lot of the guys on my shift think negative energy could be used to stablise shortcuts through space time. If that is possible, do you think if you went back in time with a hard-on it would never go soft again?

Geovanni, Morecambe

HEY, stop talking about men's bits!... it's getting a bit tiring now. As for string theory, I think must be confused because I've never heard of it. I asked some of my friends who work at the Hadron Collider and they say there is no such thing. The one string I know is Strings of Life by Derrick May, whose seminal production helped put together an early techno classic! What a tune!

Hello Brian,

i'M A professor in quantum physics and work part-time collecting trolleys at Morrisons. Why is it that space travel is measured in light years, but plasma TV's and erect penises are measured in inches whereas a defender's loss of pace is measured in yards?

Barry, Wigan

PLEASE don't say 'erect penis'. I think I know this one – Light Years was an album by Jamiroquoi. I once did the warm up for him at Manchester Apollo, it was before the Labour Party nicked our sing and made us look like twats.

TOP TIPS

MAKE it appear that you have twice as many things as you actually have by standing them all in front of a mirror.

N Bohr, London

ENGLISH Defence League members. When holding signs reading 'Ban The Burka,' you might want to reconsider wearing a balaclava so as not to appear overly hypocritical.

Johnny Adair, e-mail

MAKE passers-by think your dog is a robot by feeding it a roll of tin foil before taking it for a dump in the local park.

David Milner, Durham

FAT, balding blokes in your 50s. Don't buy Porche 911s as you may look a bit of a twat when struggling to climb out of them at Tesco petrol stations.

Nick Bullen, e-mail

LADIES. Prevent the embarrassment of accidentally tucking your dress into your knickers by sewing 5kg weights in all your dress hems.

Lemonjif, e-mail

AN AIRPORT luggage carousel is ideal is ideal for serving sushi to giants.

Tom, e-mail

CONVINCE your neighbours that you have had a bump in your car by sprinkling torn-up red and yellow fruit gums outside your house where you normally park.

Nick Gibson, e-mail

SHIFT workers. Can't get to sleep during the day because it's too light? Simply take a wind-up torch to bed, turn it on and wind the handle the wrong way.

Patrick Brogan, e-mail

MAKE it appear that you have an infinite number of things by placing them directly inbetween two mirrors parallel to each other.

N Bohr, London

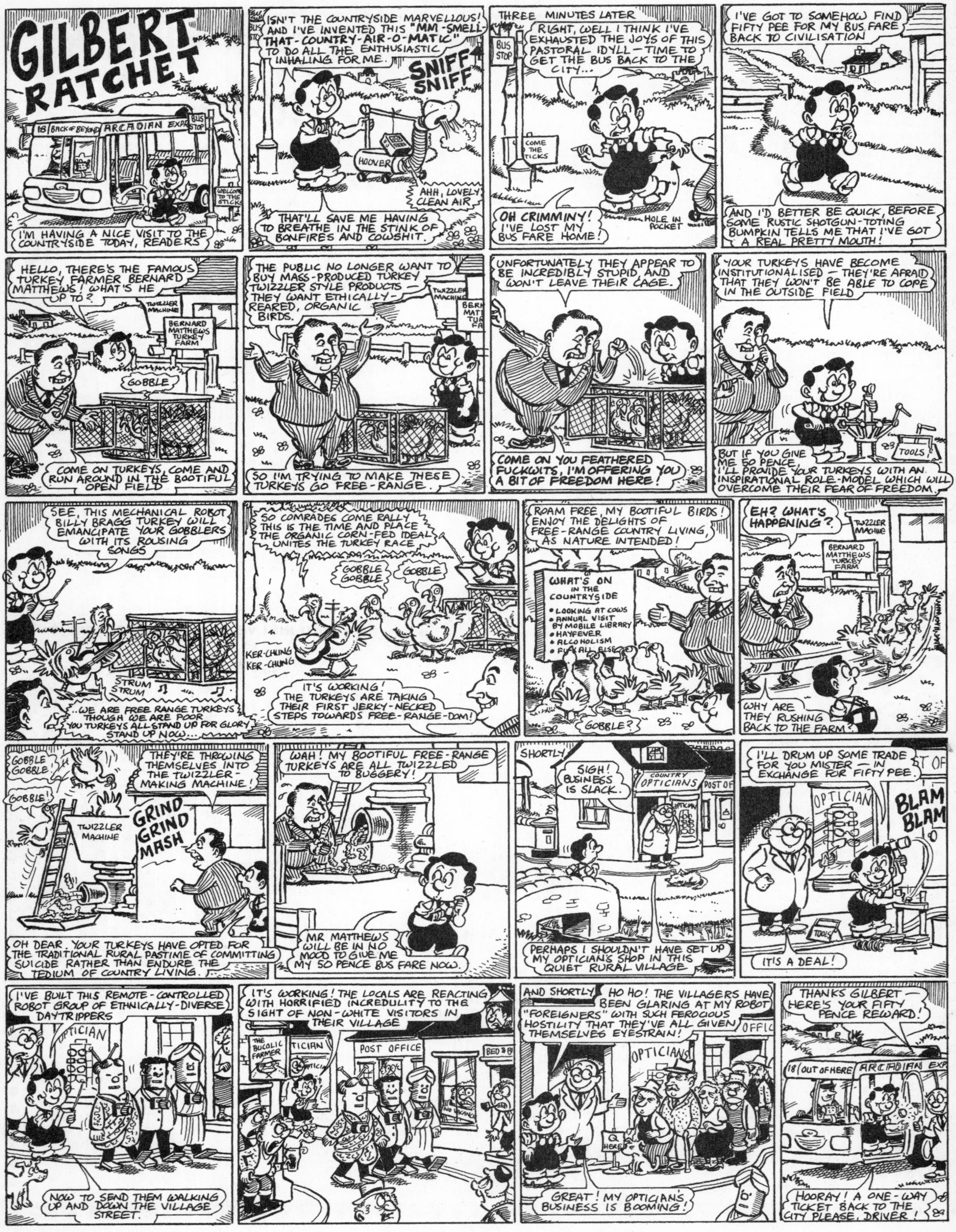
GILBERT RATCHET
18 BACK OF BEYOND ARCADIAN EXP
BUS STOP
WELCOME TO THE STICKS
I'M HAVING A NICE VISIT TO THE COUNTRYSIDE TODAY, READERS
ISN'T THE COUNTRYSIDE MARVELLOUS! AND I'VE INVENTED THIS "MM-SMELL-THAT-COUNTRY-AIR-O-MATIC" TO DO ALL THE ENTHUSIASTIC INHALING FOR ME.
SNIFF SNIFF
HOOVER
AHH, LOVELY CLEAN AIR
THAT'LL SAVE ME HAVING TO BREATHE IN THE STINK OF BONFIRES AND COWSHIT.
THREE MINUTES LATER
RIGHT, WELL I THINK I'VE EXHAUSTED THE JOYS OF THIS PASTORAL IDYLL — TIME TO GET THE BUS BACK TO THE CITY...
BUS STOP
COME THE TICKS
OH CRIMMINY! I'VE LOST MY BUS FARE HOME!
HOLE IN POCKET
I'VE GOT TO SOMEHOW FIND FIFTY PEE FOR MY BUS FARE BACK TO CIVILISATION
AND I'D BETTER BE QUICK, BEFORE SOME RUSTIC SHOTGUN-TOTING BUMPKIN TELLS ME THAT I'VE GOT A REAL PRETTY MOUTH!
HELLO, THERE'S THE FAMOUS TURKEY FARMER BERNARD MATTHEWS! WHAT'S HE UP TO?
TWIZZLER MACHINE
BERNARD MATTHEWS TURKEY FARM
GOBBLE
COME ON TURKEYS, COME AND RUN AROUND IN THE BOOTIFUL OPEN FIELD
THE PUBLIC NO LONGER WANT TO BUY MASS-PRODUCED TURKEY TWIZZLER STYLE PRODUCTS — THEY WANT ETHICALLY-REARED, ORGANIC BIRDS.
SO I'M TRYING TO MAKE THESE TURKEYS GO FREE-RANGE.
UNFORTUNATELY THEY APPEAR TO BE INCREDIBLY STUPID, AND WON'T LEAVE THEIR CAGE.
COME ON YOU FEATHERED FUCKWITS, I'M OFFERING YOU A BIT OF FREEDOM HERE!
YOUR TURKEYS HAVE BECOME INSTITUTIONALISED — THEY'RE AFRAID THAT THEY WON'T BE ABLE TO COPE IN THE OUTSIDE FIELD
BUT IF YOU GIVE ME 50 PENCE, I'LL PROVIDE YOUR TURKEYS WITH AN INSPIRATIONAL ROLE-MODEL WHICH WILL OVERCOME THEIR FEAR OF FREEDOM.
TOOLS
SEE, THIS MECHANICAL ROBOT BILLY BRAGG TURKEY WILL EMANCIPATE YOUR GOBBLERS WITH ITS ROUSING SONGS
STRUM STRUM
...WE ARE FREE RANGE TURKEYS THOUGH WE ARE POOR YOU TURKEYS ALL STAND UP FOR GLORY STAND UP NOW...
SO COMRADES COME RALLY THIS IS THE TIME AND PLACE THE ORGANIC CORN-FED IDEAL UNITES THE TURKEY RACE
GOBBLE GOBBLE
GOBBLE
KER-CHUNG KER-CHUNG
IT'S WORKING! THE TURKEYS ARE TAKING THEIR FIRST JERKY-NECKED STEPS TOWARDS FREE-RANGE-DOM!
ROAM FREE, MY BOOTIFUL BIRDS! ENJOY THE DELIGHTS OF FREE-RANGE COUNTRY LIVING, AS NATURE INTENDED!
WHAT'S ON IN THE COUNTRYSIDE
• LOOKING AT COWS
• ANNUAL VISIT BY MOBILE LIBRARY
• HAYFEVER
• ALCOHOLISM
• FUCK ALL ELSE
GOBBLE?
EH? WHAT'S HAPPENING?
TWIZZLER MACHINE
BERNARD MATTHEWS TURKEY FARM
WHY ARE THEY RUSHING BACK TO THE FARM?
GOBBLE GOBBLE
GOBBLE!
THEY'RE THROWING THEMSELVES INTO THE TWIZZLER-MAKING MACHINE!
TWIZZLER MACHINE
GRIND GRIND MASH
OH DEAR. YOUR TURKEYS HAVE OPTED FOR THE TRADITIONAL RURAL PASTIME OF COMMITTING SUICIDE RATHER THAN ENDURE THE TEDIUM OF COUNTRY LIVING.
WAH! MY BOOTIFUL FREE-RANGE TURKEYS ARE ALL TWIZZLED TO BUGGERY!
MR MATTHEWS WILL BE IN NO MOOD TO GIVE ME MY 50 PENCE BUS FARE NOW.
SHORTLY
SIGH! BUSINESS IS SLACK.
COUNTRY OPTICIANS
POST OF
PERHAPS I SHOULDN'T HAVE SET UP MY OPTICIAN'S SHOP IN THIS QUIET RURAL VILLAGE
I'LL DRUM UP SOME TRADE FOR YOU MISTER — IN EXCHANGE FOR FIFTY PEE.
OPTICIAN
BLAM BLAM
TOOLS
IT'S A DEAL!
I'VE BUILT THIS REMOTE-CONTROLLED ROBOT GROUP OF ETHNICALLY-DIVERSE DAYTRIPPERS
OPTICIAN
NOW TO SEND THEM WALKING UP AND DOWN THE VILLAGE STREET.
IT'S WORKING! THE LOCALS ARE REACTING WITH HORRIFIED INCREDULITY TO THE SIGHT OF NON-WHITE VISITORS IN THEIR VILLAGE
THE BUCOLIC FARMER
TICIAN
POST OFFICE
NO VACANCY
AND SHORTLY
HO HO! THE VILLAGERS HAVE BEEN GLARING AT MY ROBOT "FOREIGNERS" WITH SUCH FEROCIOUS HOSTILITY THAT THEY'VE ALL GIVEN THEMSELVES EYESTRAIN!
OPTICIANS
Q HERE
GREAT! MY OPTICIAN'S BUSINESS IS BOOMING!
THANKS GILBERT — HERE'S YOUR FIFTY PENCE REWARD!
18 OUT OF HERE ARCADIAN EXP
HOORAY! A ONE-WAY TICKET BACK TO THE CITY PLEASE, DRIVER!

YOUNG PUNS? GO FOR IT!

"GET BACK IN the studio and start making hits again!" That's the message from worried newspaper bosses for jailed singer GEORGE MICHAEL.

The heartfelt plea comes from tabloid editors and headline writers who fear they have now exhausted every possible pun based on the imprisoned Wham! star's back catalogue.

SEX

Michael, real name Stavros Flatley, has slowed down his musical output in recent years, last releasing an album of new material in 2004. This has forced press journalists to come up with ever more tenuous straplines when reporting his constant brushes with the law for drugs, motoring and sex offences. These usually consist of a brief description of his latest crime coupled with the suffix "before you go-go".

According to Fleet Street veteran Gary Tits, Michael now owes it to sub-editors to get back in the studio and pen some more smash hits. He told us: "We've been through every possible permutation of Young Guns, Freedom and Wham! Rap. These days, when George hits the headlines we're running on empty."

VIOLIN

"Given his track record, British newspapers need at least another two albums from him in the next five years," he added. "Preferably with song titles that ryhme with cannabis and bumming."

Sun

GEZ IS SET TO SAIL FOR WAR

BUM MY ARSE BEFORE YOU GO-GO

BATTLE FOR THE ISLANDS

TS WAR

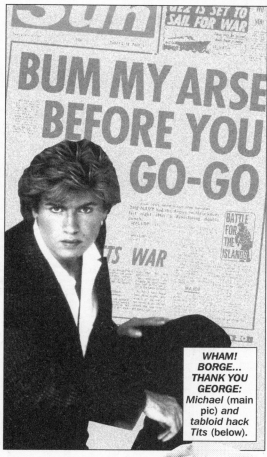

WHAM! BORGE... THANK YOU GEORGE: *Michael* (main pic) *and tabloid hack Tits* (below).

Hacks in plea to troubled pop gay

PRESS

CRIMEBOTCH UK

Govt. accused of "dumbing down" criminal standards

BAD BOYS: *Proper old-fashioned criminals* (main pic) *and* (inset) *a modern lightweight miscreant gets an ASBO yesterday.*

BRITAIN'S criminals were celebrating last night after the latest government statistics showed an increase in the crime figures for the 15th consecutive year. Recorded crime was up a whopping 5% compared with last year, with the largest number of house break-ins since 1982.

By our ***Crime Correspondent***
MR GRIMSDALE

Delighted burglar Gary Danger, 23, was one of many toasting success after he received the news that he had been credited with 8 burglaries and 2 aggravated assaults. "I set myself a target of 7 criminal acts and I've achieved that and more," he beamed.

"These results mean I can now progress further in the criminal underworld and hopefully move on to armed robberies. It's the result of a lot of hard work, planning and sneaking around at night."

Criminal opposition group, the Police, gave a cautious welcome to the results, but questioned their true worth.

hard

"We applaud the hard work of Britain's criminals but feel that these days it is all too easy to be part of recorded crime," said police spokesman Renton Standish.

"Prisons are filling up with villains who wouldn't have even spent a night in the cells twenty years ago," he told reporters.

And his accusation was backed by 1970's baddies pressure group SLAG. "It's too easy these days to commit mickey-mouse crimes like identity theft and call yourself a criminal", said spokesman Vic Dakin. "And you only have to fart in the street to be slammed up under the new anti-terror laws," he added.

violin

"Ask many of today's 'lags' to plan and execute a viscous armed robbery without using a computer and whilst wearing flares and they wouldn't know where to start."

The decline in criminal standards is also being felt on the Costa del Crime in Spain.

Once known as a refuge for hardened British villains, the area has seen a sharp rise in bars and clubs being set up by people with cautions for driving without a seatbelt and urinating in a public place.

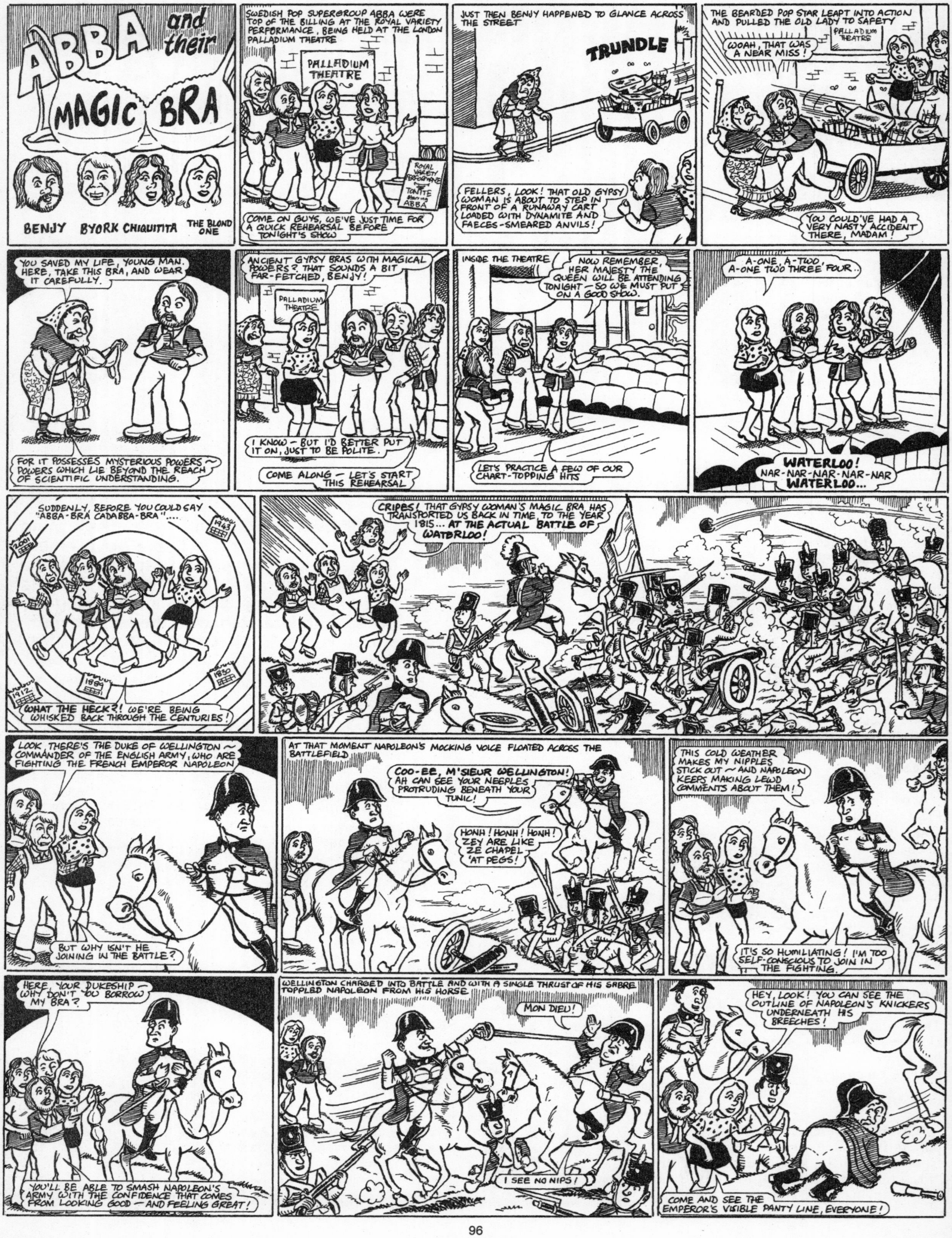
ABBA and their MAGIC BRA
BENJY
BYORK
CHIQUITITA
THE BLOND ONE
SWEDISH POP SUPERGROUP ABBA WERE TOP OF THE BILLING AT THE ROYAL VARIETY PERFORMANCE, BEING HELD AT THE LONDON PALLADIUM THEATRE
PALLADIUM THEATRE
ROYAL VARIETY PERFORMANCE TONITE starring ABBA
COME ON GUYS, WE'VE JUST TIME FOR A QUICK REHEARSAL BEFORE TONIGHT'S SHOW
JUST THEN BENJY HAPPENED TO GLANCE ACROSS THE STREET
TRUNDLE
FELLERS, LOOK! THAT OLD GYPSY WOMAN IS ABOUT TO STEP IN FRONT OF A RUNAWAY CART LOADED WITH DYNAMITE AND FAECES-SMEARED ANVILS!
THE BEARDED POP STAR LEAPT INTO ACTION AND PULLED THE OLD LADY TO SAFETY
PALLADIUM THEATRE
WOAH, THAT WAS A NEAR MISS!
YOU COULD'VE HAD A VERY NASTY ACCIDENT THERE, MADAM!
YOU SAVED MY LIFE, YOUNG MAN. HERE, TAKE THIS BRA, AND WEAR IT CAREFULLY.
FOR IT POSSESSES MYSTERIOUS POWERS ~ POWERS WHICH LIE BEYOND THE REACH OF SCIENTIFIC UNDERSTANDING.
ANCIENT GYPSY BRAS WITH MAGICAL POWERS? THAT SOUNDS A BIT FAR-FETCHED, BENJY!
PALLADIUM THEATRE
I KNOW – BUT I'D BETTER PUT IT ON, JUST TO BE POLITE.
COME ALONG – LET'S START THIS REHEARSAL
INSIDE THE THEATRE
NOW REMEMBER, HER MAJESTY THE QUEEN WILL BE ATTENDING TONIGHT – SO WE MUST PUT ON A GOOD SHOW.
LET'S PRACTICE A FEW OF OUR CHART-TOPPING HITS
A-ONE, A-TWO, A-ONE TWO THREE FOUR..
WATERLOO! NAR-NAR-NAR-NAR-NAR WATERLOO...
SUDDENLY, BEFORE YOU COULD SAY "ABBA-BRA CADABBA-BRA"....
2001
1943
1912
1889
1830
WHAT THE HECK?! WE'RE BEING WHISKED BACK THROUGH THE CENTURIES!
CRIPES! THAT GYPSY WOMAN'S MAGIC BRA HAS TRANSPORTED US BACK IN TIME, TO THE YEAR 1815... AT THE ACTUAL BATTLE OF WATERLOO!
LOOK, THERE'S THE DUKE OF WELLINGTON ~ COMMANDER OF THE ENGLISH ARMY, WHO ARE FIGHTING THE FRENCH EMPEROR NAPOLEON
BUT WHY ISN'T HE JOINING IN THE BATTLE?
AT THAT MOMENT NAPOLEON'S MOCKING VOICE FLOATED ACROSS THE BATTLEFIELD
COO-EE, M'SIEUR WELLINGTON! AH CAN SEE YOUR NEEPLES PROTRUDING BENEATH YOUR TUNIC!
HONH! HONH! HONH! ZEY ARE LIKE ZE CHAPEL 'AT PEGS!
THIS COLD WEATHER MAKES MY NIPPLES STICK OUT ~ AND NAPOLEON KEEPS MAKING LEWD COMMENTS ABOUT THEM!
IT'S SO HUMILIATING! I'M TOO SELF-CONSCIOUS TO JOIN IN THE FIGHTING.
HERE, YOUR DUKESHIP – WHY DON'T YOU BORROW MY BRA?
YOU'LL BE ABLE TO SMASH NAPOLEON'S ARMY WITH THE CONFIDENCE THAT COMES FROM LOOKING GOOD – AND FEELING GREAT!
WELLINGTON CHARGED INTO BATTLE AND WITH A SINGLE THRUST OF HIS SABRE TOPPLED NAPOLEON FROM HIS HORSE
MON DIEU!
I SEE NO NIPS!
HEY, LOOK! YOU CAN SEE THE OUTLINE OF NAPOLEON'S KNICKERS UNDERNEATH HIS BREECHES!
COME AND SEE THE EMPEROR'S VISIBLE PANTY LINE, EVERYONE!

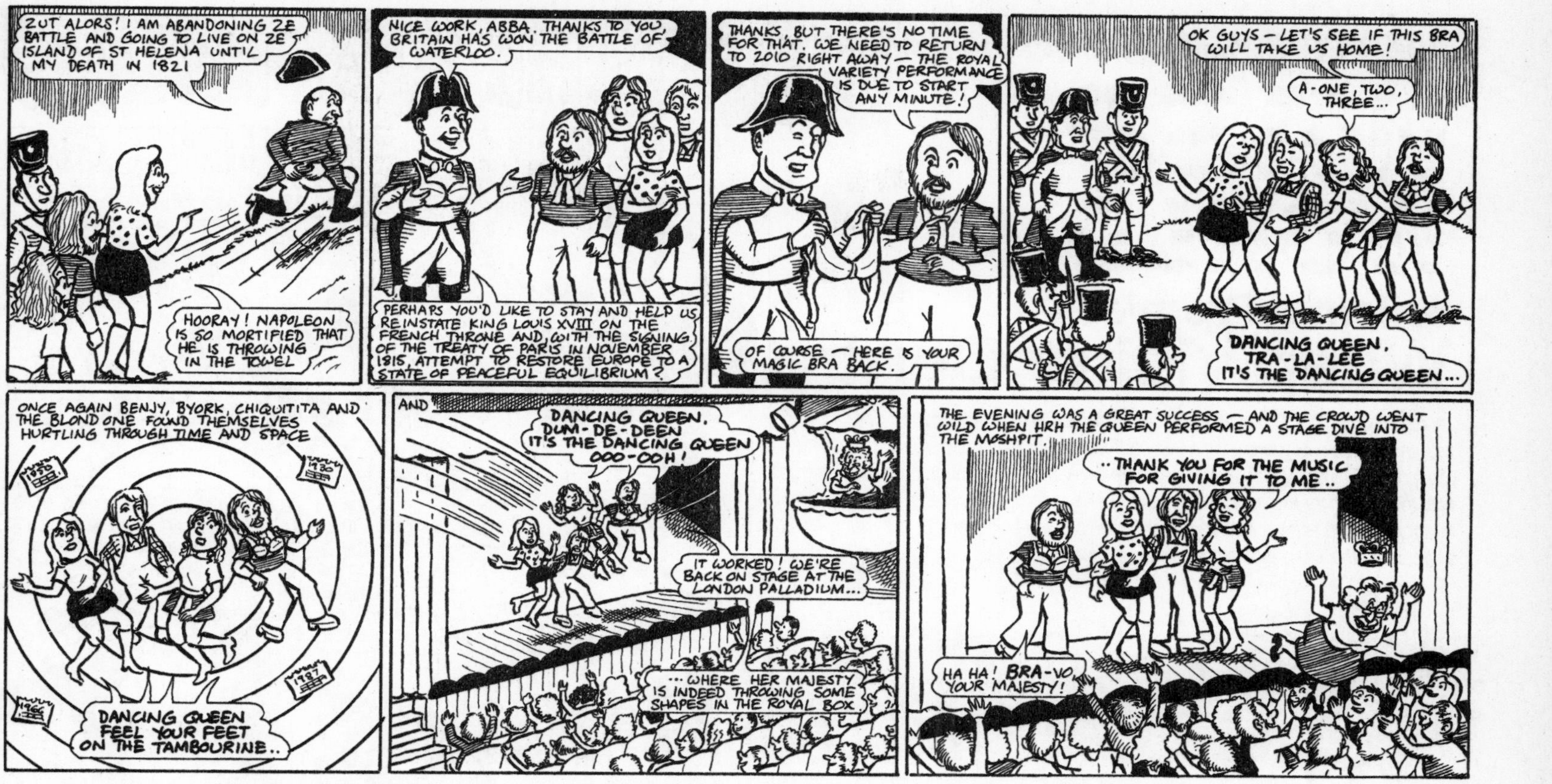
ZUT ALORS! I AM ABANDONING ZE BATTLE AND GOING TO LIVE ON ZE ISLAND OF ST HELENA UNTIL MY DEATH IN 1821
HOORAY! NAPOLEON IS SO MORTIFIED THAT HE IS THROWING IN THE TOWEL
NICE WORK, ABBA. THANKS TO YOU, BRITAIN HAS WON THE BATTLE OF WATERLOO.
PERHAPS YOU'D LIKE TO STAY AND HELP US REINSTATE KING LOUIS XVIII ON THE FRENCH THRONE AND, WITH THE SIGNING OF THE TREATY OF PARIS IN NOVEMBER 1815, ATTEMPT TO RESTORE EUROPE TO A STATE OF PEACEFUL EQUILIBRIUM?
THANKS, BUT THERE'S NO TIME FOR THAT. WE NEED TO RETURN TO 2010 RIGHT AWAY — THE ROYAL VARIETY PERFORMANCE IS DUE TO START ANY MINUTE!
OF COURSE — HERE IS YOUR MAGIC BRA BACK.
OK GUYS — LET'S SEE IF THIS BRA WILL TAKE US HOME!
A-ONE, TWO, THREE...
DANCING QUEEN, TRA-LA-LEE IT'S THE DANCING QUEEN...
ONCE AGAIN BENJY, BYORK, CHIQUITITA AND THE BLOND ONE FOUND THEMSELVES HURTLING THROUGH TIME AND SPACE
DANCING QUEEN FEEL YOUR FEET ON THE TAMBOURINE..
AND
DANCING QUEEN, DUM-DE-DEEN IT'S THE DANCING QUEEN OOO-OOH!
IT WORKED! WE'RE BACK ON STAGE AT THE LONDON PALLADIUM...
...WHERE HER MAJESTY IS INDEED THROWING SOME SHAPES IN THE ROYAL BOX.
THE EVENING WAS A GREAT SUCCESS — AND THE CROWD WENT WILD WHEN HRH THE QUEEN PERFORMED A STAGE DIVE INTO THE MOSHPIT
..THANK YOU FOR THE MUSIC FOR GIVING IT TO ME..
HA HA! BRA-VO, YOUR MAJESTY!

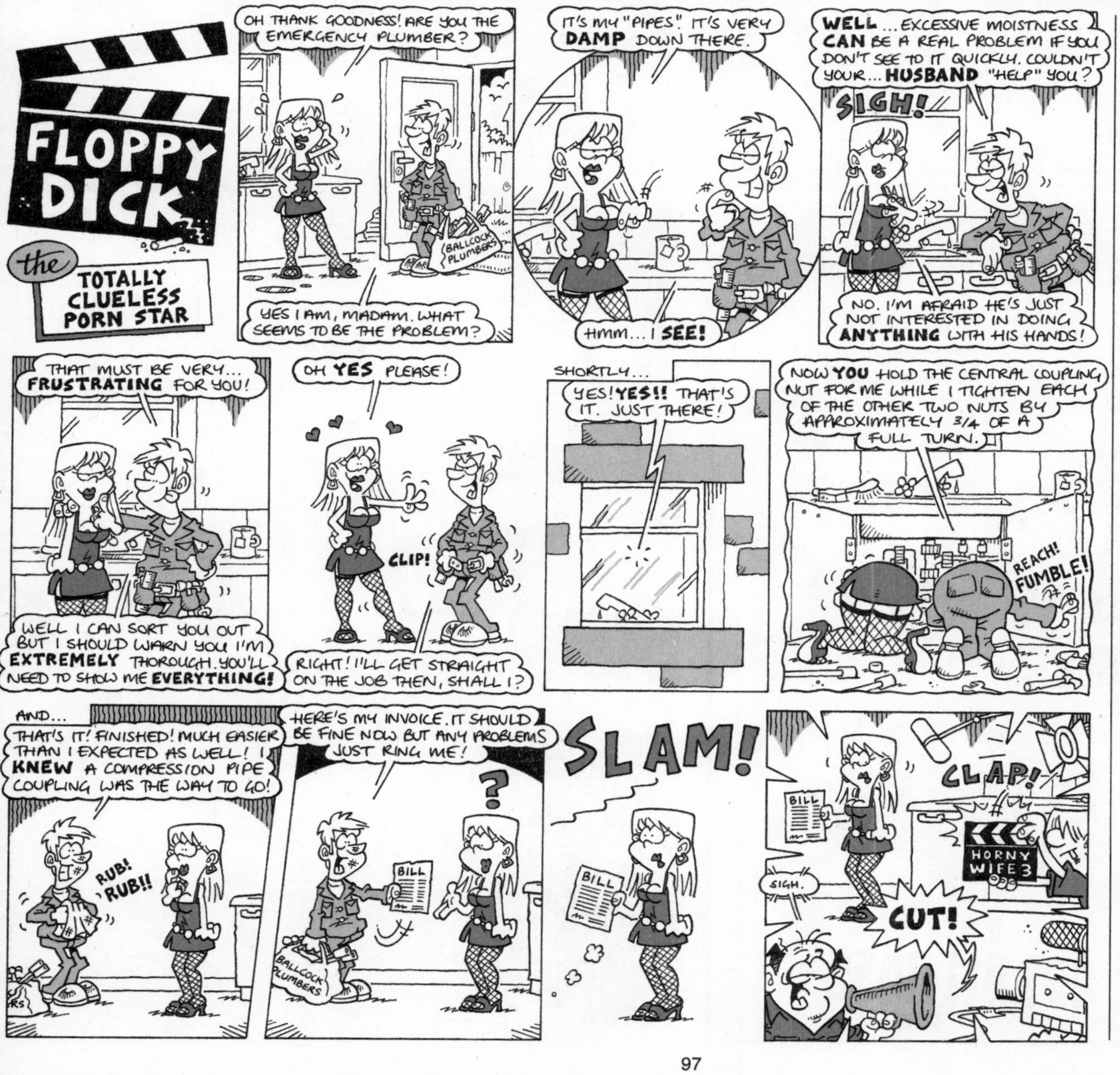
FLOPPY DICK
the TOTALLY CLUELESS PORN STAR
OH THANK GOODNESS! ARE YOU THE EMERGENCY PLUMBER?
BALLCOCK PLUMBERS
YES I AM, MADAM. WHAT SEEMS TO BE THE PROBLEM?
IT'S MY "PIPES". IT'S VERY DAMP DOWN THERE.
HMM... I SEE!
WELL ... EXCESSIVE MOISTNESS CAN BE A REAL PROBLEM IF YOU DON'T SEE TO IT QUICKLY. COULDN'T YOUR... HUSBAND "HELP" YOU?
SIGH!
NO. I'M AFRAID HE'S JUST NOT INTERESTED IN DOING ANYTHING WITH HIS HANDS!
THAT MUST BE VERY... FRUSTRATING FOR YOU!
WELL I CAN SORT YOU OUT BUT I SHOULD WARN YOU I'M EXTREMELY THOROUGH. YOU'LL NEED TO SHOW ME EVERYTHING!
OH YES PLEASE!
CLIP!
RIGHT! I'LL GET STRAIGHT ON THE JOB THEN, SHALL I?
SHORTLY...
YES! YES!! THAT'S IT. JUST THERE!
NOW YOU HOLD THE CENTRAL COUPLING NUT FOR ME WHILE I TIGHTEN EACH OF THE OTHER TWO NUTS BY APPROXIMATELY 3/4 OF A FULL TURN.
REACH! FUMBLE!
AND...
THAT'S IT! FINISHED! MUCH EASIER THAN I EXPECTED AS WELL! I KNEW A COMPRESSION PIPE COUPLING WAS THE WAY TO GO!
RUB! RUB!!
HERE'S MY INVOICE. IT SHOULD BE FINE NOW BUT ANY PROBLEMS JUST RING ME!
BILL
?
BALLCOCK PLUMBERS
SLAM!
BILL
CLAP!
HORNY WIFE 3
SIGH.
CUT!

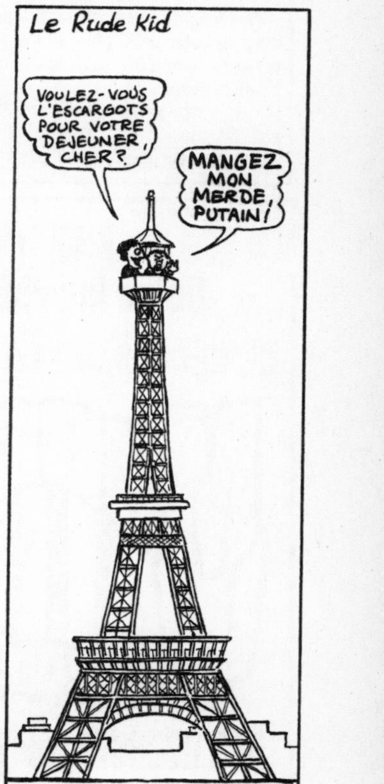
Le Rude Kid
VOULEZ-VOUS L'ESCARGOTS POUR VOTRE DEJEUNER, CHER?
MANGEZ MON MERDE, PUTAIN!

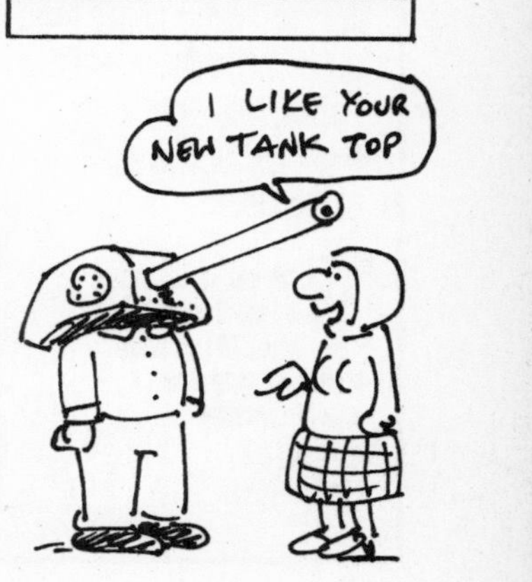
I LIKE YOUR NEW TANK TOP

DON'T RUN! You'll just make them ANGRY at

WASP WORLD

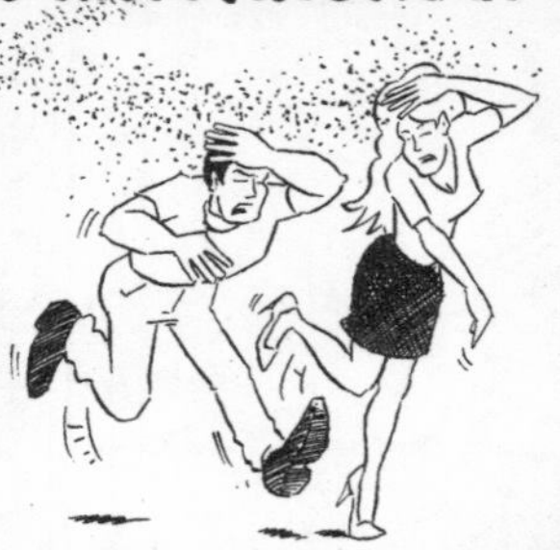

Britain's Premier Wasp Visitor Centre

There's 'SOME STING' for all the family at ***Wasp World****, so why not spend the day with these viscious, spiteful little insects? Marvel as they buzz around one of our 40 'observation bins'. Watch as they get incresingly frustrated banging against the glass. Feel their wrath as you accidentally disturb one of their paper nests. And when you're hungry, you can enjoy a troubled lunch at the Melting Lolly Café, or eat your own food al-fresco in the wasp-infested picnic area.*

A superb glasshouse complex, home to 2 MILLION WASPS!

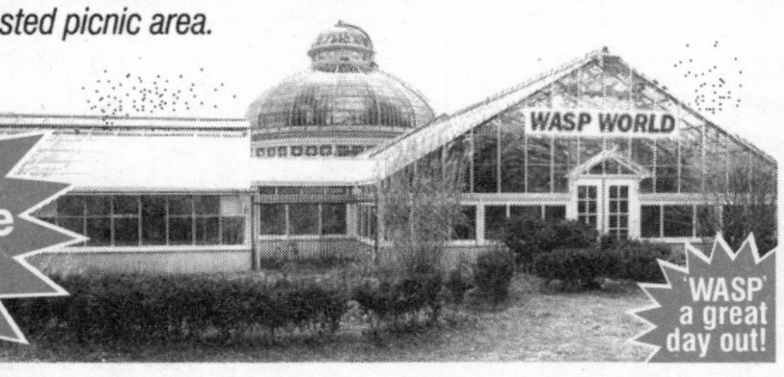
WASP WORLD

'WASP' a great day out!

"My wife and I went last year and we were stang 108 times between us. We can't wait to go again this year."
~Mr. H, Luton

"I was stang 78 times all over my body. I even took one on the bell end while I was in the toilets having a piss"
~Mr L, Chester

"Last time I visited, I ended up in hospital with anaphylactic shock. It was great!"
~Mrs Q, Hull

We are HERE

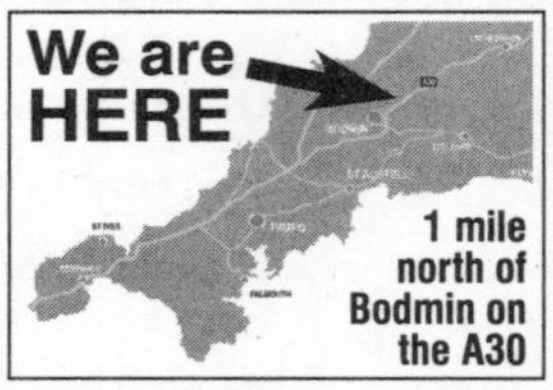

1 mile north of Bodmin on the A30

Are you walking like a right southern twat?

Quick hurried steps or an effeminate gait?

Shoulders not rocking from side to side?

Manc WALK 2000

LEARN HOW TO:

- AGGRESSIVELY approach paparazzi
- WALK through Manchester Arndale Centre
- BE A right nob at music awards ceremonies

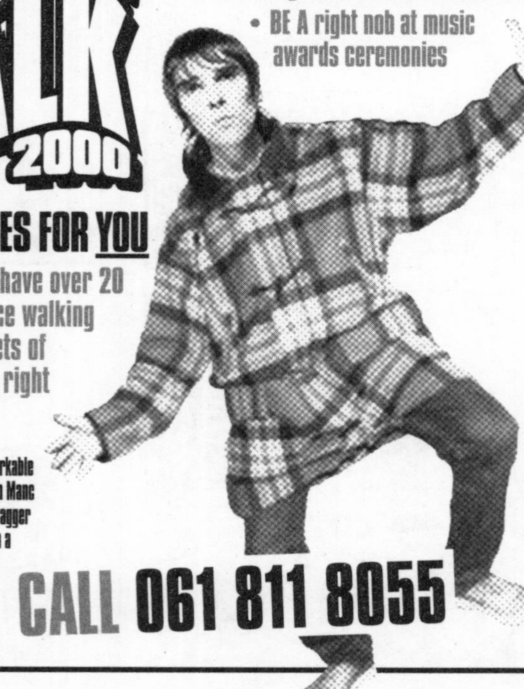

HAS COURSES FOR YOU

Our instructors have over 20 years' experience walking around the streets of Manchester like right cocky cunts

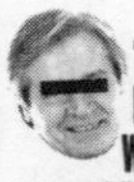

"My walk was unmarkable but after 6 weeks on Manc WALK 2000 I now swagger around like a pissed chimp in a nappy full of porridge."
K. BARLOW, MANCHESTER

CALL 061 811 8055

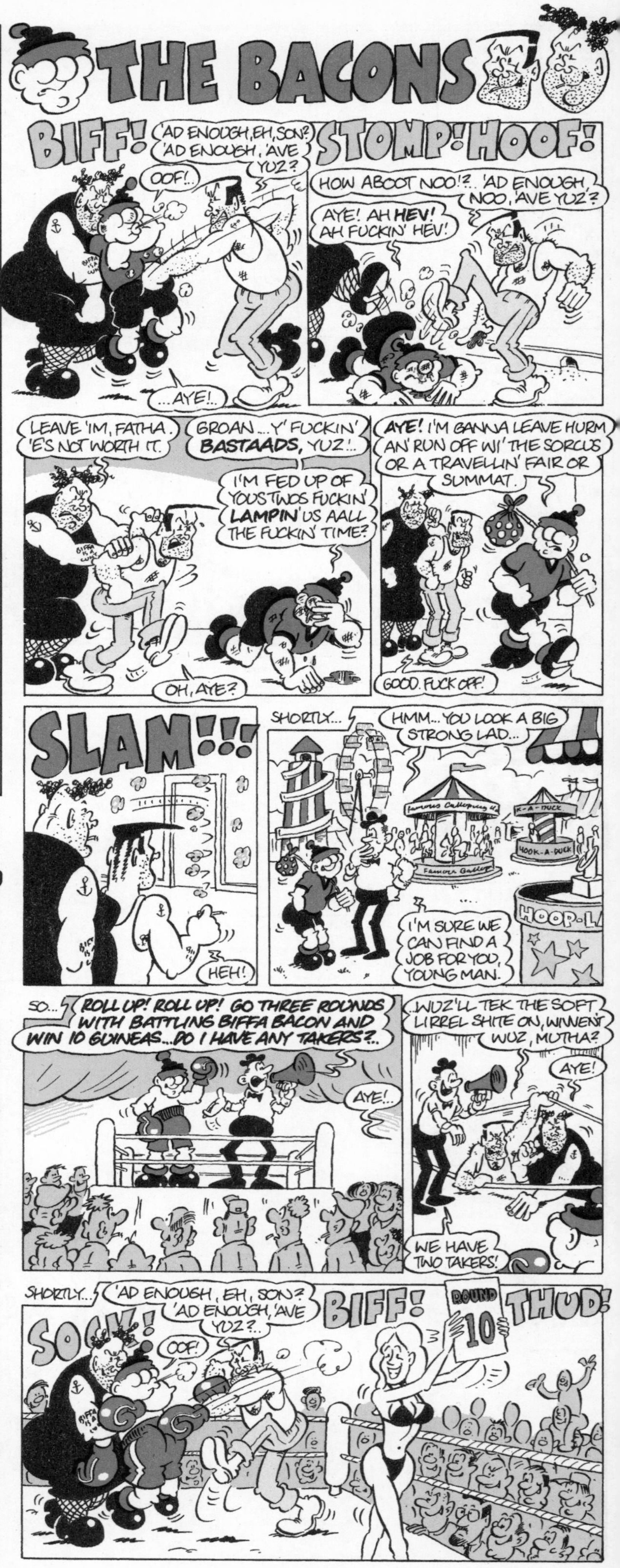
THE BACONS
BIFF!
'AD ENOUGH, EH, SON? 'AD ENOUGH, 'AVE YUZ?
OOF!
...AYE!
STOMP! HOOF!
HOW ABOOT NOO!? 'AD ENOUGH NOO, 'AVE YUZ?
AYE! AH HEV! AH FUCKIN' HEV!
LEAVE 'IM, FATHA. 'E'S NOT WORTH IT.
GROAN... Y' FUCKIN' BASTAADS, YUZ!..
I'M FED UP OF YOUS TWOS FUCKIN' LAMPIN' US AALL THE FUCKIN' TIME?
OH, AYE?
AYE! I'M GANNA LEAVE HURM AN' RUN OFF WI' THE SORCUS OR A TRAVELLIN' FAIR OR SUMMAT.
GOOD. FUCK OFF!
SLAM!!!
HEH!
SHORTLY...
HMM... YOU LOOK A BIG STRONG LAD...
HOOK-A-DUCK
I'M SURE WE CAN FIND A JOB FOR YOU, YOUNG MAN.
HOOP-LA
SO...
ROLL UP! ROLL UP! GO THREE ROUNDS WITH BATTLING BIFFA BACON AND WIN 10 GUINEAS... DO I HAVE ANY TAKERS?..
AYE!
...WUZ'LL TEK THE SOFT LIRREL SHITE ON, WINNENT WUZ, MUTHA?
AYE!
WE HAVE TWO TAKERS!
SHORTLY...
'AD ENOUGH, EH, SON? 'AD ENOUGH, 'AVE YUZ?
SOCK!
OOF!
BIFF!
ROUND 10
THUD!

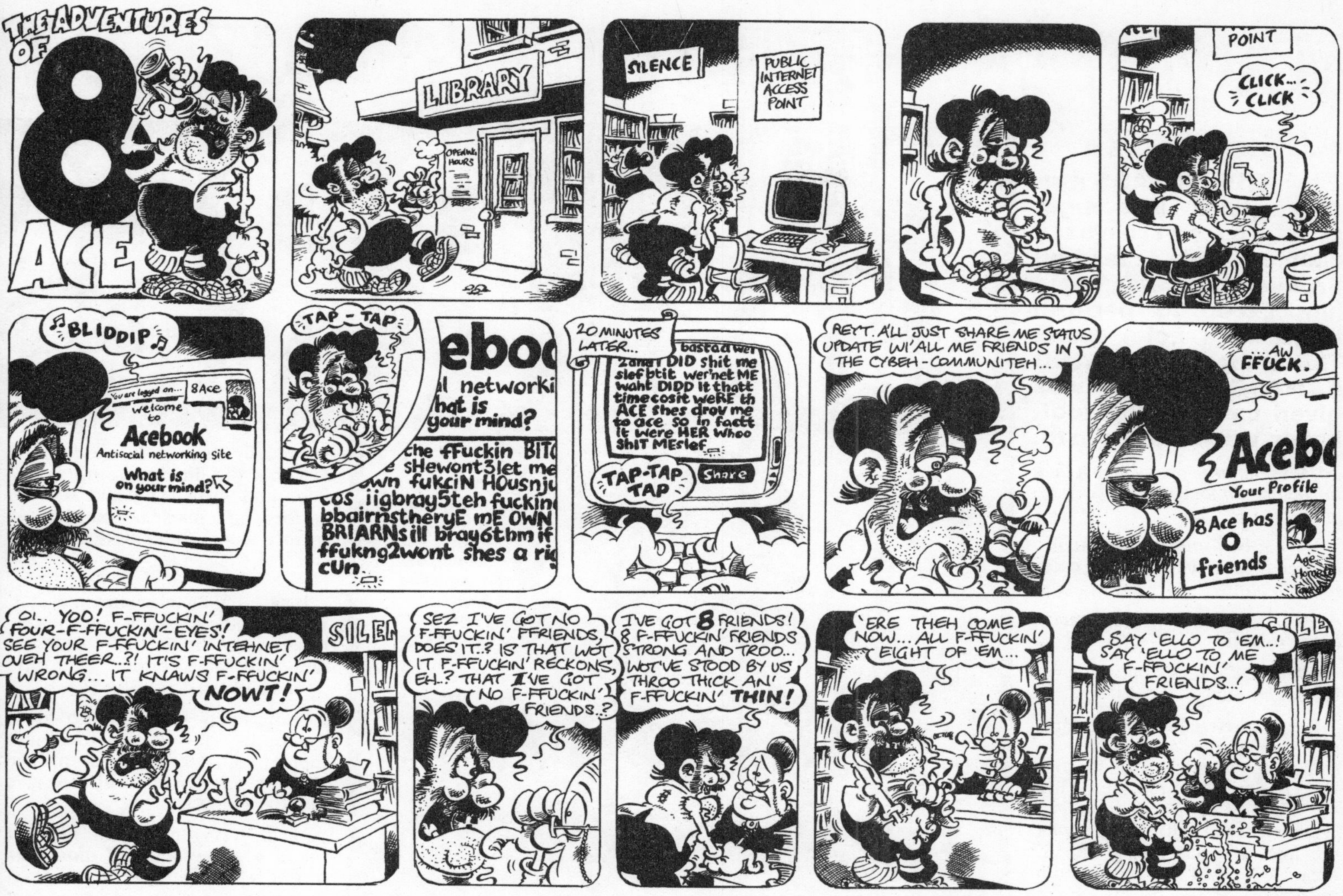
THE ADVENTURES OF
8 ACE
LIBRARY
OPENING HOURS
SILENCE
PUBLIC INTERNET ACCESS POINT
POINT
CLICK... CLICK
BLIDDIP
You are logged on... 8Ace
welcome to
Acebook
Antisocial networking site
What is on your mind?
TAP - TAP
networki
hat is
your mind?
the fFuckin BIT
sHewont3let me
own fukciN HOusnju
cos iigbray5teh fuckin
bbairnstheryE mE OWN
BRIARNsill bray6thm if
ffukng2wont shes a ri
cUn
20 MINUTES LATER...
bastaa wei
2and I DID shit me
slef btit wer'net ME
waht DIDD it thatt
timecosit weRE th
ACE shes drov me
to ace so in factt
it were HER whoo
shIT MEslef
TAP-TAP TAP
Share
REY'T. A'LL JUST SHARE ME STATUS UPDATE WI' ALL ME FRIENDS IN THE CYBEH-COMMUNITEH...
...AW FFUCK.
Acebo
Your Profile
8 Ace has 0 friends
OI.. YOO! F-FFUCKIN' FOUR-F-FFUCKIN'-EYES! SEE YOUR F-FFUCKIN' INTEHNET OVEH THEER..?! IT'S F-FFUCKIN' WRONG... IT KNAWS F-FFUCKIN' NOWT!
SILE
SEZ I'VE GOT NO F-FFUCKIN' FFRIENDS, DOES IT..? IS THAT WOT IT F-FFUCKIN' RECKONS, EH..? THAT I'VE GOT NO F-FFUCKIN' FRIENDS..?
I'VE GOT 8 FRIENDS! 8 F-FFUCKIN' FRIENDS STRONG AND TROO... WOT'VE STOOD BY US THROO THICK AN' F-FFUCKIN' THIN!
'ERE THEH COME NOW... ALL F-FFUCKIN' EIGHT OF 'EM...
SAY 'ELLO TO 'EM..! SAY 'ELLO TO ME F-FFUCKIN' FRIENDS..!

Benson & Hedges

SAMURAI FAGS

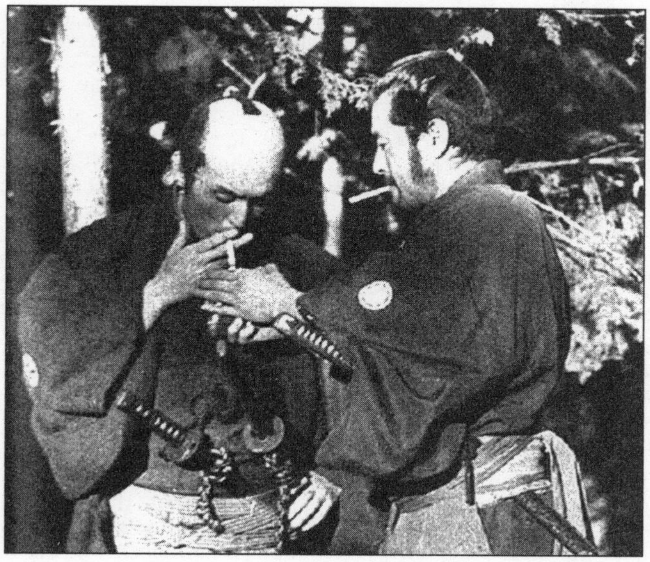

Government Health Warning

SMOKING SAMURAI FAGS MAY LEAD TO SELF-DISEMBOWELMENT WITH A RAZOR-SHARP CEREMONIAL SWORD FOLLOWING MINOR PUBLIC EMBARRASSMENTS.

6mg Tar   0.5mg Nicotine   0mg Scrutability

Have you heard the buzz at

HornetLand

Come and get stang off nature's stripey bastards all year round.

- *3 million hornets from 12 aggressive species*
- *Café and toilets*
- *Gift shop*
- *Medical treatment room*

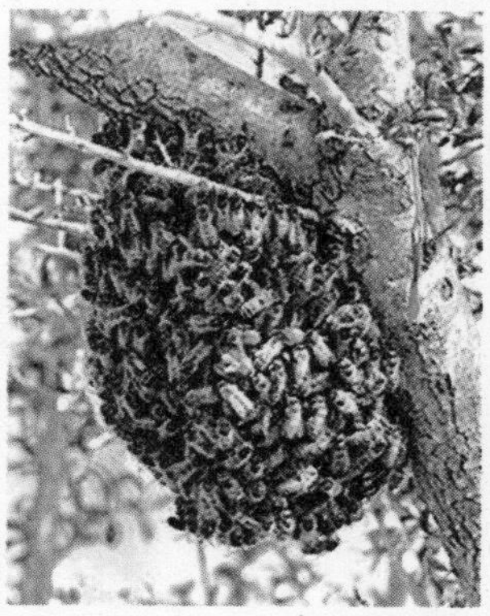

"Cornwall's Most Painful Tourist Attraction" WINNER 2010

There's always a **SWARM WELCOME** at **HornetLand**

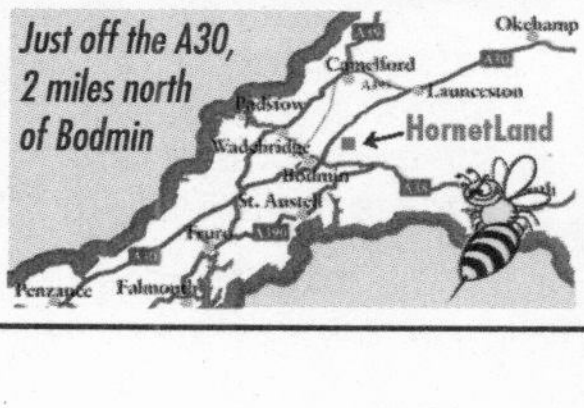
Just off the A30, 2 miles north of Bodmin
Okehampton
Launceston
Camelford
Padstow
Wadebridge
HornetLand
Bodmin
St. Austell
Penzance
Falmouth

"They stang me over and over again. They just wouldn't go away."
Mrs Bee., Essex

"Last year I visited a nearby wasp attraction. I paid £15 to get in and got stang **once** on the arse. What a rip off. From now on it's HornetLand for me."
Mr P., Crewe

MAGICIAN'S SEEDY HAT-TRICK FOR F.A. PRES

EXCLUSIVE

A HIGH-CLASS magician last night sensationally claimed that a leading Premiership star paid him £2000 to perform tricks in a hotel room. The amazing ALFONSO SANTORINI, 48, was given cash by the footballer, who asked him to:

- **CUT** *a length of rope which then miraculously joined itself back together*
- **PUT** *a ball under a cup, which he then tapped with a wand, causing it to vanish*
- **PRODUCE** *a bunch of flowers out of thin air*
- **REMOVE** *a series of coins from behind his ear*

Dark-haired conjurer Santorini met the famous sportsman, who cannot be named for legal reasons, in a London bar. "I recognised him off *Match of the Day*," he told us. "He bought me a drink and invited me into a special roped-off VIP area. He seemed very interested in my magic."

"I was just messing around, pulling rabbits out of my top hat and making some metal rings link together and then come undone. He looked amazed and kept saying he had no idea how I was doing it."

The footballer - who earns £150,000 a week playing for a leading northern club - then suggested that Santorini accompany him back to his hotel. "He said he wanted me to show him a little more," Alfonso told us. "I told him I was a professional magician and I didn't do tricks for free, and he promised he would make it worth my while."

taxi

The pair got in a taxi, where the footballer - who has represented his national side for many years - offered Santorini cash to perform card tricks in the back of the car. "I shuffled the deck and asked him to pick a card," Alfonso said. "He couldn't believe it when I correctly identified it as the three of clubs. He just sat there open-mouthed, he couldn't get enough of my sleight of hand."

"A little later on we were stopped at a red light. There was a crowd of people waiting to cross the road who could see clearly into the back of our cab, but he didn't seem to care. Not even when I reached into his top pocket and pulled out the card he had been thinking about."

"That was just close-up stuff, the sort of tricks I do at parties and wedding receptions. I was saving the grand illusions for when we got back to the hotel," said Santorini.

The taxi dropped the pair off outside a well-known five-star hotel, where rooms can cost upwards of £1000 a night. "The man at the reception desk hardly gave us a second glance as we walked past his desk," Alfonso told us. "I got the impression that I wasn't the first magician he'd taken back there."

"His suite was on the eighteenth floor, but he said he couldn't wait. He begged me to do some more conjuring for him in the lift. We agreed a price of £50 and I got a little guillotine out of the pocket of my cape, got him to check that it was genuine and demonstrated to him how it would chop a small carrot in two."

"Then I asked him to stick his finger under the razor-sharp blade and slammed it down. His eyes stuck out on stalks as the guillotine passed harmlessly through his finger. The fact that the lift could stop at any floor and someone could see me performing a magic act on him just seemed to make him more excited."

top

Inside the hotel room, the star, who plays for a leading Manchester-based club, threw a wad of notes onto the table, asking Santorini: "What will you do for that?"

"I normally charge £200 for a 45-minute set, but this was more money than I had ever seen," the conjurer told us. "I decided to give him the show of his life."

"I did everything that night. I made a silver ball roll along the top of a handkerchief, I produced five doves out of a silk scarf and sat them on a hat rack and I pushed a cigarette through a coin."

"As a grand finale, I put his £20,000 Cartier watch in a bag and smashed it with a hammer right in front of his eyes. He gasped in shock until I told him to take a look in his bedside drawer. He found an ordinary duck egg in there and when he cracked it open, there was his watch inside ... good as new!"

By the early hours of the morning, The Amazing Alfonso was absolutely exhausted. "I made to leave, but the footballer barred my way. He was insatiable, begging me to come back the next week and put on another show for him. Only this time, he wanted me to bring a glamorous assistant."

finger

The following Saturday, the magician turned up at the hotel with his partner, the Wonderful Janet, and a trunk full of props. Up on the eighteenth floor, the pair entered the footballer's suite where they were in for a bit of a shock. The Premiership star was sitting on the bed swigging from a beer bottle ... along with five of his United team-mates!

Santorini told us: "He said he hoped I didn't mind performing for this many people. I replied that I did large groups all the time, and me and the Wonderful Janet got straight down to business."

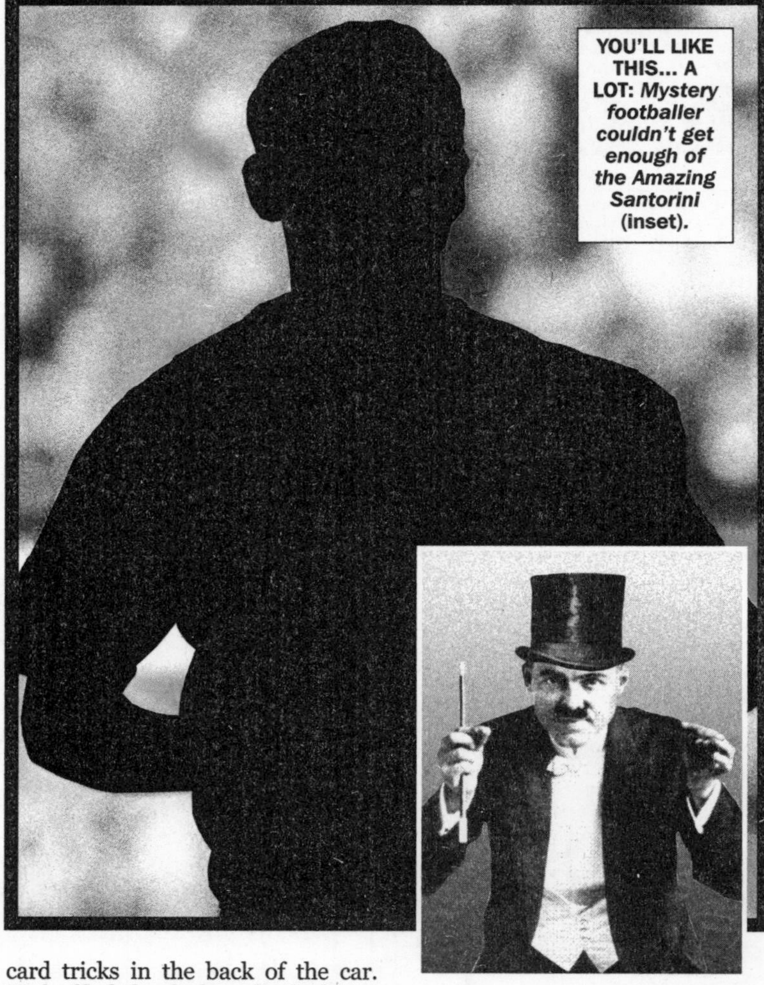

YOU'LL LIKE THIS... A LOT: *Mystery footballer couldn't get enough of the Amazing Santorini* (inset).
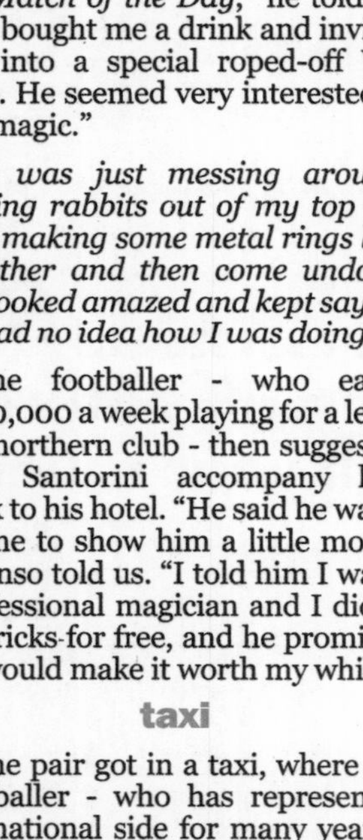

CAB RANK: *Santorini performed seedy act in back seat.*

CCER ACE

O!

"I sawed her in half, locked her in a cabinet with little doors showing her face and the toe of her shoe, and even chained her up in a wicker basket and stuck swords through it. When I pulled the blades out and she stood up out of the basket - not only unscathed but wearing a different outfit and feathered headdress - the players cheered."

"Janet then laid down across two chairs. I gingerly removed them one at a time until she appeared to be floating in mid-air. Then I invited the number eleven and his team-mates to come up and check there were no hidden strings. They didn't need asking twice!"

"Three of them started passing a hoop backwards and forwards over her body, whilst the others cheered them on. One of them filmed it on his mobile phone. None of them seemed to care that footage of them taking part in a levitation act might find its way into the wrong hands."

NEXT WEEK: **Giggs asks Alfonso to perform the ultimate act of prestidigitation:** ***"He offered me £20,000 to make an elephant disappear right before his eyes."***

GET IN TOUCH

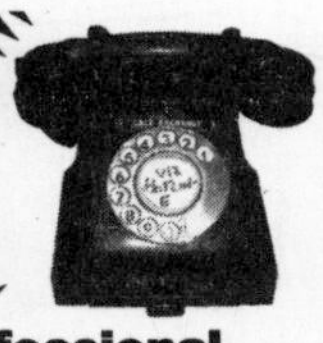

HAS A professional footballer offered YOU money to perform a service of any sort for them?

Perhaps Theo Walcott begged you to plumb in his washing machine or maybe you put a new roof on Kenwyn Jones's garage while he watched?

We've got **CASH** *waiting for the right story, preferably with blurred pictures.* **PHONE OUR NEWSDESK ON 01 811 8055.** *Don't worry, we'll ring you straight back.*

(Calls cost £85 per second and may last for five minutes or more)

SCROTS AWAY!

Kyle show fails to plug scum slick

HOMEOWNERS living near Granada TV studios feared for their safety yesterday after reports that guests from the JEREMY KYLE show had escaped.

Station bosses admitted that a lapse in security allowed several of the daytime programme's participants to find their way out of the building. However they confessed they were unable to say exactly how many had escaped and which sections of British lowlife they represented.

Insiders claim the flood of vermin continued unchecked for several hours before the breach was discovered. Concerned local residents contacted Greater Manchester Police after noticing an unusual number of overweight housewives with gambling addictions milling about in tracksuits and slippers.

EXCLUSIVE

A Granada source said that security at the studio was a major concern. "Upset guests often bolt from the set after hearing the results of their lie-detector tests," he said. "But we usually find them in a small connecting room with a couple of rubber plants in it."

BINGO

"Normally, Jeremy coaxes them out to complete their humiliation in front of the cameras and a baying audience. If they are proving a bit more stubborn, we send the fox from the Foxy Bingo advert in to flush them out."

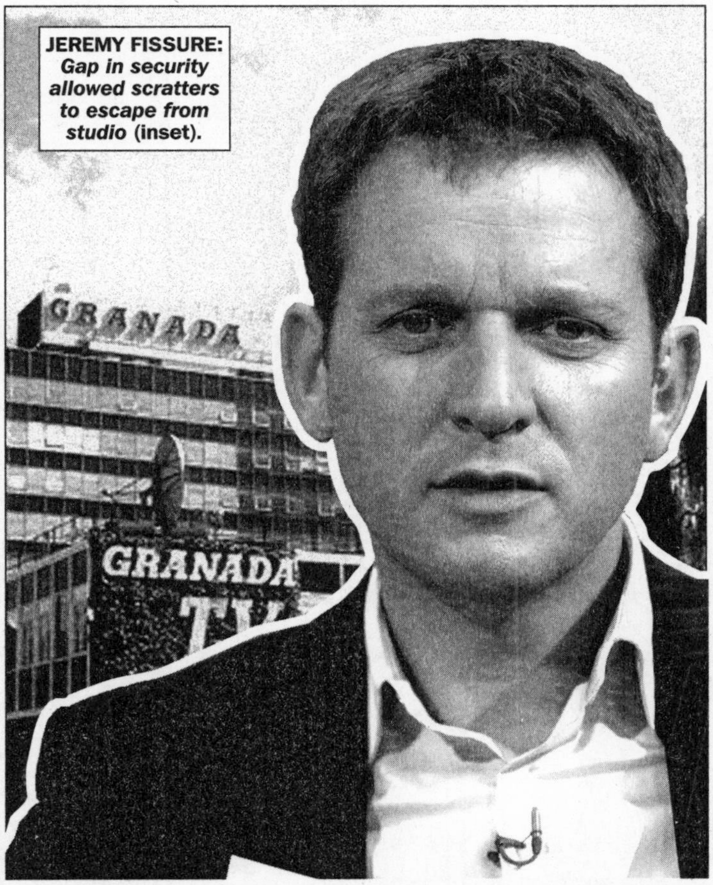

GRANADA
GRANADA TV

JEREMY FISSURE: ***Gap in security allowed scratters to escape from studio*** **(inset).**

But the spokesman insisted that this was the first time that any dysfunctional scrotes had actually made it outside the studio perimeter.

"We still don't know how many toe-rags are still at large. It's quite worrying," he added.

One local man said he'd counted at least 30 scratters, scroungers and neds emerging through a gap in a fence. And a Salford woman rang a local radio phone-in to complain that she couldn't sleep at night due to the incessant whining of an unemployed father of 9 from Leeds who had found his way into her home. "He has taken roost on my settee," she told Radio Manchester's Mike Prepuce. "He is refusing to leave or face up to his responsibilities as a parent."

TIM TIM

Producer Jezebel Wanksworth assured viewers that the leak would not affect production of further shows. "We may not manage to recapture every last guest, but there are plenty more where they came from," he assured viewers. "Trust me there is a never ending supply of vermin willing to reveal every aspect of their sorry lives on national telly in return for the bus fare to Manchester and a night in a Travelodge."

She continued: "We already recycle 80% of our guests, with many of them appearing several times to be pilloried about different aspects of their shameful lives. It might be their drink problem one week, their infidelity the next and their out of control kids the week after that."

"It's a bottomless pit of scum," she added.

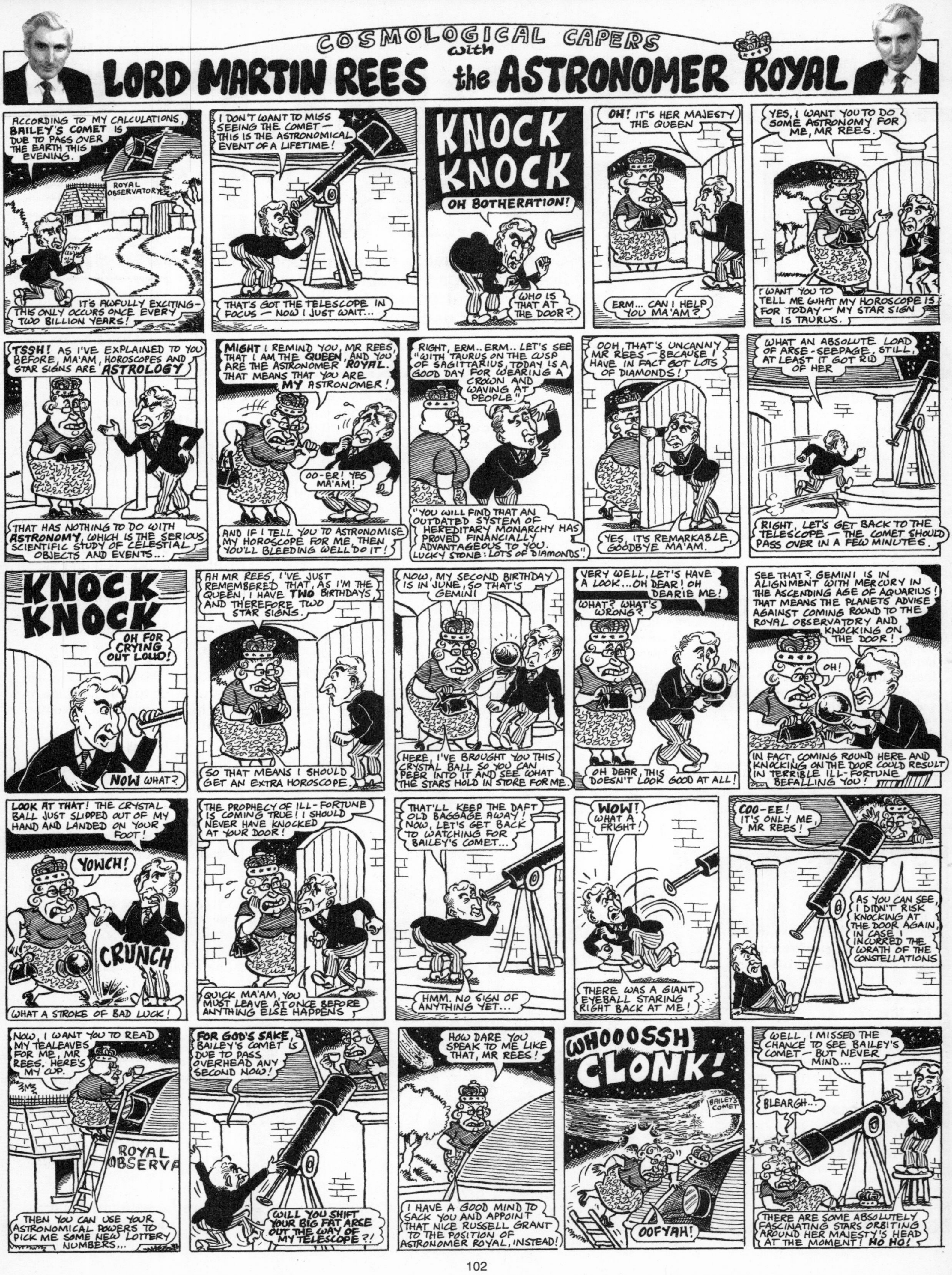
COSMOLOGICAL CAPERS
with
LORD MARTIN REES the ASTRONOMER ROYAL
ACCORDING TO MY CALCULATIONS, BAILEY'S COMET IS DUE TO PASS OVER THE EARTH THIS EVENING.
ROYAL OBSERVATORY
IT'S AWFULLY EXCITING - THIS ONLY OCCURS ONCE EVERY TWO BILLION YEARS!
I DON'T WANT TO MISS SEEING THE COMET - THIS IS THE ASTRONOMICAL EVENT OF A LIFETIME!
THAT'S GOT THE TELESCOPE IN FOCUS - NOW I JUST WAIT...
KNOCK KNOCK
OH BOTHERATION!
WHO IS THAT AT THE DOOR?
OH! IT'S HER MAJESTY THE QUEEN
ERM... CAN I HELP YOU MA'AM?
YES, I WANT YOU TO DO SOME ASTRONOMY FOR ME, MR REES.
I WANT YOU TO TELL ME WHAT MY HOROSCOPE IS FOR TODAY ~ MY STAR SIGN IS TAURUS.
TSSH! AS I'VE EXPLAINED TO YOU BEFORE, MA'AM, HOROSCOPES AND STAR SIGNS ARE ASTROLOGY
THAT HAS NOTHING TO DO WITH ASTRONOMY, WHICH IS THE SERIOUS SCIENTIFIC STUDY OF CELESTIAL OBJECTS AND EVENTS...
MIGHT I REMIND YOU, MR REES, THAT I AM THE QUEEN, AND YOU ARE THE ASTRONOMER ROYAL. THAT MEANS THAT YOU ARE MY ASTRONOMER!
OO-ER! YES MA'AM!
AND IF I TELL YOU TO ASTRONOMISE MY HOROSCOPE FOR ME, THEN YOU'LL BLEEDING WELL DO IT!
RIGHT, ERM.. ERM.. LET'S SEE "WITH TAURUS ON THE CUSP OF SAGITTARIUS, TODAY IS A GOOD DAY FOR WEARING A CROWN AND WAVING AT PEOPLE."
"YOU WILL FIND THAT AN OUTDATED SYSTEM OF HEREDITARY MONARCHY HAS PROVED FINANCIALLY ADVANTAGEOUS TO YOU. LUCKY STONE: LOTS OF DIAMONDS".
OOH, THAT'S UNCANNY MR REES - BECAUSE I HAVE IN FACT GOT LOTS OF DIAMONDS!
YES, IT'S REMARKABLE, GOODBYE MA'AM.
WHAT AN ABSOLUTE LOAD OF ARSE-SEEPAGE. STILL, AT LEAST IT GOT RID OF HER
RIGHT, LET'S GET BACK TO THE TELESCOPE - THE COMET SHOULD PASS OVER IN A FEW MINUTES.
KNOCK KNOCK
OH FOR CRYING OUT LOUD!
NOW WHAT?
AH MR REES, I'VE JUST REMEMBERED THAT, AS I'M THE QUEEN, I HAVE TWO BIRTHDAYS AND THEREFORE TWO STAR SIGNS.
SO THAT MEANS I SHOULD GET AN EXTRA HOROSCOPE.
NOW, MY SECOND BIRTHDAY IS IN JUNE, SO THAT'S GEMINI
HERE, I'VE BROUGHT YOU THIS CRYSTAL BALL SO YOU CAN PEER INTO IT AND SEE WHAT THE STARS HOLD IN STORE FOR ME.
VERY WELL, LET'S HAVE A LOOK... OH DEAR! OH DEARIE ME!
WHAT? WHAT'S WRONG?
OH DEAR, THIS DOESN'T LOOK GOOD AT ALL!
SEE THAT? GEMINI IS IN ALIGNMENT WITH MERCURY IN THE ASCENDING AGE OF AQUARIUS! THAT MEANS THE PLANETS ADVISE AGAINST COMING ROUND TO THE ROYAL OBSERVATORY AND KNOCKING ON THE DOOR!
OH!
IN FACT, COMING ROUND HERE AND KNOCKING ON THE DOOR COULD RESULT IN TERRIBLE ILL-FORTUNE BEFALLING YOU!
LOOK AT THAT! THE CRYSTAL BALL JUST SLIPPED OUT OF MY HAND AND LANDED ON YOUR FOOT!
YOWCH!
CRUNCH
WHAT A STROKE OF BAD LUCK!
THE PROPHECY OF ILL-FORTUNE IS COMING TRUE! I SHOULD NEVER HAVE KNOCKED AT YOUR DOOR!
QUICK MA'AM, YOU MUST LEAVE AT ONCE BEFORE ANYTHING ELSE HAPPENS
THAT'LL KEEP THE DAFT OLD BAGGAGE AWAY! NOW, LET'S GET BACK TO WATCHING FOR BAILEY'S COMET...
HMM. NO SIGN OF ANYTHING YET...
WOW! WHAT A FRIGHT!
THERE WAS A GIANT EYEBALL STARING RIGHT BACK AT ME!
COO-EE! IT'S ONLY ME, MR REES!
AS YOU CAN SEE, I DIDN'T RISK KNOCKING AT THE DOOR AGAIN, IN CASE I INCURRED THE WRATH OF THE CONSTELLATIONS
NOW, I WANT YOU TO READ MY TEALEAVES FOR ME, MR REES. HERE'S MY CUP.
ROYAL OBSERVA
THEN YOU CAN USE YOUR ASTRONOMICAL POWERS TO PICK ME SOME NEW LOTTERY NUMBERS...
FOR GOD'S SAKE, BAILEY'S COMET IS DUE TO PASS OVERHEAD ANY SECOND NOW!
WILL YOU SHIFT YOUR BIG FAT ARSE OUT THE WAY OF MY TELESCOPE?!
HOW DARE YOU SPEAK TO ME LIKE THAT, MR REES!
I HAVE A GOOD MIND TO SACK YOU AND APPOINT THAT NICE RUSSELL GRANT TO THE POSITION OF ASTRONOMER ROYAL, INSTEAD!
WHOOOOSSH
CLONK!
BAILEY'S COMET
OOFYAH!
WELL, I MISSED THE CHANCE TO SEE BAILEY'S COMET - BUT NEVER MIND...
BLEARGH...
THERE ARE SOME ABSOLUTELY FASCINATING STARS ORBITING AROUND HER MAJESTY'S HEAD AT THE MOMENT! HO HO!

A-*PAULIN* BEHAVIOUR

NO KECKS-CLUSIVE!

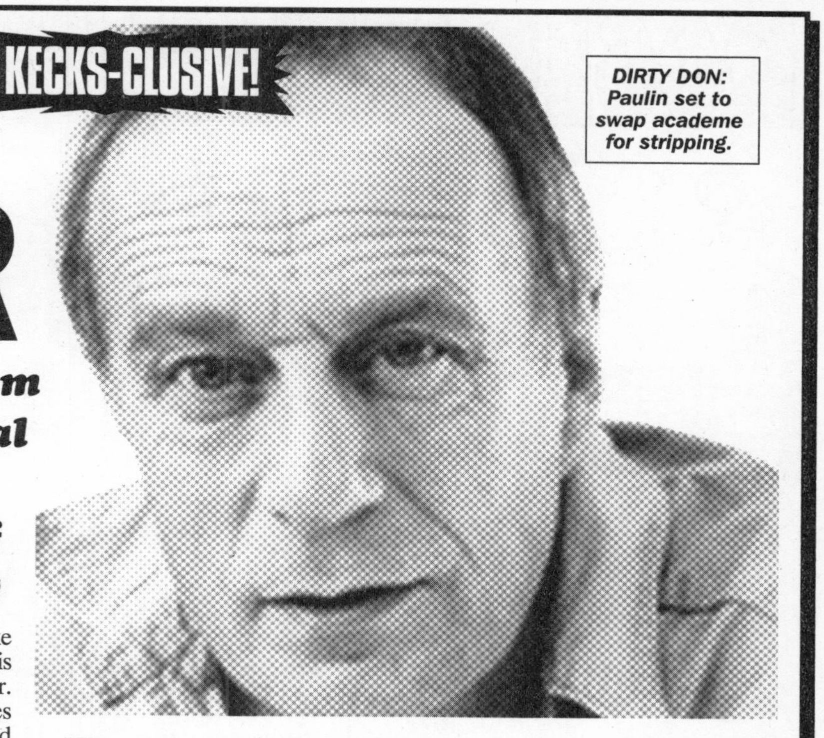

DIRTY DON: Paulin set to swap academe for stripping.

TV brainbox Tom ditches cultural criticism... ...in favour of nude dancing

Newsnight Review and *Late Show* critic Tom Paulin is set to abandon his distinguished career as an arts pundit and poet to become a *MALE STRIPPER*, it was revealed yesterday.

The opinionated university lecturer, 61, known for his warm, lilting voice, broke the news to pals last night.

"I was absolutely gobsmacked when he told me what he was planning," a close friend told us. "Tom is a great teacher, a fabulous writer and a gifted poet, and the literary and academic worlds will feel the loss of his talent keenly. But if he feels he'll be happier disrobing rhythmically in front of large groups of drunk women, then good luck to him, I suppose."

Paulin's agent, Len Slottmeyer, has already begun advertising the Northern Irishman's saucy services and is convinced his phone will soon be ringing off the hook. "Tom will make a killing in this industry because his act is so unique," said Slottmeyer. "Not only can he remove his clothes seductively and then prance around with his nuts out, but he's also able, should the party in question desire it, to chair a lively and informed discussion about the humanist philosopher and essayist Wiliam Hazlitt afterwards."

heavyweight

However, while Slottmeyer feels that Paulin's reputation as an academic heavyweight could benefit his career as a Chippendale, the man himself stresses that he is eager to leave his bookish background behind him.

"That was the old Tom," Paulin told reporters outside his Oxford home this morning. "Dry scholarship has been my bread and butter for almost four decades, but deep down I'm a highly sensual being."

He added, "I have a fabulous body and I want to show it off. That's something I was never able to do when I was sat on a sofa between Michael Ignatieff and Waldemar Januszczak, prattling on about Seamus Heaney's latest volume of poems."

pedigree

Paulin revealed he first became interested in the world of erotic dance after accidentally finding himself in popular gentlemen's club Spearmint Rhino. "I was in London to look round the new Canaletto exhibition at the National Gallery. It was a hot day and I was very thirsty so I popped into the nearest bar for a glass of water," he said.

"I was minding my own business, sipping my drink, when I looked up to see a semi-nude woman writhing frantically just inches above my groin."

Whilst such a spectacle would have had most red-blooded gents salivating eagerly, Paulin was unimpressed. "I have to say I didn't like it," Paulin told us. "It was a woefully banal and trite performance. Miserably contrived. I decided then and there that I could do a much better job myself."

bum

And Paulin's naked ambition is being justly rewarded, with commissions for his novel brand of intellectual healing already flooding in.

32-year-old bride-to-be Pam Nostradamus has booked the hunky culture vulture to strut his stuff at her Blackpool hen party next month. "Having an ageing Oxford don strip off for me and my girlfriends is not something I'd normally consider," she told us. "I was originally just planning to go out on the town for a few drinks, but when I heard about Tom Paulin's new direction, I thought: 'Why not?'"

She continued: "I've been a huge fan of his for years. I loved his modern language re-workings of Sophocles' Antigone and Aeschylus' Prometheus Unbound and I used to enjoy watching him lock horns with fellow intellectual Germaine Greer each week on Newsnight Review."

"Now I'm greatly looking forward to meeting him in person, and seeing his penis," she added.

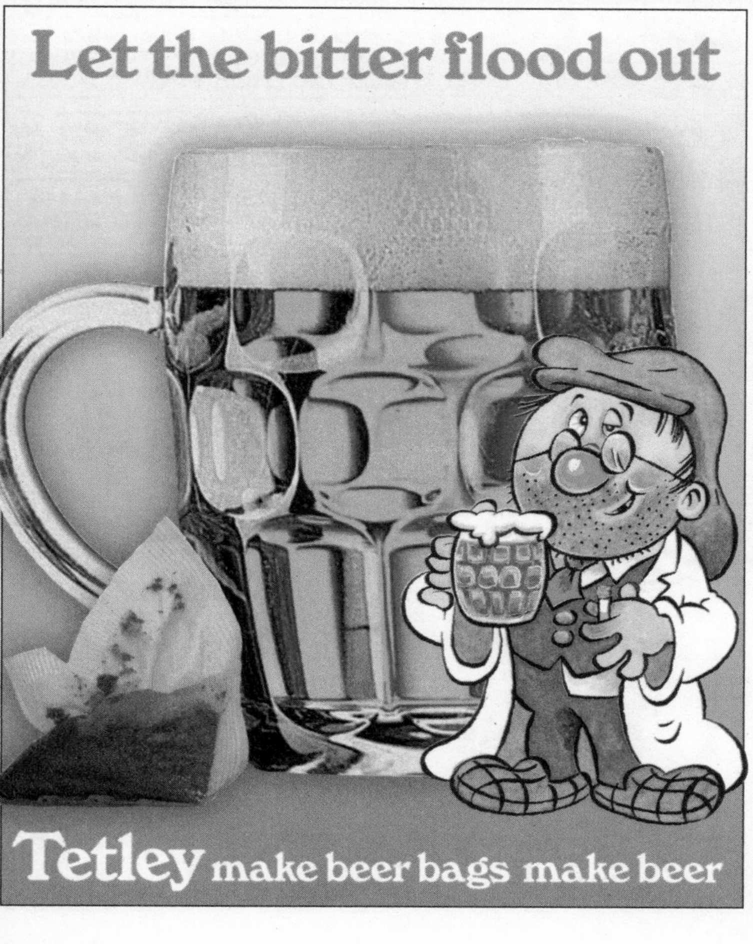
Let the bitter flood out
Tetley make beer bags make beer

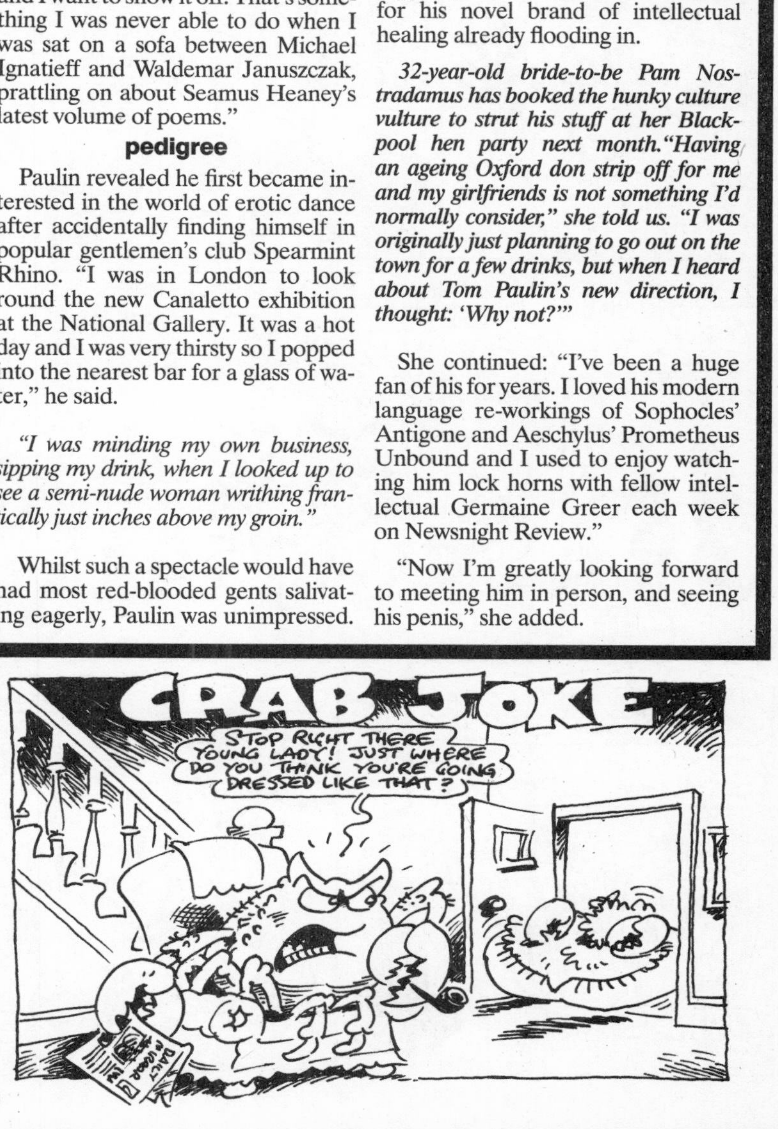
CRAB JOKE
STOP RIGHT THERE YOUNG LADY! JUST WHERE DO YOU THINK YOU'RE GOING DRESSED LIKE THAT?

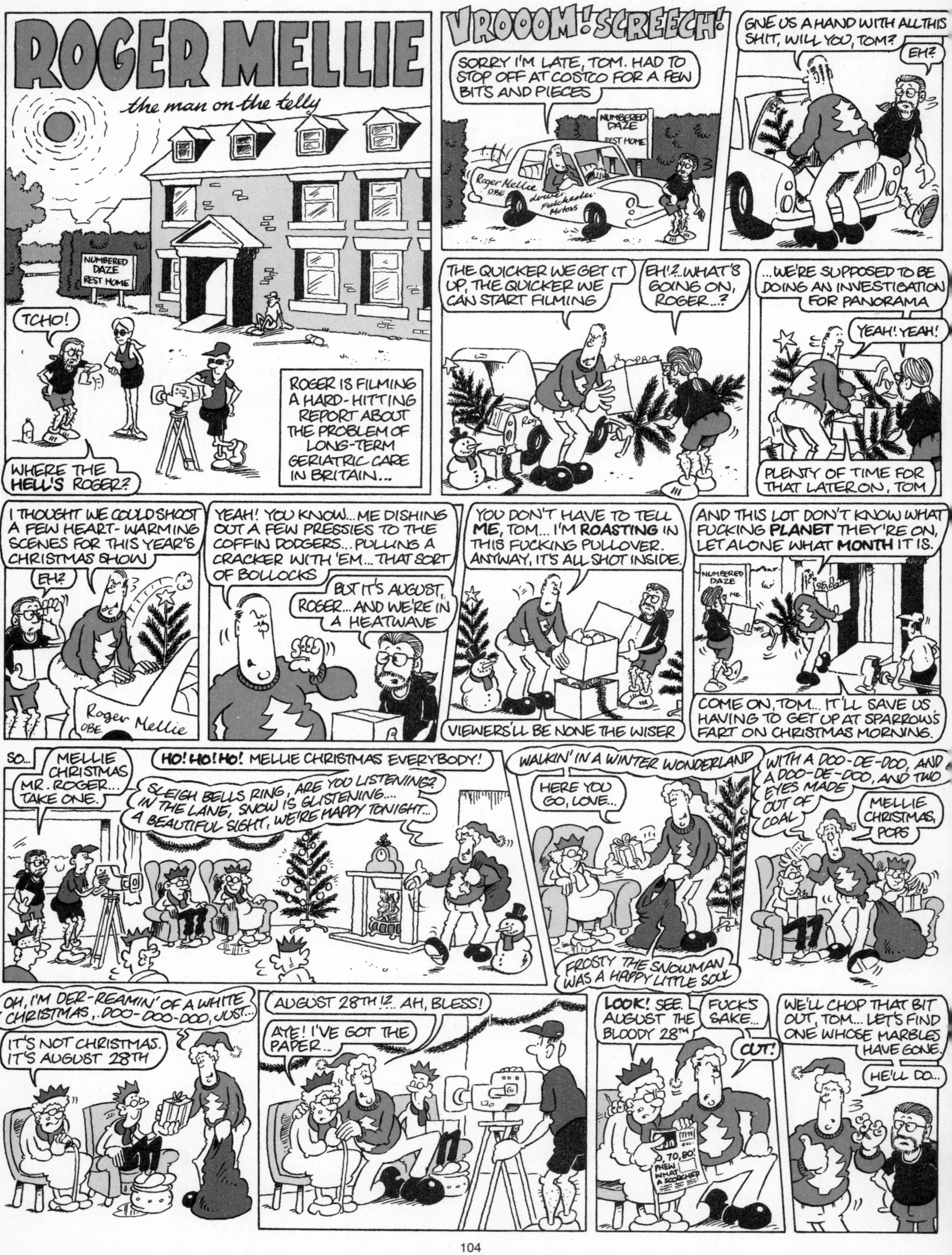
ROGER MELLIE
the man on the telly
NUMBERED DAZE REST HOME
TCHO!
WHERE THE HELL'S ROGER?
ROGER IS FILMING A HARD-HITTING REPORT ABOUT THE PROBLEM OF LONG-TERM GERIATRIC CARE IN BRITAIN...
VROOOM! SCREECH!
SORRY I'M LATE, TOM. HAD TO STOP OFF AT COSTCO FOR A FEW BITS AND PIECES
NUMBERED DAZE REST HOME
Roger Mellie OBE
GIVE US A HAND WITH ALL THIS SHIT, WILL YOU, TOM?
EH?
THE QUICKER WE GET IT UP, THE QUICKER WE CAN START FILMING
EH!?..WHAT'S GOING ON, ROGER...?
...WE'RE SUPPOSED TO BE DOING AN INVESTIGATION FOR PANORAMA
YEAH! YEAH!
PLENTY OF TIME FOR THAT LATER ON, TOM
I THOUGHT WE COULD SHOOT A FEW HEART-WARMING SCENES FOR THIS YEAR'S CHRISTMAS SHOW
EH?
Roger Mellie OBE
YEAH! YOU KNOW...ME DISHING OUT A FEW PRESSIES TO THE COFFIN DODGERS... PULLING A CRACKER WITH 'EM... THAT SORT OF BOLLOCKS
BUT IT'S AUGUST, ROGER... AND WE'RE IN A HEATWAVE
YOU DON'T HAVE TO TELL ME, TOM... I'M ROASTING IN THIS FUCKING PULLOVER. ANYWAY, IT'S ALL SHOT INSIDE.
VIEWERS'LL BE NONE THE WISER
AND THIS LOT DON'T KNOW WHAT FUCKING PLANET THEY'RE ON, LET ALONE WHAT MONTH IT IS.
NUMBERED DAZE
COME ON, TOM... IT'LL SAVE US HAVING TO GET UP AT SPARROW'S FART ON CHRISTMAS MORNING.
SO...
MELLIE CHRISTMAS MR. ROGER... TAKE ONE.
HO! HO! HO! MELLIE CHRISTMAS EVERYBODY!
SLEIGH BELLS RING, ARE YOU LISTENING? IN THE LANE, SNOW IS GLISTENING.... A BEAUTIFUL SIGHT, WE'RE HAPPY TONIGHT...
WALKIN' IN A WINTER WONDERLAND
HERE YOU GO, LOVE...
FROSTY THE SNOWMAN WAS A HAPPY LITTLE SOUL
WITH A DOO-DE-DOO, AND A DOO-DE-DOO, AND TWO EYES MADE OUT OF COAL
MELLIE CHRISTMAS, POPS
OH, I'M DER-REAMIN' OF A WHITE CHRISTMAS,..DOO-DOO-DOO, JUST...
IT'S NOT CHRISTMAS. IT'S AUGUST 28TH
AUGUST 28TH!?... AH, BLESS!
AYE! I'VE GOT THE PAPER...
LOOK! SEE. AUGUST THE BLOODY 28TH
FUCK'S SAKE...
CUT!
PHEW WHAT A SCORCHER
WE'LL CHOP THAT BIT OUT, TOM... LET'S FIND ONE WHOSE MARBLES HAVE GONE.
HE'LL DO...

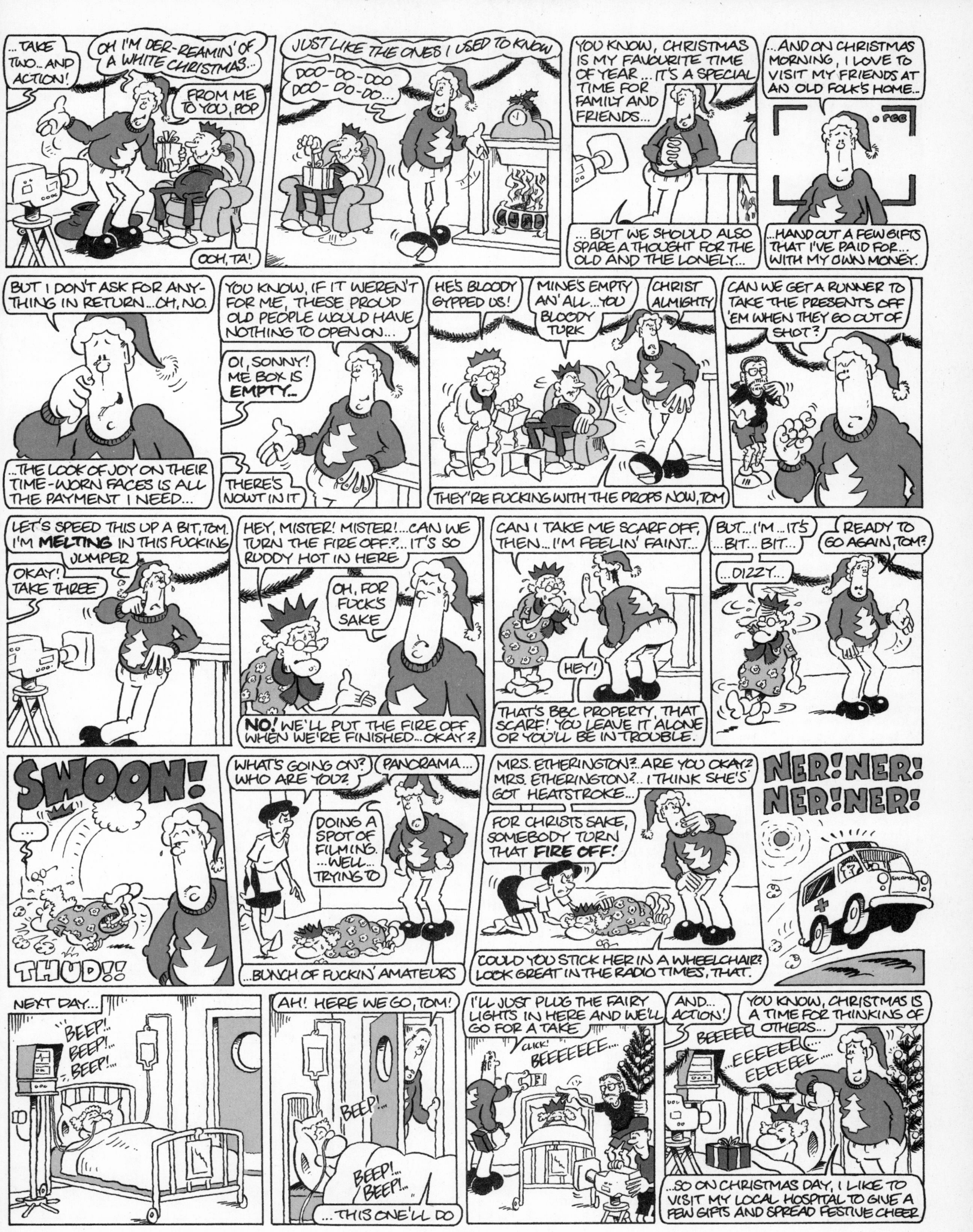

...TAKE TWO... AND ACTION!
OH I'M DER-REAMIN' OF A WHITE CHRISTMAS...
FROM ME TO YOU, POP
OOH, TA!
JUST LIKE THE ONES I USED TO KNOW
DOO-DO-DOO DOO-DO-DO...
YOU KNOW, CHRISTMAS IS MY FAVOURITE TIME OF YEAR... IT'S A SPECIAL TIME FOR FAMILY AND FRIENDS...
...BUT WE SHOULD ALSO SPARE A THOUGHT FOR THE OLD AND THE LONELY...
...AND ON CHRISTMAS MORNING, I LOVE TO VISIT MY FRIENDS AT AN OLD FOLK'S HOME...
...HAND OUT A FEW GIFTS THAT I'VE PAID FOR... WITH MY OWN MONEY.
BUT I DON'T ASK FOR ANYTHING IN RETURN... OH, NO.
...THE LOOK OF JOY ON THEIR TIME-WORN FACES IS ALL THE PAYMENT I NEED...
YOU KNOW, IF IT WEREN'T FOR ME, THESE PROUD OLD PEOPLE WOULD HAVE NOTHING TO OPEN ON...
OI, SONNY! ME BOX IS EMPTY...
THERE'S NOWT IN IT
HE'S BLOODY GYPPED US!
MINE'S EMPTY AN' ALL... YOU BLOODY TURK
CHRIST ALMIGHTY
THEY'RE FUCKING WITH THE PROPS NOW, TOM
CAN WE GET A RUNNER TO TAKE THE PRESENTS OFF 'EM WHEN THEY GO OUT OF SHOT?
LET'S SPEED THIS UP A BIT, TOM. I'M MELTING IN THIS FUCKING JUMPER
OKAY! TAKE THREE
HEY, MISTER! MISTER!... CAN WE TURN THE FIRE OFF?... IT'S SO RUDDY HOT IN HERE
OH, FOR FUCK'S SAKE
NO! WE'LL PUT THE FIRE OFF WHEN WE'RE FINISHED... OKAY?
CAN I TAKE ME SCARF OFF, THEN... I'M FEELIN' FAINT...
HEY!
THAT'S BBC PROPERTY, THAT SCARF! YOU LEAVE IT ALONE OR YOU'LL BE IN TROUBLE.
BUT... I'M... IT'S... BIT... BIT...
...DIZZY...
READY TO GO AGAIN, TOM?
SWOON!
...
THUD!!
WHAT'S GOING ON? WHO ARE YOU?
PANORAMA...
DOING A SPOT OF FILMING. ...WELL... TRYING TO
...BUNCH OF FUCKIN' AMATEURS
MRS. ETHERINGTON?.. ARE YOU OKAY? MRS. ETHERINGTON?.. I THINK SHE'S GOT HEATSTROKE...
FOR CHRISTS SAKE, SOMEBODY TURN THAT FIRE OFF!
COULD YOU STICK HER IN A WHEELCHAIR? LOOK GREAT IN THE RADIO TIMES, THAT.
NER! NER! NER! NER!
NEXT DAY...
BEEP!.. BEEP!.. BEEP!..
AH! HERE WE GO, TOM!
BEEP!..
BEEP!.. BEEP!..
...THIS ONE'LL DO
I'LL JUST PLUG THE FAIRY LIGHTS IN HERE AND WE'LL GO FOR A TAKE
CLICK!
BEEEEEEE....
AND... ACTION!
YOU KNOW, CHRISTMAS IS A TIME FOR THINKING OF OTHERS...
BEEEEEEEEEEEEE... EEEEEEE
...SO ON CHRISTMAS DAY, I LIKE TO VISIT MY LOCAL HOSPITAL TO GIVE A FEW GIFTS AND SPREAD FESTIVE CHEER

Letterbocks

VIZ COMIC, PO Box 841, Whitley Bay, NE26 9EQ

letters@viz.co.uk

STAR LETTER

I ALWAYS felt sorry for the child actors in *Grange Hill*. Not only did they have to go to a real school, but they had to spend their free time pretending to go to another.

Craig Greenhill, e-mail

I CATCH the bus to visit my sister Dolly every Wednesday without fail, and a really funny thing happened on my way there last week. A man on the seat opposite me was reading a paper, and as he crossed his legs I saw that he was wearing a pair of 'days of the week' socks. They said 'Thursday.' I hope he didn't see me chuckling.

Edna Carbunkle, Tipton

I READ that the Lord Mayor of Leicester, Councillor Colin Hall was left embarrassed after his trousers fell down during a visit to a library. The very same thing happened to Kenneth Connor when he was playing the Lord Mayor of Fircombe on Sea in the film *Carry On Girls*. If Lord Mayors are going to suffer mishaps, they should at least be original and not copied from second-rate comedy films of the 70s. Perhaps the people of Leicester should elect a Lord Mayor with a little more imagination next time round.

Cuthbert Creme, Biscuiton

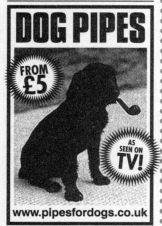

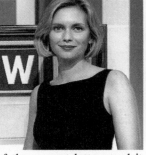

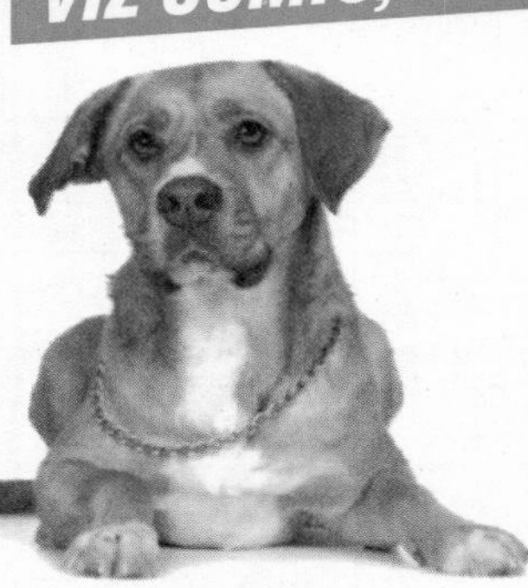

ACCORDING to Wikipedia, dogs can discriminate odours at concentrations nearly 100 million times lower than humans can. But if this is true, how come I retch when picking up my dog's turds in a scented bag at arm's length, and yet he can stick his nose in a big pile of steaming shit and not bat an eyelid. Load of old nonsense if you ask me.

Rooster, e-mail

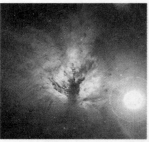

I READ that a European Space Agency probe was used to look back billions of years following the cosmic inflation. I was just wondering, if any of your readers work at the ESA, could they look at their results to see if they can see where I put my glasses last Thursday?

Justin Haddock, e-mail

IF Red Bull gives you wings, why do they sponsor a team in a sport where downforce is the most important thing?

Dean Moncaster, e-mail

THE £2.00 toll to cross the Dartford Bridge is waived after 6.00pm. So last night I drove down from Birmingham and crossed the bridge 12 times. This saved me a whopping £24, minus the fuel cost for the 212 mile round trip.

Andrew Williams Birmingham

I JUST saw a girl on *Big Brother* say "Whenever I feel a bit low, I think about that woman who got her face ripped off by a chimp." I understand that she was trying to give an example of perspective, but the clumsy wording just made it sound like chimp attacks amuse her.

Christina Martine, e-mail

WITH reference to my earlier letter. I've just remembered that last week my sister Dolly had a hospital appointment on the Wednesday, so I went to see her the following day instead. So the man had the right socks on after all. What a fool I feel for laughing.

Edna Carbunkle, Tipton

WHY is it that all the products you see advertised on daytime TV (mattresses, special shoes, etc) are all designed by NASA? You'd think that the boffins accross the pond would be more interested in sending rockets to other worlds to find out there's nothing on them.

Andy Bryant, e-mail

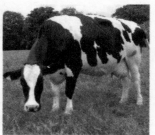

WHILST I applaud Sainsburys efforts to reduce packaging by selling milk in plastic bags, their 'Jugit' containers that conveniently hold and pierce the bag and dispense the milk need a little more research and development. As it stands at the minute, they make slightly less mess than having a cow in the kitchen.

Chester Parsnip Peterborough

ON round one of *Countdown* today, the lettersw came out as RHTCAKPIR. It was obvious that, had there been another couple of dozen

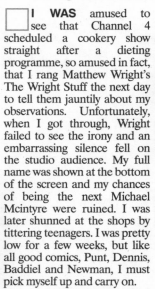

of the correct letters and it was a 31 letter game instead of 9, the contestants could easily have made 'RACHEL RILEY TAKES IT UP THE SHITPIPE.' Come on, Channel 4, this is completely vulgar and way before the watershed.

Craig Eddie, e-mail

I WAS amused to see that Channel 4 scheduled a cookery show straight after a dieting programme, so amused in fact, that I rang Matthew Wright's The Wright Stuff the next day to tell them jauntily about my observations. Unfortunately, when I got through, Wright failed to see the irony and an embarrassing silence fell on the studio audience. My full name was shown at the bottom of the screen and my chances of being the next Michael Mcintyre were ruined. I was later shunned at the shops by tittering teenagers. I was pretty low for a few weeks, but like all good comics, Punt, Dennis, Baddiel and Newman, I must pick myself up and carry on.

Peter Crumpet, e-mail

I RECKON my next door neighbour must be the hardest man in Britain. He has built himself a wall of death in his back garden, and he drives round it in a car with a lion sat on it. Can any readers beat that?

Deepworth Throatsbridge, Hull

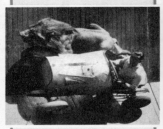

WITH reference to Deepworth Throatsbridge's letter *(above)*, that's nothing. My next door neighbour is so hard that he fights elephants.

Sexbert Boatington, Goole

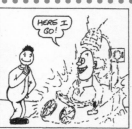

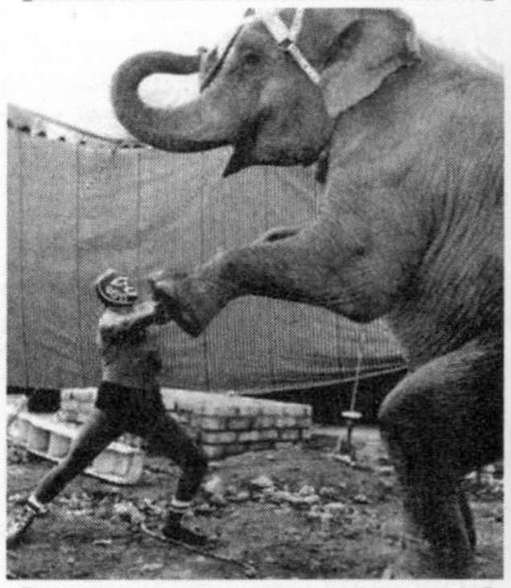

I HAVE just learned that in a Nivea poll, 57% of us admitted to being jealous of friends who tan easily. It's reassuring to know that in these times of economic uncertainty and global terrorism, Nivea has the courage to tackle the issues that really matter.

B Mooney, e-mail

Professor Piehead
RIGHT JOE. TIME TO TEST MY NEW TIME MACHINE.
HERE I GO!
IT WORKED! I'M IN DINOSAUR TIMES! NOW TO GO BACK AND TELL THE WORLD ABOUT MY INVENTION!
HMM. ANOTHER PARTIAL SUCCESS.

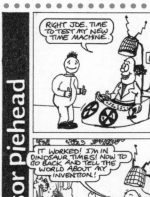

TOP TIPS

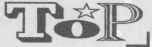

HOMEOWNERS. Don't waste money on an expensive safe. Simply keep all your valuables safe from burglars by storing them in an empty *Only Fools and Horses* DVD box set.

Yaxley Stilton, Cambridge

GOTHS. Achieve 'the look' and help society by attending several blood donor sessions in a day. For maximum effect refuse the offer of tea and biscuits afterwards.

J McGrady, e-mail

AIRBAG in your Astra gone off and can't afford to have it replaced? A Ginsters pastie fits perfectly in to the hole in the steering wheel. Not only will it give a gentle cushioning effect on impact, but it will provide you with a tasty snack while you wait for the fire brigade to cut you out of the wreckage.

Jerry Cozens, e-mail

INCREASE the size of your rooms by decorating them with thinner wallpaper.

Tony Dewey, e-mail

GENTS. Fool your penis into thinking it's having sex by shaking it vigorously whilst thinking of naked ladies.

Gary Chisholme, e-mail

DUSTMEN. Save energy by leaving my bin outside my house after you've emptied it instead of dragging it into a different postcode.

Bobby Dazzler, e-mail

SAVE money on expensive bananas by mixing cold mashed potato and banana syrup.

Lawry, e-mail

SUBBUTEO enthusiasts. Recreate the authentic World Cup 2010 atmosphere by having a paper bag full of wasps in the vicinity of your pitch.

Peter Barnes, e-mail

HIGHWAY agencies. Save warehouse space by putting what is left of your traffic cones in the gaps on the M1.

Pete Harrington, e-mail

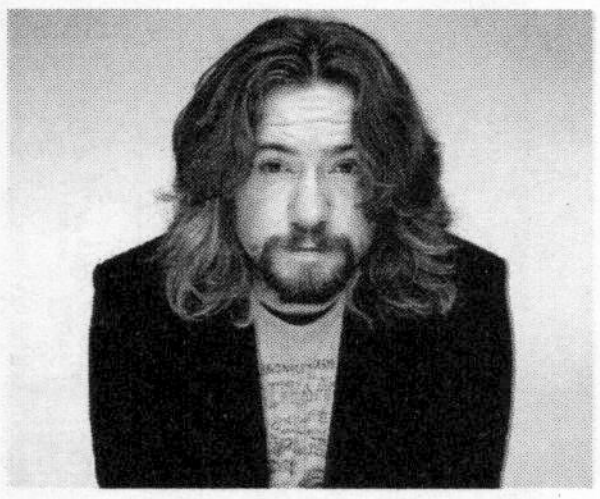

COULD someone at the BBC please tell Justin Lee Collins that having long hair and shouting in a south west accent is considerably less entertaining than he seems to think it is.

Martin Cheza, e-mail

WITH reference to my earlier two letters. My sister Dolly says it was actually the week *before* last that she went to the hospital. But I'm not sure now whether I saw the man *that* week or *last* week, so I don't know whether he had the wrong socks on or not. I'm not even sure they said 'Thursday' now, come to think of it. They might have said 'Tuesday.'

Edna Carbunkle, Tipton

I WAS driving along behind a bus recently, and saw an advert on the back which had a picture of a crying child and the slogan "You were speeding when you killed his mum." That's quite an accusation. They'll be hearing from my solicitors.

Christin Martina, e-mail

HOW come when I burn myself I can sooth it by placing something cold on the wound, yet rubbing a blunt object on a cut has little or no effect?

Craig Greenhill, e-mail

HOW is it that the people in the Churchill Insurance adverts are totally au fait with a talking dog, yet when this talking dog starts making wild claims they suddenly become cynical?

Christina Martinez, e-mail

MY mate Stan reckons that I'm a dead ringer for the actor Richard Griffiths, whereas I'm adamant that I look nothing like him. Could you print this picture of me alongside a picture of the actor and we'll let your readers decide?

S Porter, Merseysde

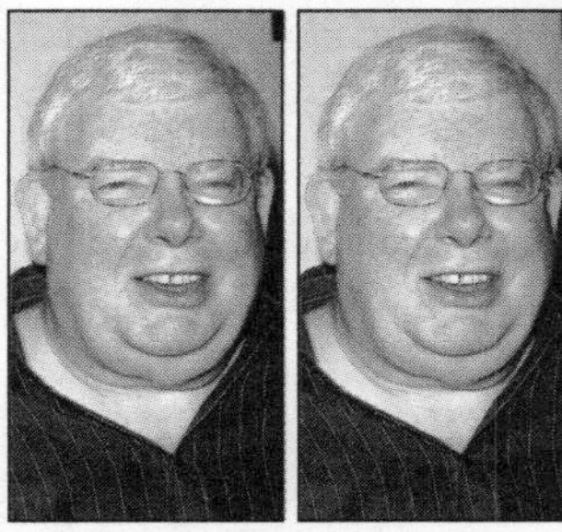

I THINK British Gas's price drop will come as a welcome relief to their customers after the coldest January for 20-odd years. I'm just surprised they didn't think of it at the start of the cold spell when we were all about to spend hundreds of pounds keeping our houses warm. Maybe next year, eh?

Jarrod, e-mail

APART from secretly purchasing surprise gifts for the wife, have any of your readers found other uses for the 'private browsing' option on their computer?

T London, e-mail

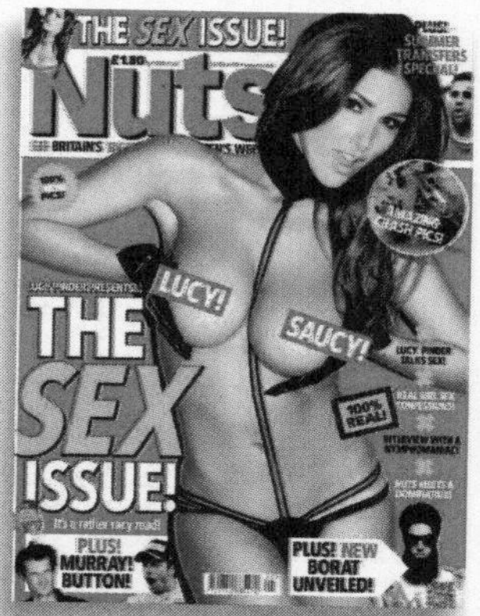

THE SEX ISSUE!
Nuts
LUCY!
SAUCY!
THE SEX ISSUE!
100% REAL!
PLUS! MURRAY! BUTTON!
PLUS! NEW BORAT UNVEILED!

I SEE that last week's edition of *Nuts* magazine was entitled 'The Sex Issue' . I must say, it's nice to see them finally tackle this subject.

Stu, e-mail

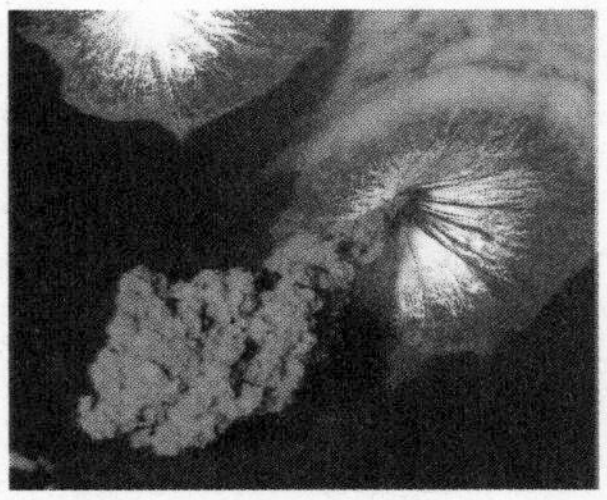

I DON'T know what all this grounding of planes is all about just because a volcano went off in Iceland. It was only a small volcano. Come on, pilots, where's your sense of adventure?

Richard Clothier, e-mail

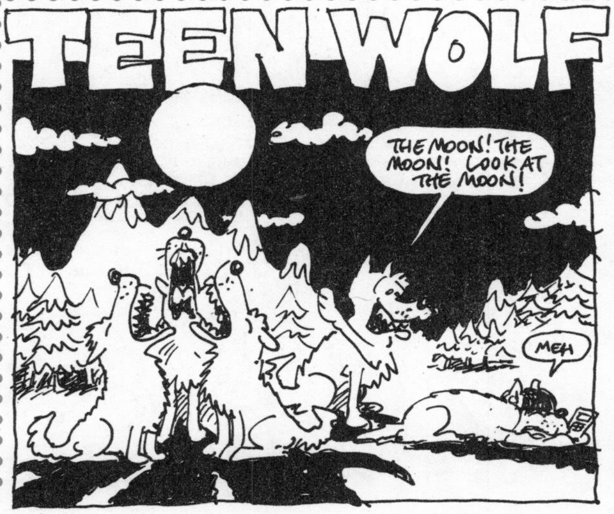

TEEN WOLF
THE MOON! THE MOON! LOOK AT THE MOON!
MEH

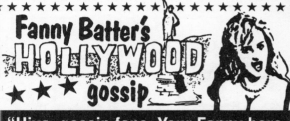

Fanny Batter's HOLLYWOOD gossip

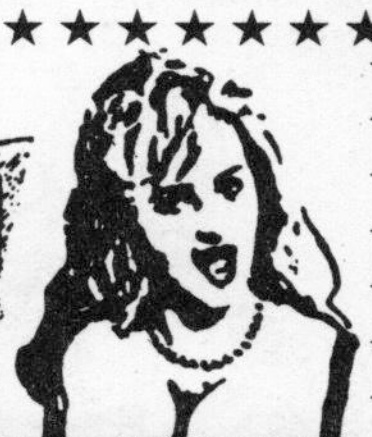

"Hiya, gossip fans. Your Fanny here with the lowdown from Tinseltown!"

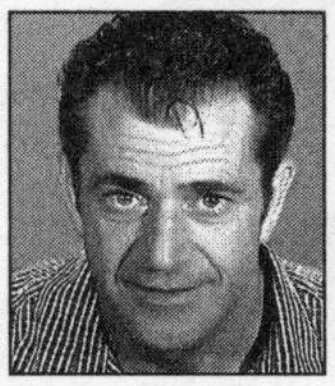

AND BIG NEWS from the Big Apple this week is that hot on the heels of his latest racist rant, Aussie beefcake ***MEL GIBSON*** looks all set to sign a $20 million deal for a sequel. The *Lethal Weapon* star is playing his cards close to his chest, but my Hollywood spies tell that the theme of the tirade will be him accusing his former girlfriend **OKSANA GRIGORIEVA** of 'comin' on like a whore' to a rabbi whilst out shopping! No date for recording has been set, but producers have slated the foul-mouthed diatribe for an August 2011 release. The question is, will the hunky *Mad Max* anti-semite be reprising his famous hyperventilating section? We'll just have to wait and see.

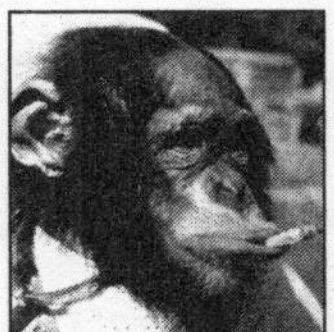

TO SAN REMO, California, where word on the street is that ex-*Friends* star ***JENNIFER ANISTON*** is stepping out with veteran *Tarzan* star ***CHEETAH***. According to sources, the 78-year-old chimp has been helping Jen cope with the break-up of her marriage to *Midnight Cowboy* star ***JOHN VOIGHT***'s *Tomb Raider* daughter ***ANGELINA JOLIE***'s squeeze ***BRAD PITT***. "Cheetah was a hairy shoulder to cry on at first, but I think it's gone beyond friendship," said a close friend of the glamtastic couple. And they were certainly close last night when they were papped at A-list restaurant Mr Vitoni's on Hollywood Boulevard. Jen looked fantastic in a Louis Vuitton off-the-shoulder dress and Jimmy Shoe choos. My spies tell me the ape kept sexy *Bruce Almighty* star Aniston entertained by doing back-flips on the table, drinking tea out of the spout and throwing his turds at waiters. Will all this monkey business end in wedding bells for the happy couple? The jungle drums aren't saying, but watch this space!

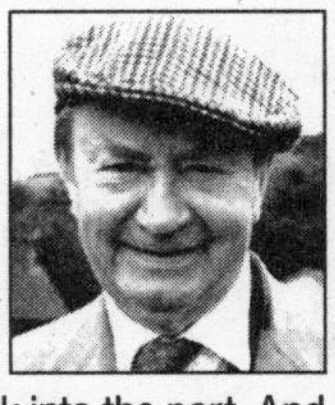

TO SILICONE VALLEY, San Fernando, where preparations are underway for a new biopic about legendary hardcore porn star ***KING DONG***. And as with every other Hollywood film, the staring role looks set to go to a Brit! But who is the actor lined up to portray the well-endowed black 70s sex machine? Step forward *Last of the Summer Wine* star ***PETER SALLIS***. "Peter is looking forward to getting stuck into the part. And parts don't come bigger than King Dong," quipped the *Wallace and Grommit* voiceover star's agent Hymen Prepuce. "Peter's 90 years old and very frail and he's a little worried that 15 hours on a plane might see him off," he continued. "But if he makes it to Tinseltown in one piece, I'm sure he'll rise to the challenge!"

"More Hot Hollywood Gossip next time, Fanny fans!"

Fanny x!x

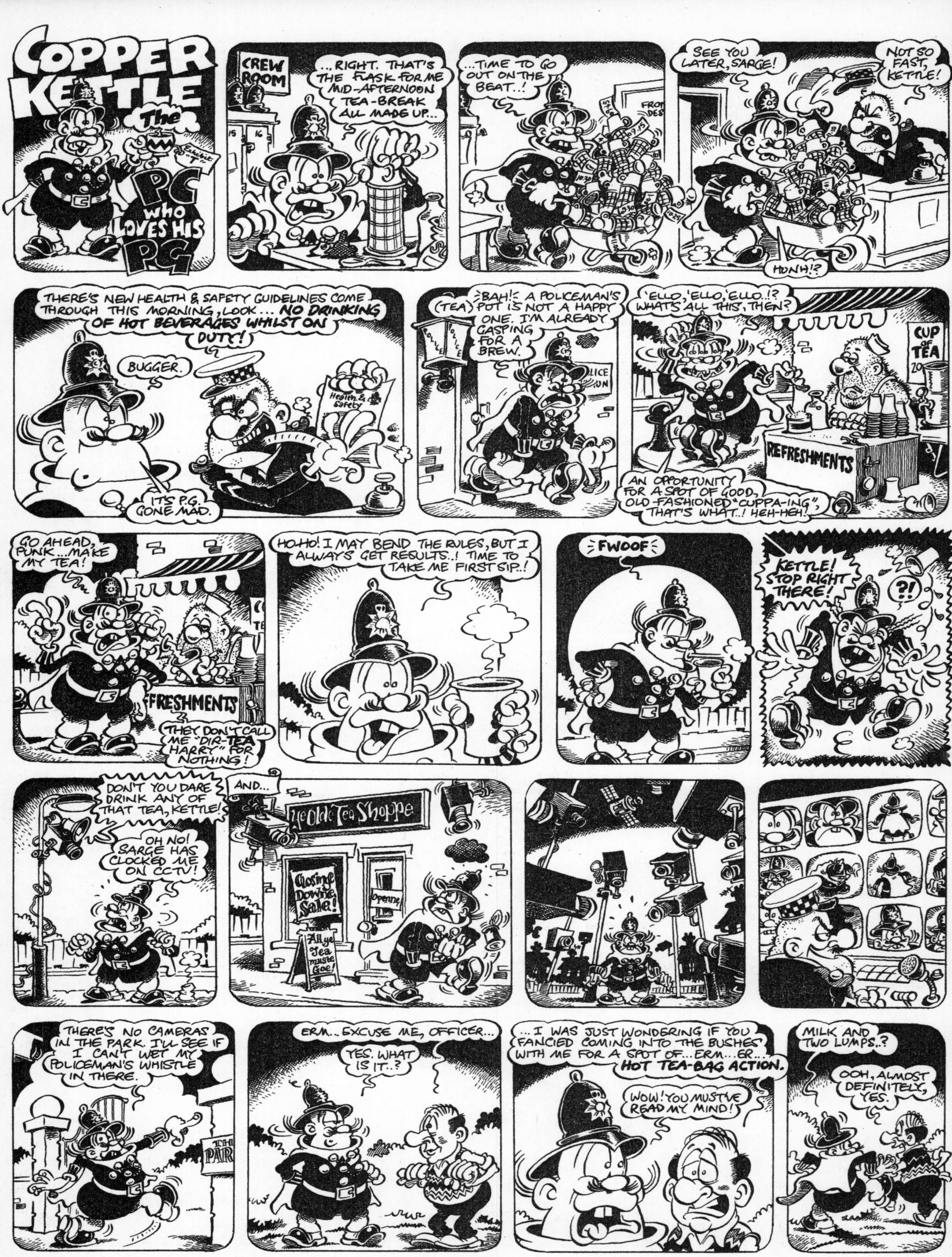

COPPER KETTLE
The PC who LOVES HIS PG
CREW ROOM
...RIGHT. THAT'S THE FLASK FOR ME MID-AFTERNOON TEA-BREAK ALL MADE UP...
...TIME TO GO OUT ON THE BEAT..!
SEE YOU LATER, SARGE!
NOT SO FAST, KETTLE!
HONH!?
THERE'S NEW HEALTH & SAFETY GUIDELINES COME THROUGH THIS MORNING, LOOK... NO DRINKING OF HOT BEVERAGES WHILST ON DUTY!
BUGGER.
Health & Safety
IT'S P.G. GONE MAD.
BAH! A POLICEMAN'S (TEA) POT IS NOT A HAPPY ONE. I'M ALREADY GASPING FOR A BREW.
POLICE
'ELLO, 'ELLO, 'ELLO..!? WHAT'S ALL THIS, THEN?
CUP of TEA
REFRESHMENTS
AN OPPORTUNITY FOR A SPOT OF GOOD, OLD-FASHIONED "CUPPA-ING", THAT'S WHAT..! HEH-HEH!
GO AHEAD, PUNK... MAKE MY TEA!
FRESHMENTS
THEY DON'T CALL ME "DIR-TEA HARRY" FOR NOTHING!
HO-HO! I MAY BEND THE RULES, BUT I ALWAYS GET RESULTS..! TIME TO TAKE ME FIRST SIP..!
FWOOF
KETTLE! STOP RIGHT THERE!
?!
DON'T YOU DARE DRINK ANY OF THAT TEA, KETTLE!
OH NO! SARGE HAS CLOCKED ME ON CCTV!
AND...
Ye Olde Tea Shoppe
Closing Down Sale!
Opening
All ye Tea muste Goe!
THERE'S NO CAMERAS IN THE PARK. I'LL SEE IF I CAN'T WET MY POLICEMAN'S WHISTLE IN THERE.
THE PARK
ERM.. EXCUSE ME, OFFICER...
YES. WHAT IS IT..?
...I WAS JUST WONDERING IF YOU FANCIED COMING INTO THE BUSHES WITH ME FOR A SPOT OF... ERM... ER... HOT TEA-BAG ACTION.
WOW! YOU MUST'VE READ MY MIND!
MILK AND TWO LUMPS..?
OOH, ALMOST DEFINITELY, YES.

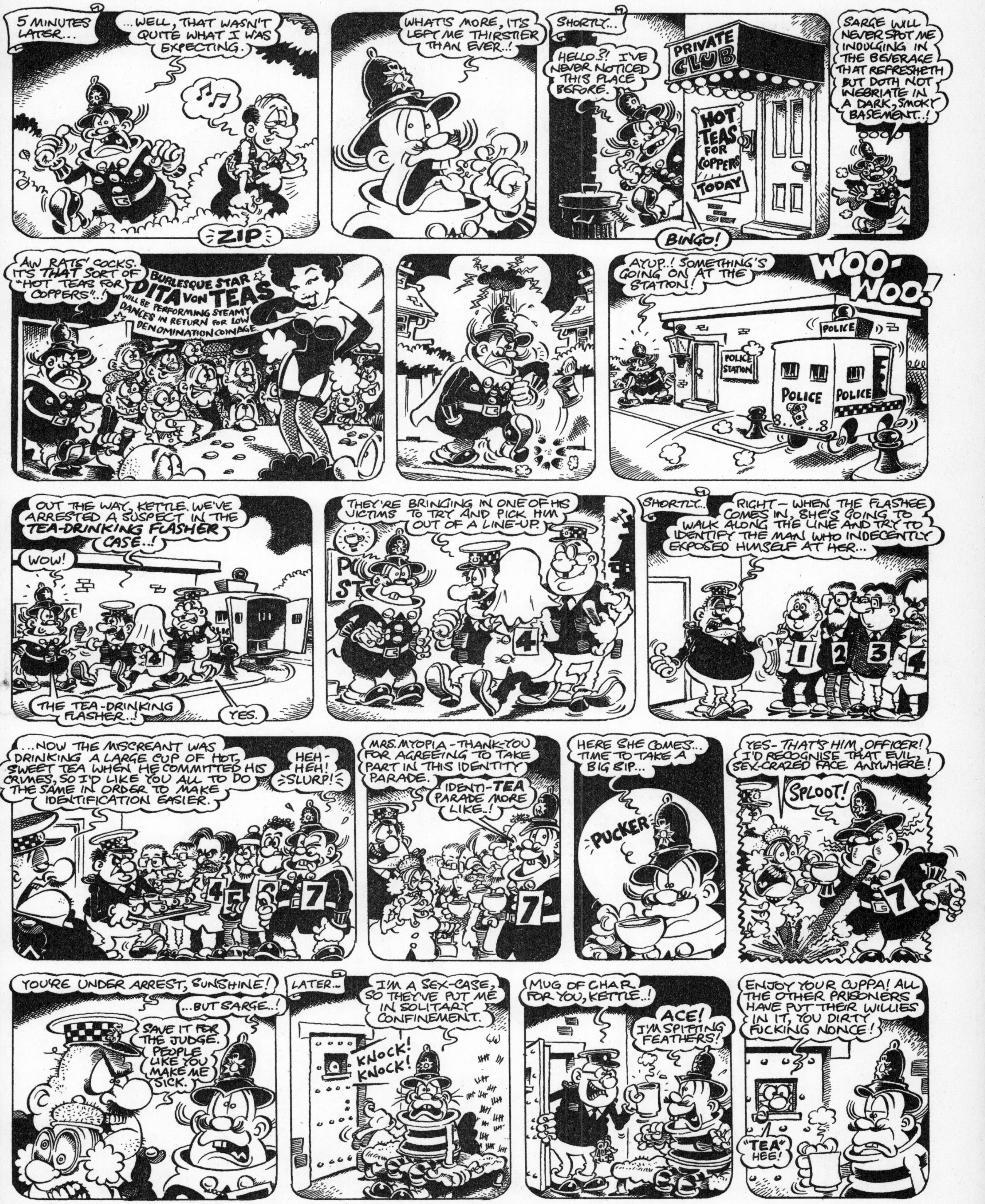
5 MINUTES LATER...
...WELL, THAT WASN'T QUITE WHAT I WAS EXPECTING.
ZIP
WHAT'S MORE, IT'S LEFT ME THIRSTIER THAN EVER..!
SHORTLY...
HELLO..?! I'VE NEVER NOTICED THIS PLACE BEFORE.
PRIVATE CLUB
HOT TEAS FOR COPPERS TODAY
BINGO!
SARGE WILL NEVER SPOT ME INDULGING IN THE BEVERAGE THAT REFRESHETH BUT DOTH NOT INEBRIATE IN A DARK, SMOKY BASEMENT..!
AW RATS' COCKS. IT'S THAT SORT OF "HOT TEAS FOR COPPERS"..!
BURLESQUE STAR DITA VON TEAS WILL BE PERFORMING STEAMY DANCES IN RETURN FOR LOW DENOMINATION COINAGE
AYUP..! SOMETHING'S GOING ON AT THE STATION!
WOO-WOO!
POLICE
POLICE STATION
POLICE
POLICE
OUT THE WAY, KETTLE. WE'VE ARRESTED A SUSPECT IN THE TEA-DRINKING FLASHER CASE..!
WOW!
THE TEA-DRINKING FLASHER..!
YES.
THEY'RE BRINGING IN ONE OF HIS VICTIMS TO TRY AND PICK HIM OUT OF A LINE-UP.
SHORTLY...
RIGHT – WHEN THE FLASHEE COMES IN, SHE'S GOING TO WALK ALONG THE LINE AND TRY TO IDENTIFY THE MAN WHO INDECENTLY EXPOSED HIMSELF AT HER...
...NOW THE MISCREANT WAS DRINKING A LARGE CUP OF HOT, SWEET TEA WHEN HE COMMITTED HIS CRIMES, SO I'D LIKE YOU ALL TO DO THE SAME IN ORDER TO MAKE IDENTIFICATION EASIER.
HEH-HEH! SLURP!
MRS. MYOPIA - THANK-YOU FOR AGREEING TO TAKE PART IN THIS IDENTITY PARADE.
IDENTI-TEA PARADE MORE LIKE..!
HERE SHE COMES... TIME TO TAKE A BIG SIP...
PUCKER
YES- THAT'S HIM, OFFICER! I'D RECOGNISE THAT EVIL, SEX-CRAZED FACE ANYWHERE!
SPLOOT!
YOU'RE UNDER ARREST, SUNSHINE!
...BUT SARGE..!
SAVE IT FOR THE JUDGE. PEOPLE LIKE YOU MAKE ME SICK.
LATER...
I'M A SEX-CASE, SO THEY'VE PUT ME IN SOLITARY CONFINEMENT.
KNOCK! KNOCK!
MUG OF CHAR FOR YOU, KETTLE..!
ACE! I'M SPITTING FEATHERS!
ENJOY YOUR CUPPA! ALL THE OTHER PRISONERS HAVE PUT THEIR WILLIES IN IT, YOU DIRTY FUCKING NONCE!
"TEA" HEE!

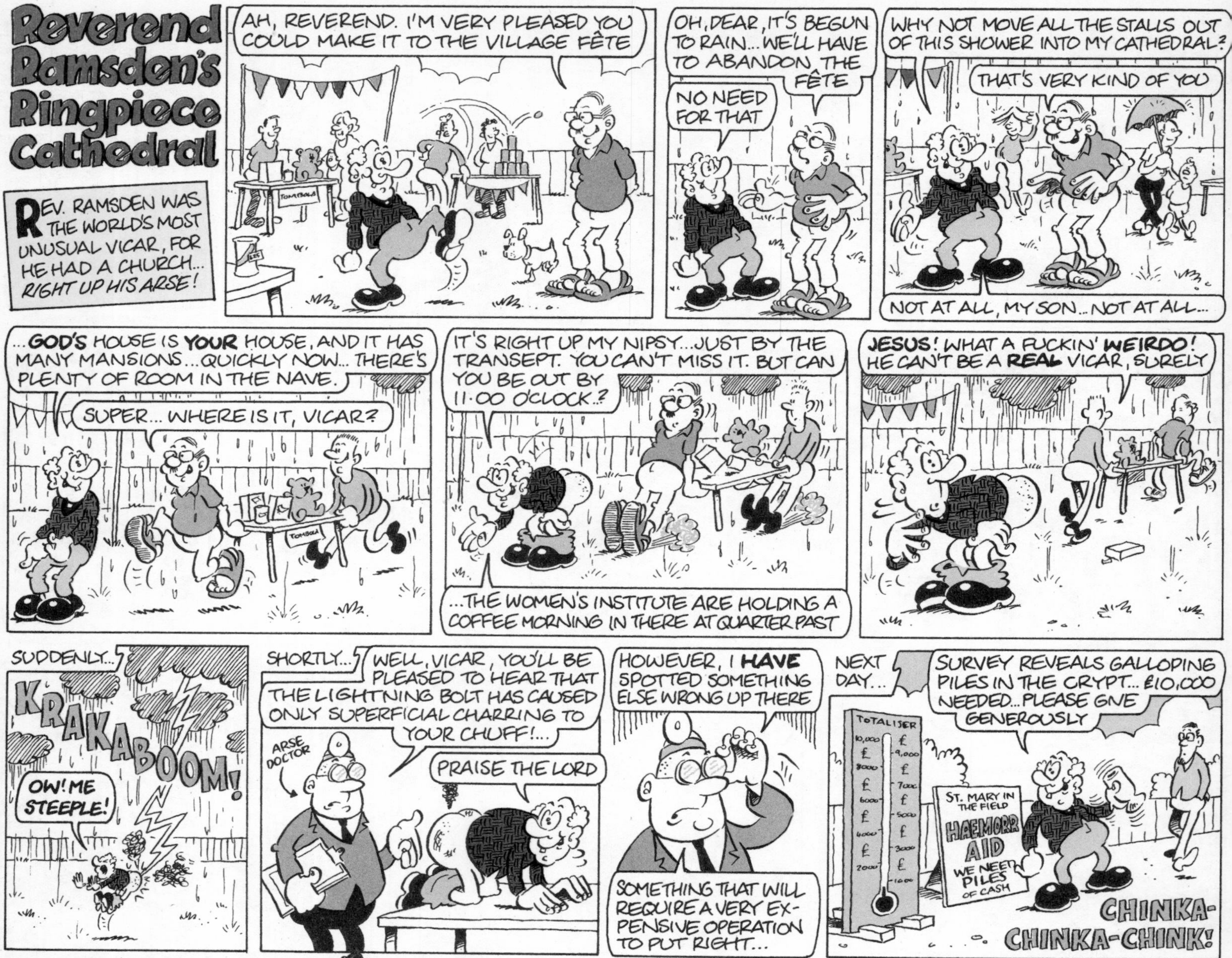
Reverend Ramsden's Ringpiece Cathedral
REV. RAMSDEN WAS THE WORLD'S MOST UNUSUAL VICAR, FOR HE HAD A CHURCH... RIGHT UP HIS ARSE!
AH, REVEREND. I'M VERY PLEASED YOU COULD MAKE IT TO THE VILLAGE FÊTE
TOMBOLA
OH, DEAR, IT'S BEGUN TO RAIN... WE'LL HAVE TO ABANDON THE FÊTE
NO NEED FOR THAT
WHY NOT MOVE ALL THE STALLS OUT OF THIS SHOWER INTO MY CATHEDRAL?
THAT'S VERY KIND OF YOU
NOT AT ALL, MY SON... NOT AT ALL...
...GOD'S HOUSE IS YOUR HOUSE, AND IT HAS MANY MANSIONS... QUICKLY NOW... THERE'S PLENTY OF ROOM IN THE NAVE.
SUPER... WHERE IS IT, VICAR?
TOMBOLA
IT'S RIGHT UP MY NIPSY... JUST BY THE TRANSEPT. YOU CAN'T MISS IT. BUT CAN YOU BE OUT BY 11.00 O'CLOCK?
...THE WOMEN'S INSTITUTE ARE HOLDING A COFFEE MORNING IN THERE AT QUARTER PAST
JESUS! WHAT A FUCKIN' WEIRDO! HE CAN'T BE A REAL VICAR, SURELY
SUDDENLY...
KRAKABOOM!
OW! ME STEEPLE!
SHORTLY...
WELL, VICAR, YOU'LL BE PLEASED TO HEAR THAT THE LIGHTNING BOLT HAS CAUSED ONLY SUPERFICIAL CHARRING TO YOUR CHUFF!...
ARSE DOCTOR
PRAISE THE LORD
HOWEVER, I HAVE SPOTTED SOMETHING ELSE WRONG UP THERE
SOMETHING THAT WILL REQUIRE A VERY EXPENSIVE OPERATION TO PUT RIGHT...
NEXT DAY...
SURVEY REVEALS GALLOPING PILES IN THE CRYPT... £10,000 NEEDED... PLEASE GIVE GENEROUSLY
TOTALISER
ST. MARY IN THE FIELD
HAEMORR AID
WE NEED PILES OF CASH
CHINKA-CHINKA-CHINK!

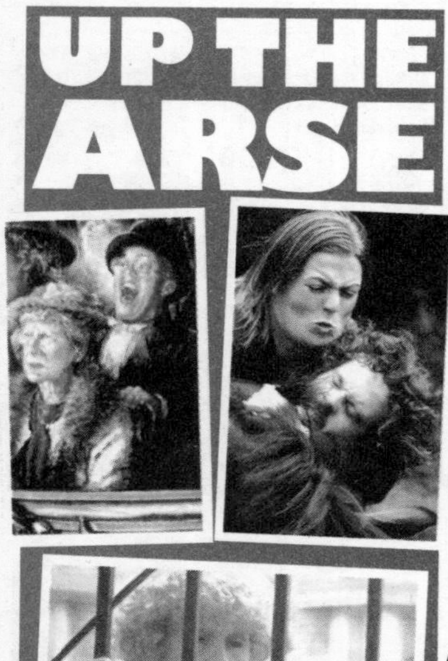
UP THE ARSE
CORNER

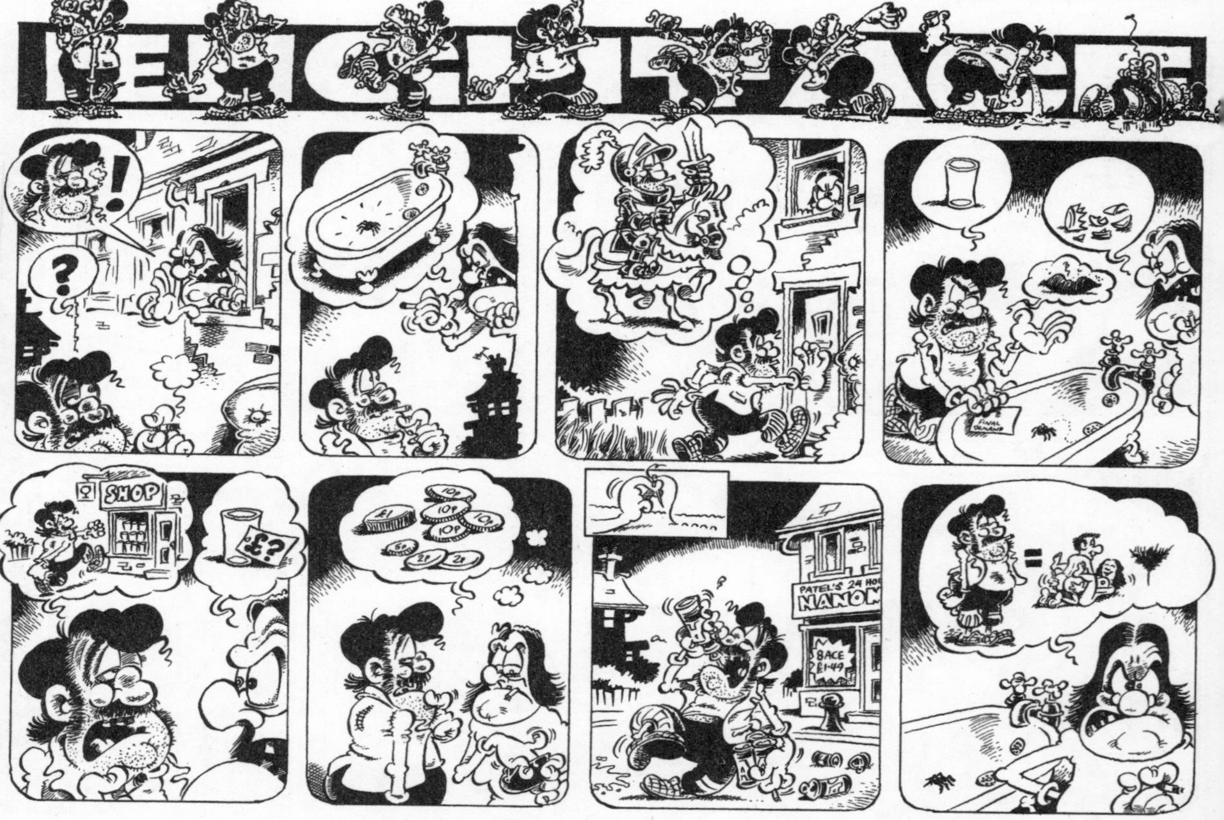

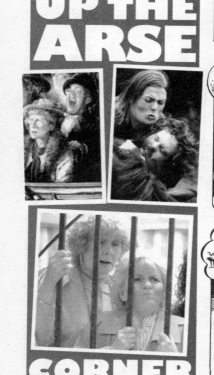

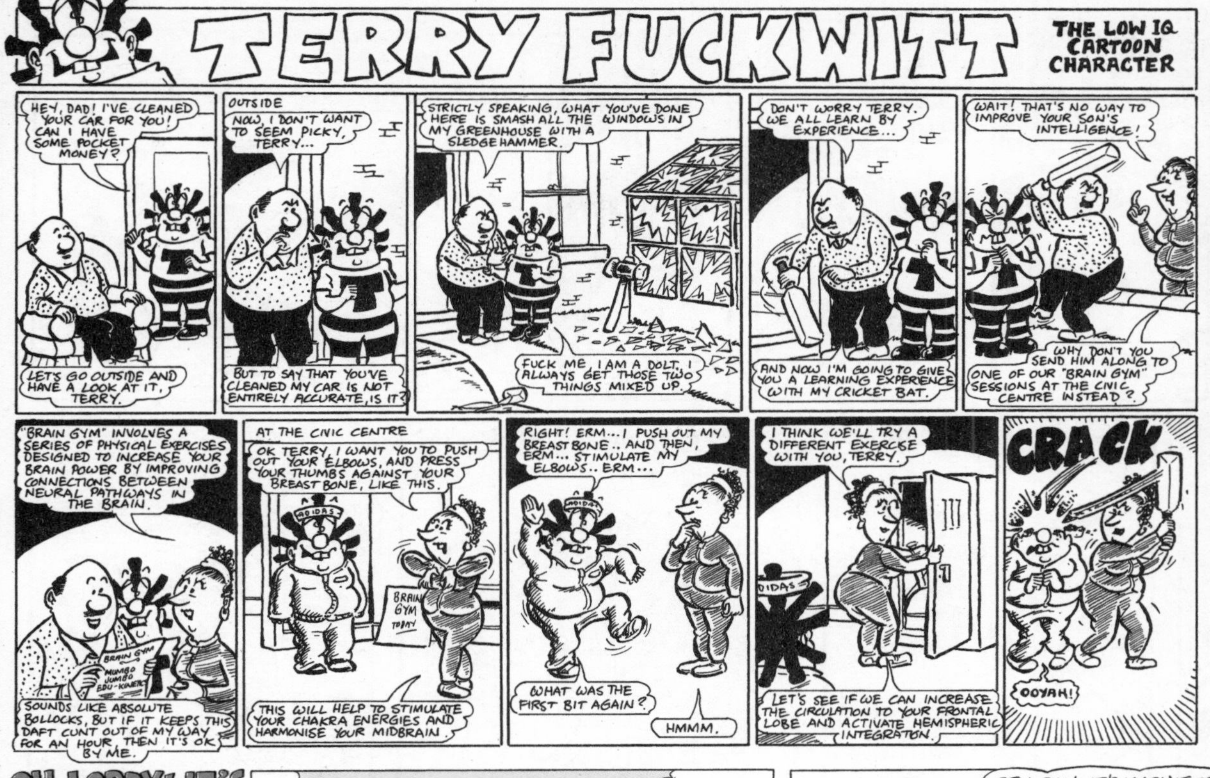
TERRY FUCKWITT
THE LOW IQ CARTOON CHARACTER
HEY, DAD! I'VE CLEANED YOUR CAR FOR YOU! CAN I HAVE SOME POCKET MONEY?
LET'S GO OUTSIDE AND HAVE A LOOK AT IT, TERRY.
OUTSIDE
NOW, I DON'T WANT TO SEEM PICKY, TERRY...
BUT TO SAY THAT YOU'VE CLEANED MY CAR IS NOT ENTIRELY ACCURATE, IS IT?
STRICTLY SPEAKING, WHAT YOU'VE DONE HERE IS SMASH ALL THE WINDOWS IN MY GREENHOUSE WITH A SLEDGEHAMMER.
FUCK ME, I AM A DOLT. I ALWAYS GET THOSE TWO THINGS MIXED UP.
DON'T WORRY TERRY. WE ALL LEARN BY EXPERIENCE...
AND NOW I'M GOING TO GIVE YOU A LEARNING EXPERIENCE WITH MY CRICKET BAT.
WAIT! THAT'S NO WAY TO IMPROVE YOUR SON'S INTELLIGENCE!
WHY DON'T YOU SEND HIM ALONG TO ONE OF OUR "BRAIN GYM" SESSIONS AT THE CIVIC CENTRE INSTEAD?
"BRAIN GYM" INVOLVES A SERIES OF PHYSICAL EXERCISES DESIGNED TO INCREASE YOUR BRAIN POWER BY IMPROVING CONNECTIONS BETWEEN NEURAL PATHWAYS IN THE BRAIN.
SOUNDS LIKE ABSOLUTE BOLLOCKS, BUT IF IT KEEPS THIS DAFT CUNT OUT OF MY WAY FOR AN HOUR, THEN IT'S OK BY ME.
AT THE CIVIC CENTRE
OK TERRY, I WANT YOU TO PUSH OUT YOUR ELBOWS, AND PRESS YOUR THUMBS AGAINST YOUR BREAST BONE, LIKE THIS.
BRAIN GYM TODAY
THIS WILL HELP TO STIMULATE YOUR CHAKRA ENERGIES AND HARMONISE YOUR MIDBRAIN.
RIGHT! ERM... I PUSH OUT MY BREAST BONE... AND THEN, ERM... STIMULATE MY ELBOWS.. ERM...
WHAT WAS THE FIRST BIT AGAIN?
HMMM.
I THINK WE'LL TRY A DIFFERENT EXERCISE WITH YOU, TERRY.
LET'S SEE IF WE CAN INCREASE THE CIRCULATION TO YOUR FRONTAL LOBE AND ACTIVATE HEMISPHERIC INTEGRATION.
CRACK
OOYAH!

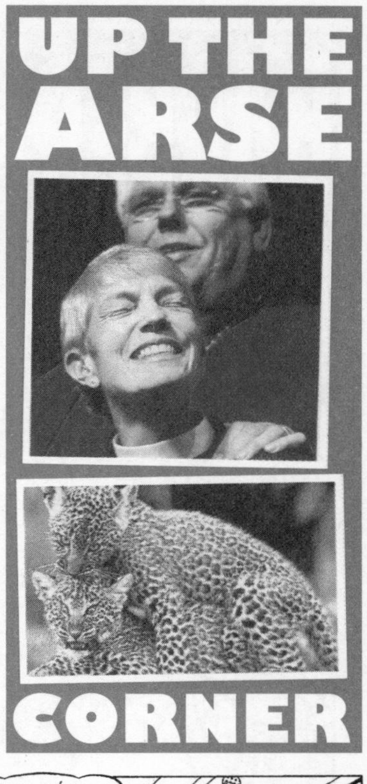
UP THE ARSE
CORNER

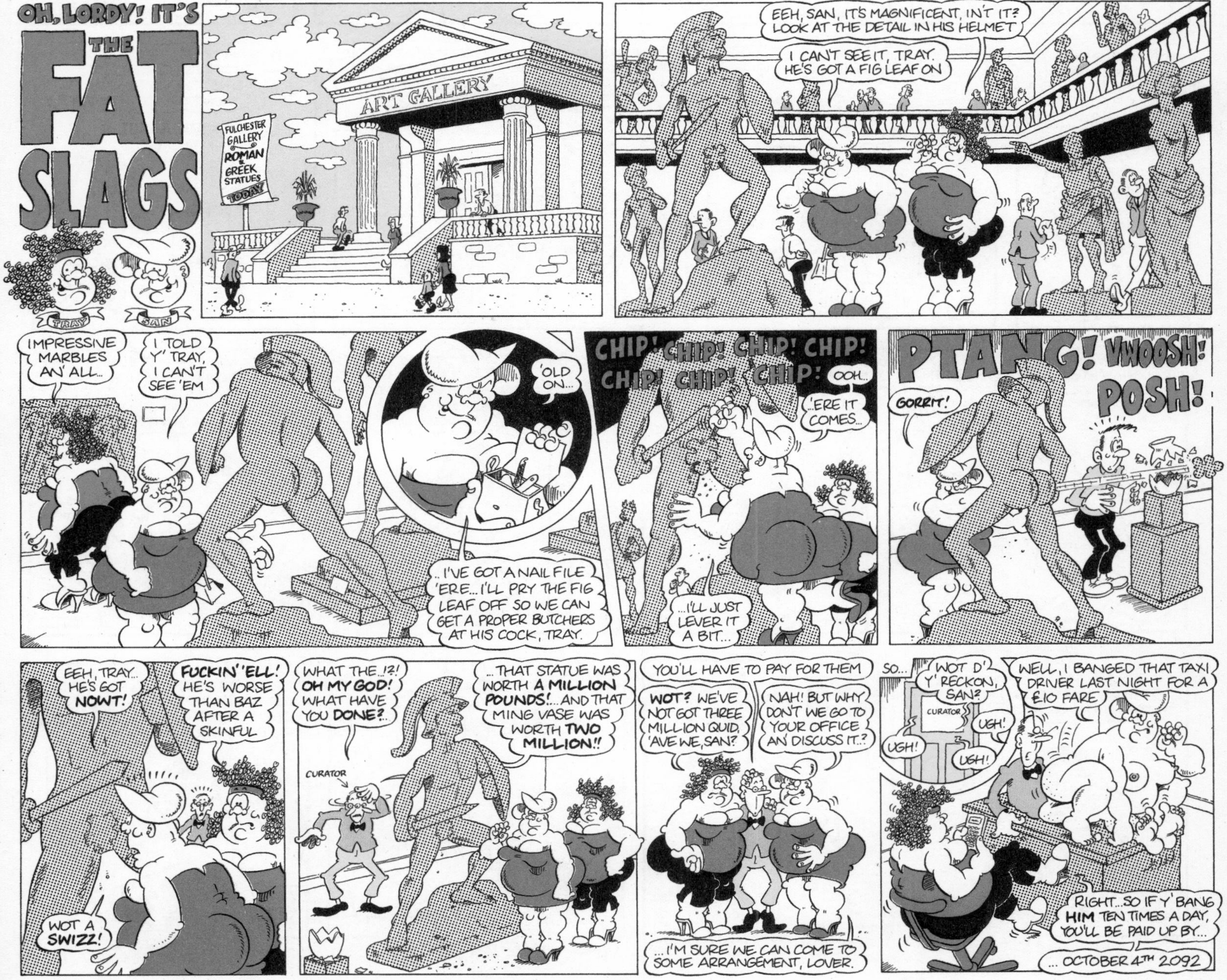
OH, LORDY! IT'S THE FAT SLAGS
TRAY
SAN
ART GALLERY
FULCHESTER GALLERY ROMAN & GREEK STATUES TODAY
EEH, SAN, IT'S MAGNIFICENT, IN'T IT? LOOK AT THE DETAIL IN HIS HELMET
I CAN'T SEE IT, TRAY. HE'S GOT A FIG LEAF ON
IMPRESSIVE MARBLES AN' ALL...
I TOLD Y' TRAY, I CAN'T SEE 'EM
'OLD ON...
..I'VE GOT A NAIL FILE 'ERE... I'LL PRY THE FIG LEAF OFF SO WE CAN GET A PROPER BUTCHERS AT HIS COCK, TRAY.
CHIP! CHIP! CHIP! CHIP! CHIP! CHIP! CHIP!
OOH..
..'ERE IT COMES...
...I'LL JUST LEVER IT A BIT...
PTANG! VWOOSH!
GORRIT!
POSH!
EEH, TRAY... HE'S GOT NOWT!
FUCKIN' 'ELL! HE'S WORSE THAN BAZ AFTER A SKINFUL
WOT A SWIZZ!
WHAT THE..!?! OH MY GOD! WHAT HAVE YOU DONE?..
CURATOR
...THAT STATUE WAS WORTH A MILLION POUNDS!... AND THAT MING VASE WAS WORTH TWO MILLION!!
YOU'LL HAVE TO PAY FOR THEM
WOT? WE'VE NOT GOT THREE MILLION QUID. 'AVE WE, SAN?
NAH! BUT WHY DON'T WE GO TO YOUR OFFICE AN' DISCUSS IT..?
...I'M SURE WE CAN COME TO SOME ARRANGEMENT, LOVER.
SO...
WOT D' Y' RECKON, SAN?
CURATOR
UGH!
UGH!
UGH!
WELL, I BANGED THAT TAXI DRIVER LAST NIGHT FOR A £10 FARE
RIGHT...SO IF Y' BANG HIM TEN TIMES A DAY, YOU'LL BE PAID UP BY...
...OCTOBER 4TH 2092

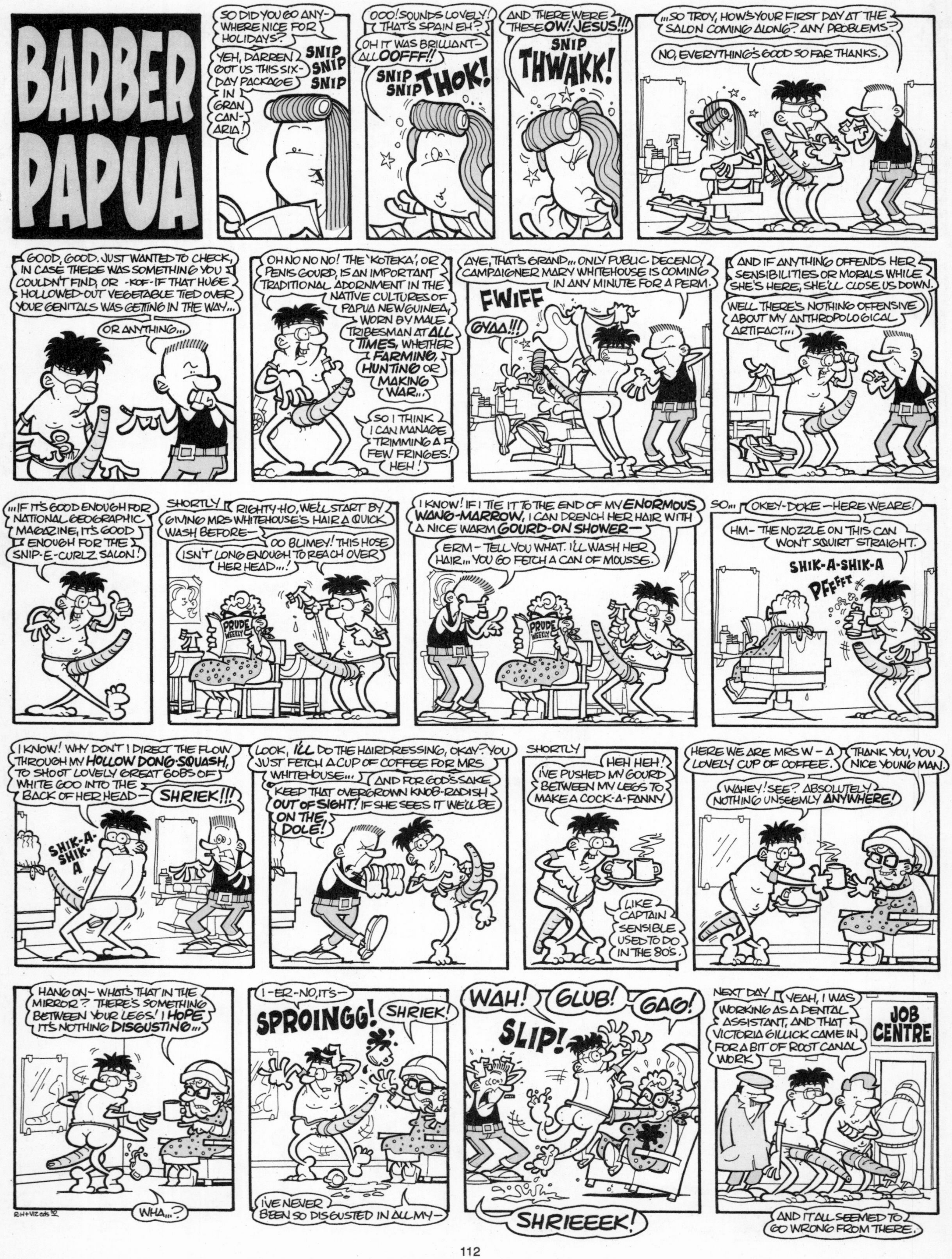

BARBER PAPUA
SO DID YOU GO ANYWHERE NICE FOR HOLIDAYS?
YEH, DARREN GOT US THIS SIX-DAY PACKAGE IN GRAN CANARIA!
SNIP SNIP SNIP
OOO! SOUNDS LOVELY! THAT'S SPAIN EH?
OH IT WAS BRILLIANT-ALL OOFFF!!
SNIP SNIP THOK!
AND THERE WERE THESE OW! JESUS!!!
SNIP THWAKK!
...SO TROY, HOW'S YOUR FIRST DAY AT THE SALON COMING ALONG? ANY PROBLEMS?
NO, EVERYTHING'S GOOD SO FAR THANKS.
GOOD, GOOD. JUST WANTED TO CHECK, IN CASE THERE WAS SOMETHING YOU COULDN'T FIND, OR -KOF- IF THAT HUGE HOLLOWED-OUT VEGETABLE TIED OVER YOUR GENITALS WAS GETTING IN THE WAY...
OR ANYTHING...
OH NO NO NO! THE 'KOTEKA', OR PENIS GOURD, IS AN IMPORTANT TRADITIONAL ADORNMENT IN THE NATIVE CULTURES OF PAPUA NEW GUINEA, WORN BY MALE TRIBESMAN AT ALL TIMES, WHETHER FARMING, HUNTING OR MAKING WAR...
SO I THINK I CAN MANAGE TRIMMING A FEW FRINGES! HEH!
AYE, THAT'S GRAND... ONLY PUBLIC DECENCY CAMPAIGNER MARY WHITEHOUSE IS COMING IN ANY MINUTE FOR A PERM.
FWIFF
GYAA!!!
AND IF ANYTHING OFFENDS HER SENSIBILITIES OR MORALS WHILE SHE'S HERE, SHE'LL CLOSE US DOWN.
WELL THERE'S NOTHING OFFENSIVE ABOUT MY ANTHROPOLOGICAL ARTIFACT...
...IF IT'S GOOD ENOUGH FOR NATIONAL GEOGRAPHIC MAGAZINE, IT'S GOOD ENOUGH FOR THE SNIP-E-CURLZ SALON!
SHORTLY
RIGHTY-HO, WE'LL START BY GIVING MRS WHITEHOUSE'S HAIR A QUICK WASH BEFORE—
OO BLIMEY! THIS HOSE ISN'T LONG ENOUGH TO REACH OVER HER HEAD...!
PRUDE WEEKLY
I KNOW! IF I TIE IT TO THE END OF MY ENORMOUS WANG-MARROW, I CAN DRENCH HER HAIR WITH A NICE WARM GOURD-ON SHOWER—
ERM - TELL YOU WHAT. I'LL WASH HER HAIR... YOU GO FETCH A CAN OF MOUSSE.
PRUDE WEEKLY
SO...
OKEY-DOKE - HERE WE ARE!
HM- THE NOZZLE ON THIS CAN WON'T SQUIRT STRAIGHT.
SHIK-A-SHIK-A
PFFFFT
I KNOW! WHY DON'T I DIRECT THE FLOW THROUGH MY HOLLOW DONG-SQUASH, TO SHOOT LOVELY GREAT GOBS OF WHITE GOO INTO THE BACK OF HER HEAD—
SHRIEK!!!
SHIK-A-SHIK-A
LOOK, I'LL DO THE HAIRDRESSING, OKAY? YOU JUST FETCH A CUP OF COFFEE FOR MRS WHITEHOUSE...
AND FOR GOD'S SAKE KEEP THAT OVERGROWN KNOB-RADISH OUT OF SIGHT! IF SHE SEES IT WE'LL BE ON THE DOLE!
SHORTLY
HEH HEH! I'VE PUSHED MY GOURD BETWEEN MY LEGS TO MAKE A COCK-A-FANNY
LIKE CAPTAIN SENSIBLE USED TO DO IN THE 80'S.
HERE WE ARE MRS W - A LOVELY CUP OF COFFEE.
THANK YOU, YOU NICE YOUNG MAN.
WAHEY! SEE? ABSOLUTELY NOTHING UNSEEMLY ANYWHERE!
HANG ON - WHAT'S THAT IN THE MIRROR? THERE'S SOMETHING BETWEEN YOUR LEGS! I HOPE IT'S NOTHING DISGUSTING...
WHA...?
I - ER - NO, IT'S—
SPROINGG!
SHRIEK!
I'VE NEVER BEEN SO DISGUSTED IN ALL MY—
WAH!
GLUB!
GAG!
SLIP!
SHRIEEEK!
NEXT DAY
YEAH, I WAS WORKING AS A DENTAL ASSISTANT, AND THAT VICTORIA GILLICK CAME IN FOR A BIT OF ROOT CANAL WORK
JOB CENTRE
AND IT ALL SEEMED TO GO WRONG FROM THERE.

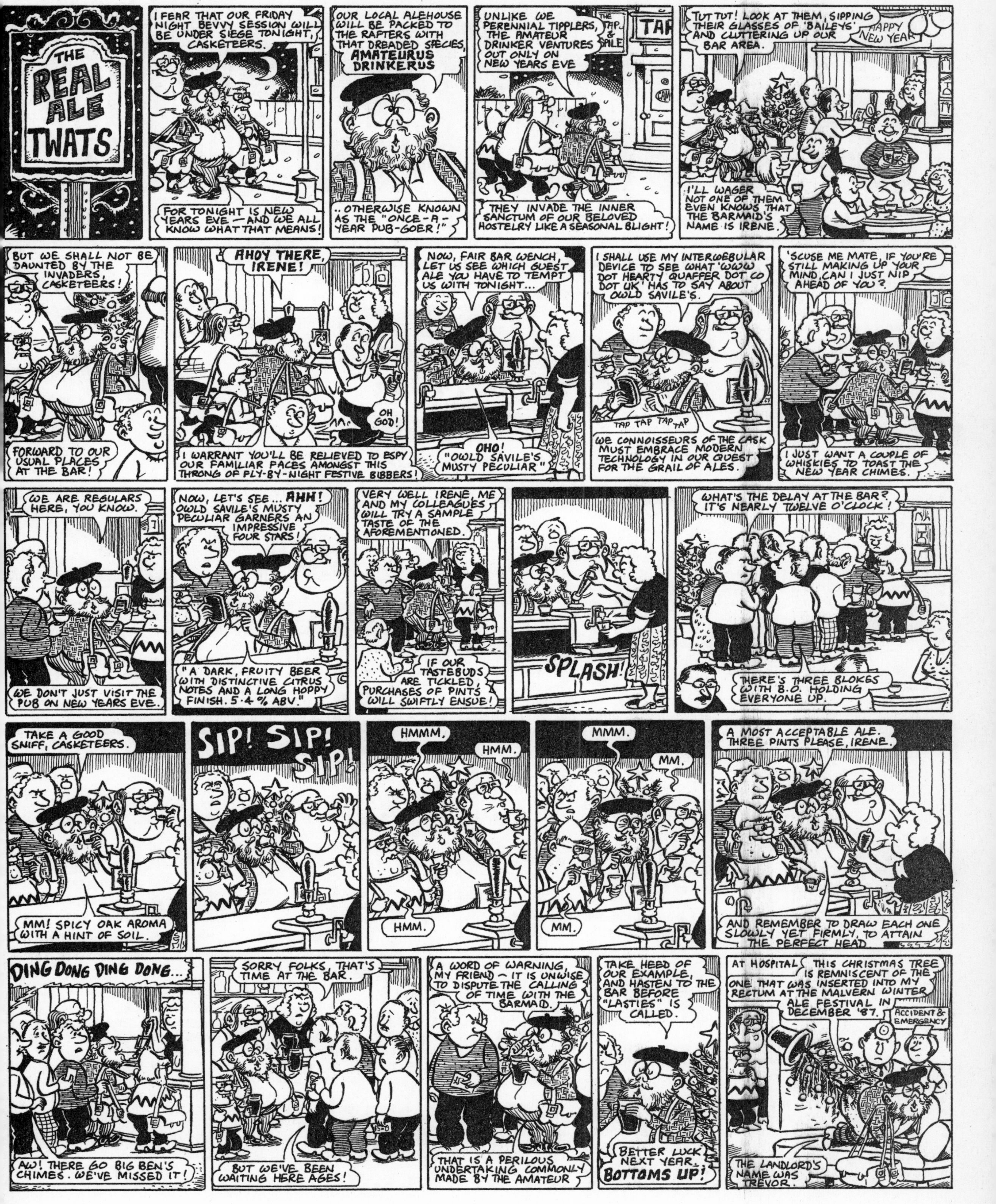
THE REAL ALE TWATS
I FEAR THAT OUR FRIDAY NIGHT BEVVY SESSION WILL BE UNDER SIEGE TONIGHT, CASKETEERS.
FOR TONIGHT IS NEW YEARS EVE — AND WE ALL KNOW WHAT THAT MEANS!
OUR LOCAL ALEHOUSE WILL BE PACKED TO THE RAFTERS WITH THAT DREADED SPECIES, AMATEURUS DRINKERUS
..OTHERWISE KNOWN AS THE "ONCE-A-YEAR PUB-GOER!"
UNLIKE WE PERENNIAL TIPPLERS, THE AMATEUR DRINKER VENTURES OUT ONLY ON NEW YEARS EVE
THE TAP & SPILE
TAP
THEY INVADE THE INNER SANCTUM OF OUR BELOVED HOSTELRY LIKE A SEASONAL BLIGHT!
TUT TUT! LOOK AT THEM, SIPPING THEIR GLASSES OF 'BAILEYS' AND CLUTTERING UP OUR BAR AREA.
HAPPY NEW YEAR
I'LL WAGER NOT ONE OF THEM EVEN KNOWS THAT THE BARMAID'S NAME IS IRENE.
BUT WE SHALL NOT BE DAUNTED BY THE INVADERS, CASKETEERS!
FORWARD TO OUR USUAL PLACES AT THE BAR!
AHOY THERE, IRENE!
OH GOD!
I WARRANT YOU'LL BE RELIEVED TO ESPY OUR FAMILIAR FACES AMONGST THIS THRONG OF FLY-BY-NIGHT FESTIVE BIBBERS!
NOW, FAIR BAR WENCH, LET US SEE WHICH GUEST ALE YOU HAVE TO TEMPT US WITH TONIGHT...
OHO! "OWLD SAVILE'S MUSTY PECULIAR"
I SHALL USE MY INTERWEBULAR DEVICE TO SEE WHAT 'WWW DOT HEARTY QUAFFER DOT CO DOT UK' HAS TO SAY ABOUT OWLD SAVILE'S.
TAP TAP TAP TAP
WE CONNOISSEURS OF THE CASK MUST EMBRACE MODERN TECHNOLOGY IN OUR QUEST FOR THE GRAIL OF ALES.
'SCUSE ME MATE, IF YOU'RE STILL MAKING UP YOUR MIND, CAN I JUST NIP AHEAD OF YOU?
I JUST WANT A COUPLE OF WHISKIES TO TOAST THE NEW YEAR CHIMES.
WE ARE REGULARS HERE, YOU KNOW.
WE DON'T JUST VISIT THE PUB ON NEW YEARS EVE.
NOW, LET'S SEE... AHH! OWLD SAVILE'S MUSTY PECULIAR GARNERS AN IMPRESSIVE FOUR STARS!
"A DARK, FRUITY BEER WITH DISTINCTIVE CITRUS NOTES AND A LONG HOPPY FINISH. 5·4% ABV."
VERY WELL IRENE, ME AND MY COLLEAGUES WILL TRY A SAMPLE TASTE OF THE AFOREMENTIONED.
IF OUR TASTEBUDS ARE TICKLED, PURCHASES OF PINTS WILL SWIFTLY ENSUE!
SPLASH!
WHAT'S THE DELAY AT THE BAR? IT'S NEARLY TWELVE O'CLOCK!
THERE'S THREE BLOKES WITH B.O. HOLDING EVERYONE UP.
TAKE A GOOD SNIFF, CASKETEERS.
MM! SPICY OAK AROMA WITH A HINT OF SOIL.
SIP! SIP! SIP!
HMMM.
HMM.
HMM.
MMM.
MM.
MM.
A MOST ACCEPTABLE ALE. THREE PINTS PLEASE, IRENE.
AND REMEMBER TO DRAW EACH ONE SLOWLY YET FIRMLY, TO ATTAIN THE PERFECT HEAD
DING DONG DING DONG...
AW! THERE GO BIG BEN'S CHIMES. WE'VE MISSED IT!
SORRY FOLKS, THAT'S TIME AT THE BAR.
BUT WE'VE BEEN WAITING HERE AGES!
A WORD OF WARNING, MY FRIEND — IT IS UNWISE TO DISPUTE THE CALLING OF TIME WITH THE BARMAID.
THAT IS A PERILOUS UNDERTAKING COMMONLY MADE BY THE AMATEUR
TAKE HEED OF OUR EXAMPLE, AND HASTEN TO THE BAR BEFORE "LASTIES" IS CALLED.
BETTER LUCK NEXT YEAR. BOTTOMS UP!
AT HOSPITAL
THIS CHRISTMAS TREE IS REMINISCENT OF THE ONE THAT WAS INSERTED INTO MY RECTUM AT THE MALVERN WINTER ALE FESTIVAL IN DECEMBER '87.
ACCIDENT & EMERGENCY
THE LANDLORD'S NAME WAS TREVOR.

Double Dec-ker!

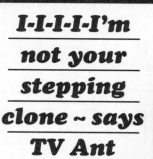

TELLY favourite ANT MCPARTLIN told yesterday how he had the shock of his life when he woke one morning to find he had turned into his double-act partner DECLAN DONNELLY!

By our Dec correspondent
SEXTON MINGE

"I couldn't believe my eyes when I looked in the mirror," the Geordie star told the *Nairobi Times*. "I had transformed into Dec whilst I was sleeping."

"I know I was definitely Ant when I went to bed the previous night," he recalled. "I remember noticing my darker hair and freakishly high forehead whilst I was brushing my teeth. I simply couldn't imagine what had happened overnight to change me into Dec."

"I immediately rushed over to the real Dec's bed and shook him awake," McPartlin told the popular Kenyan paper. *"He nearly had a heart attack when he saw I had turned into him. He must have thought he was seeing double!"*

But Donnelly's amazement soon turned to concern when the TV pair considered the implications of McPartlin's unexpected transmogrification. Ant recalled: "Looking at our multi million pound contract, we saw that we were obliged to appear in every show as Ant and Dec, not Dec and Dec."

PJ AND THE PAIR: *Ant turned into Duncan.*

"The implication was clear. Going onscreen as a pair of identical Decs could easily have got us sacked."

The pint-sized presenters were due to record an episode of *I'm a Celebrity Get Me Out of Here* at Pinewood studios that very afternoon. They had to think quickly to avoid legal action from angry ITV bosses.

McPartlin said: "I put on a large pair of sunglasses and a wide-brimmed hat which I pulled down low to hide the fact that I no longer had quite such an enormous forehead. Then I did the whole show looking down at the ground so that my face was in shadow."

"There were a few close calls during filming, such as when an emu tried to pull my hat off, but I think I got away with it," he added. *"I can laugh about it now, but I can assure you that it didn't seem so amusing at the time."*

Things weren't quite so tense once the pair finished shooting for the day. Ant told his interviewer: "Me and Dec went out to our local pub for a pint and I decided to have some fun."

"When the barmaid came over to the table to collect our empties, I pinched her bottom," Ant continued. "But it was Dec who got the slap in the face."

"Then I reached up her skirt and put my other hand in her bra ... and she kicked him in the nuts!"

"I laughed my head off, but Dec wasn't amused at all, I can tell you," Ant added.

Happily, McPartlin's Kafkaesque episode didn't last long. He woke up next day to find that he had returned to being Ant again. "It was quite a relief to see my own familiar, albeit peculiar, features staring back at me from the bathroom mirror," he said.

"I'm still none the wiser as to what bizarre process changed me into Dec. I suppose it's just one of those things that science can't explain," he added.

I-I-I-I-I'm not your stepping clone ~ says TV Ant

SCIENTISTS admit that they still can't give a rational explanation for many things that happen every day. Ghosts, Uri Geller's miraculous powers and Noel Edmonds's continued public popularity all defy rational explanation. But does McPartlin's peculiar experience fall into this category of baffling phenomena? We asked half a dozen of Britain's most eminent eggheads and boffins to hypothesise about just how Ant might have turned into Dec.

DR MAGNUS PYKE
• *Deceased windmill-armed nutritionist*

"IT'S QUITE possible that Ant left his bedroom window open during the night. A cloud of spangly gas off a meteorite or a comet may have come into the room and caused a temporary mutation in the molecules of his body, changing him into Dec."

PROFESSOR RICHARD DAWKINGS
• *God-hating biological theorist*

"A MOSQUITO could have bitten Dec whilst he was asleep, then flown across the room to Ant's bed and bitten him too. This means that some of Dec's DNAs would have been transferred into Ant's bloodstream. DNAs are so unimaginably small that you can fit fifty of them into a single mosquito, and it's not hard to imagine an accelerated evolutionary mechanism that would use these tiny springs of genetic information to turn Ant into Dec by morning. Over the course of the day, Ant's immune system would get to work attacking the foreign DNAs, turning Ant back to himself 24 hours later."

PROFESSOR STEPHEN HAWKIN
• *Computer-brained quantum physicist*

"FOR EVERY particle in the universe there is an equal and opposite anti-particle. Electrons have positrons; neutrinos have quarks; hadrons have leptrons and so on. So therefore it follows that somewhere in our universe there is an anti-universe. It may be hidden in some extra dimensions which we cannot comprehend, or it may be at night or on the Moon or somewhere. We simply don't know. But I feel sure that in this anti-universe, Ant would turn into anti-Ant - the opposite of Ant - which is Dec, and Dec would likewise turn into the anti-Dec, which is Ant. If this didn't happen, th

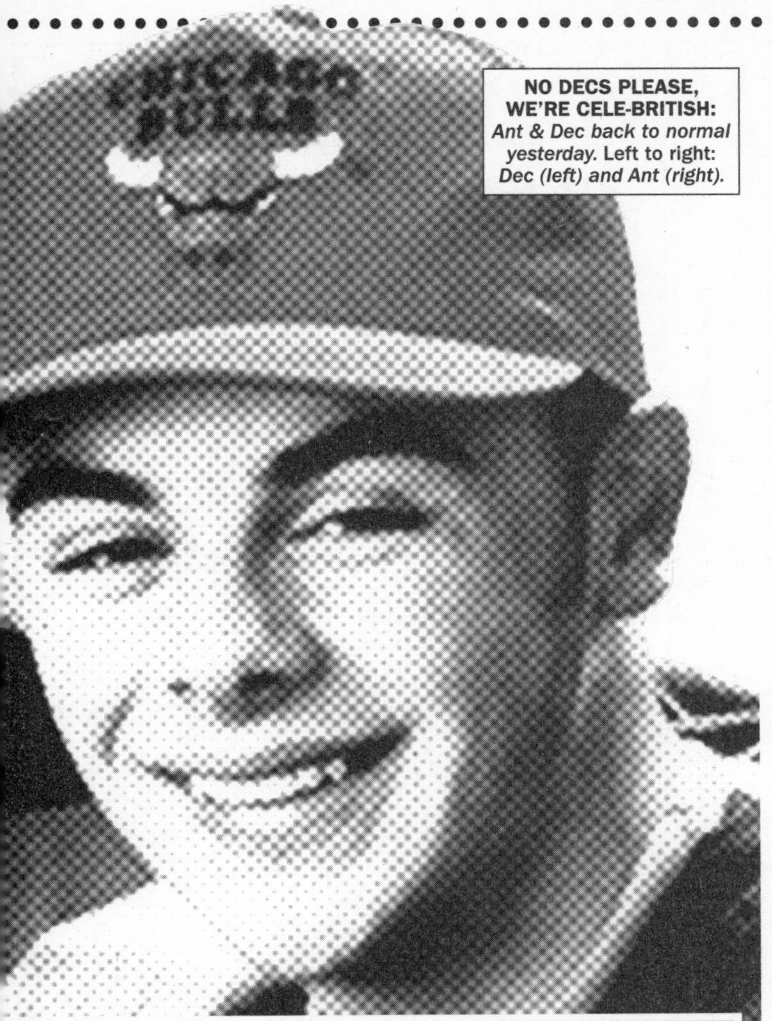

NO DECS PLEASE, WE'RE CELE-BRITISH: *Ant & Dec back to normal yesterday. Left to right: Dec (left) and Ant (right).*

/erse would be out of balance due to
urplus of anti-Ant matter, leading to
enormous "Dec-splosion" that would
the Big Bang. Either that, or Ant and
might change into Dick and Dom."

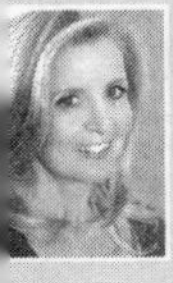

DR GILLIAN McKEITH
• Rodent-faced turd-sniffer

"IT IS A scientifically-
ven fact that you are what you eat,
I believe that Ant's transformation
Dec was a direct result of Ant eat-
Dec's dinner. Due to a mix-up at the
canteen, sandwiches intended for
nnelly may have been accidentally
to McPartlin. The niacin, riboflavin
chlorophyll in the sandwiches will
e combined with the E-numbers and
oxidants in Ant's gut and changed
into his comedy partner. The pro-
s was reversed when Ant evacuated
bowels and purged himself of Dec's
dwiches."

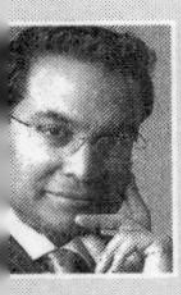

DR RAJ PERSAUD
• Poundshop psychiatrist

"IT IS WELL documented
oughout the anals of psychoanalysis
t the mind is able to affect the body in
narkable ways. For example, a person
o believes he is suffering from a par-
lar disease may develop psychoso-
matic spympton of that very disease. By a similar mechanism if, for some reason buried deep within his psyche, Ant believed he had become Dec, he could well develop the physical characteristics of his telly pal. The spymptoms could be triggered by a number of different causes: for example, a recollection of some childhood trauma, such as when he was blinded by a paintball in Byker Grove, or even by a powerful erotic stimulus, such as watching her with the big tits out of Hear'Say having a shower under a waterfall."

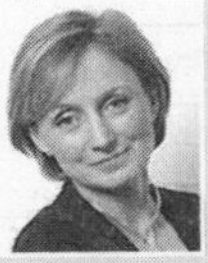

DR ROSEMARY LEONARD
• GP who you can't get an appointment with because she's always on breakfast telly

"YOU'D BE surprised how many people come into doctors' surgeries complaining of turning into Dec. The elderly are at particular risk, but pregnant women, the young and other people can also develop this condition without warning, possibly due to a virus or germs. My advice to anyone who feels themselves beginning to turn into Dec is not to panic. Wrap up warm, have plenty of fluids and take a couple of aspirins three times a day before meals. If you are at all worried, or if symptoms persist and you haven't turned back into yourself within a couple of days, give it another couple of weeks to see how things go."

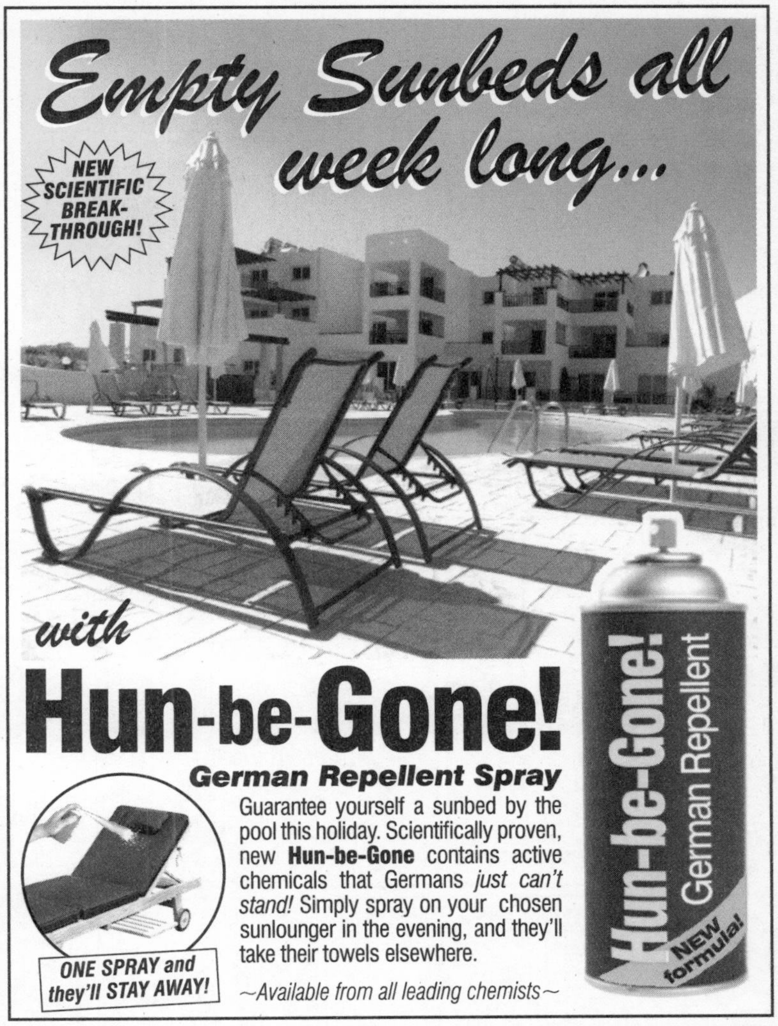

Empty Sunbeds all week long...
NEW SCIENTIFIC BREAK-THROUGH!
with
Hun-be-Gone!
German Repellent Spray
Guarantee yourself a sunbed by the pool this holiday. Scientifically proven, new Hun-be-Gone contains active chemicals that Germans just can't stand! Simply spray on your chosen sunlounger in the evening, and they'll take their towels elsewhere.
ONE SPRAY and they'll STAY AWAY!
~Available from all leading chemists~
Hun-be-Gone! German Repellent
NEW formula!

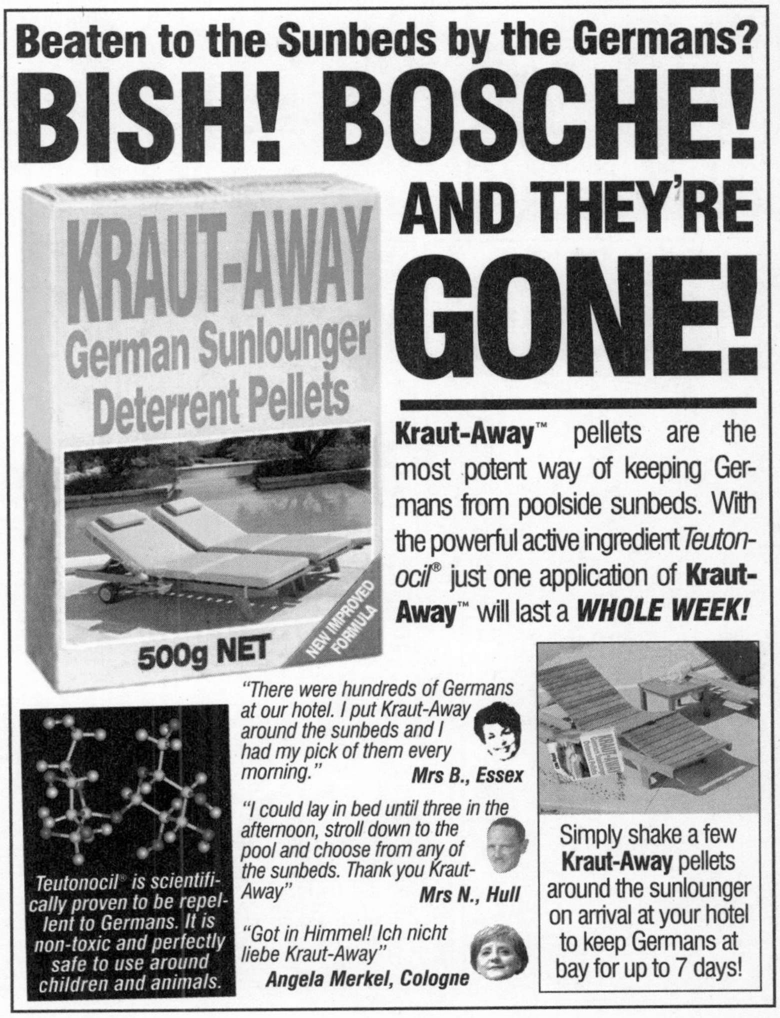

Beaten to the Sunbeds by the Germans?
BISH! BOSCHE! AND THEY'RE GONE!
KRAUT-AWAY
German Sunlounger Deterrent Pellets
500g NET
NEW IMPROVED FORMULA
Kraut-Away™ pellets are the most potent way of keeping Germans from poolside sunbeds. With the powerful active ingredient Teutonocil® just one application of Kraut-Away™ will last a WHOLE WEEK!
Teutonocil® is scientifically proven to be repellent to Germans. It is non-toxic and perfectly safe to use around children and animals.
"There were hundreds of Germans at our hotel. I put Kraut-Away around the sunbeds and I had my pick of them every morning." Mrs B., Essex
"I could lay in bed until three in the afternoon, stroll down to the pool and choose from any of the sunbeds. Thank you Kraut-Away" Mrs N., Hull
"Got in Himmel! Ich nicht liebe Kraut-Away" Angela Merkel, Cologne
Simply shake a few Kraut-Away pellets around the sunlounger on arrival at your hotel to keep Germans at bay for up to 7 days!

TINRIBS

11 YEAR OLD TOMMY TAYLOR HAD THE MOST MARVELLOUS MECHANICAL FRIEND — A REMARKABLE ROBOT WHOSE NAME WAS TINRIBS

Row 1

AT SCHOOL — MR SNODWORTHY, I'VE DECIDED TO GIVE THE CHILDREN A LESSON IN FIRST AID, TODAY. / TUT! VERY WELL HEADMASTER.

GATHER ROUND FOR YOUR FIRST AID LESSON, CHILDREN! / CLANG CLANG CL / YOW! THAT BELL NEARLY BUST MY EARDRUM!

BY A STROKE OF LUCK, MR SNODWORTHY APPEARS TO BE SUFFERING FROM A SORE EAR. / NOW CHILDREN, PUT UP YOUR HAND IF YOU CAN TELL ME THE BEST WAY OF TREATING EARACHE.

LOOK, HEADMASTER — TINRIBS KNOWS THE ANSWER! / HI, I'M BARBIE. I LOVE YOU VERY MUCH. / AHA! AND WHAT DOES YOUR FABULOUS ROBOT CHUM SUGGEST, YOUNG TAYLOR?

WELL SIR, WE CAN TAKE TINRIBS'S TOW-ROPE AND TIE ONE END AROUND MR SNODWORTHY'S AFFLICTED EAR... / THEN WE TIE THE OTHER END TO THE DOOR HANDLE.

Row 2

NEXT I SIMPLY SLAM THE DOOR SHUT, AND... / WOAH THERE, YOUNG TAYLOR! THAT'S THE CURE FOR TOOTHACHE, NOT EARACHE!

THIS REMEDY WOULD MERELY CAUSE POOR MR SNODWORTHY A LOT OF UNNECESSARY PAIN / AND WE DON'T WANT THAT, DO WE?

NO, THE MAIN THING WE HAVE TO DO IS SEE THAT THE PATIENT IS KEPT WARM AND COMFORTABLE. / MOST IMPORTANTLY, WE MUST ENSURE THAT HIS EAR IS NOT EXPOSED TO ANY COLD WIND...

SO I'LL SLAM THIS DOOR SHUT IN ORDER TO KEEP OUT ANY NASTY DRAUGHTS / YANK / YELP!

NOW THEN, BACTERIAL EAR INFECTIONS ARE BEST TREATED WITH PENICILLIN-BASED EARDROPS / UNFORTUNATELY, ALL WE'VE GOT IN THE SCHOOL FIRST AID BOX IS THIS USED RUBBER JOHNNY. THAT'S NO USE!

Row 3

HEADMASTER, PENICILLIN GROWS FROM MOULD, DOESN'T IT? / WELL THIS TIN CAN FROM MY ROBOT CHUM'S VERTICAL SUPPORT STILL BEARS TRACES OF MOULDY BAKED BEANS

GOOD THINKING, TAYLOR! / THE TIN CAN COULD ACT AS A SORT OF OVERSIZED, SHARP RUSTY METAL PENICILLIN-BASED EARDROP

HOLD STILL MR SNODWORTHY! / STAMP STAMP STAMP / I'M TRYING TO INSERT THIS EARDROP INTO YOUR EUSTACHIAN TUBE FOR YOUR OWN GOOD!

NOW, AN IMPORTANT PART OF FIRST AID IS TO REASSURE THE PATIENT WITH A FEW COMFORTING WORDS — LIKE THIS... / THERE, THERE, MR SNODWORTHY, EVERYTHING IS ALL RIGHT...

HMPH! THE STUPID FAT OAF IS TOO DEAF TO HEAR MY COMFORTING WORDS! / PERHAPS MY MECHANICAL AMIGO CAN HELP, HEADMASTER.

I'VE PLUGGED TINRIBS'S VOICEBOX INTO THE SCHOOL MUSIC DEPARTMENT'S MOST POWERFUL PA SYSTEM / THIS'LL PRODUCE COMFORTING WORDS OF REASSURANCE AT OVER A HUNDRED DECIBELS

Row 4

HI I'M BARBIE / GAH!

OHO! / MR SNODWORTHY IS DRIFTING IN AND OUT OF CONSCIOUSNESS. / THIS WILL BE AN IDEAL OPPORTUNITY FOR ME TO DEMONSTRATE MOUTH-TO-MOUTH RESUSCITATION ON HIM.

BUT BEFORE I DO I'LL JUST HAVE MY ELEVENSES... / ...A WHOLE GARLIC CLOVE AND RAW ONION SANDWICH, AND A HAVANA CIGAR. CHOMP! PUFF!

UGH! THE HEADMASTER'S BREATH IS MORE LIKELY TO FINISH ME OFF THAN RESUSCITATE ME! / I'LL HAVE TO STOP HIM GIVING ME THE "KISS OF DEATH" — AND I'LL NEED THIS ROBOT'S HELP TO DO SO.

GASP! I'VE REMOVED THE SCREWS FROM THE UNDERSIDE OF TINRIBS'S SKATEBOARD / NOW I'LL JUST — GMMF! — USE THEM TO SCREW MY LIPS TOGETHER.

Row 5

MMF-MMM-MPH-MMF! / BARRP! / *TRANSLATION: I'D LIKE TO SEE THE HEADMASTER TRY TO GIVE ME THE KISS OF LIFE NOW!

RIGHT, LET'S PROCEED WITH MR SNODWORTHY'S MOUTH-TO-MOUTH RESUSCITATION. / OBVIOUSLY I WON'T BE DOING IT MYSELF BECAUSE THAT WOULD MAKE ME A BUMMER. SO I'VE ASKED THE SCHOOL MATRON TO ADMINISTER THE KISS OF LIFE, INSTEAD!

THIS IS MISS HELGA VA-VA-VOOM, OUR ATTRACTIVE NEW SWEDISH SCHOOL MATRON / COR! / HALLO, BOYS!

OH, VOT A SHAME! MEESTER SNODVORTHY'S MOUTH EES ALL SEALED UP! / I AM UNABLE TO GEEV HIM ZE KISSY-KISSY OF LIFE!

NEVER MIND — I VEEL DEMONSTRATE ON ZEES ROBOT INSTEAD! MWAH! MWAH! MWAH! / SMOOCH! / HI, I'M BARBIE. I LOVE YOU VERY MUCH.

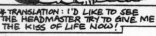

116

The BROWN BOTTLE

MILD MANNERED BANK CLERK BARRY BROWN IS MAKING HIS WAY HOME AFTER WORK...

Hmm. SEEMS QUIET. IS IT TOO MUCH TO HOPE FOR AN UNEVENTFUL EVENING?

SUDDENLY...

BANG BANG BANG!

GASP! THAT SOUNDS LIKE GUNSHOTS!

...NO REST FOR THE WICKED

BUT...

PHEW. IT'S JUST KIDS LETTING OFF BANGERS

CRACKLE FWKSSH! CRACKLE ACKLE!

I THINK IT'S ABOUT TIME SOMEONE TAUGHT THEM 'THE FIREWORKS CODE'... AND A LITTLE SOMETHING CALLED 'RESPONSIBILITY'

BARRY DRINKS FOUR BOTTLES OF NEWCASTLE BROWN TO BECOME...

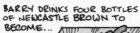

GLUG GLUG GLUG

HA-AAA! YA FUCKAAHZ!

GASP! ...THE BROWN BOTTLE!

TRIP!

BARP!

HERE, LENDS US A TAB, EH, EH, SON, EH.

...GAWAAN. BE A PAL, EH...

REET, GIZ A LIGHT OF THE FUCKAH

CAREFUL! YOU SHOULDNT RETURN TO A LIT FIREWORK!

DIVVINT TELL ME WHAT TO DO, SONN ... I'LL TAN YER FUCKIN' ARSE!

FSSSSSSS

BANG!

AAH, YAH CHEEKY LITTLE BASTAAHD

WHAT THE FUCKS THIS YUH'VE GIV US?

MALBORO FRIGGIN' LIGHTS, OR WHAT?

OOYAH... GERROOT AND WALK

AAW! HE'S PISSING ON THE FIREWORKS!

THRSSS

OH GREAT. NOW WHAT ARE WE GOING TO DO?

OOF... AAAGHH! YA FUCKAAH ... I'M GANNA FUCKINN VOMM...

SLOSH!

CRUNCH!

OOOHYAFUCKAAH!

OOU! AAH!

LOOK AT THE COLOURS

BLEEEHH!

BLAT BLAT FIZZ

CRACK BLAT

THE NEXT MORNING...

YAWN!

OH, MY POOR. HEAD... WHERE AM I

RUB! RUB!

OH NO! WHAT DID I DO?

STILL, I GUESS IF THOSE KIDS CAN LEARN FROM MY MISTAKES THEN MY JOB IS DONE

SLAP!

ACE! WE'VE GOT ENOUGH FOR A 'Mt. ETNA CHINESE MONSTA PACK'

FireWorks shop

Penny for the GUY

chink!

Penny for the Guy

CHEAP

EVERYTHING MUST GO to your EYE!

MINT! LETS STICK THEM IN NEXT DOOR'S LETTERBOX!

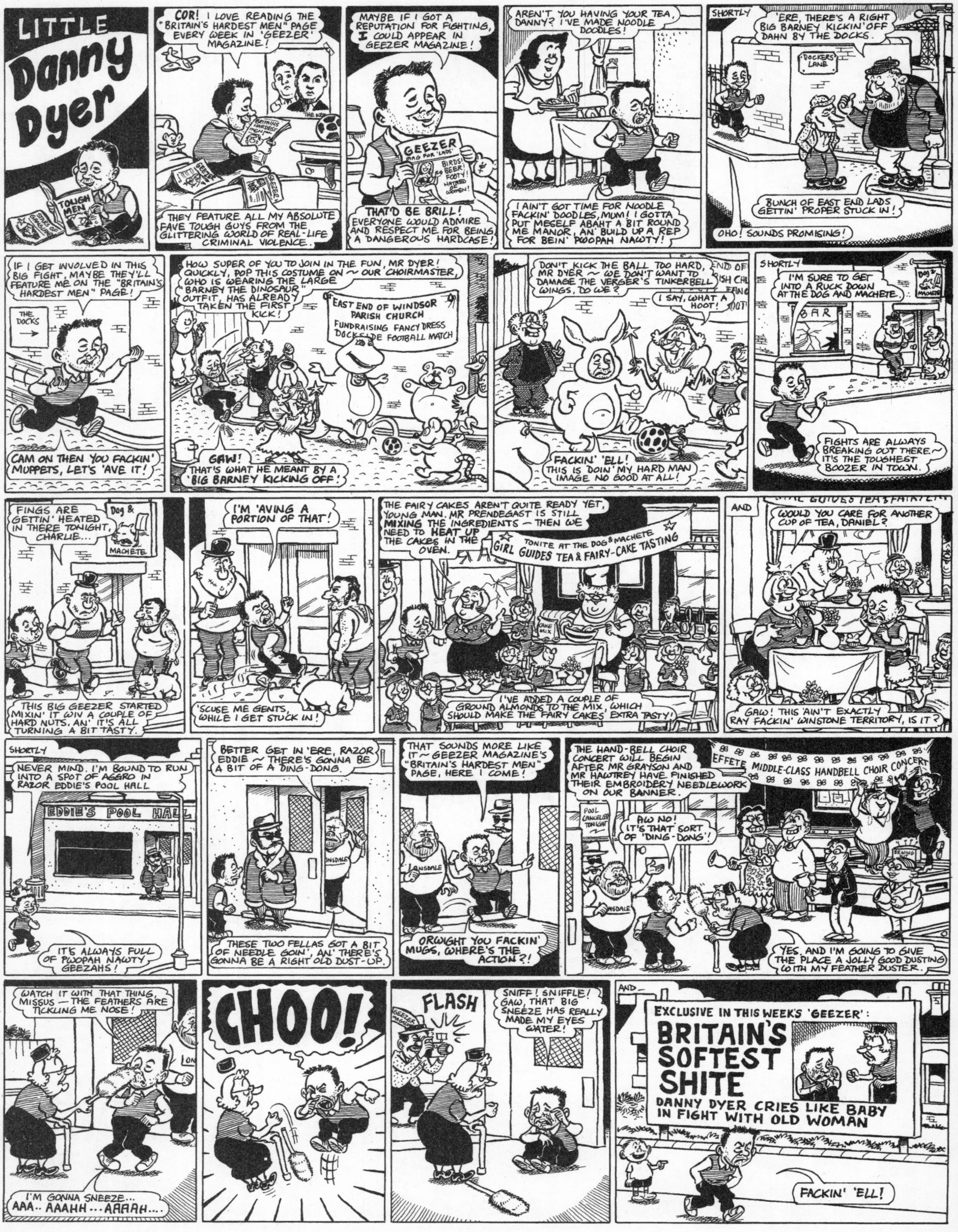
LITTLE
Danny Dyer
TOUGH MEN
COR! I LOVE READING THE "BRITAIN'S HARDEST MEN" PAGE EVERY WEEK IN 'GEEZER' MAGAZINE!
BRITAIN'S HARDEST MEN
THEY FEATURE ALL MY ABSOLUTE FAVE TOUGH GUYS FROM THE GLITTERING WORLD OF REAL-LIFE CRIMINAL VIOLENCE.
MAYBE IF I GOT A REPUTATION FOR FIGHTING, I COULD APPEAR IN GEEZER MAGAZINE!
GEEZER MAG FOR 'LADS'
BIRDS! BEER! FOOTY! HATRED OF WOMEN!
THAT'D BE BRILL! EVERYONE WOULD ADMIRE AND RESPECT ME FOR BEING A DANGEROUS HARDCASE!
AREN'T YOU HAVING YOUR TEA, DANNY? I'VE MADE NOODLE DOODLES!
I AIN'T GOT TIME FOR NOODLE FACKIN' DOODLES, MUM! I GOTTA PUT MESELF ABAHT A BIT ROUND ME MANOR, AN' BUILD UP A REP FOR BEIN' PWOPAH NAWTY!
SHORTLY
'ERE, THERE'S A RIGHT BIG BARNEY KICKIN' OFF DAHN BY THE DOCKS.
DOCKERS LANE
BUNCH OF EAST END LADS GETTIN' PROPER STUCK IN!
OHO! SOUNDS PROMISING!
IF I GET INVOLVED IN THIS BIG FIGHT, MAYBE THEY'LL FEATURE ME ON THE "BRITAIN'S HARDEST MEN" PAGE!
THE DOCKS →
CAM ON THEN YOU FACKIN' MUPPETS, LET'S 'AVE IT!
HOW SUPER OF YOU TO JOIN IN THE FUN, MR DYER! QUICKLY, POP THIS COSTUME ON ~ OUR CHOIRMASTER, WHO IS WEARING THE LARGE "BARNEY THE DINOSAUR" OUTFIT, HAS ALREADY TAKEN THE FIRST KICK!
EAST END OF WINDSOR PARISH CHURCH
FUNDRAISING FANCY DRESS DOCKSIDE FOOTBALL MATCH
GAW! THAT'S WHAT HE MEANT BY A 'BIG BARNEY KICKING OFF'!
DON'T KICK THE BALL TOO HARD, MR DYER ~ WE DON'T WANT TO DAMAGE THE VERGER'S TINKERBELL WINGS, DO WE?
I SAY, WHAT A HOOT!
FACKIN' 'ELL! THIS IS DOIN' MY HARD MAN IMAGE NO GOOD AT ALL!
SHORTLY
I'M SURE TO GET INTO A RUCK DOWN AT THE DOG AND MACHETE.
DOG & MACHETE
BAR
FIGHTS ARE ALWAYS BREAKING OUT THERE ~ IT'S THE TOUGHEST BOOZER IN TOWN.
FINGS ARE GETTIN' HEATED IN THERE TONIGHT, CHARLIE...
DOG & MACHETE
THIS BIG GEEZER STARTED MIXIN' IT WIV A COUPLE OF HARD NUTS, AN' IT'S ALL TURNING A BIT TASTY.
I'M 'AVING A PORTION OF THAT!
'SCUSE ME GENTS, WHILE I GET STUCK IN!
THE FAIRY CAKES AREN'T QUITE READY YET, YOUNG MAN. MR PRENDEGAST IS STILL MIXING THE INGREDIENTS — THEN WE NEED TO HEAT UP THE CAKES IN THE OVEN.
TONITE AT THE DOG & MACHETE GIRL GUIDES TEA & FAIRY-CAKE TASTING
CAKE MIX
I'VE ADDED A COUPLE OF GROUND ALMONDS TO THE MIX, WHICH SHOULD MAKE THE FAIRY CAKES' EXTRA TASTY!
AND
WOULD YOU CARE FOR ANOTHER CUP OF TEA, DANIEL?
GAW! THIS 'AIN'T EXACTLY RAY FACKIN' WINSTONE TERRITORY, IS IT?
SHORTLY
NEVER MIND. I'M BOUND TO RUN INTO A SPOT OF AGGRO IN RAZOR EDDIE'S POOL HALL
EDDIE'S POOL HALL
IT'S ALWAYS FULL OF PWOPAH NAWTY GEEZAHS!
BETTER GET IN 'ERE, RAZOR EDDIE ~ THERE'S GONNA BE A BIT OF A DING-DONG.
LONSDALE
THESE TWO FELLAS GOT A BIT OF NEEDLE GOIN', AN' THERE'S GONNA BE A RIGHT OLD DUST-UP.
THAT SOUNDS MORE LIKE IT ~ GEEZER MAGAZINE'S "BRITAIN'S HARDEST MEN" PAGE, HERE I COME!
LONSDALE
ORWIGHT YOU FACKIN' MUGS, WHERE'S THE ACTION?!
THE HAND-BELL CHOIR CONCERT WILL BEGIN AFTER MR GRAYSON AND MR HAWTREY HAVE FINISHED THEIR EMBROIDERY NEEDLEWORK ON OUR BANNER.
EFFETE MIDDLE-CLASS HANDBELL CHOIR CONCERT
POOL CANCELLED TONIGHT
AW NO! IT'S THAT SORT OF 'DING-DONG'!
LONSDALE
YES, AND I'M GOING TO GIVE THE PLACE A JOLLY GOOD DUSTING WITH MY FEATHER DUSTER.
WATCH IT WITH THAT THING, MISSUS — THE FEATHERS ARE TICKLING ME NOSE!
I'M GONNA SNEEZE... AAA.. AAAHH... AAAAH....
CHOO!
FLASH
GEEZER MAGAZINE
SNIFF! SNIFFLE! GAW, THAT BIG SNEEZE HAS REALLY MADE MY EYES WATER!
AND—
EXCLUSIVE IN THIS WEEK'S 'GEEZER':
BRITAIN'S SOFTEST SHITE
DANNY DYER CRIES LIKE BABY IN FIGHT WITH OLD WOMAN
FACKIN' 'ELL!

It's the battle of the Doc Coxxes!
PROFESSOR BRIAN v IVOR BIGGUN

WHETHER they're presenting ground-breaking documentary series on the wonders of the solar system, or singing cheeky songs about obsessive masturbation, Doc Coxxes are rarely out of the headlines. Ex-pop star **DR BRIAN COX** is a world-renowned physicist with a brain as big as a Higgs Bosun, whilst **DOC "IVOR BIGGUN" COX** is a failed TV presenter who spends far too much of his time thinking up rhymes for the word "wank".

But which one is the Cox of the Walk? Is it highly-qualified egghead hunk Brian, or red-nosed ukulele-plucker Ivor? It's time to decide once and for all...

Who is the Best Doc Cox?

	ROUND 1 Doctorates	
BRIAN boasts a distinguished list of academic honours. He is a Professor at Manchester University, a Research Fellow of the Royal Society and holds a first class degree in High Energy Particle Physics. But not one of his impressive-sounding qualifications permits him to prescribe even the mildest antibiotics in a GP's surgery. His claim to the title "Doctor" is therefore bogus, and he scores badly in this opening round.	**0** ROUND 1 Doctorates **4**	LIKE Brian, Ivor is not registered as a practitioner with the British Medical Association, so you might assume he would do badly in this opening skirmish. However, early in his career he worked as a teacher and it is quite likely that during his training he was required to attend a brief First Aid course to enable him to cope with simple classroom mishaps. This basic medical training nets the bespectacled low achiever a few early points.

| BRIAN has a hectic schedule, flitting between his many jobs all around the world. When he's not lecturing his students in Manchester, he's jetting to foreign locations to shoot one of his many documentaries about science, or sitting behind the steering wheel of the Large Hadron Collider underneath the Swiss Alps. As part of his jet-set lifestyle, Brian buys all his vegetables ready-cut and microwave-ready, so he would never know if they had resembled a penis before they were prepared. | **0** ROUND 2 Phallic Vegetables **9** | AS A presenter on the popular BBC TV show *That's Life*, Biggun spent a large proportion of his working life holding up cock-shaped root vegetables whilst Esther Rantzen covered her teeth. To this day, he spends much of his time on his allotment where he grows a wide variety of genital-shaped produce. Circumcised and uncircumcised carrots, beetroots that resemble scrotums and broccolis that look like fannies - complete with runner bean "clits" on the top - are all enthusiastically cultivated by Biggun. |

| BOTH Coxxes trade off their northern roots. Professor Brian was born in Lancashire. At 53°32' N, his hometown of Oldham is right in the heart of the industrial north. However, as Brian knows only too well, the earth's axis tilted at an angle of 23.5°. Once this is allowed for, Oldham actually lies at 30°N - the same latitude as Cairo! | **1** ROUND 3 Northern-ness **9** | IVOR was born in Sheffield which, at a latitude of 53°23'N, is nearly 23.5° more Northerly than the birthplace of Cairo-born Professor Brian. So flat-capped Yorkshire onanist Biggun wins this War of the Roses against southern softy boffin Brian, and scoops a steaming Yorkshire pud-ful of points into the bargain. |

| PROFESSOR Cox first shot to fame as synth player with rock band D:Ream, whose single *Things Can Only Get Better* shot to number one in the pop charts in 1994, and was later used as the theme song for Tony Blair's 1997 Election campaign. However, after this early success, D:Ream's hit dried up and Brian has been forced to eke out a living as a jobbing particle physicist ever since. | **3** ROUND 4 Pop career **9** | IVOR has enjoyed a long and successful pop career, fronting such diverse groups as Ivor Biggun and the Red-nosed Burglars, Ivor Biggun and the Left-handed Wankers, and Ivor Biggun and the D-Kups. His roll-call of hit records, such as *The Wanker's Song*, *Wanker's Rock'n'Roll* and *The Wanking Caveman*, spans more than four decades and puts his scientific rival's pitiful efforts to shame. |

| AT THE peak of their chart success, Professor Brian and his fellow D:Ream bandsters performed to packed stadiums and festivals around the globe. However, a quick phonecall to the barman at the Poacher Pub, Cratfield, confirmed that the nineties rave megastars had never sung their hit *Things Can Only Get Better* in the cramped snug of the popular Suffolk real ale hostelry. | **0** ROUND 5 Playing at the Poacher Pub, Cratfield **10** | AS PART of his latest group, Ivor Biggun and the Trembling Wheelbarrows, Doc Cox is a regular attraction at the Poacher Pub, Cratfield, and for anyone who can't believe it's true, there's even video evidence of this on the internet. When it comes to singing songs about masturbation to a bar half-full of people who aren't really listening, Biggun wins the Battle of the Bands hairy hands down! |

| OH DEAR. Brainbox Brian may reckon he knows everything about the Universe, but he's been *universally* defeated in this Doc Cox competition. His points seem to have been sucked into a Black Hole of his own making, and *things have only got worse* as the competition progressed. The Professor will be wishing this whole thing had just been a bad *D:Ream!* | **4** HOW DID THEY DO? **41** | CONGRATULATIONS Ivor, what a *Biggun*... Score that is! Doc Cox did more than *hold his own* throughout the contest. In fact, the potty-mouthed string-strummer *pulled it off* in every round to *come off* first every time and take the title *King of the Doc Coxxes!* |

NEXT WEEK: Coist or Beal - Who's the Best Ally Mc?

119

LeTTERbOcks

Viz Comic, PO Box 841,
Whitley Bay, NE26 9EQ
letters@viz.co.uk

TOP TIPS

WEAR a really big cowboy hat to impress the ladies. If your head is too small, remember to cut two eyeholes so you can see.

Tim Burke, e-mail

PICKLED onions make ideal breast implants for cats.

Mark French, e-mail

SAVE water by washing your hands in the cistern of the toilet before flushing.

Barry, e-mail

A HARD boiled egg yolk makes a cheap and effective 'golden snitch' for Harry Potter fans young and old.

Stuart Ovenden, e-mail

USED plasters make ideal chewing gum for vampires.

Dick Eggsarnie, e-mail

LIVEN up boring golf tournaments by occasionally blowing a vuvuzela just as the golfer is driving off the tee.

Jeremy of Estonia, e-mail

FARMERS. Replace grit fed to chickens with iron filings. That way, boiled eggs can be safely removed from a pan of boiling water using a large magnet.

Rob Heaven, e-mail

FOOL women into thinking you have a well paid job in the animal testing industry by throwing paintstripper over your car.

Simon Tena-Lady, e-mail

MOTORISTS. Buy four wheel clamps from Argos for £15 each, park anywhere you like and attach them to your car. Wardens will be unable to attach any more clamps and it is still cheaper than the release fee.

Pete A, e-mail

TRADITIONALISTS. Be sure to do things the way they've always been done and be sure to disregard anything new or innovative.

Rob Salmon, e-mail

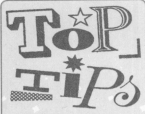

STAR LETTER

WHY oh why are we constantly forced to pay for things in shops? When are these shop keepers going to realise that if they gave stuff away for free, they would have more satisfied customers who would be more likely to visit the shop again. Furthermore, they would recommend the shop to all their friends. In my view it's simple common sense, but I'm sure these fat cat shopkeepers will carry on with their blinkered ways.

A McGuinness, e-mail

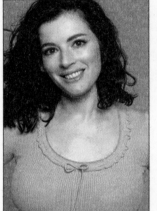

NIGELLA Lawson said on her cooking programme that with her busy schedule, she finds certain things difficult to fit in, like her kids and her husband. She forgot to mention her tits into her bra.

Grant B Warner, New Zealand

I HAVEN'T got any DVD box sets myself, but if someone has one that isn't Friends, could they send it to channel E4 so they have something else to put on?

Mr Andreaos, e-mail

I'VE never met 'the next man', but based on the miserable old bastards who claim to be as liberal, tolerant and fun-loving as him, I don't think I particularly want to.

Pete Dockar, e-mail

ON PAGE 93, Mr Burns asked if people from the south east could tell him where they planned to holiday in order that he could make other plans. Well, I'm from Clacton-on-Sea and I'd like to thank Mr Burns on two counts. Firstly for making other plans and secondly for giving me the first choice where to go. It's nice to know that a, no doubt cap-doffing northerner like him knows his place.

Mr Elsworth, e-mail

IF SUPERMARKETS have trouble with people parking in the disabled bays, why don't they simply move them to the far end of the car park. The long walk to the door would soon put them off using spaces that they weren't entitled to.

Patrick Barker, e-mail

APPARENTLY, the smell of baking bread gives a homely atmosphere in a house that may increase the chance of a sale. Well, last night I ate a Cantonese curry with a bottle of red wine, and today I farted and it smelt like a granary loaf. Individuals like myself could single-handedly create a much needed boom in the housing market.

Ross Urmston, e-mail

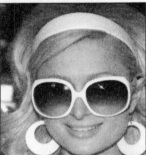

I SEE that there is a third series of Paris Hilton's Best Friend Forever. She's not really getting this 'forever' thing, is she?

Christinos Martinogalou, Greece

I THINK that if curlers want their sport to be taken seriously they shouldn't leave it till the last minute before cleaning the rink.

Huw Allen, e-mail

THESE 'Baby on Board' signs in the back of cars really get my goat. Firstly, a car is not a boat or a spaceship. And secondly, if I'm being told this so I don't crash into the back of it. then, it's a bit pointless, as I generally don't choose the cars I run into the back of.

Julian Ketcher, e-mail

THE new Halifax advert appears to be telling me that 'taking my money out' is some sort of perk. Are there other banks I don't know about that are operating some kind of finders keepers policy?

Cristian Marnit, e-mail

Twat's Life! with Esther Rantzen

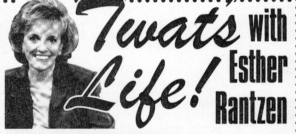

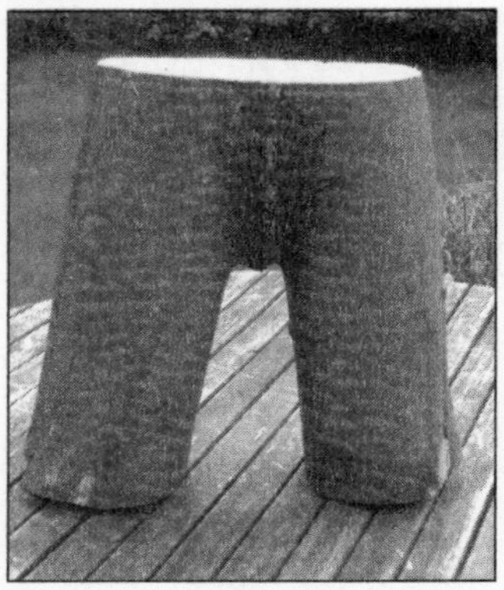

"I AM indebted to Big Ian from E-mail who, whilst cutting logs with a chainsaw, came across this celebration of the female form. I bet it gave him a proper woody.

(cue canned laughter)

Do you have a picture of something that looks like a fanny? Something that isn't a fanny, obviously, a carrot, a potato, a bit of driftwood, you know the sort of thing."

What's in a Name?

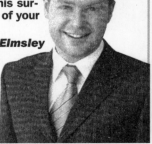

I WAS intrigued to see that the BBC had a weatherman called *TOMASZ SCHAFERNAKER*, and wondered if his surname was Polish for 'shaven knackers.' If it is, do any of your readers know whether or not he shaves his plums?

Mrs Edna Barbarian, Elmsley

***✱ THE WORD** Schafernaker probably does mean 'shaven knackers' in Polish. As to whether Tomasz does just that, who knows? Perhaps you are his doctor and he's recently been in with a snapped banjo string or boil on his bellend and you've seen if he's taken a razor to his knackers. Write to us, in the strictest confidence, and let us know.*

YOU ask, WE answer

with •••••••• Naylor Hammond

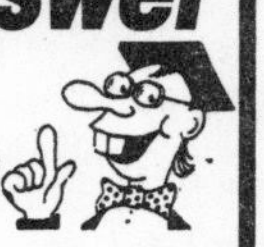

WHY is it that when you toast a cheese sandwich, the bread goes hard but the cheese goes soft?

Hector Pants, Totnes

BOTH *the cheese and the bread are made of very small things called molecules, and the way they react is all down to their structure. Cheese is made from protein, fats and water, whereas the bread is made from different molecules. When heated, the molecules vibrate around, and whilst this causes the protein in the cheese to lose its shape and go soft, it causes the bread molecules to turn into molecules of toast.*

Naylor Hammond BSc.

I HEARD on the radio today that Carol Decker out of T'Pau now runs the Cherry Tree Inn restaurant and hotel in Henley-on-Thames. I bet when they're busy or short staffed and she's pressed into being a waitress for the evening, she gets sick of people saying 'I see you've got some china in your hand' or something.

Brackstone Hicks, Luton

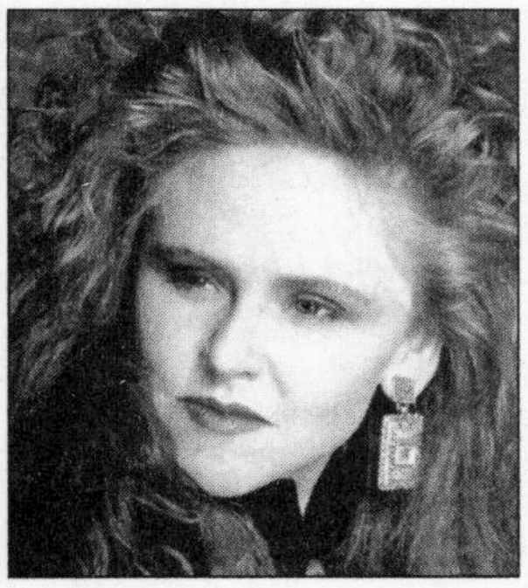

OUR LOCAL independent radio station recently asked listeners to phone in if they have ever pulled up at a fuel pump on the wrong side. Have any of your readers heard as pathetic an attempt to engage the public, other then every piece of bollocks Chris Moyles comes out with?

Mark Edwards, Leek

I TRY to pause the TV whenever the Go Compare advert comes on, and I usually catch it just before the fat cunt starts singing. However, in order to know how long I need to leave the pause on for, I have to sing the fucking song in my head. Sometimes you just can't win for losing.

Neil, e-mail

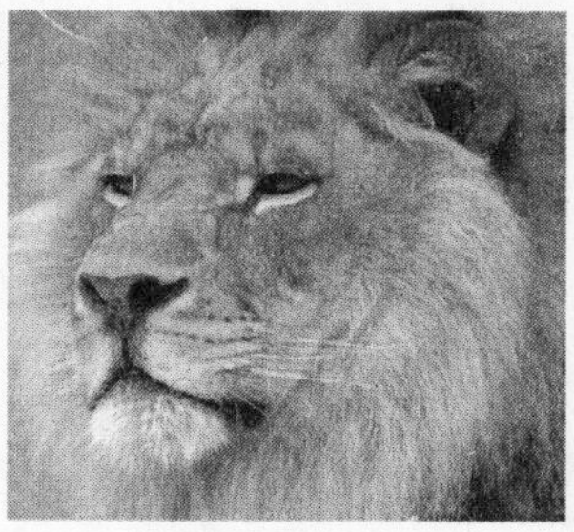

LIONEL Richie is not only rich, but I think he looks a bit like a lion too. What are the chances of that?

B Whitehouse, e-mail

HOW about a picture of a man in a top hat holding a stuffed fox above his head? If the fox could be wearing a blue and white striped scarf, even better.

Christiano Martinique, e-mail

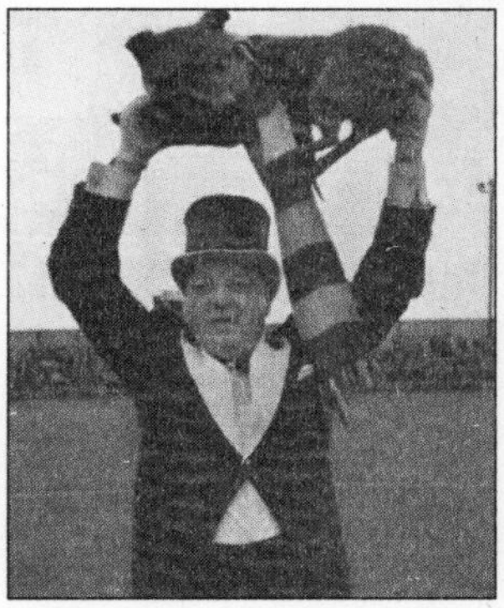

**Here you go, Christina. I mean Christiano.*

WHEN the Black Eyed Peas wrote the lyrics 'I've got a good feeling that tonight's gonna be a good night', they obviously didn't have the foresight to think the song would be played on the jukebox in the Railway Inn, Studley. Or anywhere within the Redditch area on any night.

Garry Lynch, e-mail

FAMOUS PEOPLE ON THE TOILET

No. 97 Gina G.

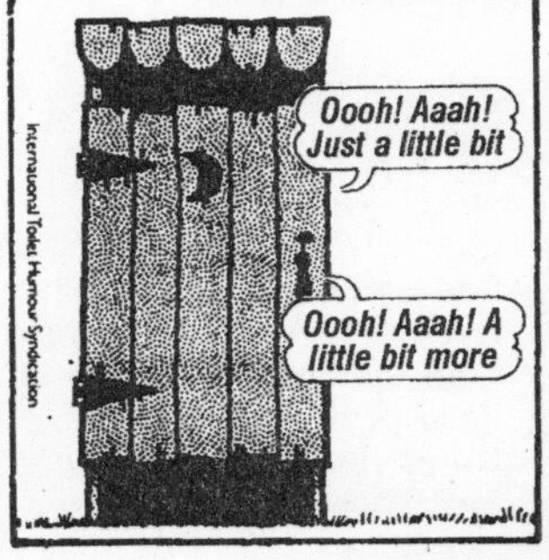
Oooh! Aaah! Just a little bit
Oooh! Aaah! A little bit more
International Toilet Humour Syndication

UP THE ARSE CORNER

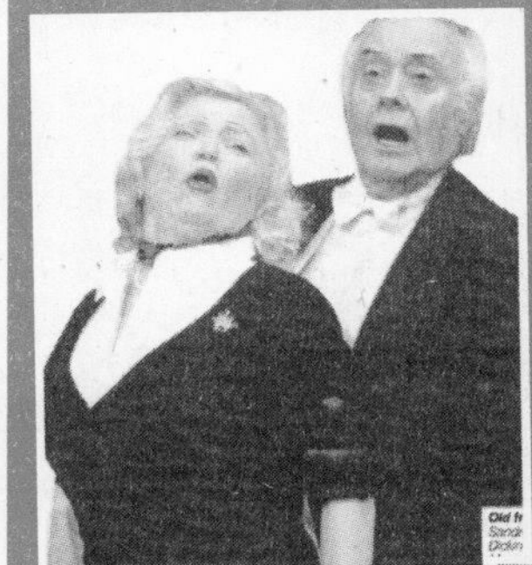

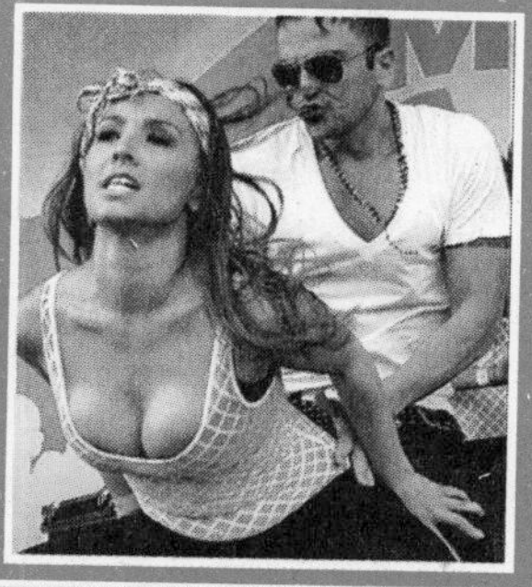

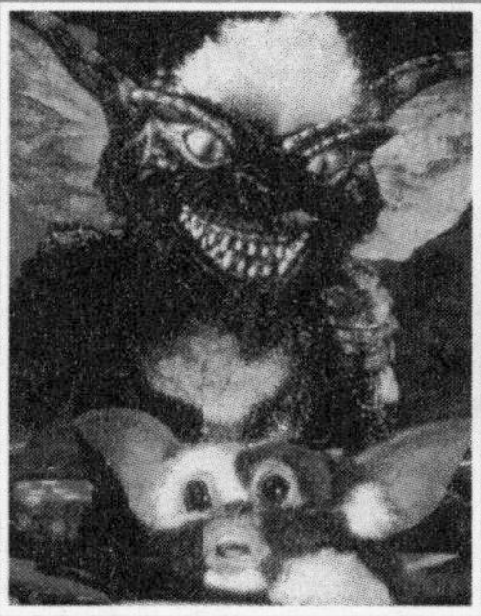

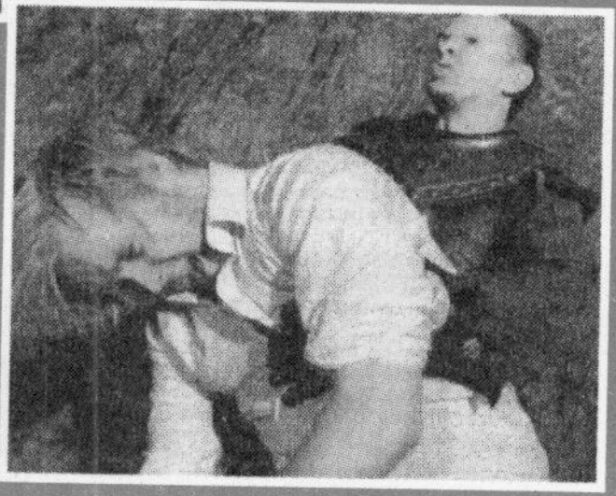

FLASH! BANG! WALLOP!

By our 43pt headline correspondent Futura Boldcondenseditalic

Brush Strokes Jacko in Hot Water

THE MAN who played *JACKO* out of *Brush Strokes*'s advertising Career as the Flash! husband hung in the balance yesterday after company management made a surprise visit to his home in South London... to find his cupboard full of... *Cillit Bang!*

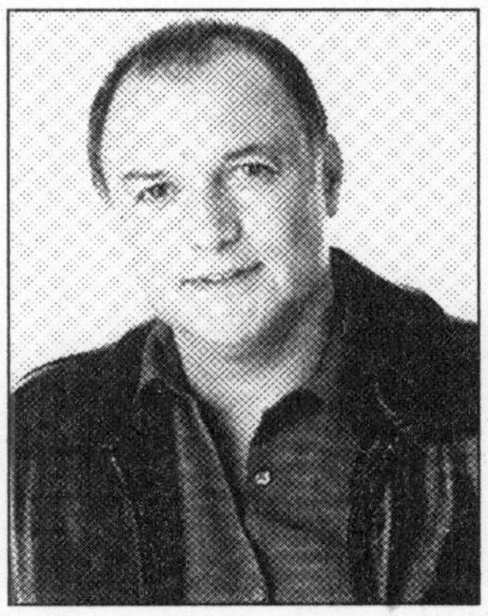

The telly favourite, famed for cleaning the house quickly whilst his wife thought it took him longer, attempted to explain the gaff to furious Flash! bosses. He told them that he was just an actor who pretended to clean the house quickly with their product, gave a cheeky smile at the camera and then watched the football.

neighbour

As part of his appearance fee, the actor was allowed to take some of the products home after filming. But bosses were tipped-off that Jacko had later swapped some of the cleaning materials with neighbour and Cillit Bang! frontman Barry Scott.

the sullivan

The actor, who is often confused with the man who played Terry the Chef in Fawlty Towers, claimed that he and Scott were merely looking after each other's cleaning products following a spate of burglaries in the area. But the detergent chiefs were sceptical and returned to Flash! headquarters to 'discuss the situation.'

We phoned Barry Scott to see if he could corroborate Jacko's story, but he was shouting so much that the telephone went all crackly.

TOP TIPS

RASPBERRIES make excellent afros for mice. They are also very tasty.

Duckin Fullard, Garforth

GIRLS. Try licking piss off a lemon before taking your profile picture. Hey presto! The perfect Facebook pout.

Brian Crabtree, e-mail

BIRD watchers. Get a closer look at birds by shooting them, then picking them up for inspection.

George Belcher, e-mail

MAKE your own snow by wafting steam from the kettle into the freezer and quickly slamming the door.

Rob Stott, e-mail

ROUND dodgers. Saying 'do you want a pint or are you alright? Makes it so uncomfortable for the recipient that they will invariably decline your 'kind' offer.

Fluff Freeman, e-mail

CYCLISTS. Re-enact the Tour de France on your commute to work by taking vast amounts of drugs, wearing a yellow t-shirt and holding your arms aloft as you reach the office car park.

Carl Norman, e-mail

ANGRY teenagers. Save time self harming by simply shaving with a Bic razor whilst getting ready for a night out.

Tony Anstis, e-mail

JEREMY Kyle. Avoid causing offence when speaking to the vermin on your showby saying 'I'm not judging you' before slagging them off. This will also enable the twats in the audience to nod in a superior manner.

Phil, e-mail

MOTORHOME owners. Instead of towing your Smart car behind your motorhome, tow your motorhome behind your Smart car as they are much more fuel economic.

Popeymike, e-mail

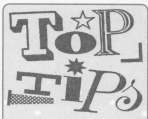

Volca-NO!

Stars hit hard in ash chaos

EARLIER this year, a plume of ash from Iceland's Eyjafjallajoekull volcano shut down the whole of Europe's airspace and left millions stranded.

As the cloud of choking lava threatened to bring down aircraft, thousands of families were forced to call off holidays and many more were trapped at holiday destinations. Even President Obama was unable to attend the funeral of his Polish counterpart as Airforce 1 was grounded by the lethal volcanic fog.

And only now, 6 months later, is the true cost of the eruption beginning to emerge. Billions of pounds were wiped off Europe's economy, and thousands of jobs were lost as airline companies went to the wall.

But above all the tales of hardship and distress for ordinary people, it is the stars who suffered the most. With their glamorous, jet-set lifestyles and luxury homes around the world, the blanket flight ban hit them hardest. Here's how some A-listers suffered at the hands of Iceland's volcano...

MRS STING............

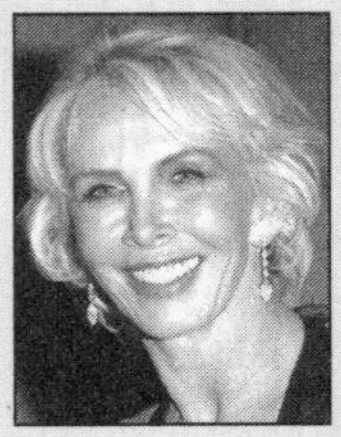

On the day of the eruption, Sting's wife Trudi Styler was booked to give a lecture to the Devizes Townswomen's Guild about reducing their carbon footprint. She was just getting ready to set off from her Wiltshire mansion to the nearby village hall when news of the flight restrictions came through. The environmentally-aware actress normally charters a jumbo jet for such visits, but due to the grounding of aircraft she had to get 50 taxis instead. "I had had 200 trees planted on another one of my estates somewhere to offset the 747 trip to Devizes village hall," the arsehole's wife said. "So when when the flight was cancelled, I realised that I had had them planted unnecessarily. I decided to offset them by burning 200 tractor tyres."

BONO.......................

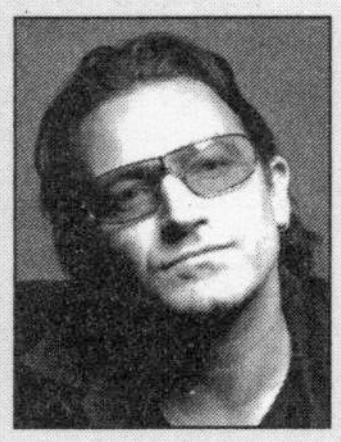

Pop megastar Bono suffered a double whammy when international travel ground to a halt. His favourite hat was relaxing in Cannes before returning to join the arsehole in Las Vegas on the next leg of U2's 360° world tour. "I can't go on stage without my favourite titfer, and I didn't want to let my zillions of fans down by refusing to perform," said Bono, real name Bonesworth Onanbridge. "I usually get it brought to where I am by private jumbo jet, but with no flights in or out of Europe, that wasn't possible. So I had a word with my pals at the United Nations, and they commandeered a fleet of US aircraft carriers which brought it over on a panda-skin cushion."

Not only was the Dublin-born shortarse inconvenienced in the hat department, but Eyjafjallajoekull cost him financially, too. "I was moving my tax affairs to Holland, but the plane taking them was grounded by the ash cloud," he told us. "So they ended up sitting on the tarmac at Dublin airport, and I was unable to legally avoid paying the full rate of duty on my earnings for nearly 12 days."

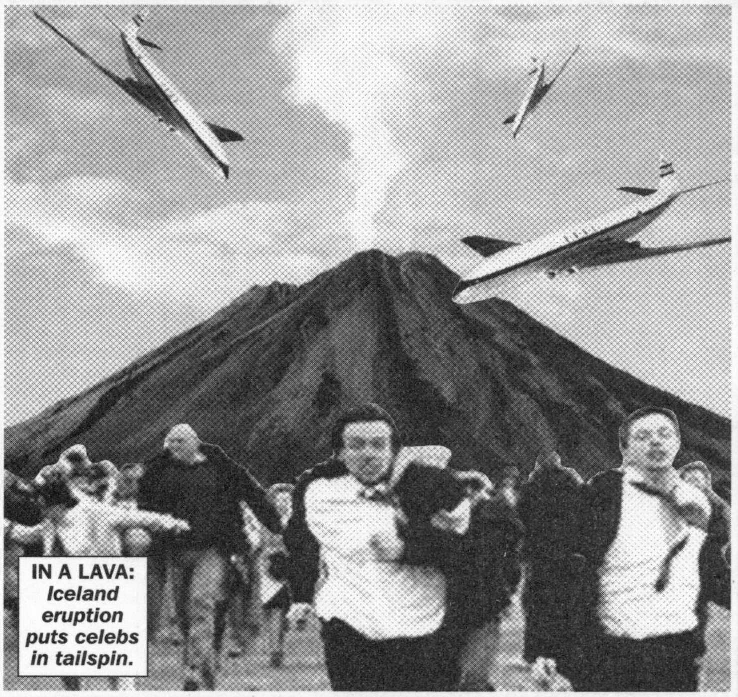

IN A LAVA: ***Iceland eruption puts celebs in tailspin.***

PETE DOHERTY.....

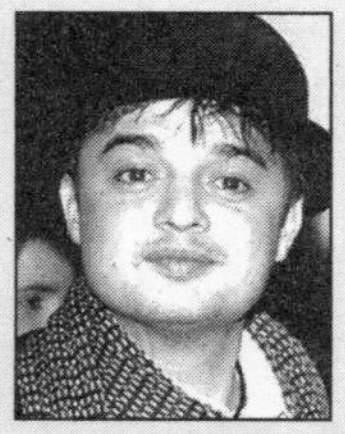

"My day is very much geared around my court appearances for various drugs-related offences," the Babyshambles frontman told us. "With airports closed by the plume of Icelandic ash, the mules that import my illegal narcotics stuffed up their arses were unable to get into the country. Consequently, I was forced to stay out of trouble."

"I remember picking up a newspaper and seeing that I wasn't pictured on the front page, falling down a courtroom steps, or punching a photographer in a lairy fashion. I was devastated," he said.

"It was a tough 12 days without any drugs to keep me in trouble, but I got through them somehow," he said. "I remember the joy of meeting my mule off the the first plane into Heathrow after the restrictions were lifted. I was such a relief to get back in the dock of Hammersmith Magistrates Court the next day, charged with illegal possession of a class A substance."

NICK BERRY............

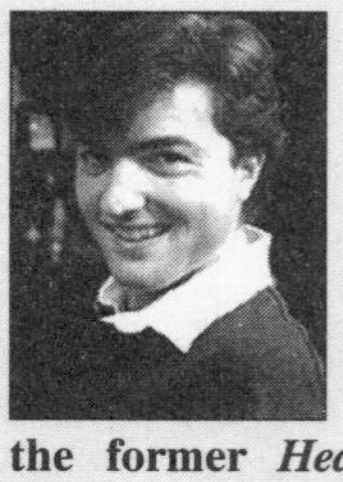

Ex-*Harbour Lights* star Nick Berry was at his Epping home as the disaster unfolded. "The flight ban may well have proved disastrous for my acting career," said the former *Heartbeat* heart-throb. "There could have been somebody coming over from Hollywood to offer me a starring role in a blockbuster movie or primetime HBO series like *Mad Men* or *Lost*. Perhaps Steven Speilberg, Frances Ford Coppola or Quentin Tarantino were looking to cast me in one of their multi-million dollar films," he mused. "But the ash cloud would have prevented them crossing the Atlantic, so they would have ended up offering the part to an American actor, such as Brad Pitt, George Clooney or Morgan Freeman."

Since they were unable to call in person, Berry suspected the Tinseltown moguls might try to contact him by phone. "I stayed in for the entire 12 days of the flight ban, sitting at the bottom of the stairs by the telephone table, but it never rang," he told us. "I occasionally called BT to make sure the line was working, and they told me it was. I can only assume that the ash from Eyjafjallajoekull must of brang the phone lines down in California."

TOMMY WALSH.....

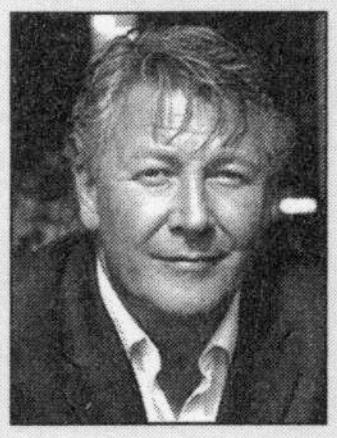

Ground Force builder Tommy Walsh and his wife were packing for a 2-week holiday in Majorca when news came through that their flight had been cancelled. But handyman Tommy wasn't going to let a little thing like a volcano get in the way of his fortnight in the sun. He decided to Do It Himself, and set about building his own Boeing 747 out of dressed timber, MDF and nails. "I nipped down my local DIY store to get the materials for the build," he told us. "When they recognised me as a celebrity, the lads at the counter gave me a pretty good deal on all the stuff."

Working on shows like *Ground Force, Challenge Tommy* and *Tommy's Ark*, Walsh is used to tight deadlines, so he had the wooden jumbo completed in a couple of days. "We were all packed and ready for take-off - I'd been given special clearance by Air Traffic Control because I'm a celebrity - and I fired up the engines. At this point I realised I'd forgotten something ... a runway!"

Walsh immediately began laying a 200-foot-wide, 2-mile-long strip of block paving. "It was backbreaking work, and very slow," he said. "Before I even picked up the first block, I had to lay an 18-inch hardcore foundation with a 4-inch layer of sharp sand tamped down on the top. I'd got the first mile-and-a-half laid when the volcano stopped and the restrictions were lifted. What a waste of fucking time."

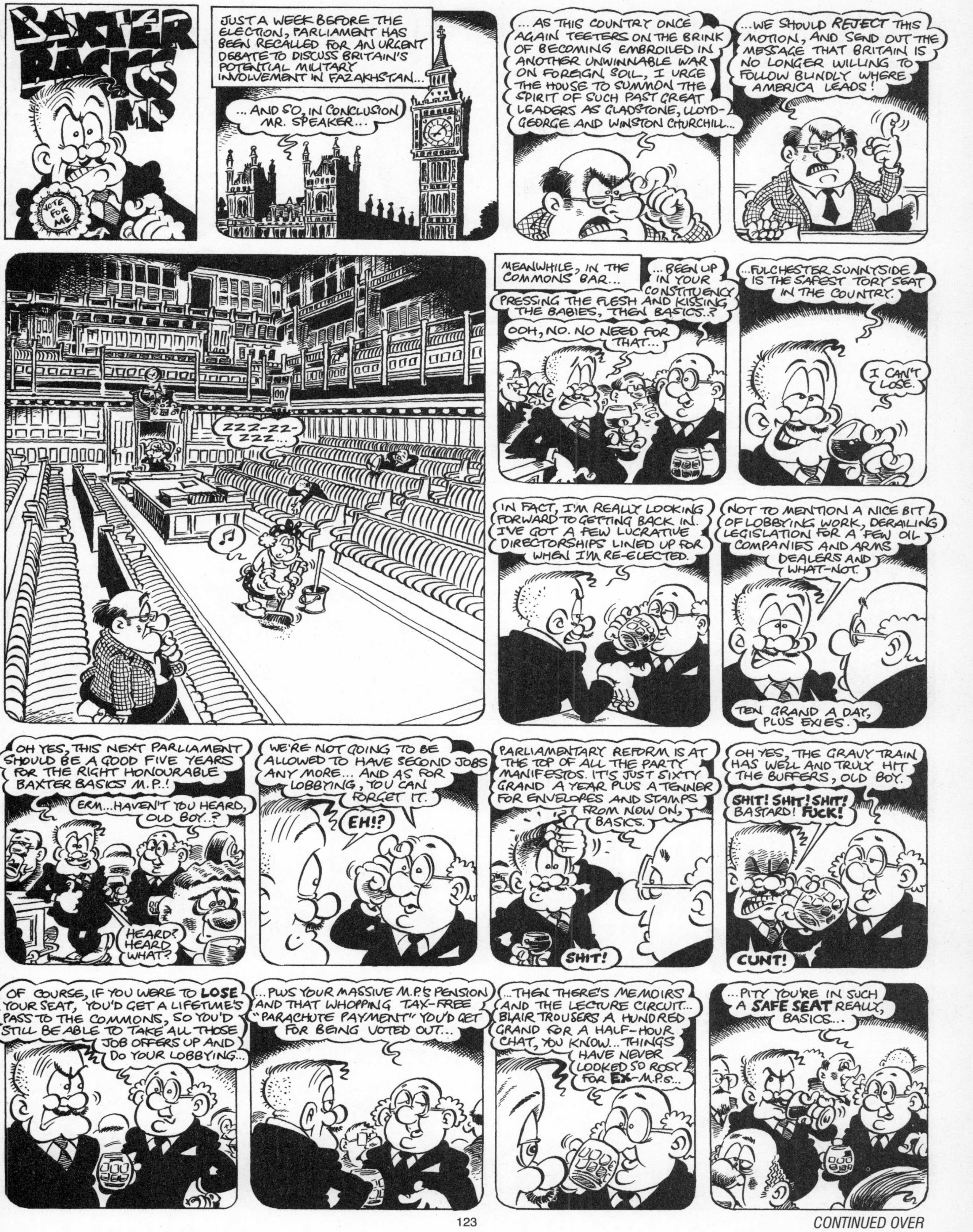
BAXTER BASICS M.P
VOTE FOR ME
JUST A WEEK BEFORE THE ELECTION, PARLIAMENT HAS BEEN RECALLED FOR AN URGENT DEBATE TO DISCUSS BRITAIN'S POTENTIAL MILITARY INVOLVEMENT IN FAZAKHSTAN...
...AND SO, IN CONCLUSION MR. SPEAKER...
...AS THIS COUNTRY ONCE AGAIN TEETERS ON THE BRINK OF BECOMING EMBROILED IN ANOTHER UNWINNABLE WAR ON FOREIGN SOIL, I URGE THE HOUSE TO SUMMON THE SPIRIT OF SUCH PAST GREAT LEADERS AS GLADSTONE, LLOYD-GEORGE AND WINSTON CHURCHILL...
...WE SHOULD REJECT THIS MOTION, AND SEND OUT THE MESSAGE THAT BRITAIN IS NO LONGER WILLING TO FOLLOW BLINDLY WHERE AMERICA LEADS!
ZZZ-ZZ-ZZZ...
MEANWHILE, IN THE COMMONS' BAR...
...BEEN UP IN YOUR CONSTITUENCY PRESSING THE FLESH AND KISSING THE BABIES, THEN BASICS..?
OOH, NO. NO NEED FOR THAT...
...FULCHESTER SUNNYSIDE IS THE SAFEST TORY SEAT IN THE COUNTRY.
I CAN'T LOSE.
IN FACT, I'M REALLY LOOKING FORWARD TO GETTING BACK IN. I'VE GOT A FEW LUCRATIVE DIRECTORSHIPS LINED UP FOR WHEN I'M RE-ELECTED.
NOT TO MENTION A NICE BIT OF LOBBYING WORK, DERAILING LEGISLATION FOR A FEW OIL COMPANIES AND ARMS DEALERS AND WHAT-NOT.
TEN GRAND A DAY, PLUS EXIES.
OH YES, THIS NEXT PARLIAMENT SHOULD BE A GOOD FIVE YEARS FOR THE RIGHT HONOURABLE BAXTER BASICS M.P.!
ERM...HAVEN'T YOU HEARD, OLD BOY..?
HEARD? HEARD WHAT?
WE'RE NOT GOING TO BE ALLOWED TO HAVE SECOND JOBS ANY MORE... AND AS FOR LOBBYING, YOU CAN FORGET IT.
EH!?
PARLIAMENTARY REFORM IS AT THE TOP OF ALL THE PARTY MANIFESTOS. IT'S JUST SIXTY GRAND A YEAR PLUS A TENNER FOR ENVELOPES AND STAMPS FROM NOW ON, BASICS.
SHIT!
OH YES, THE GRAVY TRAIN HAS WELL AND TRULY HIT THE BUFFERS, OLD BOY.
SHIT! SHIT! SHIT! BASTARD! FUCK!
CUNT!
OF COURSE, IF YOU WERE TO LOSE YOUR SEAT, YOU'D GET A LIFETIME'S PASS TO THE COMMONS, SO YOU'D STILL BE ABLE TO TAKE ALL THOSE JOB OFFERS UP AND DO YOUR LOBBYING...
...PLUS YOUR MASSIVE M.P.'S PENSION AND THAT WHOPPING TAX-FREE "PARACHUTE PAYMENT" YOU'D GET FOR BEING VOTED OUT...
...THEN THERE'S MEMOIRS AND THE LECTURE CIRCUIT... BLAIR TROUSERS A HUNDRED GRAND FOR A HALF-HOUR CHAT, YOU KNOW... THINGS HAVE NEVER LOOKED SO ROSY FOR EX-M.P.S...
...PITY YOU'RE IN SUCH A SAFE SEAT REALLY, BASICS...

CONTINUED OVER

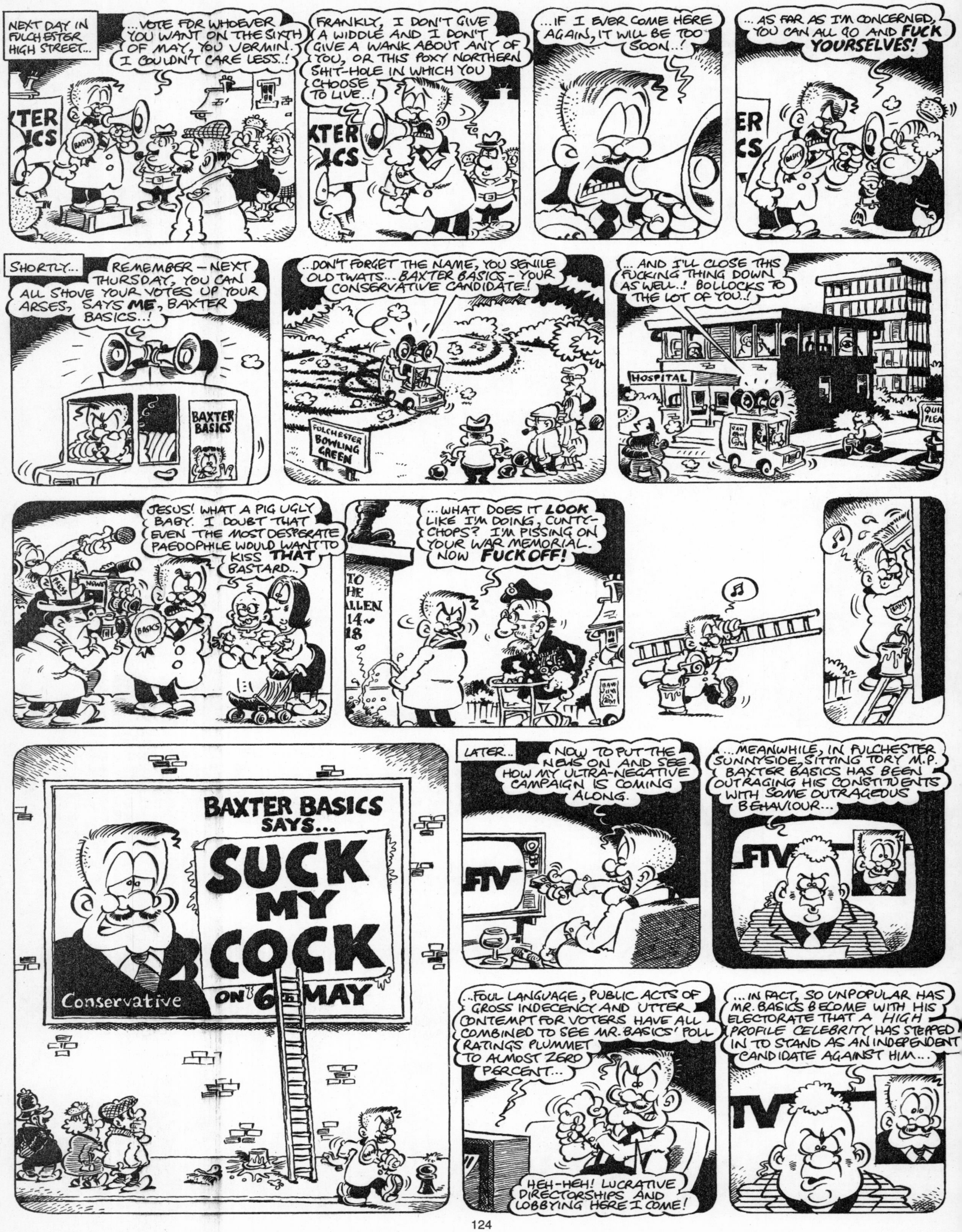
NEXT DAY IN FULCHESTER HIGH STREET...
...VOTE FOR WHOEVER YOU WANT ON THE SIXTH OF MAY, YOU VERMIN. I COULDN'T CARE LESS..!
FRANKLY, I DON'T GIVE A WIDDLE AND I DON'T GIVE A WANK ABOUT ANY OF YOU, OR THIS POXY NORTHERN SHIT-HOLE IN WHICH YOU CHOOSE TO LIVE..!
...IF I EVER COME HERE AGAIN, IT WILL BE TOO SOON..!
...AS FAR AS I'M CONCERNED, YOU CAN ALL GO AND FUCK YOURSELVES!
SHORTLY...
REMEMBER – NEXT THURSDAY, YOU CAN ALL SHOVE YOUR VOTES UP YOUR ARSES, SAYS ME, BAXTER BASICS..!
BAXTER BASICS
...DON'T FORGET THE NAME, YOU SENILE OLD TWATS... BAXTER BASICS – YOUR CONSERVATIVE CANDIDATE!
FULCHESTER BOWLING GREEN
...AND I'LL CLOSE THIS FUCKING THING DOWN AS WELL..! BOLLOCKS TO THE LOT OF YOU..!
HOSPITAL
JESUS! WHAT A PIG UGLY BABY. I DOUBT THAT EVEN THE MOST DESPERATE PAEDOPHILE WOULD WANT TO KISS THAT BASTARD...
PRESS
NEWS
BASICS
...WHAT DOES IT LOOK LIKE I'M DOING, CUNTY-CHOPS? I'M PISSING ON YOUR WAR MEMORIAL. NOW FUCK OFF!
BAXTER BASICS SAYS...
SUCK MY COCK
ON 6th MAY
Conservative
LATER...
NOW TO PUT THE NEWS ON AND SEE HOW MY ULTRA-NEGATIVE CAMPAIGN IS COMING ALONG.
FTV
...MEANWHILE, IN FULCHESTER SUNNYSIDE, SITTING TORY M.P. BAXTER BASICS HAS BEEN OUTRAGING HIS CONSTITUENTS WITH SOME OUTRAGEOUS BEHAVIOUR...
FTV
...FOUL LANGUAGE, PUBLIC ACTS OF GROSS INDECENCY AND UTTER CONTEMPT FOR VOTERS HAVE ALL COMBINED TO SEE MR. BASICS' POLL RATINGS PLUMMET TO ALMOST ZERO PERCENT...
HEH-HEH! LUCRATIVE DIRECTORSHIPS AND LOBBYING HERE I COME!
...IN FACT, SO UNPOPULAR HAS MR. BASICS BECOME WITH HIS ELECTORATE THAT A HIGH PROFILE CELEBRITY HAS STEPPED IN TO STAND AS AN INDEPENDENT CANDIDATE AGAINST HIM...
TV

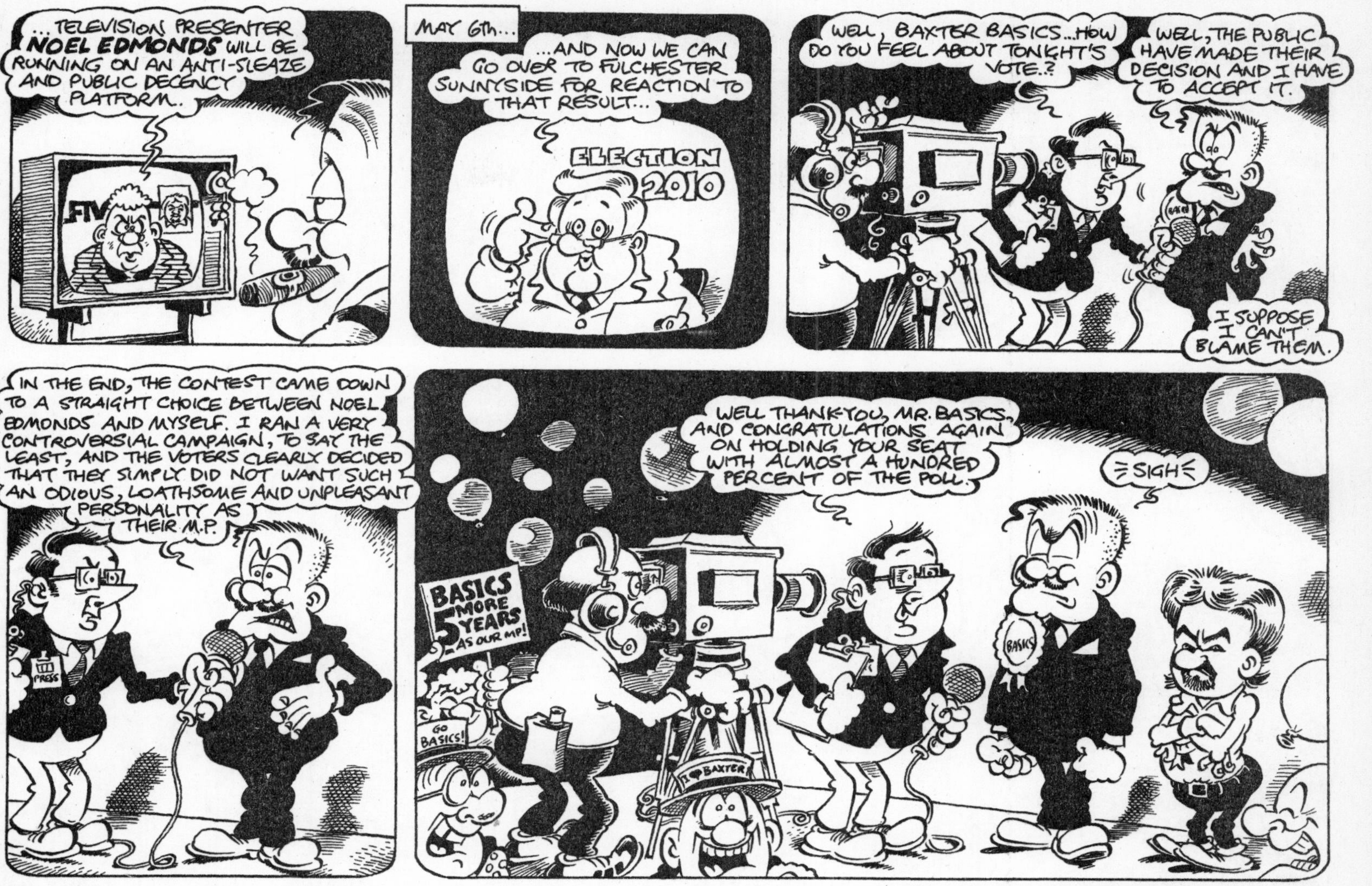
...TELEVISION PRESENTER NOEL EDMONDS WILL BE RUNNING ON AN ANTI-SLEAZE AND PUBLIC DECENCY PLATFORM...
MAY 6TH...
...AND NOW WE CAN GO OVER TO FULCHESTER SUNNYSIDE FOR REACTION TO THAT RESULT...
ELECTION 2010
WELL, BAXTER BASICS...HOW DO YOU FEEL ABOUT TONIGHT'S VOTE..?
WELL, THE PUBLIC HAVE MADE THEIR DECISION AND I HAVE TO ACCEPT IT.
I SUPPOSE I CAN'T BLAME THEM.
IN THE END, THE CONTEST CAME DOWN TO A STRAIGHT CHOICE BETWEEN NOEL EDMONDS AND MYSELF. I RAN A VERY CONTROVERSIAL CAMPAIGN, TO SAY THE LEAST, AND THE VOTERS CLEARLY DECIDED THAT THEY SIMPLY DID NOT WANT SUCH AN ODIOUS, LOATHSOME AND UNPLEASANT PERSONALITY AS THEIR M.P.
PRESS
WELL THANK-YOU, MR. BASICS, AND CONGRATULATIONS AGAIN ON HOLDING YOUR SEAT WITH ALMOST A HUNDRED PERCENT OF THE POLL.
SIGH
BASICS 5 MORE YEARS AS OUR MP!
GO BASICS!
BASICS

Bargain Hunt presenter to reveal true identity

BBC BOSSES have failed in a legal bid to prevent the mystery man who presents *Bargain Hunt* from revealing his true identity. Now the public are set to learn the man's name with the publication of his autobiography, *I'm That Bloke off That Programme*.

EXCLUSIVE

The quirky and eccentric antiques expert has become a key part of the popular daytime programme in which members of the public compete to buy and sell bric-a-brac for a profit. Yet none of the show's millions of viewers are aware who the bow-tied presenter is. Even BBC crew who work on the show are unable to put a name to his face.

guy

Wrongly identified in the past as that guy off *Flog It*, him out of *Car Booty* or even the other one off *Cash in The Attic*, persistent rumours on internet antiques discussion boards have led to a number of close calls when the man's identity was almost outed. The Beeb admits that the mystery surrounding the name of the trilby-hatted, half-moon-spectacle-wearing nonentity has been a big part of the show's success. And producers fear that the top-rated programme could lose something if viewers had the foggiest notion who he was.

garden

But the presenter says he is proud of his work on the show. He told us: "I'm not cashing in on Bargain Hunt's success. I would just like to share my secret with friends and family, all of whom work for a living and have no idea what happens on telly during the day."

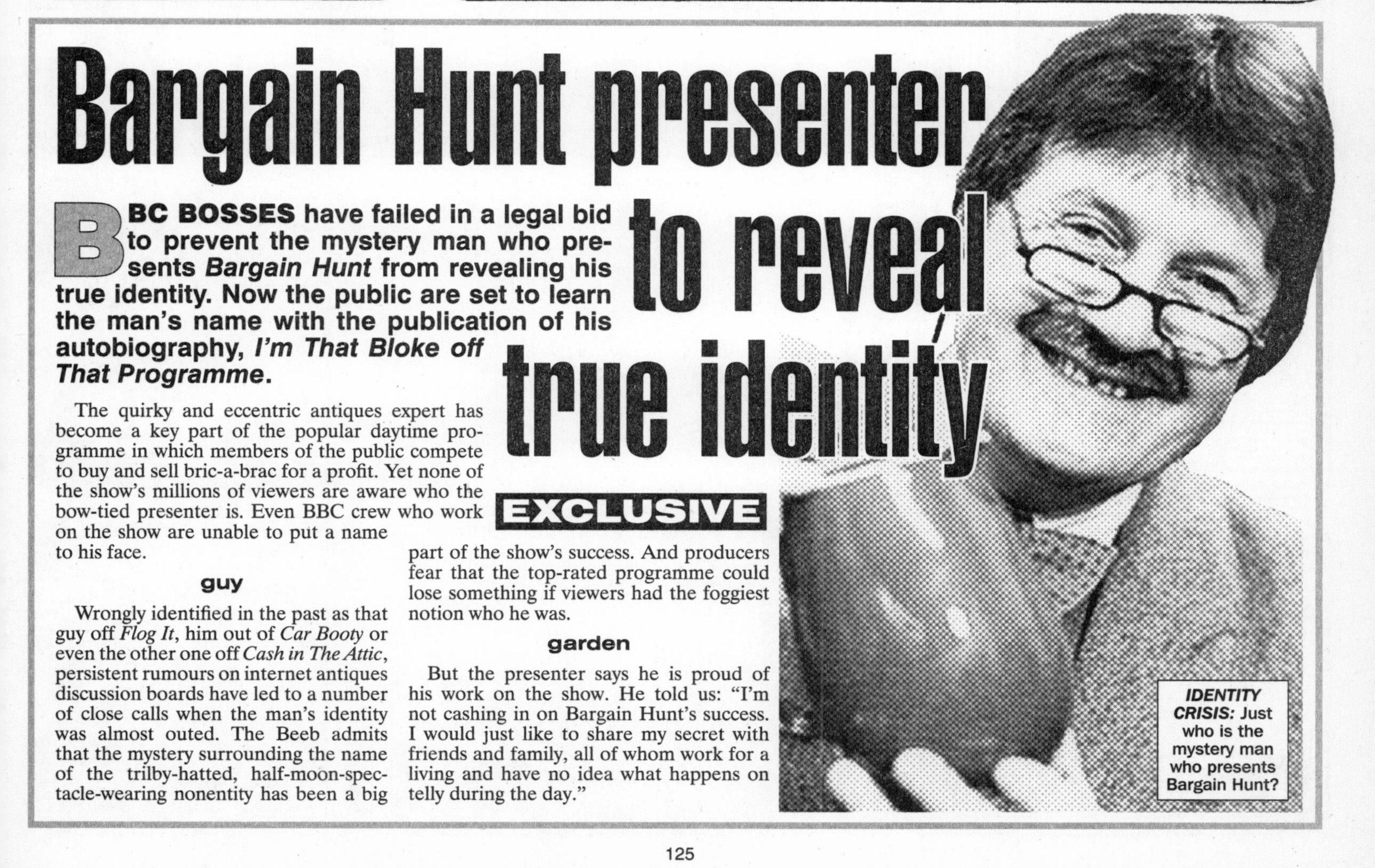

IDENTITY CRISIS: **Just who is the mystery man who presents Bargain Hunt?**

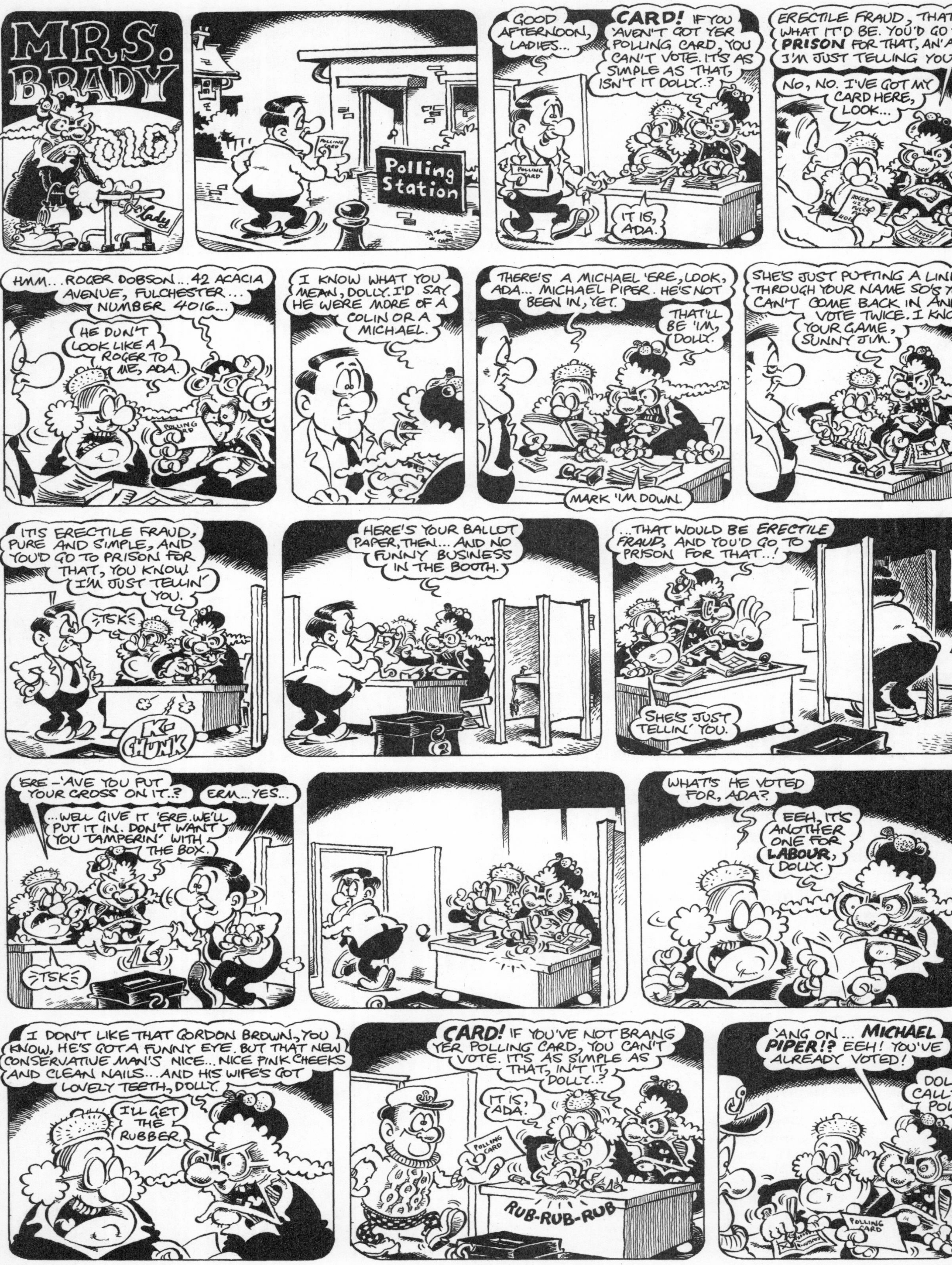
MRS. BRADY
OLD Lady
Polling Station
GOOD AFTERNOON, LADIES...
CARD! IF YOU 'AVEN'T GOT YER POLLING CARD, YOU CAN'T VOTE. IT'S AS SIMPLE AS THAT, ISN'T IT DOLLY..?
IT IS, ADA.
ERECTILE FRAUD, THAT'S WHAT IT'D BE. YOU'D GO TO PRISON FOR THAT, AN' ALL. I'M JUST TELLING YOU.
NO, NO. I'VE GOT MY CARD HERE, LOOK...
HMM... ROGER DOBSON... 42 ACACIA AVENUE, FULCHESTER... NUMBER 4016...
HE DON'T LOOK LIKE A ROGER TO ME, ADA.
I KNOW WHAT YOU MEAN, DOLLY. I'D SAY HE WERE MORE OF A COLIN OR A MICHAEL.
THERE'S A MICHAEL 'ERE, LOOK, ADA... MICHAEL PIPER. HE'S NOT BEEN IN, YET.
THAT'LL BE 'IM, DOLLY.
MARK 'IM DOWN.
SHE'S JUST PUTTING A LINE THROUGH YOUR NAME SO'S YOU CAN'T COME BACK IN AND VOTE TWICE. I KNOW YOUR GAME, SUNNY JIM.
IT'S ERECTILE FRAUD, PURE AND SIMPLE, AND YOU'D GO TO PRISON FOR THAT, YOU KNOW. I'M JUST TELLIN' YOU.
TSK
K-CHUNK
HERE'S YOUR BALLOT PAPER, THEN... AND NO FUNNY BUSINESS IN THE BOOTH.
...THAT WOULD BE ERECTILE FRAUD, AND YOU'D GO TO PRISON FOR THAT...!
SHE'S JUST TELLIN' YOU.
'ERE - 'AVE YOU PUT YOUR CROSS ON IT..?
ERM... YES...
...WELL GIVE IT 'ERE. WE'LL PUT IT IN. DON'T WANT YOU TAMPERIN' WITH THE BOX.
TSK
WHAT'S HE VOTED FOR, ADA?
EEH, IT'S ANOTHER ONE FOR LABOUR, DOLLY.
I DON'T LIKE THAT GORDON BROWN, YOU KNOW, HE'S GOT A FUNNY EYE. BUT THAT NEW CONSERVATIVE MAN'S NICE... NICE PINK CHEEKS AND CLEAN NAILS... AND HIS WIFE'S GOT LOVELY TEETH, DOLLY.
I'LL GET THE RUBBER.
CARD! IF YOU'VE NOT BRANG YER POLLING CARD, YOU CAN'T VOTE. IT'S AS SIMPLE AS THAT, IN'T IT, DOLLY..?
IT IS, ADA.
POLLING CARD
RUB-RUB-RUB
'ANG ON... MICHAEL PIPER!? EEH! YOU'VE ALREADY VOTED!
DOLLY! CALL THE POLICE!
POLLING CARD

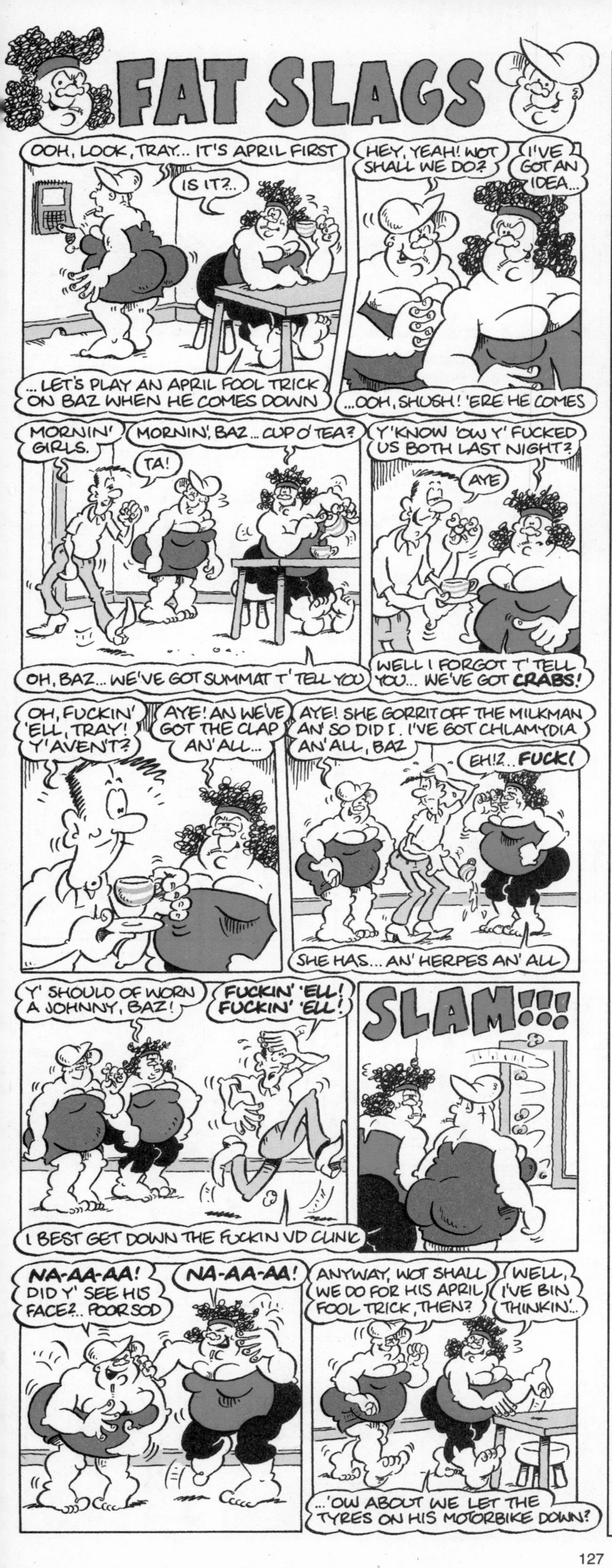
FAT SLAGS
OOH, LOOK, TRAY... IT'S APRIL FIRST
IS IT?..
... LET'S PLAY AN APRIL FOOL TRICK ON BAZ WHEN HE COMES DOWN
HEY, YEAH! WOT SHALL WE DO?
I'VE GOT AN IDEA...
...OOH, SHUSH! 'ERE HE COMES
MORNIN' GIRLS.
MORNIN', BAZ... CUP O' TEA?
TA!
OH, BAZ... WE'VE GOT SUMMAT T' TELL YOU
Y'KNOW 'OW Y' FUCKED US BOTH LAST NIGHT?
AYE
WELL I FORGOT T' TELL YOU... WE'VE GOT CRABS!
OH, FUCKIN' 'ELL, TRAY! Y'AVEN'T?
AYE! AN WE'VE GOT THE CLAP AN' ALL...
AYE! SHE GORRIT OFF THE MILKMAN AN' SO DID I. I'VE GOT CHLAMYDIA AN' ALL, BAZ
EH!?.. FUCK!
SHE HAS... AN' HERPES AN' ALL
Y' SHOULD OF WORN A JOHNNY, BAZ!
FUCKIN' 'ELL! FUCKIN' 'ELL!
I BEST GET DOWN THE FUCKIN VD CLINIC
SLAM!!!
NA-AA-AA! DID Y' SEE HIS FACE?.. POOR SOD
NA-AA-AA!
ANYWAY, WOT SHALL WE DO FOR HIS APRIL FOOL TRICK, THEN?
WELL, I'VE BIN THINKIN'..
...'OW ABOUT WE LET THE TYRES ON HIS MOTORBIKE DOWN?

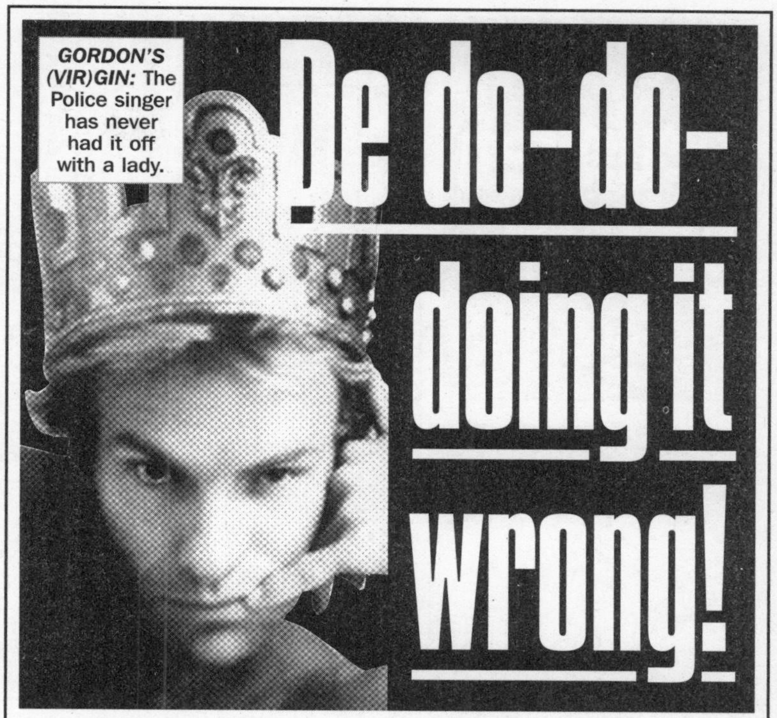

GORDON'S (VIR)GIN: The Police singer has never had it off with a lady.

De do-do-doing it wrong!

INCREASINGLY irrelevant recording artiste and complete bell-end *STING* has confessed that despite his famous marathon sessions between the sheets, he may have actually been "doing sex wrong" all his life!

In a frank interview for the *NME*, the former Police frontman confessed that he only realised his mistake last month after unexpectedly walking into his parents' bedroom when they were making love.

The singer, 58, hit the headlines in 1986 after boasting that by using tantric sex methods, he was able to make love to his wife, Trudie Styler, for up ***EIGHT HOURS***. Despite talking about his sexual prowess in every interview since then, he now admits he made the whole story up to impress some older boys he once met in a park.

PARK

"One day I was in the park and some big boys came up to me," he told *an NME reporter. "They started asking me questions about all sorts of things, drink, drugs, smoking - to be honest I didn't have the foggiest about any of them."*

"Then they started quizzing me about girls. They all said they'd 'done it' with loads of girls and asked me if I had. I was still a virgin at the time but didn't want to appear foolish in front of them. So I said I had, lots, and that I could go like steam-hammer for hours on end. After that they threw my coat up a tree and walked away."

GOAL

A confused Sting, real name Gordon, continued: "I meant to ask my mum what the boys were talking about, but when I got home she told me that my song Roxanne was number one in the charts and I had to go to London to be on Top of the Pops. By the time I got home later that night everyone was asleep and I guess I just forgot to ask."

SEXCLUSIVE!

"After a while it became too embarrassing to bring the subject up and then, somehow, the rumour got out. By this time I was a major international rock star.

I couldn't admit I was still a virgin so I just put my head down and concentrated on acting like an arsehole," he added.

POTTY

Despite being married since 1992, the Geordie millionaire admitted that he's never really fully understood what goes on in the bedroom and said he received 'the shock of his life' after noises from his parents' bedroom woke him in January.

"I could hear a lot of puffing and panting coming from their room," he said. *"At first I thought I was dreaming, but then I thought someone might be having a heart attack, so I walked in. I asked my dad what he was doing to my mummy and he replied, 'What does it look like?'"*

IT'S OWL STRETCHING

"I was so stunned I just turned around and went back to bed. After that I couldn't get back to sleep and just lay there next to my wife, Trudie Styler," he continued.

After a lengthy clear-the-air chat with his father the following morning, Sting admitted he was wrong to tell silly stories just to impress people and said he felt relieved that the truth was finally out. "I promised my parents I'd never tell stories again," the grown man concluded.

Drunken bakers

Sixteen, seventeen, seventeen-fifty –

Whoops.

tink

Come here you twat.

YMO 37F

Is that can cold?

Nah, not really.

Bloody Boozebox never put the fridge on proper.

Mind you, at a five quid for eight export I ain't moaning.

Yeah...

Where am I?

Hospital.

A car hit your head.

Just my head?

Mostly.

The copper said the driver said you bent over and stuck it out.

I remember dropping a quid...

And calling it a twat.

Why?

Twat rolled off.

I needed it for that rum offer.

What rum offer?

Boozestop.

Two bottles for twenty.

Lamb's?

Sea Dog.

Bloody rough shit like...

But litres.

Cheap.

Sea Dog.

Give us a pull on that eh?

Ow! Ow! Ow! Oww!

That feels quite cold.

On my dressings.

The doctor reckons there's a chance they might save your eye...

128

Footballers' Fury as Flights Soar

By our sports correspondent
Les Kellett

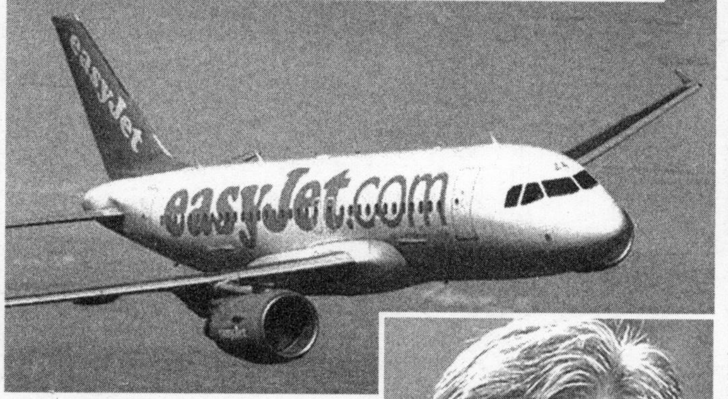

easyJet
easyJet.com

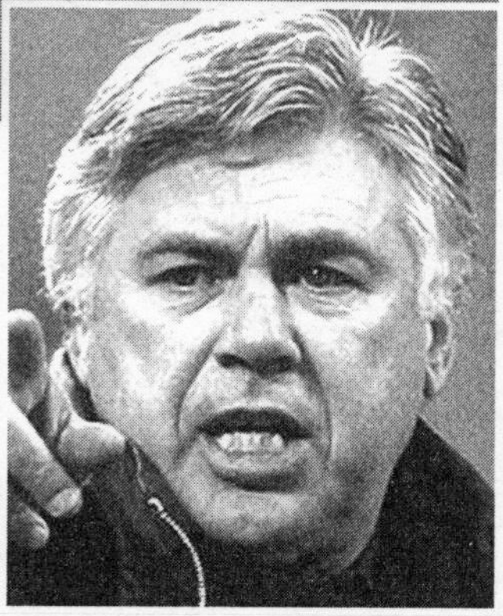

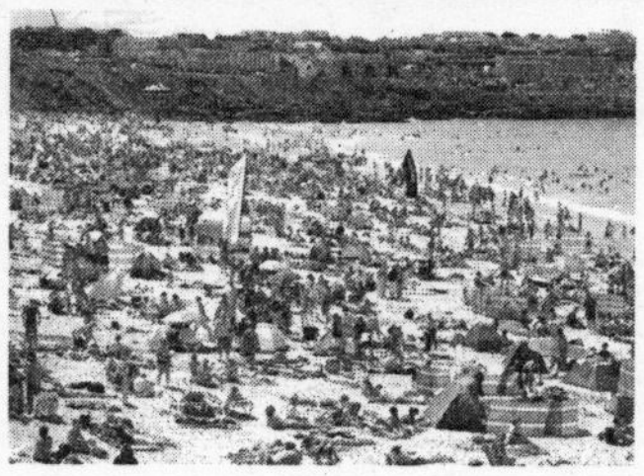

Could holidays like these soon be out of the pocket of footballers? Top: Carlo Ancelotti yesterday

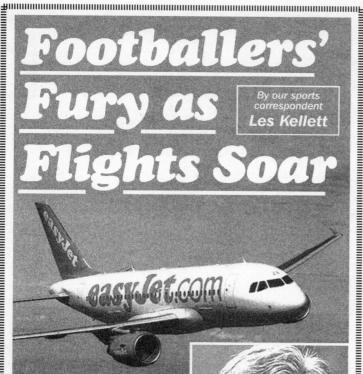

PREMIER LEAGUE footballers were last night threatening to STRIKE over FA rules that force them to take their annual holidays outside the soccer season. And they were angry that airlines, tour operators and holiday parks were cashing in by *BUMPING UP* prices the minute football clubs break up for the summer.

Current rules forbid players from taking time off during the playing season, traditionally held from August to May. But a recent poll conducted by Sky Sports reveals that many top flight players are prepared to break the rules and save money by holidaying during the season.

booked

One goalkeeper, who didn't want to be named, told reporters: "After I let that silly goal in during the World Cup, I just wanted to get away for a holiday, so I booked a week in Magaluf in July. It was £380 for the week, including transfers from the airport and continental breakfast. The travel agent told me that if I could go the third week in August, the same package holiday would be be £40 cheaper. But I couldn't, as we kicked off the season away to Aston Villa that week."

sent off

But more alarmingly, the Sky poll claims a staggering 78% of players say they are willing to "throw a sickie" in order to cash in on cheaper mid-season holidays. Lying about illnesses, pretending to pull a hamstring and faking a broken leg are all tactics used by players to get time off. And one international player even had sex with another player's wife in an attempt to be dropped for misconduct for a couple of games to take advantage of a cheap week at Butlins in Skegness.

"My squad are paid to be available to play through out the season. If any of them are too poorly to play, they have to have a doctor's note," said Chelsea boss Carlo Ancelotti. "If they are absent for any game without a note, I fine them £50 and give them a stern talking to."

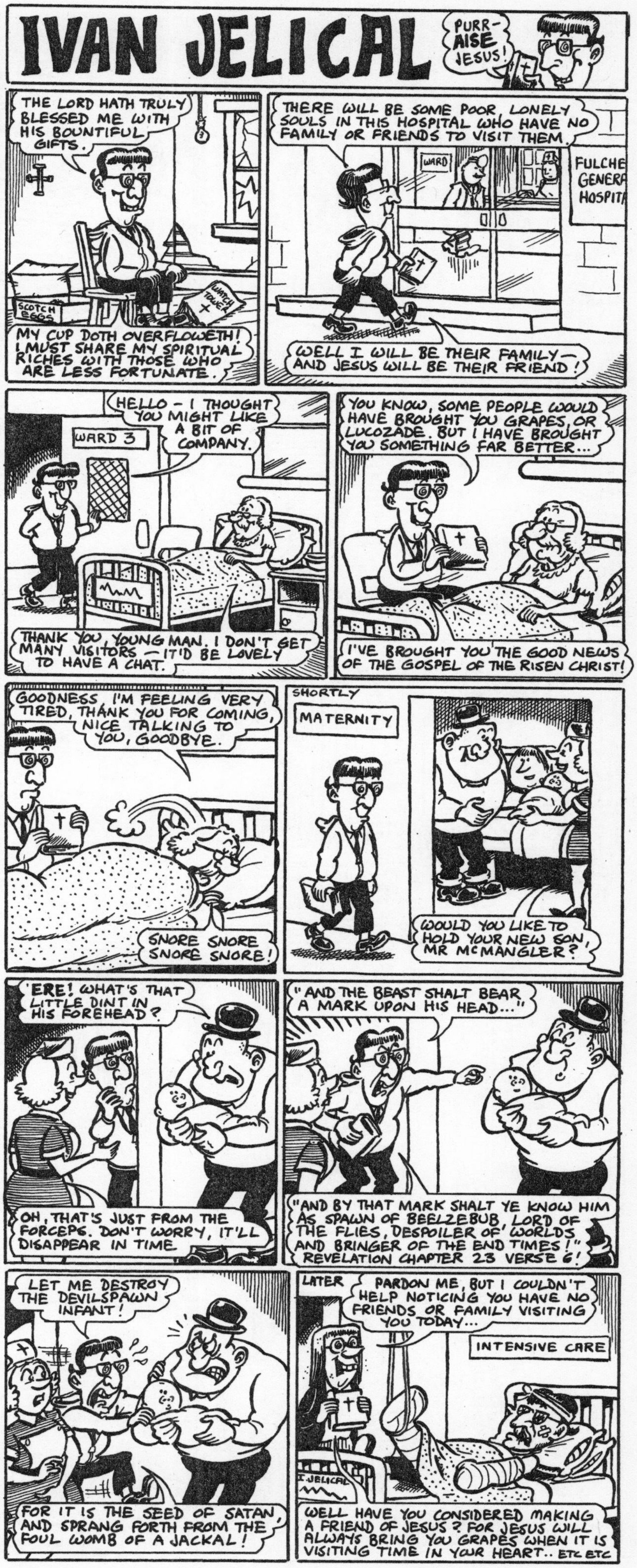

IVAN JELICAL
PURR-AISE JESUS!
THE LORD HATH TRULY BLESSED ME WITH HIS BOUNTIFUL GIFTS.
SCOTCH EGGS
WATCH TOWER
MY CUP DOTH OVERFLOWETH! I MUST SHARE MY SPIRITUAL RICHES WITH THOSE WHO ARE LESS FORTUNATE.
THERE WILL BE SOME POOR, LONELY SOULS IN THIS HOSPITAL WHO HAVE NO FAMILY OR FRIENDS TO VISIT THEM.
WARD
WELL I WILL BE THEIR FAMILY - AND JESUS WILL BE THEIR FRIEND!
HELLO - I THOUGHT YOU MIGHT LIKE A BIT OF COMPANY.
WARD 3
THANK YOU, YOUNG MAN. I DON'T GET MANY VISITORS - IT'D BE LOVELY TO HAVE A CHAT.
YOU KNOW, SOME PEOPLE WOULD HAVE BROUGHT YOU GRAPES, OR LUCOZADE. BUT I HAVE BROUGHT YOU SOMETHING FAR BETTER...
I'VE BROUGHT YOU THE GOOD NEWS OF THE GOSPEL OF THE RISEN CHRIST!
GOODNESS, I'M FEELING VERY TIRED, THANK YOU FOR COMING, NICE TALKING TO YOU, GOODBYE.
SNORE SNORE SNORE SNORE!
SHORTLY
MATERNITY
WOULD YOU LIKE TO HOLD YOUR NEW SON, MR McMANGLER?
'ERE! WHAT'S THAT LITTLE DINT IN HIS FOREHEAD?
OH, THAT'S JUST FROM THE FORCEPS. DON'T WORRY, IT'LL DISAPPEAR IN TIME.
"AND THE BEAST SHALT BEAR A MARK UPON HIS HEAD..."
"AND BY THAT MARK SHALT YE KNOW HIM AS SPAWN OF BEELZEBUB, LORD OF THE FLIES, DESPOILER OF WORLDS AND BRINGER OF THE END TIMES!" REVELATION CHAPTER 23 VERSE 6!
LET ME DESTROY THE DEVILSPAWN INFANT!
FOR IT IS THE SEED OF SATAN, AND SPRANG FORTH FROM THE FOUL WOMB OF A JACKAL!
LATER
PARDON ME, BUT I COULDN'T HELP NOTICING YOU HAVE NO FRIENDS OR FAMILY VISITING YOU TODAY...
INTENSIVE CARE
WELL HAVE YOU CONSIDERED MAKING A FRIEND OF JESUS? FOR JESUS WILL ALWAYS BRING YOU GRAPES WHEN IT IS VISITING TIME IN YOUR HEART.. ETC ETC

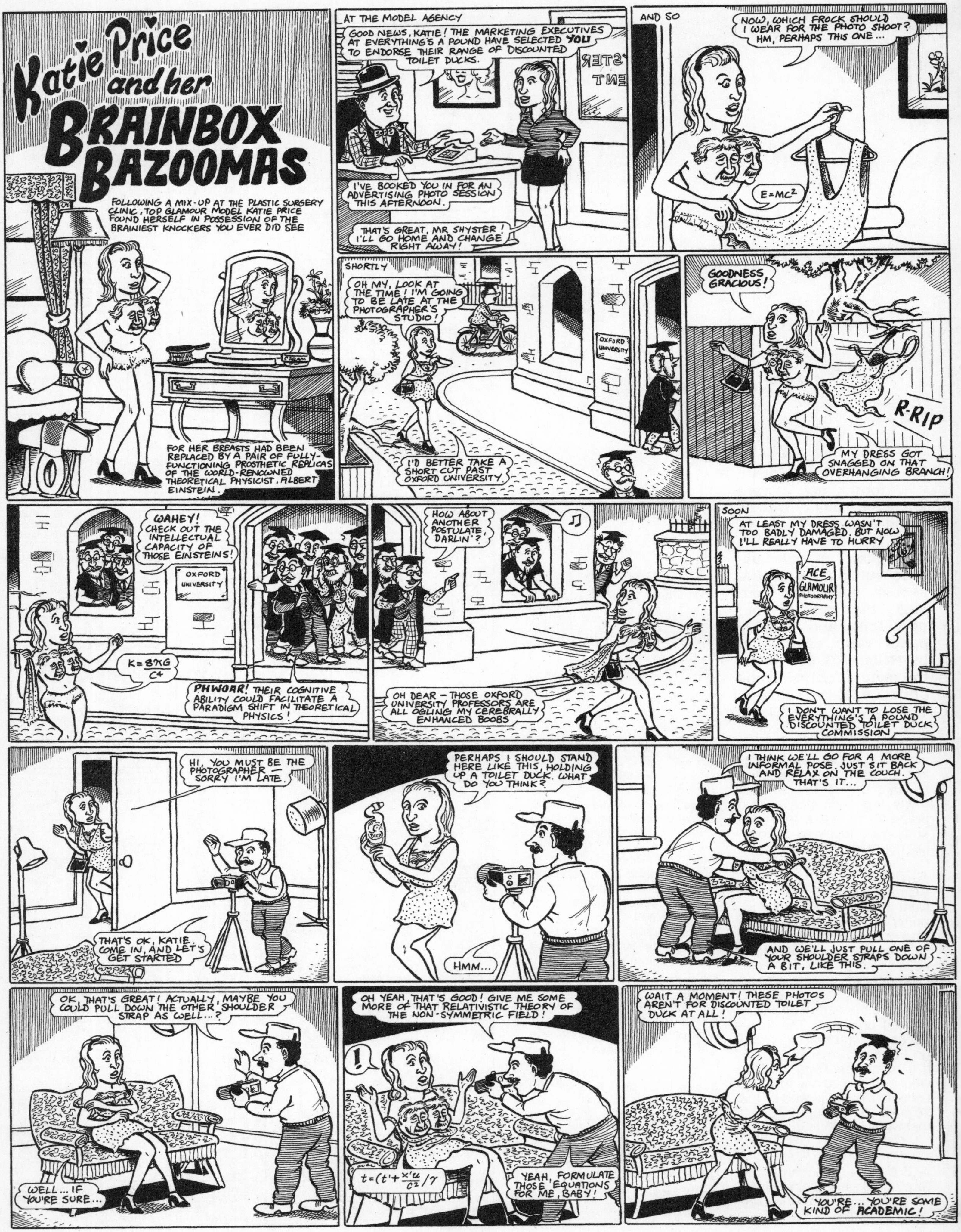
Katie Price and her
BRAINBOX BAZOOMAS
FOLLOWING A MIX-UP AT THE PLASTIC SURGERY CLINIC, TOP GLAMOUR MODEL KATIE PRICE FOUND HERSELF IN POSSESSION OF THE BRAINIEST KNOCKERS YOU EVER DID SEE
FOR HER BREASTS HAD BEEN REPLACED BY A PAIR OF FULLY-FUNCTIONING PROSTHETIC REPLICAS OF THE WORLD-RENOWNED THEORETICAL PHYSICIST, ALBERT EINSTEIN.
AT THE MODEL AGENCY
GOOD NEWS, KATIE! THE MARKETING EXECUTIVES AT EVERYTHING'S A POUND HAVE SELECTED YOU TO ENDORSE THEIR RANGE OF DISCOUNTED TOILET DUCKS.
I'VE BOOKED YOU IN FOR AN ADVERTISING PHOTO SESSION THIS AFTERNOON.
THAT'S GREAT, MR SHYSTER! I'LL GO HOME AND CHANGE RIGHT AWAY!
AND SO
NOW, WHICH FROCK SHOULD I WEAR FOR THE PHOTO SHOOT? HM, PERHAPS THIS ONE...
E=MC²
SHORTLY
OH MY, LOOK AT THE TIME! I'M GOING TO BE LATE AT THE PHOTOGRAPHER'S STUDIO!
OXFORD UNIVERSITY
I'D BETTER TAKE A SHORT CUT PAST OXFORD UNIVERSITY.
GOODNESS GRACIOUS!
R-RIP
MY DRESS GOT SNAGGED ON THAT OVERHANGING BRANCH!
WAHEY! CHECK OUT THE INTELLECTUAL CAPACITY OF THOSE EINSTEINS!
OXFORD UNIVERSITY
K = 8πG / C⁴
PHWOAR! THEIR COGNITIVE ABILITY COULD FACILITATE A PARADIGM SHIFT IN THEORETICAL PHYSICS!
HOW ABOUT ANOTHER POSTULATE, DARLIN'?
♫
OH DEAR – THOSE OXFORD UNIVERSITY PROFESSORS ARE ALL OGLING MY CEREBRALLY ENHANCED BOOBS
SOON
AT LEAST MY DRESS WASN'T TOO BADLY DAMAGED. BUT NOW I'LL REALLY HAVE TO HURRY
ACE GLAMOUR PHOTOGRAPHY
I DON'T WANT TO LOSE THE EVERYTHING'S A POUND DISCOUNTED TOILET DUCK COMMISSION
HI, YOU MUST BE THE PHOTOGRAPHER – SORRY I'M LATE.
THAT'S OK, KATIE. COME IN, AND LET'S GET STARTED
PERHAPS I SHOULD STAND HERE LIKE THIS, HOLDING UP A TOILET DUCK. WHAT DO YOU THINK?
DUCK
HMM...
I THINK WE'LL GO FOR A MORE INFORMAL POSE. JUST SIT BACK AND RELAX ON THE COUCH. THAT'S IT...
AND WE'LL JUST PULL ONE OF YOUR SHOULDER STRAPS DOWN A BIT, LIKE THIS.
OK, THAT'S GREAT! ACTUALLY, MAYBE YOU COULD PULL DOWN THE OTHER SHOULDER STRAP AS WELL...?
WELL... IF YOU'RE SURE...
OH YEAH, THAT'S GOOD! GIVE ME SOME MORE OF THAT RELATIVISTIC THEORY OF THE NON-SYMMETRIC FIELD!
!
t=(t'+x'u/c²)/γ
YEAH, FORMULATE THOSE EQUATIONS FOR ME, BABY!
WAIT A MOMENT! THESE PHOTOS AREN'T FOR DISCOUNTED TOILET DUCK AT ALL!
YOU'RE... YOU'RE SOME KIND OF ACADEMIC!

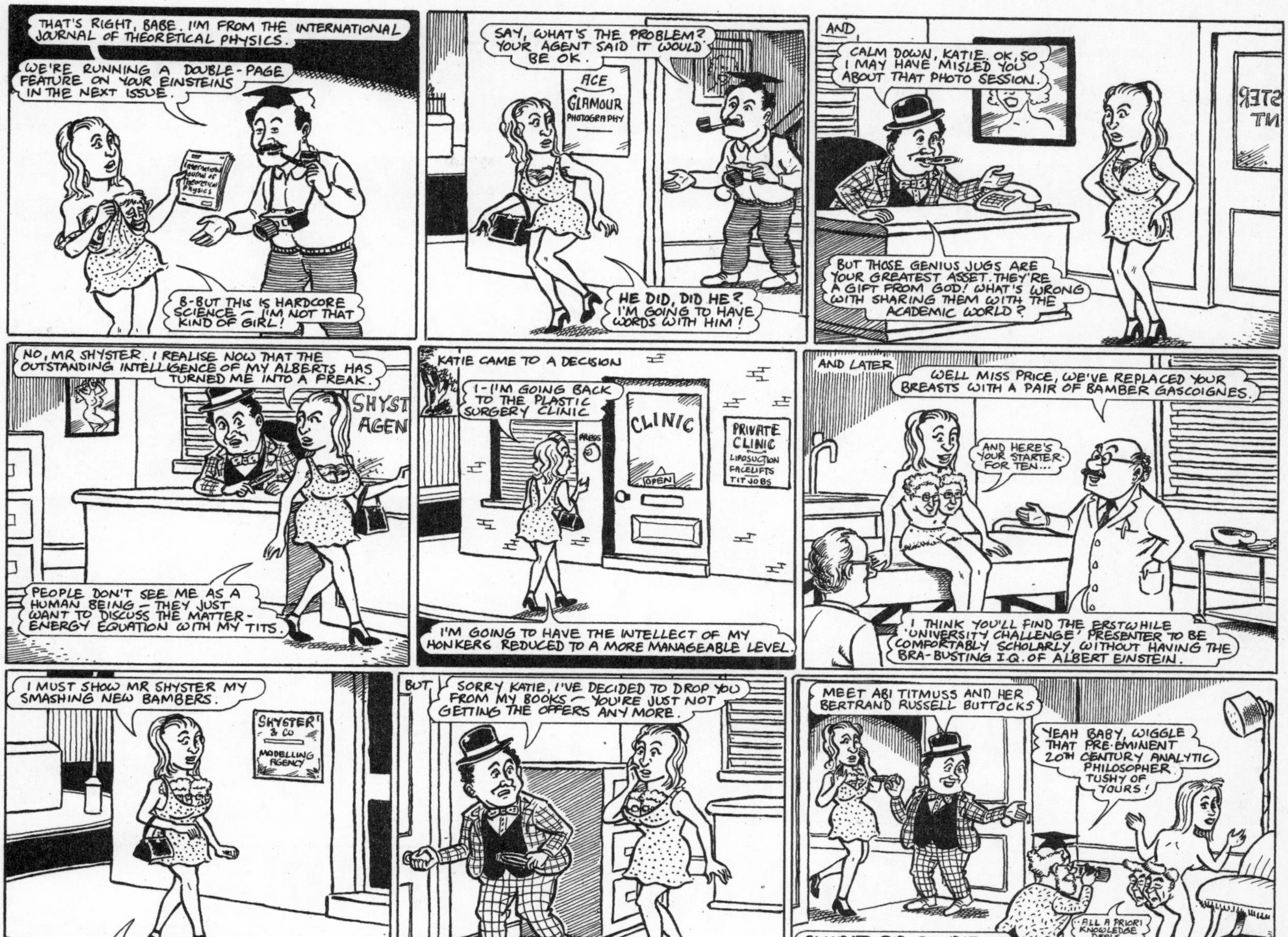
THAT'S RIGHT, BABE. I'M FROM THE INTERNATIONAL JOURNAL OF THEORETICAL PHYSICS.
WE'RE RUNNING A DOUBLE-PAGE FEATURE ON YOUR EINSTEINS IN THE NEXT ISSUE.
B-BUT THIS IS HARDCORE SCIENCE — I'M NOT THAT KIND OF GIRL!
SAY, WHAT'S THE PROBLEM? YOUR AGENT SAID IT WOULD BE OK.
ACE GLAMOUR PHOTOGRAPHY
HE DID, DID HE? I'M GOING TO HAVE WORDS WITH HIM!
AND,
CALM DOWN, KATIE. OK, SO I MAY HAVE MISLED YOU ABOUT THAT PHOTO SESSION.
BUT THOSE GENIUS JUGS ARE YOUR GREATEST ASSET. THEY'RE A GIFT FROM GOD! WHAT'S WRONG WITH SHARING THEM WITH THE ACADEMIC WORLD?
NO, MR SHYSTER. I REALISE NOW THAT THE OUTSTANDING INTELLIGENCE OF MY ALBERTS HAS TURNED ME INTO A FREAK.
PEOPLE DON'T SEE ME AS A HUMAN BEING — THEY JUST WANT TO DISCUSS THE MATTER-ENERGY EQUATION WITH MY TITS.
KATIE CAME TO A DECISION
I-I'M GOING BACK TO THE PLASTIC SURGERY CLINIC
CLINIC
PRESS
OPEN
PRIVATE CLINIC LIPOSUCTION FACELIFTS TIT JOBS
I'M GOING TO HAVE THE INTELLECT OF MY HONKERS REDUCED TO A MORE MANAGEABLE LEVEL.
AND LATER
WELL MISS PRICE, WE'VE REPLACED YOUR BREASTS WITH A PAIR OF BAMBER GASCOIGNES.
AND HERE'S YOUR STARTER FOR TEN...
I THINK YOU'LL FIND THE ERSTWHILE 'UNIVERSITY CHALLENGE' PRESENTER TO BE COMFORTABLY SCHOLARLY, WITHOUT HAVING THE BRA-BUSTING I.Q. OF ALBERT EINSTEIN.
I MUST SHOW MR SHYSTER MY SMASHING NEW BAMBERS.
SHYSTER & CO MODELLING AGENCY
NOW THE WORLD WILL TREAT ME LIKE AN ORDINARY SUPER-CELEBRITY GLAMOUR MODEL ONCE AGAIN
BUT,
SORRY KATIE, I'VE DECIDED TO DROP YOU FROM MY BOOKS — YOU'RE JUST NOT GETTING THE OFFERS ANY MORE.
I'VE SIGNED UP A NEW MODEL IN YOUR PLACE...
MEET ABI TITMUSS AND HER BERTRAND RUSSELL BUTTOCKS
YEAH BABY, WIGGLE THAT PRE-EMINENT 20TH CENTURY ANALYTIC PHILOSOPHER TUSHY OF YOURS!
ELUCIDATE THE FOUNDATIONS OF MATHEMATICAL LOGIC TO THE CAMERA!
...ALL A PRIORI KNOWLEDGE DEALS EXCLUSIVELY WITH UNIVERSALS...

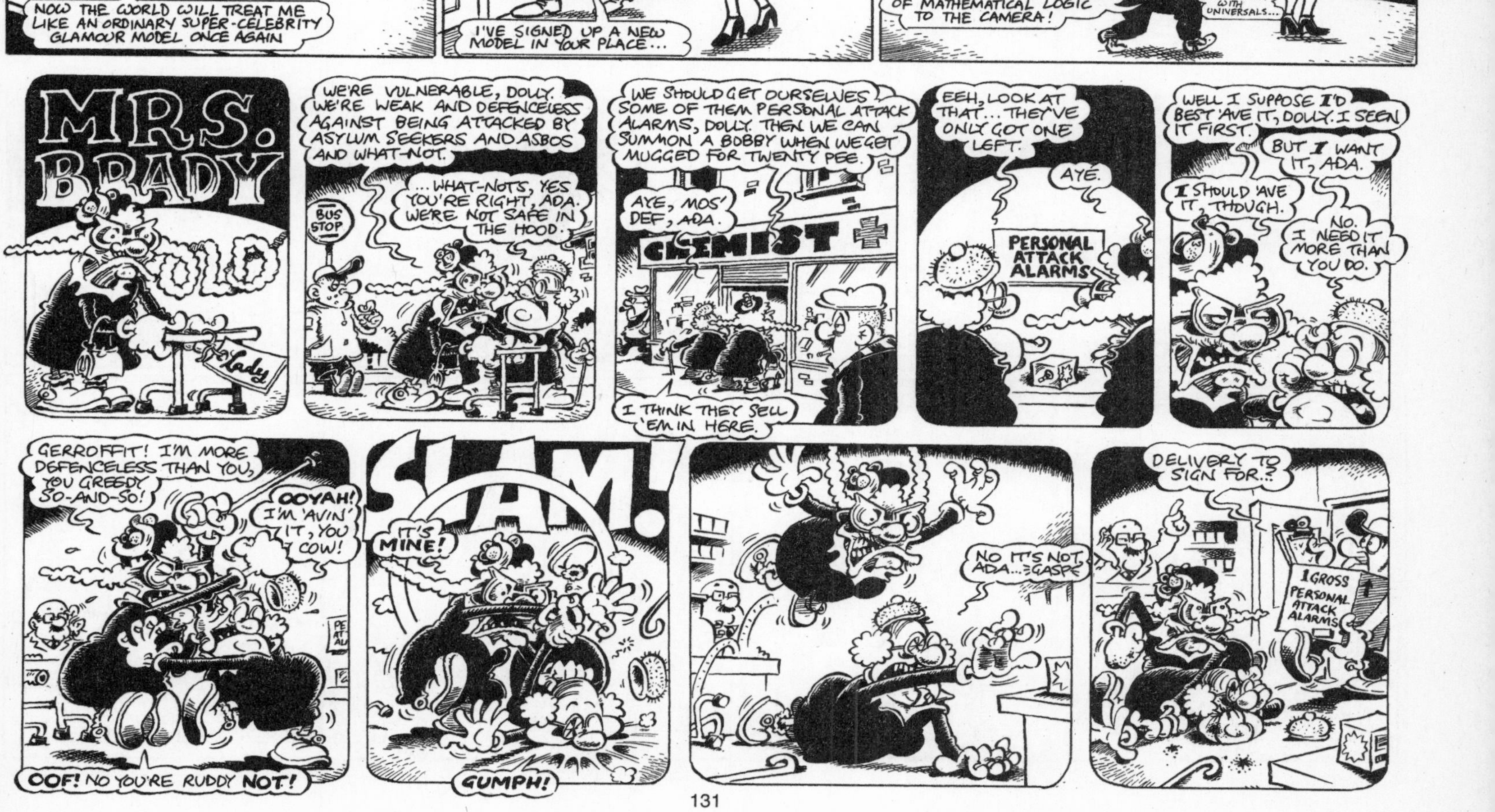
MRS. BRADY
OLD
Lady
WE'RE VULNERABLE, DOLLY. WE'RE WEAK AND DEFENCELESS AGAINST BEING ATTACKED BY ASYLUM SEEKERS AND ASBOS AND WHAT-NOT.
...WHAT-NOTS, YES YOU'RE RIGHT, ADA. WE'RE NOT SAFE IN THE HOOD.
BUS STOP
WE SHOULD GET OURSELVES SOME OF THEM PERSONAL ATTACK ALARMS, DOLLY. THEN WE CAN SUMMON A BOBBY WHEN WE GET MUGGED FOR TWENTY PEE.
AYE, MOS' DEF, ADA.
CHEMIST
I THINK THEY SELL 'EM IN HERE.
EEH, LOOK AT THAT... THEY'VE ONLY GOT ONE LEFT.
AYE.
PERSONAL ATTACK ALARMS
WELL I SUPPOSE I'D BEST 'AVE IT, DOLLY. I SEEN IT FIRST.
BUT I WANT IT, ADA.
I SHOULD 'AVE IT, THOUGH.
NO. I NEED IT MORE THAN YOU DO.
GERROFFIT! I'M MORE DEFENCELESS THAN YOU, YOU GREEDY SO-AND-SO!
OOYAH! I'M 'AVIN' IT, YOU COW!
OOF! NO YOU'RE RUDDY NOT!
SLAM!
IT'S MINE!
GUMPH!
NO IT'S NOT, ADA...GASP!
DELIVERY TO SIGN FOR..?
1 GROSS PERSONAL ATTACK ALARMS

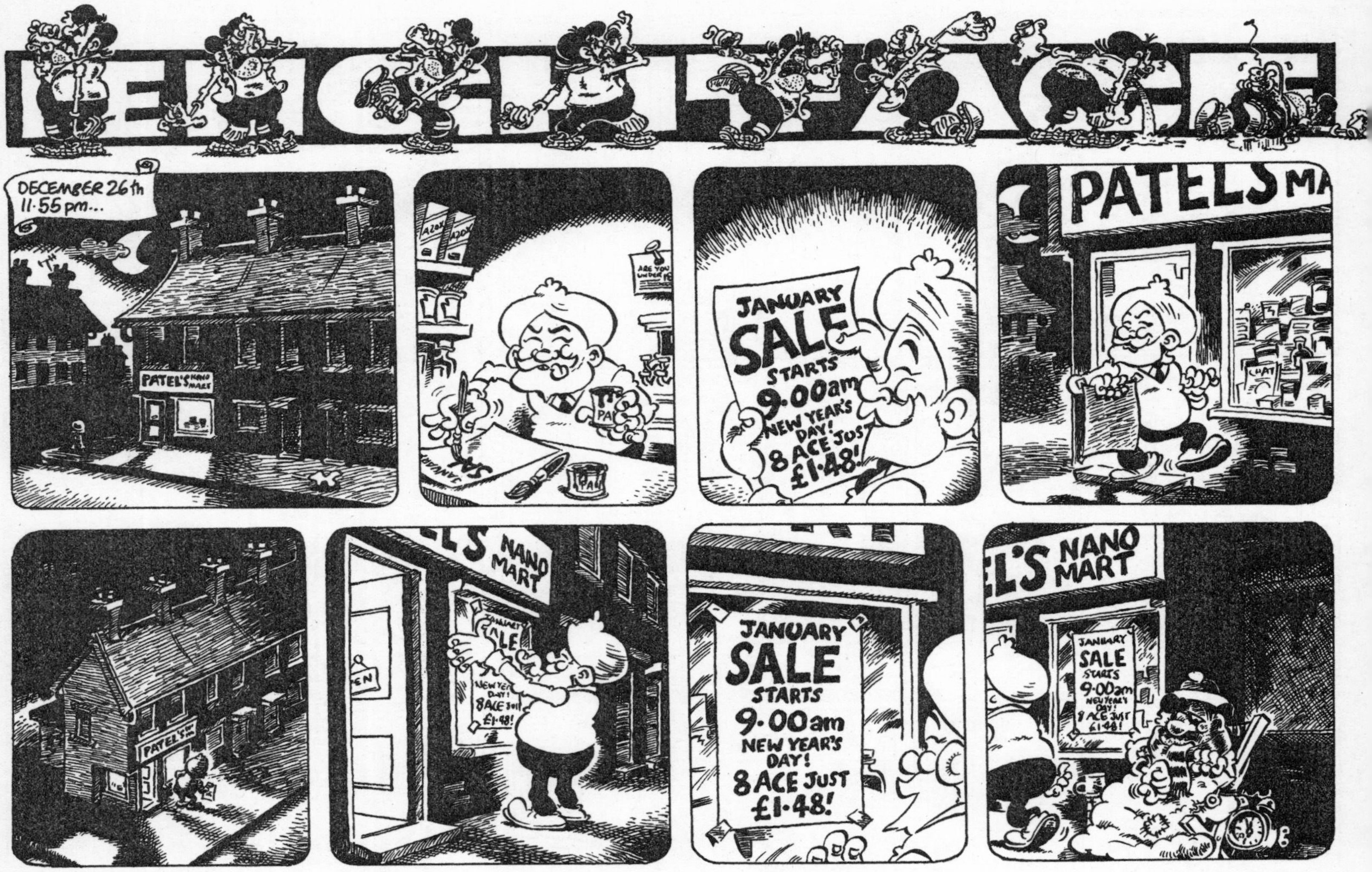
DECEMBER 26th 11.55 pm...
PATEL'S NANO MART
JANUARY SALE STARTS 9.00am NEW YEAR'S DAY! 8 ACE JUST £1.48!
PATELS MA
EL'S NANO MART
JANUARY SALE STARTS 9.00am NEW YEAR'S DAY! 8 ACE JUST £1.48!
EL'S NANO MART
JANUARY SALE STARTS 9.00am NEW YEAR'S DAY! 8 ACE JUST £1.48!
JANUARY SALE STARTS 9.00am NEW YEAR'S DAY! 8 ACE JUST £1.48!

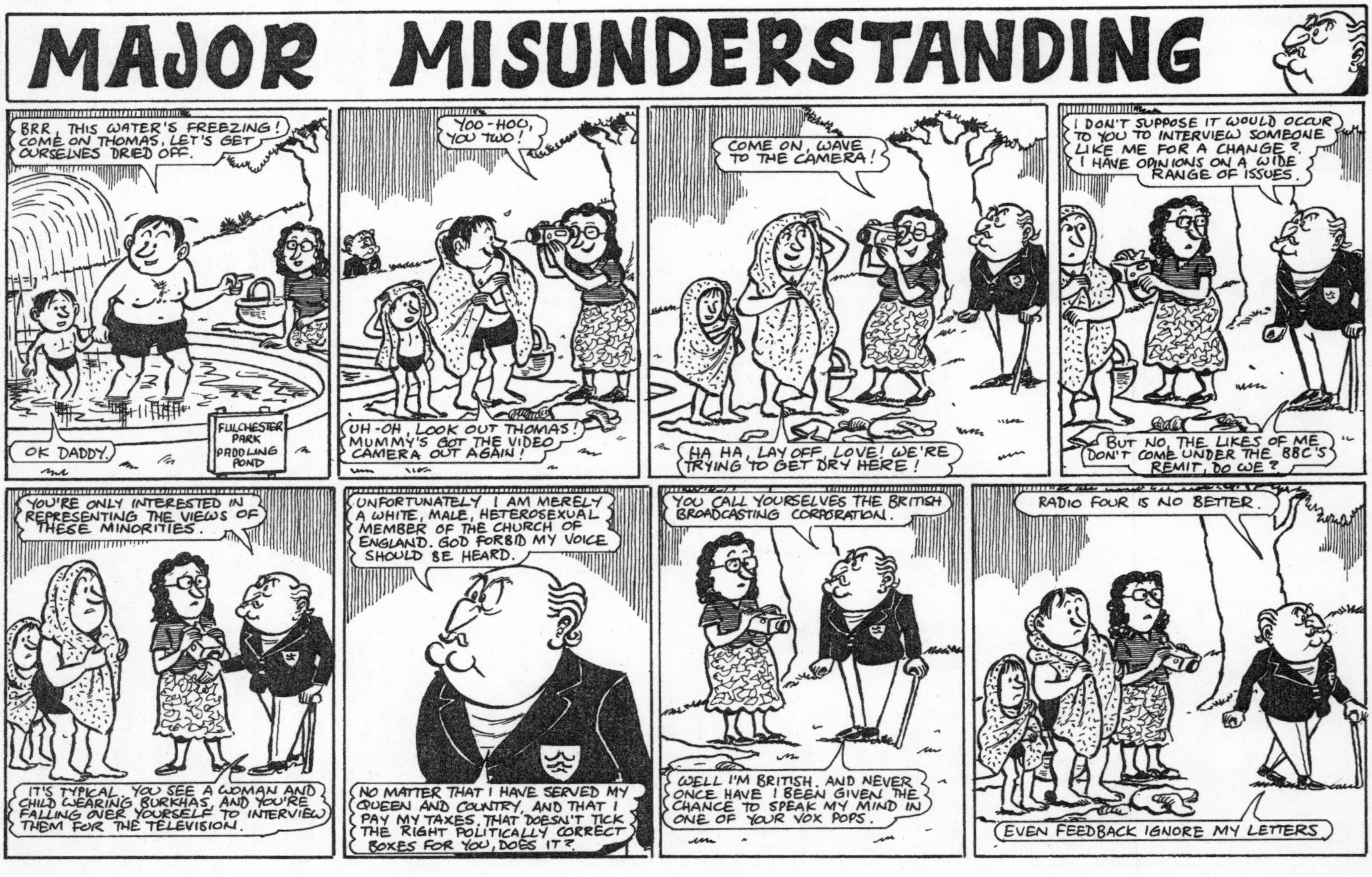
MAJOR MISUNDERSTANDING
BRR, THIS WATER'S FREEZING! COME ON THOMAS, LET'S GET OURSELVES DRIED OFF.
OK DADDY.
FULCHESTER PARK PADDLING POND
YOO-HOO, YOU TWO!
UH-OH, LOOK OUT THOMAS! MUMMY'S GOT THE VIDEO CAMERA OUT AGAIN!
COME ON, WAVE TO THE CAMERA!
HA HA, LAY OFF, LOVE! WE'RE TRYING TO GET DRY HERE!
I DON'T SUPPOSE IT WOULD OCCUR TO YOU TO INTERVIEW SOMEONE LIKE ME FOR A CHANGE? I HAVE OPINIONS ON A WIDE RANGE OF ISSUES.
BUT NO, THE LIKES OF ME DON'T COME UNDER THE BBC'S REMIT, DO WE?
YOU'RE ONLY INTERESTED IN REPRESENTING THE VIEWS OF THESE MINORITIES.
IT'S TYPICAL. YOU SEE A WOMAN AND CHILD WEARING BURKHAS, AND YOU'RE FALLING OVER YOURSELF TO INTERVIEW THEM FOR THE TELEVISION.
UNFORTUNATELY I AM MERELY A WHITE, MALE, HETEROSEXUAL MEMBER OF THE CHURCH OF ENGLAND. GOD FORBID MY VOICE SHOULD BE HEARD.
NO MATTER THAT I HAVE SERVED MY QUEEN AND COUNTRY, AND THAT I PAY MY TAXES, THAT DOESN'T TICK THE RIGHT POLITICALLY CORRECT BOXES FOR YOU, DOES IT?
YOU CALL YOURSELVES THE BRITISH BROADCASTING CORPORATION.
WELL I'M BRITISH, AND NEVER ONCE HAVE I BEEN GIVEN THE CHANCE TO SPEAK MY MIND IN ONE OF YOUR VOX POPS.
RADIO FOUR IS NO BETTER.
EVEN FEEDBACK IGNORE MY LETTERS.

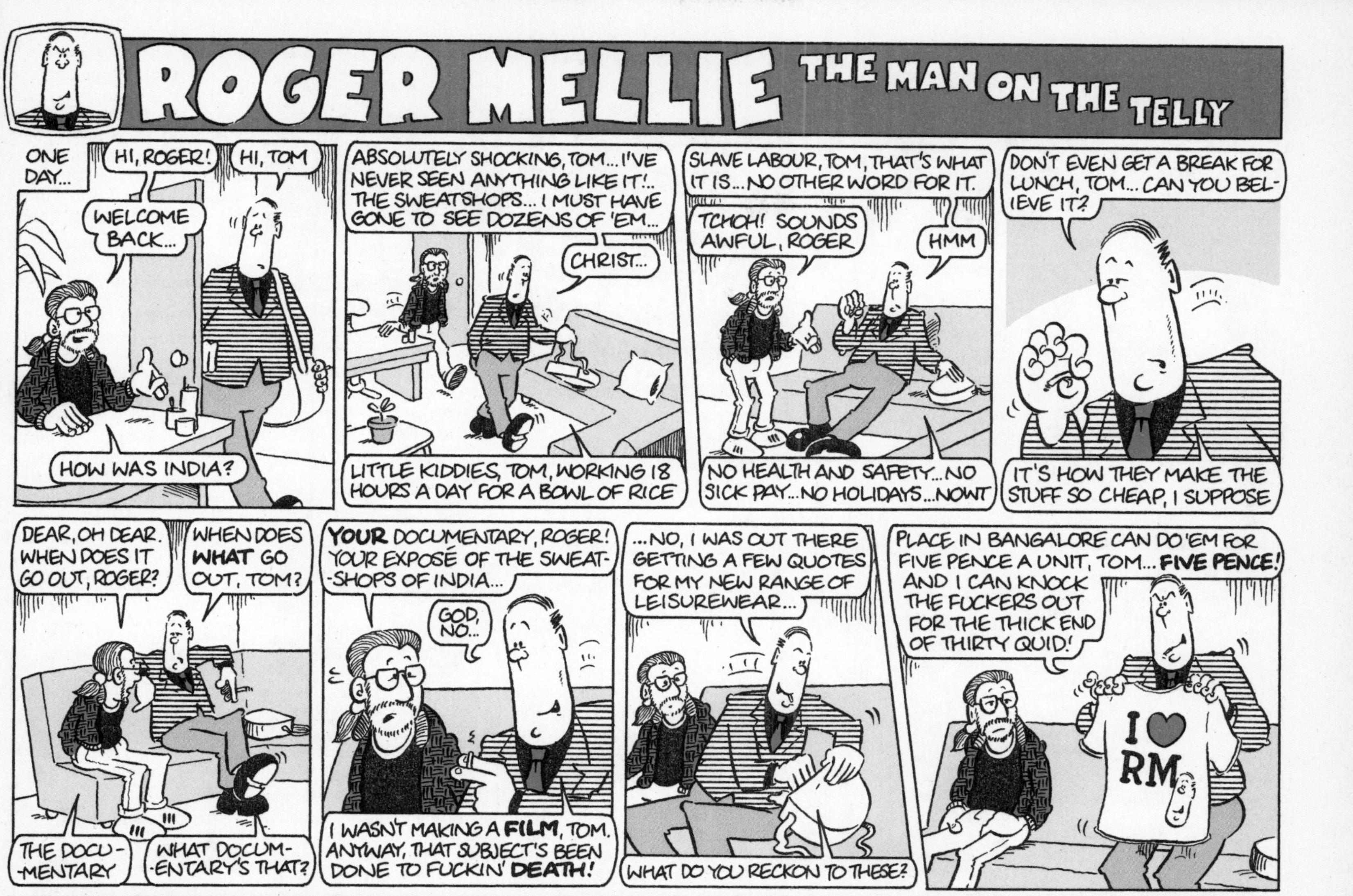
ROGER MELLIE THE MAN ON THE TELLY
ONE DAY...
HI, ROGER!
HI, TOM
WELCOME BACK...
HOW WAS INDIA?
ABSOLUTELY SHOCKING, TOM... I'VE NEVER SEEN ANYTHING LIKE IT!.. THE SWEATSHOPS... I MUST HAVE GONE TO SEE DOZENS OF 'EM...
CHRIST...
LITTLE KIDDIES, TOM, WORKING 18 HOURS A DAY FOR A BOWL OF RICE
SLAVE LABOUR, TOM, THAT'S WHAT IT IS... NO OTHER WORD FOR IT.
TCHOH! SOUNDS AWFUL, ROGER
HMM
NO HEALTH AND SAFETY... NO SICK PAY... NO HOLIDAYS... NOWT
DON'T EVEN GET A BREAK FOR LUNCH, TOM... CAN YOU BELIEVE IT?
IT'S HOW THEY MAKE THE STUFF SO CHEAP, I SUPPOSE
DEAR, OH DEAR. WHEN DOES IT GO OUT, ROGER?
WHEN DOES WHAT GO OUT, TOM?
THE DOCUMENTARY
WHAT DOCUMENTARY'S THAT?
YOUR DOCUMENTARY, ROGER! YOUR EXPOSÉ OF THE SWEAT-SHOPS OF INDIA...
GOD, NO...
I WASN'T MAKING A FILM, TOM. ANYWAY, THAT SUBJECT'S BEEN DONE TO FUCKIN' DEATH!
...NO, I WAS OUT THERE GETTING A FEW QUOTES FOR MY NEW RANGE OF LEISUREWEAR...
WHAT DO YOU RECKON TO THESE?
PLACE IN BANGALORE CAN DO 'EM FOR FIVE PENCE A UNIT, TOM... FIVE PENCE! AND I CAN KNOCK THE FUCKERS OUT FOR THE THICK END OF THIRTY QUID!
I ♥ RM

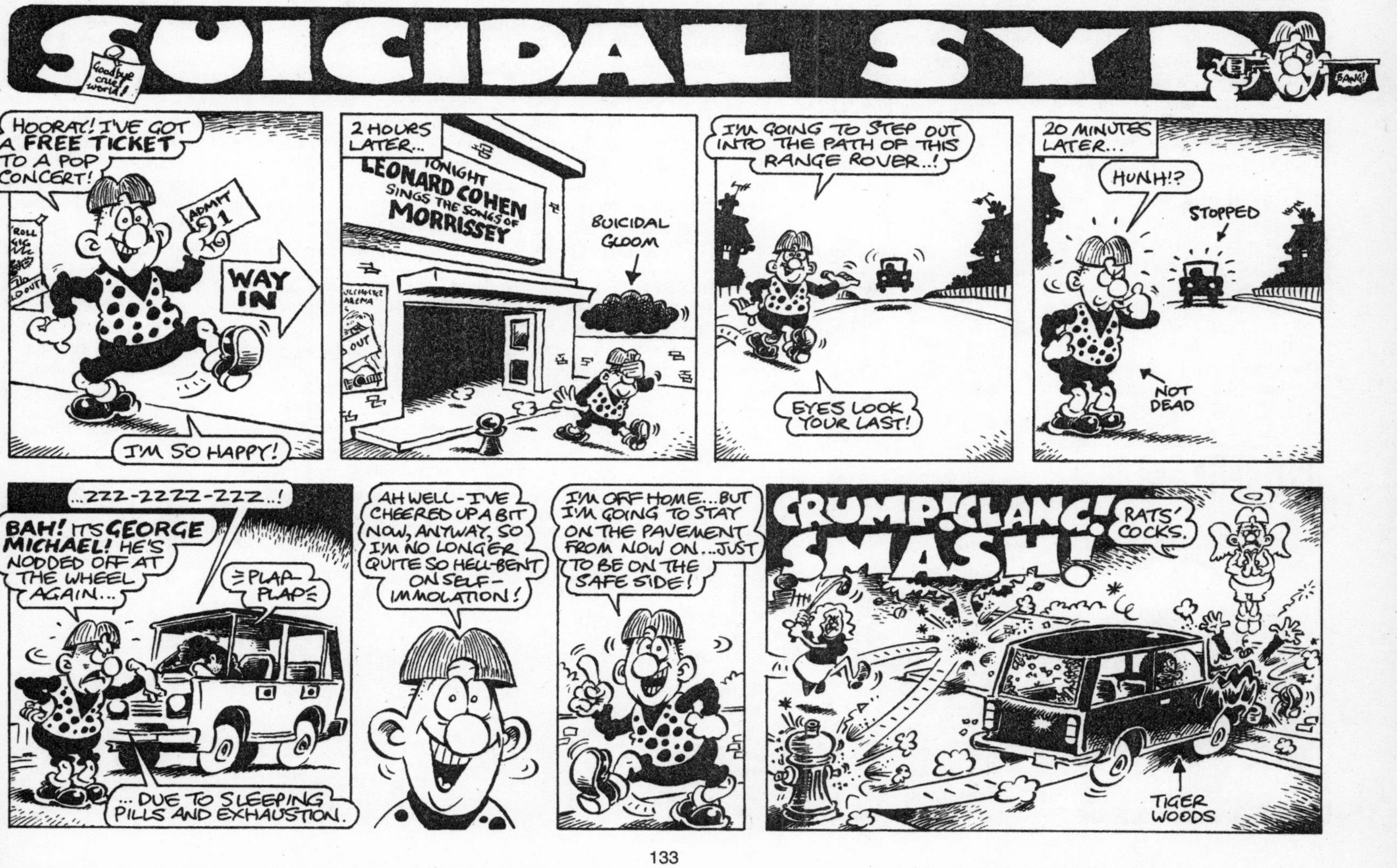
SUICIDAL SYD
Goodbye cruel world!
BANG!
HOORAY! I'VE GOT A FREE TICKET TO A POP CONCERT!
ADMIT 1
WAY IN
I'M SO HAPPY!
2 HOURS LATER...
TONIGHT LEONARD COHEN SINGS THE SONGS OF MORRISSEY
SUICIDAL GLOOM
I'M GOING TO STEP OUT INTO THE PATH OF THIS RANGE ROVER..!
EYES LOOK YOUR LAST!
20 MINUTES LATER...
HUNH!?
STOPPED
NOT DEAD
...ZZZ-ZZZZ-ZZZ..!
BAH! IT'S GEORGE MICHAEL! HE'S NODDED OFF AT THE WHEEL AGAIN...
PLAP-PLAP
...DUE TO SLEEPING PILLS AND EXHAUSTION.
AH WELL - I'VE CHEERED UP A BIT NOW, ANYWAY, SO I'M NO LONGER QUITE SO HELL-BENT ON SELF-IMMOLATION!
I'M OFF HOME... BUT I'M GOING TO STAY ON THE PAVEMENT FROM NOW ON... JUST TO BE ON THE SAFE SIDE!
CRUMP! CLANG! SMASH!
RATS' COCKS.
TIGER WOODS

Letterbocks

letters@viz.co.uk

IT'S ALL well and good Charles Darwin telling everyone about the origin of the species and how genes combine to produce individuals with superior characteristics to their parents which give them an evolutionary advantage. And then he goes and marries his cousin.

Fodron Nicolette, Leeds

MY FRIEND had never had a holiday abroad in her life as she was absolutely petrified of flying. However, last week I pointed out to her that it was actually the safest form of transport. What a fool she felt when she realised, and she immediately booked a two week break in Barbados.

Jackie Pallo, Castleford

I LOVE feeding the birds in my garden. I have a little bird table where the sparrows, blue tits, wrens, chaffinches and greenfinches all come for their dinner. I could sit and watch them all day. However, for some reason I can't stand robins. I hate the little things with their big heads, stupid red

STAR LETTER

ONE pound a week will supply water for an entire village in Tanzania, says Oxfam. So how come Yorkshire Water charge me twenty five quid a month for my three bedroomed semi? The fleecing bastards.

Norman Hunter, e-mail

breasts and thin legs. Does anyone know of anything I could put down that would poison them but leave all the other species unharmed?

Edna Carstairs, Luton

IT REALLY surprised me that the Japanese sided with the Nazis during the Second World War. They're usually so polite.

Khaled, e-mail

VIZ COMIC PO Box 841 Whitley Bay NE26 9EQ

I COULD never remember which end of a battery was the positive and which was the negative, so I made up a little rhyme to help.

*Two ends a battery does have,
One positive, the other ground,
The latter is as flat as glass,
Whilst on the first a bump is found.*

Obviously, it doesn't work for PP3s or those ones with the rabbit ear terminals, but I'm working on it.

Archie Medarno, Notts

HOW come these 'bob-a-job' kids want a pound, whatever they do? A 'bob' is a shilling, which in today's money is five pence. Okay, allowing for inflation, I'd give them ten pence. Plus a clip round the ear.

Alan Heath, e-mail

WHY is it that when birds fly south for the winter they always go to the same place? They should try somewhere new every year like me and my wife do.

M Day, Leeds

SCIENTISTS claim that spider's silk is one of the strongest materials known to man. Well how come I've just punched a hole straight through one of their webs, and I'm not even that hard?

Paul Townend, e-mail

APPARENTLY, Angelina Jolie has had an intimate tattoo done on her thigh which is 'just for Brad.' I'm guessing that it's a big arrow with the words 'This way to pissflaps' written underneath.

Stevros, e-mail

MY LOCAL travel firm, Merseyrail, bears the motto 'Merseyrail - more than just a journey,' Well after being mugged on their Wirral line service recently, I'd like to take the opportunity to thank them for their honesty.

S Porter, Merseyside

I CAN'T understand why people enter the Great North Run in fancy costume. They're never going to win dressed as an elephant or a box of cornflakes. Every year without fail, the winner has been dressed in shorts and a vest. You'd of think they would of learned by now.

M Crackerbarrel, Jarrow

'THINGS can only get better,' played D:Ream keyboardist Professor Brian Cox. But as a physicist, surely he should know that the principle of entropy points towards things becoming more chaotic and disordered, not better! Next time I see him on the television, I shall put my foot through the universe, and send him the bill.

Precious Haystacks Grimsby

HAZEL Blears MP is only 4' 10" tall, yet she pays the same council tax as a basketball player living in a similar house. This is grossly unfair, as the house will seem enormous to her and yet tiny to him. To make things fair, council tax should be divided by the person's height to get a figure of what should be paid.

Meadowlark Lemon Harlem Globetrotters

CELEBRITY SWEARS

No. 14,498
The Three Stooges

"Blow jobs"

"Rimming"

TOP TIPS

HALF a Weetabix 'erected' at the end of a mousetrap makes a dignified gravestone for any mice you've killed, and attracts a crowd of mouse 'mourners' to boot!

Ken De Mange, Leeds

BIRDWATCHERS. String up fairy lights and tinsel to give your garden that authentic 'nightclub' look. A record player covered in seeds makes an excellent revolving dancefloor, and at closing time your cat can be an effective bouncer.

Harry Cowderoy, e-mail

HAIRDRESSERS. Instead of repeatedly asking customers parrot fashion where they are going on holiday, why not charge less for a dry trim? That way, we might be able to go further than Minehead.

Bob Trimback, e-mail

CAN'T afford a camera for your holiday? Simply take along a friend with a photographic memory, then have them describe all those wonderful holiday memories when you get home.

Summerhead, e-mail

TRAINSPOTTERS. Mingle with normal people on the station platform. You can record the train numbers just as easily as you could standing on the end of the platform, which only makes you a target for scorn and ridicule.

Fat Al White, Wrenthorpe

SPRAY fish and chips with Mr Muscle window cleaner. It contains vinegar and will cut through grease, leaving your meal more healthy.

Bartram Laidlaw, Crewe

FOOL your doctor into thinking you are going on an exotic foreign holiday by making an appointment to have Malaria and Typhoid jabs.

Kevin Monster, Arbroath

CONDEMNED prisoners. Listen to Duncan Barkes's night-time Ultimate Late Show Live phone-in on Talksport during your last night before being put to death. It will make your final hours stretch out endlessly, and cause you to actively welcome the arrival of your executioner in the morning.

John Pearson, Leeds

HAIR straighteners make an ideal grill for one fish finger.

Alex Dyer, e-mail

OLD FOLK. Don't waste money on those over-sized uni-slippers, simply sellotape ' your existing slippers together. When you evening's TV viewing is finished, just cut through and remove the sellotape.

Jeremy Clarkhole, e-mail

I HAVE a small criticism to make of your map of the Shittish Isles. Pictured in South Wales are some rugby players, one of whom is doing a large shit into an old fashioned pint glass. I feel I should point out that this sort of bawdy behaviour is limited to the public school educated English rugby union players. In Wales, players like to relax after a game by indulging in some close harmony singing, visiting an Eisteddfod, or drinking 15 pints of Bains and driving a golf buggy down the M4.

Shenkin Arsecandle, e-mail

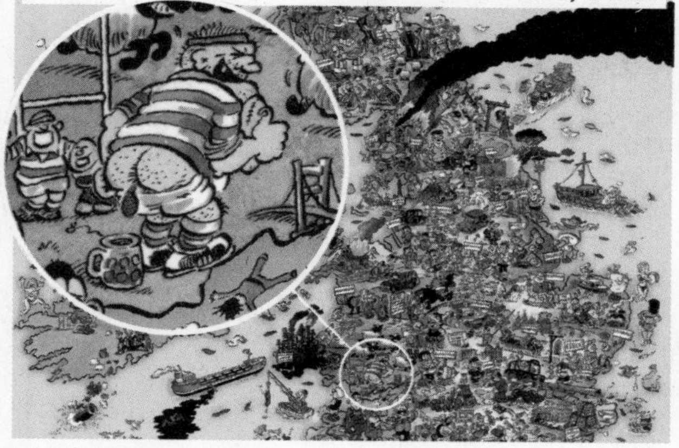

I WAS disappointed to see that Her Majesty the Queen has an Astronomer Royal for looking at big things, but she doesn't have a Microscoper Royal for looking at small things. I think it's about time she redressed the balance.

Prof Stanley Jordan British Microscopical Society

IF THE Socialist Worker is a revolutionary, anti-capitalist paper, how come I have to pay 80p for it?

Alan Heath, e-mail

WHY are rail bosses going to increase their fares above the rate of inflation? If anything, rail companies should reduce them or even give them away for free. After all, the train is making the journey anyway, so it makes no difference if people get on or not.

Dean Moncaster, e-mail

EVERY time I see the numbers 9:11 on my bedside clock radio, I get a shiver down my spine. Not because it brings back memories of the New York terrorist atrocity, but because I'm over ten minutes late for work.

Dick Baconlettucetomato e-mail

HOW come 'triple chocolate brownies' are the same size as normal chocolate brownies? If they've got triple the chocolate in them, they should be triple the size.

Richard Sewell, e-mail

THERE are no beaches in London, so presumably there are no sandcastle competitions to judge. What does Lord Mayor Boris Johnson do all day?

J Sheridan, Leeds

I HAVE had a great idea about how to solve all the world's problems, including famine and climate change. I can't say much about it at the minute as it's top secret, but as part of the research I need as many ladies as possible, aged between 21 and 31, and dress sizes 8-12 to send me their used underwear and a photo of themselves. Please hurry, as time is running out.

Karl R, e-mail

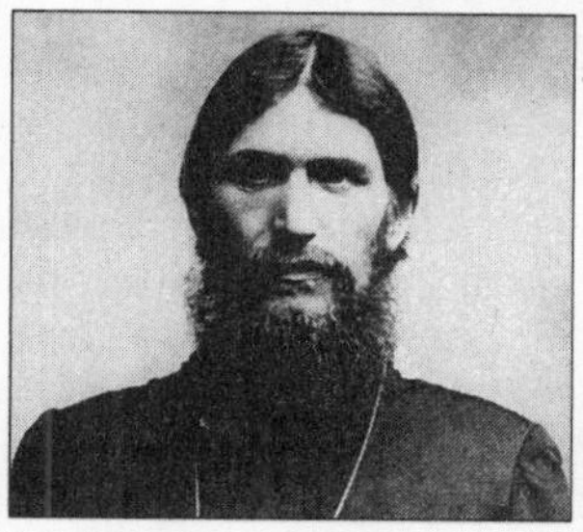

WHEN his body was found, Rasputin's testicles had been crushed flat by his torturers. How he can even have been in the top fifty Russian love machines with flat balls is beyond me. Are any other readers concerned about the accuracy of Boney M's lyrics?

Nabisco Jones, Lincoln-on-sea

I'VE recently started wanking into my ex-girlfriend's swimming hat. Have any other readers got heartwarming ways of reminiscing about old flames?

Gentleman Jim, Nivenford

I'VE BEEN looking at my feet and I reckon that most of the time I'm walking I've only got one foot on the ground, but shoe manufacturers only sell shoes in pairs, pocketing double the money. They must think I'm stupid.

Jordan Kettle, North Weald

I RECEIVED an e-mail this morning which, along with a link that read 'Surprise your wife with an enlarged penis.' I have to say, that I have an enlarged penis most nights when I climb into bed, and my wife doesn't seem the least bit surprised. I think she's rather come to expect it.

B Davison, Leeds

HOW about a picture of an old man in a tuxedo eating spaghetti, with his wife in the background holding a stuffed fox?

A Twat, e-mail

** Sorry, Mr Twat, we've run out of space.*

You Ask, I Flannel

Your Ecclesiastical Questions Waffled Over by the Archbishop of Canterbury

Dr. Rowan Williams

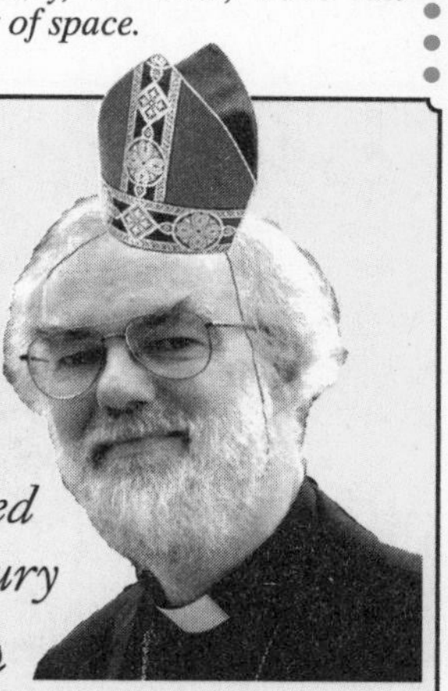

Dear A B of C,

I RECENTLY read that the Scottish Episcopal Church has removed all references to God being a man from their prayer book. They say that this is because God transcends gender, and is neither male nor female. This being the case, what sort of hermaphrodite is he? Is he like a bearded lady at the circus, or is he more like a Bangkok lady boy with tits and a cock?

Mildred Ritblat, Dover

The A B of C says...

Nobody alive has ever seen God in the flesh, as it were, so it is impossible to say what sort of genitals He has got. In the Bible, it says that He created Adam and Eve in his image, so it is likely that God has both male and female characteristics, one behind the other. Or perhaps side by side. However, you must remember that the Lords' genitals will not exist in a physical sense, as we would understand it on earth. They are probably made of the same material that halos are made of, a sort of ethereal tinsel, less dense even than a cobweb. It is my belief that God's privates may even be completely invisible to our earthly eye, leaving our creator smooth and pink 'under the bridge', a bit like an action man.

✝✝✝✝✝✝✝✝✝✝✝✝✝✝✝✝✝✝

Dear A B of C,

ON A recent visit the Sistine Chapel I saw a picture of God on the roof and was disappointed to see that he had grey hair. If God is all powerful and can move mountains, why has He allowed his hair to go white? What colour was it before, and was it the stress of having children that sent him grey, like my dad said it did with him?

Edna Bismarck, Tooting

The A B of C says...

I'm sorry that you were disappointed, Mrs Bismark. I think that God's hair looks rather distinguished. I personally would be less likely to worship God, pray to him at bedtime and follow commandments, etc. if He had a shock of black hair like the lead singer out of The Cribs. White hair is a badge of wisdom and authority, which is why Gandalf and the Headmaster out of Harry Potter are both snowy white.

✝✝✝✝✝✝✝✝✝✝✝✝✝✝✝✝✝✝

Dear A B of C,

FOLLOWING on from Mrs Bismarck's letter *(above)*, God's hair does seem to be very long. Does He ever need to get it cut, and if so, does He do it himself in front of the mirror, or does He go to a heavenly barber?

Ada Bourgeois, Scunthorpe

The A B of C says...

First of all, the Lord is all seeing, so if He did cut his own hair, He wouldn't need a mirror because He could see the back of his own head. Having said that, if God needed his hair cut, it would imply that it wasn't the ideal length. But we know from the Bible that God is PERFECT, so his hair must remain at the ideal length all the time. Perhaps God's hair can grow inwards as well as out so it can retain the perfect length. Either that or He has a tiny bit cut off every day.

Dear A B of C,

WHY DOES God wear sandals? Walking on clouds must be really comfy because they are just like big marshmallows. And presumably there are no bits of Lego or upturned plugs in heaven to step on by accident.

Dolly Gulbenkian, Croydon

The A B of C says...

That's a very interesting question, Mrs Gulbenkian, and one which the general Synod has been wrestling with for many years. Our current understanding is that animals also go to heaven when they die, and God doesn't want to step on one of the thousands of hedgehogs that are squashed on Britain's roads every year. Also, there is the risk that He might get verrucas.

✝✝✝✝✝✝✝✝✝✝✝✝✝✝✝✝✝✝

Dear A B of C,

IN YOUR previous answer, you say that animals go to heaven. Is this just nice animals, like squirrels, robins and butterflies, or do all animals go, including scorpions, tapeworms and crocodiles? I only ask, as I have a fatal allergy to wasps and I don't want to get stung in heaven and die again. Also, do angel wasps get an extra set of angel wings, or do they have to make do with their original set?

Ben Keen, Whitley Bay

The A B of C says...

Sorry, I've got to go and do a Eucharist at the cathedral, so I haven't got time to answer that, although I do know the answer, obviously.

✝✝✝✝✝✝✝✝✝✝✝✝✝✝✝✝✝✝

Do YOU have an theological question that Britain's top Holy man could spout shit about? Write to The Arch Bishop of Canterbury, Viz Comic, PO Box 841, Whitley Bay, NE26 9EQ

Ratepayers put Rocket up Council

By our space Correspondent
Evonne Goolagong

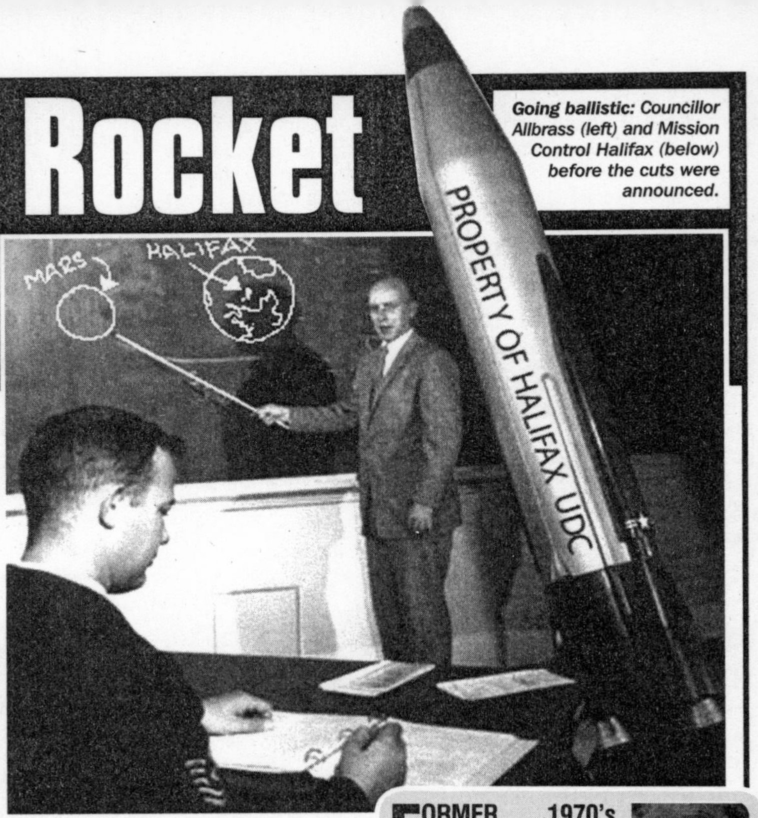

MARS
HALIFAX
PROPERTY OF HALIFAX UDC

Going ballistic: Councillor Allbrass (left) and Mission Control Halifax (below) before the cuts were announced.

THE PEOPLE of Halifax were up in arms last night as the town council announced sweeping cuts to next year's budget. Refuse collection, road repairs and meals on wheels services will all suffer under the austerity measures which will see the authority rein in spending. But it is the council's halving of its space exploration programme that has caused the most grumbles amongst ratepayers.

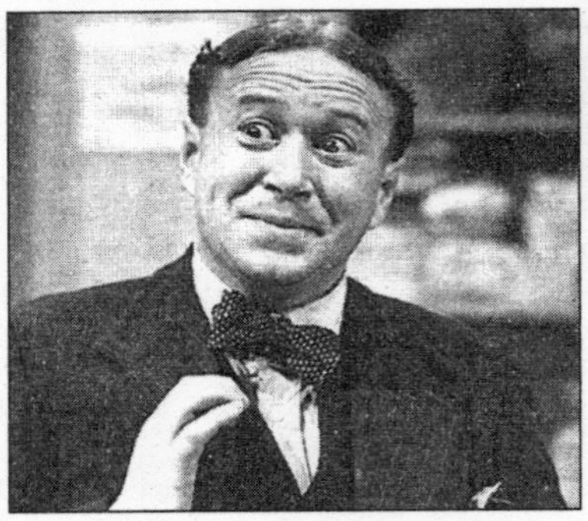

The West Yorkshire borough had intended to be the first municipal authority to set up a colony on Mars, and earmarked 78% of its income for the ambitious space programme. But last night, Councillor Fred Allbrass issued a statement blaming the u-turn on the economic recession and swingeing government cuts.

dream

"We would have liked nothing more than to continue the council's dream of delivering sustainable colonisation of the solar system," he told a packed public meeting at the Town Hall in Crossley Street. And he informed the furious crowd that a massive space exploration programme could not be undertaken without breaking the council's promise to cap rates for the next year.

"We only have so much money to play with, and the stark reality is that something has to give," he said.

But the mood of local residents leaving the meeting left councillors in no doubt as to what they thought of the cuts.

nurse

"I've never heard owt so daft," said Albert Cummings, a retired miner from nearby Shibden. "We need to be exploring the possibility of living on the red planet, not chucking money at restocking libraries and setting up playschemes and the like."

"I pay my rates, and I want to see them sending some ruddy rockets up," said dinner lady and grandmother of 12 Edna Neckbrace.

And equally disgruntled was former 70s footballer Alan Mullery. "I see they've got the money to develop the Broad Street car park, oh yes. But when it comes to sending rockets up they start pleading poverty," said the former Spurs midfielder.

"It wouldn't surprise me if there's been a few dodgy deals going on between them councillors and contractors," added Mullery, who holds the title as the first England player to be sent off in an international game.

the bed

The beleaguered council also used the meeting to try and bury other news which would not gone down well with voters. To boos and jeers, Allbrass announced that next year would see a freeze on all 'non essential' spending such as the development of a hover car for the Lord Mayor. And he also announced that planned construction of the world's first bulletproof monorail which would run councillors from the town hall to the leisure centre was to be postponed until 2012.

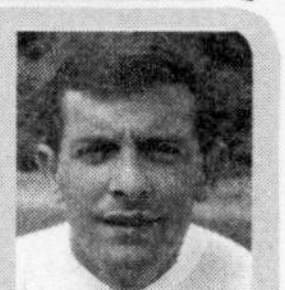

FORMER 1970's footballer *Alan Mullery* is not the only 70s soccer hero to lend his voice to the growing chorus of criticism being directed at Halifax town council.

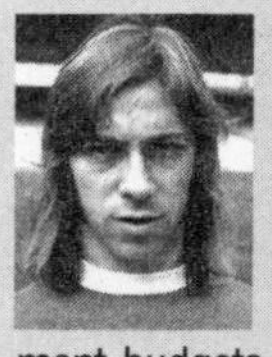

One time Arsenal forward ***Charlie George*** believes the council have got their spending priorities wrong. "I've never been to Halifax and know nothing about local government budgets, but I just turned on Sky Sports News and couldn't believe my eyes," said the lank-haired forward, best known for scoring a goal in the 1971 FA Cup and then lying down on the pitch. "How they can say there isn't money for building rockets and space probes, and then let pensioners into the North Bridge Leisure Centre free on Wednesday mornings is beyond me."

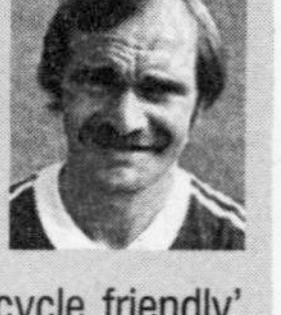

Former Ipswich Town defender ***Mick Mills*** was equally incredulous when we called him at his Spanish villa to ask for his opinion. And he blamed the council's pledge to make the city 'cycle friendly' for the cancelling of their space programme. "I don't understand this decision at all," said the slap-headed former left back. "Putting inner city cycle lanes above the colonisation of our celestial next door neighbour is short sighted in the extreme."

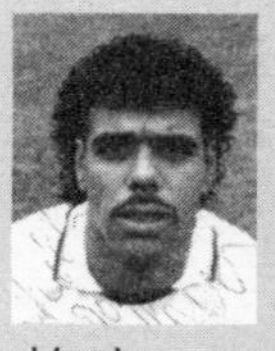

"An unbelievable decision," said former Portsmouth hard-man turned Sky pundit ***Chris Kamara***. "They've already got an advantage over the rest of Yorkshire because Halifax is high up in the Pennines, so the distance to space is shorter. These councillors need to wake up to the real world."

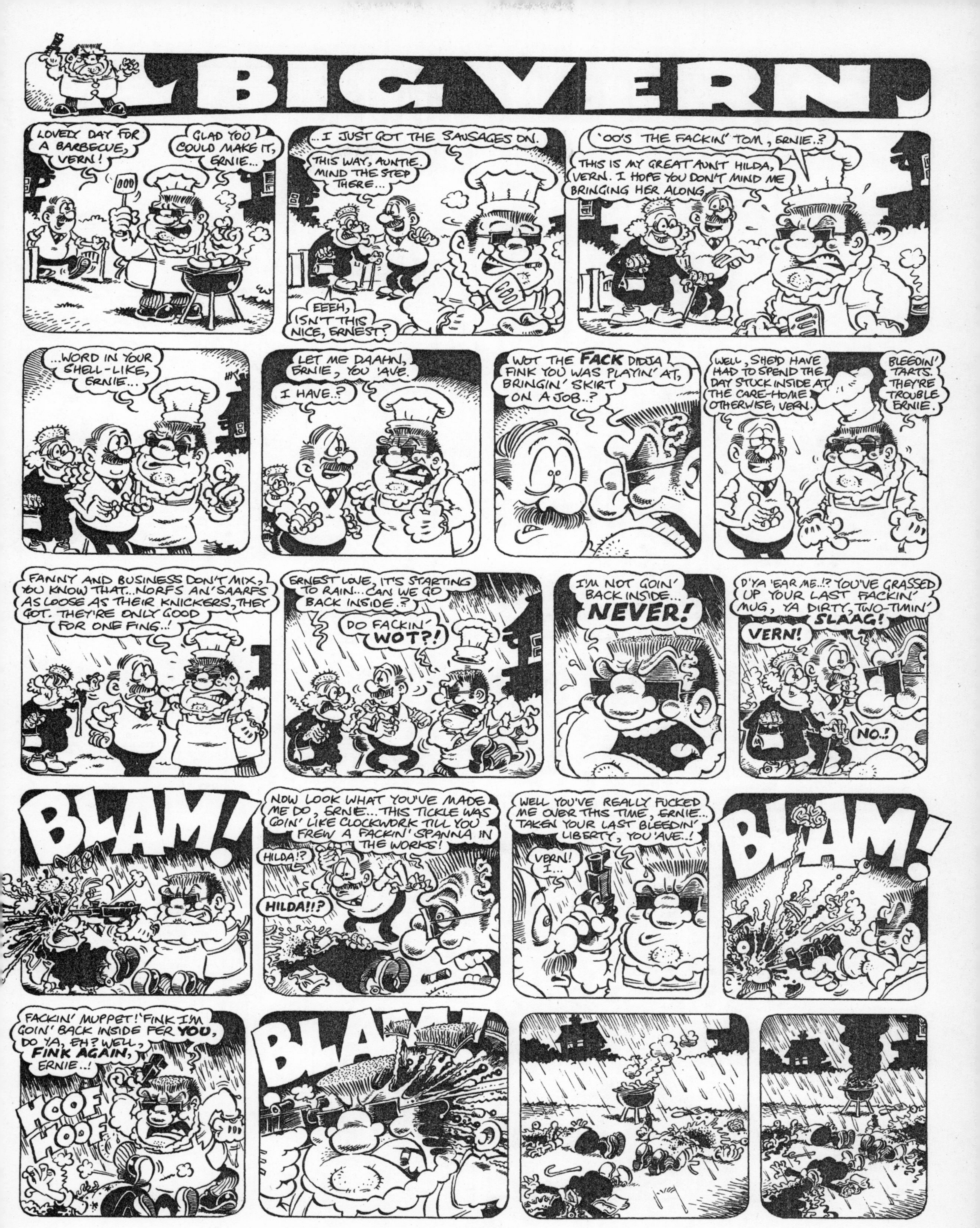
BIG VERN
LOVELY DAY FOR A BARBECUE, VERN!
GLAD YOU COULD MAKE IT, ERNIE...
...I JUST GOT THE SAUSAGES ON.
THIS WAY, AUNTIE. MIND THE STEP THERE...
EEEH, ISN'T THIS NICE, ERNEST?
'OO'S THE FACKIN' TOM, ERNIE..?
THIS IS MY GREAT AUNT HILDA, VERN. I HOPE YOU DON'T MIND ME BRINGING HER ALONG.
...WORD IN YOUR SHELL-LIKE, ERNIE...
LET ME DAAHN, ERNIE, YOU 'AVE.
I HAVE..?
WOT THE FACK DIDJA FINK YOU WAS PLAYIN' AT, BRINGIN' SKIRT ON A JOB..?
WELL, SHE'D HAVE HAD TO SPEND THE DAY STUCK INSIDE AT THE CARE-HOME OTHERWISE, VERN.
BLEEDIN' TARTS. THEY'RE TROUBLE ERNIE.
FANNY AND BUSINESS DON'T MIX, YOU KNOW THAT...NORFS AN' SAARFS AS LOOSE AS THEIR KNICKERS, THEY GOT. THEY'RE ONLY GOOD FOR ONE FING..!
ERNEST LOVE, IT'S STARTING TO RAIN...CAN WE GO BACK INSIDE..?
DO FACKIN' WOT?!
I'M NOT GOIN' BACK INSIDE... NEVER!
D'YA 'EAR ME..!? YOU'VE GRASSED UP YOUR LAST FACKIN' MUG, YA DIRTY, TWO-TIMIN' SLAAG!
VERN!
NO..!
BLAM!
NOW LOOK WHAT YOU'VE MADE ME DO, ERNIE... THIS TICKLE WAS GOIN' LIKE CLOCKWORK TILL YOU FREW A FACKIN' SPANNA IN THE WORKS!
HILDA!?
HILDA!!?
WELL YOU'VE REALLY FUCKED ME OVER THIS TIME, ERNIE... TAKEN YOUR LAST BLEEDIN' LIBERTY, YOU 'AVE..!
VERN! I...
BLAM!
FACKIN' MUPPET! 'FINK I'M GOIN' BACK INSIDE FER YOU, DO YA, EH? WELL, FINK AGAIN, ERNIE..!
HOOF HOOF
BLAM!

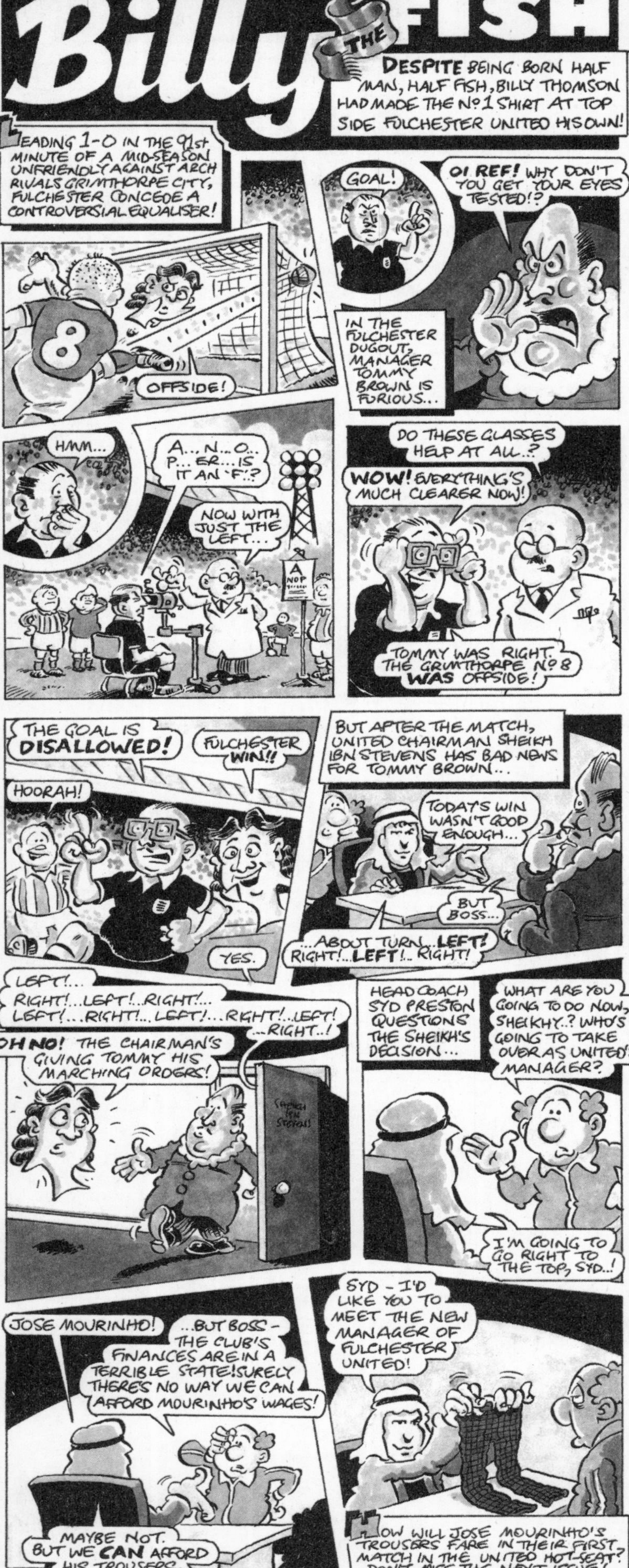
Billy the FISH
DESPITE being born half man, half fish, Billy Thomson had made the No.1 shirt at top side Fulchester United his own!
LEADING 1-0 IN THE 91st MINUTE OF A MID-SEASON UNFRIENDLY AGAINST ARCH RIVALS GRIMTHORPE CITY, FULCHESTER CONCEDE A CONTROVERSIAL EQUALISER!
OFFSIDE!
GOAL!
OI REF! WHY DON'T YOU GET YOUR EYES TESTED!?
IN THE FULCHESTER DUGOUT, MANAGER TOMMY BROWN IS FURIOUS...
HMM...
A...N...O... P...ER...IS... IT AN 'F'?
NOW WITH JUST THE LEFT...
DO THESE GLASSES HELP AT ALL..?
WOW! EVERYTHING'S MUCH CLEARER NOW!
TOMMY WAS RIGHT. THE GRIMTHORPE No 8 WAS OFFSIDE!
THE GOAL IS DISALLOWED!
FULCHESTER WIN!!
HOORAH!
YES.
BUT AFTER THE MATCH, UNITED CHAIRMAN SHEIKH IBN STEVENS HAS BAD NEWS FOR TOMMY BROWN...
TODAY'S WIN WASN'T GOOD ENOUGH...
BUT BOSS...
...ABOUT TURN...LEFT! RIGHT!...LEFT!...RIGHT!
LEFT!... RIGHT!...LEFT!...RIGHT!... LEFT!...RIGHT!...LEFT!...RIGHT!...LEFT! ...RIGHT..!
OH NO! THE CHAIRMAN'S GIVING TOMMY HIS MARCHING ORDERS!
HEAD COACH SYD PRESTON QUESTIONS THE SHEIKH'S DECISION...
WHAT ARE YOU GOING TO DO NOW, SHEIKHY..? WHO'S GOING TO TAKE OVER AS UNITED'S MANAGER?
I'M GOING TO GO RIGHT TO THE TOP, SYD...!
JOSE MOURINHO!
...BUT BOSS - THE CLUB'S FINANCES ARE IN A TERRIBLE STATE! SURELY THERE'S NO WAY WE CAN AFFORD MOURINHO'S WAGES!
MAYBE NOT. BUT WE CAN AFFORD HIS TROUSERS.
SYD - I'D LIKE YOU TO MEET THE NEW MANAGER OF FULCHESTER UNITED!
HOW WILL JOSE MOURINHO'S TROUSERS FARE IN THEIR FIRST MATCH IN THE UNITED HOT-SEAT? DON'T MISS THE NEXT ISSUE!

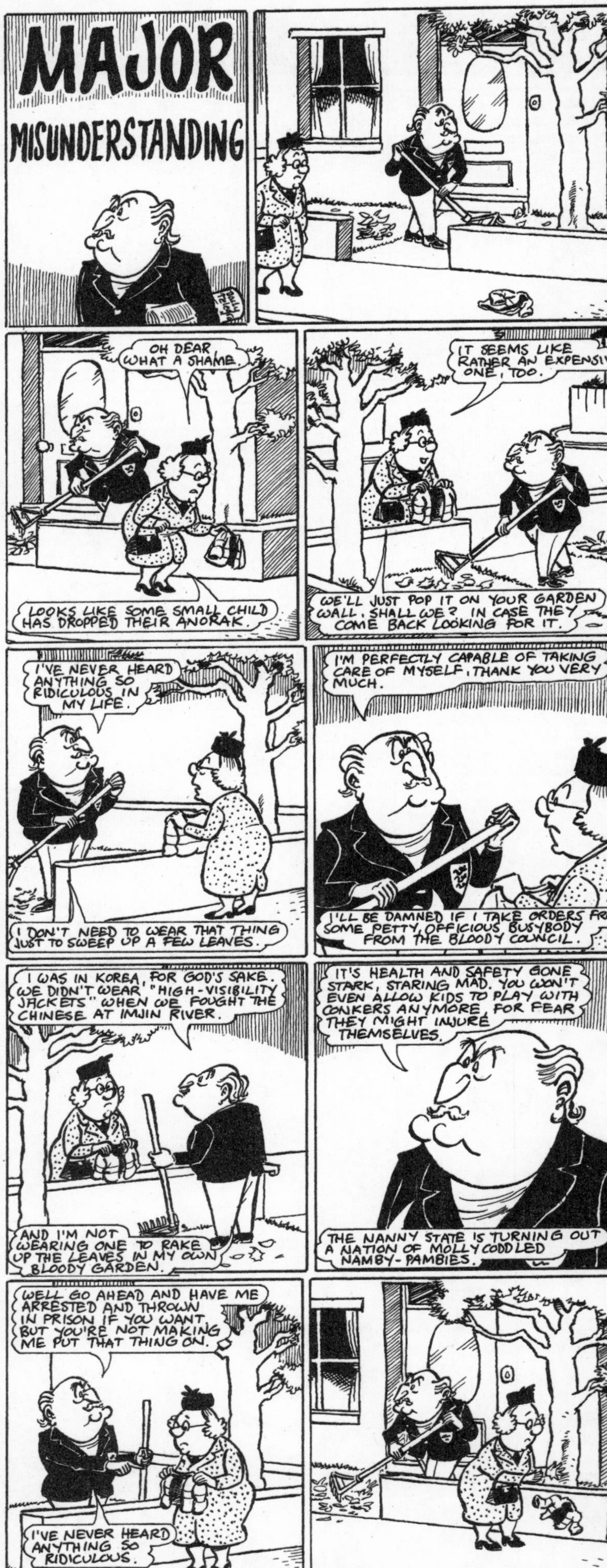
MAJOR MISUNDERSTANDING
OH DEAR WHAT A SHAME.
LOOKS LIKE SOME SMALL CHILD HAS DROPPED THEIR ANORAK.
IT SEEMS LIKE RATHER AN EXPENSIVE ONE, TOO.
WE'LL JUST POP IT ON YOUR GARDEN WALL, SHALL WE? IN CASE THEY COME BACK LOOKING FOR IT.
I'VE NEVER HEARD ANYTHING SO RIDICULOUS IN MY LIFE.
I DON'T NEED TO WEAR THAT THING JUST TO SWEEP UP A FEW LEAVES.
I'M PERFECTLY CAPABLE OF TAKING CARE OF MYSELF, THANK YOU VERY MUCH.
I'LL BE DAMNED IF I TAKE ORDERS FROM SOME PETTY, OFFICIOUS BUSYBODY FROM THE BLOODY COUNCIL.
I WAS IN KOREA, FOR GOD'S SAKE. WE DIDN'T WEAR "HIGH-VISIBILITY JACKETS" WHEN WE FOUGHT THE CHINESE AT IMJIN RIVER.
AND I'M NOT WEARING ONE TO RAKE UP THE LEAVES IN MY OWN BLOODY GARDEN.
IT'S HEALTH AND SAFETY GONE STARK, STARING MAD. YOU WON'T EVEN ALLOW KIDS TO PLAY WITH CONKERS ANYMORE, FOR FEAR THEY MIGHT INJURE THEMSELVES.
THE NANNY STATE IS TURNING OUT A NATION OF MOLLYCODDLED NAMBY-PAMBIES.
WELL GO AHEAD AND HAVE ME ARRESTED AND THROWN IN PRISON IF YOU WANT. BUT YOU'RE NOT MAKING ME PUT THAT THING ON.
I'VE NEVER HEARD ANYTHING SO RIDICULOUS.

JOHNNY LEARNS A LESSON with Peter Sutcliffe

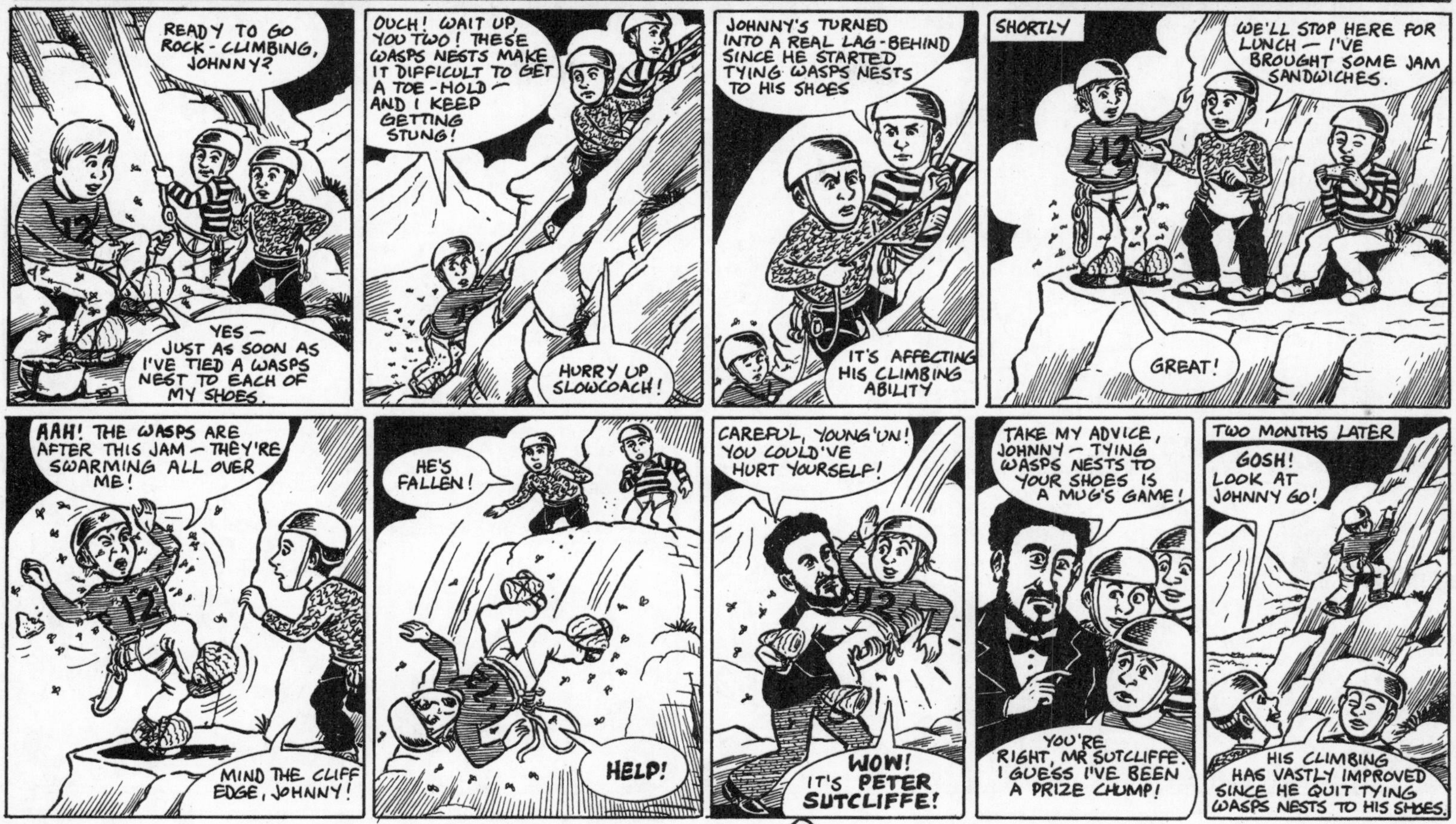
READY TO GO ROCK-CLIMBING, JOHNNY?
YES — JUST AS SOON AS I'VE TIED A WASPS NEST TO EACH OF MY SHOES.
OUCH! WAIT UP, YOU TWO! THESE WASPS NESTS MAKE IT DIFFICULT TO GET A TOE-HOLD — AND I KEEP GETTING STUNG!
HURRY UP SLOWCOACH!
JOHNNY'S TURNED INTO A REAL LAG-BEHIND SINCE HE STARTED TYING WASPS NESTS TO HIS SHOES
IT'S AFFECTING HIS CLIMBING ABILITY
SHORTLY
WE'LL STOP HERE FOR LUNCH — I'VE BROUGHT SOME JAM SANDWICHES.
GREAT!
AAH! THE WASPS ARE AFTER THIS JAM — THEY'RE SWARMING ALL OVER ME!
MIND THE CLIFF EDGE, JOHNNY!
HE'S FALLEN!
HELP!
CAREFUL, YOUNG'UN! YOU COULD'VE HURT YOURSELF!
WOW! IT'S PETER SUTCLIFFE!
TAKE MY ADVICE, JOHNNY — TYING WASPS NESTS TO YOUR SHOES IS A MUG'S GAME!
YOU'RE RIGHT, MR SUTCLIFFE. I GUESS I'VE BEEN A PRIZE CHUMP!
TWO MONTHS LATER
GOSH! LOOK AT JOHNNY GO!
HIS CLIMBING HAS VASTLY IMPROVED SINCE HE QUIT TYING WASPS NESTS TO HIS SHOES.

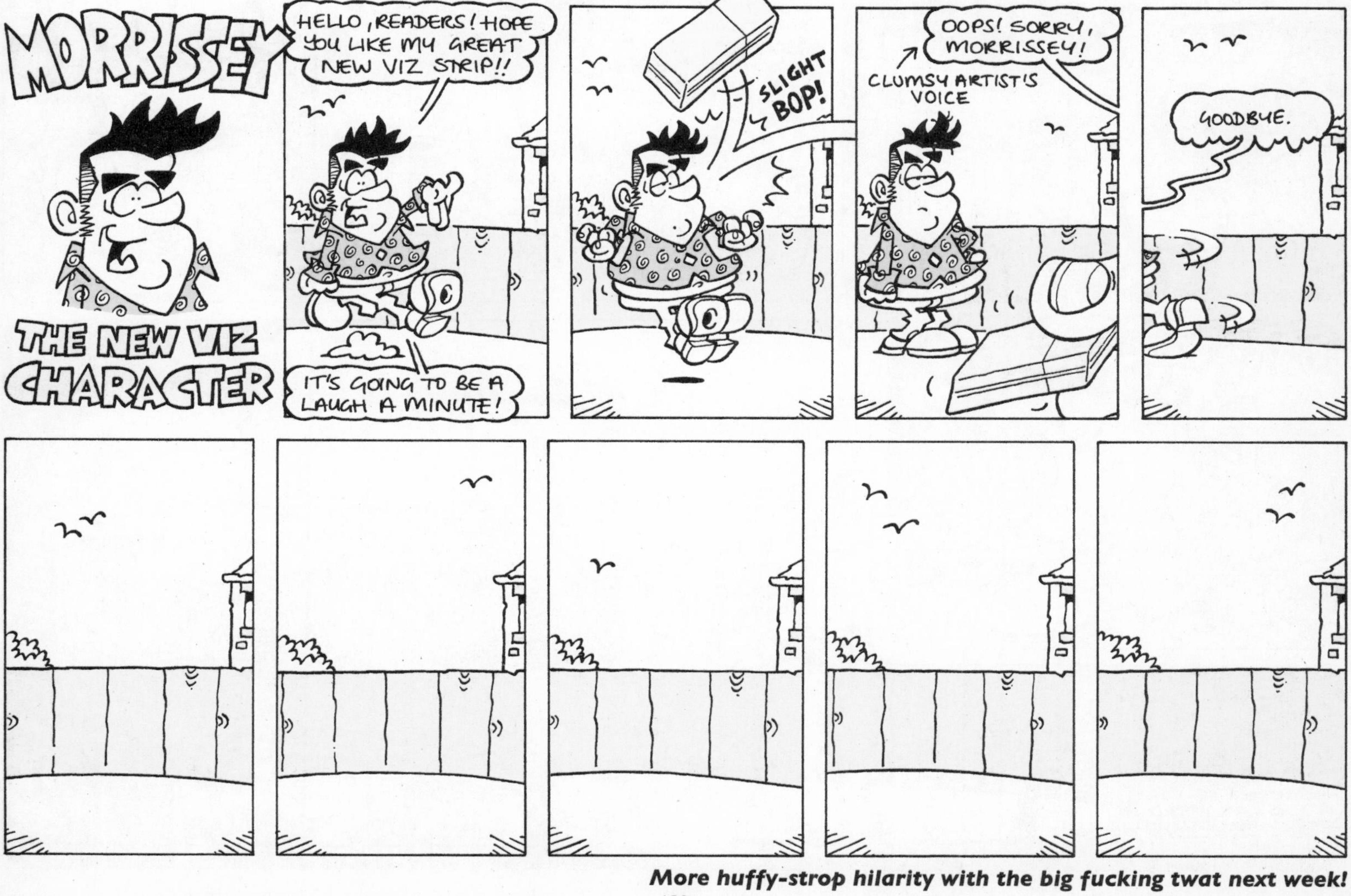
MORRISSEY
THE NEW VIZ CHARACTER
HELLO, READERS! HOPE YOU LIKE MY GREAT NEW VIZ STRIP!!
IT'S GOING TO BE A LAUGH A MINUTE!
SLIGHT BOP!
OOPS! SORRY, MORRISSEY!
CLUMSY ARTIST'S VOICE
GOODBYE.

More huffy-strop hilarity with the big fucking twat next week!

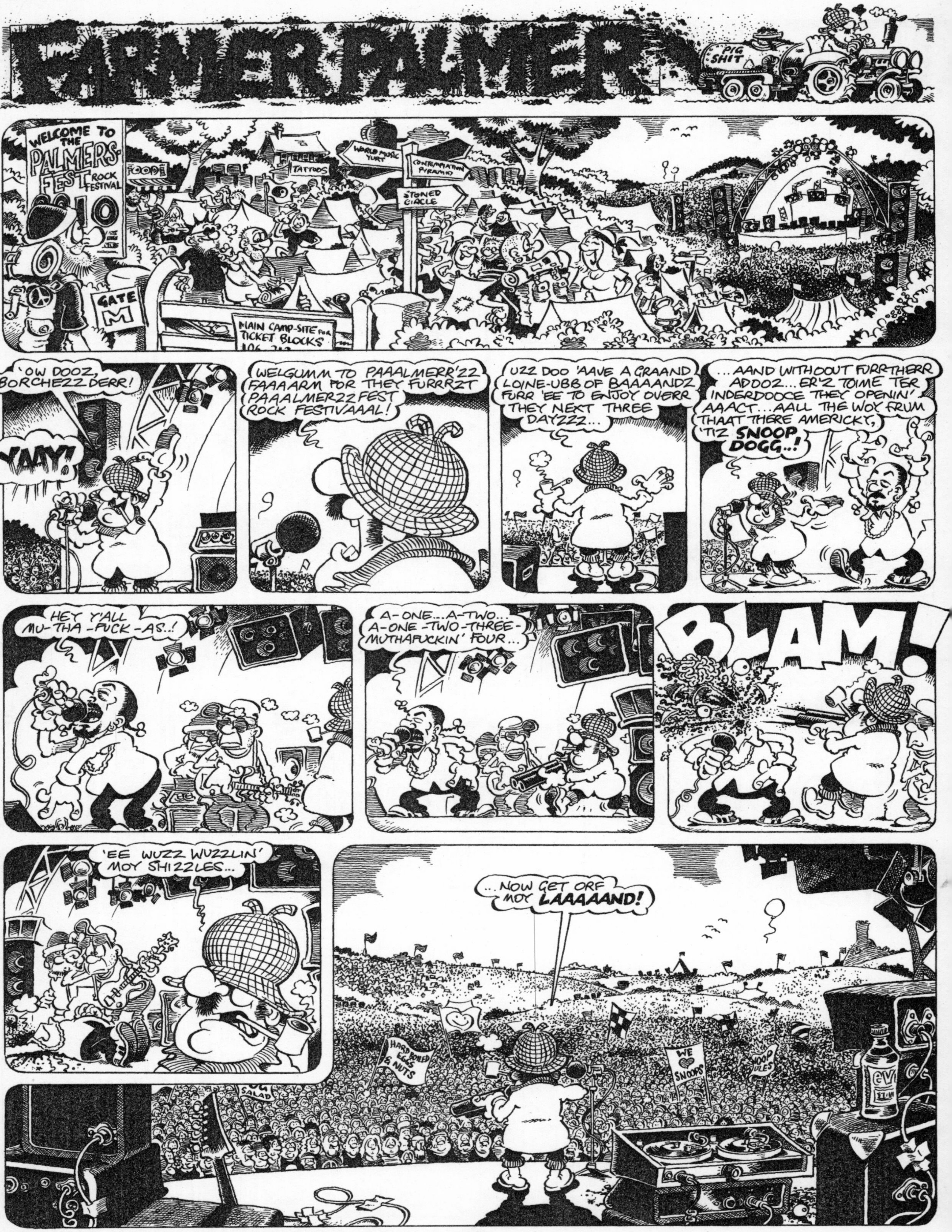
FARMER PALMER
PIG SHIT
WELCOME TO THE PALMERS-FEST ROCK FESTIVAL 10
FOOD
TATTOOS
WORLD MUSIC YURT
STONED CIRCLE
GATE M
MAIN CAMP-SITE FOR TICKET BLOCKS
'OW DOOZ, BORCHEZZDERR!
YAAY!
WELGUMM TO PAAALMERR'22 FAAAAARM FOR THEY FURRRZT PAAALMERZZFEST ROCK FESTIVAAAL!
UZZ DOO 'AAVE A GRAAND LOINE-UBB OF BAAAAANDZ FURR 'EE TO ENJOY OVERR THEY NEXT THREE DAYZZZ...
...AAND WITHOUT FURRTHERR ADOOZ... ER'Z TOIME TER INDERDOOCE THEY OPENIN' AAACT... AALL THE WOY FRUM THAAT THERE AMERICKY, 'TIZ SNOOP DOGG..!
HEY Y'ALL MU-THA-FUCK-AS..!
A-ONE...A-TWO... A-ONE-TWO-THREE-MUTHAFUCKIN' FOUR...
BLAM!
'EE WUZZ WUZZLIN' MOY SHIZZLES...
...NOW GET ORF MOY LAAAAAND!
HARD BOILED EGGS & NUTS
WE ♥ SNOOPS
SNOOP RULES

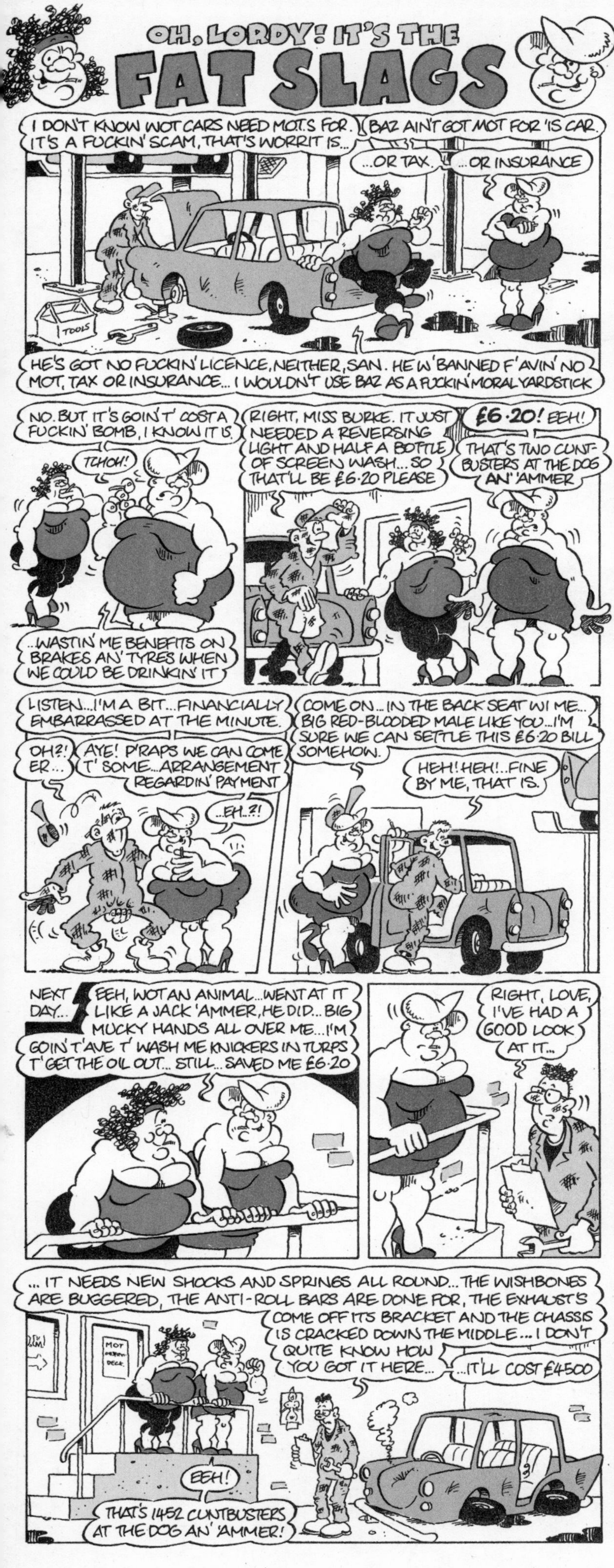
OH, LORDY! IT'S THE
FAT SLAGS
I DON'T KNOW WOT CARS NEED MOT.S FOR. IT'S A FUCKIN' SCAM, THAT'S WORRIT IS...
BAZ AIN'T GOT MOT FOR 'IS CAR.
...OR TAX.
...OR INSURANCE
TOOLS
HE'S GOT NO FUCKIN' LICENCE, NEITHER, SAN. HE W' BANNED F'AVIN' NO MOT, TAX OR INSURANCE... I WOULDN'T USE BAZ AS A FUCKIN' MORAL YARDSTICK
NO. BUT IT'S GOIN' T' COST A FUCKIN' BOMB, I KNOW IT IS.
TCHOH!
...WASTIN' ME BENEFITS ON BRAKES AN' TYRES WHEN WE COULD BE DRINKIN' IT
RIGHT, MISS BURKE. IT JUST NEEDED A REVERSING LIGHT AND HALF A BOTTLE OF SCREEN WASH... SO THAT'LL BE £6.20 PLEASE
£6.20! EEH!
THAT'S TWO CUNT-BUSTERS AT THE DOG AN' 'AMMER
LISTEN...I'M A BIT...FINANCIALLY EMBARRASSED AT THE MINUTE.
OH?! ER...
AYE! P'RAPS WE CAN COME T' SOME...ARRANGEMENT REGARDIN' PAYMENT
...EH..?!
COME ON...IN THE BACK SEAT WI ME... BIG RED-BLOODED MALE LIKE YOU...I'M SURE WE CAN SETTLE THIS £6.20 BILL SOMEHOW.
HEH! HEH!..FINE BY ME, THAT IS.
NEXT DAY...
EEH, WOT AN ANIMAL...WENT AT IT LIKE A JACK 'AMMER, HE DID...BIG MUCKY HANDS ALL OVER ME...I'M GOIN' T'AVE T' WASH ME KNICKERS IN TURPS T' GET THE OIL OUT... STILL...SAVED ME £6.20
RIGHT, LOVE, I'VE HAD A GOOD LOOK AT IT...
... IT NEEDS NEW SHOCKS AND SPRINGS ALL ROUND... THE WISHBONES ARE BUGGERED, THE ANTI-ROLL BARS ARE DONE FOR, THE EXHAUST'S COME OFF ITS BRACKET AND THE CHASSIS IS CRACKED DOWN THE MIDDLE... I DON'T QUITE KNOW HOW YOU GOT IT HERE...
...IT'LL COST £4500
MOT
EEH!
THAT'S 1452 CUNTBUSTERS AT THE DOG AN' 'AMMER!

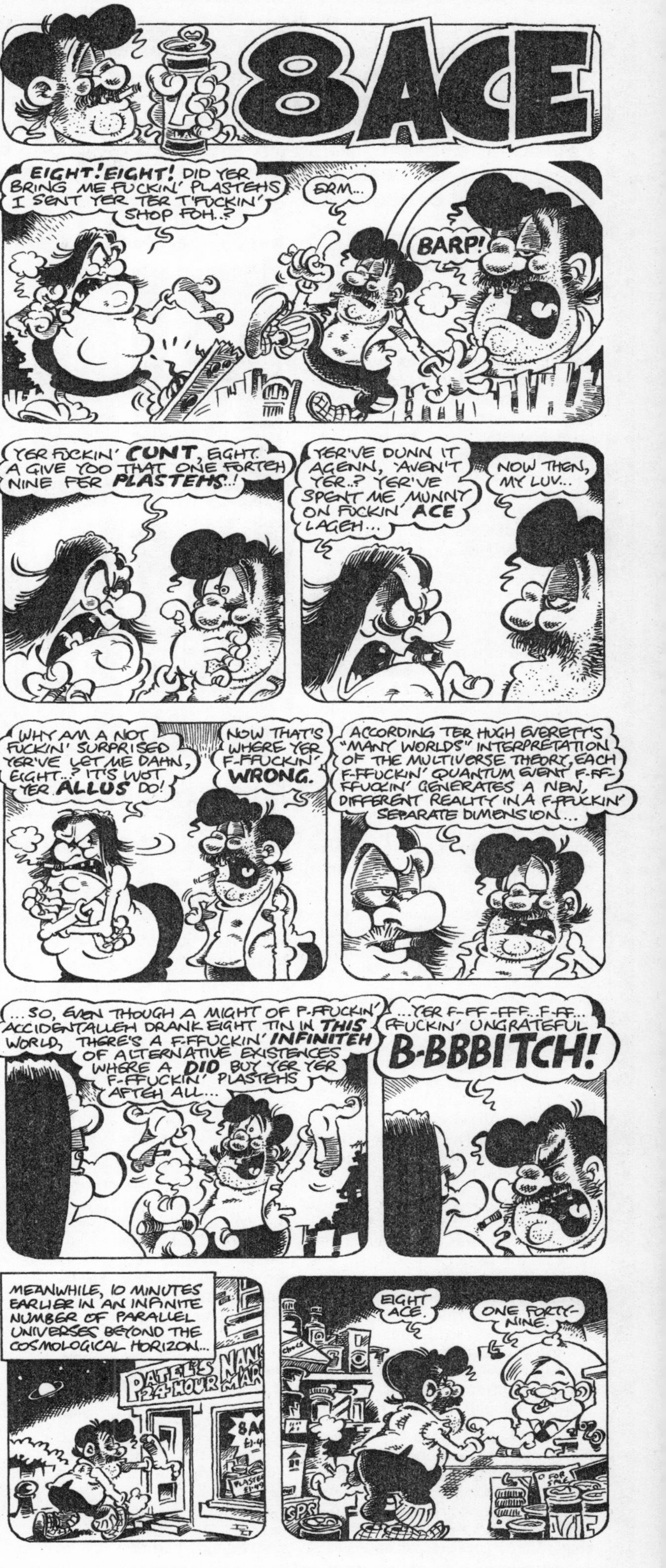
8 ACE
EIGHT! EIGHT! DID YER BRING ME FUCKIN' PLASTEHS I SENT YER TER T'FUCKIN' SHOP FOH..?
ERM...
BARP!
YER FUCKIN' CUNT, EIGHT. A GIVE YOO THAT ONE FORTEH NINE FER PLASTEHS..!
YER'VE DUNN IT AGENN, 'AVEN'T YER..? YER'VE SPENT ME MUNNY ON FUCKIN' ACE LAGEH...
NOW THEN, MY LUV...
WHY AM A NOT FUCKIN' SURPRISED YER'VE LET ME DAHN, EIGHT..? IT'S WOT YER ALLUS DO!
NOW THAT'S WHERE YER F-FFUCKIN' WRONG.
ACCORDING TER HUGH EVERETT'S "MANY WORLDS" INTERPRETATION OF THE MULTIVERSE THEORY, EACH F-FFUCKIN' QUANTUM EVENT F-FF-FFUCKIN' GENERATES A NEW, DIFFERENT REALITY IN A F-FFUCKIN' SEPARATE DIMENSION...
...SO, EVEN THOUGH A MIGHT OF F-FFUCKIN' ACCIDENTALLEH DRANK EIGHT TIN IN THIS WORLD, THERE'S A F-FFUCKIN' INFINITEH OF ALTERNATIVE EXISTENCES WHERE A DID BUY YER YER F-FFUCKIN' PLASTEHS AFTEH ALL...
...YER F-FF-FFF...F-FF... FFUCKIN' UNGRATEFUL B-BBBITCH!
MEANWHILE, 10 MINUTES EARLIER IN AN INFINITE NUMBER OF PARALLEL UNIVERSES BEYOND THE COSMOLOGICAL HORIZON...
PATEL'S 24 HOUR
EIGHT ACE.
ONE FORTY-NINE.

IF you saw ERIC POULTRY pottering round the shops, mowing his lawn or washing his car on a Sunday afternoon, you probably wouldn't give him a second glance. You certainly wouldn't think the portly, bespectacled 68-year-old Peckham resident had spent the 1970s and 80s in a haze of wild sexual abandon, strong liquor and drug-fuelled debauchery.

EXCLUSIVE

The Black & White Stuff

Eric recalls his checkered past as a Minstrel

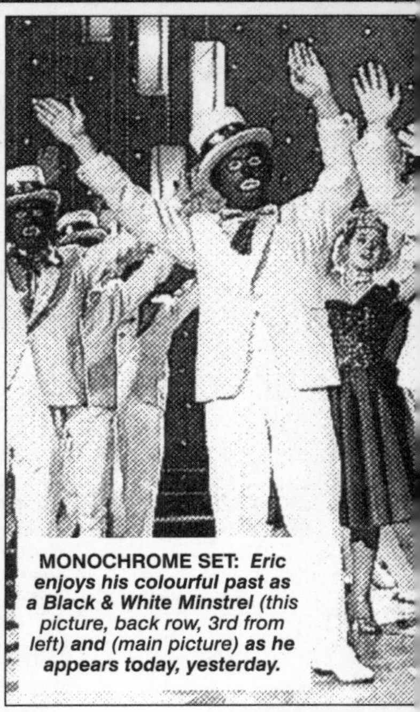

MONOCHROME SET: *Eric enjoys his colourful past as a Black & White Minstrel (this picture, back row, 3rd from left) and (main picture) as he appears today, yesterday.*

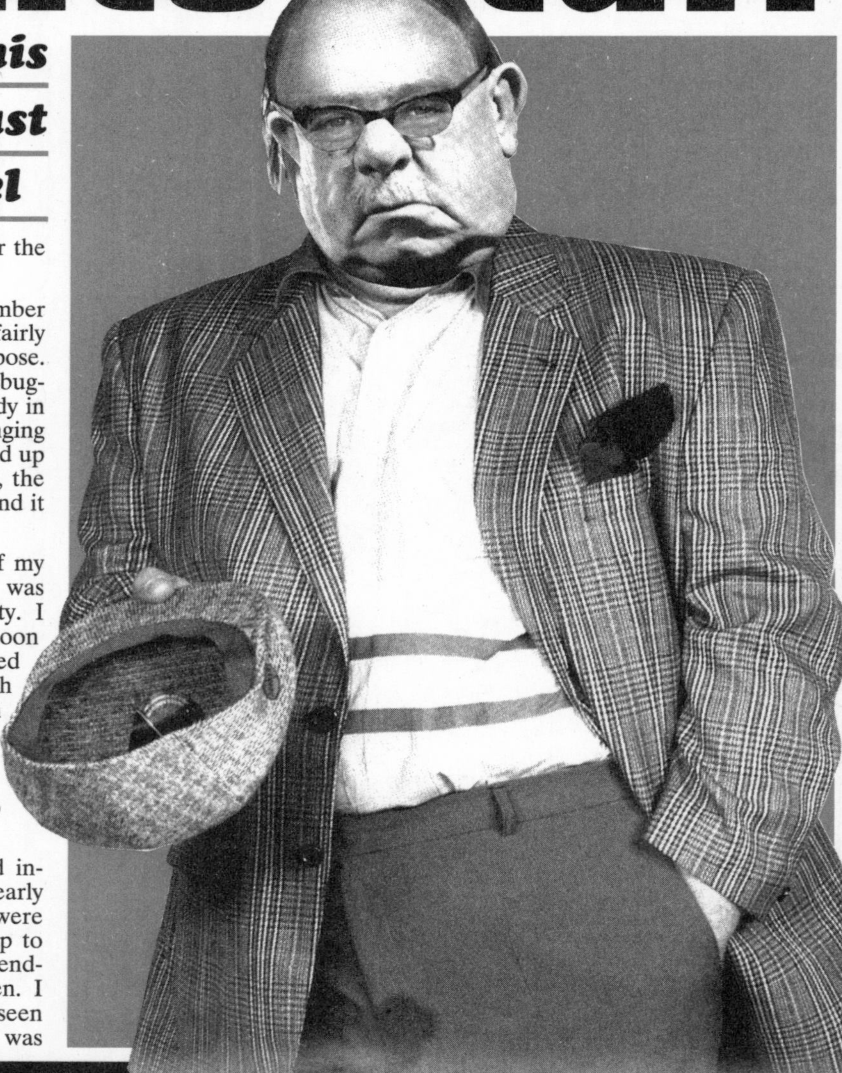

But you'd be wrong, for Eric toured the world for two decades as a member of one of Britain's top bands - *The Black and White Minstrels.* Now, as he looks back on his years of excess, he can barely believe he's the same person who used to think nothing of staying up for weeks on end, drinking catering-sized barrels of Jack Daniels every day and bedding groupies by the score. "Looking back on my years of excess, I can barely believe I'm the same person who used to think nothing of staying up for weeks on end, drinking catering-sized barrels of Jack Daniels every day and bedding groupies by the score," he says.

Now, nearly twenty years after the band broke up, Eric has handed over his life savings of £200 to a vanity publisher to see his memories immortalised in a new autobiography. ***Black & White & Read All Over*** (Lone Ranger Books, £13.99) is the story of his wild rollercoaster ride through fame and fortune, and his eventual fall from grace. "I had it all - the houses, the cars, the women - but it slipped through my fingers like fairy dust," he smiles.

"Even so, I've got no regrets. I've still got my memories, and they're worth more than all the millions I ever earned in the Minstrels."

Now, in these exclusive extracts from his 38-page memoir, Eric lifts the lid on his crazy times as an anachronistic racist stereotype.

Eric's dizzying trip on the showbiz merry-go-round began in 1973.

"I'd got some casual work, washing up in the BBC canteen. I was getting ten bob an hour, which was good money in them days, and I'd got myself some digs in a hostel just outside Shepherds Bush. Life was good, but little did I realise it was about to get a whole lot better.

One afternoon I'd just finished washing a big pile of dinner plates. My hands were wet, but because there were no towels in the kitchens, I was waving them round to get them dry. As luck would have it, the producer of the Black & White Minstrel Show had just come in for an omelette. He saw me waggling my hands about like the Minstrels did and offered me a ten year contract to join his band on the spot. I couldn't believe my luck.

To say I got thrown in the deep end would be an understatement. The Minstrels were doing a show that night ... on live TV! There was no time for rehearsals. Before I knew what was happening, I was covered head to toe in boot polish and the director was counting us down for the opening number.

To be honest, I don't remember much about the show. It was fairly straightforward stuff, I suppose. I had to wear a wear a humbug-striped waistcoat and push a lady in a frilly dress on a swing whilst singing Daisy Daisy. Then we all dressed up in white top hats for the finale, the floor manager counted us out and it was all over.

In the dressing room, one of my new bandmates asked me if I was coming to the after-show party. I didn't need asking twice, and soon found myself being whisked through the West End in a stretch limousine. I kept having to pinch myself. This was a whole new world I had never even dared to dream about. Little did I know it, but the best was yet to come.

At the venue, I was ushered inside to the party and my eyes nearly popped out of my head. There were minstrels everywhere, getting up to all sorts of hanky-panky with an endless parade of gorgeous women. I was only 31, and I'd never even seen a naked lady before, yet here I was

surrounded by dozens of women in various states of undress, and all of them gagging for a bit of Black & White action with yours truly.

What me and my fellow minstrels got up to that night would have made Caligula blush! Suffice to say, by the time the orgy finally ended in the early hours of the morning, there wasn't a woman in that room who didn't have black handprints plastered over every inch of her body... or a Minstrel who had any boot-black left on his hands... or his manhood.

Rock bands are famous for getting up to high jinks on aeroplanes, and the Black and White Minstrels were no exception. Eric recalls one wild flight which got out of hand and nearly ended in disaster.

We'd been over to the Isle of Man to film a sequence of us singing (Hold it) Flash Bang Wallop What a Picture at the Laxey Wheel for our Christmas Show. The shoot had gone well and we were all in high spirits as we piled onto our specially chartered jumbo jet at Douglas Aerodrome. But once we got up in the air, the spirits got even higher, I can tell you!

The drink started flowing before we'd even got to the end of the runway, and by the time we reached altitude, the party was well underway. The Black & White Minstrels had a reputation for being the hardest drinking act in showbiz, and we'd hardly reached cruising height before we'd drunk the duty free trolley completely dry.

We were all three sheets to the wind, but still we wanted more booze. But when you're five miles above the Irish Sea, you can't just nip out to the Off Licence for more supplies. Then one of the lads had a brainwave. He suggested we should make a start on the plane's petrol. Someone found a hose from somewhere, and rigged up a syphon from the petrol tank to the bar. We were soon necking pint after pint of aviation fuel like there was no tomorrow.

Unfortunately, we forgot to tell the pilot, and the first he knew that we were boozing our way through his petrol was when the empty fuel tank warning light started flashing in the cockpit. But by that time it was too late. The engines spluttered to a halt and the plane went into a nosedive. It should of been terrifying, but we were so far gone that we just kept partying as we hurtled towards certain death at 500mph.

Luckily, the pilot was very skilled and somehow managed to make an emergency landing on the beach at Prestatyn. We stumbled down the steps and straight into the nearest pub!

It was two weeks before that plane was dug out of the sand, refueled and ready to take off again. I don't think the pubs of Prestatyn have ever done such a roaring trade as they did in that fortnight! In fact, when we finally got back to our dressing rooms at BBC Television Centre and took our make-up off, we discovered that we all had bright red noses off all the booze!

According to Eric, the backstage excesses didn't stop at drinking. Other, illicit substances also came to play an important part in the lives of the Black & White Minstrels.

For any artist, performing live is an incredible high. It's the most amazing feeling in the world to be up there on stage, singing Swannee How I Love Ya How I Love Ya to a woman in a frilly crinoline dress and an oversized hat while the crowd goes wild. But there's a price to pay for that feeling, and it's the terrible low you experience when the show is ended.

Like lots of other bands, we picked ourselves up by going on drugs.

Drugs were everywhere. You simply couldn't avoid them. They were just part of the Minstrel culture that everyone seemed to take for granted. After a show, there'd be bowls of cocaine in amongst the plates of sandwiches and sausage rolls, and it was a common sight to see a Minstrel toking on a bong, shooting up or chasing the dragon at the dinner table.

Drugs were so freely available that we got hooked. Indeed, some of the Minstrels could only perform if they were ripped to their blacked-up tits on Charlie. I remember one night when my own coke habit nearly got out of hand. We were backstage at the London Palladium, about to do the Royal Variety Show, and I'd tooted more than my fair share of marching powder - truth be told, I'd probably had about three pounds of the stuff. As I stood in the wings and the band struck up with the opening bars of How You Gonna Keep 'em Down on the Farm, I was absolutely pumped.

Suddenly, I glanced in the mirror and noticed that it wasn't just my eyes and lips that were surrounded with white circles. My nose was snow white too ... from all the cocaine I'd just been snorting up it!

It was too late to go back to the dressing room and touch up my nose with boot polish, as we had already started to walk on the stage, waving our top hats. Thinking quickly, I pulled up my big, spotty bow tie to cover the evidence, and did the whole number like that. Fortunately, I don't think the Queen noticed what was going on.

Another time, the Minstrels got raided by the drugs squad after a performance at Blackpool Winter Gardens. We were partying with some groupies in the green room, and as usual, there was plenty of drugs about. The air was so thick with heroin smoke, you couldn't see your white cotton gloves in front of your face. Suddenly, one of my bandmates ran into the room, waggling his hands on either side of his face in alarm. 'It's the filth!' he cried.

The warning gave us just enough time to hastily hide our stash under our spangly bowler hats. Moments later, the door was kicked open and in rushed several burly policemen, who proceeded to search us for illegal substances. Needless to say, they didn't find anything, and were forced to leave empty-handed. They were pretty cross, because thanks to our gloves, they couldn't even fingerprint us!

Modern day footballers have a reputation for misbehaving whilst on tour. But, says Eric, the carryings-on of the Minstrels make them look like choirboys!

We always had a reputation as clean, family entertainers. But let me tell you, once we got off that stage, our behaviour was as dirty as our faces.

The women who came to our shows literally threw themselves at us. It was there on a plate for the taking, and more often than not, we took it! One summer season we were appearing in Leeds and I decided to cut a notch in my bedpost for every bird I brought back to my digs for a bit of how's your father.

Well, I've no idea what my final tally was, but let me put it this way. When I checked out of the boarding house at the end of six weeks, my bed was just a pile of matchwood! And all the springs in the mattress had bust too.

Anyone who thinks that the Premiership stars of today invented "roasting" is sorely mistaken. Us Minstrels were doing it every night back in the seventies before they were even born. I'll always remember one orgy we had whilst travelling to appear at Nottingham Playhouse. Our minibus had broken down on a sliproad, and we were picked up by a coachload of Page 3 models.

We hadn't got a mile up the M1 before the girls had stripped off stark naked, and a mile later we had joined them! The aisle was piled high with top hats, bras, tailcoats, knickers, bow ties and suspenders. It was two topless birds per Minstrel - the scene in that coach made the sexiest excesses of Sodom and Gomorrah look like a vicarage tea-party. Double oral, DP, DVDA, rimming, pegging and round-the-world ... you name it, it was all going on as we sped along the motorway.

At one point we overtook a Morris Minor with a load of nuns in. You should have seeen their faces when they saw what we were getting up to!

In fact, we were having so much sex that the suspension completely collapsed as we pulled into Watford Gap Services. The coach was a write-off, but fortunately we managed to hitch a lift on a double decker bus full of Miss Worlds on their way to a nymphomaniacs convention. Needless to say, that bus was also ready for the scrapyard by the time it limped into Leicester Forest East Services!

I remember thinking at the time that it was a good job there was no such thing as mobile phones with a camcorder, because if someone had filmed our mammoth motorway sex session and put it on the net, our reputation as family entertainers would of been up the Swannee River!

In 1978, the Black & White Minstrel Show was axed for being racist by politically correct BBC bosses and Eric found himself looking for work again. He took on a part-time job sorting service washes at a large London launderette, but was dismissed when lady customers complained that he'd been interfering with their smalls. "They alleged that items of underwear, such as bras and knickers, were being returned in a slightly less-than-pristine condition," he recalls. "But it wasn't me doing it, it must of been somebody else."

"Someone was probably coming in the shop after I'd locked up and doing it then," he says. "Someone who was jealous of me because I'd been in the Black & White Minstrels."

> "We hitched a lift on a double decker full of Miss Worlds on their way to nymphomaniacs convention."

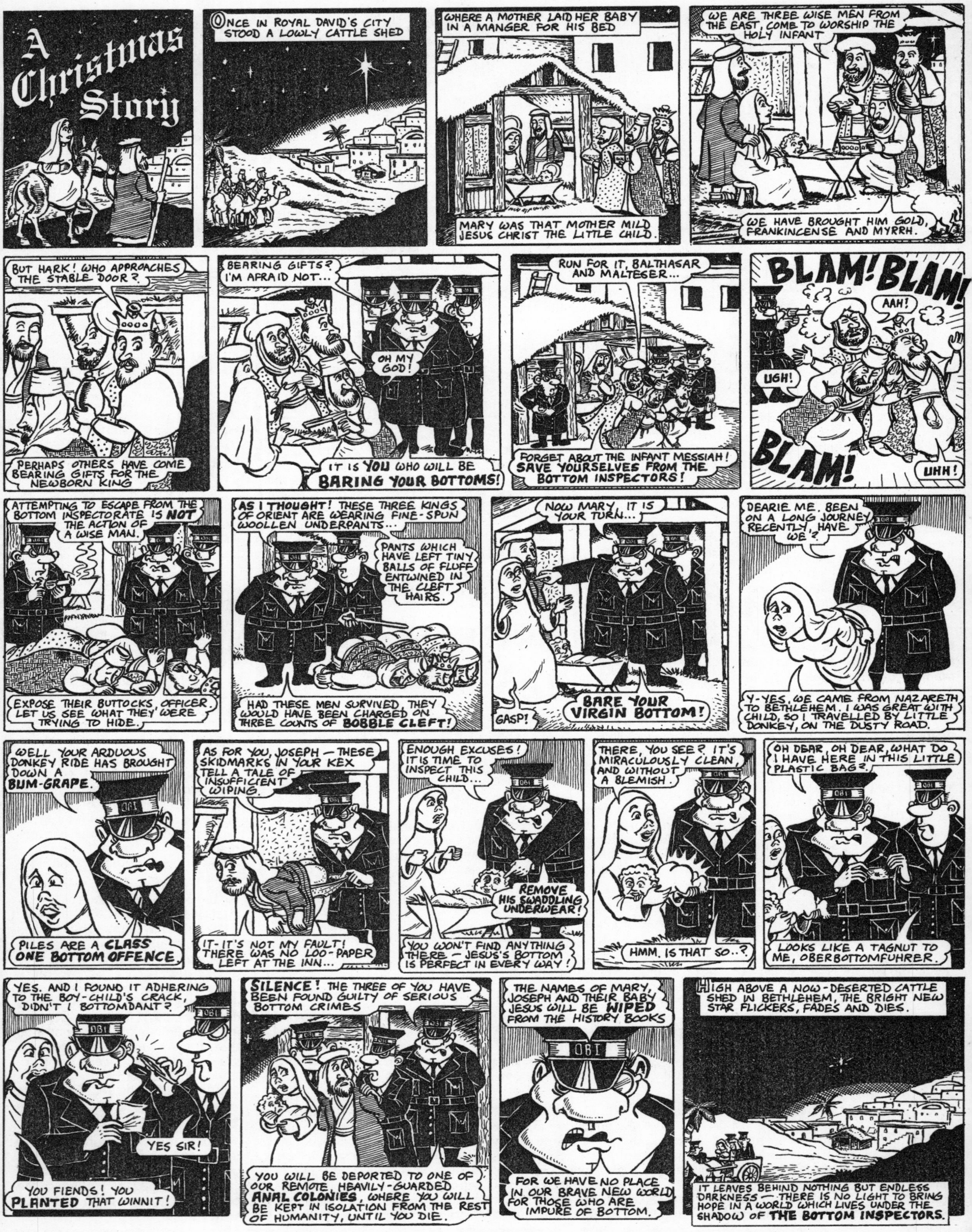

A Christmas Story
ONCE IN ROYAL DAVID'S CITY STOOD A LOWLY CATTLE SHED
WHERE A MOTHER LAID HER BABY IN A MANGER FOR HIS BED
MARY WAS THAT MOTHER MILD JESUS CHRIST THE LITTLE CHILD.
WE ARE THREE WISE MEN FROM THE EAST, COME TO WORSHIP THE HOLY INFANT
WE HAVE BROUGHT HIM GOLD, FRANKINCENSE AND MYRRH.
BUT HARK! WHO APPROACHES THE STABLE DOOR?
PERHAPS OTHERS HAVE COME BEARING GIFTS FOR THE NEWBORN KING
BEARING GIFTS? I'M AFRAID NOT...
OH MY GOD!
IT IS YOU WHO WILL BE BARING YOUR BOTTOMS!
RUN FOR IT, BALTHASAR AND MALTESER...
FORGET ABOUT THE INFANT MESSIAH! SAVE YOURSELVES FROM THE BOTTOM INSPECTORS!
BLAM! BLAM!
AAH!
UGH!
BLAM!
UHH!
ATTEMPTING TO ESCAPE FROM THE BOTTOM INSPECTORATE IS NOT THE ACTION OF A WISE MAN.
EXPOSE THEIR BUTTOCKS, OFFICER. LET US SEE WHAT THEY WERE TRYING TO HIDE.
AS I THOUGHT! THESE THREE KINGS OF ORIENT ARE WEARING FINE-SPUN WOOLLEN UNDERPANTS...
PANTS WHICH HAVE LEFT TINY BALLS OF FLUFF ENTWINED IN THE CLEFT HAIRS.
HAD THESE MEN SURVIVED, THEY WOULD HAVE BEEN CHARGED ON THREE COUNTS OF BOBBLE CLEFT!
NOW MARY, IT IS YOUR TURN...
GASP!
BARE YOUR VIRGIN BOTTOM!
DEARIE ME. BEEN ON A LONG JOURNEY RECENTLY, HAVE WE?
Y-YES, WE CAME FROM NAZARETH TO BETHLEHEM. I WAS GREAT WITH CHILD, SO I TRAVELLED BY LITTLE DONKEY, ON THE DUSTY ROAD.
WELL YOUR ARDUOUS DONKEY RIDE HAS BROUGHT DOWN A BUM-GRAPE.
PILES ARE A CLASS ONE BOTTOM OFFENCE.
AS FOR YOU, JOSEPH — THESE SKIDMARKS IN YOUR KEX TELL A TALE OF INSUFFICIENT WIPING.
IT-IT'S NOT MY FAULT! THERE WAS NO LOO-PAPER LEFT AT THE INN...
ENOUGH EXCUSES! IT IS TIME TO INSPECT THIS CHILD...
REMOVE HIS SWADDLING UNDERWEAR!
YOU WON'T FIND ANYTHING THERE — JESUS'S BOTTOM IS PERFECT IN EVERY WAY!
THERE, YOU SEE? IT'S MIRACULOUSLY CLEAN AND WITHOUT A BLEMISH.
HMM. IS THAT SO..?
OH DEAR, OH DEAR, WHAT DO I HAVE HERE IN THIS LITTLE PLASTIC BAG?
LOOKS LIKE A TAGNUT TO ME, OBERBOTTOMFUHRER.
YES. AND I FOUND IT ADHERING TO THE BOY-CHILD'S CRACK, DIDN'T I BOTTOMDANT?
YES SIR!
YOU FIENDS! YOU PLANTED THAT WINNIT!
SILENCE! THE THREE OF YOU HAVE BEEN FOUND GUILTY OF SERIOUS BOTTOM CRIMES
YOU WILL BE DEPORTED TO ONE OF OUR REMOTE, HEAVILY-GUARDED ANAL COLONIES, WHERE YOU WILL BE KEPT IN ISOLATION FROM THE REST OF HUMANITY, UNTIL YOU DIE.
THE NAMES OF MARY, JOSEPH AND THEIR BABY JESUS WILL BE WIPED FROM THE HISTORY BOOKS
OBI
FOR WE HAVE NO PLACE IN OUR BRAVE NEW WORLD FOR THOSE WHO ARE IMPURE OF BOTTOM.
HIGH ABOVE A NOW-DESERTED CATTLE SHED IN BETHLEHEM, THE BRIGHT NEW STAR FLICKERS, FADES AND DIES.
IT LEAVES BEHIND NOTHING BUT ENDLESS DARKNESS — THERE IS NO LIGHT TO BRING HOPE IN A WORLD WHICH LIVES UNDER THE SHADOW OF THE BOTTOM INSPECTORS.

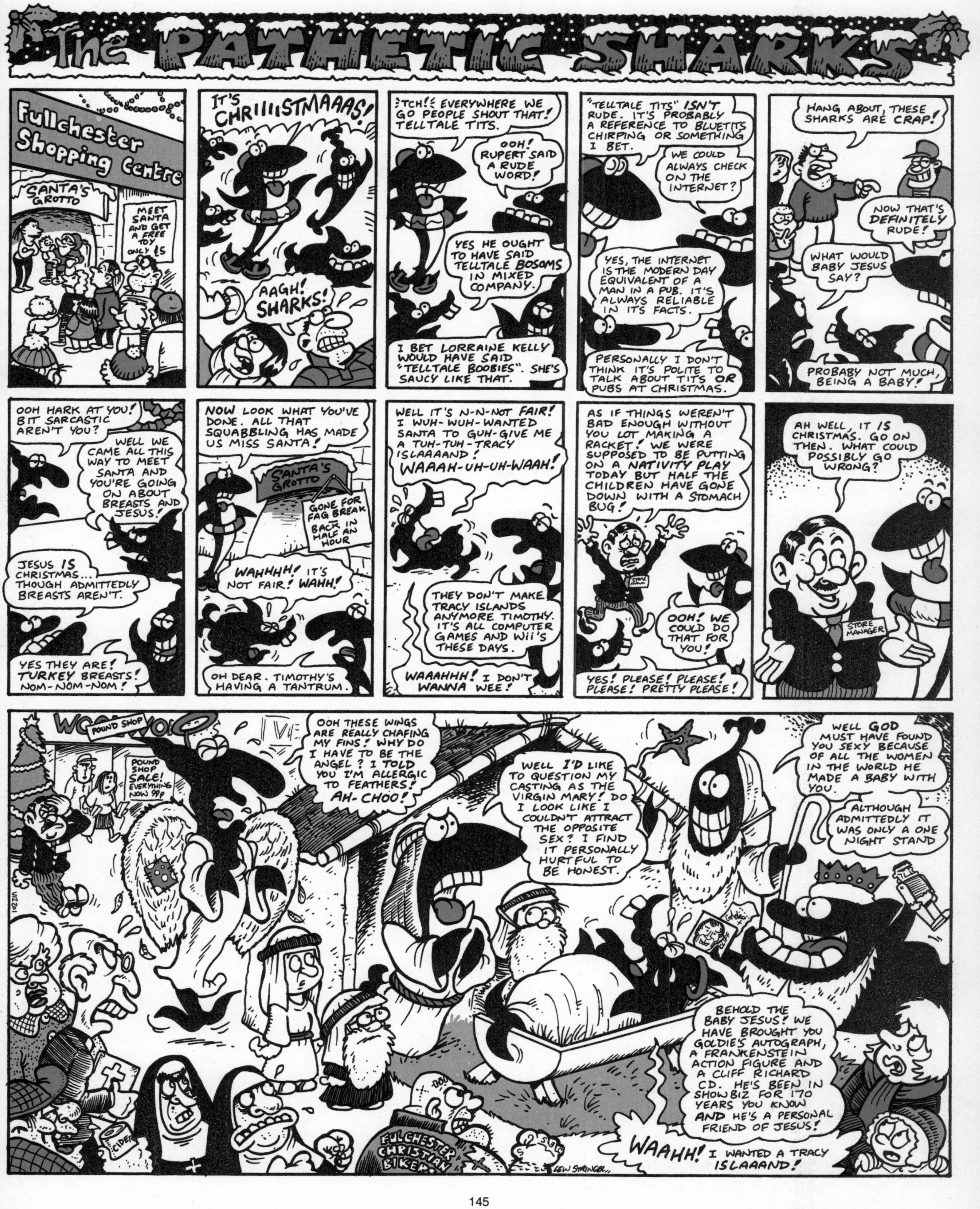
The Pathetic Sharks
Fullchester Shopping Centre
SANTA'S GROTTO
MEET SANTA AND GET A FREE TOY ONLY £5
IT'S CHRIIIISTMAAAS!
AAGH! SHARKS!
TCH! EVERYWHERE WE GO PEOPLE SHOUT THAT! TELLTALE TITS.
OOH! RUPERT SAID A RUDE WORD!
YES HE OUGHT TO HAVE SAID TELLTALE BOSOMS IN MIXED COMPANY.
I BET LORRAINE KELLY WOULD HAVE SAID "TELLTALE BOOBIES". SHE'S SAUCY LIKE THAT.
"TELLTALE TITS" ISN'T RUDE. IT'S PROBABLY A REFERENCE TO BLUETITS CHIRPING OR SOMETHING I BET.
WE COULD ALWAYS CHECK ON THE INTERNET?
YES, THE INTERNET IS THE MODERN DAY EQUIVALENT OF A MAN IN A PUB. IT'S ALWAYS RELIABLE IN ITS FACTS.
PERSONALLY I DON'T THINK IT'S POLITE TO TALK ABOUT TITS OR PUBS AT CHRISTMAS.
HANG ABOUT, THESE SHARKS ARE CRAP!
NOW THAT'S DEFINITELY RUDE!
WHAT WOULD BABY JESUS SAY?
PROBABY NOT MUCH, BEING A BABY!
OOH HARK AT YOU! BIT SARCASTIC AREN'T YOU?
WELL WE CAME ALL THIS WAY TO MEET SANTA AND YOU'RE GOING ON ABOUT BREASTS AND JESUS!
JESUS IS CHRISTMAS... THOUGH ADMITTEDLY BREASTS AREN'T.
YES THEY ARE! TURKEY BREASTS! NOM-NOM-NOM!
NOW LOOK WHAT YOU'VE DONE. ALL THAT SQUABBLING HAS MADE US MISS SANTA!
SANTA'S GROTTO
GONE FOR FAG BREAK BACK IN HALF AN HOUR
WAHHHH! IT'S NOT FAIR! WAHH!
OH DEAR. TIMOTHY'S HAVING A TANTRUM.
WELL IT'S N-N-NOT FAIR! I WUH-WUH-WANTED SANTA TO GUH-GIVE ME A TUH-TUH-TRACY ISLAAAAND! WAAAH-UH-UH-WAAH!
THEY DON'T MAKE TRACY ISLANDS ANYMORE TIMOTHY. IT'S ALL COMPUTER GAMES AND Wii'S THESE DAYS.
WAAAHHH! I DON'T WANNA WEE!
AS IF THINGS WEREN'T BAD ENOUGH WITHOUT YOU LOT MAKING A RACKET! WE WERE SUPPOSED TO BE PUTTING ON A NATIVITY PLAY TODAY BUT HALF THE CHILDREN HAVE GONE DOWN WITH A STOMACH BUG!
OOH! WE COULD DO THAT FOR YOU!
YES! PLEASE! PLEASE! PLEASE! PRETTY PLEASE!
AH WELL, IT IS CHRISTMAS. GO ON THEN. WHAT COULD POSSIBLY GO WRONG?
STORE MANAGER
POUND SHOP
POUND SHOP SALE! EVERYTHING NOW 99p
OOH THESE WINGS ARE REALLY CHAFING MY FINS! WHY DO I HAVE TO BE THE ANGEL? I TOLD YOU I'M ALLERGIC TO FEATHERS! AH-CHOO!
WELL I'D LIKE TO QUESTION MY CASTING AS THE VIRGIN MARY! DO I LOOK LIKE I COULDN'T ATTRACT THE OPPOSITE SEX? I FIND IT PERSONALLY HURTFUL TO BE HONEST.
WELL GOD MUST HAVE FOUND YOU SEXY BECAUSE OF ALL THE WOMEN IN THE WORLD HE MADE A BABY WITH YOU.
ALTHOUGH ADMITTEDLY IT WAS ONLY A ONE NIGHT STAND
BEHOLD THE BABY JESUS! WE HAVE BROUGHT YOU GOLDIE'S AUTOGRAPH, A FRANKENSTEIN ACTION FIGURE AND A CLIFF RICHARD CD. HE'S BEEN IN SHOWBIZ FOR 170 YEARS YOU KNOW AND HE'S A PERSONAL FRIEND OF JESUS!
WAAHH! I WANTED A TRACY ISLAAAND!
CIDER
FULCHESTER CHRISTIAN BIKERS
LEW STRINGER

WORLD WAR II "MAY HAVE TO BE REFOUGHT"

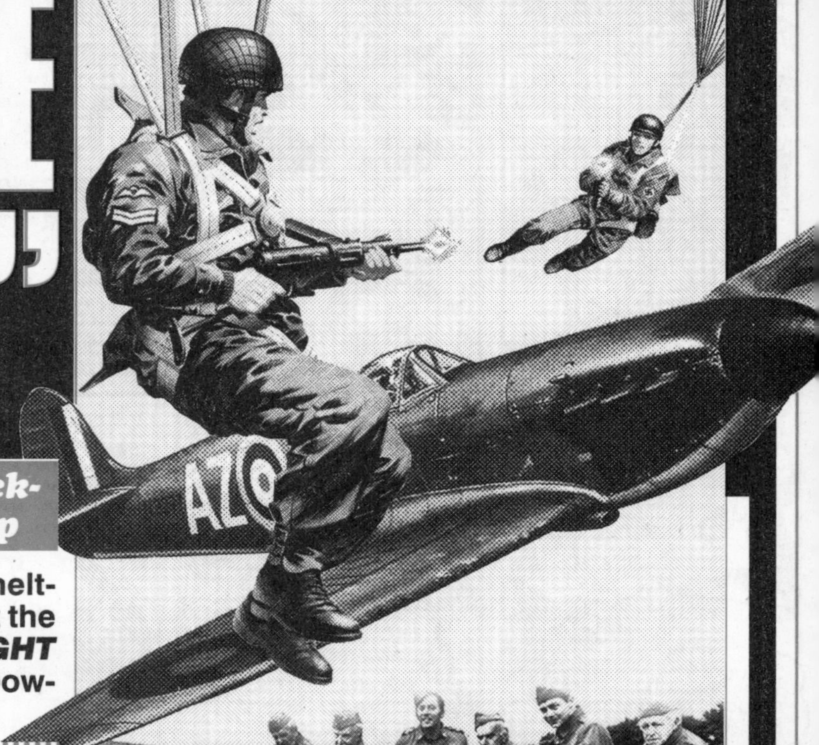

AZ

Germans have last laugh as Allied cock-up could lead to war fixture pile-up

GLOBAL geopolitics was thrown into melt-down yesterday after reports emerged that the Second World War may have to be *REFOUGHT* due to an administrative oversight by the allied powers in 1945.

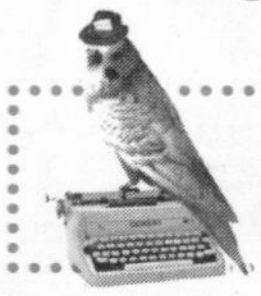

By our War Budgerigar **DEREK PATTERSON**

Conventional thinking has it that the conflict ended with the defeat and unconditional surrender of the Germans and Japanese in 1945. However, World War II revival pressure group "Fatherland for Justice" have questioned the result and called for key participants to do the honourable thing and resume the conflict from the beginning.

VICTOR

"According to the Geneva Convention, War treaties must be made in triplicate - one copy for the victor, one for the loser and one for the file," said the group's spokesman, Helmut Cheeze. "It seems that only two copies were signed for the German Instrument of surrender by General Jodl in Reims," he added.

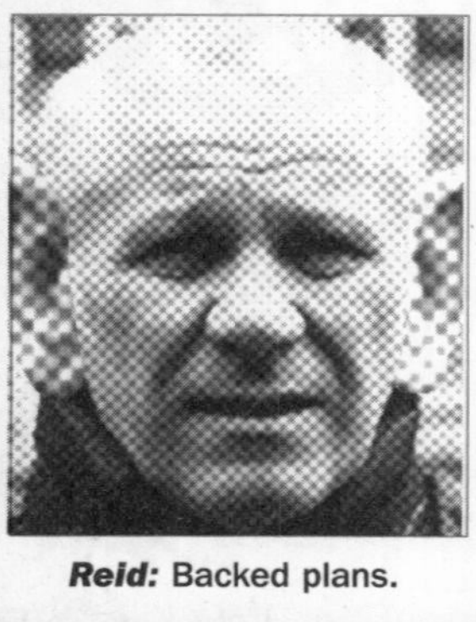

Reid: Backed plans.

And that shoddy paperwork could now be set to cost the Allies dearly. For according to Cheeze, it renders the surrender and subsequent division of territory and power in Europe, NULL and VOID.

CHEVETTE

But it is feared that the re-run of WWII would be an administrative headache for world leaders. With a busy schedule of intervention and conflict already penned in for Sub-Saharan Africa and the Middle East in the next few months, a re-run of the largest conflict in history would lead to a war fixture pile-up.

"There is just no room for a six year global conflict in our diaries at the moment," explained United Nations boss Banksy Moon. "A log jam of wars is the last thing we need. We'll have to look at the schedules and do a bit of shuffling around."

CORVETTE

One suggestion is that the return to arms could start on a Tuesday or Wednesday night to avoid clashing with Afghanistan and Iraq. But it is likely that some minor conflicts will have to be postponed to make way for a potential World War II replay.

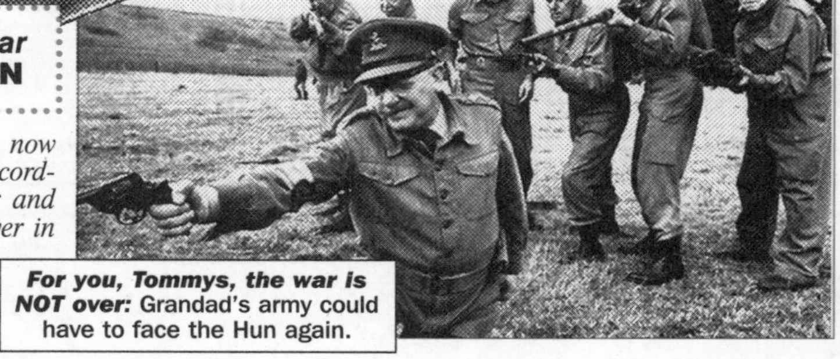

For you, Tommys, the war is NOT over: Grandad's army could have to face the Hun again.

Apart from all the logistical problems, there may be reluctance from the remaining veterans of the conflict, given their age, to re-don their uniforms and resume combat.

ROOSTER

"We are considering laying on courtesy buses to ferry the elderly troops back to France, North Africa and the eastern front as well as providing refreshments and wash facilities," said German ambassador, Reinhardt Spoffenheimer.

But British forces manager Gordon Brown said he would be appealing against any decision to hold a replay, claiming that the Germans should have flagged up the gaffe at the time. He told reporters: "We firmly believe the result should stand - there was a clear cooling off period of fourteen days after the Germans surrendered – plenty of time for them to question the result." There are also fears that the Cold War result might not stand, should Germany win the rematch.

RIDING HOOD

This is not the first time that a supposed historical result has been called into question due to an administrative botch. There have long been calls for video technology to be used when signing war treaties after the Hundred Years War had to be refought in the 18th century when it came to light that the peace treaty had been signed outside the margins of the box by the Duke of Burgundy.

Stoke City assistant manager Peter Reid backed such calls. "The technology is there and should be used, although I'm not sure exactly how", he said without swearing.

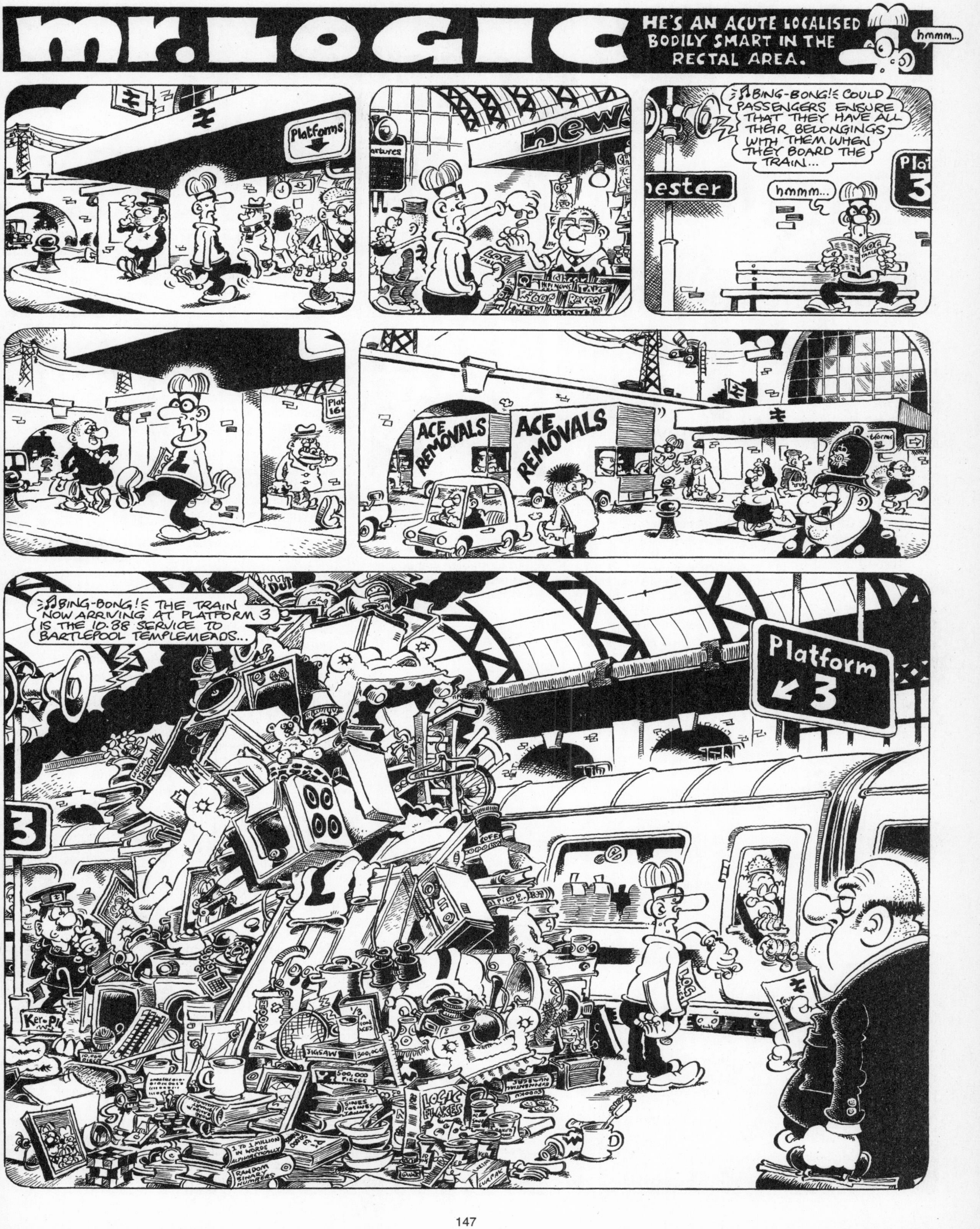
mr. LOGIC
HE'S AN ACUTE LOCALISED BODILY SMART IN THE RECTAL AREA.
hmmm...
Platforms
news
BING-BONG! COULD PASSENGERS ENSURE THAT THEY HAVE ALL THEIR BELONGINGS WITH THEM WHEN THEY BOARD THE TRAIN...
hmmm...
ACE REMOVALS
ACE REMOVALS
BING-BONG! THE TRAIN NOW ARRIVING AT PLATFORM 3 IS THE 10.38 SERVICE TO BARTLEPOOL TEMPLEMEADS...
Platform 3
LOGIC FLAKES
JIGSAW
RANDOM BINARY NUMBERS

LetteRBocks

VIZ COMIC
PO Box 841
Whitley Bay
NE26 9EQ
letters@viz.co.uk

★ STAR LETTER

✳ **THEY** say that the Bible is the greatest story ever told. They obviously haven't heard my mate's story about his recent trip to Amsterdam involving three prostitutes, an angry dwarf, a pool cue and a vibrating replica dog's foot. Honestly, it knocks all those biblical tales into a cocked hat.

James Watson, e-mail

✳ **I RECENTLY** suffered an accident at work. Yet when I called Claims Direct they told me I couldn't get compensation for shitting my pants whilst bending down to lift a pallet. Is there no justice?

Gerry Paton, e-mail

✳ **I HAVE** noticed that Trade secretary Vince Cable talks as though he is deaf. If he is actually deaf, then his rise to power demonstrates a truly heartwarming triumph over adversity in the face of overwhelming odds. However, if he is merely pretending to sound deaf to further his career, then he should be thoroughly ashamed of himself.

C Hawkes, e-mail

✳ **I SAW** with interest that Coventry University offers courses in terrorism and organised crime. Now Osama Bin Laden was pretty good at it, but he studied engineering or something similar. It just goes to show that your studies do not necessarily lead you to the right career.

Alan Heath, e-mail

✳ **IF DOLPHINS** are so clever, how come they haven't been to space, but mice have? It's a load of old nonsense if you ask me.

Sidney Sausage-Biscuit, e-mai

✳ **I'VE JUST** watched a Jewish woman on Channel 4 saying her religion forbids her from ripping up toilet paper on the sabbath, so she has to rip enough up on Friday night to see her through the next day. I must admit, I'm not sure on a Friday what my arse is going to do on Saturday. I wonder if she 'prepares for the worst' just to be on the safe side. Also, do these rules allow her to flush the bog afterwards, or does it have to sit stewing until Sunday morning?

Albert Plywood, Luton

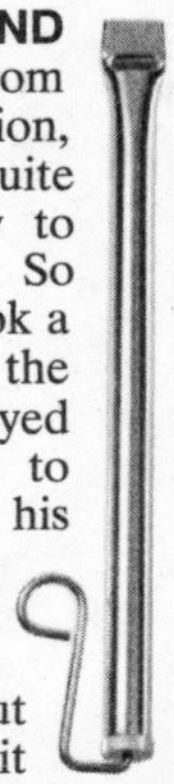

✳ **MY HUSBAND** suffers from erectile dysfunction, and he often gets quite upset when we try to have intercourse. So the other night I took a Swanee whistle into the bedroom and played it when he began to achieve or lose his erection. I thought it might put him at his ease and lighten the atmosphere, but I have to say that it didn't really help all that much.

Doreen Charlesworth, Bute

✳ **EVERY** day I buy a nice farmhouse loaf from a red-headed man at the shop in town. He is quite literally a ginger baker. Do any of your readers know of a local businessman whose profession, when preceeded with a one-word description of him, forms the name of a classic drummer?

Chris Francis, e-mail

✳ **FIRST** it was the power of juba juba, then microstrand innovations and finally anti-crimp genetic-inspired technology.

When are the Nobel Prize Committee going to consider the contributions of those scientific giants at the Laboratoire Garnier?

Ed O'Meara, e-mail

✳ **IF I WAS** Marty McFly I would go forward in time 30 minutes to check if it was raining so I would know whether or not to bring my washing in from the line. Can any of your readers think of a more mundane way of using a time machine?

Leon Hennessy, e-mail

✳ **I'VE JUST** heard that short-arsed, overhyped fuckwit Bono is coming here to New Zealand. Next time you tell him to fuck off, could you be a little more precise and not send him our way?

Ian Pedersen, New Zealand

✳ **WE WERE** told on the news that the Chilean miners would not be rescued until Christmas, and I was really looking forward to viewing the rescue whilst tucking into my roast turkey with all the trimmings. Imagine my bitter disappointment when I learned that they

TOP TIPS

ACORNS wrapped in silver paper make great Easter eggs for squirrels.

Acko, e-mail

RAIL passengers. Try pressing the button to open the door as the train pulls away. It won't magically open, but it will provide the driver with amusement as he watches on the CCTV.

A Traindriver, London

STOP blokes walking around with pitbulls and Staffordshires by simply changing the breed names to things like ladypuff marmalade terriers.

Tony Cockles, e-mail

HELP to teach kids how the government works by simply taking all their sweets off them and telling them to fuck off.

fang, e-mail

AXL Rose. If turning up at a venue within 2 hours of a pre-arranged time is too demanding for you, then why not consider a career with a more generous appointment window, such as a Parcel Force delivery driver or Virgin Media broadband installer?

J Davighi, e-mail

SOUTHERNERS. Convince everyone you are a northerner by regularly going to the foot of your stairs.

Nigel Hurll, e-mail

SAVE time when counting to 10 by starting at the number 4. If you are in a real hurry, try starting at 5.

Ian Smith, e-mail

CHILEAN miners.Take a large range of pornography and crossword puzzles to work with you, just in case.

Jason Richardson, e-mail

JEREMY Kyle show participants. 'Irregardless' is not a word. The word you are looking of is either irrespective or regardless.

Jubnut, e-mail

SHOPPERS. Use a 1 Euro coin in the trolley chain instead of a pound coin, saving yourself 11p at today's exchange rates. If the pound is suddenly devalued, simply do your shopping in Europe and use a pound coin.

Tony K, e-mail

JAMES Dyson. Increase sales of your inventions by grossly exaggerating how difficult it is to complete a simple task using existing technology.

J Davighi, e-mail

AVOID an entirely preventable court appearance by refraining from using the expression 'unrelenting shower of incompetent cunts' in correspondence with BT, Sky, O2, Vodaphone, Virgin Media, Virgin Trains, London Midland Trains, Northampton Borough Council, Scottish and Southern Energy, Npower and Microsoft.

J Davighi, e-mail

were coming up several weeks early. I would like the Chilean authorities to know that they have ruined my, and no doubt many other people's Christmas.

Chris Higson, e-mail

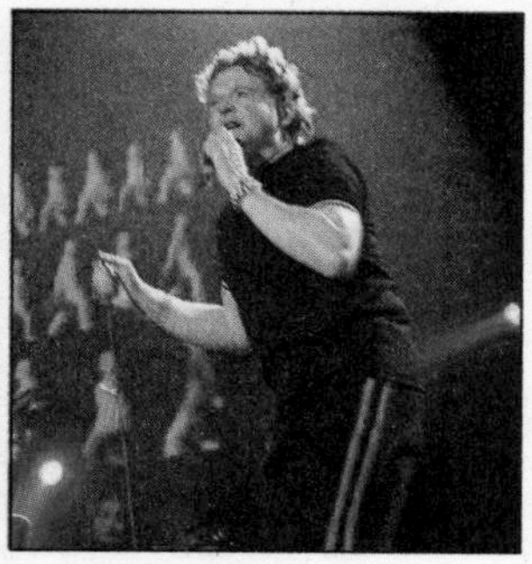

I MADE a point of watching the Simply Red farewell show the other week. I'm not a fan, I just wanted to make sure.

Christina Martin, e-mail

I RECENTLY saw an advert advising that you can now sign up for Jobseekers Allowance online 'at your convenience.' I'm glad the government has finally recognised how busy the unemployed are and are not forcing them to turn off Jeremy Kyle and put down the Jaffa cakes to go outside at an awkward time.

Tudor Sykes, e-mail

DO ANY of your readers know the correct way to dispose of a condom immediately after sex? I normally just throw it towards the bedside table, but I just had a massive row with the missus about 'not showing respect' for a picture of her mam and dad.

C Lantsbury, e-mail

UP THE ARSE CORNER

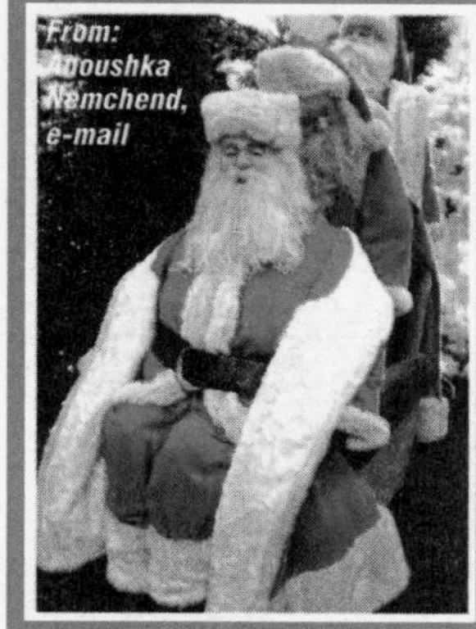
From:
Anoushka
Nemchend,
e-mail

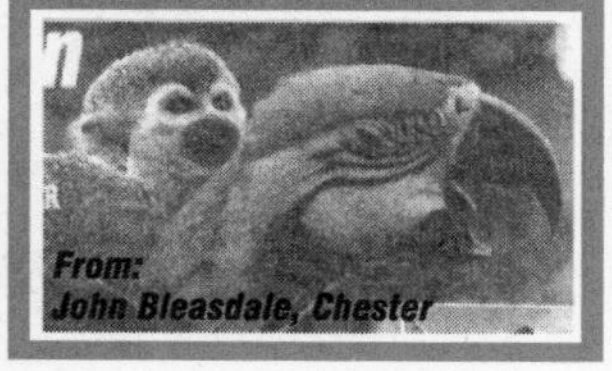
From:
John Bleasdale, Chester

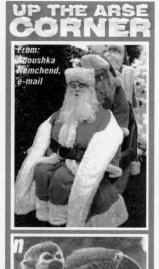

"DEDICATION, ooh! Dedication, ooh! Dedication, that's what you need. If you wanna be the best, if you wanna beat the rest. Ooooh! Dedication's what you need," sang Roy Castle at the end of each episode of *Record Breakers*. Well the world's shortest man is 2 feet 2 inches tall, while I am 6 foot 8. I don't see how any amount of fucking dedication on my behalf is going to win me that title.

Rob Shields, e-mail

WHY IS it that when someone punches a policeman, it's always described as 'a cowardly attack'? Given that coppers usually carry an extendable batton, pepper spray and a tazer, and is usually accompanied by an equally tooled-up mate, I'd say it was pretty rock to take one on.

Nick Short, Adelaide

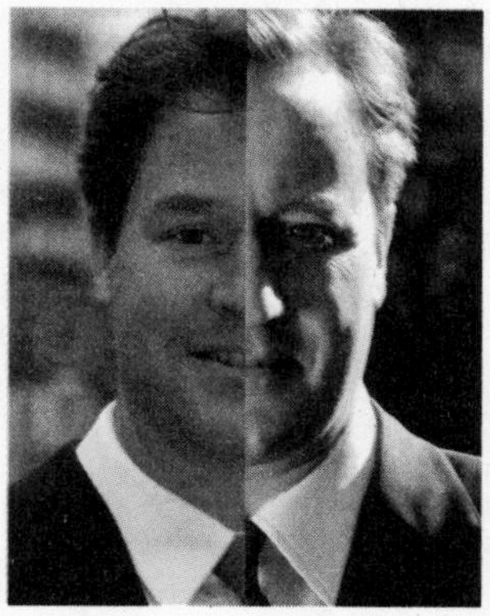

I WAS quite depressed about the new government coalition and their huge cuts. But I find it helps to imagine Nick Clegg and David Cameron as a kind of political version of that *My Two Dads* sitcom. That way, I went from being depressed about losing my job to chuckling about them being so different but, through a series of comical situations, learning to get along.

Martina Christiano, e-mail

MAY I congratulate *Heat* magazine for their recent exposé of the sham 'showmance' plot hatched between Preston and Chantelle in *Big Brother* this year in order to milk the celebrity gossip mags for a few quid. Where would this country be without such fine investigative journalism?

Adrian Newth, e-mail

IT'S A good job that Clark Kent never wore contact lenses, as his true identity would have immediately been revealed.

Dave Atkinson, e-mail

TOP TIPS

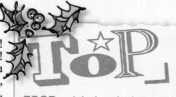

FOOD label designers. Instead of writing 'Best before end: see top of lid," why not simply replace this message with the best before end date?

Niloc, e-mail

GENTLEMEN. An erect penis makes an ideal emergency perch for an escaped budgerigar, I would imagine.

John Rhythm, e-mail

REFEREES. Keep a lie detector at the pitchside. Players know if they were offside or not, and it could sort out those tricky decisions.

Neil Vickery, e-mail

GLUE some blackcurrants to your anus and go to the doctor complaining of haemorrhoids. When he gives you some ointment on prescription, it can be saved as an 'insurance policy' should you ever develop the condition for real.

Ian Smith, e-mail

VACUUM cleaner nozzles make great intergalactic 'wormholes' for spiders and woodlice.

Woof the wolf, e-mail

GAME show and cereal enthusiasts. Recreate the madness of the end of The Crystal Maze by quickly picking all the raisins out of your museli. But for every oat you pick up, deduct a raisin.

Jonny R, e-mail

PRETEND you are at a rally for enthusiasts of normal, everyday cars by driving to a supermarket car park and sitting beside your vehicle in a folding chair, talking about it to everyone who passes.

R Belfitt, Leeds

SNOOKER players. Wear clown shoes to help get those hard-to-reach shots where you have to stretch over the table whilst keeping your feet on the floor.

Neil Mainey, e-mail

RADIO enthusiasts. Don't bother listening to commercial radio stations. Simply invite your most witless, tedious neighbour round to put records on and then talk over them.

Ed O'Meara, e-mail

RESTAURATEURS. Draw attention away from your cuisine being bland, tasteless and overpriced by serving it on an oversized, wavy oblong plate.

Stuart Achilles, e-mail

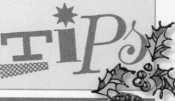

Look After the Purple Pennies

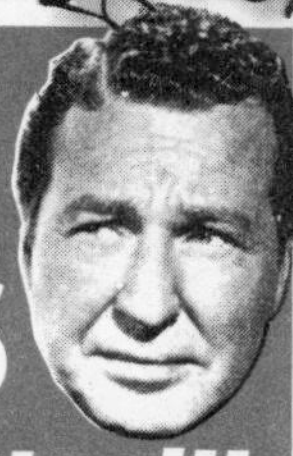

with Money Saving Sexpert Ingledew Botterill

WELL It's that time of year again when we all start to feel the pinch, and this year more so than ever. What with kids' presents to buy and that special something for the wife, it soon adds up. With the never-ending-round of Christmas parties, boozy nights out and visits to the in-laws, it's doubly important to keep a close on eye on what you are paying for sexual services.

Here are my festive tips for ensuring your sack is emptied by a pro without breaking the bank!

- ***AGREE*** what you're getting beforehand. Christmas is a busy time for everyone, especially dads, and a visit to a brothel will likely have to be squeezed in between shopping for toys and putting up the decorations. But don't be rushed. Take a few minutes to agree with the madam what services you'll be getting before handing over the cash. If you don't, you could find yourself charged extra for services that you don't want like reverse cowgirl and A-levels.

- ***ALWAYS*** have a budget in mind. It can be hard to say no to expensive face-sitting when you are 2 strokes off jizz o'clock, so always tell the pro your budget BEFORE she goes near your gentleman. It could save a lot of embarrassment and a nasty visit from her pimp.

- ***DON'T*** be greedy. Do you really need a prostrate massage with your straight sex? Say no politely - remember it's your hard earned cash. That's £15 saved already in one visit - the price of a medium-sized turkey or 2 discounted High School Musical DVDs for the kids.

- ***IMPROVISE.*** 'OWO' - parlour speak for fellatio performed without a condom - may be appealing, but ask yourself if it's really necessary. French with an ultra-thin johnny is just as good - and £10 cheaper! That's money in your pocket towards a day out in that dull time between Christmas and new Year.

- ***BE*** patient. If you can put off that cold impersonal and lacklustre handjob for just a few weeks, there are usually great deals to be had in the January sales.

- ***PAY*** up quickly. If you frequent the posher establishments where they accept plastic, then pay it for in full the following month. 3 hours of full sex plus two handjobs could mean a crazy £18.50 in interest payments alone. Paying off the full amount straight away means you have already saved half the cost of a disinterested 20 minutes ball massage.

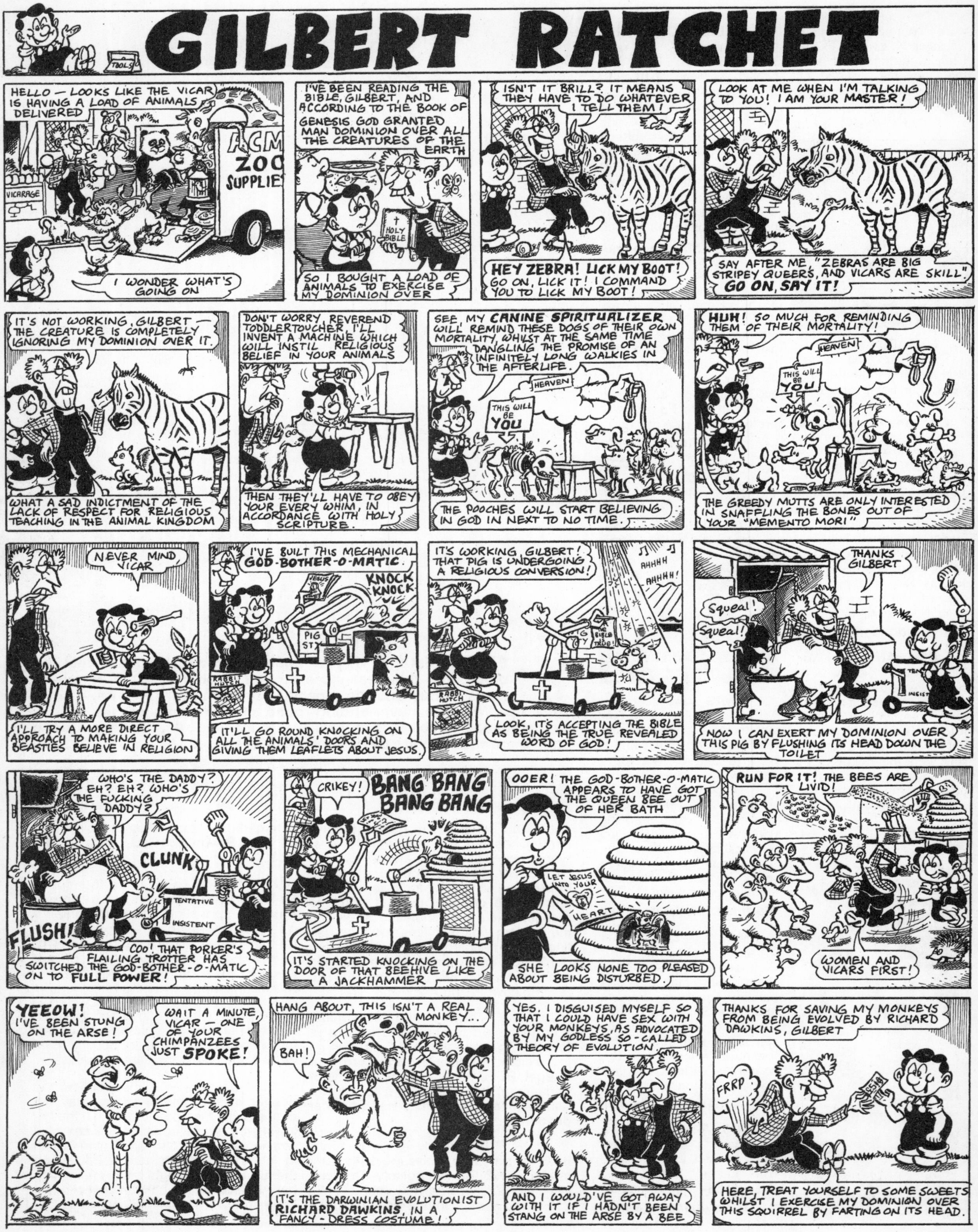
GILBERT RATCHET
TOOLS
HELLO — LOOKS LIKE THE VICAR IS HAVING A LOAD OF ANIMALS DELIVERED
VICARAGE
ACME ZOO SUPPLIES
I WONDER WHAT'S GOING ON
I'VE BEEN READING THE BIBLE, GILBERT, AND ACCORDING TO THE BOOK OF GENESIS GOD GRANTED MAN DOMINION OVER ALL THE CREATURES OF THE EARTH
HOLY BIBLE
SO I BOUGHT A LOAD OF ANIMALS TO EXERCISE MY DOMINION OVER
ISN'T IT BRILL? IT MEANS THEY HAVE TO DO WHATEVER I TELL THEM!
HEY ZEBRA! LICK MY BOOT! GO ON, LICK IT! I COMMAND YOU TO LICK MY BOOT!
LOOK AT ME WHEN I'M TALKING TO YOU! I AM YOUR MASTER!
SAY AFTER ME, "ZEBRAS ARE BIG STRIPEY QUEERS, AND VICARS ARE SKILL". GO ON, SAY IT!
IT'S NOT WORKING, GILBERT — THE CREATURE IS COMPLETELY IGNORING MY DOMINION OVER IT.
WHAT A SAD INDICTMENT OF THE LACK OF RESPECT FOR RELIGIOUS TEACHING IN THE ANIMAL KINGDOM
DON'T WORRY, REVEREND TODDLERTOUCHER. I'LL INVENT A MACHINE WHICH WILL INSTIL RELIGIOUS BELIEF IN YOUR ANIMALS
THEN THEY'LL HAVE TO OBEY YOUR EVERY WHIM, IN ACCORDANCE WITH HOLY SCRIPTURE.
SEE, MY CANINE SPIRITUALIZER WILL REMIND THESE DOGS OF THEIR OWN MORTALITY, WHILST AT THE SAME TIME DANGLING THE PROMISE OF AN INFINITELY LONG WALKIES IN THE AFTERLIFE.
HEAVEN
THIS WILL BE YOU
THE POOCHES WILL START BELIEVING IN GOD IN NEXT TO NO TIME.
HUH! SO MUCH FOR REMINDING THEM OF THEIR MORTALITY!
HEAVEN
THIS WILL BE YOU
THE GREEDY MUTTS ARE ONLY INTERESTED IN SNAFFLING THE BONES OUT OF YOUR "MEMENTO MORI"
NEVER MIND, VICAR
I'LL TRY A MORE DIRECT APPROACH TO MAKING YOUR BEASTIES BELIEVE IN RELIGION
I'VE BUILT THIS MECHANICAL GOD-BOTHER-O-MATIC.
KNOCK KNOCK
JESUS
PIG STY
RABBIT HUTCH
IT'LL GO ROUND KNOCKING ON ALL THE ANIMALS' DOORS AND GIVING THEM LEAFLETS ABOUT JESUS.
IT'S WORKING GILBERT! THAT PIG IS UNDERGOING A RELIGIOUS CONVERSION!
AHHHH
AHHHH!
AHHHH!
RABBIT HUTCH
LOOK, IT'S ACCEPTING THE BIBLE AS BEING THE TRUE REVEALED WORD OF GOD!
THANKS GILBERT
Squeal!
Squeal!
NOW I CAN EXERT MY DOMINION OVER THIS PIG BY FLUSHING ITS HEAD DOWN THE TOILET
WHO'S THE DADDY? EH? EH? WHO'S THE FUCKING DADDY?
CLUNK
TENTATIVE
INSISTENT
FLUSH!
COO! THAT PORKER'S FLAILING TROTTER HAS SWITCHED THE GOD-BOTHER-O-MATIC ON TO FULL POWER!
CRIKEY!
BANG BANG BANG BANG
IT'S STARTED KNOCKING ON THE DOOR OF THAT BEEHIVE LIKE A JACKHAMMER
OOER! THE GOD-BOTHER-O-MATIC APPEARS TO HAVE GOT THE QUEEN BEE OUT OF HER BATH
LET JESUS INTO YOUR HEART
SHE LOOKS NONE TOO PLEASED ABOUT BEING DISTURBED.
RUN FOR IT! THE BEES ARE LIVID!
WOMEN AND VICARS FIRST!
YEEOW! I'VE BEEN STUNG ON THE ARSE!
WAIT A MINUTE, VICAR — ONE OF YOUR CHIMPANZEES JUST SPOKE!
HANG ABOUT, THIS ISN'T A REAL MONKEY..
BAH!
IT'S THE DARWINIAN EVOLUTIONIST RICHARD DAWKINS, IN A FANCY-DRESS COSTUME!
YES. I DISGUISED MYSELF SO THAT I COULD HAVE SEX WITH YOUR MONKEYS, AS ADVOCATED BY MY GODLESS SO-CALLED THEORY OF EVOLUTION.
AND I WOULD'VE GOT AWAY WITH IT IF I HADN'T BEEN STANG ON THE ARSE BY A BEE
THANKS FOR SAVING MY MONKEYS FROM BEING EVOLVED BY RICHARD DAWKINS, GILBERT
FRRP
HERE, TREAT YOURSELF TO SOME SWEETS WHILST I EXERCISE MY DOMINION OVER THIS SQUIRREL BY FARTING ON ITS HEAD.

From our Education Correspondent
PAT PENDING

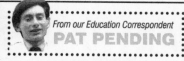

Academics' standards fall, says report

UNIVERSITY professors are in breach of their contracts by failing to meet expected standards of appearance, according to a new report by the University Codes and Standards Association. The official watchdog claims that 90% of professorial posts in British universities are held by middle-aged men with well-groomed hair styles and fashionable clothes.

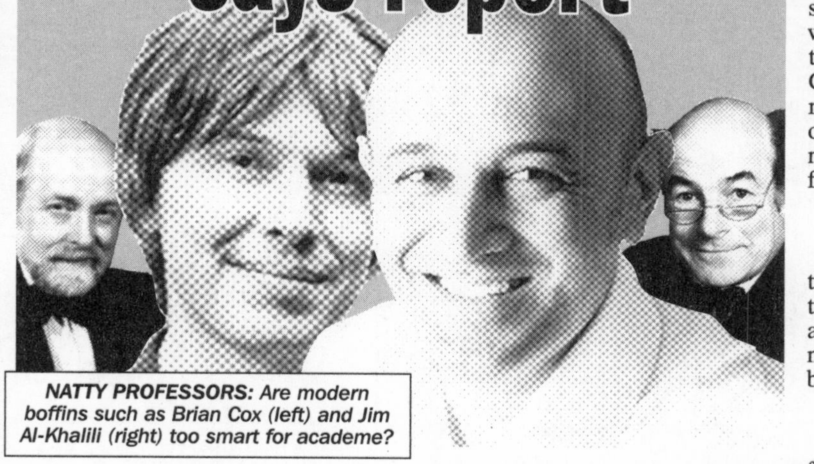

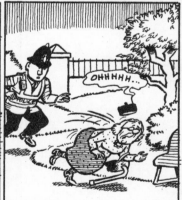

***NATTY PROFESSORS:** Are modern boffins such as Brian Cox (left) and Jim Al-Khalili (right) too smart for academe?*

"We need to get back to the days of proper boggly-eyed professors with wild hair styles, shuffling around university corridors with a bumbling detachment from reality," said Frank Pennycress, chairman of the UCSA. "These days, you are more likely to find professors striding confidently along wearing designer jeans and training shoes. Half of them wouldn't even know what a spotted dickie bow was, let alone how to put one on," he added.

PUBLIC

And Pennycress claimed that the decline in appearance has led to a lack of public confidence in Professors. "Years ago, Heinz Wolf would come on the telly in his ill-fitting suit with his hair all over the shop, babbling on in a comical German accent, and we would have confidence in what he said," he said.

The report singled out trendy media academic professor Jim Al-Kahlili, presenter of the BBCs *Chemistry - A Volatile History*. "With his Levi 501s and an open neck Prada shirt, he looks more like an interior designer than a crackpot boffin. And when he starts talking about atomic structure without waving his arms around like a windmill, you don't know whether to believe him or not. The least he could do is put on a stained lab coat and a pair of half moon glasses," said Pennycress.

PUBIC

Also slammed was inventor of the CERN hadron collider, professor Brian Cox. "This man doesn't tick any of the boxes. He's got collar length brown hair, wears a t-shirt under his jacket and has an unremarkable northern accent," said Pennycress. "He doesn't even wear glasses. And even if he did, they'd probably be Dolce and Gabbana, not three pairs of wire-rimmed ones absent-mindedly left on his pate. If anything, he looks more like the keyboard player from the late 80s synth band."

PUNIC

According to the report, fewer that 4% of professors routinely talk to themselves, and only two in a hundred regularly have experiments blow up leaving their faces blackened and their hair smoking.

TROJAN

We called professor Heinz Wolff for his reaction to the report, but the phone was answered by his hunchback assistant. he told us: "The master cannot speak to you at the moment. he is in the basement, tampering with the very fabric of life itself and unleashing forces that he will be unable to control."

MAJOR MISUNDERSTANDING

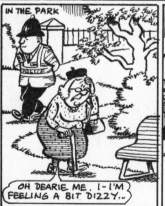

IN THE PARK
OH DEARIE ME. I-I'M FEELING A BIT DIZZY..
OHHHHH...
FOXTROT CHARLIE DELTA, I'VE GOT AN ELDERLY WOMAN JUST COLLAPSED IN FULCHESTER PARK
REQUIRES IMMEDIATE MEDICAL ATTENTION, OVER!
=CRACKLE CRACKLE= ROGER THAT, FOXTROT CHARLIE DELTA, I'M SENDING AN AMBULANCE UNIT RIGHT AWAY. CONFIRM TEN-TWENTY FULCHESTER PARK, OVER?
ROGER THAT
=CRACKLE CRACKLE= ROGER, TEN-FOUR OVER AND OUT.
DO YOU HAVE TO INFLICT THAT RACKET ON THE ENTIRE PARK?
I DON'T SUPPOSE IT'S OCCURED TO YOU THAT OTHER PEOPLE MAY NOT WANT TO LISTEN TO YOUR "RAP" MUSIC, OR WHATEVER IT'S CALLED.
NO, YOUR GENERATION DON'T GIVE A DAMN FOR OTHER PEOPLE. ALL YOU CARE ABOUT IS SATISFYING YOUR OWN HEDONISTIC APPETITES.
JUST LOOK AT THE PAIR OF YOU, ROLLING AROUND DRUNK. IT'S PATHETIC.
WELL FOR YOUR INFORMATION, THAT GIZMO OF YOURS IS SUPPOSED TO BE PLUGGED INTO YOUR EAR, ENABLING YOU TO LISTEN TO THAT CACOPHONOUS BILGE WITHOUT DISTURBING OTHERS.
IF YOU DON'T POSSESS AN EARPIECE, THEN KINDLY TURN THE VOLUME DOWN.
=CRACKLE CRACKLE= FOXTROT CHARLIE DELTA, AMBULANCE UNIT ON ITS WAY, OVER
I'M NOT ASKING YOU AGAIN. TURN THAT DOWN OR I'M CALLING THE POLICE.

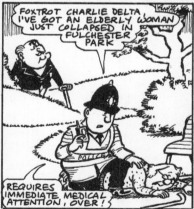

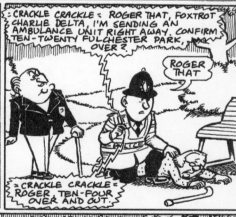

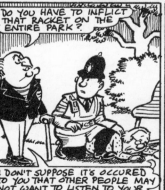

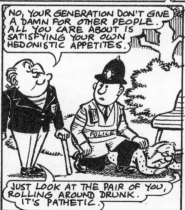

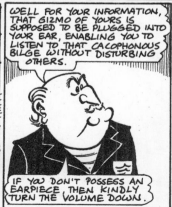

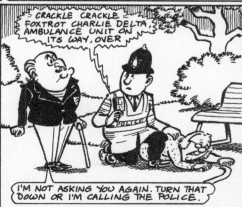

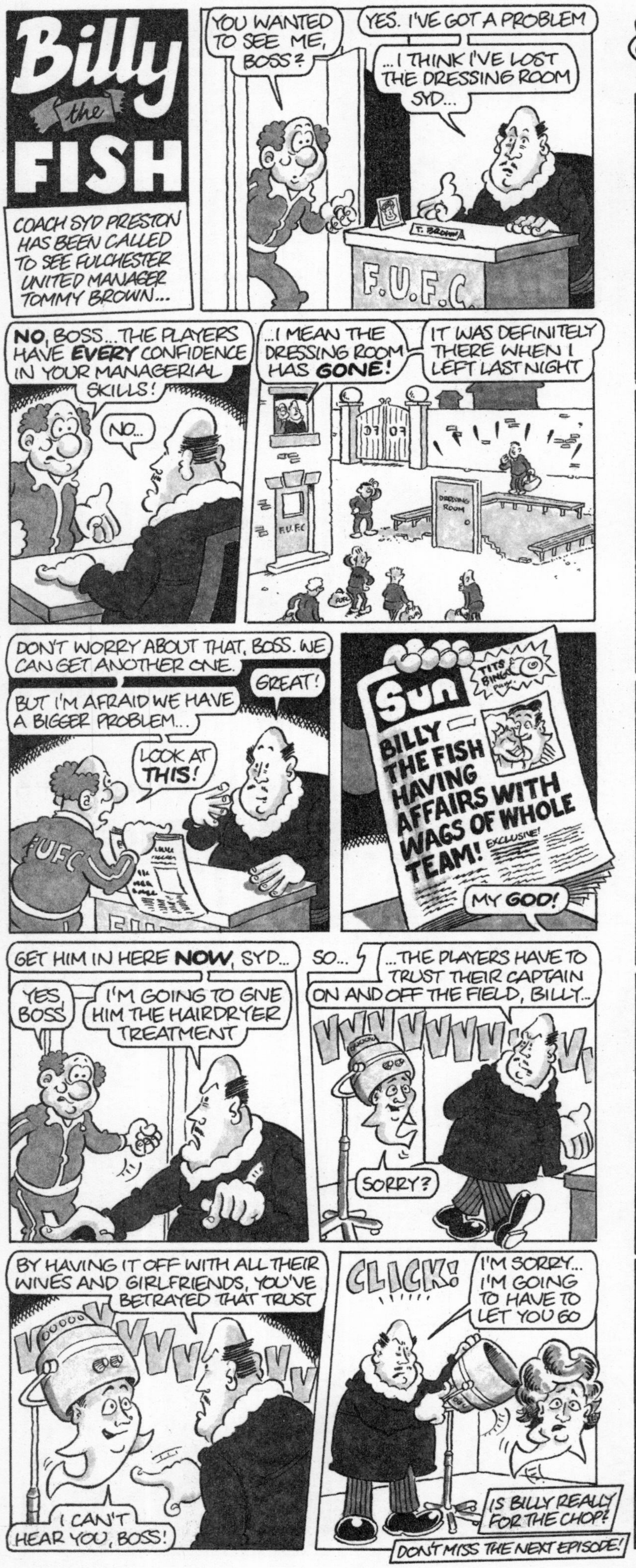
Billy the FISH
COACH SYD PRESTON HAS BEEN CALLED TO SEE FULCHESTER UNITED MANAGER TOMMY BROWN...
YOU WANTED TO SEE ME, BOSS?
YES. I'VE GOT A PROBLEM
...I THINK I'VE LOST THE DRESSING ROOM SYD...
T. BROWN
F.U.F.C.
NO, BOSS... THE PLAYERS HAVE EVERY CONFIDENCE IN YOUR MANAGERIAL SKILLS!
NO...
...I MEAN THE DRESSING ROOM HAS GONE!
IT WAS DEFINITELY THERE WHEN I LEFT LAST NIGHT
DRESSING ROOM
F.U.F.C.
DON'T WORRY ABOUT THAT, BOSS. WE CAN GET ANOTHER ONE.
GREAT!
BUT I'M AFRAID WE HAVE A BIGGER PROBLEM...
LOOK AT THIS!
FUFC
Sun
TITS BINGO
BILLY THE FISH HAVING AFFAIRS WITH WAGS OF WHOLE TEAM!
EXCLUSIVE!
MY GOD!
GET HIM IN HERE NOW, SYD...
YES, BOSS
I'M GOING TO GIVE HIM THE HAIRDRYER TREATMENT
SO...
...THE PLAYERS HAVE TO TRUST THEIR CAPTAIN ON AND OFF THE FIELD, BILLY...
SORRY?
BY HAVING IT OFF WITH ALL THEIR WIVES AND GIRLFRIENDS, YOU'VE BETRAYED THAT TRUST
I CAN'T HEAR YOU, BOSS!
CLICK!
I'M SORRY... I'M GOING TO HAVE TO LET YOU GO
IS BILLY REALLY FOR THE CHOP?
DON'T MISS THE NEXT EPISODE!

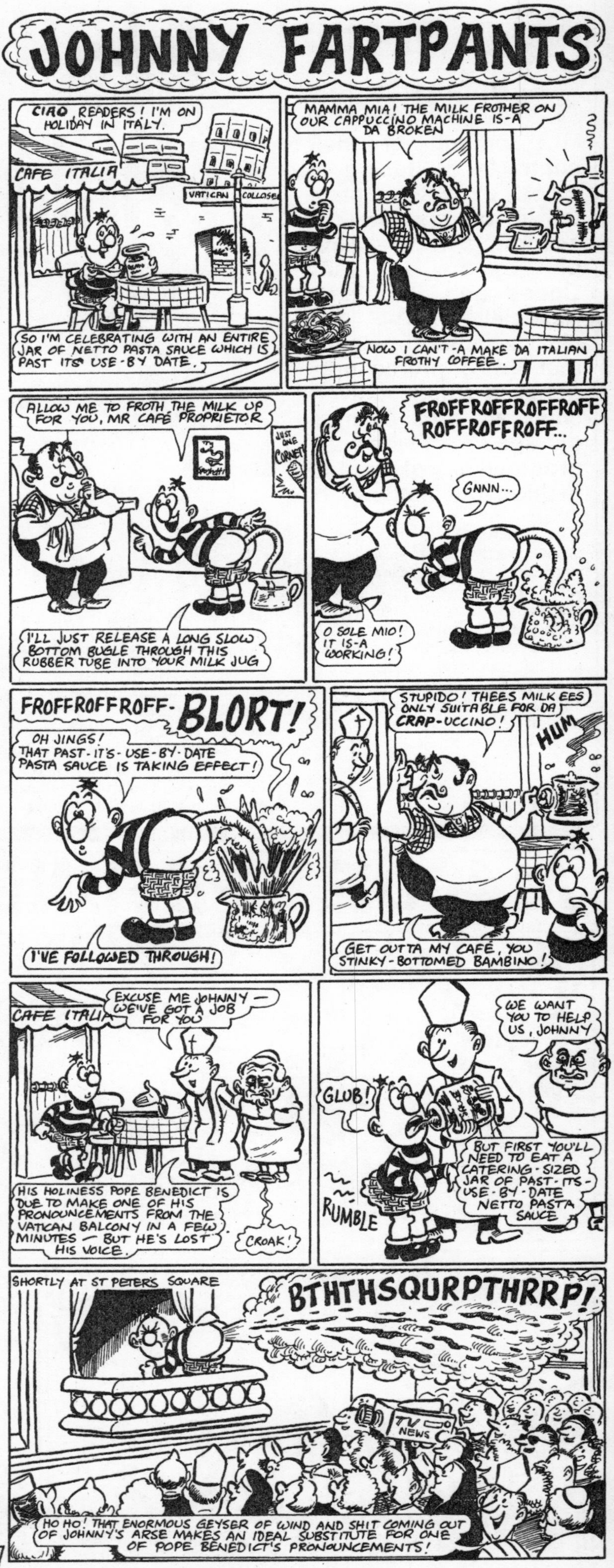
JOHNNY FARTPANTS
CIAO READERS! I'M ON HOLIDAY IN ITALY.
CAFE ITALIA
VATICAN
COLLOSEUM
SO I'M CELEBRATING WITH AN ENTIRE JAR OF NETTO PASTA SAUCE WHICH IS PAST ITS USE-BY DATE.
MAMMA MIA! THE MILK FROTHER ON OUR CAPPUCCINO MACHINE IS-A DA BROKEN
NOW I CAN'T-A MAKE DA ITALIAN FROTHY COFFEE.
ALLOW ME TO FROTH THE MILK UP FOR YOU, MR CAFÉ PROPRIETOR
JUST ONE CORNETTO
I'LL JUST RELEASE A LONG SLOW BOTTOM BUGLE THROUGH THIS RUBBER TUBE INTO YOUR MILK JUG
FROFFROFFROFFROFF ROFFROFFROFF...
GNNN...
O SOLE MIO! IT IS-A WORKING!
FROFFROFFROFF-BLORT!
OH JINGS! THAT PAST-IT'S-USE-BY-DATE PASTA SAUCE IS TAKING EFFECT!
I'VE FOLLOWED THROUGH!
STUPIDO! THEES MILK EES ONLY SUITABLE FOR DA CRAP-UCCINO!
HUM
GET OUTTA MY CAFÉ, YOU STINKY-BOTTOMED BAMBINO!
CAFE ITALIA
EXCUSE ME JOHNNY — WE'VE GOT A JOB FOR YOU
HIS HOLINESS POPE BENEDICT IS DUE TO MAKE ONE OF HIS PRONOUNCEMENTS FROM THE VATICAN BALCONY IN A FEW MINUTES — BUT HE'S LOST HIS VOICE.
CROAK!
WE WANT YOU TO HELP US, JOHNNY
GLUB!
BUT FIRST YOU'LL NEED TO EAT A CATERING-SIZED JAR OF PAST-ITS-USE-BY-DATE NETTO PASTA SAUCE
RUMBLE
SHORTLY AT ST PETER'S SQUARE
BTHTHSQURPTHRRP!
TV NEWS
HO HO! THAT ENORMOUS GEYSER OF WIND AND SHIT COMING OUT OF JOHNNY'S ARSE MAKES AN IDEAL SUBSTITUTE FOR ONE OF POPE BENEDICT'S PRONOUNCEMENTS!

MEDDLESOME RATBAG

CYPRUS — I TELL YOU ONE THING I LIKE ABOUT BEING ON HOLIDAY IN THE MEDITERRANEAN

WHEN YOU'RE AT A RESTAURANT, YOU CAN LIGHT UP A CIGARETTE AFTER YOUR MEAL AND NOBODY OBJECTS.

SNIFFFFFFFFFFFFFFFFFFFFFFFFFFFFFFF

HEY, WHAT'S HAPPENING?

IT'S AS IF MY FAG SMOKE HAS BEEN SUCKED AWAY BY SOME KIND OF GIANT VACUUM CLEANER!

FFFFFFFFFFFFFFFFFFFFFFFFFFF

MEDITERRANEAN SEA

FFFFFFFFFFFFFFFFFFFFFFFF

GREECE — OLIVES

FFFFFF FFFFFFF

LUIGI'S SPAGHETTI & BARBER SHOP — ITALY

FFFFFFFFFF

FRANCE

FFFFFFFFFFFFFFFF

ENGLAND — BUCKINGHAM PALACE — TRAFALGAR SQUARE — LONDON BU — VISIT T

FFFFFFFFFFFFFFFFF

FULCHESTER TEAROOMS — TEAS

FFFFFFF!

CREAM TEAS

COUGH COUGH COUGH COUGH COUGH COUGH COUGH COUGH COUGH COUGH

CREAM T

LONG DISTANCE TELEPHONE CALL FOR YOU, SIR.

COUGH COUGH! WOULD YOU MIND PUTTING THAT OUT, PLEASE? COUGH COUGH!

THERE'S PEOPLE TRYING TO EAT HERE, YOU KNOW. AND WE DON'T WANT TO HAVE TO INHALE YOUR FILTHY SMOKE. COUGH COUGH!

MICKEY'S MONKEY SPUNK MOPED

YOUNG MICKY MOXON WAS THE LUCKIEST BOY IN BARNTON — FOR HE WAS THE OWNER OF A SUPER MOPED POWERED BY SIMIAN SEMEN...

HI, READERS... I'M WORRIED THAT THE GOVERNMENT WILL RAISE THE FUEL DUTY ON MONKEY SPUNK. SO I'M MODIFYING MY MOPED TO MAKE IT RUN ON RENEWABLE ENERGY.

THIS WANKING GORILLA WILL PROVIDE ALL THE 4-STAR PRIMATE LOVE PORRIDGE I NEED

OO! OO! OO!

WITH A FUNNEL TO CATCH THE JUNGLE JIZZ, AND A TELLY AND DVD SHOWING A LOOP OF HARDCORE GORILLA GRUMBLE FROM DAVID ATTENBOROUGH'S 'LIFE ON EARTH', WE'LL BE MOTORING

AND THESE BANANAS WILL GIVE HIM PLENTY OF ENERGY FOR HIS ROUND THE CLOCK SELF-ABUSE

BANANAS

START THE DVD AND OFF WE GO!

HERE IN THE CANOPY OF THE TREES, THE HUGE BEASTS BEGIN THEIR MATING RITUAL, AND YOU CAN ACTUALLY SEE IT GOING IN...

AH! THERE'S NOTHING LIKE A NICE SPIN IN THE COUNTRYSIDE...

CAN'T SEE MUCH, MIND.

OO! OO! OO!

WANK! WANK! WANK!

SMACK!

AH, WELL. BACK TO THE OLD DRAWING BOARD

OO! OO! OO!

WANK! WANK!

WANK! WANK!

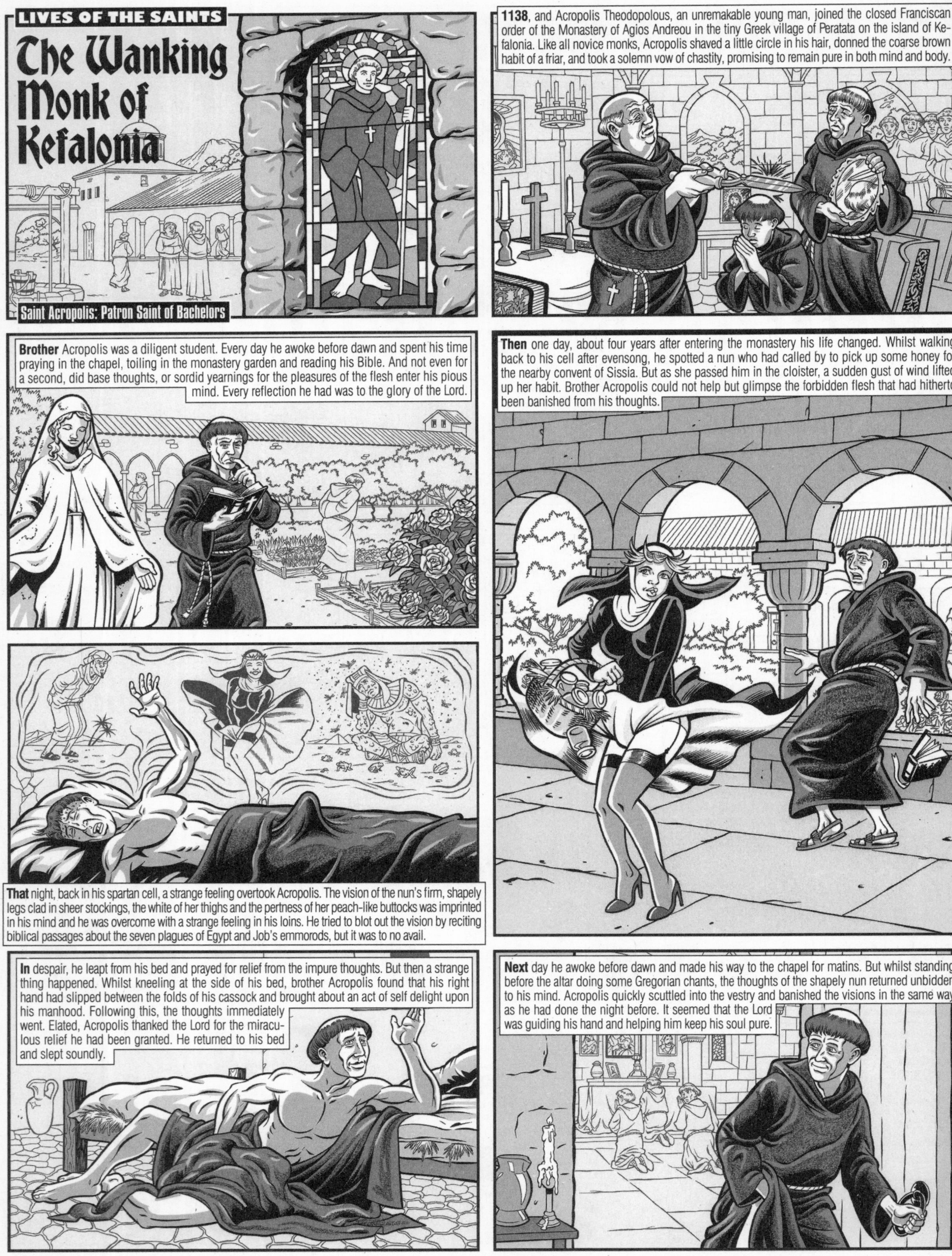
LIVES OF THE SAINTS
The Wanking Monk of Kefalonia
Saint Acropolis: Patron Saint of Bachelors
1138, and Acropolis Theodopolous, an unremakable young man, joined the closed Franciscan order of the Monastery of Agios Andreou in the tiny Greek village of Peratata on the island of Kefalonia. Like all novice monks, Acropolis shaved a little circle in his hair, donned the coarse brown habit of a friar, and took a solemn vow of chastity, promising to remain pure in both mind and body.
Brother Acropolis was a diligent student. Every day he awoke before dawn and spent his time praying in the chapel, toiling in the monastery garden and reading his Bible. And not even for a second, did base thoughts, or sordid yearnings for the pleasures of the flesh enter his pious mind. Every reflection he had was to the glory of the Lord.
Then one day, about four years after entering the monastery his life changed. Whilst walking back to his cell after evensong, he spotted a nun who had called by to pick up some honey for the nearby convent of Sissia. But as she passed him in the cloister, a sudden gust of wind lifted up her habit. Brother Acropolis could not help but glimpse the forbidden flesh that had hitherto been banished from his thoughts.
That night, back in his spartan cell, a strange feeling overtook Acropolis. The vision of the nun's firm, shapely legs clad in sheer stockings, the white of her thighs and the pertness of her peach-like buttocks was imprinted in his mind and he was overcome with a strange feeling in his loins. He tried to blot out the vision by reciting biblical passages about the seven plagues of Egypt and Job's emmorods, but it was to no avail.
In despair, he leapt from his bed and prayed for relief from the impure thoughts. But then a strange thing happened. Whilst kneeling at the side of his bed, brother Acropolis found that his right hand had slipped between the folds of his cassock and brought about an act of self delight upon his manhood. Following this, the thoughts immediately went. Elated, Acropolis thanked the Lord for the miraculous relief he had been granted. He returned to his bed and slept soundly.
Next day he awoke before dawn and made his way to the chapel for matins. But whilst standing before the altar doing some Gregorian chants, the thoughts of the shapely nun returned unbidden to his mind. Acropolis quickly scuttled into the vestry and banished the visions in the same way as he had done the night before. It seemed that the Lord was guiding his hand and helping him keep his soul pure.

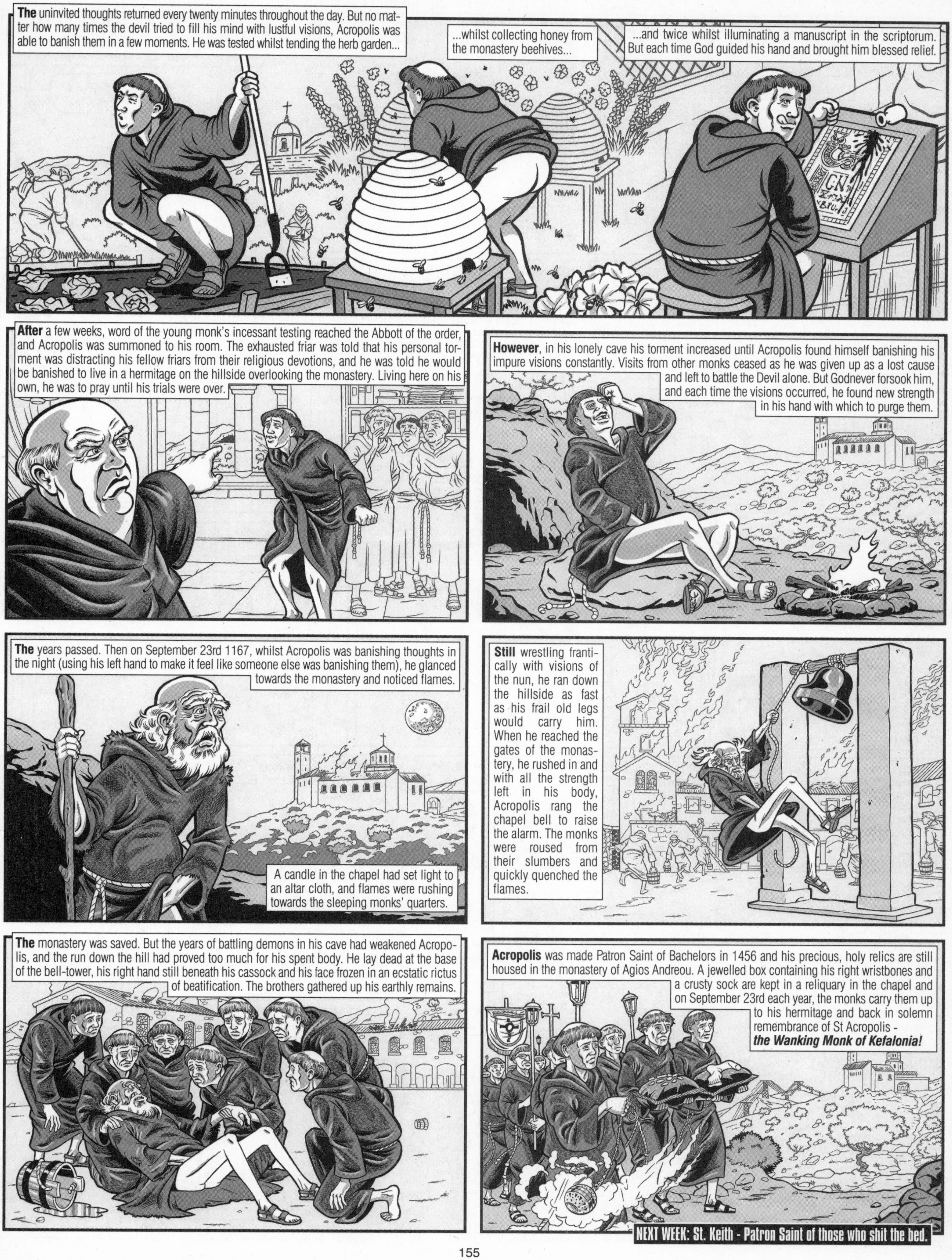
The uninvited thoughts returned every twenty minutes throughout the day. But no matter how many times the devil tried to fill his mind with lustful visions, Acropolis was able to banish them in a few moments. He was tested whilst tending the herb garden...
...whilst collecting honey from the monastery beehives...
...and twice whilst illuminating a manuscript in the scriptorum. But each time God guided his hand and brought him blessed relief.
After a few weeks, word of the young monk's incessant testing reached the Abbott of the order, and Acropolis was summoned to his room. The exhausted friar was told that his personal torment was distracting his fellow friars from their religious devotions, and he was told he would be banished to live in a hermitage on the hillside overlooking the monastery. Living here on his own, he was to pray until his trials were over.
However, in his lonely cave his torment increased until Acropolis found himself banishing his impure visions constantly. Visits from other monks ceased as he was given up as a lost cause and left to battle the Devil alone. But Godnever forsook him, and each time the visions occurred, he found new strength in his hand with which to purge them.
The years passed. Then on September 23rd 1167, whilst Acropolis was banishing thoughts in the night (using his left hand to make it feel like someone else was banishing them), he glanced towards the monastery and noticed flames.
A candle in the chapel had set light to an altar cloth, and flames were rushing towards the sleeping monks' quarters.
Still wrestling frantically with visions of the nun, he ran down the hillside as fast as his frail old legs would carry him. When he reached the gates of the monastery, he rushed in and with all the strength left in his body, Acropolis rang the chapel bell to raise the alarm. The monks were roused from their slumbers and quickly quenched the flames.
The monastery was saved. But the years of battling demons in his cave had weakened Acropolis, and the run down the hill had proved too much for his spent body. He lay dead at the base of the bell-tower, his right hand still beneath his cassock and his face frozen in an ecstatic rictus of beatification. The brothers gathered up his earthly remains.
Acropolis was made Patron Saint of Bachelors in 1456 and his precious, holy relics are still housed in the monastery of Agios Andreou. A jewelled box containing his right wristbones and a crusty sock are kept in a reliquary in the chapel and on September 23rd each year, the monks carry them up to his hermitage and back in solemn remembrance of St Acropolis -
the Wanking Monk of Kefalonia!
NEXT WEEK: St. Keith - Patron Saint of those who shit the bed.

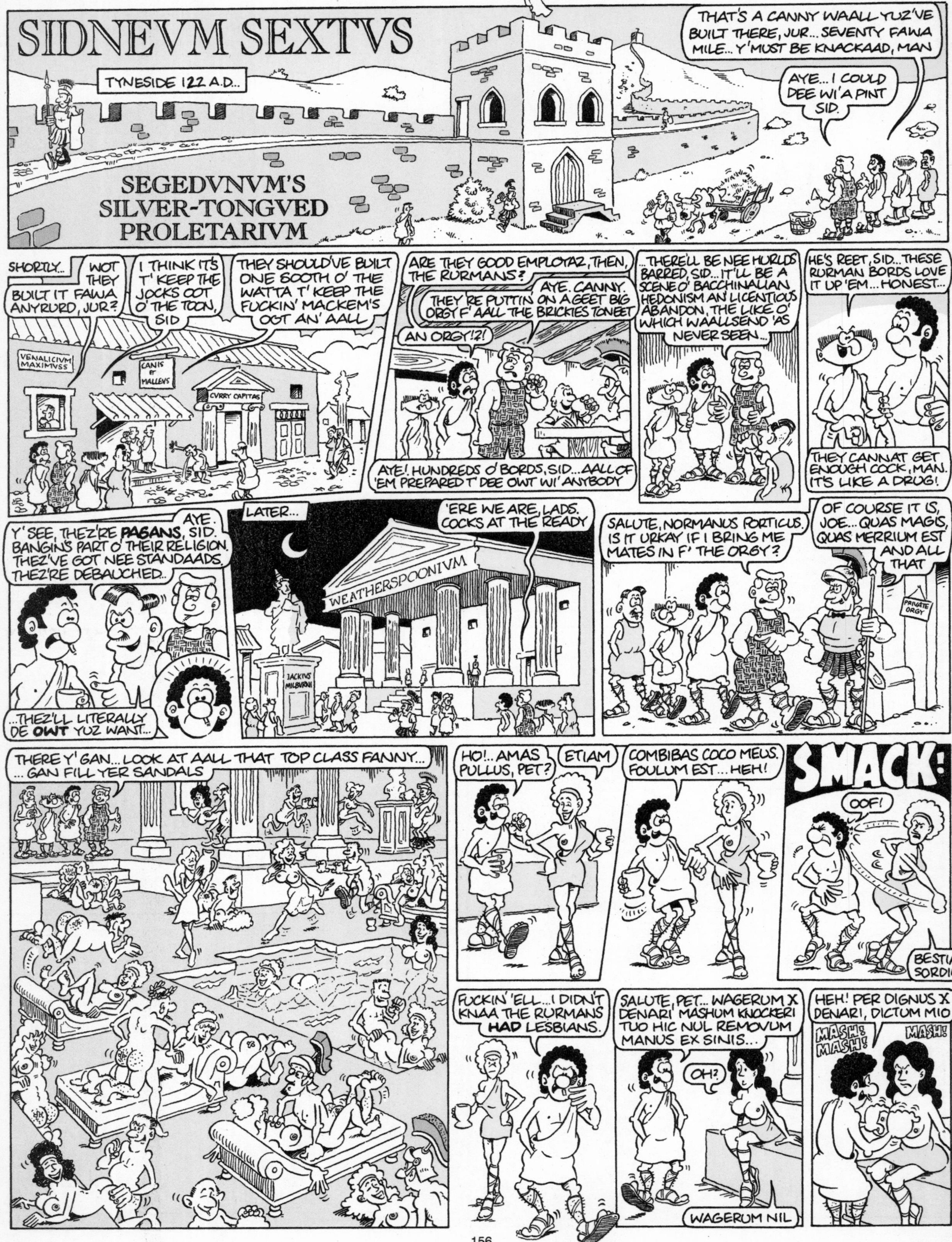
SIDNEVM SEXTVS
TYNESIDE 122 A.D...
SEGEDVNVM'S SILVER-TONGVED PROLETARIVM
THAT'S A CANNY WAALL YUZ'VE BUILT THERE, JUR... SEVENTY FAWA MILE... Y'MUST BE KNACKAAD, MAN
AYE... I COULD DEE WI'A PINT SID.
SHORTLY...
WOT THEY BUILT IT FAWA ANYRURD, JUR?
I THINK IT'S T' KEEP THE JOCKS OOT O' THE TOON, SID
THEY SHOULD'VE BUILT ONE SOOTH O' THE WATTA T' KEEP THE FUCKIN' MACKEM'S OOT AN' AALL
VENALICIVM MAXIMVSS
CANIS ET MALLEVS
CVRRY CAPITAS
ARE THEY GOOD EMPLOYAZ, THEN, THE RURMANS?
AYE, CANNY. THEY'RE PUTTIN' ON A GEET BIG ORGY F' AALL THE BRICKIES TONEET
AN ORGY!?!
AYE! HUNDREDS O' BORDS, SID... AALL OF 'EM PREPARED T' DEE OWT WI' ANYBODY
...THERE'LL BE NEE HURLDS BARRED, SID... IT'LL BE A SCENE O' BACCHINALIAN HEDONISM AN' LICENTIOUS ABANDON, THE LIKE O' WHICH WAALLSEND 'AS NEVER SEEN...
HE'S REET, SID... THESE RURMAN BORDS LOVE IT UP 'EM... HONEST...
THEY CANNAT GET ENOUGH COCK, MAN. IT'S LIKE A DRUG!
AYE.
Y' SEE, THEZ'RE **PAGANS**, SID. BANGIN'S PART O' THEIR RELIGION. THEZ'VE GOT NEE STANDAADS. THEZ'RE DEBAUCHED...
...THEZ'LL LITERALLY DE **OWT** YUZ WANT...
LATER...
'ERE WE ARE, LADS. COCKS AT THE READY
WEATHERSPOONIVM
JACKIVS MILBVRNI
SALUTE, NORMANUS PORTICUS. IS IT URKAY IF I BRING ME MATES IN F' THE ORGY?
OF COURSE IT IS, JOE... QUAS MAGIS, QUAS MERRIUM EST AND ALL THAT
PRIVATE ORGY
THERE Y' GAN... LOOK AT AALL THAT TOP CLASS FANNY... ...GAN FILL YER SANDALS
HO!.. AMAS PULLUS, PET?
ETIAM
COMBIBAS COCO MEUS. FOULUM EST... HEH!
SMACK!
OOF!
BESTIA SORDIO
FUCKIN' 'ELL... I DIDN'T KNAA THE RURMANS **HAD** LESBIANS.
SALUTE, PET... WAGERUM X DENARI MASHUM KNOCKERI TUO HIC NUL REMOVUM MANUS EX SINIS...
OH?
WAGERUM NIL
HEH! PER DIGNUS X DENARI, DICTUM MIO
MASH! MASH!
MASH!

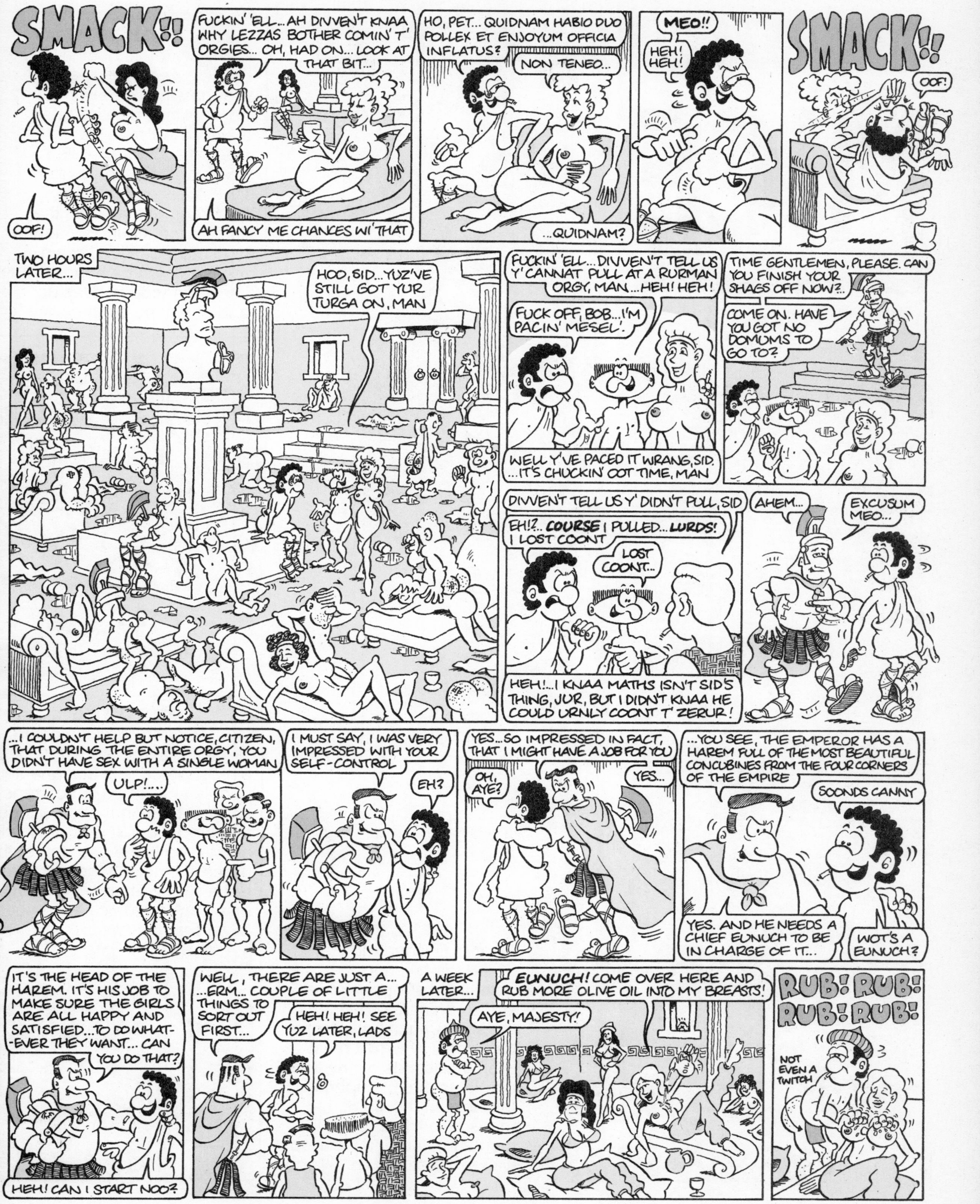
SMACK!!
OOF!
FUCKIN' 'ELL... AH DIVVEN'T KNAA WHY LEZZAS BOTHER COMIN' T' ORGIES... OH, HAD ON... LOOK AT THAT BIT...
AH FANCY ME CHANCES WI' THAT
HO, PET... QUIDNAM HABIO DUO POLLEX ET ENJOYUM OFFICIA INFLATUS?
NON TENEO...
...QUIDNAM?
MEO!!
HEH! HEH!
SMACK!!
OOF!
TWO HOURS LATER...
HOO, SID... YUZ'VE STILL GOT YUR TURGA ON, MAN
FUCKIN' 'ELL... DIVVEN'T TELL US Y' CANNAT PULL AT A RURMAN ORGY, MAN... HEH! HEH!
FUCK OFF, BOB... I'M PACIN' MESEL'.
WELL Y'VE PACED IT WRANG, SID. ...IT'S CHUCKIN' OOT TIME, MAN
TIME GENTLEMEN, PLEASE. CAN YOU FINISH YOUR SHAGS OFF NOW?..
COME ON. HAVE YOU GOT NO DOMUMS TO GO TO?
DIVVEN'T TELL US Y' DIDN'T PULL, SID
EH!?.. **COURSE** I PULLED... **LURDS!** I LOST COONT
LOST COONT...
HEH!.. I KNAA MATHS ISN'T SID'S THING, JUR, BUT I DIDN'T KNAA HE COULD URNLY COONT T' ZERUR!
AHEM...
EXCUSUM MEO...
...I COULDN'T HELP BUT NOTICE, CITIZEN, THAT DURING THE ENTIRE ORGY, YOU DIDN'T HAVE SEX WITH A SINGLE WOMAN
ULP!....
I MUST SAY, I WAS VERY IMPRESSED WITH YOUR SELF-CONTROL
EH?
YES... SO IMPRESSED IN FACT, THAT I MIGHT HAVE A JOB FOR YOU
OH, AYE?
YES...
...YOU SEE, THE EMPEROR HAS A HAREM FULL OF THE MOST BEAUTIFUL CONCUBINES FROM THE FOUR CORNERS OF THE EMPIRE
SOONDS CANNY
YES. AND HE NEEDS A CHIEF EUNUCH TO BE IN CHARGE OF IT...
WOT'S A EUNUCH?
IT'S THE HEAD OF THE HAREM. IT'S HIS JOB TO MAKE SURE THE GIRLS ARE ALL HAPPY AND SATISFIED... TO DO WHATEVER THEY WANT... CAN YOU DO THAT?
HEH! CAN I START NOO?
WELL, THERE ARE JUST A... ...ERM... COUPLE OF LITTLE THINGS TO SORT OUT FIRST...
HEH! HEH! SEE YUZ LATER, LADS
A WEEK LATER...
EUNUCH! COME OVER HERE AND RUB MORE OLIVE OIL INTO MY BREASTS!
AYE, MAJESTY!
RUB! RUB! RUB! RUB!
NOT EVEN A TWITCH

HOW THEY'RE MADE

This Week...

MICE

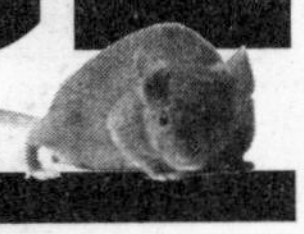

MICE have been scurrying around our houses for hundreds of years. Whether they're gnawing holes in the skirting board, nibbling through electrical wires, or making ladies scream on chairs, these little furry critters are never far away. But have you ever stopped to think where they come from? Let's go behind the scenes at one of Britain's oldest mouse factories to see how these intricate, cheese-eating wonders are made.

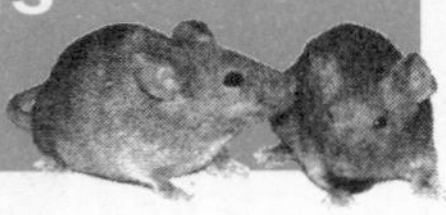

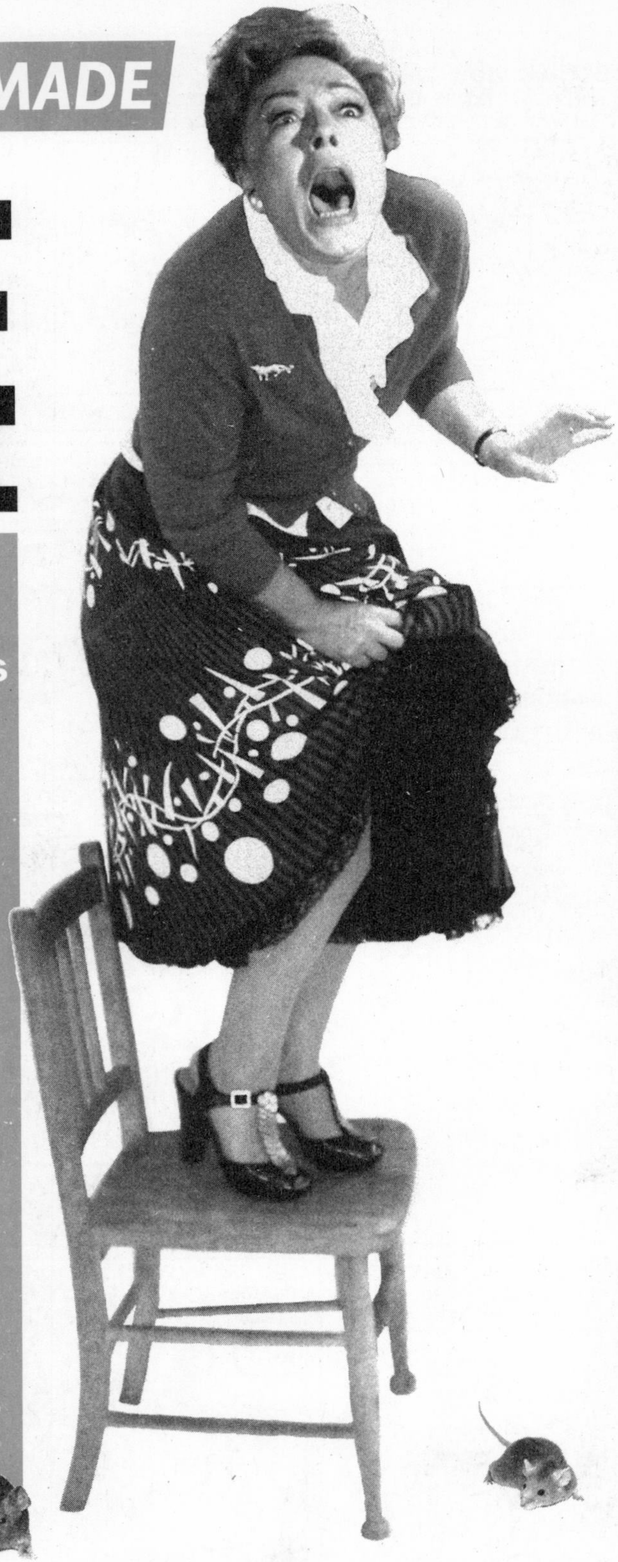

1 **EACH TYPE** of mouse begins life as a sketch on a draughtsman's drawing board. Once the designer is happy with the plans, a set of accurate, scaled up blueprints is prepared for the workshop. Here, the draughtsman puts the finishing touches to a new type of long-tailed brown mouse which he hopes will infest terraced houses up and down the country.

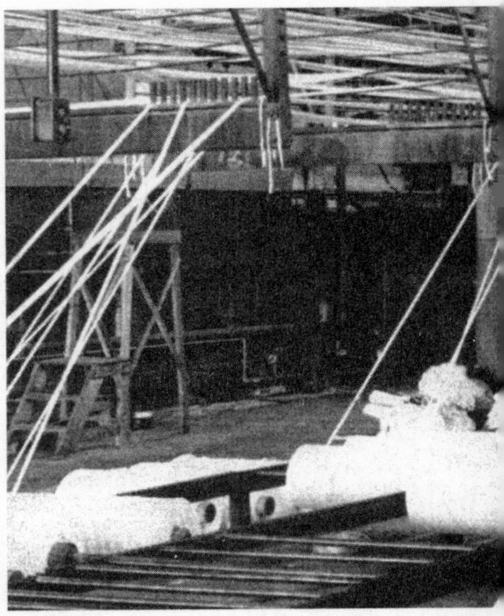

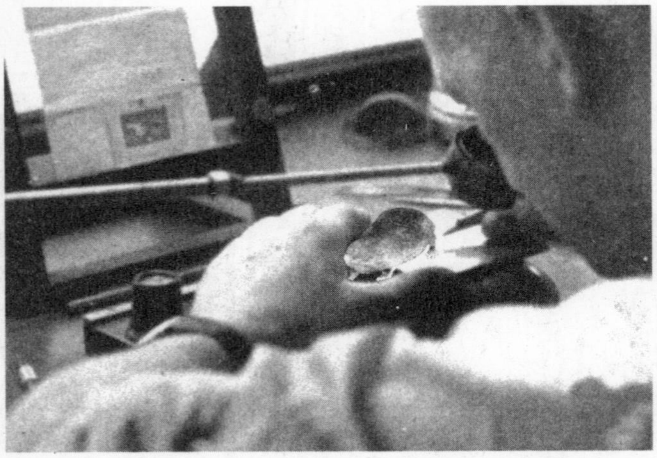

4 **NEXT,** the half-finished mouse is taken to the defecation shop, where a craftsman carefully inserts the shitting unit between its back legs. This unit must drop thousands of tiny turds on plates and in cupboards throughout the life of the mouse, so it has to be manufactured and inserted with extraordinary precision.

5 **ON TO THE** tailing shop, where workers insert the characteristi pink, hairless tails that enable people to lift mice out of traps and put them in the bin withou touching them. It is fiddly work and tailing is the one part of th process that isn't mechanised. But a skilled fitter can tail as many as 1000 mice in an hour. faster than any machine!

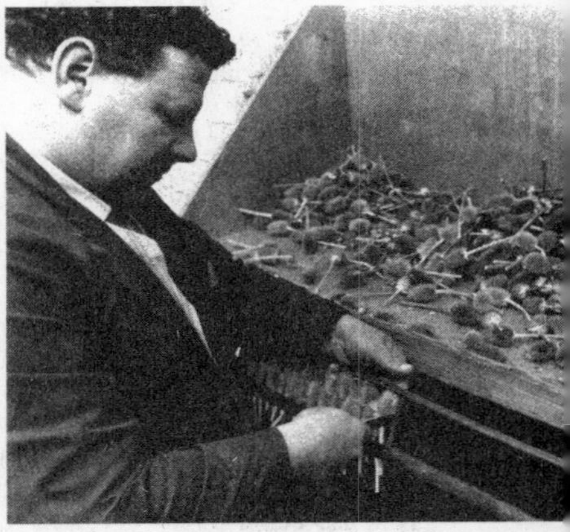